Standards Policy for Information Infrastructure

Standards Policy for Information Infrastructure

edited by Brian Kahin and Janet Abbate

A Publication of the Harvard Information Infrastructure Project

The MIT Press, Cambridge, Massachusetts, and London, England

This book was printed and bound in the United States of America.

Library of Congress Cataloging-in-Publication Data

Standards policy for information infrastructure / edited by Brian
  Kahin and Janet Abbate.
        p.   cm.—(A Publication of the Harvard Information Infrastructure
  Project)
   Includes bibliographical references and index.
   ISBN 0-262-11206-X (alk. paper).—ISBN 0-262-61117-1 (pbk. : alk. paper)
   1. Internet (Computer network)—Standards.   2. Internet (Computer
network)—Government policy.   I. Kahin, Brian. II. Abbate, Janet.
III. Series.
TK5105.875.I57S73   1995
384'.042'0218—dc20   95-8809
                                                            CIP

Contents

Contents

Foreword

Arati Prabhakar

When people talk about "building" a National Information Infrastructure, it is important to remember that we already have an information infrastructure. In fact, we have several, dating back to a time when humans began to communicate with each other. That's the problem. Today, every time we transmit and process information, whether by newspapers, broadcasting, cable, telecommunications systems, or other means, we are using some kind of infrastructure. But these systems evolved separately, so transferring information from one to the next is difficult.

We have a unique opportunity, not just to improve how we communicate, but to use technology to enrich our lives. As a nation, we have a chance to develop a single information infrastructure that will produce useful information, provide equity of access, protect privacy and security, and enhance competitiveness, education, and national well being.

Technology is producing dramatic and pervasive change. Already the evolution of the NII is beginning to touch the lives of many people, not just the technologists and engineers. Evolving applications for manufacturing, health care, commerce, education, libraries, and the environment are challenging many traditional roles and boundaries within the information industry.

The NII cannot be built by one company or one industry alone. The NII can only be achieved through cooperation between the private and public sectors and through discussions to resolve the issues that cross traditional industry and national boundaries.

While it is clear that the private sector will build and operate the NII, the role of government in supporting the smooth evolution of the NII must be defined.

The Information Infrastructure Task Force under Secretary of Commerce Ronald H. Brown is working with the private and public sectors through many committees and working groups to guide the evolution of the NII. Task Force participants are exploring how the government can coordinate its policies, stimulate competition, support research and development, and use technology to advance the NII.

On the Committee on Applications and Technology (CAT), we have been identifying both the applications that people will use on the information infrastructure and the barriers and enablers that affect those applications. The Technology Policy Working Group, under the CAT, is taking a look at the technical issues of scalability and interoperability, the architecture for the NII, the standards process, and where the NII technologies are going.

It's no surprise that the issue of standards underlies every application area that we have identified. Without standards, we cannot achieve our goals for an integrated, transparent, and interoperable information infrastructure that the user perceives as seamless and without boundaries. We have a long way to go, but we are making strides in the right direction.

One important step was the workshop on Standards Development and the Information Infrastructure, which the National Institute of Standards and Technology was pleased to cosponsor with the Science, Technology and Public Policy Program at Harvard University and with the Technology Policy Working Group of the Information Infrastructure Task Force. The Science, Technology and Public Policy Program proposed this workshop to us as a way to stimulate discussions and to identify options for the Federal government on standards and the information infrastructure. I believe that the workshop discussions and papers have given us a better understanding of the complexity of standards development issues and the challenges that they present.

The workshop addressed fundamental questions about the procedural, economic, and policy issues that arise when we talk about developing standards. Now we must build on those discussions and make the government a strong partner with the private sector in the national effort to advance the development of the NII.

My thanks to all who participated and contributed to the discussions on standards, and to Lewis Branscomb and the staff of the Science, Technology and Public Policy Program at Harvard University who did a superb job of organizing and conducting the workshop.

Preface

The Harvard Information Infrastructure Project began five years ago with a small workshop on "Commercialization of the Internet" (summarized in the online document RFC 1192). Held right after the first commercial Internet services were announced, that workshop asked how the subsidized Internet should evolve toward commercialization. The Project's first book, *Building Information Infrastructure* (McGraw-Hill Primis, 1992), was an early effort to scope out the broader vision of a digital infrastructure. In September 1993, the National Information Infrastructure initiative was officially launched. Envisioned as a heterogeneous collection of hardware, software, and services that are interconnected to create, transport, and manipulate information, the NII presents immense technical and policy challenges in its complexity and rapid pace of change.

This volume looks at the issue of standards development for the emerging National Information Infrastructure. It considers the crucial role of standards in providing interconnection and interoperability, possibilities for optimizing the standards process, and a spectrum of policy options for balancing the often conflicting interests involved in standards issues. Most of the papers were first presented at a workshop held on June 15–16, 1994, and subsequently revised and updated.

The workshop and this volume were sponsored by the National Institute for Standards and Technology, and the workshop was held jointly with the Technology Policy Working Group of the

Information Infrastructure Task Force. We want to thank the contributing authors as well as those who helped in the production of the workshop and this volume, especially Shirley Radack at NIST and Veronica McClure at the Science, Technology and Public Policy Program. We also express our appreciation to Bob Prior and Larry Cohen at The MIT Press.

A collaborative effort between the Harvard Information Infrastructure Project and The MIT Press has made possible this series of volumes on information infrastructure issues. The series began with *Public Access to the Internet,* and others are planned. It is our intention to create volumes that reflect the judgments and research of practitioners and scholars from a wide range of areas and fields. We hope that they will collectively make a contribution to both policy and practice.

Lewis M. Branscomb
Director
Science, Technology and Public Policy Program

Overview

Standards Processes and Objectives for the National Information Infrastructure

Lewis M. Branscomb and Brian Kahin

There are many visions of the National Information Infrastructure (NII).[1] No doubt it will eventually incorporate capabilities that we do not foresee today and support applications yet to be conceived. But the model that is emerging is a heterogeneous constellation of networks, services, and applications that are interconnected and, for many purposes, interoperating. It is the prospect of widespread interconnection combined with a high degree of interoperability that makes the promise of advanced information infrastructure so different from the stovepiped systems for delivering information that are familiar and well-established today.

The concept of interconnection is already clearly embodied in the global telephone system. The lines that compose it interconnect, but they interoperate only in a limited sense by providing simple conduit for voice, fax, and data communications. Interoperability is a measure of the power and variety of functions that add value to interconnection, providing platforms for evolving services and applications. The significance of interoperability derives from the positive economic externalities of aggregating an ever larger number of interconnected users while, at the same time, aggregating the services and applications that computer technology makes possible and economically practical. In other words, it builds the potential user base while enlarging the scope of market demand.

Achieving interoperability in the presence of diversity, heterogeneity, and change calls for the widespread adoption of common standards. Ideally, this is accomplished with a minimum of coordination and therefore with minimal constraints on innovation. This requires timely identification and articulation of the issues the standards need to address—and a process through which they are to be realized. To this end, interoperability is often facilitated by allocating functionality to different "layers" and specifying the interface between layers. This allows the technology within layers to evolve independently but with the interface as a stable reference point. For example, supporting communications services can be evolved without disrupting overlying applications—and vice versa.[2]

The American approach to information infrastructure development places the government in the role of enabler and the private sector in the role of investor and innovator. The government has no intention, or indeed capability, of imposing a system-level architecture on the NII. The standards are expected to emerge from the experimentation, competition, and market acceptance of services, many of which have yet to be conceived and tested. At the same time, traditional standards development procedures and institutions that ensure consensus among producers and users about how mature technologies should be specified do not fit well with the rapid development of digital information technology.[3] Ratification by international standards development organizations is clearly not a prerequisite for rapid deployment of the NII.

The purpose of this book is not to think about how formal *de jure* standards might best be developed, but to consider how standards work as a dynamic, living process—a dialog about technology and how limited common implementations of technology may be useful to enable interoperability and spur market development.[4] Under this view, the test of effectiveness is not the achievement of a consensus that allows a standard to be published by a standards development organization (SDO). The test lies in the market response to the standards process and its expressions—reference models, architectures, draft specifications, or standards—and in the further response of the standards process to the market. The challenge is to determine how this process can effectively bootstrap the evolution of a technology, from conceptualization and innovation to commoditization.

Three Models for NII Standards Development

This expanded view of standards activity was not occasioned by the NII but has been evolving out of experience in the computer industry and the Internet over many years. However, the initiative for an advanced digital NII and the critical importance of interoperability give new urgency to understanding, improving, and expediting standards processes. This task requires first taking the special technological, institutional, and policy characteristics of the emerging NII into account. To this end, it may be useful to consider the three distinct models for standards development converging in the NII: the competitive, market-driven model of computer software and applications; the collaborative, flexible and innovation-based model of the Internet; and the more traditional and formal practices in the telecommunications industry, now pushed by deregulation and the prospect of intense competition.

The Applications Model: Intense Competition and Ad Hoc Consortia

Computer programs are in themselves notoriously susceptible to interoperability problems: debugging one function may induce unexpected behavior in another function, and an inadvertent incompatibility in interface code may result. The more complex the program, the greater the challenge of ensuring internal consistency.

The democratization of computing over the past fifteen years has lead to an extremely competitive market for software applications that integrate an increasingly complex set of functions while remaining highly reliable. (In fact, designers seek to hide this complexity from the user, which makes the software as a whole even more complex.) Fueled by the promise of greater and greater rewards as the size of the market grows, intense competition has spurred short product cycles and extremely rapid technological change.

In this fiercely competitive environment, consumer loyalty is highly inelastic because of the time invested in learning one vendor's system and the difficulty of migrating either one's data or one's abilities to a competitor's system. Companies with proprietary interests in specific products and their interfaces recognize these "network effects" as well as the extraordinary scale economies in software. Such powerful market dynamics are an inducement to set *de facto* standards, either cooperatively or competitively. Alliances, consortia, and other ad hoc efforts come and go as firms seek to expand the market or to defend against market dominance by others.

The Internet Model: A Cooperative Platform for Fostering Competition

The Internet is another arena of rapid technological change central to the evolution of the NII. Unlike microcomputer software, which builds on standalone computers and their operating systems, the Internet has developed around the exigencies of communications among disparate computers over disparate networks. The Internet achieves its interoperability through a series of consensus-based protocols, which have enabled the implementation of a software- and dataset-defined constellation of networks. These logically defined networks overlay a heterogeneous physical infrastructure of computers, LANs, campus-area networks, leased lines, and routers.

The dramatic growth of the Internet testifies to the network economics that underlie the development and adoption of its standards. The Internet demonstrates the powerful externalities of commoditized interconnection leveraging off sunk investments in private infrastructure, and of virtual interconnection leveraging commoditized physical interconnection.[5] More importantly for our purposes, the Internet demonstrates the remarkable potential (although perhaps the outer limits) for standards development and implementation in concert with rapid technological change.[6]

The success of the Internet can be attributed in part to the long-term involvement of a relatively small community of computer scientists who saw the Internet as a collaborative enterprise in which they served as designers, developers, and users. They understood that the large number of alternative paths for technological evolution meant that standards must be open to new technology,

anticipate future innovations, and either accommodate anticipated innovations or minimize the cost of accommodating them
later. Experimentation prior to formal standards adoption has
been key. It was part of the culture, and it has been facilitated by the
openness of UNIX operating system that was a common tool for
most of this community.[7]

The challenge of commercialization is squarely presented by the
convergence of the Internet with the market for applications
software, now formalized by the bundling of Internet connectivity
into operating systems for personal computers. As the Internet
grows and the technology develops, the standards processes and
the communities working them naturally become more heterogeneous and diverse. Interoperability becomes harder to achieve as
the functionality of the NII expands and draws in more and more
vendors, and it remains uncertain how well Internet-style standards
processes will scale.[8]

Interoperability has been achieved on the Internet because it has
been continually tested in the interplay between anticipatory
standards development and implementation. In the experimental
and open environment of the Internet, innovations have been
routinely made available to a large number of computer-literate
users eager to explore new ideas and tolerant of imperfection.
Feedback from experience has flowed quickly and freely. This
pragmatic learning by doing combined with public dialog on long-
term architectural issues must be encouraged, even though there
is growing interest in acquiring and maintaining proprietary advantage.

Quite likely, the procedures of the Internet Engineering Task
Force (IETF) will not work as well with a multitude of stakeholders
in a commercialized environment where large investments are at
stake. While testing for interoperability in an environment as
heterogeneous and complex as the NII threatens to be nearly
impossible, it is doubtful whether users of the NII, most of whom
will be technically unsophisticated and accustomed to telephony
levels of service, will accept NII technology that has not been
thoroughly tested across the many competing but interoperating
systems it may invoke. Thus conformance testing for interoperability,
which is unreliable, expensive, and difficult to implement using

standard commercial product assurance methods, will have to depend on collaboration between vendors and both private and government users cooperating as they have in the Internet. Indeed, for such reasons, testing is often put forward as a candidate for government support.

Rapid digitization and growing demand for new value-added services are pushing different industries onto the Internet and into contact and competition with each other. This industry convergence makes it very difficult, indeed inappropriate, for standards to be dealt with in traditional industry-specific fora.[9] It also threatens to politicize the standards process by elevating self-interest above shared interest in technology and market development.

The Telecommunications Model: From National-Level Management to Open Competition

Facilities-based telecommunications, the "superhighway" aspect of the NII, has characteristics of both the applications and Internet models. Like the Internet, it is fundamentally oriented to two-way communications and issues of interconnection and interoperability. However, the telecommunications industry was built as a classic mass-market provider—an omnipotent monopoly providing a simple, undifferentiated universal service. Indeed, historically, the telecommunications industry was well-suited for the traditional standards development process. Motivated by the need for internal and external interconnection, nationwide monopolies (generally owned by the government, except in the U.S.) found that international standards development organizations allowed the industry to adapt to change on its own terms.

There is every expectation that the Congress (and governments in other countries) will proceed with progressive deregulation of this industry. This means that the importance of standardization will grow, while the government's authority to dictate standards will weaken. Yet these standards must not only accommodate the market failures of a deregulated industry; they must support the much more complex networks of the NII.

These three models—applications, Internet, and telecommunications—each of which is in some respects inherited as a model for the NII, circumscribe the principal issues in the standards landscape. All increasingly confront a common environment of complexity and rapid change in which an array of strategic elements must be evaluated and balanced by a growing and unstable mix of stakeholders. All face the paradox that standards are critical to market development but, once accepted by the market, standards may threaten innovation, inhibit change, and retard the development of new markets. These risks require standards processes to be future-oriented.

Traditional standards development, in which standards emerge when vendors and users have formally agreed that the time for commoditization of the technology has arrived, is poorly suited to anticipate unrealized technologies and their untested uses. Since the rules for traditional standards require supermajorities of voting representatives of users as well as producers, it is very difficult to create standards in anticipation of applications not yet widely practiced. The traditional process may get high marks for fairness but is often criticized for being time-consuming and for enshrining past practices that no are longer state-of-the-art.

The applications, Internet, and telecommunications models all embrace anticipatory standards development, but in very different ways. In the 1970s, the International Standards Organization (ISO) developed a top-down vision for Open Systems Interconnection (OSI), premised on a seven-layer reference model intended as an architectural framework for digitized telecommunications. Internet/IETF practice, which is often contrasted with the long-term, committee-driven OSI vision, breaks down the dichotomy between anticipatory versus reactive standards by promoting an iterative standards development with concurrent implementation. The applications model is actually a constantly changing field (sometimes a battleground) of players: dominant firms that set *de facto* standards on their own; strategic alliances of two or more firms; and consortia, which may look like anything from large alliances to trade associations to something approaching the traditional SDO.

Increased Prominence and Sophistication of Users

In the world of analog telecommunications, before users were allowed to attach their own equipment to the network, it was clear who was a vendor and who a user. In a digital information infrastructure, users in one context are likely be vendors in another. Users may include resellers, integrators, publishers, value-added networks, libraries, or companies with private networks, as well as individual end-users. Except for the end-users, all of these are also vendors. For example, an MIS department is a vendor to individual end-users within the company. Thus, the vendor/user distinction is of less value for classifying stakeholders than it is for describing relationships within a complex infrastructure.

Although users are likely to understand the technology less well than vendors, they are likely to have a better sense of their requirements, more so as they gain experience with the technology, either on their own or through outsourcing. Over the past two decades, users have become more numerous, more sophisticated, and very wary of being locked in by vendors offering proprietary technologies. Although users generally demand open systems, vendors naturally want to secure their customer base as much as possible. While most vendors claim that their systems are open, they may try, usually in non-explicit ways, to keep them from being fully open and nonproprietary.

In addition to the expanded universe of users, providers of complementary products and services may also have a major interest in standards activity.[10] Such third-party providers include information systems consultants and services, specialized hardware and software producers serving niche markets, and even government agencies investing in public service applications. In fact, technically, most users other than mere end-users provide products and services that complement the products and services they acquire from vendors, even if they are not immediately adjacent to each other on the distribution chain. This interrelationship of activities in different areas and niches of the infrastructure is further complicated by substitution effects, e.g., the substitutability of compression for bandwidth. It is also complicated by the difficulty of drawing fixed functional boundaries in the digital environment. For example: what can be implemented in software can also be implemented in hardware; operating system software may accrete features formerly found in applications software.

Complements and substitutes create a skein of interdependent relationships that influence the evolution of *de facto* standards. In an NII in which interoperability and openness are essential architectural features, virtually every subsystem affects and is affected by the entire complex of systems. Indeed, this is why it now makes sense to speak of a digital information infrastructure quite distinct from the collection of self-contained systems that convey analog information.

Emergence of Standards Consortia

The most striking change in the institutional arrangements for standardization in the information industry is the emergence of a large number of consortia assembled, principally by vendors, to address issues of compatibility and interoperability that impede the aggregation and growth of markets.[11] Some consortia consist of only a few companies, and might be more properly described as ad hoc alliances. At the other extreme, the Object Management Group (OMG) has some 500 members, 40% of which are headquartered outside the United States. In the OMG case, a broad acceptance of *de facto* standardization is required to create a market for reuse of software "objects."[12]

The push for standards-oriented software consortia has many roots. The dramatic slowdown in growth of the U.S. computer industry at the end of the 1980s led many vendors to respond to customer frustration over lack of interoperability and the high cost of applications development by promoting open systems. Another factor was the emergence of distributed systems based on the client-server model as the dominant mode of computation. This created opportunities for systems software houses, drove IBM and Apple to collaborate on end-user software compatibility, and triggered the UNIX "wars" when UNIX was seen as the interoperability environment of choice. Other factors included the loss of dominance of mainframe-based software systems architecture and the emergence of RISC architecture chips to drive high-speed work stations.

Consortia come in many flavors. They may be horizontal (among competitors), vertical (between integrators and suppliers), or comprised of firms providing complementary products and services. They may develop specifications, patentable technology, or tools and platforms. They may be structured as stock companies, exclusive non-profit organizations, open trade associations, or ad hoc interest groups. They may assert varying degrees of proprietary interest in the technology they develop and, subject to antitrust constraints, may license rights in many different ways. Consortia may seek to accelerate the process for a formal standard by some form of agreement among key producers, which then enables SDOs to invoke their consensus process in a much shorter time than usual. If, however, a consortium can succeed in obtaining *de facto* market acceptance of its technology, it may bypass the formal standards process altogether.

Because of their flexibility and ad hoc nature, consortia enjoy a number of advantages over SDOs. In many cases, management commitment to the objectives of the consortium is much higher. The financial commitment, whether in the form of fees or equity interest, is usually higher, sometimes much higher. On the other hand, consortia that are operated like businesses run into a complicated set of strategic concerns about how they may compete with or otherwise relate to the business interests of their members.

There are some policy problems with consortia. Bypassing the standards development organizations may sacrifice the benefits of a consensus process that addresses the concerns of users (including the government) and other affected parties. However, some consortia, such as PDES, Inc., are user-based, and there are ways that consortia can be designed to address these concerns. A related matter is antitrust liability, particularly when vendors constitute a dominant share of a market and are developing standards outside the formal process. In today's more permissive antitrust environment this has not been a serious limitation, but given the scope for interpretation in antitrust law, this will always be a concern both as a matter of public policy and as a risk for consortium participants.

Competition from consortia may actually stimulate SDOs to shape up and accelerate their work. Indeed, there may be a symbiotic relationship of sorts. Consortia may be well-suited to the early stages of the standards process, where they may compete with each other or with non-member companies. SDOs may be well-suited to vetting and refining the work of consortia and to extending and solidifying a consensus as an international standard.

There is some concern that consortia are diverting funds that might otherwise have been made available for participation in formal standards processes. While that may be possible in the computer industry, it is probably much less so in telecommunications, where it is difficult to bypass the SDOs and regulatory bodies.

Rethinking the Role of Government

Governments may affect standards processes in many ways:

• By procuring information technology for government purposes or as part of a public sector service, such as education;

• By conducting or investing in research, whether on generic technologies or on specific applications;

• By seeding development of resources or services as a strategic investment (e.g., the NSFNET);

• By mediating private sector competition through regulation (such as FCC mandates) or legislation (e.g., intellectual property laws);

• By convening diverse interests and facilitating cooperation across industry and sectoral boundaries.

These functions have been performed under very different circumstances by agencies operating under a variety of programmatic and policy frameworks. With no coherent framework for standards policy per se, standards have been viewed as a strategic issue within applicable policy domains.[13] The convergence of these traditionally distinct policy domains can result in conflict. For example, rather than adopting a single set of network protocols for government use, the research agencies were involved in developing the TCP/IP protocols while the federal information resource management (IRM) community was directed to procure OSI-capable products.[14]

While the divergence of OSI and Internet within the Executive Branch agencies vividly illustrates the problem, it goes far deeper. Not only is there no coherent body of law or directives, there is no common venue or forum for standards policy at the federal level. The executive branch standards-setting agencies (NIST, the General Services Administration, and the Defense Information Systems

Agency) only support the government's own procurement needs. The policy-making interests of the federal government may in themselves be too balkanized to oversee development of standards policy.[15] Of course, the lack of venue only reflects a long-standing assumption that standards are a private sector responsibility except as specific public interests—health, safety, telecommunications, government procurement, and international trade—are involved.

Until the past fifteen years, there has been remarkably little literature on standards from either a strategic or public policy perspective. The major international standards bodies, the International Standards Organization and the International Electrotechnical Commission (now merging), saw their role as maximizing efficiency in trade, not addressing innovation and systems relationships in very rapidly evolving technologies. Sensitivity to strategic aspects of standards has come only with the pervasiveness and ongoing challenges presented by information technology. Awareness of policy issues is of even more recent origin, spurred by observation of powerful network effects and externalities.[16] Today, the major standards bodies are struggling to define how they can play a more active and constructive role in international technology policy.[17]

Accordingly, it is only relatively recently that agencies have begun to grasp the full strategic importance of standards within their traditional programmatic domains and to realize that these concerns are shared to varying degrees across agencies. In the case of procurement, a coordinating perspective was fashioned in the "Brooks Act," which charged NIST with the development of the Federal Information Processing Standards.[18] At the same time, the growing sensitivity of the FCC to the subtleties of deregulation led to a greater understanding of the interplay between politics and economics in the standards process. The dogmatic refusal of the FCC to provide leadership in setting standards for AM stereo in the early 1980s provided an object lesson that stands in contrast to the restrained but determined strategic role the agency played in the HDTV proceedings a decade later.[19] In the HDTV case, the agency helped maneuver industry away from the analog MUSE standard developed by the Japanese and toward a digital standard, and nudged the several proponents of particular digital standards towards a cooperative "Grand Alliance."[20] In effect, the FCC engaged industry in a dialog that moved firms to agree on a voluntary standard, since they knew that otherwise the FCC would mandate a standard.

During this same period, the federal research agencies played a major role in supporting the evolution of the Internet and its protocols. The success of the TCP/IP protocol suite for commercial internetworking and the success of the Internet itself demonstrate the potential of strategic investment in platform technology, even if the results cannot be fully anticipated. Furthermore, the standards processes developed by the IETF and supported in part by the government stand as an important paradigm for evolving standards and technology together in an open, efficient, and highly effective manner.[21]

It is only with the NII initiative and the formation of the Information Infrastructure Task Force that these diverse policy domains begin to converge in practice. Standards are now identified as a common element in major components of the initiative: standards for competitive interconnection in support of telecommunications policy reform; standards to enable the reengineering of government's own operations and public services; standards to advance high-speed networking, to support "grand challenges," and to enable widespread applications in health care, manufacturing, and education.

Interoperability and the Focus on Openness

During the past year, a growing attention to interconnection and interoperability as central characteristics of the NII has forced a public examination of how interoperability can and should be achieved. Is interoperability best achieved through the application model developed under market forces with strong influence from a single well-capitalized provider (such as Microsoft)? Or is it better achieved through a public process that results in nonproprietary specifications (as in the case of the Internet)? Or through the use— or threat of use—of government regulatory authority, as in the case of HDTV? Or some mix of all three? Does the answer depend on what interface or what level of infrastructure? Some interfaces might be deemed more "critical" than others, or at least more politically sensitive. Alternatively, it might be argued that proprietary incentives are more important for certain aspects of the infrastructure—operating systems, for example—than others.[22]

A thoughtful paper issued by the Computer Systems Policy Project (CSPP) in February 1994 took a stab at some of these questions.[23] The CSPP paper identifies four critical interfaces— appliance to network, appliance to application, application to application, and network to network—and asserts that specifications for these interfaces should be "open." CSPP's definition of "open" allows for proprietary specifications provided they are licensed on reasonable, nondiscriminatory terms. However, to be considered open, proprietary specifications can be changed only with notice and opportunity for public input. While the CSPP paper is remarkably specific in this regard, it does not explain how this degree of openness could or should be enforced.[24]

The CSPP requirement of notice and public process is an ambitious effort to strike a balance between proprietary control and competitive fair play. On one side of CSPP, Microsoft claims that its Windows applications program interface is open because it is published and freely available; on the other side, Sun maintains that critical interfaces should be "barrier-free," i.e., completely nonproprietary, like Internet protocols.[25]

Should different aspects of the NII be viewed differently on the basis of historical differences? Or on the basis of economic differences? Telecommunications networks, especially at lower levels (basic services, facilities, rights of way, spectrum), have traditionally been subject to regulatory oversight. Operating systems, by contrast, are protected as intellectual property and not subject to institutionalized oversight. Like networks, operating systems may be subject to antitrust scrutiny, and in some circumstances operating systems could conceivably be viewed as "essential facilities" that, under antitrust law, must be available to all comers on reasonable, nondiscriminatory terms.[26] Some would argue that the threat of antitrust action is not enough and that powerful network effects, economies of scope, and practical advantages accruing to providers of operating systems require close, ongoing oversight.[27]

Standards and Intellectual Property

The debate around critical interfaces in the NII reveals the growing tension between the push for widely implemented standards to support interoperability and the desire to retain incentives for proprietary investment. This is not a simple matter. There are complex strategic issues on the standards side, and unresolved and controversial issues of both substantive law and policy and administrative process on the intellectual property side.

One aspect of the conflict is illustrated in the recent attempt by ETSI (the European Telecommunications Standards Institute) to require members, including American manufacturers, to declare in advance intellectual property rights, including patent applications in process, that might affect standards work to be undertaken by ETSI.[28] If a company wanted its proprietary technology to be considered for a standard, the company would have to commit to licensing it on specified terms. The manufacturers protested and ETSI was forced to back down. However, the risk of unanticipated proprietary rights holding up standards processes remains and seems likely to grow, especially in the United States, where patent applications are not published prior to grant and can suddenly issue with a priority that predates the standards work.[29]

Standards activities have expanded to encompass the development of complex, technologically advanced platforms, while in the United States, at least, patents have become easier to enforce and costly to defend against. A wide variety of patents on software processes have been granted (many improvidently, but nonetheless endowed with a strong presumption of validity), and the availability of patents for software processes has led many small firms, even individuals, to pursue strategic patenting. Unlike the large firms that traditionally dominated telecommunications technology, these patentees may have little interest in cross-licensing because they are focused exclusively on licensing rather than manufacturing and provision of services. They are unlikely candidates to participate in standards processes but may have the power to stop them cold. In any case, these non-manufacturing patentees are likely to be more aggressive and unyielding in their demands than the large, established companies. The large companies are not only accustomed to cross-licensing, they have ongoing relationships with each other, a stake in the stability of the market and standards processes, and a reluctance to engage in behavior that invites public scrutiny and government intervention.

There is continuing uncertainty about the extent to which interface specifications can be controlled by either patents or copyright: if not directly, then by patents on underlying functionality or copyright on implementations that have resulted in *de facto* standards. The scope of copyright protection is unclear in several areas, including the user interface and the structure, sequence and organization of computer programs. A particularly persistent and emotional controversy concerns whether it is permissible under copyright to decompile software to understand how it functions.[30] There is U.S. case law to the effect that decompilation is permitted, at least if decompilation is done to develop a complementary (interoperating) product rather than for a substitute (competing) product. However, there are major stakeholders who are concerned about the risks of unauthorized decompilation and believe fervently that it should never be permitted.[31]

Uncertainty about the scope of control provided by intellectual property law may work to promote defensive standardization. This can take many different forms, from new collective standards activity to relatively open *de facto* standards, such Microsoft's freely licensed common user interface for Windows. The dynamics of this process, and the public policy implications, may get quite complicated. For example, if the decompilation issue were resolved so that any decompilation is clearly prohibited, this would strengthen proprietary *de facto* standards. This might lead to lasting control of the standard by the owner or to costly and risky countervailing efforts to develop an alternative standard. From a public policy standpoint, these outcomes might be less desirable than a weaker form of proprietary control that fostered a less adversarial evolution of the standard.[32]

These issues need to be understood in terms of system dynamics. We have observed that there are many forms of standards activity short of the formal international standards processes—corporate alliances, standards consortia, and other forms of voluntary cooperation among firms to achieve interoperability as a means of expanding or stabilizing markets. Similarly, there are many other ways to maintain proprietary advantage short of prosecuting patents and asserting copyright. Trade secrets, employee contracts, lead time, trademarks, embedded knowledge, goodwill and reputation, and employee skills are all elements of proprietary strategy that, if not "property" in the strictest sense, also serve as intangible capital of more or less predictable value.[33]

An Enabling Strategy

Visions, rather than plans, should guide public/private NII strategy. Public policy should enable the evolution of demand for new applications and the supply of new technologies to create yet more opportunities. Mixed and balanced demand- and supply-driven strategies are needed: Demand cannot be expressed for emerging applications until they are realized, and many NII technologies offer new opportunities as well as more efficient ways to address today's demand.

The goal embodied in most NII visions is a dynamic evolution of national capabilities to satisfy a great range of economic, social, educational, and security needs. The role of standards strategy is to identify those elements whose standardization will not just commoditize the NII (as might be expected from a traditional consensus product standards process), but will keep open the maximum range of opportunities for realizing public benefits. An efficient enabling strategy seeks the minimum number of agreements needed to facilitate the maximum number of public applications and opportunities for private business growth. This is analogous to the technology strategy pursued by some high tech manufacturing companies, such as NEC in Japan.[34] In short, standards strategy for the NII should be enabling, not prescriptive.

A More "Projectized" and Staged Process

Timely standardization for the NII cannot be expected from traditional standards development organizations (SDOs).[35] The checks and balances in their processes are intended to ensure against premature, market-distorting standardization and provide

time for sufficient marketplace experience so that users' views can
be strongly represented in the standards development process.
While lack of user input remains a risk in NII standardization, it is
a risk that must addressed by open lateral communications, not by
procedural hurdles in a confined process.

Because of the difficulty of achieving interoperability in a complex heterogeneous infrastructure involving different industry
segments with different technology bases, NII standardization
must be addressed as a concurrent engineering problem. It requires the coordinated engagement of SDOs, industry standards
consortia, government policy makers, regulators and implementors.

More generally, the standards process has to be concurrently
integrated into a complete strategy for innovation and implementation—i.e., "projectized."[36] It must anticipate and encompass a
number of distinct phases, from research and reference modeling
at one end to deployment at the other.[37] The critical issue, of
course, is how this concurrent approach can be brought about. If
standards are to evolve and diffuse from the interplay of market-
based applications interfaces, Internet-style cooperative protocol
development, and telecommunications standards, some institutional mechanism for coordinating this interplay is necessary. The
government will have to suggest how this will come about and
participate in it, both from the perspective of its own operational
interests and its stewardship of the public interest in the development of the NII.

A More Automated Process

The success of Internet standards has been attributed in part to the
fact that they are developed using the Internet itself as a communications medium. This speeds communications, substitutes for
some meetings, and broadens input and participation. Many SDOs
have at least adopted electronic mail to facilitate their work. A
related issue is electronic publication of standards, which can
reduce the cost and inconvenience of accessing standards documents. However, some SDOs rely on sales of paper copies as
important source of income and have been reluctant to move to
electronic distribution.[38] On the other hand, free electronic dis-

semination accelerates deployment and use, providing important and timely feedback to standards development process. Where there are competing standards, as in the case of Internet and OSI protocols, this will likely afford a strategic advantage.

Financing Standardization Activities

The "voluntary" consensus standards process is entirely dependent on the willingness of firms to finance the participation of their engineers in standards activities. However, such participation is costly, and only firms that have clearly perceived strategic interests in the technology are likely to participate. All other firms who benefit from their work, whether vendors or users, are "free riders."[39]

This free rider problem means that there is chronic under-investment in standards activity.[40] As indicated above, many SDOs try to address this problem by selling standards documents to help recover overhead and other costs. But if standards deployment is a concern, as it certainly is in an infrastructural context, then this, too, is economically suboptimal.

Thus, in both development and deployment, there is a classic public goods problem in funding standards processes. This problem is by no means unique to standards needed to support the NII, but in the NII the powerful network externalities at work leverage and disperse the benefits in many different directions. In general, the more open the standards and systems of the infrastructure, the more the benefits go uncaptured. So there are strong arguments for public subsidy of standards processes, especially at an early stage where the technology is generic and the payoff in marketable applications is most remote. There is also justification when significant public interests (such as management of government information) are directly involved.

In fact, the government has played an important role in indirectly funding standards processes through R&D investments, including work on Internet protocols and other specific needs of the Department of Defense and other mission agencies. In recent years, ARPA has shown strong interest in funding in standards work in the "services" level of information infrastructure (i.e., security, accounting, directory management, and other functions that are needed by a wide variety of applications). Recently, a seventy-million-dollar consortium, the National Information Infrastructure Industrial Protocols, was set up with substantial funding from the Technology Reinvestment Project. But despite the economic arguments and the recognized importance of interoperability to NII development, no coherent rationale for federal government funding of information infrastructure standards processes has yet been articulated.[41]

Identifying and Engaging Users

Some believe that vendor interests are ultimately incompatible with open systems, which are seen as the best path to interoperability. To the extent that this is the case, provision must be made for a standards process that is strongly representative of user interests. But in an advanced information infrastructure, there are multiple levels of users with varying interests, some established, some inchoate. The government is itself a major user, or more accurately, collection of users. Individual agencies may represent different user perspectives, and the government as a whole may have conflicts between its interests as a consumer and its public policy responsibilities.

Access to government information, participatory democracy, improved schools, health care delivery, and library services are featured in many discussions of NII benefits. Librarians, clinics, school officials, enthusiasts for community access, and, of course, NII policy-makers from all sectors are surrogates for the consumer interest in these areas. But these surrogates all depend on third parties for technical knowledge on how their interests can best be reflected in standards. By contrast, for the electronic commerce and enterprise integration applications of the NII, the end-users include many large companies that are directly represented by their own technologically sophisticated employees.

Clearly, standards processes need surrogates for the general public. But who are those surrogates? How do we give them legitimacy when they come up against well-established commercial interests? Over many years NIST and its predecessor, the National

Bureau of Standards, have balanced the agency's role as an independent technical support for a rational process of give and take among producers and between producers and consumers and its role as a surrogate for the public in the standards process.[42]

Connecting Standards Policy and Intellectual Property Policy

Just as standards development is commonly viewed primarily as a set of technical problems and not as a matter of public policy, so intellectual property is commonly viewed as a set of rights to be interpreted in court primarily by the application of precedent to particular facts. However, standards and intellectual property should be seen as complementary systemic functions, both of which are responses to market failure. Standards processes attempt to minimize redundancy, waste, and transaction costs by articulating a common public approach to technology and market development. Intellectual property systems address appropriability problems by creating and enforcing private interests in technology and market development. "Standards" are best viewed as a process, not merely as officially sanctioned and published end-products; similarly, intellectual property should not be seen as a set of preordained rights protecting particular technologies, but as a system to promote investment and a body of public knowledge. Predictability is an essential feature of both standards and intellectual property.

Ideally, standards processes, intellectual property, and market competition should operate in dynamic equilibrium. In practice, this has not always been the case. As information technology has developed, there has been confusion and controversy about the relationship between the value of anticipatory standards and incentives needed for private innovation, a problem that becomes all the more pressing in the context of a widely interconnected and interoperating infrastructure. However, there is no framework for dealing with anticipatory standards policy in disputes between two private parties in a precedent-oriented legal system. Indeed, the strategic and policy environments for standards and intellectual property are addressed by two different communities—engineers in the standards arena and attorneys in the intellectual property arena—with little common language.

Conclusion

The debate about critical interfaces has helped focus the larger questions about the role of government in standards processes. The network/appliance interface (commonly associated with the "set-top box") seems to call for the closest scrutiny because it is the locus of convergence for so many industries, regulated and unregulated. There is widespread concern that control of this interface, whether through vertical integration, intellectual property, or sheer market power and positioning, would grant extraordinary leverage in many directions.

How real are these possibilities? And, to the extent they are real, what policy tools do they call for? There is clearly reluctance to trust the government to step in as a regulator absent some demonstrated economic dysfunction. With all its resources, the FCC is struggling conspicuously in efforts to reregulate cable. Can it be entrusted with a far more complex and extensive infrastructure? FCC regulations are frequently appealed and often overturned. Such regulatory and legal processes add yet another dimension of uncertainty to the volatility of the market and changing technologies.

Nonetheless, the "set-top" is the entry point into the home, where the government's role as surrogate for the general public is most apparent. It is also a microcosm of the NII, a focal point for heterogeneity and diversity. As in the HDTV proceeding, perhaps the threat of intervention should be the big stick that is carried but never fully used. But here the challenge is greater than herding four or five competing technological perspectives toward a clearly envisioned goal. It is inducing cooperation among a half dozen industries with different business and regulatory models in the pursuit of a vision of interoperability that has not yet found its full expression in public policy.

De facto NII standards will emerge whether or not the government plays a significant role in organizing and leading standards activity. However, full realization of Internet-style interoperability requires institutionalized, technically insightful, industry-spanning capacity to develop anticipatory standards. This capacity must accommodate the strategic applications interfaces emerging through highly competitive markets (moderated by antitrust restraint). It also depends on artful negotiations by the Congress and the FCC in the deregulation of facilities-based providers. It calls for both public-private consensus and leadership to help the consensus come about. Here government appears to have a critical, if restrained, role.

Does the balkanization of standards policy require a remedy? As long as interoperability remains the key technology and market development issue in the NII, we believe it needs to be addressed in a more focused and coherent manner than present institutions allow. Furthermore, even though standards development will continue to be carried out in a variety of organizations already engaged in standards making—the IETF, ANSI X committees, and other non-governmental bodies—standards policy requires federal leadership. Where might this leadership be most effectively institutionalized?

The Information Infrastructure Task Force is a logical venue. However, standards policy cuts across the three principal committees of the IITF. Furthermore, the private-sector NII Advisory Council is not structured in a way that could usefully address standards strategy. It would be possible to set up another virtual agency like the IITF along with its own private sector advisory council, but it would likely be perceived as competing with the IITF and the schedules of its meeting-weary members. It would be preferable to set up new working groups to address cross-cutting issues such as standards policy within the IITF, in effect providing a matrix structure.

The Commerce Department is another logical home, but here again standards policy cuts across well-established divisions. NTIA, NIST, PTO, and the Office of Technology Policy all have important interests in different aspects of standards. Of the four agencies, only NTIA and NIST have economists on staff, and only NIST has experience with standards processes. NIST's mission does not preclude policy development, but NIST has seen itself as a technical research agency that does not attempt to resolve major interagency policy issues. In addition, standards policy has traditionally been handled by the Commerce Department's secretarial staff, with NIST in technical support. (It should be noted that NIST and the Office of Technology Policy are both part of the Technology Administration, while NTIA and PTO are on their own.)

The FCC, an independent agency that implements legislation enacted by Congress, probably has the resources and depth to address standards policy effectively, but primarily within the domain of the facilities-based service providers, i.e., only the lower levels of the NII. The 1994 telecommunications regulation reform legislation that passed the House with near unanimity would have had the FCC undertake a broad investigation of interoperability in interactive communications services.[43] While the FCC has a competent professional staff, the agency is primarily concerned with implementing legislative policies. For example, in the reform legislation, the FCC was specifically charged with using the study to shape regulations for cable converters and other consumer premises equipment, as well as reporting to Congress on the overall study.[44]

There are groups outside government but having government participation that might be candidates for a leadership role. The Information Infrastructure Standards Panel launched by ANSI in June 1994 is designed to oversee and help coordinate NII standards activities in the private sector. The IISP does not develop policy, but to the extent it succeeds in its goals, it will obviously minimize the need for institutionalized private sector involvement in standards policy. Government could decide to place heavy reliance on this group and participate more extensively.

It is hard to tell where the still growing focus on interoperability will lead. It may be difficult to generate political concern for standards policy unless there is a prominent crisis around set-top devices, or an antitrust case, or a patent problem. Rather than deal with standards policy in a context of crisis or prolonged litigation, we would rather see a concerted proactive effort, endorsed by the Administration and chartered by Congress, to assess the value and role of interoperability in information infrastructure. Chartered by Congress with a modest budget for independent research, a National Commission on Interoperability Standards could combine the perspectives and insights of the public and private sectors and reflect the array of converging industries and users. A four-year charter should get us through the most critical phase of NII development. The secretariat for such a commission (and the venue for appropriations to support the government's role in the commission) would have be vested in a single agency. Given the locus of the NII Initiative, our suggestion would be the office of the Secretary of Commerce, with NIST and NTIA tasked to provide supporting analysis.

Notes

[1] Although this chapter draws from the contributed papers and the discussion at the June 1994 workshop, it does not attempt to derive any consensus from the workshop. The views expressed are solely those of the authors.

[2] For an explanation of layered architecture for the Internet, the opposite of the "stovepipes" mentioned above, see Computer Science and Telecommunications Board and National Research Council, *Realizing the Information Future.* Washington DC: National Academy Press, 1994, pp. 47–51.

[3] See Martin C. Libicki, "Standards: The Rough Road to the Common Byte," in this volume.

[4] Through FCC regulatory processes, telecommunications standards may have the force of law, while other NII standards will emerge as formal published documents from the traditional voluntary consensus-based process. Both types of standards are called "*de jure*" by many people, while some prefer to limit "*de jure*" to legal mandates, referring to the second category as "formal" standards. "*De facto*" standards do not enjoy either the force of law or the legitimacy of the traditional formal processes, but derive their status from market power. Because of the extreme inelasticity of customer demand for those *de facto* standards that enjoy very wide market acceptance (such as Microsoft's Windows or IBM's CICS transaction software), their effect may be close to that of *de jure* standards.

[5] The market for the provision of public Internet services is still very small, probably less than $300 million in 1994. The capitalization of Internet service providers is even less impressive because the Internet is constructed of leased lines. The real costs of the Internet are in the billions of dollars invested in private networks that were typically justified for internal purposes, not for public interconnection.

[6] See William Lehr, "Compatibility Standards and Interoperability: Lessons from the Internet," this volume.

[7] UNIX is almost unique among the popular computer operating systems in that when it first appeared its source code, written in a highly functional language, was widely available. Users, especially those in universities, were permitted to modify it experimentally. UNIX is supported by virtually every hardware platform in the computer industry and is used for interoperations among heterogeneous systems. The TCP/IP protocol was added to Bell Laboratories' original UNIX by scientists at the University of California and was popularized by Sun Microsystems.

[8] Internet protocols are developed by the Internet Engineering Task Force, which is now part of the Internet Society.

[9] ANSI has addressed this problem by inaugurating the Information Infrastructure Standards Panel, which is designed to ensure that all necessary NII standards are effectively addressed by industry. The Cross-Industry Working Team, housed at the Corporation for National Research Initiatives, works to develop inter-industry consensus on the architecture of generic services.

[10] D. Teece, "Capturing Value from Technological Innovation: Integration, Strategic Partnering, and Licensing Decisions," in Guile, Bruce R. and Harvey Brooks, *Technology and Global Industry: Companies and Nations in the World Economy*. National Academy Press, 1987. pp. 65–96. See especially pp. 65–75 and discussion of complementary assets.

[11] See Andrew Updegrove, "Consortia and the Role of the Government in Standard Setting," this volume.

[12] See Richard Soley, "OMG: Building Industry Consensus," this volume.

[13] See Robert Mark Aiken and John S. Cavallini, "When Are Standards Too Much of a Good Thing? Will They Provide Interoperability for the National Information Infrastructure?", this volume.

[14] See *Report of the Federal Internetworking Requirements Panel* 31 May 1994. The set of protocols known as TCP/IP (Transmission Control Protocol/Internet Protocol) was originally developed by the U.S. Department of Defense for the ARPANET and is now the standard for communication on the Internet. The Open Systems Interconnection (OSI) model was created by the International Standards Organization in an effort to prospectively define international networking standards.

[15] These include the FCC (an independent agency), the National Telecommunications and Information Administration (NTIA), the State Department, the U.S. Trade Representative, the Congress, and the federal courts.

[16] Some core works on standards include Berg and Schumny (1990), Besen and Farrell (1991), Bonino and Spring (1991), Cargill (1989), David (1987), David and Greenstein (1990), Farrell and Saloner (1986), Farrell (1989), Gabel (1987), Garcia (1993), Kindleberger (1983), Lehr (1992), Libicki (1993), OECD (1991), OTA (1992), Weiss and Cargill (1992), and Weiss and Sirbu (1990). See bibliography for this volume.

[17] *A Vision for the Future: Standards needs for emerging technologies*. Geneva: ISO/IEC 1990, page 5–9.

[18] NIST has independent authority to develop standards for federal computer systems under the Brooks Act (P.L. 89-306). As amended by the Computer Security Act of 1987 (P.L. 100-235), the Brooks Act charges NIST with "developing standards, guidelines, and associated methods and techniques for computer systems" and for "developing technical, management, physical and administrative standards and guidelines for the cost-effective security and privacy" of unclassified, sensitive information processed by federal computer systems. NIST works with many national, international and regional organizations to develop

standards which become the basis for Federal Information Processing Standards (FIPS). FIPS are approved by the Secretary of Commerce and issued for use by federal government agencies in their information technology activities. This includes Department of Defense activities that process unclassified information.

[19] See, e.g., Klopfenstein, Bruce C., and David Sedmen. "Technical standards and the marketplace: The case of AM stereo." *Journal of Broadcasting and Electronic Media* 32(2):171–194.

[20] See Suzanne Neil, Lee McKnight and Joseph Bailey, "The Government's Role in the HDTV Standards Process: Model or Aberration?" this volume.

[21] See William Lehr, "Compatibility Standards and Interoperability: Lessons from the Internet," this volume.

[22] See Jim Isaak, "Information Infrastructure Meta-Architecture and Cross-Industry Standardization ," this volume.

[23] *Perspectives on the National Information Infrastructure: Ensuring Interoperability.* Computer Systems Policy Project, February 1994.

[24] In an alternative view, *Realizing The Information Future* (see note 2) envisions an "open data network architecture" with four layers: bearer service, transport, middleware, and applications (pp. 44–52). The bearer service, a bit conduit located between the physical infrastructure and the higher-level services, is identified as the site where open standards are most crucial for interoperability. The report defines an "open" data network as one that permits universal connectivity for users, competitive access for service providers, interconnection by network providers, and change over time. It does not specify how companies would be persuaded or obliged to follow this vision.

[25] See Jonathan Band, "Competing Definitions of 'Openness' on the NII," this volume.

[26] Indeed, the common thread running through many civil antitrust suits against IBM in the 1970s (mostly resolved in IBM's favor) was competitors' demands that IBM share operating system interfaces to input-output equipment before IBM's own I/O products were put on the market. Similarly, applications software developers have argued that Microsoft's advance knowledge of changes in its Windows applications program interface gives Microsoft an unfair advantage in the development of applications software. Recently Microsoft has been subject to antitrust investigations by the Justice Department and Federal Trade Commission for this and other reasons.

[27] See Joseph Farrell, "Arguments for Weaker Intellectual Property Protection in Network Industries ," this volume.

[28] See Mark Shurmer and Gary Lea, "Telecommunications Standardization and Intellectual Property Rights: A Fundamental Dilemma?", this volume.

[29] It is not surprising that such issues came to the fore first in Europe, as ETSI has a very ambitious standards development program in trying to create a common market for telecommunications services. Both ETSI and CBEMA (the Computer and Business Equipment Manufacturers Association, recently renamed the

Information Technology Industry Council) contributed position papers to this book shortly before the ETSI policy was withdrawn. CBEMA advocated the position of the American manufacturers.

[30] See Band.

[31] It is unclear, however, how such a prohibition could ever be effectively enforced.

[32] See Farrell.

[33] Patents are thought to be the strongest form of intellectual property because they protect against any kind of use and against independent creation. However, the value of software patents is likely to be more unpredictable than some of these other intangible assets because it so difficult to locate and definitively assess prior art, the nonobviousness standard is difficult to apply, claims are often abstract and nontechnical and therefore hard to interpret, and the law on the scope of patentable subject matter is confusing and unsettled.

[34] The NEC strategy is to look at all the possible technologies and to identify the minimum number of technologies necessary to support the maximum number of market opportunities. NEC R&D executives focus their R&D effort on that minimum number of technologies and say to the marketing people: "Your problem is to figure out what markets to address with this core competence." See Lewis Branscomb and Fumio Kodama, *Japanese Innovation Strategies: Technology Support for Business Visions* (Lanham, MD: University Press of America, 1993). In the case of the NII, of course, the issue is not strictly the minimum number of technologies requiring investment, but the minimum number of common denominator constraints on freedom of action.

[35] Some standards groups rooted in the telecommunications community, such as JTC-1, have been effective in providing a diverse set of standards that enhance options for addressing system diversity. There are also techniques to expedite channeled processes, which should not be overlooked. Since bargaining over differences can be very protracted, successful SDO committee chairs sometimes seek initial commitment on willingness to act on agreed key principles by forcing a vote on whether it is time to vote on the unresolved issues. This agreement to agree, not unlike the approach used in the Montreal Protocols for international limits on production of chlorofluorocarbons, structures and expedites the process.

[36] The need, and the term "projectize," was articulated by James Crawford at the June 1994 workshop.

[37] See Carl Cargill," A Five Segment Model for IT Standardization," this volume.

[38] The 1992 OTA report, *Global Standards—Building Blocks for the Future,* expressed concern about the possible impact of this dependence on publication revenue on the objectivity of the standards process.

[39] See Michael Spring and Martin Weiss, "Financing the Standards Development Process," this volume.

[40] This is a problem in all market economy countries, where national standards development is a private sector activity, but U.S. firms seem to be more reluctant to invest in formal standards activities than are their counterparts in Europe and Japan.

[41] One workshop participant noted that his Federal research grant had words in it that expressly forbade him from using funds for standards work.

[42] Technical experts from NIST and other federal agencies serve on hundreds of voluntary consensus standards development committees. Through their expertise on test methods and other aspects of standardization they work to resolve or reduce technical disputes. But to varying degrees over past history the government has expected these public servants to serve as surrogates for unrepresented elements of the affected public. The extent to which this is an appropriate role for NIST in the NII is basically a political question.

[43] See H.R. 3626 (incorporating H.R. 3636), "Antitrust and Communications Reform Act of 1994," 103rd Congress, June 30, 1994, Section 405(b), p. 181.

[44] Ibid, Section 405(c).

The Standards Problem

Standards: The Rough Road to the Common Byte

Martin C. Libicki

Introduction

The proliferation of digital devices—each with its own way of representing and communicating information—has heightened the importance of getting these devices to talk to one another, to their applications, and to their users in mutually comprehensible tongues. Success—speaking the common byte—is prerequisite to building organizational and national and, ultimately, global information infrastructures. Failure leaves islands of connectivity, keeps systems expensive, difficult to use, and inflexible, and retards the flow of useful technology into society.

Information technology standards have been touted as a means to interoperability and software portability, but they are more easily lauded than built or followed. Users say they want low-cost, easily maintained, plug-and-play, interoperable systems, yet each user community has specific needs and few of them want to discard their existing systems. Every vendor wants to sell its own architecture and turbo-charged features, and each architecture assumes different views of a particular domain (e.g., business forms, images, databases). International standards founder on variations in culture and assumptions—for example, whether telephone companies are monopolies—in North America, Europe, and Asia. Protests to the contrary, the U.S. government is a major, indeed increasingly involved, player in virtually every major standards controversy.

This paper looks at the growing but confusing body of information technology standards by concentrating on seven areas: The

UNIX operating system, Open Systems Interconnection (OSI, for data communication), the Department of Defense's Continuous Acquisition and Life-cycle Support program (CALS), the Ada programming language, Integrated Services Digital Networks (ISDN, narrowband and broadband), multimedia standards (text, database, and image compression), and five specialized standards (encryption, electronic chip design, machine tools, maps, TRON). Each realm is examined from several viewpoints: the problems that need to be solved, the degree of success of standards, the role of public policy in the standards process, and major trends in each area. A subtheme throughout is the persistent divergence between the perspective of the commercial user (standards are but one possible solution to the problems of interoperability) and that of government as both customer and policymaker.

What Standards Do

Good information technology standards are common conventions for representing information as data so that finicky but increasingly indispensable machines may speak the common byte. Standards play a key though poorly understood role in the Information Era. Without them, the trillions of bytes on the Net would make little sense, intelligent machines would lose much of their brainpower, one type of equipment could not work with another, and all the data being so busily created would be accessible only to the creators.

In many ways standards are technical matters of little obvious significance; mention them and listeners' eyes glaze over. Most standards arise with little fuss, while others feature tedious Tweedledee-Tweedledum conflicts of no real import. Yet fights over the important standards matter, because the outcomes affect the architecture and politics of information. Standards require convergence on the correct question as well as the correct answer.

The fundamental issues of standards are reflected by the most basic information standard: human language. A good language has certain properties. It represents meaning efficiently and avoids unnecessary ambiguity but is robust against noise and error, ensures that a word can group like concepts, and, finally, remains alive, that is, flexible enough to absorb new meaning. Language has an architecture; it reflects and reinforces the ways by which societies construct human discourse. Thus results the extensibility of English, the logic of French, the lyricism of Italian, the fluid formality of Japanese, and the social range of Russian. Language can make particular concepts easy or difficult to convey. Life would be simpler if everyone spoke the same language, but they will not, and for good reasons.

Information technology standards exist to solve three problems. The first is interoperability, that is, getting systems to work with one another in real time (for example, telephone systems). Failure could prevent communication, but most of the time a kluge to glue systems together is sufficient. The second problem is portability, which permits software to work with heterogenous systems (for example, a consistent computer language). Again, failure could lead to closed systems, but most of the time software can be ported if more code is written to accommodate each system (or functions are dropped). The third problem is data exchange among different systems (for example, wordprocessing files). Failure could mean loss of access to information, but most of the time translators work, although with a cost in effort and dropped details. Successful standards share the ability to facilitate plug-and-play systems and induce competition among potential software and hardware providers, thus lowering costs and raising choices.

Interoperability, portability, and data exchange are usefully distinguished from one another when evaluating the need for and reach of specific standards or the consequences of their absence. Standards have costs. A convention that fits the general may be inefficient for the specific. When standards enable certain functions they inhibit others. A standard often limits efforts to extend and maintain what is standardized. The wait for standards may cause technologies to miss their markets.

All good standards go through two steps: invention and proliferation. Most are also formalized in standards bodies (sometimes prior to proliferation). Proliferation is usually more important than formalization (which is too often the focus of standards studies). De facto standards offer many of the virtues of de jure ones, particularly if the latter are a waste of time (or, worse, yet one more check-off in a government bid). But formalization has advantages: it opens the review process to outsiders (e.g., users, small vendors, and third parties), generally improves definition, and aids the inclusion of the standard in government purchases.

At the international level, communications standards come from two committees of a treaty organization, the International Telecommunications Union (ITU): the ITU-T for telecommunications and the ITU-R for radio. Computer standards come from the voluntary International Organization for Standards (ISO). NATO standards often subsume those of the United States Department of Defense (DOD).

At the national level, the American National Standards Institute (ANSI) charters committees, trade groups, and professional societies (such as the Institute of Electrical and Electronic Engineers [IEEE]) to write standards. Government standards are set by the National Institute of Standards and Technology (NIST). The DOD, the largest U.S. buyer of goods and services, is influential, as is the Federal Communications Commission (FCC), the spectrum regulator.

Often proliferation is driven by strong bandwagon effects. A standard that appears to be winning will garner more support in the form of software, training, expertise, and drivers. Potential winners offer users the possibility of interacting with an increasing number of other users. Growing sales mean lower costs for conforming products. All these make the standard more appealing and lengthens its lead. Accidents of birth or early support, by starting a virtuous circle, can make a large difference in a standard's success. Can a targeted government purchase constitute sufficient early support to drive the market toward convergence on a standard? In theory, yes, but it is risky. If the market pulls away from the government (e.g., Ada, OSI), government users may be stranded. Alternatively, convergence may be forced before the embedded technology has been proved superior.

Correct comprehensiveness, timing, and family relationships influence the success of a standard. Figure 1 shows some choices involved in choosing a standard's scope. A standard may cover only the core of a solution—that is, the functions supported by all vendors. In this case, proprietary ways of dealing with peripheral functions can frustrate interoperability for years. An overly comprehensive, perhaps anticipatory, standard, however, may cost too

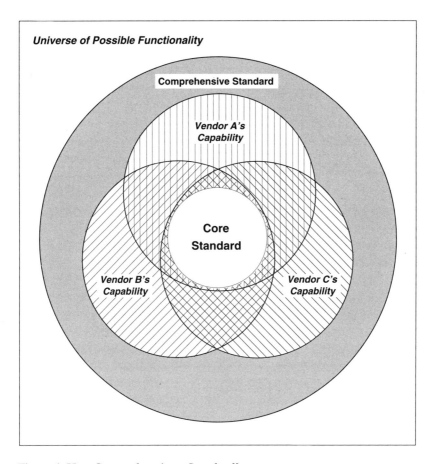

Figure 1 How Comprehensive a Standard?

much to implement. By supporting alternative ways of representing essentially similar functions, such a standard can frustrate unambiguous translation between two systems. An intermediate solution is to take a large problem and divide it into layers, standardizing each. This is easier said than done, particularly if, as with data communications, standard solutions at one layer and nonstandard solutions at another do not interact well.

When should standardization occur? Premature standardization leaves no time for the market to smooth the kinks and separate out nice-to-have from need-to-have features. Late standardization yields

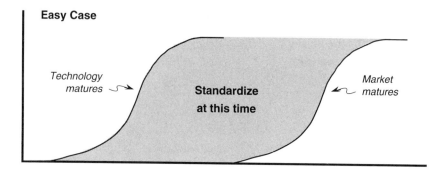

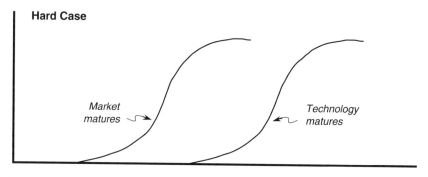

Figure 2 When Should a Technology Be Standardized?

years of market confusion and the need to cope with a proliferation of variants that arise in the interim. If the technology matures before the market takes off (see Figure 2), standardization can occur smoothly in between. What if the market threatens to take off before the technology matures? With image compression, technology keeps getting better; a premature standard may either forestall further progress or itself be swept away by better but nonstandardized solutions.

Figure 3 shows standards clustered in families. Because a member's takeoff often carries another along, a coherent standards strategy pushes related standards. In contrast, the federal government has promoted the Ada computer language, the UNIX operating system, the OSI data communications model, and the Standard General Markup Language (SGML) text formatting system, all from competing families. Ada competes with the C computer

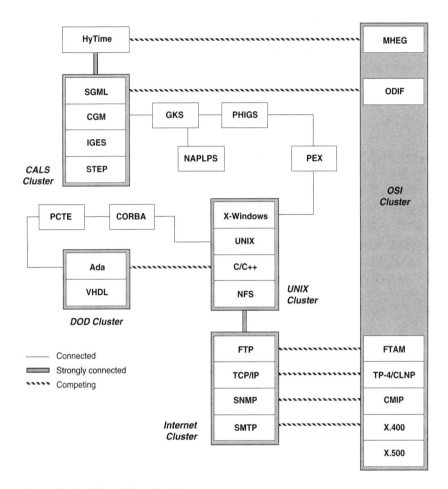

Figure 3 Families of Standards.

language from the UNIX family; UNIX is strongly associated with a specific transport protocol (the transmission control protocol/ Internet protocol [TCP/IP]) that conflicts with OSI's, while the OSI community is associated with an open document interchange format (ODIF) that competes with SGML.

Beyond technical issues, standards influence the architecture of information. A choice of computer languages implies a relationship of programmers to their managers and to one another. Compared with a top-down communications protocol, a bottom-up one facilitates different flows of information and different social relations. Standards that make it easy to exchange and annotate computer-aided designs are related to the status of manufacturing engineers relative to that of design engineers. Because the problems standards solve are not always perceived the same way, choices among solutions influence who is connected to whom, what is expressed easily and what requires effort, whose needs matter, and who exercises influence. Standards have been touted as a way to avoid the Scilla of chaos and the Charybdis of monopoly; they shape the struggles of competing vendors and their technologies and the power of vendor versus user.

Standards also affect larger issues:

• The timing, shape, and potential of the national (and international) information infrastructure

• The internal structure of organizations (for example, from hierarchical to horizontal) and their external relationships (for example, virtual corporations)

• Choices among systems designs, from tightly integrated (which tends to be efficient) to tightly interfaced (which needs standards but is more flexible)

• The form information is likely to be seen in—linear (such as text), linked (hypertext), or lateral (database)—with further effects on the changing roles of writer and reader in providing coherence

• The speed with which new technologies come into use

• The competitiveness of the U.S. software and systems integration sector

Indeed, there are very few information issues standards do *not* affect.

Each of the seven topics presented below illustrates a theme that sets the virtues of standards against obstacles to the realization of standards. The openness of UNIX (for example, source code in public domain), for instance, has made standardization difficult. Users rejected OSI in favor of a protocol with fewer features that worked by the time they needed a standard. The DOD's Continuous Acquisition and Life-cycle Support program is impeded, because its computer-aided design (CAD) standards attempt to bridge competing paradigms of spatial information. Ada was invented for managers but rejected by programmers. The narrowband integrated services digital network (ISDN) has a known architecture and slow-to-settle standards, while broadband versions are the opposite. Multimedia standards to bring together tomorrow's digital libraries have been called for, while the requisite technologies are still jelling. Five specialized standards (encryption, electronic chip design, machine tools, maps, and TRON) illustrate the weakness of public standards policy in the face of market forces.

The Open Road

Standard interfaces between layers of software—whether to run programs or to communicate data—permit the construction of systems from mix-and-match parts and free users from dominance by a single vendor. In the 1990s, all vendors pay lip service to open systems, but agreement ends there. The computer industry needs as many words for "open" as Eskimos need for snow.

Is the PC DOS architecture open? Although its well-defined software and hardware interfaces and hundred million plus user base make it a proved mix-and-match technology, one company controls the operating system and another the microprocessor. Most applications markets are dominated by a single vendor, and software struggled for years against the (640K) memory limitation that resulted from early standardization. In some respects the Macintosh, whose box and operating system come from one company, Apple, is more closed than the PC DOS system, but a well-defined user interface freed customers to switch among competing software applications without sinking time into becoming familiar with each.

Even though IBM opened its mainframe architecture by the early 1980s to allow development of plug-compatible machines, third-party peripherals, and a robust software base, many defined open as any system that would get them out from under IBM's thumb. The UNIX operating system is available from open sources but comes in so many flavors that an era of mix-and-match software is still years away. Proponents consider OSI open because it was developed in a formal process in a public forum, yet the scarcity of applications in the United States forces users to pay a premium for conforming products. To advocates of high-definition television (HDTV), open means "capable of absorbing new technology within the standard," while to the federal government, open systems mean those that can be specified in a request for proposals (RFP) without the need to mention either specific vendors or branded products.

UNIX. Open and standard, although apparently synonymous, can conflict. Openness helped UNIX spread: UNIX was the first operating system in use not exclusive to any one brand of computer (antitrust rulings kept its parent, AT&T, from selling computers). That plus the availability of its source code made UNIX popular in universities, an environment where writing and sharing code are common. When the government needed an operating system to use as a test-bed for artificial intelligence (AI) and networking, UNIX (in the version refined at Berkeley) was there to benefit. As computer scientists and engineers flowed from academia into business, they brought with them their fondness for UNIX, opening a large market for UNIX-based minicomputers and workstations. By the mid-1980s UNIX was the dominant operating system on workstations and by the end of the decade had driven most proprietary minicomputer operating systems (and many of their vendors) out of the market. UNIX is poorly suited for mainframes and microcomputers, which make up two-thirds of the market, but it dominates the remainder: supercomputers, minicomputers, and workstations.

The features that made UNIX fun to play with led to a proliferation of dialects, inhibiting the creation of a mass applications market. Personal computer users enjoy a consistent applications binary interface (ABI) that lets any software run on any machine. The absence of a dominant architecture for workstations or minicomputers (or of any successful architecturally neutral distribution format [ANDF]) limits the odds of a shrink-wrapped UNIX software market. The standardization of UNIX can, at best, foster a common applications portability interface (API), so that when source code is compiled on different machines it will act in similar ways.

Formal UNIX API standards include POSIX from an official body (IEEE) and XPG from an unofficial body (X/Open, a consortium of vendors active in Europe). XPG is more comprehensive than POSIX, but POSIX, developed in a neutral forum, has been chosen by the federal government to define UNIX. POSIX compliance, however, can be claimed by many non-UNIX systems, which allows those system to compete for government contracts when UNIX is what is really wanted.

The search for a de facto common UNIX has been a busy mating dance. Through the mid-1980s UNIX was split between versions based on AT&T UNIX and Berkeley UNIX. In 1988 AT&T united with Sun (whose co-founder helped write Berkeley UNIX) to create what was hoped would be a standard UNIX. The rest of the industry, in opposition, formed the Open Software Foundation (OSF) to develop its own version. Although the new split stalled unification, it prompted each group to compete in complementing UNIX with graphical user interfaces, network file systems, distributed computing environments, and multiprocessing architectures. In 1993, under the threat of Microsoft's Windows NT, UNIX vendors banded to support a common open systems environment (COSE).

UNIX illustrates several themes in standards:

• Standards reflect the communities they come from. UNIX's growth among small machines and within the academic environment gave it enduring characteristics: well-understood building-block function calls, cryptic names, poor documentation (UNIX users do not need user-friendly), good communications, but generally weak operational and database security.

• A respected but disinterested developer makes becoming a standard more likely. AT&T played that role for UNIX. (MIT played it for X-windows, a machine-independent graphical user interface associated with UNIX.)

• A standard does well to start small. Vendors (or their consortia) can compete to add functionality; surviving features can later be massaged into standard form.

• The openness of a technology can be inimical to standardization if vendors can tweak the source code in different ways to meet specific needs.

If Windows NT makes UNIX extinct (a prospect that seemed more likely the year before Windows NT was released), UNIX's lack

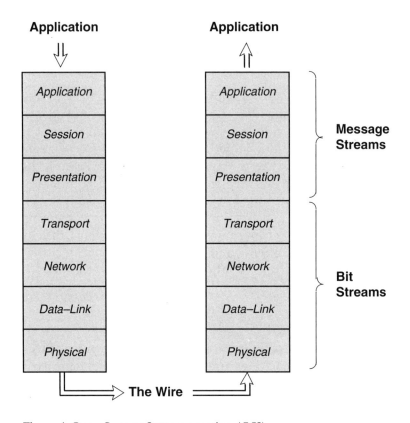

Figure 4 Open Systems Interconnection (OSI).

of standardization will have been a contributing factor. Otherwise, even though UNIX is not standard, it still hosts most work on the cutting edge of computer technology; it is the operating system on which even microcomputer operating systems are converging.

OSI. In contrast to UNIX, which started off in a corner, OSI saw life as a comprehensive reference model for data communications that only needed to be filled in by actual standards to thrive.

The OSI reference model breaks down the problem of data communication into seven layers; this division, in theory, is simple and clean, as shown in Figure 4. An application sends data to the *application layer*, which formats them; to the *presentation layer*, which specifies byte conversion (e.g., ASCII, byte-ordered integers); to the *session layer*, which sets up the parameters for dialogue; to the *transport layer*, which puts sequence numbers on and wraps check-sums around packets; to the *network layer*, which adds addressing and handling information; to the *data-link layer*, which adds bytes to ensure hop-to-hop integrity and media access; to the *physical layer*, which translates bits into electrical (or photonic) signals that flow out the wire. The receiver unwraps the message in reverse order, translating the signals into bits, taking the right bits off the network and retaining packets correctly addressed, ensuring message reli-ability and correct sequencing, establishing dialogue, reading the bytes correctly as characters, numbers, or whatever, and placing formatted bytes into the application. This wrapping and unwrap-ping process can be considered a flow and the successive attach-ment and detachment of headers. Each layer in the sender listens only to the layer above it and talks only to the one immediately below it and to a parallel layer in the receiver. It is otherwise blissfully unaware of the activities of the other layers. *If* the stan-dards are correctly written, the services and software of any one layer can be mixed and matched with no effect on the other six.

Intent on inventing an optimal protocol, OSI's developers ended up with something not so much optimal as invented. They created standards that detail a wealth of functionality, with little market feedback on what features were worth the cost in code or machine resources. OSI standards were a long time in the making, complex with options, difficult to incorporate into products, and a burden on system resources such as memory and clock cycles.

The standards took time to fill in. The IEEE provided local area network (LAN) standards; the ITU-T supplied both the X.25 standard for public packet switching and the X.400 electronic mail standard. The rest of the OSI standards were laboriously written during the early to mid-1980s.

Because many layers of the OSI model featured several OSI standards and because the standards were laden with options, profiles of standards (e.g., one from layer A, two from layer B) were needed to ensure interoperability within an OSI architecture. In the early 1980s General Motors sponsored a profile, the Manufac-turing Applications Protocol (MAP), with a top layer that format-ted instructions to automated factory equipment and two bottom layers that shuttled bits along a token bus factory LAN. Profiles were also developed for the electric utility industry and air-ground communicators. The most complete profile, shown in Figure 5, is the government's OSI profile (GOSIP), which became mandatory for federal purchases after August 1990.

With a reference model, standards, and profiles in hand, advocates took their show on the road—or the promise of a show; what with late standards spelling later products, they entered a world many of whose needs had been met by other standards. Most were proprietary (e.g., IBM's Systems Network Architecture [SNA], introduced in 1974). OSI's most serious competition, however, came from another open suite, the Internet's, which covered core application functions (e-mail, file transfer, remote terminals) plus transport and address mechanisms. The standards process for the Internet was completely different from that for OSI. For every new problem engineers would hack together a solution and put it out on the Internet for users to try out. If the responses were favorable, the solution was a standard.

Thus the problem of transition strategies was born: how to build a new network protocol suite in place of, around, or between existing suites. Figure 6 illustrates four strategies: bridging, gateway, dual-host, and encapsulation, each serving a different function.

Bridging places feature-rich OSI application layer protocols atop proven TCP/IP networks. It works by slipping in a layer of code to translate OSI's application function calls into terms the transport layer understands.

Gateways allow existing networks to communicate with other networks in a lingua franca. For every X.400 native e-mail system, for instance, there are ten X.400 gateway translators to glue other e-mail systems together.

Dual-host (more commonly, multihost) computers permit machines on heterogenous networks to use their own protocols to access a common resource (such as a supercomputer).

Encapsulation lets machines on two OSI LANs talk to each other through a TCP/IP wide area network (WAN). OSI address and transport information are treated as raw bits by the TCP/IP network, which wraps its own envelope around the data.

The four, billed as transition techniques, became in practice accommodation techniques (or general glue methods for any two protocols). OSI appears valuable primarily for its e-mail and direc-

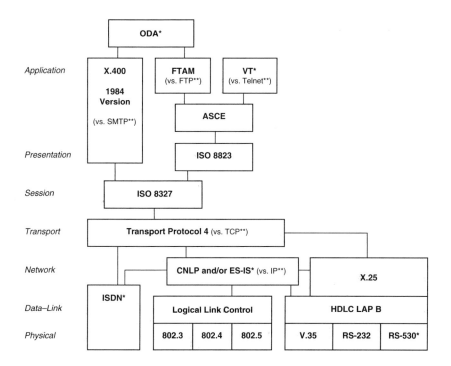

*Requirements of GOSIP 2, but not GOSIP 1. ODA, although not an ISO protocol, was included in GOSIP, because it provides services the OMB feels are required by federal agencies. Another protocol, CONS (connection-oriented network service, ISO 8878), is not shown, because it is *optional* and may be specified to link systems directly connected to X.25 WANs and ISDNs (and systems not GOSIP-compliant).

**Indicate Internet equivalents for some GOSIP standards.

Figure 5 The GOSIP 2 Stack.

tory standards (X.400 and X.500). Of the four strategies, bridging and gateways will probably garner the most attention.

Most experts initially felt that the triumph of OSI, though slow, was inevitable. A study done in 1985 for the DOD, for instance, recommended a move to OSI not for technical reasons but because everyone else was headed there. Since about 1990 the tide has turned. Few believe OSI will do well in the U.S., and even Europe may reexamine its commitment.

What went wrong? First, contrary to theory, one size does not fit all. OSI was too heavy for personal computers and their networks but less efficient than IBM's SNA for supporting the mainframe as the data pump. OSI was left with the middle market and the glue

Bridging

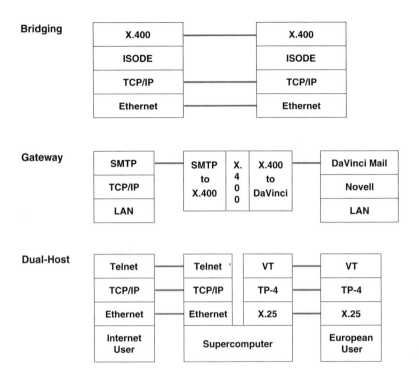

Gateway

Dual-Host

Encapsulation

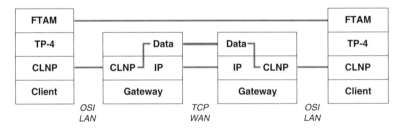

Figure 6 Infiltration Strategies.

market (sticking heterogenous platforms and networks together). The middle market went to UNIX, and thus to TCP/IP (which, for historical reasons, is free in most UNIX systems). The glue market might have gone to OSI, but when such needs surfaced in the late 1980s, OSI products were either late or too new to inspire confidence. The momentum built up by available, tested, and ready TCP/IP products and their presence on the growing Internet could not be overcome. Between 1989 and 1991 the big computer vendors, hitherto committed to OSI, backed away; by 1993 even the government was reconsidering its earlier exclusion of TCP/IP from GOSIP. The contest between rough and ready Internet standards and formally constructed OSI standards was repeated in network management (OSI's Common Management Interface Protocol [CMIP] versus the Internet's Simple Network Management Protocol [SNMP]) and path routing (OSI's Intermediate System to Intermediate System [IS-IS] protocol versus the Internet's Open Shortest Path First [OSPF] protocol), with much the same results.

Tomorrow's integrated data communications networks are likely to be a complex patchwork of proprietary protocols built around mainframes and servers (e.g., SNA and Novell's) plus Internet standards (for internetworking and systems management) and some OSI protocols (e.g., X.400 and X.500). Had the major computer companies and the government thrown their weight behind TCP/IP rather than OSI, perhaps much of the complexity might have been avoided.

Front Line Manufacturing

During the 1980s the DOD took a hard look at how information technology could promote better software and hardware, and it concluded that standards would be the core of its approach. One set of standards, CALS, was to govern the production of documentation associated with weapons systems, while another, Ada, would be the language in which defense software was written.

With standards as with any specification, the DOD always has three choices: (*i*) it can lead, by creating difficult but worthwhile challenges and supporting the search for their solution; (*ii*) it can lag, by scouting the commercial realm for good solutions and encouraging their adoption by the DOD's workers and suppliers; and (*iii*) it can mandate a separate convention that differs from what others do. The third choice is often the unintended result of seeking the first (leadership for improved interoperability) and laying claim to the second (taking standards stamped in commercial forums). Separate conventions are often worst, because they further divide the defense production base from the commercial production base. The DOD's leadership is also vitiated by mixed signals (its standards mandates compete with many more urgent internal mandates) and long development cycles (so that its standards are often out of date).

Continuous Acquisition and Life-cycle Support (CALS). The CALS initiative, begun in 1985, specifies a set of standards used in formatting text (see the next section) and images of technical data. CALS was intended to meet three goals. The first was to move from paper to write-once, read-many bytes. The second was to collect product data in CAD form for post-production support (i.e., recompeting, redesigning, and remanufacturing subsystems and spare parts). The third, concurrent engineering, was looked on as the most important goal. A common CAD file format would facilitate early and frequent exchange of information between prime contractors and their vendors, thereby injecting the considerations of manufacturing engineering into those of design—a way to raise quality and lower life-cycle costs.

Table 1 shows the DOD's four-level schema to represent technical imagery; each level permits increasing abstraction. Raster standards are for pictures, computer graphics metafile (CGM) for technical illustration, Initial Geometric Exchange Specification (IGES) for CAD data, and STEP for CAD/CAM (computer-aided manufacturing) data.

CALS requirements slowly seeped into contracts; the DOD's project managers wanted digital data without the expense of mandating conformance to complex standards. Only programs started since the late 1980s (thus unlikely to yield fielded systems this century) will get delivery of data in IGES form; the rest will rely on less manipulable deliverables.

The DOD had several choices in specifying how it wanted CAD data. It could have mandated delivery of all CAD data either in a format that was de facto a standard (e.g., Autocad's DXF) or one

Table 1 CALS Standards

Standard	Purpose	IOC	Standardized
Raster	Images	Early 1990s	1980, 1984
CGM	Technical drawings	Late 1990s	1981–1986
IGES	CAD	Early 2000s	1979–1982
STEP	CAD/CAM	Maybe never	1984–1994

from a selected vendor (e.g., Navy's systems commands buy all CAD stations from a single vendor). It could have specified two or three formats (e.g., GM's C4 program). It could have ignored the issue and purchased format-to-format translators as needed. Instead, it chose IGES, a standard labelled as commercial but one the DOD had actually sponsored in 1979.

IGES is generally disparaged by the DOD's customers. Although prime contractors respect the IGES mandate when dealing with the DOD, they rarely pass it down to their subcontractors, preferring to get data in the CAD format they themselves use. Failing that, translators are preferred. Only paper is less popular than IGES. IGES mandates almost never cross over from military to commercial operations of prime contractors, and IGES stands no chance of becoming any vendor's native file format.

Why has IGES done so poorly? In part because the standard was too broad and ambiguous. Internal loop tests (from a vendor's CAD format to IGES and back) drop a tenth of the data; external loop tests (one vendor's file format to another vendor's via IGES) drop a quarter. Thus, IGES requires the use of flavored CAD files— that is, files written with subsequent translation in mind. In addition, IGES files are ten times as large as native CAD files. Perhaps no neutral format could have worked. The underlying paradigm for CAD modeling is still evolving and therefore unsettled. IGES did not keep up.

Many observers, critical of IGES, aver that the Standard for the Exchange of Product (STEP) data will fix all of IGES' problems and more. At the very least, since the late 1980s the imminence of STEP inhibited the development of IGES. STEP is not just a better IGES, it is a completely new way to manage the data life-cycle of manufacturing, from design to production to maintenance. Advocates claim STEP avoids many specific mistakes of IGES and includes many general advances: built-in product conformance testing, the Express programming language (to ease building translators to CAD systems), and support for hierarchical decomposition of images. Most important, it supports object-oriented feature-based modeling. STEP represents a cement pipe differently from a shirt sleeve or a glass column, even though all are cylinders.

It would be easier to be optimistic about STEP if only it did not echo OSI. The standard has been ten years in the making but is still not a superset of IGES; its document exceeds 2,500 pages. Few products reify the technology STEP is supposed to standardize. Between the unpopularity of IGES and the vapor of STEP, it is difficult to see how CALS can promote concurrent engineering.

Since roughly 1990 the electronic delivery of technical data under CALS has been officially linked with the electronic delivery of business data under electronic data interchange (EDI). As a standard for business documents, the ANSI's X12 series has succeeded. When EDI was invented in the early 1970s, major buyers imposed their own proprietary forms, which were followed by forms developed by industry groups. The ANSI drew the best of these together so that, as the mid-1990s near, proprietary forms are nearly gone and applications for standard forms are now submitted by groups previously disinclined to merge their forms with those of truckers and grocers. X12, however, is a domestic standard; the international standard EDI For Administration, Commerce, and Transport (EDIFACT), little used in the U.S., is slated to supersede X12 starting in 1997.

The success of X12 may be ascribed to two factors. First, X12 did not try to solve everything at once. It started with a few forms and grew. Second, the paradigms for business data (e.g., invoices) are common and mature. Electronic representation follows closely from standard business forms. In promoting EDI, the DOD (thanks to restrictive contracting law) has not been a leader but seems, to its credit, to be following in well-plowed paths.

The contrast between the success of EDI standards and the difficulties of CAD standards illustrates the greater importance of common notions over common notations in predicting a standard's success. As Figure 7 illustrates, translation between an Ottawan's "winter" and a Quebecois "l'hiver" is easy if both refer to the same months. Similar translation between the experience of Houstonians (with their short winters) and Edmontonians (with their longer winters) is more difficult even though both use the same language.

Ada. The search for a standard computer language has been going on since the late 1950s, beginning with the development of three fundamental families. FORTRAN (formula translator) became a standard over time as the multitude of algorithms written by early users required later users to work with the language. ;Common Business-Oriented Language (COBOL) became a standard for business computation, in part because of federal pressure. Both Fortran and COBOL are based on old technology and have not spawned new languages in almost thirty years. Algol, an elegant language widely used only in Europe, spawned JOVIAL (an Air Force standard prior to Ada), Pascal (Ada's progenitor), and C and then C++, which in the 1990s is becoming the standard for applications development.

Ada was invented when the DOD found its software costs escalating partly because it was supporting more than three hundred computer programming languages. Rather than converge on an existing language, the DOD spent the eight years from 1975 to 1983 developing one of its own. Standardization followed in lock-step order.

Any analysis of Ada must address two question: Was it a good language? Has it become a common one?

Ada was designed for the large, long-lived projects that characterize defense systems. It benefits from a solid analytical foundation and supports object-oriented design and strong type checking. But it is large, prolix, and ponderous; it produces object code that tends to run slowly and tax computer resources (although the problem is lessened with newer compilers).

Ada brought unique strengths to the realm of embedded systems. It featured exception handling (so that faults do not shut down all operations), concurrence, standard interrupt handling and protection against real-time bugs, and very high host-target portability

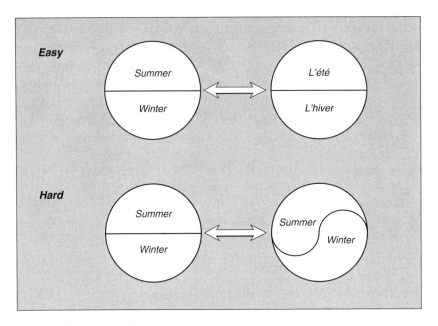

Figure 7 Translating Notations and Notions.

(Ada code is often transported from development environments to weapons). The DOD hierarchy is generally satisfied with Ada's contribution to software engineering.

As a common language, the story is different. Ada's acceptance within the DOD was assured by about 1987. Many of those forced to use Ada grew to like it, and the DOD made it hard to get exceptions. Ada has also become the language of choice for non-Defense aerospace projects (e.g., the Federal Aviation Administration (FAA), the National Aeronautics and Space Administration (NASA), Boeing, Beechcraft). Outside that community it has spread poorly; advocates enumerate its users, a fact that speaks for itself.

What hurt Ada outside the DOD? Too much time was taken determining requirements, too little fieldtesting the desirability of its features. It was solidified just before object-oriented technologies caught on. Worse, Ada's model of programming was inimical to programmers. The language implicitly assumed that programmers never document code adequately, take too many short cuts, make too many sloppy errors, and look over everyone's shoulders. Managers might agree, but programmers are put off by the restrictions in the language prompted by such perceptions.

Ada's newest incarnation is Ada 9X, a mere six years in the making (1988–94). This time around managers at least recognize the need to market Ada aggressively, exploit the established vendor base, and appeal to business users. The last focus stems from efforts to make Ada a standard language for business applications within the DOD. This is a less obvious need than supporting embedded systems; standard languages already exist in these areas (such as COBOL, or MUMPS for health applications), and Ada does not hook well to database languages and user interface tools common in such environments.

Ada's fate is in doubt. Computerdom is converging on C and its object-oriented descendent, C++. In contrast to supersafe Ada, C and C++ empower the programmers, some soaring to great heights while others crash. C is what programmers learned in school (partly because UNIX programs are written in it) and so like working in after they leave.

As the emerging standard, C/C++ is the language that today's tools support, tomorrow's microprocessors are optimized for, and the global network objects of the future will be written in. Ada users, in contrast, will always be late getting new tools (e.g., computer-aided systems engineering [CASE]), new technologies (such as object-oriented programming), hooks to operating systems features (such as windows environments), and, in the thin times of the 1990s, new jobs in commercial enterprises. Ada's vendors are retreating, and the Ada mandate is being questioned more frequently at the military's highest levels.

To the Gigabit Station

The great promise of the National Information Infrastructure (NII) is the individual's ability to access all the information in the universe—data, text, image, audio, and video (both real-time and archived)—with only a computer and a telephone. The technology to realize this promise exists; its economics are not prohibitive (fiber to the home is neither necessary nor sufficient). Two types of

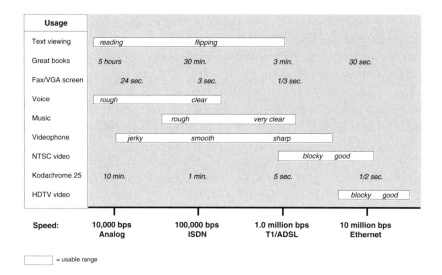

Figure 8 What Various Communications Rates Permit.

standards are necessary for realization: those that specify how users are plugged into networks and those that format the information users receive.

As an indication of potential policy choices involved in construction of the NII, Figure 8 illustrates capabilities that become available with increases in bandwidth, from today's analog telephones (equipped with a 14,400 bit per second [bps] modem), to dual-line ISDN phones (128,000 bps), to T1 rates (1.5 million bps), to Ethernet rates (10 million bps). Different uses require different bandwidths; even low-bandwidth digital networks (such as ISDN) enable powerful services.

ISDN. In the early 1980s the road to the gigabit station appeared obvious. Public telephone systems worldwide would install an integrated services digital network with circuits containing two 64,000 bps B lines (for voice, videotelephony, facsimile, and modems) and one 16,000 bps D line (for call-control information and packet-switched data).

ISDN could have been the second stage of the personal computer revolution. Its digital lines would have permitted major increases in data throughput. The D-channel services would have presented the nation's central office (CO) switches as just another personal computer device. The packet-switching capabilities of ISDN would have permitted remote command and control of the many smart machines that surround us. ISDN's compatibility with the nation's local loops makes it relatively inexpensive. The current cost of roughly $1,500 per connection (about $500 for each phoneset, CO-line card, and CO-switch software) could have dropped sharply had U.S. installations exceeded the present paltry rate of ten thousand a month.

As with many formal standards, ISDN took time. After a decade of discussion, in 1984 the ITU-T cobbled together enough specifications to make a standard. Implementation was to have followed quickly. In 1985 chipsets hit the market, then in 1986 ISDN-compatible CO switches, and in 1987 the first trials. On the heels of the trials surfaced the first reports of widespread incompatibilities among versions supported by the various CO vendors. The 1984 standard was too fuzzy, and, in its place, a tighter 1988 standard had to be specified. At about the same time, in 1987 Bellcore began to sponsor intensive discussions with individual switchmakers to develop compatible call control specifications. As Bellcore's ambitions were steadily pruned, in 1991 the talks resulted in the National ISDN-1 specification (demonstrated in installed switches a year later).

Yet ISDN has come to mean It Still Does Nothing. Progress remains slow, particularly in North America. Residential and small business services began only in 1992–93, and as yet there are few long-distance clear-channel lines. Corporate customers, which were expected to create initial volumes for ISDN deployment, could not wait, and they developed their own networks instead. Most D-channel services are now available on analog lines (although via a very complex user interface). Although ISDN may yet prevail in the absence of easy alternatives for user-driven digital communications devices, its success is hardly assured.

Its problems can be ascribed to two factors: mistargeted services and slow standardization. ISDN was sold on the basis of its services to very large customers (predominantly those with Centrex service), but their complex needs do not need ISDN to be satisfied. Instead, ISDN shines as a service for small and home offices, where workers rely on public infrastructure (rather than a corporate LAN). Phone companies ought to have thought of ISDN as wires and specs to link personal computers (for a fee) to the world; attic entrepreneurs of the sort that powered the personal computer revolution would do the rest.

Deliberately paced standards setting, although once appropriate for monopoly networks, was ill-suited to the far faster realm of computers. The divestiture of AT&T—erstwhile supplier of local service, long lines, switches, phonesets, and technology—deprived the standards community of its leader, whose mantle has only recently and not completely been assumed by Bellcore. The ISDN standard is extremely complex: providing B-line service was a snap; most of the difficulty was with the D-line switch-control functions (e.g., those targeted for large customers). The complexity of ISDN was also exacerbated by its goal of unifying phone systems around the world, yet ISDN calls require translations at many levels (trunk line speeds, analog-digital conversion, rate adaptation, interface levels) to cross the Atlantic.

The hoopla over the looming information highway has suggested to some that ISDN deployment might have been, at best, a brief rest stop on, and, at worst, a detour from that road. Broadband ISDN remains a mix of technologies, standards, and architectures that is far from convergent. In the early 1990s Bellcore demonstrated a technology, asymmetric digital subscriber line (ADSL), that, compared with ISDN, can transport more than ten times the bits (inbound only) on the same wires to the same distance (18,000 feet without signal regeneration) or, in its discrete multi-tone version, forty times as much to nearly the same distance (12,000 feet). Cable companies have the bandwidth to offer video-on-demand and even shared Ethernet-like services, although internal switching architectures and standard connections to long-distance services are still to be worked out.

For business communications ISDN defined the Primary Rate Interface (PRI), a 1.5 million bps service. Lacking a standard way to synchronize lines (as AT&T's Accunet does in a proprietary implementation), PRI is a bundle of 64,000 bps straws (good for PBX traffic, which has low growth rates) rather than a single pipe (which is more appropriate for data traffic, which grows far faster).

Since the mid-1980s business users have met their expanding needs for data communications by building private telephone systems from leased lines, notably T1 (at 1.5 million bps). Since 1991 quasi-public systems have been introduced to offer similar services. Two of them, frame relay and switched multimegabit data services (SMDS), were expected to take off, but their ascent has been slow, even though their standards processes, while leaving some holes, have been swift. Architectural issues plague acceptability. Frame relay is marketed as a virtual private system, and SMDS traffic is limited to single metropolitan areas. Neither frame relay nor SMDS effectively permits large data transfers outside pre-defined walls.

Broadband's great hope is a cell-switching technology, asynchronous transfer mode (ATM), which promises the ability to mix constant bit-rate voice, variable bit-rate video, and bursty data traffic. Its standards process has been very fast (once computer vendors perceived the LAN interconnect market and took over from the phone companies). The combination of hype (extreme even for the information industry), dozens of potential switch suppliers, a lack of serious interoperability testing among their switches, and the varied uses for which ATM is touted (campus LANs, private WAN interconnection, internets, telephone trunk lines, cable switching) warrant caution about its prospects.

If the NII can be defined by its services rather than by its switches, the Internet, whose standards became its architecture, has succeeded as a model by any measure. It reaches twenty million people on two million hosts in more than a hundred countries. To become the global information infrastructure, the Internet will need to overcome two deficiencies. First, its orientation to packet switching (coupled with nontrivial message delays and heterogeneous access rates) inhibits its support of real-time voice and video. Second, a system built to support subsidized academic and government uses is having difficulty coping with growth. New standards need to be created to expand its address space, enlarge its routing tables, and separate paying customers from free riders. To complete the circle, as Internet access becomes widely available to users outside institutions, it may drive a demand for ISDN-type access speeds and thus propel the ISDN along.

Narrowband ISDN had a settled architecture, but its standards were too long getting settled. The broadband version seems to have standardized faster, but its architecture remains in flux. Time—and success—will tell which, stable standards or settled architecture, matters more.

The Congress of Libraries. The standards that would organize the formatting, accessing, and compression of information within tomorrow's congress of libraries are in various states of repair; many are attempting to coalesce before the technology behind them has settled.

One problem is how to go past ASCII's standard for text in order to represent documents that also contain metatext (e.g., italics), hypertext (even footnotes), and images. Two approaches are possible. The first represents layout and other metatext directly; the second specifies a grammar to separate text and metatext (to be processed separately).

The DOD's CALS program selected the second approach, in the form of SGML, a standard way to define and mark nontext features. SGML technology has advantages for CALS beyond ensuring a consistent organization (and look) for DOD manuals and other publications. Formatted documents are essentially free-form databases; a marked-up document can be sliced and diced into a variety of reports. SGML also lends itself to hypertext, which many consider the best electronic expression of a maintenance manual.

By removing formatting decisions from authors, SGML supports many-to-one publishing well, but it supports peer-to-peer exchange of documents poorly. Because it is a metastandard, two systems must support a standard tag set to interchange documents. The DOD has an official tag set for technical manuals; book publishers, classicists, and airlines, among others, each have their own. All of these are different and not interoperable. Such differences may not matter initially (few classicists read tank repair manuals), but interdomain exchange and software portability require a convergence of tag sets, something less likely with every new set invented. Documents must contain (or reference) not only the material itself but also the tag set and the output specifier (to convert mark-up into page-printing instructions) before they can be exchanged.

Widespread adoption of SGML, by making one cluster of functions easier, inhibits the rise of alternative standards to facilitate other clusters. A standard extended ASCII for metatext is likely to be preempted by Unicode, a 16 bit extension to represent every language's alphabets. Other methods of direct format representation include Microsoft's Rich Text Format (which primarily supports fonts), Adobe's Postscript page-description language, and its successor, the Portable Document Format. The last may achieve de facto status for representing pages (as unrevisable images), but its use requires purchasing Adobe's software. In the absence of a common format, direct translation among popular wordprocessing formats leaves much to be desired.

Query systems for the digital congress of libraries—or, at least, the fraction kept as databases—have been successfully standardized. Following the invention of the relational database in 1969, IBM released the specifications for its structured query language (SQL) in 1976, which it commercialized for mainframes in the early 1980s. Because IBM boxes ruled the corporate data warehouse, every other major vendor of database management software felt required to follow suit and support SQL, which they did between 1985 and 1988.

Like UNIX, SQL has continued to evolve with deeper and richer colors. In 1986, SQL received ANSI imprimatur, with subsequent versions appearing in 1989 and 1992. Each successive version is more complex—sometimes following and sometimes inducing corresponding features in products. Again like UNIX, the portability of SQL, never perfect, continues to improve for the core functions, as other functions, less well standardized, are added. In 1989, the SQL Access Group was formed to tighten the standard (X/Open and NIST, too, worked on the issue). The group also sought to promote SQL's companion in interoperability, remote database access (RDA), so that clients using one database management system could access data managed by another.

Image compression is necessary for the digital library, because the picture worth a thousands words needs fifty thousand words' worth of bytes to be transmitted. Technology permits lossless compression at ratios of 10:1, acceptable lossy compression at 30:1, and workable compression at higher rates. A surfeit, not a lack, of standards is the problem. Fax machines support two standards; videophones, one; still and motion pictures one each; television, several; and the list does not include either de facto standards or efficient but unstandardized approaches.

For real-time videophone compression, the ITU-S's H.261 standard provides least-common-denominator interoperability. Every major vendor of encoder-decoder (codec) boxes claims its proprietary algorithms can support twice the data rate H.261 does at the same level of quality. They will keep the videoconferencing market, while H.261 is expected to prevail on personal computer-based systems (where clarity is less an issue because video windows are smaller than full screen).

Official standards for still and motion picture image compression (JPEG and MPEG, respectively) are gathering support. Yet, newer technologies, wavelet and fractal compression schemes (both funded by the DOD's Advanced Research Projects Agency [ARPA]), are frequently better (because they produce less objectionable artifacts at high rates of compression). Other schemes, such as Intel's Indeo and Media Vision's Captain Crunch, are less efficient but work without a dedicated hardware chip. Standardization before the technology was fully developed may be premature.

The search for a television compression standard was buffeted by two unexpected developments. The FCC's 1989 dictate that HDTV signals must fit within the narrow spectrum now allocated for analog television effectively ended the front runner status of Japan's MUSE analog technology in favor of a digitally compressed signal. In 1992, aggressive cable companies announced they could use compression to offer five hundred channels (mostly for video on demand) along existing coaxial wiring. In contrast to terrestrial service, which uses many broadcasters (each of them necessarily using the same standard), neighborhoods tend to be served by a single provider that can impose a compression format on its subscriber base. Standards are not necessary, although they can keep costs down.

Lessons and Prognostications

The search for better standards (or better paths to what standards provide) continues. The quest can be summarized by looking at five areas that illustrate the limits of government standards policy, exploring a future for standards, and drawing some lessons.

Limits of Standards Policy. Although in theory public policy can promote growth in particular sectors by adroit backing of standards, in practice its influence is circumscribed. For example:

• As the major buyer and developer of encryption and digital-signature technology, the federal government can be expected to be a large influence on creating standards, but public policy has not resolved the tension between the government's desire to support commercial security and its desire to tap into private and foreign data streams. Thus, the government's standards efforts are increasingly suspect.

• The DOD financed an electronic CAD standard, the very-high-speed integrated circuit (VHSIC) hardware description language (VHDL), and mandated it for a certain class of chips, but the standard did not catch on. Unexpectedly, however, a private firm, Cadence, boosted its own proprietary language, Verilog, to de facto status. Cadence's competitors, in response, rallied 'round VHDL, available as a de jure standard, which then took off.

• The DOD has also supported development of a standard for machine tool controllers, in part to support machine tool builders competing with Japan, which had a single controller vendor. U.S. companies earlier unable to unite on a de facto standard, however, appear unable to unite on one supported by the DOD.

• As the world's largest collector and archiver of map data, the U.S. government ought to be able to set standards for its archived data and, by so doing, influence how everyone represents map data. The government's spatial data transfer standard (SDTS) was a trifle too long in the making. In the early 1990s private repackagers of geographical data began to use incompatible approaches based on older formats.

• Japan tried to counter U.S. dominance in microprocessors and operating systems by having electronic firms adopt a single standard, The Real-time Operating Nucleus (TRON). But a standard by itself appears unable to help Japanese producers in this area.

The Future of Standards. If microcomputer markets are any indication, the conflict between closed and open architectures may be settled by the rise of owned architectures (see Figure 9). In a

Libicki

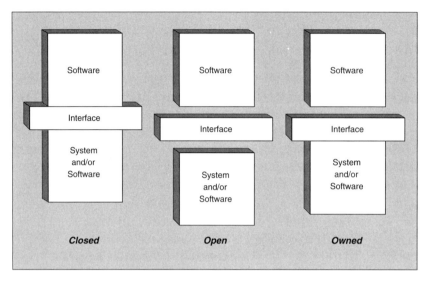

Figure 9 Closed, Open, and Owned Architectures.

closed architecture (e.g., IBM or AT&T circa 1975) a single vendor defines and sells most of the basic systems on one side of the interface and the software on the other side. In an open architecture, the interfaces are externally defined, often in open forums, and vendors compete in the segments delineated by the interfaces. In an owned architecture, a single vendor sells all or most of a segment and by its dominance establishes an interface whose specifications are released to the public. Other vendors develop products that support that interface, and thus the interface becomes entrenched as the de facto standard. The architect nevertheless retains control, either by owning the technology needed to make the interface work (e.g., Adobe) or by using a deep knowledge of the interface to stay a generation ahead of rivals (e.g., Intel).

Sometimes the architect profits solely through its market clout in the basic segment (e.g., Hewlett-Packard in laser printers). Occasionally a vendor that dominates one segment uses knowledge of the interface to dominate another. Microsoft's knowledge of its Windows environment, for instance, allowed it to jump off to an early (and perhaps sustainable) lead in Windows-compatible applications software. In contrast, its knowledge of DOS provided no

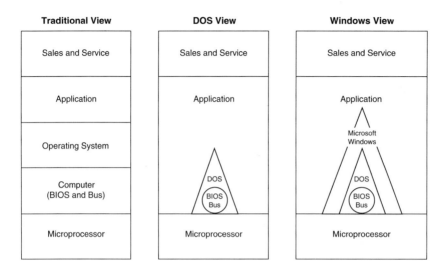

Figure 10 Altering the Interfaces of the Microcomputer World.

such advantage. Figure 10 suggests why Windows had a greater effect. Computer markets are typically shown as segmented by one-dimensional interfaces. The interface between DOS and an application tends to be short, that is, information-poor; applications write directly to the chip. The interface between Windows and typical applications is long, that is, information-rich (the applications make many calls on Windows functions). If Microsoft's object-linking and embedding technology proves functional and popular, the interface will be richer yet. The richer the interface, the more difficult to master and thus more important to control. Other vendors compete with owners of dominant interfaces, not by breaking into the original architecture but by developing new uses—such as network operating systems or groupware—that establish alternative interfaces as more important.

How useful is the layer model for comprehending standards? The OSI's travails should have suggested that layers may be misleading. Perhaps software should be understood as clusters of objects—packages that combine data-structures, data, and operations defined on the data. Such packaging provides well defined but extensible interfaces. Accessing these objects requires both standard ways to call them and standard ways to package them so they

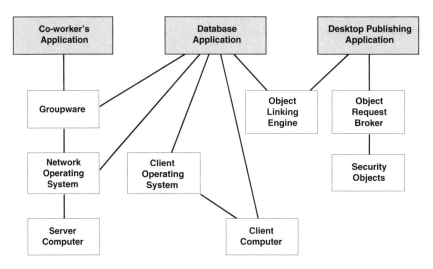

Figure 11 Objects Rather than Layers.

behave predictably. To this end, a consortium, the Object Management Group (OMG), developed a common object-request broker architecture (CORBA), which enjoys wide support but needs far more definition to be truly useful.

Powering the challenge of integration is the increasing convergence of the entire information industry. The personal computer model of a lone user on a stand-alone machine running a single application is giving way to networked groups running applications that must work with one another (Figure 11 shows a typical profile). The scale of integration is rising from the user to the office, the institution, and, sooner rather than later, the universe. With increases in scale comes a shift in the purposes of standardization, as Figure 12 shows. For the lone user standards provided familiarity with systems built from plug-and-play components made cheap through competition among clones. For the institution familiarity matters less and interoperability more; standards help users knit heterogenous legacy systems into a functioning whole. At the global level plug-and-play declines in importance, while political issues of architecture influenced by competing standards assume importance.

Interoperability is often understood as a way of making two parallel systems (e.g., workstations on two networks) talk to each

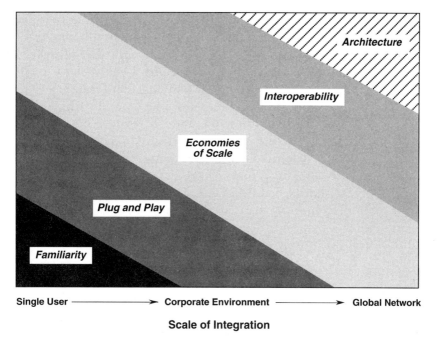

Figure 12 As the Scale of Integration Grows, What Standards Are Good for Changes?

other. Yet conversion or translation is always possible with enough work; what matters is how much. Rival products, each attempting to own an architecture, cover territory differently, and gluing them to create, say, an open database architecture may require varied methods: front-end APIs; gateways, structured and open; SQL routing; and database encapsulation. Each method emphasizes another standard, some more formal than others. The OSF melds suites in many ways at once—by incorporation, extension, hooks above, hooks below, and, if all else fails, by gateways and translation. Parts of this can always talk to parts of that, but which parts varies by case. Putting virtual layers (e.g., hardware abstraction layers) above real ones is another way standards can glue systems together. CASE, as another example, is looked to as a way to surmount problems caused by multiple computer languages, but its tools must be inter-operable—calling for yet more standards (e.g., the portable common tools environment [PCTE] from Europe).

Standards become critical for the external systems integration necessary to building tomorrow's networks, which will unite users, instruments, sensors, and software with contributions from governments, corporations, and other institutions. One network might monitor the earth's environment, trading data and rules back and forth; another may do the same for personal health, linking medical sensors with monitoring stations, expert systems, and doctors. Microstandards are needed to ensure that data (the nouns and adjectives) are defined in mutually comprehensible ways while functions (the verbs) can interact predictably.

So Many Standards, So Little Time. The worth of or rationales for information technology standards are empirical: Do conventions work? Are they common? Are they sufficient to meld heterogenous applications, products, and systems smoothly?

For those who cannot tell the standards without a scorecard, Tables 2–4 summarize standards in three ways: their status as common conventions, their origins and spread, and the influence of standards groups and the government on their development. Forty-one standards are classified according to whether they promote interoperability, portability, or data exchange, an imprecise trichotomy (many interoperability standards, for instance, promote software portability and data exchange).

Table 2 places standards in one of eight groups (largely on the basis of how they fare in North America). *Winners* are well accepted conventions subdivided into *stable winners, unstable winners* (which may be overtaken, particularly by microcomputer conventions), and *chaotic winners* (which may spawn multiple versions at higher speeds). *Niche* standards are stable within a well-defined segment but failed to penetrate the entire market; some (e.g., Ada, ISDN, CMIP) may, for that reason, be considered *losers*. *Comers* are not well accepted but seem to be growing toward that status. *Babies* have yet to emerge strongly into the market; they are divided into *healthy* and *sick* on the basis of their prospects. *Losers* are self-explanatory.

The volatility of information technology, and thus, supposedly, its standards, may call such judgments into question, yet the stability of the fate of these standards over the two years since initial assessments were made is remarkable. The few shifts worth noting include:

Table 2 The Status of Specific Standards

	Interoperability	Portability	Data Exchange
Stable winners	SNMP, Group 3 Fax, SS7, Fanuc Controller	BIOS/DOS, SQL, VHDL	Postscript, TIFF
Unstable winners	TCP/IP, X-Windows	UNIX	EDI X.12
Chaotic winners	802 LAN, Modem		
Niche	CMIP, MUSE, Z39.50, X.400/500, ISDN	Ada	Group 4 Fax, DES/DSS, EDIFACT
Comers	H.261		SGML, CGM, SDTS, JPEG/ MPEG
Healthy babies	FCC-HDTV, ATM, Frame Relay		
Sick babies	NGC, SMDS	PCTE	STEP
Losers	OSI Organic	TRON	IGES

• De facto microcomputer standards may put winners from the UNIX cluster at risk

• Two CALS standards, CGM and SGML, are becoming popular more quickly than seemed likely earlier

• Official compression standards are facing a tougher fight from software-based methodologies and new technologies

• ATM may eclipse the emergence of frame relay and SMDS

   Table 3 sorts standards by origin and spread. Of the forty-one listed, twenty-four originated in the U.S. (broadly defined to include U.S.-based multinationals, imports such as Ada in response to U.S.-generated requirements, foreign nationals based in the U.S., and the now global Internet community). Although many of these forty-one are used overseas, ten are confined mainly to North America. Another twelve (eight from ITU) are considered global in origin, with strong U.S. input. Of the five distinctly Japanese in origin, two are unlikely to see much use outside Japan. As a rough generalization, the U.S. originates perhaps two-thirds of all soft-

Table 3 Source and Spread of Standards

	Interoperability	Portability	Data Exchange
U.S. origin, not exported	SNMP, NGC, TCP/IP, FCC-HDTV, Frame Relay		EDI X.12, HyTime, IGES, DES/DSS, SDTS
U.S. origin, exported	X-Windows, Modem, Z39.50, 802 LAN, SMDS	BIOS/DOS, UNIX, Ada, SQL, VHDL, CORBA	SGML, Postscript, TIFF
Global	CMIP, SS&, H.261, OSI Organic, ATM, X.400/500, ISDN	PCTE	STEP, CGM, EDIFACT, JPEG/MPEG
Japan	Group 3 Fax, Fanuc Controller, MUSE	TRON	Group 4 Fax

ware and the same share of its standards. The U.S. chairs only one-fifth of the ISO's computer subcommittees, however, and has only one vote in the ITU.

The search for the one true standard and the process of formal standardization are not the same (see Figure 13). Consensus standards may be unnecessary in some situations; where they are needed, informal arrangements may suffice. The Internet and X/Open produce workable and robust standards, and vendor consortia (such as the ATM Forum) have proved capable of filling gaps and tightening loose ends left by more formal efforts. Conversely, some formal efforts result in competing standards (e.g., SGML versus ODIF) or standards that need considerable refinement to be useful.

To supply a de facto standard a vendor does not need to be the industry gorilla. The influence of IBM on some standards has varied greatly: from positive (SQL, DOS/BIOS PCs), to neutral (its Extended Binary Coded Decimal Inter-Change [EBCDIC] alternative to ASCII, its Distributed RDA), to counter-positive (OSI and UNIX were favored to limit IBM's dominance). Will Microsoft, often viewed as IBM's successor, be more successful? User-written standards (e.g., Ada, MAP) are not necessarily winners either.

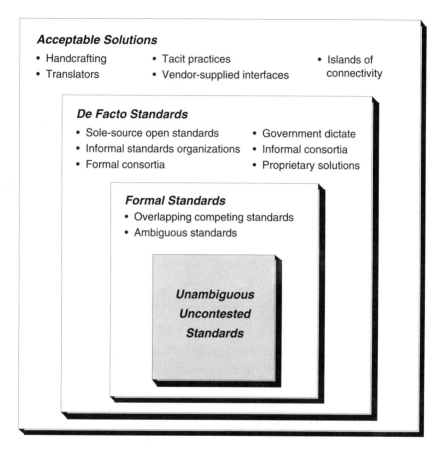

Figure 13 Standards and Standardization.

Table 4 presents standards in five categories according to the importance of formalization to their spread. *Nil* means that formal standards bodies have yet to play: personal computer standards, Internet-based standards, and those where government efforts are ongoing. For five standards, formalization came *after the fact*, that is, after development, and affected spread only modestly. Five were developed outside standards bodies and taken inside for *imprimatur*, which then became critical to their credibility. The rest, labelled *critical*, were deliberately and specifically developed in standards bodies and are mostly interoperability standards. The U.S. government has played a major role in almost half of the forty-

Table 4 The Role of Standards Organizations

	Interoperability	Portability	Data Exchange
Nil	SNMP, NGC[a], TCP/ IP[a], FCC-HDTV[a], X-Windows, SMDS, Fanuc controller	BIOS/DOS, TRON[b], CORBA	DES/DSS[a], Postscript, TIFF, SDTS[a]
After-the-fact		UNIX[b], Ada[a], SQL, VHDL[a]	SGML[b]
Imprimatur	Group 3 Fax, Z39.50[a], 802 LAN, MUSE		IGES[a], Group 4 Fax
Essential	CMIP[b], SS7, Modem, H.261, X.400/500[b], ATM, Frame Relay, ISDN, OSI Organic[b]	PCTE[b]	EDI X.12, HyTime, STEP[b], CGM[b], EDIFACT, JPEG/MPEG

a. Sponsored by U.S. Government.
b. Other U.S. Government involvement.

one standards. Nine were created by government policy or program. Three others were strongly supported by GOSIP, another three by CALS.

In spite of so much government activity, public policy does not merit high marks. NIST's emphasis on open systems, software portability, and vendor independence accurately and wisely presaged the market, but execution has been less stellar: GOSIP did little good, POSIX was a poor vehicle for UNIX standardization, and NIST lost credibility in cryptology controversies. The emphasis of the DOD on the portability of software and documentation was wise, although the uniqueness of the Department's problems are often unrecognized. The DOD to its credit has promoted TCP/IP, SGML, and CGM, but IGES is universally disparaged and the failure of Ada to win support outside aerospace (while otherwise a good language) has left its users out on a technological limb. The free market shibboleths of the FCC prevented the emergence of AM stereo and left ISDN without support, but its mandate that HDTV must fit into existing bandwidths spurred image compression. The government, lacking the heavy handedness of its European counterparts, has at least let the native U.S. genius at software proceed unimpeded.

So why has public policy not been better? First, because government is ponderous; it gets under way slowly and once a course is set plods on, well after everyone else may have taken a different path. Second, because federal policy has an inordinate respect for international standards bodies, even though the U.S. is underrepresented in them. Third, because public policy often responds to the peculiar needs of users in the government in general (such as vendor neutrality) or in the DOD in particular (such as the need to support large, centralized projects). Federal standards policy is inescapably an aspect of economic strategy: deliberate choices are made (passing the buck to an international organization is still a choice) whose success would create winners and losers and has ramifications for the entire economy (as proponents might wish, even though such efforts are technically oriented to government users only).

If the rough road to the common byte teaches anything, it is that successful standards start small and grow with consensus on the core. The linked standards of UNIX, the C programming language, and TCP/IP all started as simple, elegant solutions to problems that grew to meet increasingly complex needs; SQL or X12 started life much smaller than they stand today.

The OSI edifice, in contrast, is large, complex, and notoriously unsuccessful in North America; the parts that did well—X.25 and X.400—were not written by the ISO. ISDN has been similarly retarded by its bulk. Technologies that become standards without being tested in working products that are accepted by the market are risky. Ada is a prime example of specifications preceding realization.

Although any specific approach to standards must be sensitive to particulars of the relevant technology, applications, and markets, the one emerging from the standards community reflects these lessons: collect a small group of vendors, write a small, simple specification that covers the important functions, omit nonessentials, leave room for both new technologies and possible backtracking, identify real-world test-beds for the standard, and get it out the door as soon as possible. This approach suggests government standards policy concentrate on the following questions:

- What problem is standardization needed to solve?
- Must the problem be solved through collective means; must it be solved internationally?
- What is the smallest solution, and can it be broken into manageable chunks?
- What are the best tools (e.g., imprimatur, research and development, targeted purchases, regulation) to promote convergence that also permit backing off if they fail?
- Should a domestic solution be exported?

Are standards ultimately irrelevant? Given enough time, faster hardware and smarter software will, if not end the standards problem, reduce it to very low levels of discomfort. Yet the architecture of information that today's standards permit will persist, because the social relationships they create reinforce themselves. Decisions on who can say what to whom about what have both explicit and implicit dimensions, and standards play a powerful role in the implicit ones. Getting the architecture right is what matters; standards policy then accommodates it, not the other way around. The vision of the international information infrastructure should persist; the communion of bytes should follow.

Appendix: Acronyms

ABI	applications binary interface
ADSL	asymmetric digital subscriber line
AI	artificial intelligence
ANDF	architecturally neutral distribution format
ANSI	American National Standards Institute
API	applications portability interface
ARPA	Advanced Research Projects Agency (under the DOD)
ASCII	American Standard Code for Information Interchange
ATM	asynchronous transfer mode
BIOS	basic input-output system
BPS	bits per second
CAD	computer-aided design

CALS	Continuous Acquisition and Life-Cycle Support
CAM	computer-aided manufacturing
CASE	computer-aided systems engineering
CGM	computer graphics metafile
CMIP	Common Management Information Protocol
CO	central office
COBOL	COmmon Business-Oriented Language
CODEC	encoder-decoder
CORBA	common object-request broker architecture
COSE	common open systems environment
DOD	Department of Defense
DOS	disk operating system
DXF	Digital Exchange Format
EBCDIC	Extended Binary Coded Decimal Inter-Change
EDI	electronic data interchange
EDIFACT	EDI for Administration, Commerce, and Transport
FAA	Federal Aviation Administration
FCC	Federal Communications Commission
FIPS	federal information-processing standards
FORTRAN	Formula Translator
GOSIP	Government Open Systems Interconnection Protocol
HDTV	high-definition television
IGES	Initial Geometric Exchange Specification
IOC	initial operational capability
IS-IS	intermediate system-intermediate system
ISDN	integrated systems digital network
ISO	International Organization for Standards
ITU	International Telecommunications Union
ITU-R	ITU, radio standards subcommittee
ITU-T	ITU, telecommunications standards subcommittee
JOVIAL	Jules' Own Version of International Algebraic Language
JPEG	Joint Photographics Experts Group
LAN	local area network
MAP	Manufacturing Applications Protocol
MPEG	Motion Picture Experts Group
MUMPS	Massachusetts's General Hospital Utility Multi-Programming System

MUSE	MUltiple Sub-Nyquist Encoding
NASA	National Aeronautics and Space Administration
NATO	North Atlantic Treaty Organization
NII	National Information Infrastructure
NIST	National Institute of Standards and Technology
ODIF	Open Document Interchange
OMG	Object Management Group
OSF	Open Software Foundation
OSPF	Open Shortest Path First
PBX	private branch exchange
PCTE	portable common tools environment
POSIX	Portable Open Systems Interface for computer environments
PRI	primary rate interface
RDA	remote database access
RFP	request for proposals
SDTS	spatial data transfer standard
SGML	Standard General Markup Language
SMDS	switched multimegabit data services
SNA	Systems Network Architecture
SNMP	Simple Network Management Protocol
SQL	Structured Query Language
STEP	Standard for the Exchange of Product
TCP/IP	transmission control protocol/Internet protocol
TRON	The Real-time Operating Nucleus
VHDL	VHSIC hardware description language
VHSIC	very high-speed integrated circuit
WAN	wide area network
XPG	X/Open Portability Guide

A Five-Segment Model for Standardization

Carl F. Cargill

Introduction

The present Information Technology (IT) standardization process is predicated upon the concept that practitioners and users of a discipline and skill are better qualified to create a standard relating to that skill or discipline than are those who are only peripherally involved. This is reasonably self evident. The corollary to this is that the participants in the process—either Standards Developing Organizations (SDOs) or consortia—believe that they understand the market for their products better than do non-participants and therefore can best judge when a standardization effort is necessary as well as what form the effort should take. Because there is an implied intuitive understanding of the market ("We will write no standard before its time"), the concept of planning is not especially strong in the current standardization arena. For that matter, it is probably safe to say that there is no serious planning in standardization, other than that achieved by the market, which is external to current standardization efforts. This paper analyzes the ability of both formal SDOs and consortia to meet the new and emerging market characterized by the term "open systems," and then postulates a new approach to standardization that may fit the high technology arena better than the current model.

Standards-Developing Organizations

Within the IT industry, creation of standards is largely left to the technologists. Most standards committees are driven by technically trained practitioners. Senior committees are composed—usually—of technical practitioners who either have risen within the system (from technical committee to administrative committee) or who are accepted by the system because of an imputed technical background. To facilitate the development of technical standards (as well as to hold the participants free from anti-trust), standards-developing organizations (SDOs) have been formed to create de jure standards. SDOs operate under a defined set of rules that codify the steps necessary to achieve broad consensus. Consortia, the other major factor in the growing standardization movement, operate under less explicit rules, but these rules are as firmly rooted in each separate consortium as the rules for consensus are for SDOs. Both types of organizations, however, stress the technical aspect of their work and the fact that they are creating the technical responses to market requirements. The "standardization process" deals only with these rules and is the justification for the structure of the organization.

Accredited Standards Committee (ASC) X3 is (depending upon how you count membership and participation) the largest national IT standardization committee in the United States (and possibly the world), producing the lion's share of IT standards. (Unofficial estimates indicate that X3 produces up to 85% of all IT standards. Verification of this would be a simple task for either ANSI or X3, but it appears never to have been done.) The standards process, as it is generally described by X3, details the rules for actually writing a standard, balloting that standard, and then having it approved.[1] This is the arena in which many theorists concentrate their research. The best documentation of the process of writing a U.S. National voluntary standard is contained in Standing Document 2 (SD2) of the Accredited Standards Committee X3, entitled "X3 Standardization Process for Type D Projects" (dated September 27, 1990). This flow chart shows the entire stream of activities involved in ensuring that a standard reaches consensus and follows all of the ANSI rules about being open to all possible participants. It includes 18 significant milestones along the way. This is, for many standards participants, "as good as it gets."

However, in the late 1980s, ASC X3 decided that it needed to do more planning. It developed a Strategic Planning Committee

(SPC) in 1988 to begin to do "planning." From the start, the committee had serious flaws, since its charter was never clearly defined. It had turf wars with the other two management committees of X3, the Standards Planning and Requirements Committee (SPARC) and the Standards Management Committee (SMC). Additionally, it was never clear on its mission—whether it was to chart a future course for technology or to chart a future course for the discipline of standardization. The technology faction was endorsed by some of the heavier technology companies, and the author was the champion of the "discipline improvement" school. The hapless chair was caught between the two factions.

To bolster the claims of the "discipline improvement" school, the author proposed a five-stage model for standardization. The description in the paper was a personal opinion of what I felt the process should be about, rather than being about the "rules of the process." The contention was that the actual process of standards creation begins much earlier than the process described in the SD2, and consists of five steps. The five steps break into three stages of unequal length but of equal importance. Each stage must be completed before the next stage can be entered and each stage anticipates the next stage, telegraphing the intent of the process so that there is an anticipation of future activity. These five steps are:

Preconceptualization

The Formal Standards Process:

  Conceptualization

  Discussion

  Writing the Standard

Implementing the Standard

Preconceptualization occurs constantly. It is not unique to the standards process, but rather is part of the nature of business, and is where innovation begins. It is in this stage that a proponent of an idea first comes to believe that there is a potential standardization solution to a problem and begins to create a large support base that needs and wants the standardized solution. Additionally, the standard being proposed must work within the bounds of practical technology—or technology that the market can use. While ideas that rely upon leaps in technology are not uncommon, standardization must use implemented or only slightly advanced technology. Finally, the proposed solution should not overwhelm the problem for which it is being offered as a solution. There must be an examination of the problem to ensure that it is not a transient problem, a problem that stems from a misapplication or misunderstanding, or a problem that is chronic, and thus probably not capable of being dealt with by a standard.

The preconceptualization stage continues until the proposal is formally submitted to a Standards Developing Organization (SDO) or until the proposal dies. If the proposal makes it to an SDO, then the formal process of standardization can begin.

The first step of the formal process is the conceptualization phase. It is in this phase that the concept is given its first formal structured review by an SDO and is examined to see if it has potential merit as a standard and if it can be standardized (that is, lies within the capability of technology to implement). There is an implicit assumption—never verified—that the proposal that makes it to an SDO solves a real problem and has a degree of economic viability. At the same time, the SDO reviews the proposal to insure that there is not a jurisdictional problem with the proposal—that is, that the proposed standard falls within the expertise of the SDO. This step may be overlooked, since some SDOs make a good deal of money by publishing standards, and a potential "best seller" is hard to refuse. Again, rules mandate an examination, though it is often only cursory.

Once an SDO has accepted the proposal, it will be rigorously described, and a call for volunteers to work on the committee will be initiated. If no one comes to the committee to work on the proposal, the proposal will die—and the originator will have a good idea that the industry segment that populates standards committees doesn't care; whether or not this is indicative of the market at large is a problem for the originator. There is always the possibility that the larger market may be willing to accept something for which the standardization community is not ready.

The second stage of the formal process is the discussion stage, where the concept is fleshed out, generalized, and made part of the current IT environment. It is in this stage that the proposed standard is subjected to some analysis of the market demand for the proposed technology. The organization of the committee takes place and the goal(s) of the committee are created. This is the planning stage for many standards, where the intent of the standard is decided upon and a methodology for achieving successful completion—within the context of the standardization committee—defined.

The writing stage is the stage with which most people are familiar. It is the time when a technical idea is translated into native language in a manner that provides a non-ambiguous interpretation of the designers' intent. The standard must be written in a way that allows multiple implementations of the standard but only a single interpretation of the language of the standard. It is also where the consensus process becomes important, since it is here that the checks and balances begin to take hold—insuring that there is consensus, but with the potential side effect of slowing the process down. At the conclusion, the standard will be named, and the appellation of American National Standard will be assigned. (The cynical reader might enjoy the idea of two dozen brilliant engineers sitting in a room wordsmithing a document into clear and easily understood English, given the questionable ability of many engineers to write a coherent English sentence on a simple subject, let alone a complex one.)

The final stage, before which all is prelude, is the implementation of the standard. This is where the worth of the standard becomes known. A standard written for the sake of being printed serves no one, not even the publishers. There must be a demand for the standard—either on the part of the providers or on the part of the users. There is no guarantee that what the vendors have provided the users will employ.

The problem with this model is that it is descriptive, not predictive. It describes a scenario that was known by the SDOs, but which had not been documented. The effort to do more languished in the SPC since it was felt that we somehow all understood the concepts and knew how all of them interacted. The technologists refocused SPC on a technical strategic plan.

Then, in 1990, Dr. Michael Spring of the University of Pittsburgh School of Information and Library Science presented a paper to the committee entitled "Models, Musings, and Managers." In addition to the concepts contained in the paper, he pointed out that planning is usually done by mature organizations facing an external threat, and that the SPC had not—in the strategic plan that they had written—identified this external threat. Additionally, he explained that it is usually necessary to define the process you currently have before you can initiate improvements to that process. (Intuitively obvious, but somehow overlooked by the committee. We all thought that we understood the process, until we tried to explain it to him.)

Based on this session, SPC initiated and completed their document entitled "Standards Life Cycle." The intent of the document was to expand the understanding of standardization beyond both the SD2 document and the narrative description contained in the *Five-Stage Conceptual Model*. Figure 1 is the summary diagram from the document, which represents the best attempt by SPC to structure the standardization—not just standards—arena. It recognizes the influencers in standards creation as they define the requirements for standards, and proceeds through the creation stage to the profile development stage and then to the testing and implementation stage.

It is a much more comprehensive document than the SD2, and is more complete than the *Five-Stage Conceptual Model*. It suffers from the same flaws as the Cargill document in that it is a narrative statement of how things work on a large scale and is unable to be used to predict the success of any discrete effort.[2] However, it does represent the first (to my knowledge) attempt by an SDO to understand their complete environment, including activities that are not considered a part of the "consensus" process.

The life cycle document was the last and major output of the X3 Strategic Planning Committee. With the reorganization of X3 and the renaming of the various committees, X3's members decided that planning by an SDO was not a viable task. The members of X3 decmitted from planning, and put the Strategic Planning Committee into hibernation (1993).

During the same time, X3's active membership declined from over 3000 members to slightly less than 2000. The rationale given by X3 members for the decline was that companies could not afford to fund the activities, that there was an economic downturn, and

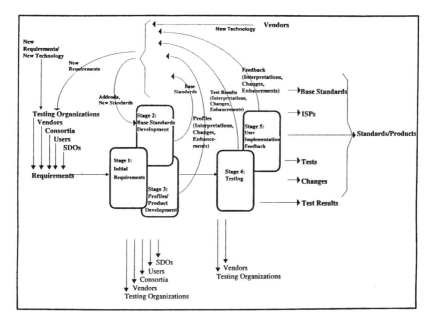

Figure 1 Standards Life Cycle Summary Model.

that major areas of interest were completed. In reality, the same companies that were decommitting from X3 were continuing to fund standardization consortia. Approximately one major new consortium per quarter is being created. (A major consortium is defined as a consortia which costs over $50,000 per year to join; minor consortia appear even more quickly.) That creation rate continues today (June 1994). One must wonder why major corporations were pouring money into these consortia if the "interesting" things were done and if there was an economic downturn.

To compound the problem, there was an explosion of standardization organizations. Within the United States, there are over 250 formally recognized SDOs. While only a handful of these organizations actually dealt with IT standardization (ASC X3, Accredited Organization (AO) IEEE, EIA/TIA, NISO, and ASC T1), other organizations began to preempt some of the territory previously considered the domain of IT standards. The formal structure was essentially powerless to stop the increasing fragmentation of the SDO arena, since many members on the management panels represented providers—and the providers were frantically trying to increase sales by any means possible, including using "open systems."

Consortia

The rationale for inclusion of the consortia and testing organizations in the Standards Life Cycle was that it was necessary; they had become increasingly important within the IT industry in the late 1980s. The advent of anticipatory standardization (that is, creation of a standard from existing technology without an existent commercially available reference implementation) had given rise to a what I refer to as "maybe bits" in standards. "Maybe bits" are options within standards, established to admit of multiple implementations, and usually put in place to ensure participant consensus. The options are sometimes contradictory, so that it is possible to have products that conform to standards but which do not interoperate. The first—and still the classic case of this type of standard—is the Open Systems Interconnection (OSI) model. To solve this problem, the vendor community created a new type of organization— testing consortia to test and validate multiple profiles being created from standards. The consortia could, it was hoped, encourage the use of vendor products by providing some assurance of interoperability. The first of these consortia was the Corporation for Open Systems (COS), whose function was to create test suites and profiles that would both ensure—and legally insure— interoperability. Unfortunately, COS failed in its primary mission, but did succeed in beginning a new phenomena—the rush to consortia to help the standardization process meet user needs.

The need to placate (if not satisfy) users came about because users had been largely dispossessed in the standardization process by the mid-1980s. The problem for the standardization industry was the lack of demand for the standardized products that were being produced to standards written by the SDOs. The vendors were spending large amount of money creating and implementing standards because it was held, as an article of faith, that users wanted them. There was no empirical data to support this proposition; what academic studies had been done were largely in support of the theory of economics of standardization.[3]

To solve the problem of demand creation, providers began to look for ways to capitalize on their production of standards. The answer came in a 1986 European Institute of Business Administration (INSEAD) conference entitled "Product Standardization as a Tool of Competitive Strategy." The conference proceedings are fairly esoteric,[4] and were not really applicable to business—except that the title of the proceedings seemed to unleash a desire by marketing managers to "use standards" to prove openness. As a result, there was a movement to "popularize" standards, usually in association with the open systems concept. Secondarily, there was a provider effort to prove that users wanted standards.

In order to compensate for the "maybe bit" confusion that was being generated by the SDOs, as well as the user desertion of the SDOs, the consortia took up the role of both creating demand and market definition. Unfortunately, in order to do this, the consortia had to constantly invent newer and better standardized solutions in order to both justify their existence and legitimize the open systems that they were creating. New consortia began to be created to deal with nearly every aspect of marketing, all focused on creating a clear "open system." The users, even disregarding the obvious hyperbole of these groups, suddenly found they had to decide among multiple, usually incompatible, technologies, all of which promised a brighter future and open systems.

It is my contention that this is one of the fundamental reasons for the incredible growth of consortia. Many of them were originally designed to be vendor marketing tools, devoted to providing support for specific vendor "openness" claims. The best known were the Open Software Foundation (OSF), UNIX International (UI), X/Open Company, Ltd., and the Object Management Group (OMG). All of these consortia were focused on providing an "industry-wide standardized solution" to the problem of open systems, and all were heavily funded by the providers. All of the consortia initiated major campaigns to prove that they—and implicitly, their members—were open because they built products that conformed to specifications generated by consortia, which the users needed. (Because the need was obvious, it never required proof.)

Summary of the SDO and Consortia Activities

Standardization figures prominently in all of the open systems activities; without it, open systems do not exist. From a provider point of view, the key to open systems has been a better technology, which went from plug compatible to OSI to POSIX to objects. An underlying assumption in all of this activity is that users want and need technical standardization—and are willing to pay for it. Most current activities of SDOs and most consortia support the view that providers create technical standards, which are in turn implemented in products, which are then sold to users, who are willing to pay for the standard as part of the product. The problem is that the alpha and omega of IT standardization today are the providers. Users—that is, the non-technical business, academic, and governmental users of IT equipment—are largely absent from standardization. Standards are technical documents that the vendors use to build products that are supposed to be compatible—but that, because vendors "add" things, become non-interoperable. It is safe to say that providers are the creators of their own woes. Most important, it is necessary to understand that the standards deal only with computers, not with computing. The fascination with the tools has deprived the industry of the chance to look at the uses to which the tools are being put—except as it relates to the creation of faster and "neater" tools.

Understanding and appreciating this "computer-centric" focus is essential to understanding the "computer open systems" movement—and the standardization that accompanied it. The discipline of standardization is very complex and not well understood. As noted above, there are few theoretical writings on the subject that have received widespread acceptance among the provider community. Because the providers were trying something new—that is, creating a discipline where none existed before—it was natural that they would continue an evolutionary course. Small modifications—such as the changes among the various iterations of the open systems movement—were about as daring as the IT industry could accept.

The concept of small modifications might have been acceptable to the industry—users and providers—had they not lost sight of the fact that the IT industry had become ubiquitous, and the very nature of the ubiquity demanded that *vendors cooperate, not compete, in defining systems that were open.* The standardization process tried to feed dual streams by using both SDOs and consortia—by creating more and more massively open systems in the SDOs, while having the consortia tell the users that standards were vital and that each vendor was "uniquely open."

Very simply, what has happened is that as the standardization movement fed the two divergent streams of the open systems movement, it satisfied neither. The vendors never agreed on common implementations, and never agreed upon what it was that they were doing. The users, after being patient for a decade, finally decided that standardization of technology, as it was being implemented, was a failure, and began to look for other, more productive, options.

Toward a New Standardization Open Process

The user community began a revolutionary movement that changed the face of the IT industry substantially, forcing (and continuing to force) a break with the past rules and governance, including those offered by standards and standardization. This movement came from an entirely different direction than did the traditional open systems movement; its focus was on using computing resources. This shift from computer focus to computing focus is key to understanding the revolutionary branch of the open systems movement.

The key to the revolution was not "open systems" in the sense of the computer environment. Instead, there is a "general systems theory " that combines organizational structure and information usage so that the organization begins to collapse the managerial hierarchy. The highly structured Weberian bureaucracy is giving way to a situational management that is task and goal oriented, rather than structure oriented. The dislocation that is caused by the non-traditional structure of work is politely referred to as "rightsizing;" those who have suffered through it know it as "downsizing." In many cases, the wrenching reduction is meant to make the corporation lean—but a lean hierarchy. The triangle that typifies management structure is moving from equilateral to acute isosceles to scalene in a search for stability.

The standardization that the "open organization" movement requires is not standardization of the tools (i.e., the computers) but rather a standardization of attributes of the information system. The construct has changed from the mechanism (computers) to the goal itself (computing). In an organization that is driven by both situational computing and by the knowledge worker, the greater knowledge of a situation does not necessarily flow up the organization, and the CEO of a corporation—theoretically—can be subordinated to a junior engineer who is situationally capable of committing large amounts of organizational resources. This is an unexpected result of "open organizations"—and results in a Jacksonian leveling of the organization.

The User Alliance for Open Systems, before it became technically driven, defined an open system as "a system that allows a worker access to information necessary to do one's job." While the UAOS was a short lived phenomenon, it was a form of consortia activity that marked the first—and possibly most significant—user revolt against the continued technological movement orchestrated by the vendors.

The standards creators—usually vendor employees or vendor agents—see standards as entities in their own right. Users, on the other hand, do not see standards as a product, but rather as a bundle of attributes that they want. While both have a degree of validity, there is a conflict that the market presently does not have the ability to resolve.

The conflict can be viewed in the following manner:

1. Standards are usually created by vendors in standards committees with little user help.

2. Standards (and open specifications) are meant to describe a bundle of attributes desired by a user.

3. Standardization is the act of specifying common interfaces for which the industry can create implementations, which takes time.

4. Users specify standards in their procurement documents only if the specification answers a current need.

5. Vendors create standardized implementations based on interface specifications.

6. Standardized implementations are then employed to solve a user problem only if they meet business criteria.

Looking at the situation from a process point of view, the following becomes clear:

There are no sustainable connections between the specification and the creation (paragraphs 1 and 2). This indicates that the specification process is fundamentally flawed.

There are no logical connections between 3 and 4; users and vendors have a fundamentally different time scale when dealing with standardization.

There are no logical connections between 5 and 6. The implementation is usually done without regard to the cost of the solution to the user—and the user rarely determines the economic value of a standard in a procurement situation.

The disconnects that exist do so for a reason, and the reason lies in the dual nature of standards. The actual technical creation of standards is a skilled and reasonably difficult act. The providers must try to determine exactly how to provide a set of capabilities to the market, and standards must be expressed in terms of a particular technological interface that allows implementations to be built. But these capabilities must also be needed and used, a function that user participation provides—or should have provided.

And this is where the providers fail to understand the full nature of standardization. The specification of standards by users falls short because users, in many cases, fail to include standardization in their plans. *This is caused by either a failure of the planning process (that is, not planning with a long enough horizon) or simply not believing that a standardized product or service will be available.* This makes the vendors, on the other hand, disbelieve in the standardization process because they see users demanding standards be included in the products that they specify—but then failing to buy these products, and choosing less expensive non-standard products.

These trends were apparent during the "open systems" controversy. The advocates of open computer systems tended to favor the odd-numbered positions, while the open organization advocates tended to favor the even-numbered items. The odds are technology focused, while the evens are solution focused.

The solution that I propose is somewhat radical within the confines of the standardization system. It is, I believe, legal within the constructs of the current rules, and would require no changes to the U.S. system of checks and balances. It is not especially elegant, and will no doubt offend many purists in the process who are "standards professionals." It also requires that users learn to cooperate and that vendors give up "innovation for innovations' sake." The model is reasonably simple, but does change the way that standardization occurs.

The first step is admitting that the SDOs do produce a legitimate product. Standards that go through the formal process have an aura of moral legitimacy. That is, in order to achieve the appellation of National or International Standard and be allowed into government procurements (in the United States, accordance with the Office of Management and Budget Circular A119), they must conform to certain creation rules. It is obvious that these cannot be thrown away, or chaos would likely result.

However, it is also true that SDOs are poor at producing a standard in a hurry. ASC X3 claims to have reduced the cycle time for writing a standard to 18 months—which is laudable, but only part of the solution. (Writing a standard is only one part of the five stages that are described in the X3 life cycle planning document.) The other stages, from initial requirements through development and testing to user implementation and feedback, can and usually do add up to an additional four years to the cycle. There are advantages to this approach, but they are tied not to standards, but to a general spirit of cooperation that can be created within standardization committees. (This last part is not especially true of certain committees, especially the IEEE Technical Committee on Operating Systems (TCOS, part of the POSIX effort) where a full time expert on Robert's Rules of Order was necessary to maintain a veneer of civility.) The problem is that consensus—full and complete consensus—requires time, and may add little significant benefit to the results of the process. It is however, a carryover from the days of power brokering interests—and still may be viable in industries that are liable to monopoly.

The solution to the problem of writing slowness is to provide a "pre-writing" focus group that produces "open specifications" for use by the SDOs. The idea is not as radical as it sounds, fortunately; it has been used in Europe for some time by the Comité Européen de Normalisation (CEN). The difference between this and CEN's implementation, however, comes from the requirements stage, which precedes the specification stage. As noted above, the problem with requirements is that they are usually written by the IT industry in a somewhat confused daisy chain fashion after hearing what users "sorta say they want." In this mode, no one really is at fault if the process fails—and everyone can (and usually does) complain. (Note that in the X3 Life Cycle, the section on user requirements is extremely nebulous. I was involved in creation of the original document, and the sad truth is that the Strategic Planning Group of X3 could not really say why a majority of standards projects started or who wanted them when.) The specification writing group could be a technical industry consortium (Object Management Group), a consultant hired for the purpose, or an individual. The intent of the group would be to produce a specification that was a "pre-standard" that represented the needs of some interest group that wanted a standard. The specification would be technically correct; that is, it would represent implementable technology in some form. The specification would be passed to an SDO for approval—that is, the SDO would become an approval group, not necessarily a writing group. The SDO would not re-write the specification, but would rather endorse it and remove—if necessary—any egregious vendor bias.

The left hand side of Figure 2 represents the state of the model as described thus far. However, to be viable, the model needs a simultaneous validation—the proof that products are being created that meet the standard. The work in this arena would be carried out by testing organizations, such as X/Open in the IT arena or other test houses as they come on line and are able to test the complexities of software and hardware. I imagine that the specification producing groups would be closely linked with such firms—after all, if the SDO is able to issue the standard in less than 12 months (which is possible, if the specification is presented on a fully written basis) then the test would have to be ready within a 12

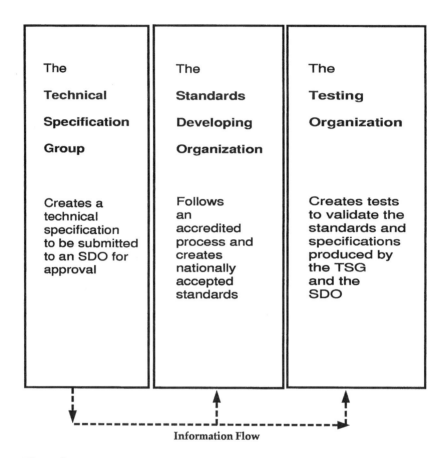

Figure 2

month time frame after the specification was completed. The real challenge would be to ensure that the two groups acted in coordination, and not in collusion.

To make the model succeed, two more vertical segments need to be added. These are illustrated in Figure 3. The left-hand column labeled "User Requirements" is where the users provide business specifications for the specification writing group. The farthest right-hand column, labeled "User Procurements," is where the user procurement of systems occurs—using the tests created in the previous column.

Would this approach have solved the "open systems" wars? I believe that it would have, although there is little empirical evi-

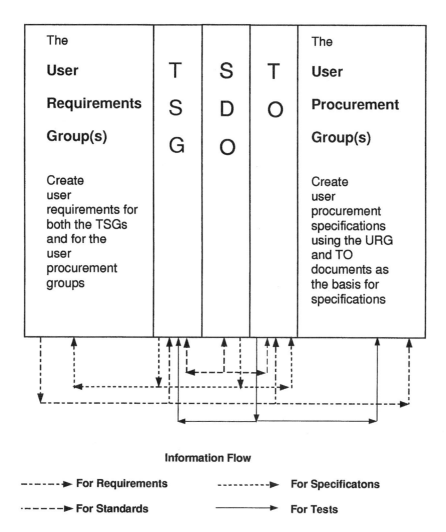

Information Flow

------▶ **For Requirements**   --------▶ **For Specificatons**

·-----▶ **For Standards**   ───────▶ **For Tests**

Figure 3

dence to prove this assertion. The simplest test is to examine the
market, which is no easy task. However, a single broad trend is
distinguishable—in the users' eyes, Microsoft is the dominant
player in the "open systems" market. If you examine the five
columns of the model, you will see that Microsoft followed four of
the columns, excepting the SDO column. They engaged in extensive marketing to understand user needs, and then put together

specifications that resulted in a product that was testable for conformance. They made the specification of their product in the procurement cycle very easy, and made the use of their product equally easy through good human-interface engineering. Most importantly, they redefined the "open systems" question so that it was nearer to the needs of the market. The definition of "open systems" that Microsoft embraced was "inexpensive, ubiquitous computing." Compare this to the UAOS "access to information to do one's job" and the similarity is much closer that that of POSIX— "application portability, interconnectivity, and interoperability."

The ability to move in the direction that is suggested by the five columns is not lacking. There exist user consortia (such as UniForum) that could, if properly prepared, create user functional requirements. There are competent consortia who could, without too much trouble, draft a competent technical specification for submission to an SDO. SDOs—especially in the United States—are reasonably easy to find. There are test houses willing to test and brand various solutions. For the last stage—the unified buyers— the precedent is the automotive industry, which has published joint requirements.

What appears to be missing is the will to drive in this direction— and to make the change. The intent of the new process that has been described is not so much to change the current process as it is to re-engineer the ideas and the concepts that go into the current process. What both users and providers have forgotten in the standardization issue is that standardization is a bundle of at-tributes that users use and that providers provide. How these solutions are provided should make little difference to the user community—as long as basic user requirements are met. On the other hand, providers must stop second guessing users, who really can invent new and novel ways to use products. The current process seems to try to force the two groups to merge interests—and their interests are no longer capable of being united.

The way to the solution—if the vendors won't and the users can't—is direct or indirect governmental intervention to legitimize an overarching organization that can begin to make the changes necessary to actualize this type of responsive standardization struc-ture. The nature of this organization, is not clear: whether it should be a quasi-governmental public-private corporation, the creation of a pan-American standardization organization, or the legitimization of an already existing structure. However, what is clear is that if the private sector cannot provide the technological infrastructure that supports standardization, then governmental intervention to move the process out of its current paralysis is not only necessary but vital.

Acknowledgment

Portions of this paper have appeared in the March 1994 edition of *StandardView, the ACM Journal of Standardization.*

Notes

[1] See Cargill (1989a). Chapters 7 and 8, provide an extensive overview of how an SDO such as X3 operates. Linda Garcia (1992) and Dorothy Cerni (1984) also offer excellent descriptions of how the standardization process works with in the United States. All of these descriptions look at the process as a phenomena that occurs in a context of business and a social structure, rather than in the technical domain. The work by X3 (the SD) does not cover this aspect, but rather focuses on the actual act of gaining consensus within the committee writing the standard. The process adopted by most other standardization groups — from other national body SDOs to international bodies to consortia — tends to mimic the intent, if not the form, of these rules. Consortia tend to de-emphasize consensus at the price of governmental acceptance, since nearly all consortia have a "pay to play" policy to ensure that they make money and pay their staff members.

[2] Cargill, Carl F., "A Five Stage Conceptual Model for Information Technology Standards", 31 October 1988. Unpublished and unnumbered paper submitted to the X3 Strategic Planning Committee. The basis of the paper was a conversation with Gary S. Robinson, then Director of Standards at Digital Equipment Corporation, now Director of Standards at Sun Microsystems. Gary and I were trying to understand why some standardization efforts never seemed to come to closure, why some came to closure slowly, and why some coalesced very quickly. The paper was the result of analyzing the process from a group psychology, rather than technical standardization, point of view.

[3] The paper was presented to the SPC but was not assigned a number by that committee at Dr. Spring's request. The paper (which carries the tag line of Msspring/4-90/#1, and is dated April 25, 1990) contains some excellent insights into the nature of the standards process and its evolution. Several concepts that were exposed in the "Models paper" have since been incorporated into the body

of thought that is fundamental to the growing body of literature on standardization.

[4] ASC X3/93-0884-L, 12 February 1993.

[5] The best description of the nature of the Brownian activity of a standardization committee can be found in a paper by Marvin Sirbu and Martin Weiss entitled "Technological Choice in Voluntary Standards Committees: An Empirical Analysis of the Economics of Innovation and New Technology." The paper reviews the possible causative factors of a standards success and concludes that there is not single dominant factor in ensuring successful standardization. It is the only empirical study of which I am aware that looks at this possibility.

[6] See Weiss and Cargill (1992) for a further description and an interesting taxonomy of consortia which still appears valid as these organizations begin to collapse.

[7] The works by Paul David, Joseph Farrell, Brian Arthur, and Stanley Besen, while excellent for their rigor, all tend to emphasize the more generalized and abstract economic approach to standardization, based largely on telecommunications, a regulated discipline. This made them somewhat problematical for use by the IT industry, which is largely unregulated, except by market economics. (See Cargill [1989] for a discussion of the deeper cultural and economic differences that distinguish the telecommunications and information technology standardization disciplines.) The difference between regulatory and voluntary standardization masks a deeper cultural difference that derives from the competitive (IT) and cooperative (telecommunications) genesis of the two disciplines. Other academics—notably Garth Saloner—have done analysis of the IT arena and standardization process from an outside observer's point of view, relying on inferences and reports rather than upon actual participation. A newer group of academics—led by Michael Spring, Martin Weiss, William Lehr, Marvin Sirbu, and Shane Greenstein (University of Pittsburgh, Columbia, Carnegie-Mellon, and University of Illinois [Urbana]) have done excellent and useful work that was not available in the early and mid-1980s. Of significant importance to the field, however, is the fact that nearly all of this last mentioned group are also educating students in the discipline of standardization. Among the major consultants in the field, I have found the writings and presentations of Robert Toth (R. B. Toth Associates of Alexandria, Virginia) to be of the most help. Toth's *The Economics of Standardization* (SAS) is a practical guide to internal standardization that is most helpful to the general practitioner. He is also the editor of the ANSI handbook on standards management (Toth, 1992).

[8] Gabel (1987).

References

ASC X3/93-0884-L, 12 February 1993, "Standards Life Cycle." Available from the X3 Secretariat, 1250 I Street, Suite 200, Washington D.C. 20010.

Berg, J.L. and Schumny, eds., 1990, *An Analysis of the Information Technology Standardization Process,* Amsterdam: North-Holland.

Cargill, Carl F., 1989a, *Information Technology Standardization, Theory Process and Organizations,* Bedford, MA: Digital Press.

Cargill, Carl F., 1989b, "A Clash of Cultures: ISO/IEC and the ITU," Auerbach 61-10-20, Warren, Gorham, and Lamont, Publishers.

Cargill, Carl F., 1994, "Evolution and Revolution in Open Systems," *StandardView, the ACM Journal of Standardization,* Vol. 1, No. 3, pp. 3–12.

Cerni, Dorothy M., 1984, *Standards in Process: Foundations and Profiles of ISDN and OSI Studies,* NTIA Report 84-170, U.S. Department of Commerce.

Frenkel, Karen A., 1990, "The Politics of Standards and the EC," *Communications of the ACM,* Vol. 33, No. 7, pp. 40–51.

Gabel, H. Landis, ed., 1987, *Product Standardization and Competitive Strategy,* Amsterdam: North-Holland.

GAO/IMTEC-91-52A, 1991, *U.S. Communication Policy: Issues for the 1990s, Results of a GAO Roundtable,* Gaithersburg, MD: USGAO.

Garcia, D. Linda, 1992, *Global Standards: Building Blocks for the Future,* Office of Technology Assessment Study OTA-TCT-512, Washington D.C.: U.S. Government Printing Office.

Garcia, D. Linda, 1994, *Electronic Enterprises: Looking to the Future,* Office of Technology Assessment Study OTA-TCT-600, Washington D.C.: U.S. Government Printing Office May 1994.

Jespersen, Hal, 1993, *Your Guide to POSIX; A Uniforum Technical Guide,* Santa Clara, CA: UniForum.

Toth, Robert B., ed., 1992, *Standards Management—A Handbook for Profits,* New York: American National Standards Institute.

Weiss, Martin and Carl Cargill, 1992, "Consortia in the Standards Development Process," *Journal of the American Society for Information Science,* pp. 559–565.

Information Infrastructure Meta-Architecture and Cross-Industry Standardization

Jim Isaak

The information infrastructure on either a national or global level is currently the focus of marketing, political, and practical investments and interest.[1] Many of the visions elaborated today are not new,[2] nor is the call for standards to accomplish them,[3] and much of the future capability exists in some form today, although not in a fully integrated way. The Information Highway, just like the Interstate Highway, will build on the existing network of information paths, streets, and roads. We will see an evolution, not a revolution, but with quite revolutionary impact on other aspects of society. Just as automobiles and roads restructured our cities and our ways of doing business, so the Information Infrastructure will impact these and more. The meta-architecture discussed here is the way we structure industry organizations and government to accomplish the required standardization.

Much of the current infrastructure depends on voluntary, industry, or regulatory standards that have been essential to creating a viable service or market. Simple examples of these include television broadcast band allocation (regulatory), VHS video tape formats (industry), and video cable connectors (voluntary). This paper will look at the need for standardization as we seek to build an integrated infrastructure from the diverse components of the telephone, television, utility, and information processing industries. The role that government plays in this process is most significant, since government policy and practice will have a massive impact. The value to the public in terms of services needs to be balanced with the freedom of the industry to create and compete. Standards are a prerequisite for service delivery, innovation, and even competition. Timely delivery of the key standards is therefore essential. This is a challenge to industry and government to collaborate. How to do this and also foster an environment that can embrace future innovation is a critical aspect of this challenge.

The Need for II Standardization

In their interoperability report[4], the Computer Systems Policy Project makes the case for standardization, presents a high-level architectural view, and identifies areas where standardization is necessary. This paper also provides some useful presentation of related concepts like "open," "non-proprietary," and "standard."[5] I will try to be consistent with these terms. However, in the term "standardization" I include the concept of voluntary standards, and also the concepts of consortia, industry, and vendor specifications.

A given segment of the market will only adopt the infrastructure on a broad basis as the services that segment requires become available in a standardized form. In the case of machines, this was an ISO standard, and in the case of personal computers it has been specific vendor products. If consumers perceive that standardization is insufficient, then they will be reluctant to buy products, and the benefits of the infrastructure will be delayed. Note that voluntary standards, like any other form of standardization, must also reach the status of being "de facto" to be sufficient. (See Figure 1.) The appearance of significant divergence in the market, limiting "interoperability," will discourage consumer investment. Domination of the infrastructure by a single vendor product could provide sufficient specification, but also may introduce many potential constraints on open competition, although there are many vendors who are currently seeking such architectural franchises.[6] Consumers and suppliers alike will benefit from a clear picture of where architectural franchises will be permitted and where standards will be the norm.

The government could eliminate ambiguity here by creating regulatory standards. For example, the mandating of a common electrical outlet eliminates divergence, and creates a mass market

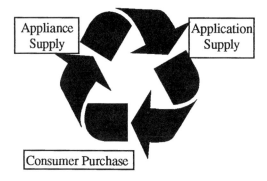

Figure 1 Standards Dependency Spiral.

for appliances and the associated benefits for consumers. Mandating that coal-powered generating plants be the method for delivering power to that outlet would be a problematic regulation, precluding any number of alternative methods that might improve the service or lower the costs for consumers as well as provide other social benefits. A similar issue exists for government regulation in the information infrastructure: Where is regulation appropriate and necessary? Today's regulatory environment for communications is one of the factors that is inhibiting innovation and growth of the infrastructure. With the rapid rate of advances in technology this is not surprising, but it is a warning about the downside of regulation.

CSPP identifies four areas in their architecture where standards are essential (see Figure 2). These include:

1. The interface between the appliance and the network
2. The interface between networks
3. The interface between the application and the appliance
4. The interface between applications

In each of these cases a suite of standards is needed to describe the interface fully. And in each case, the decisions at that point are fairly independent of the suite selected for one of the other areas. These are points where CSPP has determined that architectural franchises must yield to the benefits of open competition in order for the information infrastructure to attain its objectives.[7]

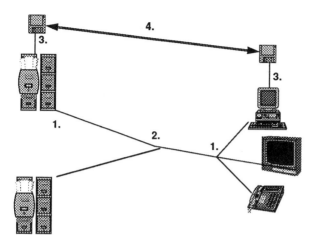

Figure 2 CSPP NII Interfaces for Standardization.

Clearly there are communications standards required here. Connector, signal specifications, multiplexing, protocols, and even data formats are part of this. Compression and security encoding are an aspect of this as well. Not so obvious are data exchange formats and protocols between applications, and also the portability of applications between appliances.

The area of applications portability is one in which I have particular expertise, and since it is not commonly identified as a key infrastructure standard, I will expand on this example. Existing infrastructure appliances (VCR, TV, telephones, etc.) already have microprocessors in them, and the potential for downloading critical computer program elements as well as the data associated with a service expands the range of services and future evolution dramatically. Appliance software can select services of value to the consumer (screen calls, sort mail, monitor a financial market, locate products that meet specific purchasing criteria, or identify preferred movies, games or news items), provide services directly to the consumer (perform calculations, initiate a purchase order, prepare an expense report, leave a message for the kids), or adapt the appliance to a new function.

Historically, application portability has been accomplished by designing applications for a specific combination of a processor and an operating system. Broadly used environments like IBM's MVS, Digital's VAX/VMS, and the PC x86/MS-DOS all reflect this approach. However, standardization in this area based on a specific operating system or processor would create a significant limitation on competition and innovation, while actually providing a lesser degree of portability for consumers, since applications would not be able to move to future generations of systems. In the last ten years a new paradigm for portability has been emerging. This started with access to services like databases (SQL)[8], currently covers operating system services (POSIX)[9], and is expanding to displace dependencies on processors as well (ANDF[10]).

There is a good example here of how government can (and has) encouraged standardization, and what can be done in the future to make this more effective. In the case of POSIX, the government has acted as a major user interest, driving that work forward toward results. FIPS 151[11] encourages a government market for conforming systems, which creates an economic incentive for suppliers. NIST has developed a conformance test suite and certification program that provides a level of confidence in conforming systems. Unfortunately, there is not as strong an incentive program for applications suppliers, so currently most computer systems conform to the standard, but few applications programs do. Here is government involvement in a standard that has resulted in widespread adoption, leveraging the volunteer standards program and non-regulatory methods. The initial POSIX standard, based on work from UniForum, was approved in eighteen months, with a more comprehensive standard delivered two years later (1988), providing some hope that the volunteer process can deliver quickly.

Application portability, like the other critical areas of the architecture, requires multiple standards that work together in a coherent fashion. POSIX may be one of the base standards here, but the selection of programming languages, data access, interchange formats, windowing management, and multimedia control at least will also be required. The industry has limited experience in defining comprehensive sets of specifications that work together to provide an applications environment. This issue is addressed below in the context of "profiles," where Standards Users align suites of standards with an area of applications. The following is an example of an application profile:

A Partial Set-Top Appliance Application Portability Profile

Load & Execute Applications—multi-processing

POSIX (IEEE 1003) & windowing (IEEE 1295)

SQL for database, w/multi-media addendum

ANDF for "platform-independent executables"

Communications

POSIX .12 for protocol stack independent API

IEEE 1224 for email & directory services

Stack based on TCP/IP or OSI

Data Exchange

EDI for commerce

MPEG, JPEG, etc. for entertainment

We have some experience in developing architectures and the associated profiles in the area of OSI. The development of a top-down architecture in this situation required a number of years; this was populated with standards at each level; and from these profiles have been identified of specific suites of standards, along with the appropriate parameters and options, to accomplish specific functional objectives. The disadvantage of this approach is the pressing need for capability on the part of users, which resulted in the widespread use of TCP/IP and marginal use of the OSI profiles. The information infrastructure environment will not wait for "top down" architectural development and deployment of the resulting standards. A second example exists in the POSIX community, where much of the effort has been "bottom up." The base standards[12] have been developed and concurrently an architecture[13] has been defined, and profiles[14] have been developed based on these. A significant difference between these two approaches is the concurrent engineering approach used in the POSIX work, which might result in less optimal solutions, but also yields results in terms of procurement standards in less time.

The same type of decomposition can be made for each of the four critical areas from the CSPP report. Moreover, there will be additional areas where similar suites of standards will be needed. The potential for the Information Infrastructure will not be realized until the resulting appliances are as essential and ubiquitous as the telephone, and easier to use than a VCR. This cannot happen without a coherent set of appropriate standards for all segments of the communications and information technology industry.

Obtaining Viable Results in a Timely Fashion

Some number of the interface standards required for the infrastructure already exist. ANSI and other SDOs are establishing information infrastructure focal points to help identify existing standards responsive to II requirements and feed new requirements into the appropriate working groups. In ANSI this group is called the Information Infrastructure Standards Panel[15]. In addition to the work inside the SDO bodies, there are a wide variety of consortia and industry collaborations. Some of these efforts are testbeds[16], prototyping applications on a local or national scale to help the participants gain experience in what is required to implement infrastructure applications. Others are looking at specific application areas[17] and determining what common elements are needed to make it possible for applications in this area to work. Finally, there are groups looking at the broad picture and the policies, specifications, and overall architecture[18] of the information infrastructure. In each of these cases the participants have some mental image of an overall information infrastructure architecture, which most have not tried to document in detail. This yields a dialogue much like the proverbial blindmen and the elephant. The ANSI effort will provide a forum where the diverse affected industries can establish a common vocabulary, dialogue, and set of priorities with respect to formal standardization.

The standardization process for II must leverage the strengths of both the existing volunteer standards process and the consortia processes. The volunteer standards process provides a key "infrastructure" and experience dealing with "mundane" but essential considerations such as common definitions, document formatting, life cycle management, interpretation, revision, deprecation,[19] withdrawal, due process, and a channel for international approval. This process also has its drawbacks, including the delays associated with its checks and balances, the influence of corporate interests, and at times failure for lack of corporate interest. Consortia often start with focused objectives that allow them to put aside these considerations, and then "re-invent" mechanisms to accomplish these over time. (When they reach "process parity," oddly enough they tend to have the same disadvantages and delays as the volunteer standards process.)

Consortia have a value that can benefit this process as well. They offer focus, commitment, and often a diversity of scope and purpose that can be essential to establishing a beachhead in emerging areas. Given the right players, the consensus gained in consortia can accelerate subsequent volunteer standards acceptance. There is a downside here as well: getting off the ground entails overhead and time delays. Much of the initial efficiency can be lost as additional participants become involved and issues related to due process, consensus/acceptance, and the "life cycle" of the effort become apparent. Consortia have the additional overhead of building an organization while also trying to focus on problems; if they choose to create a paid staff, then personnel management and staffing become distractions, and with a paid staff, job continuation may take precedence over the founders' objectives.

There is a way to get the best of both channels, but it requires collaboration between them, and a recognition of the value that each brings to the process. Using focused consortia to test concepts and gain both a common view of the requirements and perhaps some consensus on the required specifications (or at least the areas where standards are required), then feeding this information into a volunteer standards process where the mechanisms exist for formalization, is one way to do this. Consortia developing specifications can use the same formats as ISO, and produce documents that can be brought more quickly through the system.

The POSIX effort has done this with materials out of UniForum, X/Open, and other organizations. While some of the "formalities" were only that, the POSIX group found that the broader participation, and the more meticulous approach to content, resulted in a more definitive specification. Specifications that eliminate ambiguity, accommodate diverse international concerns, and yield testable results require a discipline that is a key value of the formal process. In any case, experts from the consortia perspective, as well as users with a sense for the requirements, are both essential participants in the standardization process.

There are opportunities to accelerate standardization beyond those mentioned above. The key result of standardization is to have a reference document that represents the basis for building products and purchasing them. Investing in the technical editing of the document is a key area for process acceleration (this is one of the things that yields quick results out of the consortia process). A core element of formal "due process" is the ballot review and response, and again, funding sufficient person-hours to get this done quickly will accelerate that process. One obvious application of the infrastructure is distributed development and review of documents, and this is a place where funding can help accelerate standardization. ANSI is working on an automation system, and IEEE has launched its Standards Process Automation system (SPAsystem[20]) along these lines. The conversion of the applicable existing documents into "on-line" format is another opportunity for greater efficiency. This will allow emerging efforts to take full advantage of existing work, pursuing questions like "but where else is that mentioned," which often are discovered "after the fact." It is important to recognize that the II calls for a level of coherence in standards that has not existed in the past, and emerging methods like hypertext may be the only way to accomplish this. Finally, the methodical job of defining the requisite test methods and associated test processes, not just for the individual standards but for integrated sets of these, is non-trivial, and an important opportunity for investment to encourage rapid deployment of competitive but compatible products and to establish consumer confidence.

Methods for Coordination and Collaboration

High-level industry-driven coordination of the diverse standardization bodies is needed to maximize the effectiveness of investment in standards and to direct user requirements and testbed conclusions to appropriate forums. The wide range of technology required for the infrastructure, and the proliferation of organizations addressing various aspects of this, requires a new level of coordination. Collaboration will be most effective if all of the parties concerned focus on how to deliver specifications and standards that are responsive to the requirements in a timely fashion and that avoid turf battles (see Figure 3).

An example is the previously mentioned Information Infrastructure Standards Panel (IISP) in ANSI. The key function of this group is "cataloguing" of requirements and of standards and specifications that are responsive to these requirements. IISP creates at ANSI a central point in the United States for communicating the need for II-related standards. Similarly, a coordinated response can be provided by bringing responses to those requirements up through the same ANSI organization. It is significant that this organization is not "competing" with the distributed development organizations that exist both as accredited bodies and as consortia. Instead, it is providing a focal point for communications.

A second key role that this group could play is to identify priority areas where resources can be applied to accelerate the process. As noted above, money and editorial resources can be applied to work at key points, moving that work forward quickly. If the IISP identifies these opportunities, will the government or other beneficiaries of the results put forward the resources to accelerate it?

A similar group has been formed in IEEE (an Information Infrastructure Standards Coordinating Committee[21]), which will perform a parallel activity in IEEE and participate in the ANSI forum. Hopefully all of the ANSI SDOs will formulate an appropriate way to coordinate their activities in collaboration with ANSI. Also, the consortia need to be included in this process: where these are accelerating work, that should be utilized. The formal processes can embrace the results of the more focused groups, and these groups can release control as needed to meet the open process requirements of the volunteer standards bodies. Some of these focused groups may wish to use the ANSI canvass method, or seek ANSI accreditation if they wish to retain total control of their documents. Quite properly, one of the challenges of IISP will be to help identify forums to do development work, and help organizations that have not used the formal processes to understand these and use them effectively.

How do we identify the areas where standardization is needed to move the infrastructure forward? There are two approaches that need to be applied: models and profiles. Models reflect a top-down

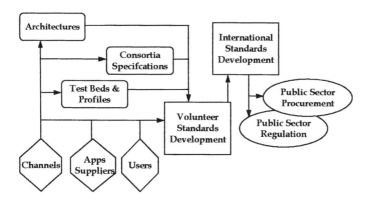

Figure 3 Cross-Industry Standardization Meta-Architecture.

approach. The CSPP "Interoperability" document provides a simple model, which can then be used to describe points where standardization is needed. More detailed models or architectures can be used to identify additional elements. Profiles approach the problem from the "bottom up," focusing on a specific application area. The prototype and testbed activities are creating "informal profiles"[22] that describe a suite of capabilities that are needed to accomplish a specific application objective. Getting these groups to document their experience and submit these environment descriptions will also help identify where additional standards are needed. One lesson learned from the OSI work is that strictly top-down operations may result in significant delays in both standards and products. Similarly, Internet, which was built from the bottom up, reflects some of the limitations of that approach (such as the constrained address space). We need both approaches, and we need collaboration between these and the specification, product development, testing, and procurement processes.

Ultimately we need profiles for key areas of the infrastructure. One or more profiles for "appliances" would be one example. Such a profile would define the standards that an appliance must support in terms of application program interfaces, user interfaces, data handling, protocols, and connectivity with the infrastructure. A profile for a interactive voice appliance (telephone) would differ in some ways from the profiles for a asymmetric video display appliance (TV), but they might have more in common that the current devices in these categories, and some appliances would provide both services by conforming to both profiles. Notice that these profiles span industries and SDOs, selecting electrical interfaces in some areas and programming interfaces in others. Initially these profiles will reveal gaps as well as standards that meet the requirements. These gaps reflect requirements that need to be fed back into the standardization process.

Fully formed profiles become the specifications that are useful in purchasing. When we get a VCR we expect it to meet many standards: mechanical tape standards, video signal reception and tuning standards, tape format/interchange standards, cable and TV connectivity standards. Efforts in the multimedia arena, applications portability arena, and networking arena to "brand" systems with labels that imply conformance to a suite of standards reflect this same logic. Such a suite in the formal process is called a profile, and these are the end product of information infrastructure standardization. They are also useful stepping stones, since the process of building a useful profile, and verifying that it works, will expose "gaps" and areas where standardization is needed.

Within the United States, one key forum for profile collaboration is the Open Systems Environment Implementors Workshop (OIW), which is hosted by NIST. OIW recently expanded its domain of concerns from communications to the full range of Open System Environment issues (interoperability, portability, and consistency of user interfaces, parallel to the IEEE 1003.0 Guide), although no II specific projects have been defined for OIW yet. OIW is the regional workshop for the Americas, collaborating with parallel bodies in Asia (AOW) and in Europe (EWOS). Together these groups have the authority to forward documents for approval by JTC1 as "International Standardized Profiles," which reflects the ideal status for information infrastructure specification: *a coherent suite of well-defined standards adopted by the international standards community.*

Roles of Key Players

Suppliers, users, application developers, government, test beds, and prototype developers all are key sources of the requirements that need to be addressed in infrastructure standards. In some cases these folks will also have the expertise needed to define those standards, as well as existing practice in many areas that can be used as a starting point. There is a real risk for users in leaving the standardization process in the hands of vendors. The results may not meet the real user requirements, or may introduce unexpected compatibility or consistency problems for users. Rarely are user requirements stated with sufficient completeness and clarity that the user perspective is not needed in the subsequent development process.

The government must play multiple roles, and can contribute more as well. Some of the issues facing II implementation are policy issues only the federal government can address. Changes in regulatory standards are also an area reserved for the federal government. However, the government is also a user, a source of requirements, a critical participant, and a catalyst towards appropriate standardization. By encouraging participation in the process by both government experts and consumer interest groups, the government can provide an essential user perspective in standards development. Application of government buying power, both for implementations and even more so for applications that conform to the standardized environment, will help establish a market. Government can also play a key role in the establishment of conformance test methods, again accelerating the confidence level of industry and consumers in the environment. Note that conformance testing can be applied to both sides of any interface; for example, to the applications as well as the applications program interface.

One key point is for government to provide sufficient but minimal incentives, both negative and positive, to get the job done. For example, the threat of government intervention in the standards process is a negative incentive that has already created a level of response; and government purchasing of conforming applications would be a positive incentive. The POSIX experience has a lot to offer here as an example, both positive and negative. The unique power[23] of the federal government to select one-and-only-one standard from among competing alternatives needs to be used with great discretion, if at all, since it pre-empts industry and constrains innovation. Procurement based on specifications created outside of the international volunteer standards process creates incentives for competing alternatives. This will generate a broad array of specification processes with varying degrees of due process and commercial bias, which will force the public sector to invent new methods for accrediting specification bodies, generating significant duplication and expending substantial resources in both development and marketing of alternative specifications. In short, government is best advised to invest in helping to improve and accelerate the existing processes, thereby focusing industry resources on the established channels. The government's role is summarized below:

The Role of Government in II Standardization

Participate as a user

Identify requirements and priorities

Support international industry consensus process international standard conforming implementations and applications

Invest in acceleration

Provide document editors

Fund conformance test development

Invest in standards infrastructure

Email access and online development support

Fund online access to key standards

Users are a difficult but necessary group to draw into participating in standardization. There must be driving sets of user requirements; without this, we will end up with an NII environment that does not respond to real user interests. Internet is an interesting example: being designed by engineers who were using the facility, the process has been very responsive to a certain level of needs. However, it breaks down as you go beyond the engineering community. Internet is a channel for computer experts to communicate; it is not a friendly environment where the public can access services. Many consumers cannot operate the record function on their VCRs, certainly not the programmable versions. Tools like Mosaic are starting to reverse this characteristic, as is the broader access from commercial network services (such as America On-line). Users must buy the results, not just in the sense of acceptance, but in terms of purchasing demand. Without this carrot, vendors of appliances, applications, and communications will not build the products.

Applications developers[24] are a critical interest group that must adopt and use the standard environment or the infrastructure will not deliver value to users. These developers will target the largest volume environments, and shy away from any that are too small. Applications developers are the most aware of the requirements that affect the standardization process since they are often the most affected expert users of the standardized interfaces.

A quick checklist of the things that must be accomplished by the standardization process:

It must engage affected and interested parties

It must be user and application developer requirement driven

It must reflect due process

The results must be well formed, unambiguous, and provide for a coherent whole

It must be driven by a commitment to business value

It must have vendor implementation commitment

It must establish confidence in conformance

It must attract a critical mass of purchasing for both implementations and applications

The resulting documents must meet the volunteer standards process criteria for release or access to intellectual property rights (IPR), though they might not be approved standards in the short term. These requirements are not too demanding, essentially calling for release of appropriate copyrights, and where patents apply, access to these on a non-discriminatory basis at a reasonable fee. This retains a level of incentive for innovation, even in areas where standardization is required, and at the same time prevents any single corporation from obtaining an exclusive franchise in these areas. There is no evidence that this level of acceptance of IPR leads to abuse or any decrease in consumer acceptance.

Similarly, the process must lead to acceptance on an international basis. The U.S. market for appliances and applications will be a target for international competition, with all of the implications of trade battles, if the results of U.S. standardization become a trade barrier. Moreover, if compatible environments are adopted on an international basis it will create new opportunities for global business operations, and a much larger market for appliances and applications built by U.S. suppliers.

Conclusions

U.S. industry is rapidly creating the forums and environments to bring the information infrastructure into existence. This includes high level standards coordination activities as well as a multitude of consortia. These must be brought together and encouraged to collaborate to generate timely results in terms of specifications, test mechanisms, products, and applications. Suites of standards (profiles) will be needed to define the complex sets of standards in terms that consumers can use. All of the affected parties—vendors in various industries, applications and data suppliers, beneficiaries, and government—need to clearly see the "gold at the end of the rainbow" as well as intermediate points on the way, and to understand the need to collaborate to attain that gold.

Notes

[1] See Information Infrastructure Task Force (1993); High Level Group on European Information Society (1994); Computer Systems Policy Project (1993).

[2] See Nelson (1974).

[3] See Isaak (1978).

[4] Computer Systems Policy Project (1994).

[5] The CSPP descriptions of these concepts are:

•Open: specifications available for implementation by any interested party, reasonable license fees may apply

•Proprietary: patent, copyright, or trademark rights apply

•Standard: adopted by an accredited standards body

Note: you can mix these terms in almost any combination, except a "non-open standard."

[6] See Ferguson (1993). I disagree with key conclusions of this book, which views the market as being constrained by the ISO standards as opposed to having a market created by standards. I agree that architectural franchises are a key business objective; the challenge here is to provide business with this opportunity in areas and ways that benefit the public.

[7] These principal points in short form are: universal access, First Amendment freedoms, privacy, security, confidentiality, affordability, intellectual property protections, encourage new technologies, interoperability, competition, limited carrier liability; see Computer Systems Policy Project (1993) for details.

[8] SQL: Structured Query Language, a US and ISO/IEC standard for database access that is widely used from personal systems to mainframes. The most recent generation includes multimedia data types.

[9] POSIX: Portable Operating System Interface, an IEEE and ISO/IEC standard for application portability based on the popular UNIX operating system (UNIX is a trademark of X/Open Company).

[10] ANDF: Architecturally Neutral Distribution Format—a concept being developed by OSF (Open Software Foundation) in the United States and OMI (Open Microprocessor Initiative) in Europe—permits transfer of applications between systems with different instruction sets or architectures without exposing the application source code "trade secrets" or opening the code to modification.

[11] FIPS 151: Federal Information Processing Standard, a U.S. Government procurement standard based on the voluntary POSIX standard, so that conformance to the FIPS requires conformance to the industry standard.

[12] POSIX base standards cover: System Interface (IEEE 1003.1), Shell and Utilities (1003.2), and Systems Administration (IEEE 1387), with a number of extensions for real time, security, distributed operations, etc.

[13] An overview of an Open System Environment architecture is described in IEEE 1003.0, "Guide to the POSIX Open System Environment," which also outlines how users can develop profiles to take advantage of this environment.

[14] POSIX profile projects include: Supercomputing (IEEE 1003.10), Real Time (1003.13), Multiprocessor (1003.14), and a general purpose environment (1003.18).

[15] The ANSI IISP terms of reference are accessible via: gopher:/stdsbbs.ieee.org/00/pub/NII.GII/ansiiisp.htm

[16] Examples of testbeds include: National Information Infrastructure Testbed (NIIT), which is implementing applications in Environment/Earth Sciences, Health Care, and Astrophysics on a nation-wide basis; or Smart Valley, testing applications in the Silicon Valley.

[17] Examples of application-focused efforts include: InfoPort, a UN sponsored effort to encourage the development of international electronic commerce, or US West's Omaha project, providing video-on-demand services.

[18] Examples here include the CSPP, which has a simple model but is primarily

focused on policy issues; and the Cross Industry Work Team (XIWT) , which is developing a more detailed architecture.

[19] Deprecation is used in the standards process to indicate specifications that are considered out of date, and are expected to be eliminated in the future.

[20] The SPAsystem can be accessed via: gopher:/stdsbbs.ieee.org/

[21] For information on the IEEE SCC, see: gopher://stdsbbs.ieee.org/00/pub/ NII.GII/giiintro.htm via the Web.

[22] Lewis et al. (1994).

[23] In this case the constitutional power of regulating interstate commerce and implementing treaties.

[24] Another way to view a standard is as an agreement between some "user" and some "supplier." The network to network interfaces may entail peer agreements between "suppliers," the application-to-appliance interface engages appliance suppliers with application developer "users," and so forth.

References

Computer Systems Policy Project, 1993. "Perspectives on the National Information Infrastructure: CSPP's Vision and Recommendations for Action," January 12.

Computer Systems Policy Project, 1994. "Perspectives on the National Information Infrastructure: Ensuring Interoperability," February (CSPP documents are available by calling 202-393-0220).

EDUCOM et al., 1994. "R&D for the NII: Technical Challenges," May (order information via nii-forum@educom.edu).

Ferguson, Charles H., 1993 *Computer Wars.* New York: Random House.

High Level Group on European Information Society, 1994. "Report to the European Council," 25 June

IEEE 1003.0, 1995. "Guide to the POSIX Open System Environment," currently in draft form.

Information Infrastructure Task Force, 1993. "The National Information Infrastructure: Agenda for Action," September 15 (gopher://gopher-server.nist.gov/ file is: niiagenda.asc in DoC Documents).

Information Infrastructure Task Force, 1994. "Intellectual Property and The National Information Infrastructure," July (http//iitf.doc.gov).

Isaak, Jim, 1978. "Standards for the Personal Computing Network," *Computer,* Vol. 11, No. 10.

Lewis, Kevin, et al., 1994 *Open Systems Handbook.* Piscataway, NJ: IEEE Standards Press.

Nelson, Theodor, 1974. *Dream Machines/Computer Lib.* Privately published.

NIST, 1994. "Framework for National Information Infrastructure Services," 1994 (http//iitf.doc.gov)

NRC Computer Science and Telecomunications Board, 1994. *Realizing the Information Future,* Washington, DC: National Academy Press.

This paper is available on-line at: http://www.digital.com/info/ whitepaper/nii.txt.html

Current Practice

Compatibility Standards and Interoperability: Lessons from the Internet

William Lehr

Introduction

The purpose of this paper is twofold. First, I will argue that the common presumption that the ultimate goal of compatibility standardization is or should be to achieve interoperability is misguided. Second, I will explain why, although it is both appropriate and feasible to employ a process in the Internet community that assures that interoperability will be achieved, it remains desirable in other contexts to accept incomplete standards that fail to guarantee interoperability.

These two questions are related because in recent years disappointment with traditional standardization fora such as ISO, CCITT, and ANSI have led critics to consider procedural reforms that mimic the approaches of what some analysts view as more successful efforts, such as those of the Internet community.[1] The traditional Standards Development Organizations (SDOs) identified above are perceived as too slow and often approve standards that fail to guarantee interoperability. Even once specifications emerge from these bodies, producers and customers often need to expend significant resources on conformance testing to assure interoperability.[2]

In contrast, standardization in the Internet community has proceeded relatively quickly and the process is designed so that multiple independently designed, interoperable implementations must be demonstrated before a standard may advance through the approval process. The evolution of global electronic communications and efforts to promote a National Information Infrastructure (NII) in the United States have focused interest in the Internet both as a management model and as a technical base on which to construct the "Information Superhighway." This paper considers the question of whether the Internet provides an appropriate forum in which to develop the steady stream of communications protocols and compatibility standards that will be needed to glue the whole mess together. I believe the answer is yes if we are concerned with software-based internetworking protocols; however, I am less sanguine about the validity of the Internet approach when applied to more traditional questions of hardware standardization.

The success of the Internet's approach derives from three factors: historical accident, which blessed their efforts with a less contentious environment thatn today's; the nature of the technologies that they addressed (i.e., software-based communications protocols); and strong user involvement in the development process. These factors are not universally applicable, however. In other environments, it may not be advisable to require that interoperability be demonstrated before a standard may be approved. In addition, it is not always beneficial to increase customer involvement in the process. Finally, many of the Internet's historical advantages are disappearing as the community grows and diversifies.

The Goals of Standardization and Conformance Testing

Compatibility standards make vendors' products more alike. The technical specifications that compose these standards constrain firms' product design decisions by specifying allowable ranges for a variety of design parameters. These specifications may include physical dimensions (e.g., size and configuration of plugs and sockets), electrical, optical or logical parameters (e.g., voltages, transmission wavelengths, or protocol structures), or functional requirements (e.g., what services must be supported). Conceptually at least, it is possible to imagine a specification that is so complete as to guarantee that any two products that conformed to the specification would be identical and hence fully interoperable.

In practice, compatibility standards are never so complete. Often specifications are incomplete because the engineers fail to anticipate all technical options or fail to anticipate how users might interpret the language of the specification. Although such errors of omission are no doubt common, most specifications are incomplete by design. By purposely failing to specify restrictions for particular parameters or by allowing sufficient flexibility, the engineers who frame the standard can permit compliance without guaranteeing interoperability. Since controlling the degree of interoperability is akin to controlling the extent to which vendors' products are perceived by customers as substitutes, one may interpret the decision to permit variable interoperability as a decision to allow vendors to product differentiate.

I will present below a model that shows why a conflict of interest between producers and consumers can lead to different conclusions about the desirability of standardization with or without interoperability. Before pursuing this line of argument, however, it is worthwhile considering several alternative explanations for why compatibility specifications may remain incomplete and why costly investments in conformance testing may be required even after the approval of a base standard.

First, standards may be incomplete because of timing issues. Delaying the decision of what technology to adopt postpones the realization of the consumer surplus and firm profits produced by an active market. This creates an incentive to decide early. On the other hand, if the technology is still evolving, a later decision will allow firms and consumers to take advantage of improvements that lower production costs and increase product functionality. It may be possible to specify the technology incrementally. Viewed in this light, we can interpret standardization as a complex dynamic optimization problem where developers balance the trade-off between waiting for a better technology (e.g., lower cost) against the costs of delaying the benefits of adoption. These decisions need to be made at each stage along the critical path from product conception to market implementation. Farrell and Shapiro (1992) focused on these timing issues in their analysis of HDTV standardization and concluded that United States consumers are likely to benefit from the government's decision to postpone specification of a transmission technology.

Second, standards may be incomplete in order to economize on bargaining costs. When participants have heterogeneous preferences, it may be impossible to generate consensus on every issue. For example, it may be possible to get firms to agree on the physical dimensions of a plug or the voltage drop across an interface, but they may not be willing to agree on whether the first or last bit should be the most significant. Developers may expedite the process of reaching consensus by narrowing the scope of formal standards, excluding issues that generate disagreements. Although this may result in a "lowest common denominator" standard, it may be a worthwhile compromise. This is a form of hybrid standardization (Farrell and Saloner, 1988) in which a partial agreement is reached in the standards committee and outstanding issues are resolved through market competition.

Timing and bargaining issues may overlap when participants' preferences are evolving over time. It may be easier to reach agreement early, when firms and consumers are ignorant about the cost/benefit calculus associated with alternative technologies. Moreover, early decisions that pre-commit participants to particular ex post bargaining allocations but leave sufficient flexibility to adapt technologies to accommodate new information may increase the attractiveness of incremental, sequential standardization. I explore these issues in related work on anticipatory standard setting (Lehr, 1994).

Even if the standard is complete in the sense that full conformance to the specification guarantees product compatibility, there may be an economic role for conformance testing standards subsequent to the specification of the base standard. First, even if vendors know that their products are compatible, they may need to signal this fact to consumers. If the quality/compatibility of products is not directly observable at the time of purchase, conformance testing may play a certification role, reducing consumer search costs by identifying which products are interoperable. Third-party, independent conformance testing could help discourage firms from making exaggerated compatibility claims and could help enforce compliance.

Second, if the standard is incomplete because firms differ in their interpretation of the specification, then conformance testing can provide a mechanism for discovering whether products are interoperable. This may be especially important in the case of software compatibility, where identifying bugs is difficult and the number of potential implementation permutations is large. When the interpretation of the standard is evolving, conformance tests can be used to determine who is out of compliance, assigning the blame (and cost) for design modifications.

In either of these two roles, however, we do not need to equate conformance testing with assuring interoperability. The tests may focus solely on the issue of compliance with the existing standard, without addressing the issue of interoperability. When multiple, partially incompatible technologies co-exist in the market at equilibrium, conformance and/or interoperability testing can help signal to consumers each class of products' compatibility characteristics.

The above rationales for incomplete standardization depend on heterogeneous preferences among otherwise similar agents and/ or asymmetric information. Even if the sources of the above problems could be eliminated, however, it would not necessarily be true that full interoperability should always be the goal for compatibility standardization. Although heterogeneous preferences, technical uncertainty, and asymmetric information may cause greater problems for standardization efforts in the Internet and elsewhere, let us temporarily ignore these problems to focus specifically on the relationship between the economic effects of standardization and interoperability.

Compatibility standards can have three types of economic effects: they may lower supplier costs, increase consumers' willingness-to-pay, or alter the competitive dynamics among suppliers. Product development costs may be reduced, for example, when compatibility standardization provides a mechanism for firms to share information about an emerging technology, thereby reducing collective uncertainty and enhancing the efficiency of industry R&D. Or, by coordinating their product design decisions, suppliers may realize scale or scope economies in factor markets, leading to lower fixed and variable production costs. An agreement to adopt a common screw size, type of fiber optic cable, or programming language can produce such gains. To the extent that lower supplier costs lead to lower equilibrium prices, consumers also will benefit from standards that facilitate these types of design coordination.

In addition to lowering supplier costs, compatibility standardization may increase consumer willingness-to-pay (w-t-p) both directly and indirectly. For example, direct benefits are common in network technologies wherein the value of adoption to an individual increases with the size of the population that adopts the same technology. Telephone services are more valuable to all subscribers when compatibility between adjacent facilities allows interconnection of user communities. Indirect benefits accrue when compatibility enhances the supply of complementary products (e.g., computer software or peripherals) or services (e.g., maintenance services and used equipment markets). Once again, the benefits of the increases in aggregate demand are likely to be shared between consumers and producers.[3]

The third effect of standardization is more problematic. Compatibility standards may alter competitive dynamics by making vendors' products closer substitutes[4]. As products become closer substitutes, price competition intensifies. In the absence of capacity constraints and in the extreme where products become perfect Bertrand substitutes, firm operating profits are reduced to zero. The success of the IBM PC as a de facto industry standard helped encourage the emergence of a clone market wherein products compete largely on price. Although aggregate demand has increased, profit margins are quite low.

The threat of aggressive price competition, which occurs when products are perceived as close substitutes, may induce firms to adopt partial standards that allow them to capture some of the cost and demand benefits of compatibility while still allowing them to differentiate their products. Consumers and firms are likely to differ on the degree of compatibility that is desirable when increased compatibility leads to market equilibria that allocate a larger share of total surplus to consumers. On the other hand, consumers may accept decreased compatibility if the alternative is to adopt less valuable (e.g., lower quality) or more expensive technologies, or if excessive competition would lead to insufficient profitability to ensure producers' willingness to continue servicing the market. This latter incentive to accept incomplete compatibility arises because imperfect competition may be necessary to produce sufficient Schumpeterian rents to recover the fixed/sunk costs of product development.

As long as standardization is voluntary, consumers cannot compel firms to adopt a particular technology. However, if they participate actively, they can influence the choice of technologies that are adopted. Requiring multiple interoperable implementations as a pre-requisite for approval bundles the question of interoperability and technology choice. In the next two sections of this paper, I will explore the circumstances in which consumers find it desirable to require that these two decisions be bundled.

A Model of Incomplete Standardization

Imagine a four stage game of standards adoption. In the first stage, consumers choose a set of institutional rules that will govern how firms choose technical compatibility standards. In the second stage, firms choose a technology to adopt, $s \in S$, with an eye toward maximizing the profits they will earn competing for consumer demand. Assume that there is a continuous range of technologies $[0, s_{max}]$. The choice of technology will determine each consumer's intrinsic willingness-to-pay for the technology, $v(s)$, and the production costs that firms will face servicing the market, where these costs include the fixed costs $f(s)$ of developing the technology and the constant marginal costs $c(s)$ of producing the goods demanded by consumers.

Let us assume there are two firms that will compete to service a continuum of consumers distributed uniformly along the unit interval $[0, 1]$. In stage 3 of the game, the firms will choose their locations L_1 and L_2 along this interval, and in stage 4 the firms will choose prices (P_1 and P_2) for their two goods. A consumer located at x will face quadratic transportation costs, $t(L_i - x)^2$, if she decides to purchase from the firm located at L_i. Each consumer will seek to maximize her net surplus by choosing among the following three alternatives:

Consumer surplus for consumer $x \in [0, 1]$

Purchase from firm 1: $\quad v(s) - t[L_1 - x]^2 - p_1$

Purchase from firm 2: $\quad v(s) - t[L_2 - x]^2 - p_2$

Purchase from neither: $\quad 0$

The last two stages of this game are a classic Hotelling spatial differentiation game that yields the following symmetric equilibrium (see, for example, Tirole [1988], page 279)[5]:

(1) Firms locate at $L_1 = 0$ and $L_2 = 1$

(2) Firms set prices $p_1 = p_2 = p = t + c(s)$

(3) Firm profits are $\Pi_1 = \Pi_2 = \Pi = (t/2) - f(s)$ (≥ 0, by assumption)

(4) Firms split the market such that the surplus of the marginal consumer who is indifferent between purchasing from either firm, $x = 1/2$, is $CS_{1/2} = v(s) - c(s) - (5/4)t$ (≥ 0, by assumption)

(5) Total Consumer Surplus, $CS = v(s) - c(s) - (13/12)t$

(6) Total Surplus $= CS + 2\Pi = v(s) - c(s) - 2f(s) - (1/12)t$

In this equilibrium, the firms locate so as to maximally differentiate themselves and thereby minimize the intensity of the price competition they would face otherwise. The outcome that would maximize total surplus would be to locate the firms at $1/4$ and $3/4$ in order to minimize total transportation costs, so an inefficient degree of product differentiation occurs in equilibrium.[6] In the present application, think of the transportation costs as the costs of achieving interoperability whenever $t > 0$.

This is the equilibrium that firms will anticipate when they choose a technology s at the second stage. Since the firms are identical, they will have identical preferences over the set of potential technologies and if we identify the status quo ex ante with $s_0 \in S$, then the firms will prefer to adopt a new technology $s \in S$ if $\Pi(s) > \Pi(s_0)$. Or, if we hold t constant, whenever $f(s) < f(s_0)$. Let us assume that the set of technologies S can be ordered so that $s' > s$ implies that $f(s') > f(s)$ and $c(s') > c(s)$.

This means that fixed and variable costs move in the same direction. I will interpret s as measuring the degree of compatibility such that lower s implies that the designs of the firms' products are more closely coordinated and hence both fixed/sunk product development and variable production costs are lower for the reasons cited earlier. Other things being equal, firms will always prefer lower s and, assuming that the status quo is not the minimum s (i.e., $s_0 > 0$), will prefer some technology to the status quo.

I will say consumers and producers "agree" in their ranking of technologies whenever $s' > s$ implies $v(s') \leq v(s)$; and conversely, will say consumers "disagree" whenever $v(s') > v(s)$.[7] Irrespective of the degree of interoperability obtained, it may be the case that technologies that increase consumer w-t-p are more costly. When firms and consumers agree, holding t constant, both will prefer lower s; however, when they disagree, consumers may prefer increasing s even though prices will increase with variable costs. Finally, I will interpret t as measuring the degree of interoperability. In this model, bundling standardization and interoperability decisions is equivalent to requiring that in addition to choosing a new s firms choose a new t with the stipulation that $s = t$. When the two decisions are not bundled, assume that the firms choose s independently and t remains equal to its status quo value of t_0.

In the first stage, consumers choose whether to require firms to bundle the interoperability and standardization decisions and whether to participate in the standards process. Although consumers cannot constrain firms to choose a particular technology, if they choose to participate, they can veto any choice of s that they find less attractive than the status quo. Similarly, firms can always decide to adopt the status quo if there is no other technology they prefer more. Since there are no costs to participation, consumers will always weakly prefer to participate and have the potential of exercising their ability to block acceptance of new technologies that are less preferable than the status quo.

The ability of both parties to enforce the status quo unless a mutually preferred alternative is available captures the essence of the consensus decision-making process employed by voluntary standards development organizations. These procedures are designed to prevent approval of a standard that attracts significant minority opposition. Neither the traditional SDOs nor the Internet community would approve a standard that was opposed by either all consumers or all producers.

If consumers and producers agree and in the absence of fixed costs, the equilibrium that maximizes total surplus is for consumers to require bundling of the standardization and interoperability decisions and to set $s = t = 0$ and $p = c(0)$.[8] This corresponds to choosing the minimum cost technology with perfect substitutes. In this equilibrium, consumers would capture all of the surplus. In the presence of fixed costs, however, t must be greater than 0 or else firms' profits will be negative and they will refuse to participate in the market. Deviating from the least cost technology ($s > 0$) is necessary as long as product development expenditures are funded out of firm operating profits. These Schumpeterian rents are a necessary cost of using the market to decentralize technology development.[9]

If the decisions are not bundled, then firms unambiguously prefer the least cost technology ($t = t_0$, $s = 0$) to the status quo (t_0, s_0); however, consumers may prefer the status quo if they disagree with firms regarding the ranking of technologies.[10] Letting $s^* = t(s^*)$ designate the level of compatibility/interoperability selected by producers when the two decisions are bundled, consumers will unanimously prefer to require bundling whenever

(1) $CS_{1/2}(s^*, s^*) > CS_{1/2}(t_0, 0)$ or

$[v(s^*) - v(0)] + [c(0) - c(s^*)] + (5/4)[t_0 - s^*] > 0$

and

(2) $\Pi(s^*, s^*) \geq \Pi(t_0, s_0)$ or $(1/2)[s^* - s_0] + [f(s_0) - f(s^*)] > 0$

The first condition guarantees that consumers prefer the bundled to the unbundled outcome, and the second condition guarantees that producers prefer the bundled to the status quo outcome. If the latter condition fails, then even when consumers prefer the bundled outcome, they prefer settling for partial standardization in the form of the unbundled outcome rather than maintaining the status quo. Thus, it may be a second best solution to accept partial standardization even when full interoperability is preferred, if attaining the latter is not feasible.

Whenever w-t-p increases with decreasing costs such that the most desirable technologies are also the lowest cost and most interoperable, it will always be efficient to increase interoperability (decrease $t(s)$), but consumers and producers will disagree. By bundling the two decisions, producers can be induced to accept increased competition in return for lower fixed costs. However,

even when both conditions are satisfied, it may be socially inefficient to require the two decisions to be bundled. If $f(s_0) - f(0) > 0$
is sufficiently large, then consumers may prefer the bundled
outcome even if the unbundled yields higher total surplus. Therefore, we cannot be certain that better (more efficient) standardization decisions always result when interoperability is included as
part of the standardization decision. When consumers and producers disagree regarding the ranking of technologies, then although
consumers always prefer to participate, it is possible that their
participation reduces total surplus. Consumers may veto adoption
of a standard that would improve total surplus.[11] Moreover, when
consumers and producers disagree, both may prefer adopting a
technology that offers reduced compatibility (i.e., $s^* > t_0$). In light of
these results, it is clear that in order to determine whether it is
desirable to require that standardization and interoperability decisions be bundled, one needs to consider how the costs and benefits
of adopting alternative technologies are likely to be allocated.

Standard Setting in the Internet

The Internet is a network of autonomous data networks that
electronically links host computers at universities, research centers, government offices, and corporations around the globe.
Today's Internet evolved from the ARPANET, which was created in
1969 under the aegis of the U.S. Department of Defense as the first
wide-area packet-switched data network linking a few prominent
research universities and defense contractors within the United
States[12]. The Internet permits users on its sub-networks to transfer
files, exchange electronic mail ("e-mail") and access remote host
computers. These functions require a collection of networking
protocol standards that guarantee that communications between
hosts on disparate networks will be compatible. During the 1970s,
the family of TCP/IP protocols were developed for use in the
Internet.[13]

The continuing evolution of the TCP/IP suite of protocols is
managed by the Internet Engineering Task Force (IETF), which is
one of the two task forces under the supervision of the Internet
Architecture Board (IAB)[14]. The IETF is organized into collections
of working groups in ten functional areas, each of which is under

the supervision of an area director. Each area director supervises the work of from five to nine working groups that are actively engaged in developing new or revising existing protocol standards. The IETF is itself managed by the Internet Engineering Steering Group (IESG), consisting of the IESG Chairman and the ten area directors. The members of the IESG and IAB and the chairpersons and participants in the working groups are all volunteers, who participate as individuals (rather than as representatives of their employers).[15]

The actual standards are developed in the IETF working groups, where anyone who is interested may participate, although typically draft documents are produced by a few dedicated engineers[16]. Each working group must have a charter approved by the IESG and IAB. These charters limit the technical scope of a working group, and working groups are usually disbanded once their chartered task is either completed or abandoned. The willingness to carefully constrain the scope and lives of working groups distinguishes the Internet process from other Standards Development Organizations (SDOs) such as ISO where working groups often have longer lives.

In addition to working group meetings and several annual IETF plenary meetings, where all of the working groups discuss their progress, draft standards are debated on electronic bulletin boards that are accessible to anyone with access to the Internet. To further facilitate communication within the Internet community, the IAB maintains the "Request for Comments" (RFCs) document series. These RFCs report important IAB positions, official standards documents, and statements of procedures. The RFCs, meeting minutes for the IAB, IESG and the various working groups, and all of the working drafts are electronically accessible at no cost via the Internet.[17]

The ability to communicate electronically dramatically lowers the costs of remotely tracking and monitoring the activities of the IETF. This distinguishes the IETF from more traditional SDOs like ISO or ANSI. Other SDOs usually sell copies of standards and documents that describe their procedures, and seldom, if ever, use e-mail and electronic file transfers to facilitate geographically dispersed communications. Although the cost of standards documentation from traditional SDOs may be unlikely to deter those who are directly involved in implementation of the standards, these costs make it more difficult for peripherally interested parties to keep informed. The IETF is more "open" than traditional SDOs in the sense that it is much easier for outsiders to keep abreast of the IETF's activities and to contribute comments.[18]

When it comes to decision-making power, however, the IETF process is in some respects less open than the more formal SDOs. First, the IETF does not have formal voting rules. Voting rules are a mechanism for establishing property rights to decision-making power. Other SDOs usually require supramajority voting before major decisions are approved. Also, participants usually vote by firm or organization to prevent vote-packing.[19]

Second, the IETF's implementation of consensus decision-making is far less bureaucratically constrained than in other SDOs. For example, in the ANSI Accredited X3 Committee for Information Processing Systems (X3), standards must progress through a series of 18 "milestones." Supramajority voting (usually two-thirds) is used for most decisions and there must be a documented attempt to reconcile *all* negative comments. In practice, ANSI approval procedures require multiple ballots and time-consuming comment and review cycles before achievement of consensus can be demonstrated. By contrast, in the IETF, WG chairs are permitted far greater discretion in how development proceeds. Rather than demanding that consensus be convincingly demonstrated, as under the ANSI procedures, the IETF process presumes that consensus exists in the absence of vocal opposition.

Historically, most of the important positions in the IAB, IETF, and various working groups were controlled by the same academics, network researchers and consultants who participated in the development of the original ARPANET technology.[20] All of the key participants were experts in networking technology with long working relationships. In this small, relatively homogeneous community, an informal decision-making process worked quite well. It afforded the flexibility to adjust to changing circumstances, and the common level of expertise reduced problems associated with asymmetric information. Long-term relationships (à la Axelrod (1984)) reduced the threat from short-term opportunistic behavior and created opportunities for inter-temporal side-payments ("I'll yield today and you'll yield tomorrow"). Moreover, small groups are often better able to achieve consensus (Olson, 1965).[21]

It is also noteworthy that users have been and continue to be prominently represented among the key participants in Internet standards development. This is an important difference vis a vis traditional IT hardware standardization efforts, which have tended to be dominated by vendors. Although users have been and continue to be encouraged to participate in SDOs such as X3 and the IEEE, their participation tended to be less active in times past. As will be discussed more below, greater user participation helps explain some of the advantages of the Internet process.

Over the years, however, the Internet has grown dramatically: from 213 hosts in 1981 to 80,000 hosts in 1989 to over 700,000 hosts in 1992.[22] As of April 1994, the Internet supports an estimated 20 million users with network growth at 10% per month![23] The TCP/IP protocols are the most widely used vendor-independent family of networking standards publicly available.[24] Analysts have estimated that the worldwide commercial market for TCP/IP products and services was $607 million in 1990 and expect it to grow to over $1.8 billion by 1995[25].

In recent years, both the U.S. Congress and the Executive Office have proposed a number of initiatives that would dramatically affect the future evolution of the Internet.[26] In December 1991, President Bush signed a $1 billion authorization for establishment of a National Research Education Network (NREN), which will be based on the Internet. In light of these events and the growing commercial importance of the TCP/IP suite of protocols for corporate wide-area "enterprise" networks,[27] the Internet community is in the process of rapid change.

Participation in IETF meetings keeps growing, and many of the new participants come from heterogeneous backgrounds.[28] They do not have long-term relationships with each other or with the present leaders of the IAB and IESG. Many are much less well informed than previous participants regarding the engineering technicalities. According to Lyman Chapin, the chairman of the IAB in 1992,

In size and extent, it [the Internet] has grown beyond what any of us envisioned 10 years ago. It's easily the largest telecommunications network in the world. At last count, 110 countries were connected. . . . There is also the difficulty of management. There is a much broader group of interests using the network and the issue of commercialization. The scope of interest in the Internet community is broader now and you can no longer manage it as you used to, by calling up a few graduate students. . . . The biggest long-range problem is how the internet will be managed. Before, it was sort of an insiders' club and there was no formal structure. (see Messmer, 1992)

In recognition of these problems, the IAB and Internet are changing. In order to create a new institutional home for the IAB that would be less beholden to the U.S. government and in recognition of the increased internationalization of the Internet, the Internet Society (ISOC) was created and held its first meeting during the summer of 1992 in Kobe, Japan.[29] The ISOC is a professional society with membership open to anyone who is willing to pay the dues.[30] In addition, a new IETF Working Group entitled POISED was formed to discuss proposals on how (and if) the IAB and IETF should reform their decision-making rules.[31] The beginnings of this trend are apparent in the new IAB charter, which specifies election voting rules and term limits for IAB and IETF officers.[32] The increased formalism is required in order to educate new participants and convince them that their longer term interests will be protected. In the absence of long-term relationships, new participants seek assurance that IAB and IETF decisions will not be capricious.

As the rents that are at stake have grown, so has the threat of opportunistic behavior and conflict. Increased bureaucracy and procedural rules are likely to slow the standards process, but this slowing is partially intentional. When the potential for conflict and strategic rent-seeking are large, bureaucratic red tape creates "early-warning" systems, reducing ex ante expected gains from opportunistic behavior. The increased difficulty in creating new standards provides greater weight to the technological "status quo." Since the adoption of a standard often requires specialized investments, the willingness-to-adopt is reduced if adopters fear future attempts to expropriate their quasi-rents. If it's too easy to overturn the status quo with a new standard, then there's little incentive to cooperate in today's adoption decision. In Lehr (1992a, 1992b), I argued that the procedures employed by traditional SDOs should be understood, in part, as a rational response to the collective choice problem of standardization when private and collective interests conflict. Based on recent trends in the Internet, I would expect the IETF to become more like traditional SDOs both in terms of structure and in terms of the difficulties faced in developing standards quickly. Thus far, however, procedural changes in the standards process have been relatively minor. These have consisted primarily of attempts to better codify and explain the process to newcomers. This reflects a conscious attempt by IETF'ers to preserve the perceived advantages of greater speed and flexibility that attend the reduced bureaucratic formalism of their approach.[33]

In addition to the differences cited above, the IETF's approach differs from the approach followed by traditional SDOs in two other very important respects. First, the IETF embeds a requirement to demonstrate interoperable implementations into its lifecycle model. An Internet standard is supposed to progress through three states: proposed standard, draft standard, and Internet standard. Associated with each standard is a status, which may be either "required," "recommended," "elective," or "not recommended." Before the IESG will recommend advancing a standard from proposed to draft status, the IETF requires that there be at least two independent implementations interoperating on the Internet.[34]

Second, the IETF process is designed to accelerate standards development. The minimal time that must elapse before a proposed standard may be elevated to draft status is six months, and the minimal time before a draft standard may be approved as an Internet standard is four months. Draft standards that are not reviewed within 6 months are removed from the draft directory, and the IESG reviews the charters of working groups that have not produced a standard in 24 months. You either "move it, or lose it."

The success of the TCP/IP suite of protocols and the continued growth of the Internet, coupled with the perception that other, more traditional SDOs are less effective, has attracted interest to the Internet process. Proponents of the IETF's approach argue that it may be worth imitating elsewhere. In the following section, I will attempt to interpret the sources for the Internet's success and the appropriateness of extending these benefits to other standardization fora.

Why Does the Internet Standards Process Work?

One of the most important explanations for the IETF's success to date is historical accident. As discussed above, the IETF community was relatively small, dominated by users/developers who shared similar levels of expertise and preferences about the set of technologies being developed. In this environment, standardization is much less contentious. As the Internet's standards environment has changed, the IETF has adopted some of the features that are familiar from more traditional SDOs, although it has tried to retain its most important distinguishing traits.

The IETF focuses on internetworking protocols for a diverse collection of heterogeneous networks, which by the very nature of the standards under consideration places an extremely high premium on interoperability and ubiquity. Thus IETF standards tend to emphasize supporting minimal functionality at least cost, as opposed to supporting specialized services.[35] In terms of the model presented earlier, imagine a situation where $v(s)$ changes little if at all with s, but customers are extremely sensitive to the costs of attaining interoperability (t matters a lot). Moreover, since the protocols are embodied in software, the marginal costs of production, $c(s)$, are close to zero. What consumers care most about is inducing firms to accept as low a t as possible, so they will prefer to bundle the interoperability and compatibility decisions, hoping that development costs fall sufficiently so that $s^* < t_0$.

In contrast, when one considers hardware standards, the potential for significant cost savings from adopting a standard that fails to improve interoperability may be sufficiently promising that consumers prefer an unbundled standards process (i.e., $c(s_0) - c(0) > 0$ and large). Although this need not be the case, it seems more likely in the context of hardware standardization.

Furthermore, since communication protocols are implemented with software technologies, there is a very short lead time between when a standard is accepted and when it can be deployed by customers in the market place. With hardware standards (e.g., a design for a fiber optic coupler), there is a longer lead time between when the technology is developed and when product can be made available.[36] The IETF's extremely aggressive timing rules discriminate against technologies with longer development lifecycles. Also, the requirement to demonstrate interoperable implementations may increase the difficulty of reaching agreement on a standard. It is easier to modify a software design than a hardware design. By the time product developers are ready to demonstrate working implementations they may already be too committed to their particular design to be willing to compromise. Finally, since it is more difficult to identify bugs and determine the performance characteristics of software, the requirement to demonstrate multiple working implementations is more important with software technologies than with hardware.

A second reason the IETF process works is that from its inception, users have been the dominant participants in the IETF. In the model presented above, standardization may be inefficient because the development costs of new technologies, $f(s)$, are recovered via the operating profits of producers. If producers and consumers are merged—so that consumers directly incur the development and production costs—then consumers can control the choice of s and t directly and will adopt an efficient solution.

Although user participation helps explain why the IETF process bundles the standardization and interoperability decisions and why this is successful when applied to the development of communication protocols, such participation may be less beneficial in the case of hardware standardization. Even within the abstract model, consumer participation does not always lead to more efficient solutions since consumers may prefer the status quo to a less costly, and perhaps more interoperable, technology. Also, as noted earlier, hardware vendors need to commit to investments in particular technologies, $f(s)$, well in advance of when consumers commit to purchasing products. This creates the potential for hold-up problems if consumers refuse to approve standards that will support an adequate level of product differentiation and hence prices sufficient to recover the costs of development if these costs are largely sunk.

A third advantage for IETF is that the Internet's existence as a communications medium to facilitate the dissemination of information about ongoing and complete standards significantly lowers the costs of participating in the process. Since other SDO fora could avail themselves of the Internet, this is not an advantage that is peculiar to the Internet. I believe that part of the reason that more traditional fora have resisted adopting electronic communications is twofold: (1) a significant source of funding for their development activities derives from the sale of published standards;[37] and (2) the greater bureaucracy of traditional SDOs becomes even more unwieldy the larger the number of active participants. With electronic communications making it easier to copy and distribute documents, it would be more difficult to protect revenues from the sale of standards. With lower participation costs, it would become easier for participants who wished to slow down the development of a standard to manipulate the bureaucratic procedures toward this end. Moreover, it would become more difficult to conclusively demonstrate that consensus had been achieved.

The implications of these arguments are twofold. First, if other SDOs adopt electronic communications they will probably need to streamline their procedures and develop formal participation limits to help assure that only stakeholders who are interested in seeing the development process proceed are included. Otherwise, the consensus rules will be vulnerable to participants who wish to stop or slow down the process (e.g., vendors of proprietary systems who are threatened by a new standard or who want additional time to come up the learning curve). Similarly, the IETF's open-access means that they should be very cautious in introducing additional formalism. The most obvious step in this direction—which I would advise against—would be to adopt supramajority voting requirements. In addition to being difficult to implement electronically (e.g., how to prevent vote-packing with individual participation, how to verify identity), these would significantly slow down the process.

The Internet is also valuable as a test bed for demonstrating the feasibility of interoperable implementations. Other things being equal, lowering the costs of interoperability testing increases the benefits from improved interoperability. This is important when considers extending the requirement for demonstrating multiple working implementations to other fora. In the absence of a test bed, one would need to be created. These are expensive, and introducing a requirement to fund conformance/interoperability testing would strain resources that are already scarce for the basic development process.

A final reason for IETF's success is that once one accepts that it is a good idea to require working implementations as a prerequisite for advancement within the standards process, one eliminates much of the need for the enhanced bureaucracy (voting rules, proposal review procedures, public notice requirements, etc.) observed in traditional SDOs. With multiple working implementations available for review, it becomes much less likely that interested parties would fail to detect an attempt by a crafty minority to force adoption of a standard that adversely affected their interests. When this threat is reduced, the need for built-in early warning alarm systems—one of the advantages of a more bureaucratic process—is reduced. Moreover, the characteristics of communications protocol design (emphasis on interoperability, willingness to accept lowest-common-denominator solutions, and shorter product development lifecycles) further reduce the need for bureaucracy.

Countering these trends is the growing heterogeneity of tastes that attends the growing diversity of the Internet communities. Although these effects are not addressed in the model presented above, they help explain the moderate movement toward increased formalization of the process noted above.

Summary

This paper has examined why the Internet standardization process appears to have been more successful than other SDOs in producing timely standards. The analysis focused particularly on the Internet's strong emphasis on achieving interoperability as the goal for standardization. In light of the growing need for more timely IT compatibility standards and the growing importance of the Internet in infrastructure planning, it is worthwhile considering what the implications might be for adopting IETF procedures in other fora and for the IETF itself as IT markets continue to evolve.

Several conclusions emerge from this analysis. First, much of the IETF's prior success is owed to historically favorable circumstances, which produced a less contentious standards environment. As these change, we should expect Internet standardization to become more difficult and to suffer more of the same problems that plague other SDOs. However, although its earlier history as a small community of like-minded, publicly spirited experts contributed significantly to its record of success, there are other features of the Internet process that are worth considering.

The IETF's approach appears especially well suited to the project of designing software-based communications protocols. These place a high premium on interoperability by their very nature, so stressing this goal is appropriate, even though it is less appropriate in other circumstances. This emphasis on interoperability is encouraged by strong user participation. Also, the lifecycle timing attributes of software standardization seem more amenable to the IETF's aggressive timing schedule.

Finally, the Internet itself proves a valuable asset that complements the IETF's less bureaucratic approach. If the IETF responds to increased contentiousness by mimicking the procedures of traditional SDOs, then the open participation supported across the Internet may present a problem. The Internet is also valuable as a test bed for new technologies that lowers the costs of interoperability testing and enhances the feasibility of stressing the demonstration of working implementations.

Even though the IETF's procedures work well in the case of internetworking protocols, we cannot presume they will be equally successful in other venues. The model presented here demonstrates that it is possible for consumer participation to be inefficient; for decreased interoperability to be efficient; and for partial standardization that admits variable interoperability to be optimal.

Acknowledgment

A preliminary version of this paper entitled "Compatibility Standards and the Internet" was presented at the Twentieth Annual

Telecommunications Policy Research Conference, Solomons Island, September 1992.

Notes

[1] All of these organizations are involved in the development of technical compatibility standards for the computer and telecommunications industries. In structure and procedures these organizations are all more similar to each other than to the Internet. ISO is the International Standards Organization; CCITT is the International Telegraph and Telephone Consultative Committee; ANSI is the American National Standards Institute. See Cargill (1989) for a description of these and other standards institutions or Lehr (1992a) for analysis of structure. See McQuillan (1990) for a claim that the Internet process works better, and Vasquez (1990) or Moad (1990) for critiques of other fora.

[2] For example, conformance tests for FDDI, Ethernet and ISDN were funded, developed and implemented in fora subsequent to and different from those in which the original base standards were developed. The separation of conformance testing and standards development processes is recognized in the X3 Strategic Planning Committee's five stage model of the standards lifecycle (see X3 Lifecycle Model Draft Report).

[3] The allocation of the benefits between consumers and producers will depend on how the market equilibrium shifts. In general, we would expect both consumer surplus and producer surplus to increase at least weakly if w-t-p increases (which manifests itself as an outward shift in aggregate demand). However, it is possible for either consumer surplus or producer surplus to actually decrease. For example, consumer surplus may decrease if the new equilibrium involves serving a smaller market at a higher price (e.g., if marginal costs are decreasing and intersect marginal revenue from above at the old equilibrium).

[4] Compatibility standards also may make vendors products closer substitutes when they facilitate customer bundling of products from vendors at different points along the vertical value chain for complex systems. In this paper, I am focusing on the effect of compatibility standards on firms which make similar products. For a discussion of the competitive effects of standards which allow customers to mix-and-match multiple vendor components see Matutes and Regibeau (1988) or Economides and Lehr (1994).

[5] Assuming $v(s)$, t, $f(s)$, and $c(s)$ are suitably bounded such that the entire market is served in equilibrium and both consumer surplus and producer profits are bounded.

[6] This yields $TS = v(s) - c(s) - 2f(s) - (7/96)t$.

[7] To simplify the analysis, I assume these rankings are monotonic.

[8] Assume $v(0) > c(0) + 2f(0)$ for simplicity.

[9] In this model, a single monopolist would locate at $x = 1/2$ and would choose $t = 0$ and $p^m = v(0) - c(0) - f(0)$, which would offer even higher surplus than under the duopoly solution.

[10] When consumers disagree with producers regarding the ranking of technologies, it is possible that the gains from adopting a lower cost technology are more than offset in terms of the losses in w-t-p, or $v(s_0) - v(0) > c(s_0) - c(0) > 0$.

[11] For example, suppose the reduction in fixed costs is sufficiently large that $s^* < t_0$ and that $TS(t_0, 0) < TS(s^*, s^*) < TS(t_0, s_0)$ but that consumer w-t-p increases sufficiently with increasing s that $CS_{1/2}(t_0, s_0) > CS_{1/2}(s^*, s^*) > CS_{1/2}(t_0, 0)$. In this case, the most efficient outcome is the unbundled outcome but consumers prefer the status quo to either alternative.

[12] See Cook (1992) or Kahin (1992) for histories of the Internet. The ARPANET was finally phased out in 1988 and its traffic was shifted to NSFnet, the network funded by the National Science Foundation (NSF) to provide backbone services to the Internet.

[13] TCP/IP stands for Transport Control Protocol and Internet Protocol. See Rose (1990, 1991) or Tannenbaum (1988) for an introduction to networking protocols. Vinton Cerf and Bob Kahn co-authored the first paper describing the Internet architecture in 1974. The TCP/IP protocols were formally adopted for use in the ARPANET in 1983.

[14] The Internet Architecture Board is the descendant of the Internet Activities Board, which was the governing body of the Internet until the formation of the Internet Society (ISOC) in 1992. The Internet Activities Board was formed in 1983 from the re-organized Internet Configuration Control Board (ICCB), which was originally formed in 1979 by Vinton Cerf, who at the time was the Defense Advanced Research Projects Agency (DARPA) program director. The IETF was formed in January 1986. The other important task force is the Internet Research Task Force (IRTF) which supervises experimental networking research in the Internet. See Cerf (1989) or Huitema (1994).

[15] The Internet Society approves the operating rules and procedures under which the IAB, IETF and IESG operate. The trustees of the Internet Society provide the charter for and approve the membership of the IAB, which in turn approves appointments to the IESG from those nominated by the IETF. The nominating committee for membership in the IAB and IESG is drawn from the active membership of the IETF (Huitema, 1994).

[16] Membership in the ISOC is not required in order to participate in the IETF WGs.

[17] These documents, including the RFCs, are available by anonymous FTP from ds.internic.net. For descriptions of the Internet standards process, see especially RFC1600 "Internet Official Protocol Standards" (Postel, 1994), RFC1601 "Charter of the Internet Architecture Board" (Huitema, 1994), RFC1602 "The Internet Standards Process—version 2" (IAB) and RFC1603 "IETF Working Group Guidelines and Procedures" (Huizer, 1994).

[18] During the course of this research, I have reviewed the e-mail archives from several working groups and have seen many comments from obviously technically unsophisticated would-be participants.

[19] The SDOs differ on voting rules. In the IEEE, participants vote as individuals, whereas in the ANSI X3 Committee, ISO, and ETSI votes are by organization or firm. In the CCITT, votes are by country. Besen (1990) discusses why ETSI decided to relax its supramajority voting requirements to make it easier to pass decisions. Although vote-packing might be perceived as a threat when participants vote as individuals, this does not seem to have been a major problem for the IEEE. See Lehr (1992a,b) for further discussion of the procedures employed by other SDOs.

[20] See Malkin (1992), which provides the curriculum vitae for 24 of the IAB and IESG members. Most of the members have long backgrounds either in academics, research centers or university computer centers. Most are Americans. A number of prominent participants were associated with SRI or Bolt, Beranek and Newman, two of the original ARPANET contractors.

[21] With a fixed total benefit, private gains decrease as the size of the group that must share the benefits increases.

[22] See Lottor (1992).

[23] According to an ISOC FAQ document entitled "What-is.txt" available by anonymous FTP from ds.internic.net in the ISOC sub-directory: "At April 1994, the Internet consisted of more than 30,000 networks in 71 countries. Gateways that allow at least Email connectivity extend this reach to 146 countries. At the end of 1993, 2.217 million computers were measured as actually reachable—with an estimated total of 20 million users. Network growth continues at around 10 percent per month."

[24] IBM's proprietary System Network Architecture (SNA) is the most widely used protocol suite. Digital Equipment Corporation's DECnet is another vendor-specific architecture which is in wide use. The only significant public standards competition for TCP/IP comes from the ISO-sponsored OSI standards (see further discussion below).

[25] See Cook (1992).

[26] In 1989, the White House Office of Science and Technology Policy published its High Performance Computing Plan which called for an upgrading of the National Science Foundation's (NSF) NFSnet, which provides backbone services for the Internet. In 1991, Congress passed the High Performance Computing Act (S.272), which calls for the creation of a National Research Education Network (NREN). See Cook (1992) and Kahin (1992).

[27] Personal computers became prominent in the first half of the 1980s. These were interconnected into Local Area Networks (LANs) during the latter half of the decade. Corporations are now in the process of inter-connecting LANs into "enterprise-wide" networks spanning both the country and the globe.

[28] According to Clark (1991), "over the past few years, there have been increasing

signs of strains on the fundamental architecture, mostly stemming from continued Internet growth. Discussions of these problems reverberate constantly on many major mailing lists."

[29] According to Lyman Chapin: "The effort now is to try to promote the Internet Society (a nonprofit organization formed this January) as an overall umbrella to include the IAB as well as the IETF and the IRTF, both chartered by the IAB" (Messmer, 1992). According to Kozel (1992), "the Internet Society is an attempt to impose structure on the Internet's loose confederation of interconnected networks. In a formal way, this global professional society will be an Internet institution answerable to those outside the Internet. It will set broad policy and standards, sponsor conferences."

[30] As of February 1994, the annual dues for individuals were reduced from $70 to $35. Information on the ISOC and Internet is available via anonymous FTP from ds.internic.net.

[31] In an August 13, 1992 e-mail announcement to the IETF mail list, Phil Gross, the chairman of the IETF, reported that "the IAB has recommended that the most effective means available to the Internet Community for gathering recommendations for refining our existing procedures is to request that an IETF Working Group be formed."

[32] See Huizer (1994).

[33] The most important substantive reform that was recommended was to clarify the role of the IAB vis a vis the IESG and the IETF. Previously, there was some ambiguity regarding the IAB's ability to over-rule IESG recommendations. This reached a head in the spring and summer of 1992 and led to the decision that final authority to approve a standard must reside with the IESG and that the IAB's role would be to help adjudicate appeals and when necessary to refer IESG recommendation to further study. In addition, the POISED committee recommended formal appeals procedures (including referral to the IAB) and policies towards external standards and intellectual property issues. The publication of the IETF Working Group Guidelines (RFC1603) and the Internet Standards Process (RFC1602) and the reorganization of the FTP access sites are all part of the effort to better explain IETF operations.

[34] See Postel (1994), p. 3.

[35] According to this argument, we should expect Internet protocols to be more tolerant of lowest common denominator solutions. Users choose their primary network affiliations to form coalitions to economize on the costs of meeting their most important specialized communication needs. However, when users on these specialized networks communicate with users on different networks across the Internet, presumably their need for and willingness-to-pay for special, custom-tailored protocol support is lower.

[36] For example, hardware production requires the set-up of a production line.

[37] See Garcia (1992) for a discussion of the economic effects of SDOs dependency on the sale of standards for funding development activities.

References

Note: A number of the documents below are referenced as "RFCxxxx," which means they are part of the series of on-line documents maintained by the Internet community. They may be accessed via anonymous FTP in the subdirectory RFC on the host ds.internic.net.

Axelrod, R., 1984. *The Evolution of Cooperation* (New York: Basic Books).

Besen, S., 1990. "The European Telecommunications Standards Institute," *Telecommunications Policy*, December, 521–530.

Cargill, C., 1989. *Information Technology Standardization: Theory, Process and Organizations* (Boston: Digital Press).

Cerf, V., 1989. "The Internet Activities Board," RFC1120, September.

Clark, D., 1991. "Toward the Future Internet Architecture," RFC1287, December.

Cook, G., 1992. *The National Research and Education Network: Whom Shall It Serve?*, privately published.

Economides, N., and W. Lehr, 1994. "The Quality of Complex Systems and Industry Structure," in W. Lehr, ed., *Quality and Reliability of Telecommunication Infrastructure* (Hillsdale, NJ: Lawrence Erlbaum).

Farrell, J., and G. Saloner, 1988. "Coordination through Committees and Markets," *Rand Journal of Economics*, Vol. 19, No. 2, 235–252.

Farrell, J., and C. Shapiro, 1992. "Standard Setting in High Definition Television," *Brookings Papers on Economic Activity, Microeconomics*, 1–94.

Garcia, L., 1992. *Global Standards: Building Blocks for the Future*, Office of Technology Assessment, U.S. Congress, TCT-512 (Washington DC: GPO).

Huitema, C., 1994. "Charter of the Internet Architecture Board," RFC1601, March.

Huizer, E., 1994. "IETF Working Group Guidelines and Procedures," RFC1603, March.

IAB and IESG, 1994. "The Internet Standards Process—Revison 2," RFC1602, March.

Kahin, B., ed, 1992. Build*ing Information Infrastructure: Issues in the Development of the National Research Education Network* (New York: McGraw-Hill Primis).

Kozel, E., 1992. "Commercializing the Internet: Impact on Corporate Users," *Telecommunications (International Edition)*, Vol. 26, No. 1 (January), s11–s14.

Lehr, W., 1992a. "The Political Economics of Voluntary Standards," mimeo, Columbia University, March.

Lehr, W., 1992b. "Standardization: Understanding the Process," *Journal of the American Society for Information Science*, Vol. 43, No. 8 (September), 550–556.

Lehr, W., 1994. "Economics of Anticipatory Standards," mimeo, Columbia University, January.

Lottor, M., 1992. "Internet Growth," RFC1296, January.

McQuillan, J., 1991. "Setting a Faster Standards-Setting Pace," *Network World* (March 11), 35.

Malkin, G., 1992. "Who's Who in the Internet: Biographies of IAB, IESG, and IRSG Members," RFC1336, May.

Matutes, C., and P. Regibeau, 1988. "'Mix and Match': Product Compatibility without Network Externalities," *Rand Journal of Economics*, Vol. 19, No. 2, 221–234.

Messmer, E., 1992. "Internet Architect Gives Long-Term View," *Network World* (May 18), 37, 46.

Moad, J, 1990. "The Standards Process Breaks Down," *Datamation*, Vol. 36, No. 18, 24–32.

Olson, M., 1965. *The Logic of Collective Action* (Cambridge: Harvard University Press).

Postel, J., 1994. "Internet Official Protocol Standards," RFC1600, March.

Rose, M., 1990. *The Open Book: A Practical Perspective on OSI* (Englewood Cliffs, NJ: Prentice-Hall).

Rose, M., 1991. *The Simple Book: An Introduction to Management of TCP/IP based Internets* (Englewood Cliffs, NJ: Prentice-Hall).

Tirole, J., 1988. *The Theory of Industrial Organization* (Cambridge: MIT Press).

Vasquez, W., 1990. "Standards Groups Have Their Work Cut out for Them," *Network World* (January 15), 37.

Information Infrastructure Standards in Heterogeneous Sectors: Lessons from the Worldwide Air Cargo Community

Paul W. Forster and John Leslie King

Introduction

The United States already has a robust and highly sophisticated national information infrastructure. This infrastructure is built upon a large number of standards that are the product of socio-technical regimes in telecommunications and computing that have, until recently, been rather stable. In particular monopolistic or oligopolistic service providers such as the telephone companies and broadcasting networks and product suppliers such as the large computer and software companies have been extraordinarily successful at creating and enforcing uniformity in the communications infrastructure of the nation and, to a considerable extent, the world. As a result, these standards have also tended to guide the kinds of traffic that use the infrastructure and the kinds of activities that result or benefit from that use. These standards have constrained the space of possible innovations, but they have also provided operational efficiency through economies of scale and allocation of resources. Early agreement on such standards can be seen in retrospect as part of a national competitive strategy to build capacity. Having such standards *ex ante* has arguably provided a head start for US businesses competing in a rapidly growing worldwide environment of suppliers and customers.

The future prospects for the NII depart significantly from this earlier era of anticipatory and authoritative standards. The emerging world of information management is dynamic and evolving, building on rapid technical and social change. The importance of the "new NII" will not derive from the engineering origins of the technologies, such as multimedia or wireless communications, but from the diversity of work that will be conducted upon it. The NII has never been relegated to servicing a single homogeneous community. It serves a 'meta-community' through a shared technical infrastructure that supports the work activities of local, national and international communities in all sectors. Each community has its own institutional characteristics and conducts its operations in an environment of competing interest groups within the community. The existing information infrastructure has facilitated the most homogenous and rudimentary aspects of information management across these heterogeneous organizations and communities by serving a "lowest common denominator" purpose. The new NII will penetrate more deeply into the idiosyncratic features of the communities it supports. In the process, it will itself become less homogenous, less predictable, less controllable, and most important, less standardizable.

The decline of anticipatory standard setting in the new NII is a symptom of a welcome change. This change is not inevitable—it is possible to reduce any case of social heterogeneity to homogeneity given enough power and resources to overcome all resistance. Nevertheless, heterogeneity has always been and will likely continue as an essential attribute of economic and social activity for four reasons:

• Diversity is inherent in the structure of each community and the work it performs. Cultural differences both cut cross and characterize group, intra-organizational, inter-organizational, sectoral, regional, and national boundaries. Practices, conventions, and meanings have evolved at each level to coordinate work.

• Technical, economic, and social circumstances are themselves dynamic, creating heterogeneity within each community and motivating adaptive behavior.

• Variety and experimentation with new behaviors and techniques create the opportunities for extraordinary benefits from innovation.

• Periodic lapses and failures of will and organization in even the most authoritarian and centralizing power structures bring opportunities for diversity to break loose.

Suppressing heterogeneity can lead to premature convergence on non-optimal solutions, stifle creative alternatives, and exacerbate conflict between interest groups. Information infrastructure can aid in such suppression, as illustrated by the rapidly built and highly effective centralized telephone system Stalin installed in the USSR during the 1930s. Long before citizens had access to a telephone network, Stalin was linked with his political and military minions throughout his far-flung empire, and this network played an influential role in his consolidation and maintenance of power. The new NII will not necessarily take shape in a manner that supports the activities of heterogeneous communities. To serve such a role, the new NII must emerge not from concerns about engineering standards, but rather from a concern over how best to support the coordination of work within heterogeneous communities. Standards must be developed less to dictate the *way* in which work should be done, and more to indicate *what* needs to be done, with the details unspecified and left to the direction of the communities themselves.

This paper provides observations about information-handling standards derived from one highly heterogeneous sector of work, the worldwide air cargo community. This community has properties that make it attractive for this purpose. First, it is truly a community, and a global community at that, with powerful institutional conventions at work that impose constraints on the behavior of the participants within the community. Second, there are substantial benefits anticipated for those who are able to exploit the network externalities of a transnational information system for air trade. And third, to date, no individual or collaborative attempt to take advantage of these opportunities has been successful. This singular anomaly sets the stage for our investigation. In the remaining sections we will introduce information management practices in this community, concentrating on the practices and technology used for that purpose. We then discuss the broader sectoral conditions that shape the practices and technologies, explaining why much of the conventional NII-oriented wisdom about what "should" facilitate the work of the community simply will not do so. In conclusion, we discuss alternative infrastructure visions with attendant standards that could, at least in principle, facilitate the work of the community as it actually functions.

Information Management in the Air Cargo Community

The international air cargo community is made up of three broad segments: ground transport that moves cargoes from origin to airports and airports to destination; air transport that moves cargoes between airports; and agents that coordinate and perform some or all of these services plus the handling of institutional requirements such as customs, insurance, and so on. The simplest example of air cargo is passenger luggage, which is delivered by the passenger to the air transport carrier and picked up for final delivery by the passenger. The traditional air cargo community consists of three broad functional domains: airlines (including passage/cargo carriers and cargo-only carriers), ground transport companies (truck and rail transport companies), and freight forwarders that coordinate the door-to-airport and airport-to-door activities at each end. Some forwarders are vertically integrated to the extent that they coordinate and perform all functions at each end, consigning the cargoes only to the air carrier for flight.

Recently, a new kind of organization has emerged in the air cargo community. This is the "integrated" carrier, such as Federal Express, that does everything, including fly the cargo in its own aircraft. The integrators grew very rapidly by transporting small, high-value, time-critical packages, usually documents. In the short space of twelve years, from 1978 to 1990, the integrators grew in revenues to equal the size of the traditional air cargo community. Since then, despite efforts to take an even larger share of the air cargo market, the integrators have run into serious difficulties as the limits to the economies of homogenization and integration have been reached. These limits are closely linked to the underlying heterogeneity of the air cargo sector, and form part of the story we engage later in this paper.

Like any complex work world, the air cargo sector has well-established information processing practices. Some of these make use of the long-standing standards of the existing information infrastructure. The air cargo community was an early and enthusiastic diffusion site for telegraph, telex, telephone, cable, and fax technologies. Surprisingly, however, technologies such as electronic document interchange (EDI) and cargo community systems (CCSs) that depend on much more elaborate standards touching on work practices have fallen far short of expectations in this community. This failure is not from a lack of trying or interest; the opportunities for reducing uncertainty in the process of trade and increasing reliability and enabling new services are widely recognized. Nor are the failures technical in nature. The failures are due to the unwelcome intrusion of standards for such technologies on the work worlds of the inherently disaggregated, dis-integrated structure of the cargo community. As important, the functions that would be served by these newer technologies are already well served by a highly effective technology called the air waybill. This technology, which basically is implemented with carbon paper and ball point pens, embodies a set of standards and social conventions for the processing of critical cargo-related information that is vital to the functioning of the community.

We should note that EDI, CCSs and other support technologies might well be adopted widely in the air cargo community of the future. But this adoption is unlikely unless either the air cargo community itself changes drastically or the standards and conventions behind the technologies change to conform to the community as it is. To date, information infrastructure building for the air cargo community has been misled by ideals appropriated from apparent successes in other sectors, such as the passenger airlines, that have fundamentally different institutional characteristics. Translation of such experience to the heterogeneous and disaggregated political structure of the air cargo industry has proven difficult and basically misguided. Unilateral imposition of such standards is unworkable because there is no authority with sufficient power to impose such requirements, and given the nature of the air cargo community, such requirements would be quickly diverted from their original purposes to suit the conventions and economics of the community's participants. If the new NII is to meet the needs of the air cargo community, the design of the technologies to be used must be built around the varied interests and activities of the participants in heterogeneous communities. They must, in other words, be standardized around diversity.

The Integration of Work Practices through the Air Waybill

Replacing an existing work practice with a new, standardized one can unintentionally transform the structure of the community and destabilize relationships between participants. We present for exploration of this assertion the humble air waybill, which we will contrast with its information-age counterpart, the electronic air waybill. The air waybill has persisted in the air cargo community since its inception and quietly sustains the interests of the air cargo community worldwide. Every piece of cargo carried by air carries an air waybill, including every package carried by Federal Express, DHL, UPS, and so on. (A careful reading of the fine print on any integrator's standard shipping form will find the words "air waybill.") Carriers, forwarders, brokers, consolidators, packagers, warehousers, and integrators alike use this highly stable and enormously potent device that has survived despite dramatic changes in its economic environment. It survives because it supports the way work is done in the industry, which in turn reflects the physical and economic realities of air cargo.

The air waybill is a contract between the shipper and the air carrier for passage of goods, and is similar in function to a passenger ticket.[1] With every shipment it routinely crosses the technical, social, and political boundaries between carriers and intermediaries such as forwarders, ground transportation, consolidators, and warehousers. The immediately observable waybill on a parcel is the *master waybill.* This is always attached to the parcel itself throughout transit, and at each stage in a multi-stage trip it contains enough information to make the local transactions go right. It is not the purpose of the master waybill to coordinate the full trip of the shipment or dictate the many local work activities that get the shipment to its destination, but at each stage it provides sufficient information to inform the next work activity at that particular site. It doesn't say *how* the activity is supposed to happen, but just *what* is supposed to happen as a result.

The master waybill is the only waybill attached to the parcel unless the parcel is a consolidated shipment, which is a bundle of shipments packaged into fixed-sized pallets or containers for transport by carriers. The service of consolidation is most frequently used by shippers with variable-size or occasional loads. Consolidation may be performed by a forwarder or by an agent that performs only the consolidation function. Consolidators make their profits on the margin between the carrier's bulk freight rates and the rates they themselves charge the shippers. The consolidator prepares a *house air waybill* for each shipper's freight that shows the details of that shipment and the charges payable by the consignee (or that were prepaid by the shipper). The house air waybills are bundled together in a sealed envelope that is attached to the master air waybill. The master air waybill shows only the published International Air Transport Association (IATA) bulk freight rates charged by the carrier to the consolidator. The established agreement in the industry is that the house air waybill remains sealed throughout the journey to be opened *only* by the 'break-down' operator or other agent of the consolidator, who presents the appropriate house air waybill to the consignee.

The house air waybill can be physically opened on a journey, and the information contained therein has been used to undercut the competition. But there is a general unwillingness in the air cargo world to violate a community standard. The consolidators serve an important brokerage role, leveraging the discount obtained from providing the carrier with guaranteed revenue for a fixed consolidated load to provide shippers with access to passage at lower prices than would otherwise be available if their parcels were shipped unconsolidated. The mechanism by which the consolidators are paid is highly efficient and rational, because it forces the consolidator to drive a hard bargain with the carrier while passing on the minimum workable discount to the shipper. Competition among consolidators based on stealing information from competitors cannot bring lasting advantage because both supply and demand adjust constantly. Each consolidated load consists of a unique set of deals done with a carrier and N shippers. Consolidations are not commodities, and the information hiding inherent in the house/master waybill arrangement reflects the essence of the business.

The air waybill persists because it protects the interests of the shippers, consolidators, and carriers by providing essential information for the one thing that absolutely must occur—getting the shipment where it's going—without confusing the issue with bargaining. The conventions surrounding its use further support the continuation of the air waybill by hiding shipment-sensitive pricing information. It is highly robust in that the information and conventions are sufficient to handle the many unanticipated situations encountered by a shipment through the air cargo system. The air waybill is not only always "up," which computers are not, but it is literally attached to the cargo, which a computer record cannot be.[2]

Problems in the Vision of the Electronic Air Waybill

From a technical perspective computerizing the air waybill is an easy task. A number of standard-developing organizations such as the UN have already embedded air waybill features into standards for EDI. In cargo community systems, the air waybill is usually the primary document in the computerization of the system and the waybill number is the unique identifier for identifying a shipper's shipment. All these systems have the same conceptual architecture: a network of computers and telecommunications capabilities allow an electronic version of the air waybill to "follow" the shipment through its travels. In principle, a parcel would need only a unique identifier that could be used at each point along the way to access this electronic waybill.

The electronic information infrastructure required for such a system must provide transparency of at least some data, such as origin and destination, backwards and forwards through a shipment's life-cycle in the shipper-consignee pipeline. This kind of information is readily, cheaply, and reliably provided by the paper air waybill, so implementing an electronic air waybill would not provide recognizable benefits. The only way to reap the benefits of making an electronic air waybill system would be to exploit the opportunity to use the full range of data in the constantly-growing record on each shipment for improved service and performance. This is precisely the use made of electronic air waybill systems by the integrators: the systems can track wayward parcels, not to reassure customers[2], but to enforce strict performance expectations on employees by identifying who last handled a wayward parcel. Such data transparency in an integrator might affect power relationships between, for example, senior managers and parcel delivery personnel.

In the traditional air cargo sector, an electronic waybill system would transform power relations by changing information asymmetries. "Access to or control over information flows and power are two sides of the same coin. Most participants in the network are well aware of it, and those who are not suffer the consequences."[3] Forwarders and air carriers, for example, are co-dependent, but not in inherently stable ways. Carriers can and have attempted to displace forwarders by providing to-airport and to-door service, and a nice on-line data base of a forwarder's shippers and their cargoes could be a useful marketing tool for such services. Forwarders and consolidators will not (willingly) participate in a system that reveals their cost structures to the carriers, exposing the deals they have cut with their shippers at the carriers' expense. Once this information is revealed, the carriers or other parties can use it to adjust their pricing structures to match the costs of the consolidators to either steal business from the consolidators (if they want it) or at the very least to reduce the bargaining power of the consolidators with the carriers. Information is power, and in this case the power would rest with the carriers. As will be seen, the forwarders play an essential role in this industry, and are in a position to resist coercive attempts by the carriers to subjugate them. Turning the interests around, carriers fear that forwarders could use access to data in an integrated system to drive competition on rates among the air carriers. At the broader level of consumer welfare, it is not clear how an electronic air waybill system would improve the consumer surplus. Most of the successful firms in the industry do not want competitors to be able to probe their operating procedures in ways that would eliminate organizational efficiency as a strategic competitive factor.

Cargo Community Systems

The cargo community system exemplifies the new NII of the air freight sector, at least if constructed according to conventional expectations. CCSs are basically computerized systems operated at major nodes of the larger air cargo physical/social network (mainly near airports), serving as clearing houses of information in a public utility model. They are envisioned as facilitating timely exchange of cargo information among participants in the worldwide cargo community to the benefit of all. The rationale is that pre-defined document standards will reduce data entry and re-keying of information and that coupling cargo systems and accounting systems will speed billing processes and reporting procedures. In the rhetoric of the system designers, the systems will span countries and organizations while remaining neutral and unbiased toward any of the many interest groups. Some of the benefits desired by the participants:

• Shippers want increased control of their total logistics and services more appropriate to their particular niche. This means knowing the shipment status and being provided with tracking, documentation, and value-added services. For many firms the hope is that forwarders can take over the headaches associated with international shipping, leaving them to focus on their businesses.

• Carriers want to be able to compete internationally door-to-door with the integrators by providing reliable time-dependent service between countries. They want to use CCSs to maintain a high bi-directional load factor on long-haul routes by locking-in large suppliers whose regular freight will reduce uncertainty in load factors.

• Forwarders foresee an increase in their world services by reducing search costs and providing opportunities for optimizing logistical solutions for their customers that will secure closer ties to the shippers.

• National interests would be served if CCSs reduced the regional transaction costs associated with import and customs clearance, creating a favored port status. Other social benefits would be the overall increase in usage of a more efficient trade system and the possibility of new services. Computerization of trade also raises the possibility of coordinating import and export with the revenue and taxation systems.

The two basic coordinating features of every cargo community system are a message switching system and an international database of supply and booking information. EDI is used for inter-organizational transfer of documents such as invoices, shipment status notices, and bills of lading. There are standard messages for party-to-party data exchange, such as space allocation, air waybill, flight manifest, accounting, status, discrepancy, embargo and customs information. The systems generally provide an intra-organizational communication standard, a standard for communication with external parties, and conversion of messages to other EDI standards. The creation of the database requires the participation of an quorum of ground and air transportation participants at source and destination to provide meaningful door-to-door cargo information.

The reality of cargo community systems is quite different from the vision. Technically, the implementation of a cargo community system is relatively easy and cost effective. Message switching protocols already exist such as UN EDIFACT, IATA's Cargo-IMP, and others. The underlying telecommunications infrastructure is already in place for most communities or can be easily provided by value-added networks. The hardware and software expertise are already available to the large carriers and forwarders. The difficult part has been getting people to get onto the highway. To succeed, a CCS requires that participants enter their supply and booking information into the system and make it available for others to use. This is not an inexpensive task, even assuming that the smaller forwarders without technical expertise are not on the system. There are many different types of cargo services available, all requiring entry into the database and EDI support. The higher the cost of entering information, the higher and longer is the expected payback for those that went through the trouble of getting the information in and updating and putting together their internal infrastructure. As the cost of putting together the system increases, the number of transactions required to make it break even increases proportionately.

There is also a large installed base of internal systems in use by the larger firms. While the carriers have been longtime adopters of new technologies, only the larger forwarders have made similar investments. For those that have systems, adopting CCSs means trusting a standard to remain stable long enough to make it worthwhile to provide the investment in interfaces and translators or even change their systems. For the majority of the smaller forwarders that don't have their own systems, CCSs mean entering a new world filled with threats of lock-in and other new concerns. Having endured the aggressive expansion of the integrators and witnessed the use of passenger reservation systems to impose switching costs on travel agents, forwarders look suspiciously upon CCSs as attempts by powerful alliances to either lock them in or to bypass them entirely by placing terminals in the offices of their shippers.

The major CCS projects are shown in Table 1. There is considerable diversity of participants in the projects; represented in the ownership of the systems are the interests of airlines, forwarders, governments, and industry associations. The same organizations may also participate in more than one CCS. The adoption of CCSs has been far slower than anticipated. The largest system claims about 2,000 forwarders (air, rail, and ocean) in a worldwide population of 25,000 freight forwarders. It is likely that the other systems focus mainly on air forwarders, of which there are estimated to be about 4,000.[4] None of the systems has generated the number of subscribers required to create network externalities in the larger community or the number of transactions needed to achieve economies of scale in processing. Even if some of these systems have captured the largest forwarders, which as a group dominate the largest cargo routes, the nature of the air cargo enterprise remains so heterogeneous that even a lock-up of the large forwarders would not touch much of the air cargo community's operations. Reactions to the slow adoption of CCSs and EDI standards have been to increase exhortations for a global standard and to criticize countries and companies that adhere to their own proprietary standards.

A good example of a large-scale CCS is Encompass, an enterprise under the ownership of AMR Corporation (American Airlines). The vision of the system was ambitious: "By using the system, shippers can manage inventories; carriers can relay information to shippers; consignees can be alerted as to what shipments are coming and their sizes; and third parties can supply their customers with freight information throughout every step of the process. Freight forwarders can be the travel agents of the cargo industry, providing customers with up-to-date information within minutes."[5] In interviews with senior air cargo management it has been reported that Encompass has been forced to scale back to far more modest goals. Instead of a door-to-door logistical control system, it appears that it will be more of an air cargo Official Airlines Guide. The reason is that other participants see this as a control system in the hands of an undesirable controller—American Airlines.

Table 1 Cargo Community Systems (*IATA Cargo Community Systems Directory*, 1993)

Year of operation	Name	CCS owners	Geographical region	Number of users
1992	Aviation Exchange	Teledyne ICARUS	North America	—
1989	Bruncargo CS	Belgian Airport Authority, Belgian customs	Belgium	22
1992	Cargo Community Network	SIA Ltd., TMB Holdings, SAAA Cargo Services	Singapore (Linked to TradeNet)	98
1993	CCS-UK	BT Customer Systems	UK	697
1992	Cargo Switch AG	Swissair, forwarders, other airlines and private investors	Switzerland	29
1988	Cargonaut	Schiphol Airport Authority	Netherlands	109
1992	Encompass	AMR, CSX, Netherlands PPT	America, Europe, Far East	—
planned	Fretair	British Airways, IBERIA, KLM, Swiss Air Transport	France	704
1990	Icarus	Irish Community Airlines, forwarders	Ireland	58
1990	Tradevision	SAS, other airlines, Swedish customs	Copenhagen	125
1989	TDNI	Airlines, forwarders, customs brokers	North America	44
1991	Traxon Asia	Cathay Pacific, Japan Airlines, Traxon Worldwide	Asia	210
1991	Traxon Europe	Air France, Cargolux Airlines, Lufthansa Japan Airlines, Korean Air	Europe	285
1992	US-CCS	SCITOR/SITA	United States	97
planned	Trade-Van Taiwan	Taiwanese government	Taiwan	n/a
planned	ZA-CCS	Airlines, agents	South Africa	n/a
planned	COSAC	HACTL, airlines, customs, agents	Hong Kong	n/a
planned	Nippon Air Cargo Clearance System	Customs, Minister Finance, airlines	Japan	n/a
1989	Tradegate Australia	Government, Qantas, forwarders, shipping, road, rail	Australia	2,032

The problems faced by Encompass, and by the Cargo Community Systems vision generally, are embedded in the nature of air cargo as a physical and social phenomenon. Only by understanding air cargo as a business can the shortcomings in this naive construction of the new NII be made clear.

The Business of Air Cargo

The heterogeneity of the cargo community prevents the unilateral imposition of uniform standards across all communications between participants. Although such simplification may be desirable for reasons of efficiency, it is unattainable in the case of the worldwide air cargo community. In this section we examine the business of air cargo and present the following observations in support of this argument:

• The opportunities for CCSs to increase trade efficiency are real and widely recognized. The poor performance to date of CCSs is not a tale of an information technology failing because of an inappropriate match between the technology and the business reality.

• The game is about time-definite delivery and not speed. If it were simply speed, why not just scale up the national systems developed by the integrators? But international time-definite delivery requires reducing uncertainty along the entire international value chain. This is a problem because there are no single organizations that span the value chain from shipper to consignee, so any system designed to facilitate the process must coordinate activities between groups with different incentives. And systems developed to move only cargo 'as fast as possible' do not work for time-definite delivery.

• The heterogeneity of the industry is rooted in the nature of cargo itself. The diversity of the goods transported by air freight fosters specialized activities and relationships between carriers, agents and shippers. These relationships are very important to maintaining the cargo industry and any standards must facilitate the formation and maintenance of these relationships.

• The international regulatory environment and documentation requirements constrain and complicate air cargo processes and reinforce the disaggregated nature of the industry by creating regulatory boundaries. The forwarders play an essential role in reducing the apparent complexity for shippers.

• Long-haul flights are the battleground in international air cargo. High fixed costs and the over-capacity of the combination carriers plague the integrators and all-cargo carriers. For the combination carriers, cargo plays second fiddle to passengers, and their pricing policies have made it difficult for the integrators to enter into global time-definite delivery. It is on these flights that the carriers need higher load factors and bi-directional traffic. The carriers thus have an incentive to attempt to 'lock-in' large shippers either with or without the forwarders. The airlines were successful in increasing load factors with the passenger reservations systems and are tempted to use the same strategy again for cargo.

This sets the background against which we can see how it is possible for the forwarders, in protecting their interests, to resist attempts to impose standards on the community that reduce their leverage with the carriers or the shippers.

Of the total $200 billion in world scheduled airline operating revenues[6], the air cargo industry represents a relatively small share at around $30 billion[7]. Air cargo moves only a small fraction of world goods but a high fraction of the value of the goods shipped. Table 2 shows that in 1990, the value of goods shipped by air was almost half that of ocean shipping, yet the weight was only a fraction of the weight of that shipped by sea. In the United States in 1990, the average value of a kilogram of goods shipped by air was $63, while for sea vessel it was $0.50. It is because of this high value-to-weight ratio and the types of goods shipped by air that air trade plays an important role in the national economic strategy of countries. In addition, air transport contributes a trade surplus for the United States, while ocean transport yields a net trade deficit.

It has been recognized by many nations that reducing inefficiencies in trade can benefit the host nations. U.S. trade transaction costs are an estimated 5% of the value of goods sold, with some estimates putting the costs of trade as high as 10%. The differential in transaction costs between regions will affect the volume of trade

Table 2 Total U.S. Exports and Imports by Mode of Transportation[9]

	Ocean		Air	
	Weight (bkg)	Value (bUSD)	Weight (bkg)	Value (bUSD)
1970	489.4	49.4	0.7	9.5
1980	806.8	286.0	1.6	74.1
1985	679.2	300.1	2.1	103.6
1988	828.6	381.8	2.9	169.1
1989	885.3	416.2	5.9	186.3
1990	868.7	434.2	3.2	201.4

in the regions. Singapore's TradeNet system reduces transaction costs (primarily documentation) to increase speed and throughput, while Indonesia's SGS system smoothes the pre-inspection system. Since 1970, there has been an 800% increase in cross border trade flows[8], which underscores the tremendous opportunity for growth and the motivation for government interest in the outcome of CCSs.

There has been a misconception about air cargo that speed has been the key to success for the integrators, and that the purpose of CCS and EDI is to get more speed. There has been a shift from competition on the basis of weight and price, but the shift has been to time-definite delivery and not to speed. "Buyers of air-cargo services are telling their carriers, 'I may not absolutely positively need it overnight, but I absolutely, positively need it on time.'"[10] Firms that can provide reliable delivery have a competitive advantage over those who can't. There are large benefits to be gained from small improvements in efficiency and reliability in international service. But, especially in international time-definite delivery, the sources of potential delays and uncertainties lie along the entire process from shipper to consignee, which is not necessarily under the control of any single actor. The integrators were able domestically to gain control of the entire door-to-door system logistics, but internationally the problems become more difficult as borders, languages, cultural boundaries, and national regulations are crossed.

The heterogeneity of the air cargo sector is a reflection of the involvement of government and inter-government regulation, diversity in the cargo itself, the underlying economics for the shippers, and the special problems of trade routes that span many economic and political boundaries in developed and developing countries. As a result of the many varied interests of the participants, the air cargo processes themselves are complex, intersect many institutional boundaries, and are difficult to intentionally change in predictable ways.

Several characteristics of international air cargo shape the industry and the behavior of its players. The first is that cargo itself is highly diversified and the contents of the shipments matter. There are special requirements for care of the shipment, special regulations for customs, special inspection requirements and so on. The second is that air cargo is a derived demand and is dependent upon the underlying economic welfare of its users for its own survival. Many service providers directly or indirectly involved in air cargo, such as forwarders, packagers, and warehousers, are highly specialized around a particular set of client needs ranging from the transportation of live animals to emergency equipment. The third is that trade is always transnational and inter-organizational. These characteristics create the heterogeneity of the industry and the need for local specialization.

Shipping is a very personal activity. Cargo is precious to shippers since their livelihoods usually depend on its safe and timely arrival. Air cargo is used for goods that have a high value-to-weight ratio or cannot survive a long ocean trip. Live animals, emergency parts, drugs, fresh-cut flowers, sensitive equipment—these goods can't be handled by just anyone. It's the expertise of the forwarder or carrier and their close personal relationships that keep their business. The assurance that once the cargo has been delivered into the hands of the agent, that agent knows where it is and can work through any problems or delays along the route is a valuable service to the shipper.

International shipping is a complex business and the nature of the process and the actors involved depend on the origin and destination countries, the nature of the goods, and the size of the shipment. At the very least, an international shipment involves ground transportation, forwarder, carrier, customs brokers, and warehousing, at both source and destination before final delivery to the consignee. The process may also involve consolidators/ deconsolidators, independent warehousers, inspection, government import and export agencies, and value-added services such as packaging and product assembly. The regulations for hazardous goods, perishable goods, live goods, agricultural goods, and so on change from country to country, requiring knowledgeable participants to ensure a smooth passage.

The complexity of the process is also visible in the supporting documentation process. Since the documents and forms of the process are the artifacts of negotiated agreements between actors of the industry in their various institutional 'bubbles' their form and presence is important to our discussion. The documentation reflects the varied interests of the participants. Shippers need confirmation that their goods are delivered on time, intact, and correctly processed by the receiver's customs. Governments require trade data to monitor economic performance, compliance with international policy decisions, and protection of borders against illegal imports. Forwarders, carriers, customs brokers, warehousers, and any value-added service providers need to know the whos, whats, whens, wheres, and charges for their services. Documentation is time-consuming, complicated, costly to perform, and expensive in opportunity costs.

Regulatory interests in the transportation of air cargo between countries are complicated by the involvement of at least two governments, with their foreign policies and bilateral agreements for import and export; national interests in safety for passengers and cargo (including hazardous goods, live animals, and perishable foods); limited resources such as airport access and landing slots; and environmental issues such as agriculture, noise abatement, and emissions. The regulatory environment of the belly-cargo and combination carriers not only inherits the regulatory restrictions of the passenger industry, but is subject to special regulations of its own industry. The regulation is manifested in the volume of documentation required to ship internationally.

Government regulation domestically and internationally has profoundly affected the shape of the air transport industry. Perhaps one of the most dramatic illustrations of the impact of regulatory events in recent times is the deregulation of U.S. airlines and the consequent rise of the big integrators such as Federal Express, UPS, DHL, and Emery. Deregulation allowed airlines to organize themselves in a hub-and-spoke design rather than the point-to-point design required under the previous regulatory regime. Federal Express from its modest beginnings in 1971 invested heavily in infrastructure, providing pick-up, delivery, transportation, customs clearance, paperwork processing, computer tracking, and invoicing. By 1992 the integrators carried 92% of domestic shipments, leaving the airlines with the remaining 8%.

On international routes, however, the integrators have not been as successful. Time-definite international delivery is much more difficult than domestic shipping. A high load factor is essential, the hub-and-spoke system doesn't scale well, and the lower yields on international routes make it more price competitive than the domestic market. Federal Express cut back its operations in Europe in 1992 after a $1.2 billion loss.[11]

Knowledge of the processes, documentation, and regulation associated with international air cargo is too great a load for any but the largest shippers. The shipper's demand for logistical management and a sensitivity to their business needs has pressured specialization in the industry. For instance, it is the forwarders who provide expertise in handling the complexity of moving freight across borders. Forwarders, because of the amount of cargo they tender, have considerable power with the carriers, playing them off one against the other to get bulk discounts. Their expertise in reducing complexity for the shippers also allows them considerable bargaining power with the shippers (especially the small shippers). There are about 25,000 forwarders worldwide (1991), dealing with 600 or so airlines to increase their geographical coverage and to offer the best deals to their customers.

To the passenger airline industry, which has seen only marginal profitability over the last decades,[12] air cargo has increased in importance in terms of overall contribution to profits. On international routes, where the distances are greater and load utilization is more important, freight is a greater percentage of the output. Because freight and passengers share the same physical structures, the practice has been to have overhead costs covered by the passenger revenues, with cargo making a direct contribution to the profitability of the carrier. In the past this has led to flexible pricing of freight on the international routes and charging whatever the market will bear. The incremental benefit of flying both passengers and freight has provided an advantage to the belly and combination carriers that the integrators do not have. These practices impede the integrators' and all-cargo carriers' (of which few remain) ability to enter the international market using the same strategies as have proved successful domestically, for these industries require higher load factors and more balanced bi-directional traffic than the combination carriers.

For the pure belly-hold carriers, cargo is viewed as a supplement to their normal passenger operations, with the result that it has not been exploited to is fullest potential and price-cutting is used to steal business from the cargo-dependent combination carriers and integrators. This, in fact, has stymied the integrators on the international routes.

In global terms 75% of the world's air freight is international, 25% is domestic, and of that 25% one-half is transported within North America. The international yields[13] are significantly lower than domestic yields as a result of over-capacity and pricing policies. Over-capacity has plagued the international market because of the increased capacity of the newer wide-body long-haul passenger airlines and the necessity of running the passenger flights regardless of the load factor for the sake of the service reputation. It is along these highly visible international routes that the battles for the passenger traffic are fought, with the consequence that the combination of over capacity and "anyways" pricing of belly cargo has produced lower revenues for all the carriers of cargo.

Discussion

The opportunities are there, the technical capability exists, and still the systems aren't delivering. Why? We suggest that the CCSs are based upon monopolistic or oligopolistic models successful in other sectors but inappropriate for the inherent heterogeneity of the worldwide cargo community. Successful standards become powerful attractors for the designers of other standards wishing to replicate their success. In the case of CCSs, the exemplars are the computerized passenger reservation systems (CRSs), the integrated information systems of the integrators, and national systems such as Singapore TradeNet. We maintain that these exemplars are based upon an underlying economic rationality or political reality that does not exist in the world of air cargo, and that attempts to replicate their success will fail because they conflict with the institutional apparatus of air cargo.

The success of CRSs such as American Airline's Sabre and United Airline's Apollo has become part of the folklore in strategic information systems development. These systems created barriers to entry for competitors, increased the switching costs of customers, and "locked-in" travel agents, reducing their bargaining power with the airlines. For system owners the CRSs have been tremendously profitable, often producing earnings while the passage operations themselves have been losing money. Given the close association between the passenger and cargo business in the belly carriers, which carry the majority of international cargo, not to mention the political dominance of the passenger business among these carriers, it seems logical that efforts would be made to overlay the successful CRS model on cargo. The results of such efforts have foundered on the fundamental differences between the passenger and cargo institutions even within the same firm.

Passage and cargo do share aircraft, airports, and the broad institutional apparatus of air transport. But the similarities end there. Passengers are a relatively homogeneous commodity that allows the development of homogeneity in the design of services and ways of competing. Passengers as "packages" are rather homogenous. Passengers see the flight itself as the product; they are self-directed, sensitive to routing and time of travel, and usually return on the carrier on which they left. Cargo packages, on the other hand, can be highly idiosyncratic (small or large, inert or explosive, etc.) and often require special handling of a kind seldom needed for passengers. Cargo packages are insentient: they are not customers to be kept happy, are not sensitive to timing or routing, and usually go one way. For all practical purposes, airlines can treat passage as a commodity business because the passengers deliver themselves to the aircraft and disappear at the destination. Cargoes, in contrast, cannot be self-directed, and require such extensive pre-flight and post-flight handling that specialized handling skills must be acquired to offer complete forwarding services. Few airlines wish to offer such services, so they revert to offering what amounts to commodity haulage for whatever cargoes appear on their docks, leaving the rest to forwarders.

These characteristics are not in themselves institutional differences—they are differences in the business requirements of passenger and cargo services that *lead to* institutional differences in the nature of work and the distribution of power in the social networks of the cargo community. The freight forwarders are fully aware of the consequences of becoming locked-in to a carrier, and through their powerful position in the community (most airlines depend on forwarders for 80% of their loads) are capable of resisting any efforts to lock them in. Their bargaining power with the carriers rests upon their being able to select routes and prices from among many carriers to meet shippers' needs. Any forwarder that sole-sources from a carrier is likely to lose bargaining power and, if locked-in, become subject to monopolistic pricing practices of the carrier that controls them. A CRS-like cargo information system will be seen instantly by forwarders as a tool of the carriers, and forwarders can sabotage any such CRS effort through the simple mechanism of refusing to join the network. Without significant participation by forwarders, the brokerage of space on the aircraft will break down and the carriers will have to either try to capture the shippers directly (something few carriers have ever been able to do) or extend service to non-network forwarders, thus eliminating any advantage in using the CRS-like system. The most sensible strategy for any given forwarder to follow when deciding whether to join a CRS-like cargo information system is to wait until enough others join. Such anticipatory retardation is visible in the low participation rate in CCS projects and the consequent slow growth of the cargo systems.

The success of the integrators provides a different lesson. The integrators grew very rapidly by offering a highly specialized and needed service—rapid, guaranteed-time delivery of valuable small parcels. The trick was to lower costs for providing this expensive service enough to allow significant profits at the price point customers were willing to pay. Lowering costs was accomplished through economies of scale gained from standardizing packaging, handling, and billing procedures. By providing customers with packaging materials and addressing devices (specifically, air waybills), the integrators gained control over the physical characteristics and processing parameters of all parcels they handle. Automation using bar coding and hand-held scanners enabled the integrators to enforce standardized handling protocols that would ensure on-time delivery and to initiate the automated billing processes. The rest of the integrators' advantage was in exploiting the simplicity of having a single or just a few massive sorting facilities in which all inbound parcels were put in queues outbound for destination cities. What the integrators were selling was completely predictable delivery of a standardized package through a highly optimized and enforced production system.

The integrators in the US succeeded phenomenally, and many of the traditional air cargo participants feared the integrators would take over the air cargo community. The integrators gained 92% of the total US domestic air cargo shipments with relative ease, leaving only 8% to the belly carriers. However, these statistics are misleading in that the 8% remaining with the traditional carriers proved to be worth 25% of the total air cargo revenues. Moreover, much of the integrators' growth was due to a great increase in document and small parcel shipment that the integrators stimulated. The actual position of traditional air cargo, while threatened by the integrators, was not fundamentally altered. When the integrators began to move offshore from the US, where their peculiar niche advantages were less important, they experienced much greater resistance from the established air cargo community. Wide-body passenger aircraft on scheduled international routes were able to carry large volumes of cargo at very competitive prices, and efficient forwarding operations in other countries made the advantages of the integrators less noticeable. The integrators recently have made changes in tactics, expanding the range of parcels they will carry and offering a variety of price-discriminated delivery options. But these changes are likely to erode their traditional advantages from standardization and economies of scale, and put them directly into competition with both international and domestic forwarders and carriers.

In an important sense, the integrators appear to have exploited a very lucrative niche, but a niche nonetheless. For CCSs and their designers, attempts to duplicate the integrators' approach to automation in expectation of direct international door-to-door competition are probably misguided. Such systems would likely produce conflict within the community and, perhaps more important, would fail to exploit the proven opportunities in offering specialized services to smaller, established markets. There are two ways to gain control of "the system" in air cargo. The first is to attempt to integrate and optimize the entire system, as the integrators have done, excluding in the process a large and profitable sector of the market that requires specialized services. This has worked well for the US small parcel market, but is not likely to have the same potential in other markets, as recent events have shown. The second is to follow specialized pathways through the larger system, creating locally optimal solutions for sub-communities. Such solutions cannot be centrally determined, and the resulting system will be by necessity decentralized.

As a final example, it is occasionally possible to construct trade-related information infrastructure that binds together most or all members of a community and provides real performance benefits. A case in point is the Singapore TradeNet system, a value-added network that links together all of the 3,000 or so air, land and sea forwarders, carriers and agents doing business in Singapore.[14] Among other things, the TradeNet system reduced the number of documents to be completed by shippers from as many as twenty to a single electronic form. The system has reduced processing time for trade applications (i.e., import/export approvals) from between two to four days to as little as 15 minutes, and according to rough estimates by forwarders using the system, reduced the trade documentation processing costs by 20% or more.

As successful as it is, TradeNet is an unusual case because Singapore is an unusual country. Conflicts with existing institutional arrangements in Singapore are often eliminated through a powerful authoritarian government working in close cooperation with major business interests. Singapore also has extensive experience with large-scale information system building and established capability in information technology among many members of the trade community. Singapore's commitment to information infrastructure development is tied to a political willingness to displace interest group power to attain social externalities. TradeNet also illustrates an important dilemma with respect to network externalities, technology diffusion rates, and "critical mass" of adopters. Singapore's system works at only one end of Singapore's international trading routes. It does facilitate local trade activity, but it cannot easily be used to coordinate activities across national boundaries when other members of the community are not playing. Singapore has been successful in establishing a model system that works in Singapore, but it cannot be expected to impose its solution on other members of the international trade community.

Conclusions

The inability of cargo community systems endeavors to capture a substantial hold in the work life of the air cargo community stems from a misconception that externally-imposed standards will "rationalize" the community. In fact, they will not, and members of the community know it. The air cargo community already operates in a highly rational manner, predicated on a heterogeneous and flexible network of alliances and competitive practices. Likewise, any attempt to set standards for new NII solutions derived from the monopolistic and oligopolistic traditions in the computing and telecommunications industries will almost certainly fail.

The relationship between institutional conventions and standards is a useful conceptual starting point from which to rethink the development of NII standards in heterogeneous communities. Conventions embody and are subject to the economic rationality of the sector in which they operate. Conventions are not exactly economic or technical standards, but they often give rise to standards, and they are vitally important to the success of standards. Conventions determine who will play, as well as the rules, the penalties for violators, and the propensities for fellow players to seek retribution. Standards take their meaning from conventions.

For the standards makers of the NII we draw several observations, based on our assessment of the air cargo community. First, it must be recognized that heterogeneity arises in the economic, social, and political structures of a community of work, and gives rise to important institutional differences across communities. The disaggregated and decentralized nature of the air cargo industry is rooted in the diversity of the goods that are shipped and the importance of the social relationships that support the activities. Where proposed standards do not support this disaggregation and decentralization, the implementation of standards is blocked by the nature of the work itself and by anticipatory retardation by the potential losers under the new system. Standards for heterogeneous communities must be designed to support these differences or be prepared to do battle with powerful institutional forces.

Second, it is possible that changing the underlying economic structures that support a community can produce a mandate for new standards, but such change require institutional forces capable of exerting strong influence across the whole community. The air cargo community is remarkably free from such institutional forces, and the few that exist are becoming less interested in interfering with a highly complex system that already works. The complicated, multi-lateral network of regulation that has achieved a precarious stability in IATA has already proven incapable of a role as the vehicle of such change. To the extent that new standards emerge, they are very unlikely to be imposed on the air cargo community, either from without by an external institution, or from within by the actions of one or more strong players. Standards will no longer be set, but will evolve in a manner consistent with the consortium approach now common in fast-changing technical fields such as computers and communications.

Third, in designing standards for heterogeneous sectors, it is best to aim low—below the level of the work itself. This recommendation arises from a standard that already exists and persists, i.e., the air waybill. The air waybill survives precisely because it is a standard that does not interfere with the work that has to be done. It doesn't specify how the work is to be done, just that it is to be done. The success of the new NII as applied to the air cargo community, and by extension to other heterogeneous communities, rests upon enabling coordination in and among community members without forcing any members to suffer. At stake are socio-technical issues, not just technical issues. There is already a surfeit of technical standards available to make the machines and wires function. The challenge is to make the technology function at the core of business activity in established communities of work. This requires looking at the social organization of work activity and noting where and when technological aids are adopted and applied to make that organization function more effectively.

A potentially useful model for developing the new NII for heterogeneous communities is the history of TCP/IP as it evolved to support private communications and information sharing among large numbers of computer users in universities, research laboratories, and government agencies. The TCP/IP protocol was never intended to be a standard everyone should follow, but rather a common practice that would permit interested parties to join an evolving network. Efforts were made to ensure that nearly any group could join, and it was a hallmark of the TCP/IP development community that no proprietary or exclusive technical enablers would serve as barriers to entry by interested parties. TCP/IP is not particularly sophisticated or feature-filled; it stays well below the level of the work that those who use the system do. It essentially supports lowest-common-denominator text exchange (ASCII format, literally in card images), but because it enables rapid movement of such text among all members of the network, it has tremendous communication utility. With TCP/IP it is possible to create multiple networks and gateways between the networks, allowing local optimization and the development of unique functionalities unconstrained by an imposed standard. Participants define their working relationships and negotiate the nature of the work they do among themselves, but they must live within the limits of the lowest-common-denominator network.

It is quite possible that electronic mail, as embodied in Internet and other emerging network utilities, will find a ready audience with the air cargo community's diverse membership. This technology facilitates but does not control communication among the community's members, in the same way that earlier technologies such as telegraph, telephone, cable, telex, and fax have done. This approach could provide a platform for evolution of new utilities that can be run at diverse sites by mutual agreement, processing information passed through the network. In this way, each member of the community could establish processing protocols and practices with other community members, using for communication an uncontrolling exchange network. Such a design would contribute considerably to the ability of the air cargo community to move information in the text mode it has traditionally preferred, but with sufficient local autonomy and control to ensure that the long-standing heterogeneity of the community is maintained.

Design of successful NII standards, we assert, cannot be done in isolation or ignorance of a community's work practices. Those who seek to establish new NII standards should understand the institutional character of the community, which is rooted in its social, economic, and political structure. As communities evolve, especially within a rapidly changing technological environment, the dynamism of the community must be matched by a standards-setting process that is equally dynamic.

Notes

[1] Although there is some small variation, the information provided by the air waybill specifies: the parties involved in the transaction, the nature of the goods, the number of packages, weight, freight charges and the liable party, and any other expenses.

[2] Very few parcels are ever tracked for customers among the integrators. Tracking is used mainly to enforce work rules and ensure social conformity to norms and expectations. Tracking capability for customers, touted in advertising, is a side benefit.

[3] See Huigen (1993), p. 337

[4] It has been difficult to obtain precise estimates of the number of forwarders. The estimate of 25,000 forwarders of all types is from Ives, 1991; the estimate of 4,000 air forwarders is from Malkin (1990), based on IATA statistics of 1989.

[5] Barreto (1992), p. 18

[6] Air Transport World (1993).

[7] McCarthy (1990) estimate.

[8] Trunick (1992), p. 32.

[9] *Statistical Abstract of the United States* (1993).

[10] Bradley (1992), p. 62.

[11] Hawkins (1992).

[12] Members of IATA lost $11.5US billion from 1990 to 1992.

[13] In 1990 IATA reported international yield as $0.39 and domestic yield as $0.64 per ton mile.

[14] King and Konsynski (1991); Neo, King, and Applegate (1993).

References

Air Transport World, 1993. World Airline Report. June.

Barreto, Dawn, 1992. Opening Lines of Communication. *Air Cargo World,* July, 18–19.

Bradley, Peter, 1992. Time Defines Air Freight. *Purchasing,* March 5, 62–64.

David, Paul, 1985. Clio and the Economics of QWERTY. In *AEA Papers and Proceedings,* May, 332–337.

David, Paul, 1994. Standardization Policies for Network Technologies: The Flux between Freedom and Order Revisited. In R. Hawkins, R. Mansell, and J. Skea, EDS., *The Politics and Economics of Standards in Natural and Technical Environments* (London: Edward Elgar).

David, Paul, and W. Edward Steinmueller, 1989. The ISDN Bandwagon Is Coming—Who Will Be There To Climb Aboard?: Quandries in the Economics of Data Communications Networks. Center for Economic Policy Research, High Technology Impact Program Conference, Palo Alto, California, February 24–25.

Doganis, Rigas, 1991. *Flying Off Course: The Economics of International Airlines.* London: Harper Collins.

Hawkins, Chuck, 1992. FedEx: Europe Almost Killed the Messenger. *Business Week,* May 25, 124–125.

Hopper, Max, 1990. Rattling Sabre—New Ways To Compete on Information. *Harvard Business Review,* Vol. 68, No, 3, May–June, 118–125.

Huigen, Jos, 1993. Information and Communication Technology in the Context of Policy Networks. *Technology in Society,* Vol. 15, pp. 327–338.

International Air Transport Association, 1993. *Cargo Community Systems Directory and Guidelines,* 2nd Edition.

Ives, Blake, 1991. MSAS Cargo International: Global Freight Management. Case study, Graduate School of Business, University of Texas at Austin, p. 4.

Keisling, Max, 1993. Trends of Traffic Generated by Passenger Airline Air Cargo Activity. Institute of Transportation Studies, University of California, Berkeley, Draft.

King, John L., 1993. Institutional Factors and Air Support Networks in Air Cargo Operations. Manuscript.

King, John L., and Benn Konsynski, 1991. Singapore Trade Net: A Tale of One City. CAse study, Harvard Business School.

Malkin, Richard, 1990. Don't Count out the Air Forwarders. Distribution, November, pp. 78–82.

McCarthy, Denis, 1986. Airfreight Forwarders. *Transportation Quarterly,* 97–108.

Neo, Boon-Siong, John L. King, and Lynda Applegate, 1993. Singapore TradeNet: The Tale Continues. Case study, Harvard Business School.

Saloner, Garth, 1989. Economic Issues in Computer Interface Standardization. Center for Economic Policy Research, High Technology Impact Program Conference, Palo Alto, California, February 24–25.

Statistical Abstract of the United States, 1993. Washington, DC: U.S. Department of Commerce.

Trunick, Perry, 1992. Cargo Reservation Systems Move Ahead. *Transportation and Distribution,* June, 29–32.

Open Systems Standards in Manufacturing: Implications for the National Information Infrastructure

Caroline S. Wagner, Carl F. Cargill, and Anna Slomovic

Introduction and Thesis

Government planners anticipate large efficiency gains for manufacturers from a National Information Infrastructure (NII).[1] Although standards of interoperability or interconnection are essential to providing open product data exchange for industry, the process for providing the standards of interconnection that will support the NII is nearly non-existent, in large part because the current voluntary standards process is driven by vendors who have little interest in creating open system standards. For its part, the government has neither the know-how nor the infrastructure to provide these standards. After many years of watching groups of vendors attempt but fail to provide open system standards based on technology links, users have begun a quiet revolution in standards setting by establishing cooperative groups to define open computing standards independent of the constraints of available technology. This cooperative, user-based activity may act as a model for supporting the development of standards for the NII.

NII Promises Benefits for Manufacturers

The National Information Infrastructure, among other applications, is designed to:

A. Support manufacturing in a widely accessible and interoperable communications network

B. Provide easy-to-use applications over an open system

C. Contain a diverse collection of digital libraries, information databases, and services

D. Tap trained operators and support people.

This application is designed to support government manufacturing outreach programs like the National Institute of Standards and Technology's Manufacturing Extension Program and to interconnect with state programs and other business support services. Anticipated benefits are the ability to access best practice information, to achieve seamless manufacturing from concept design to product support, and to create flexible alliances within and across industries.

Creating Open Systems: From Plug Compatible to UNIX

The technology to provide open product data exchange services to industry is available, and sometimes interoperates, but the standards for data conversion are lacking. As shown in Figure 1, much of the discussion of open systems has occurred at the level of technology interface, not at the data conversion level. While vendors tend to focus on the bottom half of the 5 Cs of interoperability (communication and connection), users/manufacturers are concerned with the top half: conversation, conversion, and comprehension. Accordingly, a discussion of open systems for the NII should not focus on whether open systems will be achieved by plug compatibility, interoperability, or applications portability. Given the fact that these functions are already being addressed by vendor-led efforts, we assume that they will be available. The focus for the future should be on the top half of the 5 Cs, but the area is getting only haphazard attention, as the following history demonstrates.

The movement towards open systems has been active since the early 1970s, and has gone through several stages as it continues to create hardware "open systems." The movement was motivated in part by the increasing investment in computing being made on manufacturing shop floors. As investment in computing increased through the 1960s and 1970s, manufacturers became dismayed at

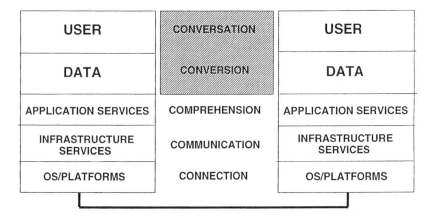

Figure 1 The Five Cs of Interoperability. Source: Curtis Royster, DOD/DISA/ Center for Standards.

the inability of their computer systems to transfer information, both within the company and with suppliers and customers. With this challenge in front of it, the IT industry began addressing open systems as the standards needed to create the technology to enable the interconnection or interoperability of heterogeneous computer systems. Attempts in the IT industry to achieve open systems have included plug compatibility, interoperability, and application portability, all of which have had some limited adoption, none reaching the shop floor. (See Figure 2.)

The open systems movement began in the 1960s and 1970s with a vision of plug compatible components. The motivation behind the plug compatible movement was to reduce the cost of computing to the user by allowing multiple providers to supply interoperable components. The idea was that increased competition would lower prices and/or increase innovation. Both happened. The plug compatible movement was hardware focused and intended to lower the cost of computers. The standards community responded with the creation of hardware interfaces, which today are seen in the PCMCIA, SCSI, EIA RS 232D, and others, that were focused on creating hardware that could interconnect. In this, the plug compatible movement was successful. It is now possible to physically connect components. The logical (software) connections are much less assured, as anyone who has ever attempted to buy a printer for

Open Systems Standards in Manufacturing

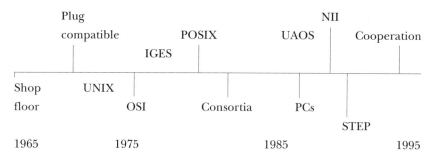

Figure 2 Open Systems Time Line.

a system can assure you. This logical connection of devices—where there was interaction among the physical devices—is only now coming to closure, nearly 30 years after the movement started.

The next stage in the open systems movement produced the Open Systems Interconnect (OSI) model for enabling interconnection of data between systems. OSI was a software communications model based upon a seven layer scheme of transferring data. It was very complex, significantly expensive, and required large amounts of computing overhead to make it work. It was also designed in international committee, and contained a large number of "options," some of which were contradictory. (As a result of these incompatibilities within the standards, and the slowness of the providers to supply OSI compliant products, the market has become disenchanted with the OSI set of standards and the market for OSI has yet to materialize. Profiles—that are selected sets of OSI standards in which incompatibilities have been minimized, are beginning to appear in procurements, especially in the European Union.) However, the OSI experience added interoperability—the ability of disparate systems to "cooperate" with one another—to the glossary of "computer open systems."

The next major movement in computer open systems, the Portable Operating Systems Interface (POSIX) movement, began as a user-group standards committee. The model for this idea was the then AT&T-proprietary UNIX operating system. The POSIX movement was driven by the successful demonstration by AT&T of a UNIX operating system. UNIX was perceived by the market to achieve applications portability by allowing programs written for one platform to be run on multiple platforms. However, none of the major vendors was willing to replace proprietary operating systems with UNIX. The intent of the initial POSIX effort was to build a series of calls to any operating system that were machine and implementation independent. Programs written using these standards calls could then be used on a large number of machines that had operating systems that also used these calls. The POSIX committee has worked for ten years defining the calls, and are now in the process of finishing the task.

Of course, the industry has changed over these ten years, and POSIX is not the solution that it was hoped to be when it was first implemented. The force that motivated the industry—the proprietary nature of UNIX—has changed with the acceptance of UNIX by nearly all of the major vendors. Additionally, the UNIX trademark and specification has been given to a consortium by Novell, which had purchased it from AT&T. This has led to the creation of the "UNIFIED UNIX" (or SPEC 1170); it represents a new form of cooperation among the UNIX providers. At the same time, a new operating system for PCs has emerged, completely changing the dynamics of the market and reducing the demand for applications portability. The major vendor of PC software—Microsoft—threatens to become a near-monopoly provider of operation systems software barring the creation of a viable alternative—which is what the vendors who are unifying around UNIX are trying to provide.

The Rise of Consortia

At the same time that manufacturers were trying to squeeze value out of installed computers, and the SDOs were discussing the technology for open computer systems, the vendors—in an effort to hedge their bets—began forming consortia. Consortia formed because there was a market need that was not being answered by the SDOs. The need was for more efficient and more widely accessible standardization efforts, with responsible program management that could set and keep a schedule. Additionally, the rapidity of technological change was making it difficult for the SDOs to keep up with the work that was needed. Finally, consortia (composed largely of the same companies that supported SDOs) are perceived to be more glamorous and exciting than SDOs, which had (and may still have) a stodgy reputation. Standards development consortia—which have become the dominant body creating IT specifications—generally take on one of three characteristics defined by Weiss and Cargill:

A. *Implementation consortia*, such as the SQL Access Group, implement standards that the formal SDOs have created but that lack the complete detail—or have too many options—to be implemented and used

B. *Proof of concept consortia*, such as the Object Management Group, prove that a technical concept is valid enough to standardize, and then are supposed to hand the idea off to an SDO when there is an adequate body of expertise to begin formal standardization

C. *Application consortia*, such as Open Software Foundation International, lobby for market acceptance (and hence the increased rationale for standards creation) of the technology of the consortia's sponsors.

Because vendors do not know which technology will eventually dominate the competition, they have participated in many SDOs and consortia in the hope that they would be able to capture some advantage when a standard emerged. Multiple SDOs and consortia have greatly raised the cost of standards setting for large vendors. Cost increases, and the difficulty of keeping track of mushrooming standards-setting meetings, also act as a barrier to participation by small and medium-sized companies. (See sidebar "Understanding the Process: SDOs versus Consortia.")

User Alliances: From Interoperability to Information Exchange

After years of investing in hardware and software, by the early 1980s, manufacturers began to realize that they were still not able to transfer information in context within and between companies. Since solutions were not forthcoming from vendors, they started creating their own solutions that focused on getting the job done. (See sidebar: "User Alliance for Open Systems.") At this point, manufacturers faced two different approaches to ensuring data exchange:

Understanding the Process: SDOs versus Consortia

It is important to understand the nature of the activity that occurs in an SDO. (The consortia were modeled after the SDOs, so their process, in large part, mirrors that of the SDOs, although usually without the rigor that the SDOs employ in their search for openness and consensus. Consortia, but for the nature of their "pay for play" roots, are less open than are SDOs.) The entire process is geared towards internal satisfaction of the rules of openness and consensus that the American National Standards Institute (ANSI) enforces. SDOs cannot reject a proposal or idea for a standard for the lack of "market" demand; their charter is to standardize technology for the good of the industry. On the other hand, consortia know exactly where their requirements come from, since they are usually generated by the sponsors who support the consortia. The problem with the consortia is that their demand may not reflect the reality of the market—but rather the reality of the sponsors. The difference between the two organizations is seen in the ability of the SDO to produce an accredited "standard;" a consortium cannot. This distinction becomes important in government procurements, which can require accredited standards, but usually cannot require consortia specifications.

A. Mandate that all divisions and suppliers use a proprietary CAD system such as CATIA or AUTODESK. This approach can be successful for large companies to a certain extent, but it places an enormous burden on lower-tier suppliers who might end up with a multitude of CAD systems, each system preferred by a different OEM

B. Allow all divisions and suppliers to have their own preferred system, but mandate a common exchange format, e.g., Initial Graphics Exchange Standards (IGES).

Between the two alternatives, designing a common exchange format appeared to users to be the most feasible approach: the installed, proprietary base of computer-aided design equipment could not be cheaply replaced. Nor should it be. Manufacturers report that it is not practical to use one vendor to supply all corporate functions.[2] Interconnection would be a more efficient application of resources.

Sometime in the late 1980s, user alliances began to form around the idea of exchanging information regardless of the hardware or software configurations involved. These activities have been based on an examination of the nature of the computing-based informa-

---

An Early Pathfinder: User Alliance for Open Systems

One of the first groups to attempt to re-define open systems was the User Alliance for Open Systems (UAOS)—a short-lived consortium that spun out of an earlier group called the "Houston Thirty." The UAOS, formed in 1990 by Boeing, Kodak, GM, and DuPont, redefined open systems as "those that permit users to obtain the information necessary to do one's job." There are, of course, all sorts of interesting implications of this statement, but we believe that it stands as a turning point for the definition for an open computing system. The UAOS recognized that open systems transmit information, and that the information is transmitted for a reason—and the reason is usually that one has a job to do. This definition of open systems is technologically neutral: a pen and paper could be just as effective an open system as a massive computer system. Soon after its formation, UAOS began attempting to define the technology needed to achieve open systems. This undoable task finally led to the organization's demise.

---

tion resource, and include groups such as the DOD's CALS program, IGES, and the Standard for the Exchange of Product Data (STEP), and their sponsoring organizations like the National Initiative for Product Data Exchange and U.S. Product Data Association (USPRO). This user-driven activity has gone largely unnoticed by vendors and consultants to the industry, but is having a significant impact on the definition and implementation of open systems, particularly in manufacturing.

Initial Graphics Exchange Standards (IGES)

Initial Graphics Exchange Standards (IGES), developed in the 1980s, is the most widely used format for exchanging Computer Aided Design/Computer Aided Manufacturing product data between dissimilar systems. IGES supports various kinds of CAD model transfers as well as drawing transfers. Types of models that can be exchanged include wire frame, surface, and solid. The primary application areas for IGES are in the architectural-engineering-construction area, and in mechanical and electrical disciplines. IGES was developed at first for a U.S. Department of Defense need and later adopted by manufacturers to provide productivity enhancements. IGES is an American National Standards Institute accredited standard developed and maintained by the IGES/PDES Organization (IPO). The IPO works together with the National Computer Graphics Association to help develop product data exchange technologies.

IGES translation software is plagued by a significant degree of ambiguity: It does not cope well with several different kinds of information (e.g., marginal notes on drawings), and sometimes omits rather than flags what it cannot translate. As a result it can take hours to recreate a transmitted drawing in its original form. The originator can anticipate problems caused by ambiguity in the way IGES translates technical data by knowing the details of the target software system and creating drawings that would be more fully translatable, but this effectively defeats the purpose of having translation software. Some of the bigger problems plaguing IGES have been solved as succeeding generations have appeared on the market (now, version 5.2), and accuracy now exceeds 98 percent. Even at this level of accuracy, however, an enormous amount of clean-up time may still required for any large project involving thousands of drawings, like a design of an automobile or an aircraft.[3] While IGES may be the only translation game in town, its limitations add large efficiency costs to data transfer.

Product Data Exchange Using STEP

The limitations posed by IGES for manufacturers led to the formation in 1984 of the Product Data Exchange Using STEP (PDES) group. PDES/STEP was formed by users from the IGES organization to support the development and implementation of international product data exchange standards.[4] The IGES/PDES organization is a voluntary activity involving predominantly users (and some vendors) from both the public and private sector. PDES took on the issue of integration of product data exchange standards in part out of frustration with the inability of CAD vendors to provide open solutions and in part in recognition of the limitation of IGES for both current and future applications. Because interoperability is a user need, the Standard for the Exchange of Product Model Data (STEP) is being promoted by users who are demanding that CAD suppliers include STEP capabilities in their software. Large manufacturers like GM, Ford, and Boeing are leading the effort to test and promote STEP. Several of these large users joined together to form PDES Inc., a consortium that provides resources to accelerate the development of the standard, but has implementation as its primary focus. A major pilot test, AEROSTEP, is being conducted by Boeing Aircraft in order to test one of the STEP applications protocols. Another pilot, AUTOPILOT, is being conducted in the automobile industry. PDES acts as a facilitator, helping competitors exchange data from pilots without fear of jeopardizing their competitive positions.[5]

STEP attempts to solve the problem of data conversion and comprehension: once a supplier gains access to data, that supplier must interpret and manipulate the data in a meaningful way. In order for different disciplines to contribute to the creation process as a product is designed, tested, and manufactured, a set of interfaces must be defined that allow unambiguous definitions relevant to each discipline. The solution proposed by STEP is a common database which includes geometric information used by all. Beyond that, STEP plans a set of application protocols that translate the relevant data into the language used by the specific discipline. The methodology underlying the development of STEP includes the use of reference models, a framework for product data modeling, formal definitions languages, and an architecture that separates applications requirements from physical implementations. STEP plans to create a complete representation of a product, not simply a graphical or visual representation like those transferred through IGES.

STEP is yet to be proven a viable technology, but it is intended to allow for advanced product modeling and to provide the ability to implement a unified manufacturing database that will include all the information necessary to manufacture a part, as well as necessary business information associated with the part. In order to incorporate information and technical terms relevant to manufacturers of different types of products, STEP contains many different application protocols (i.e., "libraries") applicable to different disciplines. Reaching agreement on the minimum common information requirements that will allow different disciplines to exchange information has constituted one of the principal issues in the process of developing the STEP standard.[6]

The difficulty of the undertaking goes beyond the need to accommodate different professional requirements. Different activities during the manufacturing cycle for a single part require different levels of detail and information. For example, a designer may omit some dimensional information that is not critical to the design phase, but this omission could make it impossible for the mold manufacturer to produce a mold. The mold manufacturer must then re-do the drawing to include relevant information.[7] STEP is supposed to provide the capability to create a CAD model that can incorporate all relevant technical and business information for the next step in a part's creation, as well as a complete history of the part from the time of its creation.

Enormous resources have been invested in the creation of STEP. Two to three hundred professionals in the United States and Europe meet quarterly for a week to discuss progress, and then return to their organizations to continue working on the standard.[8] They also have a brisk e-mail dialogue on standards making, and feed an on-line repository of information on emerging STEP standards. In 1991, a public-private coordinating organization, National Initiative for Product Data Exchange (NIPDE), was created because of the large number of individual activities taking place simultaneously with little, if any, coordination. NIPDE's Implementation Plan includes a representative (incomplete) list of STEP-related activities (that numbered 48 total in 1993) directed at the creation and promotion of STEP. Commercial software development is part of only seven of these. The rest of the organizations were involved in research, testing, and promotion of the standard.[9] NIPDE is scheduled to disband in 1995. Various organizations are forming now, with USPRO (created in 1993) scheduled to assume a coordinating role after NIPDE is disbanded. Corresponding bodies exist in other countries.

The first technically complete specification of STEP was submitted to ISO in 1988 and successive balloting and modifications led to a draft international standard in February 1993. The draft was approved in early 1994 and STEP is now an official standard, ISO 10303.

U.S. Product Data Association (USPRO)

The U.S. Product Data Association (USPRO) was established in 1993 by industry product data users to provide a forum for standards development, and to allow exchange of information and product specifications. USPRO evolved out of the IGES/PDES organization steering committee, and will assume the role of organizing and funding activities for the development, implementation, and testing of product data standards and specifications. USPRO supports several product data exchange initiatives and plans to sponsor research and development, standards development, testing, and specifications for product information. USPRO will also serve as the parent organization to IGES/PDES, the U.S. Technical Group TC184/SC4, and the National IGES Users Group.

Manufacturing and the NII

If the NII is going to benefit manufacturers, an open computing system needs to be defined in a way that addresses the problems of conversion and comprehension as well as providing support to vendors to continue efforts to improve communication and connection. As the need for STEP and other user-based standards groups shows, the voluntary standards process has difficulty providing standards at the user and data level (see Figure 1). The participants in the voluntary standards process are largely vendors who are suppliers of CAD systems. Vendors want to create proprietary systems that would give them a market advantage. Little incentive exists to make their systems exchange data with other systems. In fact, they have an incentive not to provide these standards.

The PDES/STEP case represents an attempt by a group of vendors *and users* to create an open environment for manufacturing product data exchange. Translation of product data information between proprietary systems was the original goal. The outcome is a highly complex set of layers of protocol translation that, after ten years of intense activity, is still in the early test stages. Whether STEP succeeds in becoming universally accepted as an interface standard between computer manufacturing protocols is in fact less interesting than the phenomenon of STEP's existence: it grew up outside of the voluntary standards process but has now evolved into an accredited standards activity.

The emergence of PDES/STEP to fill a void in the standards-setting and dissemination process points to a larger shortcoming that must be addressed on a public policy level. Like paying taxes, controlling pollution, and supporting research, everyone agrees that enabling standards like open systems are good and are necessary for commerce. Nevertheless, vendors will often fail market expectations for standards like open systems because of the high public good content.

There is a high cost associated with participating in the standards setting process, including not only the direct costs of attending meetings, but an even higher cost of associated technical development. Vendors can see sufficient benefits from potential future product sales to pay these costs, so they participate in the standards process. While the benefits of open systems to manufacturers as a group and to the economy as a whole are enormous, the benefits to any individual user may be such that the user cannot justify the effort of participating in the standards process. Hence, the classic market failure in which costs are concentrated but benefits are diffuse, so those who benefit the most have no incentive to participate in the process. As manufacturers start realizing greater benefits from networking and computer-based design and manufacturing, they are also taking on the costs of standardization in these areas, forming user-led bodies like PDES.

Does it matter whether vendors or users control the process for setting standards? Although open standards may empower users more than vendors by allowing "plug and play," the true test of standards is how well they meet the needs of both vendors and users. Both inputs are necessary. Similarly, the input of both the private sector and the public sector are necessary—both are players and customers. This is especially true in the creation of standards for the NII, where public and private sector groups are actors in creating and using the product.

The standards issues facing manufacturing applications for the NII are fundamentally different from standards issues that have challenged U.S. government and industry in the past. The voluntary standards process, controlled by industry and supported by government, grew up around and supported a production function based on generalized machinery in a rigid system for high-volume production. As Tassey (1992) has observed, technological change and the possibility of networking has transformed that production function to one of specialized machines organized into flexible systems. The complex nature of these interactions, and the need to involve many actors in design, creation, and dissemination of standards, require a different approach to standards setting in the information age.

Proposal for Change: Cooperation

The existence of a disincentive for the IT industry to provide open systems standards, the need to integrate the interests of users in the standards-setting process, the high public goods content of open systems standards, and the importance of incorporating small and medium-sized manufacturers into any benefit provided by the NII, all argue for a more active role for government in the process of facilitating standards for the NII. Open computing standards can be expected to provide a basis for productivity and economic growth, as planners have stated.[10] If networks fail to deliver needed information due to lack of standards that deal with the content of information transmitted over the networks, rather than merely the physical and logical devices that compose the network, there exists a high probability that the United States could suffer considerable economic harm. As it exists now, the providers of integrated manufacturing execution systems, rather than the users, are currently controlling the usage by controlling the structure.

The changed landscape for industry also changes the rules for government. No IT standard should be decreed by government. Instead, government should become a partner with vendors and users in promoting the most efficient and effective standards process for open systems, providing a concentration of voices for those who benefit from open standards to balance the voices of those who bear the cost. Accordingly, a cooperative model of standards activity, similar to that being undertaken by PDES/ STEP, may be the best model for future IT standards setting, and perhaps for standards-setting across a number of industry sectors.

The most efficient and effective way to meet these needs may be to create a joint venture between government and the private sector to coordinate standards setting activities in those areas having a high public good content. While it may be useful to have a national standards policy for all industries that are dependent upon standards, information technology would be a good place to experiment with a cooperative venture. Such an organization would help to facilitate transitions among the various phases of the standards-setting process (see Figure 3). As envisioned here, the joint venture would not develop standards: the actual development of standards would continue to be performed by the private sector, but where appropriate, government actors could take a role in helping to set and then promoting a standard. In addition, the joint venture could provide needed and useful type testing and conformity assessment services.

A joint venture between government and the private sector—perhaps in the form of a government-chartered corporation—would create a governing board of all interested parties that could approach the coordination of NII standards setting activities in a disinterested manner. Such an organization would not be funded solely by vendors or by government agencies. Funding could be provided by a government endowment and contributions from participants. Grants would be made available to small companies that could not afford to participate in the standards process. Control of the organization could alternate yearly or every other year from say majority government/minority industry to the reverse, with the chairmanship held by a representative from the minority group. A number of spaces could be held on the board by small business and the user community.

A cooperative public-private venture would provide the mediator for complex interactions among the many players who hold a stake in the outcome. It would allow participation by users and vendors, and by public and private sector agents. It would provide a common ground for groups that normally compete to meet and set the ground-rules for that competition. Moreover, it would allow representation and participation by groups currently under-represented in the standards process, such as small business, academic institutions, and non-computer literate citizens. It would provide the forum for groups to establish standards setting activities with any of the U.S. SDOs as appropriate. Finally, a cooperative joint venture could act as the official representative of the United States on an international level, receiving queries and speaking in one voice for the U.S. This function would further provide the incentive for

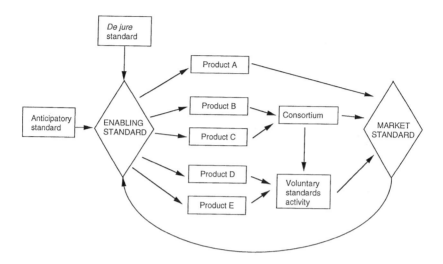

Figure 3 Map of Standards Creation.

vendors to participate in a cooperative standards-setting process.

Specifically, this cooperative body might perform the following functions:

A. Provide broad information about existing standards, their location, and on-going standards-setting activities on a regional, national, and international basis, in the form of electronics bulletin boards, databases, and libraries by actively seeking out parties judged by the board to have interest in a particular standards setting activity

B. Identify and coordinate standards-setting activities in cases where the outcome has a high public goods content—as judged by the board—convene meetings in these cases to consolidate or coordinate any standards setting activities relevant to this standard question, and in cases where standards-setting becomes contentious, provide a mediating role or otherwise help to reduce redundant and costly standards setting activities

C. Ensure adequate representation of and participation by small and medium-sized manufacturers in the standards development process by using the Department of Commerce's Manufacturing Extension Program and contact with small business associations and chambers of commerce, this joint venture could help provide the information and means to allow and encourage the broadest possible participation by small and medium-sized manufacturers. This could perhaps be accomplished electronically by providing an audio or video conference or by allowing network access to an end point for comments from small and medium-sized business people.

D. Advise government procurement, regulation, and trade activities on the role, function, and impact of standards on government activities and on economic growth.

This proposal might appear to be adding another layer of bureaucracy onto an already overburdened system, or perhaps appear to be the camel's nose under the tent for government control. This is particularly so because the American National Standards Institute already provides some of these functions. Why duplicate what already exists? As envisioned, a joint coordinating group would actually reduce the amount of bureaucracy in the standards world. The joint venture would become a "one stop shop" for companies seeking information about standards, reducing anxiety about "missing something" in on-going standards developing activities. Moreover, a joint venture would actually reduce the likelihood of government control by involving the government as a full partner and a stakeholder in the standards development process. As for duplicating ANSI's role, the intent is not to duplicate but to complement by looking at the usage of standards rather than the creation of standards. A group focused on NII standards, for example, would be aimed not at creating standards but at creating usage guides.

Conclusion

The key to standardization activity is the definition of the proper common elements to begin the process. The market, we believe, would reward cooperation and sharing at all five levels of interoperability (see Figure 1); however, the current IT standardization process within the United States is the wrong model for this approach, as it tends to focus only on the infrastructure services and the OS/platforms. This makes the current process product focused—this is, specifications are created by providers so that they can use them to create products for their markets. In nearly every case of which we are aware, the groups that stand to profit from a standard constitute the majority of contributors to the standardization activity. While private incentive can sometimes maximize public good, in the case of IT standards of interconnection, the incentive actually increases investment in proprietary systems rather than encouraging open systems. While private incentive often works, and voluntary standards activity is acceptable for the creation of product standards, it is not a viable approach to standardization for the user and data conversion levels of interoperability. Cooperation between the public and private sector to create an institution to support and facilitate this process offers the greatest opportunity for success.

Notes

[1] U.S. Department of Commerce, Technology Administration (1993).

[2] Ibid. This concept of shared manufacturing information is also reflected in the definition of manufacturing outreach contained in S.4/H.R. 820, The National Competitiveness Act of 1992.

[3] This type of occurrence is not unusual in standardization. The use of standardization activities to counter a successful *de facto* standard (or potential *de facto* standard) was especially noticeable in the case of LANs, where 87 competing varieties of LAN coalesced to three, in OSI, as a response to IBM's SNA, and in standardization of the SPARC ship set (IEEE 1754) as a counter to the Intel x86 success.

[4] Weiss and Cargill (1992).

[5,6] Libicki (1995).

[7] promoted by PDES, Inc. an international consortium of major corporations, established in 1988 to accelerate the development and implementation of PDES. PDES, Inc. works closely with NIST, the IPO, and the ISO. Its activities are consistent with NIPDE activities.

[8] Interviews.

[9] Interviews.

[10] Interviews.

[11] Interviews.

[12] U.S. Department of Commerce (1991), Appendix 1.

[13] U.S. Department of Commerce, Technology Administration (1993).

References

Cargill, Carl F., 1989. *Information Technology Standardization: Theory, Process, and Organizations.* Boston: Digital Press.

Carver, Gary, and Howard Bloom, 1991. "Concurrent Engineering Through Product Data Standards." Gaithersburg, MD: National Institute for Standards and Technology.

David, Paul A., 1987. "New Standards for the Economics of Standardization in the Information Age", in Partha Dasgupta and Paul Stoneman, eds., *Economic Policy and Technological Performance* (Cambridge: Cambridge University Press).

Farrell, Joseph, and Garth Saloner, 1985. "Standardization, Compatibility, and Innovation," *Rand Journal of Economics*, Vol. 16, No. 1, pp. 70–83.

Fleischer, Mitchell, et al., 1991. "CAD/CAM Data Problems and Costs in the Tool and Die Industry: Final Report on a Study Conducted for the Michigan Modernization Service." Ann Arbor, MI: Industrial Technology Institute.

Industrial Technology Institute, 1993. "Standards Development for Information Technology: Best Practice for the United States: Summary of Workshop Deliberations." Ann Arbor, MI: Industrial Technology Institute.

Kindleberger, Charles P., 1983, "Standards as Public, Collective and Private Goods," *Kyklos*, 36 (Fasc. 3), pp. 377–396.

Libicki, Martin C., 1995. "Standards: The Rough Road to the Common Byte," this volume.

Morell, Jonathan A., et al., 1992. "Improving the Deployment of Open Systems Technology: Lessons From the Manufacturing Automation Protocol." Ann Arbor, MI: Industrial Technology Institute.

Payne, Judith E., 1991. "A Change of Course: The Importance to DOD of International Standards for Electronic Commerce," RAND, R-4099-P&L.

Payne, Judith E., and Robert H. Anderson, 1991. "Electronics Data Interchange (EDI): Using Electronic Commerce to Enhance Defense Logistics," RAND, R-4030-P&L.

Schrage, Daniel, 1993. "Concurrent Design: A Case Study," in Andrew Kusiak, ed., *Concurrent Engineering: Automation, Tools, and Techniques* (New York: John Wiley).

Tassey, Gregory, 1992. Technology Infrastructure and Competitive Position. Norwell, MA: Kluwer.

Tassey, Gregory, 1994a. "Advanced Manufacturing Technology Policy." Gaithersburg, MD: National Institute for Standards and Technology.

Tassey, Gregory, 1994b. "The Role of Standards as Technology Infrastructure." Unpublished draft.

U.S. Congress, Office of Technology Assessment, 1992. *Global Standards: Building Blocks for the Future*, TCT-512. Washington, DC: U.S. Government Printing Office.

U.S. Congress, Office of Technology Assessment, 1994. *The Electronic Enterprise.* Unpublished drafts, March.

U.S. Congress, 1992. The National Competitiveness Act of 1992, S. 4, H.R. 820.

U.S. Department of Commerce, 1991. "National Initiative for Product Data Exchange (Implementation Plan)." Gaithersburg, MD: National Institute for Standards and Technology.

U.S. Department of Commerce, 1993. "National Initiative for Product Data Exchange Road Map Planning Guide." Gaithersburg, MD: National Institute for Standards and Technology.

U.S. Department of Commerce, Technology Administration, 1994. "Putting the Information Infrastructure to Work: Report of the Information Infrastructure Task Force Committee on Applications and Technology." Draft for comment, May.

Weiss, Martin, and Carl Cargill, 1992. "Consortia in the Standards Development Process," *Journal of the American Society for Information Science* (September), pp. 559–565.

Standards Development for Information Technology: Best Practices for the United States

Jonathan A. Morell and S. L. Stewart

Background

On July 8–9, 1993, a workshop was held under the title "Standards Development for Information Technology: Best Practices for the United States." (Appendix A contains a list of participants.) Sponsors were the National Institute of Standards and Technology (NIST) and the Industrial Technology Institute (ITI), through its Center for Electronic Commerce (CEC). This document is a synthesis of discussions that began during the workshop, and that continued among participants and others after the workshop ended. To maintain focus, conference deliberations were framed in terms of a small set of assumptions:

• Enterprise integration (EI) and electronic commerce (EC) are important for the competitiveness of industry in the United States[1]

• Deployment of new technology in support of EI and EC requires a standards process that is responsive to market needs and time constraints.

• The fundamental nature of the standards-making process is likely to be changed little in the foreseeable future. Thus, standards will be developed through the actions of standards committees working under ANSI/ISO sanction, industry groups and consortia, and market forces.

• Within the context outlined above, the process of standards making can be improved through a knowledge of best practice and continuous improvement.

- Companies (and individuals within companies) are often involved in multiple standards activities.

Also to help maintain focus, best practices were evaluated relative to four questions:

- Where in the standards life cycle will the best practice operate?
- How will the best practice affect products that will be standards conformant?
- What conditions and resources are needed for the best practice to work?
- What are the weaknesses of the proposed best practice?

Workshop organizers and attendees recognized the international nature of standards for information technology, and the consequent difficulty with the notion of "best practices for the United States." Our intention was not to confine the best practices to this country. Rather, we believe that in order to be competitive internationally, the United States must play a leading role in standards development, so as to have leading edge knowledge to produce products that support EI and EC.

The group also realized that many of our conclusions may relate to the entire realm of standards, and not just to information technology. We did, however, come to our task with a particular purpose, orientation, and experiential base, all of which oriented us toward the specific case of information technology. We believe our conclusions are relevant to that domain, and leave it to others to generalize to the larger case.

The Challenge of Improving Standards Making

Efforts to improve standards making must be sensitive to the peculiar nature of the organizational, political, business, and technical factors which constitute the standards-making environment. We present Figure 1 as a visual aid to these complexities.

Important characteristics of the standards environment depicted in the figure include:

- The entire standards-making world is subject to very strong forces over which it has little or no control. Some of these forces

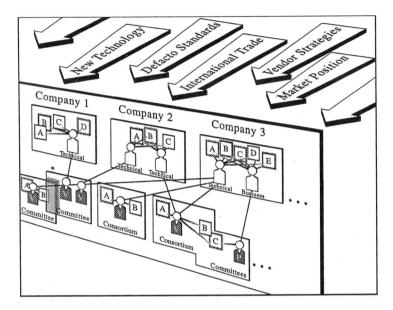

Figure 1 The Standards-Making Environment.

include existing de facto standards, the advent of new technologies, national positions on trade policy, and the market position of existing vendors.

- Most company representatives to standards committees come to their task with technical rather than business perspectives.

- Business processes within companies are often ill-defined and imprecise. More important, there is often weak coordination between representatives to standards groups and those business processes.

- Representatives to standards groups are often "volunteer labor" rather than people whose dedicated paid position is to work on standards development.

- There are a few major organizational contexts for standards making. Most formal national and international standards are developed by committees sanctioned under the ANSI/ISO structure. Also, the IEEE has its methods of standards making, as does NIST for federal information processing standards. Finally, many standards are developed by industry consortia such as X/Open, OMG and OSF.

• The work of different standards groups is often related. Sometimes those relations are recognized, while in other cases the
relationships are unknown. To complicate matters, fusions of
various technologies may generate relationships among standards
that did not exist when the standards were first conceived.

• While some processes in standards making are well defined and
explicit, others are imprecise and lacking in management control.
For example, the process for balloting and approving draft standards is well defined in most standards activity, but needs assessment and testing methodologies are left to the discretion of the
individuals involved.

An Overall View of Best Practice

The challenge is to develop a set of practices for standards that will
work within the economic and organizational context portrayed
above. Participants agreed that those practices would display three
characteristics:

1. Best practice should be seen in terms of a well-managed overall
process flow for standards, with appropriate metrics at critical
points.

2. Within the process, specific tools and methodologies are needed.
That is, an array of "micro-level" best practices must be inserted to
assure quality for specific activities.

3. The fundamental purpose of a standards effort is to support the
development of products that are economically viable for technology vendors, and whose use will support the business needs of users.

   The group recognized that this process can be applied to either
anticipatory standards (i.e., standard setting prior to the availability
of the technology being standardized), or to the formal standardization of a technology that has already been subject to a de facto
market standardization process. The application of the recommended process will have to be adjusted to these separate circumstances. As an example, anticipatory standards may require a much
more rigorous business justification than would standards for a
technology that has already been proved in the marketplace.

A series of increasingly detailed illustrations explain the view of best practice that emerged from the workshop. The highest level view of this process is contained in Figure 2.

Characteristics of best practice depicted in the figure include:

• The unbalanced arrow between the major sections of the diagram demonstrates that there is an important distinction between establishing a standards activity and developing the standard. While activities in each section can affect the other, the presumption is that important preliminary activity *must* precede the beginning of technical work.

• An effective standards process requires that a considerable amount of work be carried out prior to the start of actual development.

• Early work consists of developing the business foundation for a standard and planning at both strategic and organizational levels. These activities are concurrent and interacting, but there is a logical order for the start of each.

• The plan must be sold to critical stakeholder groups (technology vendors, end-users of standards-conformant products, and third parties.) Rather than planning and then selling, continual efforts are needed to include the views of stakeholders as part of a process that synthesizes both activities. In essence, the standards effort is sold by assuring that it is carefully crafted to meet users' needs.

• Success of the actual work of developing a standard requires strong linkages among three concurrent activities:

  • the technical work of developing the standard

  • market development for standards-conformant products

  • coordinated management of all work.

The following sections explode Figure 2 into its constituent parts and describe critical aspects of each.

Establishing a Standards Activity

The most important point about this part of the diagram is that it exists at all. There was strong agreement among participants that

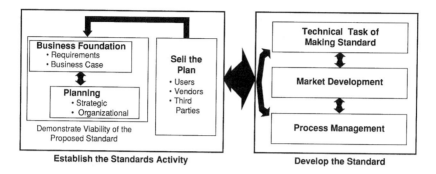

Figure 2 High Level View of the Standards Process.

in contrast to the present state of affairs, a standards effort should start only if it can be justified in business terms, even though in reality many standards efforts begin primarily for technological reasons. Two processes make up the business justification:

- Developing a "business case"
- Thorough planning

Based on beliefs about the importance of business considerations as a primary driver of standards, the following view emerges (see Figure 3):

- An extra measure of assurance can be gained by separating need definition and need validation. While these activities must be separate to maintain a validity check on data, strong iterations between them are required to assure that correct needs and requirements are determined.

- We should never assume that just because a standard can meet a set of needs, it is the *only* standard that can meet those needs. Hence the importance of a competitive analysis.

- The ability to meet needs is a necessary but not sufficient condition for commencing work. There are also issues of available resources, ability to meet windows of opportunity, likelihood that needs will remain stable, and many other issues that may affect a decision to proceed. The basic message is that needs and a competitive analysis are critical ingredients of a business case, but do not constitute the totality of that case.

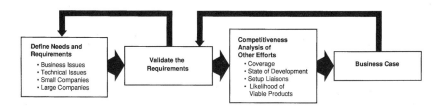

Figure 3 Business Foundation.

• Circumstances that justified a particular standard may change. (In fact, a successful standard may be a powerful contributor to that change.) Thus, ongoing feedback is needed to assure that requirements are current and that necessary adjustments are (in so far as possible) carried out.

• Special attention must be paid to the fact that small companies may have technology needs that are quite different from large companies. These considerations are particularly important with information technology because the value of that technology is so often dependent on its ability to promote inter-company cooperation among a set of trading partners.

As business issues are considered, detailed planning must commence, as depicted in Figure 4:

• Again, the process is characterized by activities that overlap and interact, but that have a natural lag for the beginning of each.

• A strategic planning activity is needed which articulates three guidelines for all those who work on developing the standard:

    • The *business problem* the work is trying to solve (e.g., slow production because of poor communication among factory floor devices)

    • The *technological objectives* (e.g., interfaces for distributed data bases)

    • The *management philosophy* (e.g., all tasks will be managed relative to deliverables, resources, and specific deadlines).

Throughout, there must be an emphasis on developing a standard that is reasonably stable over time, thus providing vendors with lower product development costs, and both users and vendors with some protection for their investment.

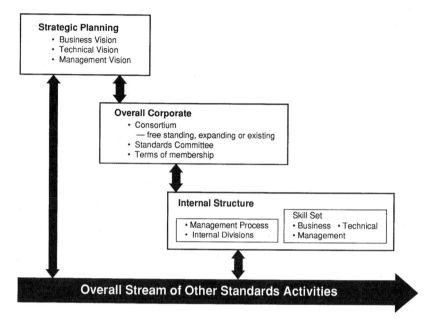

Figure 4 Planning for Standards.

• Standards work can be done either by formal standards committees or by industry consortia. The choice depends on a combination of opportunities presented by circumstance, and deliberate calculation about the impact of structure on the final outcome. There was a consensus at the workshop that a combined committee/consortium approach would be ideal. Consortia are needed to assure rapid development of standards that are tied to industry needs, and also to assure that the proper level of dedicated personnel are available. Standards committees are needed to provide formal sanction to the standard and dissemination services. The group's sense was that the work of consortia should be used to help define work items, and inserted into the International Standards Organization (ISO) process at the working draft stage.

• Corporate structure exerts incomplete control over how a standards effort will be managed. As an example, an ANSI sanctioned activity requires a balloting procedure, but ANSI says nothing about working group structure or the requirements for expertise in individual members. As overall structure begins to constrain operational practice, wise choices about internal operations must be made.

• An important part of developing an internal structure for standards work is attention to the skills needed. At a high level, those skills can be divided into three categories:

  • Standards management
  • Business objectives for the standard
  • Technical skills required to produce the standard.

The more detailed the skill assessment, the better. Ultimately such an assessment should get down to precise skills, e.g., consensus building, formal modeling, or test system development.

• Any particular standards effort is nothing more than a small part of a much larger set of related efforts that existed prior to the work in question and that will continue into the future. Thus, it is important to assure appropriate liaison with other relevant work, and to lay the groundwork for continuing coordination. One small but important element of this coordination would be some means of registering standards developed by consortia within the formal standards process. Registration would be a minimum requirement. In addition, three other tactics were suggested: formal analyses of relationships among standards; a reference model to provide public understanding of those relationships; and common definitions of terms across standards efforts, thus allowing easier comparison of diverse activities. All of this coordination is critical because product conformance testing must often be carried out relative to profiles (i.e., groups of standards) rather than to any single standard.

In addition to having value in their own right, the tasks of "developing a business foundation" and "planning" must also be seen as parts of a larger effort to sell the proposed standards efforts to critical stakeholders. Those groups must be included in the business and planning activities so that upon completion of those tasks the "sell" phase should be little more than a formality.

The process outlined above can be seen as a best practice in its own right. The group also believed that specific best practice methodologies and tools must be sought out and inserted into that process to assure success. Consider the following examples. Quality Function Deployment (QFD) can be used to do needs and requirements analysis. Total Quality Management (TQM) and Continuous Improvement (CI) approaches can keep the process functioning well, and can assure ongoing incremental improvement. Discussions at the workshop did not reveal the entire set of useful approaches, but they did establish the principle that such approaches exist, and that they should be systematically inserted into the standards-making arena.

Inserting new methods into standards making implies that a process exists to train standards makers in the appropriate knowledge. The objective would be to take generic techniques, customize them for the particulars of standards making, and deliver that knowledge to the appropriate individuals. Unfortunately, no adequate process exists to deliver the necessary training. One recommendation made was to develop training tools and programs that could then be widely disseminated, perhaps through existing standards organizations.

Metrics

We agreed that two types of metrics are important: metrics to assess how well the process is unfolding, and measures of the quality of the standards that are produced. The quality metrics are important, even at early stages, because knowledge of those metrics can be used to set objectives and to instill a sense of mission. To assure the value of metrics, we propose that they be chosen with the following criteria in mind:

- The metric must be:
  - *easily observable* (not require elaborate or special means of data collection)
  - *reliable* (different observers should get approximately the same result under similar circumstances)
  - *well defined* (general agreement on what the indicator means)
  - *useful* (knowledge of the indicator must be able to lead to practical action in a reasonable time).
- Data collection must be able to be systematically integrated into

ongoing activity, thus removing the possibility of measures being used too infrequently.

- Data must be in a form and location where it is easily available to those who can make use of it.

- The data must be useful at reasonably gross levels of approximation. Otherwise, too much effort will be expended at data quality assurance.

- Metrics must make sense when used jointly rather than individually. The problem is that any process can be distorted to meet any given metric, but joint metrics tend to preserve the intent behind the measure. The classic example is the automobile industry, which would produce a very undesirable product if it aimed *only* for low cost or *only* for high quality. Taken together, pursuit of these metrics has profoundly changed the entire world-wide automobile industry.

One important domain of process metrics is simply whether the steps in the process diagrams presented above are present. Was there a formal needs analysis? Was there feedback between "planning" and "selling" activities? Was a business vision developed? And so on. Once fidelity to the process is assured, a set of process-specific measures can be invoked. The candidate metrics generated by the group include:

- Was a product specification put forward as a basis for the standard?

- Is there multi-vendor interest in the standard?

- Was there an assessment of standard development time relative to the window of opportunity in the market?

- How good is the management of end-user expectations relative to when vendors can actually deliver product?

- Are there redundant or competing standards?

Moving from process to product, the group suggested a variety of criteria for a successful standard.

- Are vendors building products?

- Do the products meet user needs?

- How large is the installed base?
- Are products priced in terms of commodity costing?
- What impact has the standard had on the viability of the vendors' industry?
- Are diverse products interoperable?
- Were standards-conformant products on the market before the standard was finalized?
- Does the standard allow applications that are *portable* to different platforms, *scalable* in size, and *interoperable* with other applications?

If these criteria are to be of value, their use must be embedded in a system that has two features. First, it must trace the success of a standard to various aspects of the standards process, thus providing information on how the process might be improved. Second, it must provide information to new standards efforts so that mistakes of the past are not repeated.

Developing a Standard

Technical Work

As a framework for understanding best technical practice, workshop participants employed a model of the standards life cycle depicted in Figure 5.[2,3] A variety of best practices are implicit within this model.[4]

- Standards production is best viewed (and managed) as activity among three related domains—*standards* per se, *implementation*, and *testing*. Each is critical if a useful standard is to emerge. Simply writing a standard, no matter how well constructed, is not sufficient.

- Testing often lags behind other aspects of standards development, thus delaying the entire process. One value of the life cycle is that it relates specific testing activities to specific activities concerning standards and implementation. This micro-level linking may make it easier to develop management plans that keep test development on schedule.

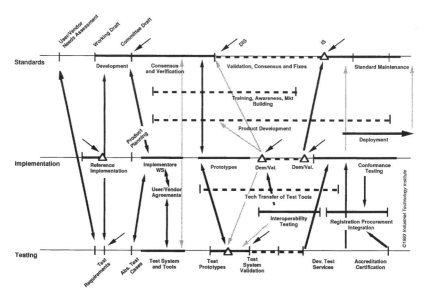

Figure 5 The Standards Life Cycle. Building requirements: QFD (technical, strategic, business, and organizational). Legend: thinner solid rules indicate tracking requirements; thicker rules indicate coordination points; stippled rules indicate feedback.

• Prototypes and demonstrations must occur quite early in the process because as we shall see in a later section, many critical market development activities must begin early, and are keyed to the availability of prototype products. In our experience, some vendors, in some situations, will commit to product development when a standard is in the working draft stage. Most, however, seek the assurance afforded by progress to the committee draft stage. We believe that as more cogent needs assessments and business cases are built for a standard, vendor commitments earlier in the process will increase. In order to assure the necessary commitments, implementors workshops must be carefully managed to provide maximum useful feedback to standards developers.

• Conformance test tools should be used by vendors as design tools, thus assuring conformance of final product. As a result those tools must be developed quite early in the process, and careful attention must be paid to the transfer of tool technology to the vendor community. It is also critical to assure fidelity between the tool and the standard because in essence, the tool will *become* the standard.

• Because consensus building is so important throughout so much of standards development, support for good group process is critical. To provide that support, both soft technology (e.g., group facilitation training) and hard technology (e.g., groupware) should be systematically deployed.

• Within an overall standards activity, each working group should write its own test assertions, thus assuring that the assertions are (1) in fact written and (2) match the intended use of the standard. This link between standards and testing needs to be established early in the process. Ideally these tests would be described through the use of formal languages and methods, thus inserting needed rigor into the testing process. Finally, it would be highly desirable to have automatic generation of test cases. Doing so, however, requires a carefully drawn specification constructed within a reference model that defines the scope of the standard. This need for specifications and reference models creates yet another important link between testing and actual standards development.

So far the discussion has centered only on standards rather than on groups of standards, i.e., profiles. This may be a serious oversight because many products must conform to an entire suite of standards. Reliance on profiles emphasizes the need for coordination among standards activities because there is a need to integrate testing. Profiles also put an added burden on test developers because their tests must account for interactions among standards.

Market Development

From the beginning workshop participants agreed that standards were valuable only if they could spur the development of products that were actually bought, installed, and used to good advantage. Thus the concept of "market development" was elevated to an important position, and was discussed in terms of a set of activities that ran throughout the standards development process.

Market development begins early, when the business case is originally built. The process then continues throughout the standards development phase of the work. As market development proceeds, it must be conceptualized and managed as a coherent process that has discrete activities that are integrated into technical work. Just as one should have a plan for reference implementations, conformance testing, or draft production, so too must one have a plan for market development.

Within this structure, the workshop yielded a variety of specific activities that must be integrated into market development. Figure 6 places these activities on a simplified version of the standards life cycle.[5]

When setting market development plans, the following issues are noteworthy:

• Standards representatives from end-user organizations often do not fully understanding what their company will actually do when acquiring technology. This is hardly surprising, as internal corporate standards are often honored more in the breach than in the observance. The reasons for the problem are no less frustrating for being well known. Corporate policy makers often do not have operational control over the Division and Facility managers who allocate budgets to technology. Those managers, in the meantime, are operating in business, economic, and technological environments that may be quite different from what existed at the time work on a standard began. Finally, standards committee members often have incomplete communication with those critical Divisional and Facility managers. The essential problem is that representing one's company in a standards committee requires considerable skill in technology assessment (What will be needed in the future?) and in organizational consensus building (How can I fashion commitments that others in the company may live by?).

• As early in the process as possible (at the latest, before development actually begins), mechanisms are needed to assure that committee members are able to represent the most likely position of their companies. One mechanism may be how a standards effort is staffed, as it may be possible to assure that personnel with the requisite skills are included. In addition, training may be useful for committee members who are not expert in technology assessment or consensus building. The point of such training would not be to

User/Vendor Needs Assessment	Begin Development	Prototypes	Demonstration Validation	Conformance Testing	
• Recruit user needs experts	•Determine windows of opportunity	• Awareness training	•Reference implementation	•Availability of commercial products	•User feedback to standards makers
•Standards training			•User training		
			•Implementation tools		

Figure 6 Market Development.

give people a new specialty, but to help reduce the likelihood of gross miscalculation.

• Schedules for the completion of technical work must take careful account of windows of opportunity in the market. As an example, the expected life of existing technology may determine the next wave of technology acquisition. Or it may be public knowledge when an industrial sector will need new technology to support its next generation product development. In both cases these events have considerable importance for when new standards-conformant products need to be available. Such knowledge must be factored into standards development plans prior to the beginning of work.

• About the time that prototypes are ready, serious awareness building for the standard must begin. This can take the form of articles in trade magazines, talks to professional groups, and demonstrations. The essential point is that awareness efforts cannot be haphazard. Target audiences must be explicitly defined based on careful assessment of where interest would best support the standards effort. Awareness is needed among both users and vendors. Users must be prepared to acquire the new technology. Among vendors, interest must be generated to get as many niche products as possible on the market, thus increasing the value of the base technology for all.

• The group emphasized that this phase of the work is extremely delicate and dangerous. On one hand, the more awareness building, the better. On the other hand, success can inflate expectations beyond what can reasonably be delivered, thus dooming the entire effort.

• As the life cycle progresses, two market-related milestones must be in place by the time public product demonstrations are held. First, there must be a "reference implementation" to give potential users confidence that claimed interoperability is a fact. In the best case the reference implementation will be part of the demonstration. At a minimum, the results of testing against that implementation must be made public. Such publicity will boost public confidence in the standard, in the standard makers, and in the vendor community.

• Also about the time of public demonstrations, training must be available for potential users of standards-conformant products. Training is needed for several reasons. By providing expertise, it lowers the cost and risk of product implementation. It helps to publicize products. Finally, it begins to develop informal networks of experts who can rely on each other for assistance.

• Another method of reducing risk is to produce tools to assist with technology adoption. As examples, tools may help manage technical aspects of use (e.g., network management), help build a business case for technology acquisition, guide business process change to help exploit the technology, or identify new personnel needs. In all these cases, technology adoption becomes faster, more valuable, and less risky.

• Real products must follow conformance testing in very short order. Particularly with anticipatory standards, it is essential that products be available as soon as possible after the value of the technology has been proven. The difficulty is that anticipatory standards represent an unfulfilled promise to users that at some point in the future products will become available to help solve business problems. Because business problems are involved, users will wait only so long.

• It is reasonable to assume that technology adoption (i.e., use for routine business) will accelerate after conformance testing is satisfactorily accomplished. Thus about that time a communication mechanism must be established to assure that real world experience is fed back into standards development and maintenance.

The critical point is that initial needs assessments and business cases are dynamic, and this reality must be systematically included in the standards process.

Management Process

We have developed a complicated process of continually linked tasks and sub-tasks that take place along four dimensions: standards development, implementation, testing, and market development. We have also claimed that evaluation and corrective action must take place continually. Effective management is needed to make this process work.

A general sense pervaded the group that much improvement could be obtained from the application of basic principles of good management, i.e., vesting responsibility in clearly defined groups and individuals, use of checkpoints for go/no go decisions, and attention to issues such as timelines, human and financial resources, milestones, and coordination. The real question is why this simple and well accepted prescription has been followed so infrequently.

We had general agreement that much of the problem is founded on two pillars. First, we have a standards committee structure that relies on "volunteer labor"—people whose income and professional advancement is not directly related to the success of the standard being built. Second, people engaged in this "volunteer labor" pursue a misguided mission. Standards committee members view their job as making a standard, when in fact they should be seeking reliable implementation of a standard in a commercial setting. Thus, a proposed (and enthusiastically accepted) best practice was to rely more heavily on a fusion between industry consortia and formal standards committees. The idea was to use industry consortia to bring a standard up through a draft phase. The advantage of doing so is that an industry consortium is likely to have a relatively high level of industry funding, and thus the dedicated resources that would allow the standards process to be "run like a business," because essentially it would be a business. Once developed, the formal standards process could be used to legitimize and disseminate the standard internationally. The group also felt that the plan proposed here would have the additional advantage of assuring closer alignment between the standards activity and true industry needs.

A major problem with the above suggestion is that it is impractical for many important standards efforts to take place within industry consortia. For better or for worse, much traditional standards committee work will continue, thus returning us to the question of how to effectively run a volunteer effort. Three suggestions emerged to address this problem:

1. Very strong champions are needed. While strong leadership is always desirable, it is particularly important in this case.

2. Personnel recruitment is critical. In volunteer efforts there is always a temptation to "take whomever one can get." We have determined, however, that a variety of skills is needed for developing a powerful standard, and that developing that skill profile must be one of the early stages in any standards effort. Leaders of a standards effort should use that profile as a recruiting tool, thus at least providing a clear statement to companies about what kind of volunteers should be detailed to the standards group.

3. Electronic technologies (e.g., video, electronic mail, moderated bulletin boards) can be used to lower the cost of committee participation and to increase the richness of contact among members. This is desirable in any standards effort, but it is particularly important in volunteer efforts, which are subject to turnover in membership and to uncertain levels of participation by people and companies.

Summary

Very powerful forces combine to subject standards making to a high degree of uncertainty:

• Factors such as changing technology and market dynamics have unpredictable affects on standards making.

• Standards require many years of effort, thus increasing their vulnerability to unpredictable events.

• Standards are produced within an organizational environment that makes coordination very difficult:

- Individuals have a hard time coordinating their standards work with related activities in their companies.
- Standards groups find it difficult to coordinate their internal processes.
- Inefficient mechanisms exist to coordinate the vast range of distributed standards activity that is taking place world-wide.
- Because consensus is such a critical element of standards making, the system is prone to argument, delay, and counter-productive compromises.

Workshop members came to the conclusion that process improvement can take place under these trying circumstances, and that such improvement can result from a traditional view of quality improvement:

- Action must begin with a keen understanding of the business reasons for a standard. In recognition of this belief, workshop members placed a very heavy emphasis on powerful business planning as a prerequisite to beginning a standards effort.
- Improvement requires a knowledge of the process of standard making. We must know what the elements of the process are, their respective time lags, what the feedback loops are, and how various elements affect each other. To this end a detailed standards life cycle played an important role in guiding deliberations and conclusions.
- Process improvement can emerge from changes in:
  - *technology* (e.g., testing methods or groupware)
  - *organization* (e.g., coordination mechanisms or the use of consortia)
  - *people* (e.g., personnel selection or training in consensus building).
- Metrics are important because we need to measure change and assess product quality.
- Continual incremental improvements can aggregate to make large improvements. This initial assumption was reinforced by the number of incremental improvements suggested by workshop members.

Despite the emphasis on incremental improvement to an existing system, it was also clear that some more fundamental change is required. The prime example of this need was the strong desire of workshop members to begin developing more standards through industry consortia, and to use the work of those consortia to define and validate both proposed work items and standards. Another example is the need for coordinating mechanisms among diverse standards activities. Both of these require changes that cannot be fairly characterized as "incremental."

The workshop was the beginning of an experiment that is still in progress, and is but one of a variety of activities aimed at improving standards making. As these activities progress and coalesce, standards-based products will better serve the business needs of the end-users of information technology.

Appendix A: Participants, Standards Development for Information: Best Practice for the United States, July 8–9, 1993

Mr. Howard Bloom NIST	Mr. Bob Boykin CAM-I
Mr. Bill Conroy NIST	Ms. Elizabeth N. Fong NIST
Dr. Stephanie Gajar U.S. Congress	Dr. Catherine Howells Boeing
Mr. Richard Hovey Digital Equipment Corp.	Mrs. Marilyn Kraus DISA/JIEO/TB
Dr. Margaret Law NIST	Mr. Roger Martin NIST
Dr. Jonathan Morell Industrial Technology Inst.	Dr. K.H. Muralidhar Xycom
Mr. Mark E. Palmer NIST	Mr. Patrick Price USAF
Dr. Ugo Racheli 3-M Company	Mr. Thomas Rhyne Atlas Standards Laboratories
Ms. Carol Rozwell Digital Equipment Corp.	Ms. Jane Schweiker American Natl. Standards Inst.

Mr. Chuck Stark
NIST
Mr. Greg Winchester
NEMA
Ms. Barbara Youngert
AIAG

Dr. Selden Stewart
NIST
Mr. Jack White
Industrial Technology Inst.

Notes

[1] *Enterprise Integration* refers to a condition in which information flows smoothly within a manufacturing company, and between the company and its suppliers, customers, and partners. The value of EI lies in its potential to help companies speed the development of better products and services that capitalize on opportunities, and reduce operating costs. EI is a broad concept that sets the technology of integration within the context of an integrated organization and an educated workforce. *Electronic commerce* is the use of digital data to support new business relationships by improving routine operations, facilitating new kinds of transactions, and allowing the establishment of products and services that require digital representation in order for them to exist.

[2] An early version of this model was developed by ITI staff and presented to the workshop. Based on suggestions made at the workshop, the model was harmonized with a similar life cycle developed by the X.3 committee. The merged version is presented here.

[3] The model employs the common parlance of ISO to lay out the standards life cycle. The process depicted, however, is generic to a wide variety of standard-making venues.

[4] Throughout this discussion we are assuming the more problematic case, i.e., that an anticipatory standard is being built. If standards are being built around existing technology, appropriate adjustments must be made with respect to when milestones should be placed and the importance of the activities discussed.

[5] Again, we are assuming the more difficult and problematic case, i.e. that an anticipatory standard is being built.

Improving the Standardization Process: Working with Bulldogs and Turtles

Michael B. Spring, Christal Grisham, Jon O'Donnell, Ingjerd Skogseid, Andrew Snow, George Tarr, and Peihan Wang

Introduction

Standards, particularly information technology (IT) standards, have been the subject of much attention over the last few years. The proliferation of computing devices, the dramatic increase in network connections, and the varied applications of information technology have all intensified the need for a comprehensive and consistent set of standards. The importance of standards has been highlighted in the planning for the National Information Infrastructure and by the High Performance Computing and Communications Initiative. Increasing attention to global commerce—in particular, the success of the GATT talks in eliminating many traditional trade barriers—has also increased interest in standards as a mechanism by which free global trade can be restricted or enhanced (Garcia, 1992).

Along with this increased attention to IT standards has come discussion and debate about the processes by which the standards are developed. Standards such Open Systems Interconnection (OSI) and Integrated Service Digital Network (ISDN) have raised questions about whether it is possible in an era of rapidly evolving information technology to develop standards in anticipation of markets for them. The emergence of consortia and other ad hoc mechanisms replacing the traditional Standards Development Organization (SDO) processes has raised questions about the importance of due process and end user involvement in standardization. Finally, while there is some evidence that Europe is moving away from government controlled standardization toward a more free market (i.e., industry controlled) approach to setting standards, discussions continue in the United States about the need for more government control of the process to reduce inefficiencies. All of these developments have been noted by the traditional information technology SDOs in the United States—X3, IEEE, T1, X12, etc. These organizations and the American National Standards Institute (ANSI) have engaged in strategic planning efforts with an eye to determining what standards will be needed over the coming years and how they might be most efficiently developed.

In April 1993, the Long Range Planning Committee of X3 met at the University of Pittsburgh.[1] The committee decided to undertake a study of the characteristics of successful technical committee chairpersons, with a goal of improving the standards development process, particularly through the training of chairpersons and members.[2]

The study seeks to identify ways to improve both the quality of the standards developed and the efficiency of the process. Data was gathered from four sources: experts in the field of standardization, existing and former chairpersons of technical committees, members of X3 technical committees who could be contacted by e-mail, and readers of selected internet newsgroups who had participated in standards development efforts. Data was gathered from technical committee chairs and experts via structured phone interviews and from committee members via an electronic survey. Analysis of the interviews and the surveys generally confirms the belief that the process is very dependent upon personal styles and yields insights into several mechanisms that might improve the process. The study strongly suggests specific foci for training of chairpersons and members of standards committees and highlights mechanisms by which the traditional SDO process may be modified, within the constraints imposed by due process, to improve both the speed and quality of the development process. [3]

Background

Standards may be achieved through market forces (de facto standards), government regulation (de jure standards), or voluntary consensus. Early on, IT standards were dominated by de facto standards—those set by IBM. Over the last twenty years, X3, the Consultative Committee on International Telephony and Telegraphy (CCITT), International Organization for Standardization (ISO), and the IEEE have played a major role in the development of voluntary consensus standards. Over the last few years, the standards development process has been impacted by changes in the market fueled by rapid technology progress, an increasingly open global market, increasing participation in the process by user groups, and competition between traditional and new standards development organizations (Rutkowski, 1991, Besen and Farrell, 1991, Farrell, 1993).

Voluntary consensus standards are usually developed by a small group of individuals representing the vendors of the technology. In the United States, the Standards Development Organizations (SDOs) in the information technology area include X3, X12, Z39, IEEE, and the Internet Engineering Task Force (IETF); internationally, the CCITT, and ISO are the dominant SDOs (Cargill, 1989, Spring, 1991a, Weiss and Cargill, 1992). These SDOs operate in an open, voluntary public fashion (Greenstein, 1992), observe a form of due process, and make decisions through consensus (Besen, 1990, Farrell and Saloner, 1988). The process is a hybrid of a technical discussion and a political negotiation (Farrell, 1993).

Standards development processes based on due process and the consensus principles are time-consuming. The average time to develop an IEEE standard is seven years. Months of public reviews and successive ballots within X3 produce standards in three to seven years. The development time for an ISO standard may exceed seven years. In the CCITT, the use of quadrennial meetings for processing proposals has now been streamlined by changing circulating and voting procedures (Farrell, 1993, Besen and Farrell, 1991). Beyond the time delays, SDOs have experienced attrition of voluntary participants. Presumably, this is due the current fee structure, requisite travel, and other expenses associated with participation in the traditional standards development process (Cargill, 1989, David and Greenstein, 1990, Lehr, 1992).

Each of the SDOs has a structure within which technical standards are developed. For example, the X3 development process involves technical committees (TCs) and subordinate technical groups (TGs) preparing draft standards within assigned areas of expertise (Cargill, 1989, Lehr, 1992). The X3-style of standardization incorporates open participation by volunteers and the enforcement of "due process" and "consensus" (Robinson, 1988). This is done to ensure the creation of functional standards that address market needs and user requirements. The formal negotiation process also minimizes the possibility of adopting standards that are incompatible with each other. Traditionally, in the IT industry, vendors have self-certified standards compliance. Thus standards developed by traditional SDOs are not developed with testing in mind. It is usually left to providers or some other third party such as the National Institute for Standards and Technology to implement testing and confirmation.

While this study focuses on improving the efficiency of the traditional SDO process, other approaches to standards development are emerging:

1. The technologically based approach to network standards development used by IETF has been looked at as a new model, particularly in light of the growth of the Internet and the acceptance of the standards on which it is based. IETF has guidelines for validation and extensive testing of draft standards prior to adoption. It is based on a predominantly electronic mode of operation with very open membership and participation rules.

2. Consortia created by vendors and industry-specific special interest groups have accelerated the standards-setting process by limiting membership and by working within a limited area. A consortium recently formed by Intel, Microsoft, Novell, HP, IBM, and other large firms (Didio, 1993) recognizes the need to prevent duplication of efforts and promote consistency in product development. The proliferation of consortia may signal a move toward the development of product oriented-standards in this manner.

3. As demonstrated by X/OPEN, a consensus process involving vendors and users may be used to efficiently develop and adopt commercial de facto standards (Dolberg, 1993). X/OPEN has been particularly successful incorporating specifications from Microsoft in this fashion.

While these and other mechanisms are attractive, they are not without detractors. When consortia become involved in the development of base standards, or grow in size, some of the same delays noted in the traditional process begin to emerge. Similarly, while IETF has been very successful in development of the Internet through its standards, it is important to note that these standards did not appear overnight. IETF and its predecessors have been at work for more than 25 years on the development of the Internet standards, with much of the initial cost borne by the Department of Defense in the initial stages of the ARPANET.

The traditional SDOs have initiated several efforts to improve their processes. Recognizing the duplication of effort in developing parallel national and international standards, they have adopted "fast track" procedures to move national standards to the international arena or international standards into the national arena. To overcome the difficulties of developing consensus, the European Telecommunications Standards Institute (ETSI) has successfully employed a "weighted majority voting" rule to expedite the setting of standards (Besen, 1990). SDOs have shown an increased interest in using public specifications (e.g. Microsoft's Windows).[4] Government involvement in strategic planning for standards has been considered as a means to insure timely standardization with minimal duplication of effort.[5] Anticipatory standards have been suggested as a way to place standards development before product development (Meek, 1988); X3's FDDI (Fiber Distributed Data Interface) standard and CCITT's ISDN are examples of anticipatory standards.[6] Finally, there are mechanisms aimed at improving the efficiency of the process. Electronic meetings, videoconferencing, computerized group decision-making laboratories, and electronic mail are all means that allow wider participation on a more timely basis. Somewhat less discussed are methods that would structure the standard and testing process more formally. Formal Description Techniques (FDTs) may be used to specify standards unambiguously and aid the development of conformance tests. On the other hand, the high level of expertise needed for FDTs may hinder and further delay the development process.

As traditional SDOs address the issues of coordination and collaboration to ensure the timely development of standards in line with market needs and user requirements, all of these mechanisms are being considered. A number of authors (Spring, 1991b, Cargill,

1989, Garcia, 1992) point to the importance of improving the traditional SDO process in light of new demands. This study focuses on improving the technical committee process as it is used by traditional SDOs. The questions addressed are:

1. What can be done to overcome the slow pace of committee work that delays the introduction of new services? (Besen and Farrell, 1991)

2. What can be done to insure effective coordination of committee activities, avoiding sabotage by participants harboring hidden agendas to serve their own market segments and protect or promote vested interests (Farrell, 1993, Farrell and Saloner, 1988).

3. What can be done to avoid the introduction of irrelevant standards due to inappropriate strategy and management? (Besen and Farrell, 1991)

Methodology

The Long Range Planning Committee of X3 suggested a study of the characteristics of chairs of IT standards committees in order to determine how to improve the quality and efficiency of standards and the standardization process.[7] The broad goal was to better understand the factors and processes that contribute to successful standardization efforts within the traditional SDOs. It is hoped that the results of this study will guide the development of a training program for chairs and participants.

The study focuses on the human dimensions of standards development (e.g., behavior, skills, group dynamics) with the goal of determining which characteristics of human behavior and standards development steps contribute to the effective generation of quality standards. Quality implies such factors as: shortest possible development time, a focused endeavor that results in widely-used products based on the approved standards, and a high degree of satisfaction among the standards participants and the organizations that sponsor them. The data was analyzed to find mechanisms for improving management skills and personal characteristics through training.

In consultation with Donald Loughry of the X3 Long Range Planning Committee, it was decided that it would be inappropriate at this point to attempt to identify standards committees that might be labeled "successful" and "unsuccessful" and then conduct a comparative analysis of the members, chairpersons, and processes. It was agreed that at this early stage it would be more useful to select successful chairpersons and to try to capture data about what made those efforts particularly successful. It was also decided that the study should be expanded to include representatives from IETF and IEEE.

In order to capture more broad based data about problems with the standardization process, it was decided to interview several individuals who had made significant contributions to the theory and practice of standardization. Because such a small sample is susceptible to bias, we decided to gather survey data from a broader community of individuals involved in the standardization process that could be used to corroborate or qualify the views of experts and chairpersons.

Questions were designed to solicit information in the following areas:

- Roles in the committee
- Characteristics of the process
- Committee composition
- Member characteristics
- Chairperson characteristics
- Decision making processes
- Conflict resolution
- Training and preparation

The research groups developed questions for each of the audiences with this general framework in mind. The interview questions intended for the experts were the least structured. Those intended for technical committee chairpersons were focused on specific techniques they used or had had experience with. The survey instruments were structured to provide demographic data and the perspective of committee members.[8]

Results

The study generated a wealth of data for analysis. While the diverse data sources make it difficult to establish clear parallels between the responses to questions that were tailored to the various interviewees, the places where there was intense disagreement or significant agreement stand out clearly. In the discussion that follows, we commend to the reader five points that were emphasized again and again in the study. They form a set of themes that permeated the interviews and questionnaire comments:

1. The success of any given standardization effort is tightly coupled with the quality of the leadership provided. While it is possible that this leadership will come from an individual other than the chair of the committee, it is most likely that this responsibility will fall to the formally appointed or elected chair.

2. The characteristics expected of the chairperson of a standards committee differ significantly from the characteristics expected of members of the committee. While it is anticipated that members will be technically competent, this characteristic is subservient in the chairperson to leadership, diplomacy, and negotiating skills. In general, committee members have a positive view of the chairs of their committees.

3. The single most important problem that must be addressed by the chairperson is the resolution of conflicts that may be technical, political, or personal in nature. The approaches suggested for resolving conflicts are as diverse as the personalities of the chairs.

4. There was little agreement about the role or importance of users in the process. While it may reflect biases of the investigative teams, we did note that "users" were less of an issue for technical committee chairs than for the expert group. This is not to say that TC chairs didn't care about users. Rather, while experts had strong opinions about the value of users, chairs simply accepted users as members of the committee, albeit members who had less to contribute if they were not technically oriented.[9]

5. There was general agreement that technology is being underused as a tool to overcome the slowness and generally unstructured nature of the standardization process.

There were fifty-four responses to the survey from individuals participating in nineteen standards committees, the majority of which were from X3 committees. The most represented committees dealt with computer language standards, with twelve from X3.J16-C++, six from X3.H2-SQL and five each from X3.J4.1-Cobol and X3.J11-C. There were four or less responses from each of the other fifteen committees. The distribution represents a fairly diverse response, with the possible exception of the twenty two percent response of the C++ group. While the survey sample was small, a few observations can be made about the responses. In general, these confirm anecdotal data:

1. Committee meetings occur with an average frequency of four times a year.

2. Seventy-five percent of the respondents describe their job function as either research and development (20/54) or product development (20/54).

3. Ten percent identified themselves as users (6/54). The other categories having responses included marketing/sales (1), operations (1), system integration (3), consultant (2) and government representative (1).

4. About fifteen percent of the participants (8/54) devote fifty percent or more of their time to standards development. Conversely, about seventy-two percent of the participants (39/54) devote less than twenty percent of their time to standards development. (Complete data is shown in Figure 7.)

5. The most often named personal contribution to the process is "attention to technical detail."

6. Standards participants are fairly senior, with about seventy-five percent having more than ten years experience. Also, on average, one-half of this experience is directly related to the standard.

7. Stated motivations for participation are strikingly personal, with fifty percent of the respondents indicating "curiosity" or a "desire to influence the future" as a major motivation.

8. Leadership, diplomacy and monitoring are the most desired and observed combination of chairperson characteristics.

9. Technical skills, doing the work themselves, and killing ideas are

the least desired and observed combination of chairperson characteristics.

10. Participants are generally satisfied with the product quality and chairs and somewhat dissatisfied with the efficiency of the standards process.

The Development Process

The chairs agreed that more structure would help the committee process. Whether this would take the form of formal meetings—Robert's Rules of Order—or simply agreement about the goals of the activity was less clear. Almost all chairs agreed that an effective practice is to first define the problem and then work on the solution. The scope and purpose of the group should be set before any hard bargaining begins; generic objectives should be established and incremental reviews and milestones set up with the focus on the pertinent issues. In order to run the meeting in a more business-oriented fashion, there is a need to set priorities, identify resources, establish agendas, assign homework, and set periodic review dates. It was also suggested that a decision log should be kept of all major issues, including the reasoning behind any resolutions.

Roger Fujii of IEEE defined five stages in the development process. The first is the "courtship dance" where each member tries to figure out the others' position and their hidden agendas while the chair outlines the scope of the project. The second phase involves creating a draft outline of the document structure. The third step is to generate a first complete written draft. The fourth stage is "quality time." Here various levels of flexibility and generality are added to the standard. The final stage is the "lawyer phase," where the legality of the document must be studied phrase by phrase and any visible ambiguities resolved. By one estimate, a standard that is produced over four years actually includes only four months of work, including the preparation and research time. The remaining time could be eliminated, to a large extent, if meetings could be scheduled more often (perhaps bi-monthly) or quarterly meetings could last longer (perhaps two weeks).

The primary strength of the traditional SDOs is a consensus-based process with the assurance of due process in development, approval, and publication. While the interviewees were clear about the importance of due process to ensure consensus, participation, and adoption, there seemed to be some feeling that strict adherence to due process rules is largely responsible for slowing standards development. Paper- and signature-based processes limit the ability to distribute information and perform balloting in a timely fashion and ultimately limit the ability to meet more often.[10] The process of development, approval, and publication is also too long relative to current technology evolution. As a result of this slowness, there has been an increase in the number of consortia bringing standards to market; as the number of consortia grow, the influence of the traditional standards making bodies is weakened. It may well be that SDOs will respond to this by using a "fast track" approach to recognize the work of the consortia while maintaining due process in the final approval.

The dichotomy between remaining staunchly consensus oriented and reducing time to market limits the realm of possible recommendations for process improvement. However, there is growing agreement that the pendulum must swing more to favor speed, even at the expense of some due process rules. For instance, if a factual or grammatical error is found once a draft standard has been approved by open balloting, the chair and editor of the standard should be trusted to make the change. They would decide on whether or not another formal ballot is necessary before publishing.[11] Streamlining the process for minor corrections could save a year in the development process.

Committee Composition

In general, the consensus was for small committees, meaning a group of 10 to 20. It was recognized that when the standard is of significance to a particular constituency, a smaller group will tend to be more successful, while for a standard of general interest a larger number of people will need to be involved. With larger committees, factions can form; smaller committees, on the other hand, may be easily dominated by one person. Some suggested that committees in the range of 20-40 members are able to accomplish significant amounts of design work if they are homogenous. There should be some divergence of opinion, but at the same time

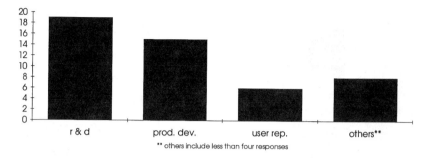

Figure 1 Job Functions of Committee Members.

enough commonality so that all work toward a goal. However, it was generally agreed that communication becomes very difficult once size exceeds 40. As indicated previously, and as shown in Figure 1, the committees tend to be dominated by technical personnel.

Survey respondents were asked to pick a statement that best described their personal contribution to the standards process. The statements were selected to correspond to characteristics of leaders, diplomats, perfectionists, doers, obstructionists and observers. As shown in Figure 2 thirty-two percent may be characterized as perfectionists ("attention to technical detail") while eighteen percent may be characterized as doers ("ability to initiate proposals to get things moving"). Sixteen percent viewed themselves as leaders ("ability to focus on objectives") and twelve percent viewed themselves as diplomats ("ability to forge consensus"). Fourteen percent of the respondents characterized themselves as observers ("ability to listen attentively and monitor activities to ensure process is going in the right direction") and another eight percent described themselves as obstructionists ("ability to actively head-off bad ideas"). Although human beings often defy one dimensional characterization, these results generally confirm other observations about the existence of "intelligence gatherers" and obstructionists. The optimal mix for a committee is not clear and may be dependent upon the point in the development life cycle. Further, it is not clear that group composition can be controlled. However, understanding the composition of a committee will be important to the chairperson in developing strategies to improve the efficiency of the standards process.

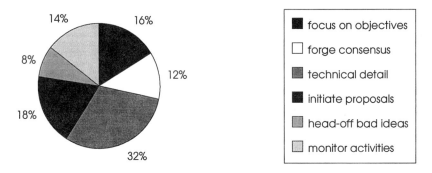

Figure 2 Most Important Contribution of Committee Members.

The stated motivations for participation were quite varied. As shown in Figure 3, personal prestige, curiosity, and the desire to positively influence future events accounts for sixty-six percent of the stated motivation for participation. Boredom, desire to travel, and forced participation accounted for only nine percent of the stated motivation. Participation for the purpose of benefiting one's employer was the response of only twenty-five percent. This would appear to be a favorable situation for standards development, as the participants tend to take a broad altruistic view.

As shown in Figure 4, the most important skill for individuals participating in the standards process is technical expertise. With thirty-six percent selecting it as the most important skill, technical expertise was selected twice as often as any other category. At the same time, 43% of the important skills are in non-technical areas such as time management, negotiation, and meeting participation. This suggests that training for standards participants in areas such as effective strategies for participation and negotiation would probably be well received. It is interesting to note that technology forecasting was given a ranking of only seven percent. Others including less than five percent each include formal presentations, marketing, international relations, foreign language proficiency, and product management. This suggests that it would be more difficult to convince participants that training in these areas was important.

Experts and chairs had suggestions about committee composition and the training of committee members. First, there was

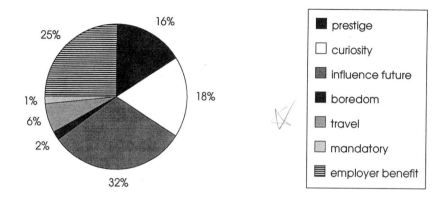

Figure 3 Motivation of Committee Members.

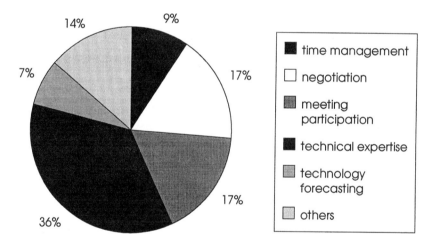

Figure 4 Skills Required of Committee Members.

strong agreement among the TC chairs that all members must be educated on what standards are and are not. Training should stress that a good standard is a victory for all companies and not just a marketing tool for one or even a few. Every member should understand how to accept and hold views without being judgmental or critical too early in the "idea" stage. In addition to these general observations, there were specific suggestions about the role of editors and users on a committee.

Several interviewees mentioned the importance of the editor and the editorial process. The position of editor seems to have particular importance in today's standards arena. Some suggested that the real delay in standard's development lies not in the balloting procedure, but in the intervening period when the document is supposedly coming together. A good editor or editorial group greatly enhances the standards process and should therefore be sought out and encouraged. Unfortunately, it seems that the task of correcting hundreds of pages of material between committee meetings is causing high attrition among editors, as they have trouble defending to their superiors at home additional time spent working on the document. It is not easy to identify individuals with a mastery of language and a desire to oversee the assembly of a report. They need a degree of freedom that allows them to work diligently towards completion of the document. It would seem that training in editing might be offered to interested members along with appropriate recognition in the process. Chairs should be alert for candidates for the editorial role.

Representation of "users" was an issue on which there was little agreement. Most of interviewees agreed that manufacturers dominate the process, and that users involve themselves only peripherally. Some concern was expressed about representation by a special class of users, standards "bagmen," who carry a consumer company or government position into committee meetings. Because of their partisan interest, these types tend to impede consensus. Some of the chairs interviewed felt that they displace knowledgeable people who could make a worthwhile contribution. The most serious observation made about users related to voting. One of our experts indicated that the "intelligence gatherers" have a tendency to vote "yes" on ballots merely to avoid justifying their answers, thereby skewing results. Thus, whereas most see the "intelligence gatherers" as fairly harmless, this observer considers them a danger and feels that the standards process would be better without them.

It was generally agreed that many end users lacked the technical knowledge to participate in the standards development process in a meaningful way. Some would suggest that engineers dominating "is a feature, not a bug." With few exceptions,[12] academic involvement in the process was seen as too idealistic. In general, there was a feeling that users should be more involved, but not at the expense of slowing down the process.

There was some sentiment for a specified role for users. Users need to be consulted in the conception of a specification and in periodic review to insure that development stays on track. One chair suggested creating the committee according to a planned distribution; he indicated that a distribution of sixty percent implementors (vendors), thirty percent users, and ten percent government has worked for his committee.

The Chairperson's Role

The process of developing standards is one of getting highly educated, highly opinionated people to agree on trivial things. The chair of the committee acts as a facilitator with little power to legislate. While there are rules and procedures related to the approval process, there are no absolute rules for running meetings. The chair must be knowledgeable about the subject and also know how a standard may be used by various segments of the industry. It is important for the chair to know what does and does not belong in the standard and to think in generalities rather than specifics.

Respondents were queried as to their views on necessary chairperson characteristics. In contrast to the skills expected of a committee member (see Figure 2) the surveys identified a very different skill mix for the chairpersons as shown in Figure 5. A chairperson should forge consensus, focus on objectives, and monitor activities in equal proportions. A chairperson should be less concerned with technical detail, heading-off bad ideas, and initiating proposals. This is consistent with the view of the chairperson as a skilled leader with strong negotiation skills who delegates.

There was a close match between ideal (Figure 5) and observed (Figure 6) characteristics of the chairperson. The greatest deviation between ideal and observed characteristics was a slight tendency of the chair to attend to technical detail: while only 10% identified attention to technical detail as a characteristic of the ideal chair, 14% identified it as a characteristic observed in chairpersons. The responses indicate that most members have the kind of chairperson they want.

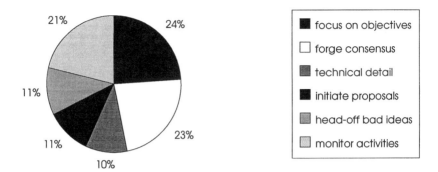

Figure 5 Characteristics of an Ideal Chairperson.

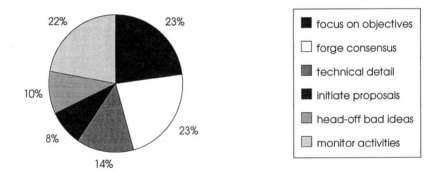

Figure 6 Characteristics of the Actual Chairperson.

The interviews suggested several skills that might be developed in chairpersons:

1. Skills in problem definition, so that underlying issues are uncovered without forcing excessive constraints that favor a given solution.

2. Skills in avoiding conflict, such as identifying the problem before proposing solutions, maintaining open communications, and avoiding back-room decision making.

3. Skills in group dynamics to help identify:

   a. when to rein things in and avoid conflicts,

   b. how to develop win-win situations by getting agreement on pieces of the problem and then piecing their way back to a solution,

c. how and when to coax shy members into giving their opinions and when to control others so they do not disrupt the rest of the group.

There was also a suggestion that a mentoring program should be available for chairpersons that would involve an "expert" (perhaps an experienced peer) sitting in on meetings to provide advice.[13]

Conflict Resolution

Far and away, the number one issue that emerged in the discussions and written comments on the survey was the matter of conflicts in the committees and the role of the chair in avoiding or managing these conflicts.[14] It was not surprising that differences in technical opinions served as the basis for some conflicts. There were widely varying opinions about the value of these conflicts: some saw them as valuable to the process, others saw them as disruptive. Another source of conflict mentioned was "hidden agendas" which were most often related to corporate interests. The final and most often mentioned source of conflicts was unprofessional behavior or personality clashes. A sense of the extent of negative feelings about this behavior is provided by a sampling of comments from the surveys:

• "Frequently this would end in bad faith accusations against other committee members. A threat that 'I will take my marbles and go home' seemed to pervade the thinking of most attendees from this one company."

• "One alternate suffers from a lack of BASIC manners."

• "A very few influential individuals had an abrasive interpersonal style, which hurt progress greatly."

• "At times, some members suggest that other member's motives are 'impure' or perhaps simply foolish, to varying degrees. At other times, some members infer such ad hominem attacks where none was intended."

• "Some (few) members have had a tendency to engage in personal attacks on and challenge the motivation of some other members."

- "Failure to Listen! Inability to Cooperate!"
- "Refusal to negotiate; stubbornness; hanging onto and re-discussing an idea after it has been rejected by the rest of the working group."
- "The need to perfect something that is good enough. The personal need to make a noticeable contribution."
- "People who criticize other peoples' proposals, but have none of their own."
- "Inability to compromise; egotistical; too political."

A person who dominates and disrupts a meeting against the majority opinion of that group is termed a "bulldog." It was estimated that between eighty and ninety percent of TC's include at least one bulldog. At best they have a disruptive effect on the process. At worst, these individuals will destroy the "team" approach and discourage attendance at meetings. This is a particular problem for IETF where there is no formal vote on the acceptance of a standard. An energetic bulldog can completely implement their own ideas. The resulting standard, not developed by consensus, may be ignored. In the X3/IEEE process, a vote can stop a bad standard moved by a bulldog, but at the cost of valuable time lost.

In part, committee members attend meetings to guard the financial interests of their sponsoring organization. Usually, their interests are not mutually exclusive. A problem arises when there are products already being developed, perhaps by more than one organization, that are not compatible with the standards favored by the rest of the committee. Some organizations use the standardization process to gain advantage over their competition. Representatives of an organization who want to slow down the development of a standard to let their product gain market share are termed "turtles." It was estimated that twenty-five to thirty percent of the committees include turtles at some point in the development process. This estimate is consistent with the twenty-two percent of participants who saw their contribution as observers or obstructionists (see Figure 2) and the twenty-five percent who identified their major motivation as employer benefit (see Figure 3).

Whether conflicts are personal, organizational, or technical in nature, it falls to the chairperson to address them. Although most chairs are highly competent in technical areas and many are skilled diplomats and negotiators, it is likely that a high percentage would benefit from training that enabled them to identify and address various sources of conflict. At one level, it may be enough for the chairs to be sensitive to the fact that these conflicts will likely arise and need to be dealt with. The interviews suggested that while each chair is different, all are highly skilled individuals who have developed techniques for working with people over the years. On the other hand, recognizing that most technical committee chairs have a strong technical background and orientation, it may be important to offer them an opportunity to learn and hone a set of skills in the areas of group dynamics and organizational communications.

Casual Participants

Most committees, regardless of their size, are directed and driven by a small group of individuals, usually ten percent or fewer. As shown in Figure 7, the vast majority of those responding to our survey indicate a very small percentage of the committee's effort devoted to development. In most committee meetings, approximately twenty-five percent of the members are attending for the first time. This is true four meetings per year, year after year. With that much turnover, it is difficult to maintain momentum. It is also necessary to take time at every meeting to explain some of the rules of order and bring new members up to date on progress and passed decisions. One estimate was that 40 minutes of every meeting was required to orient newcomers on past topics and outcomes.

In the earlier discussion of the process, mention was made of the suggestion that a decision log be kept. One important use of such a record could be to provide background to new members. In some committees, a new member is not permitted to speak until they have read the review log. This avoids the time wasted at meetings rehashing prior decisions. This log could be made available to new members prior to the first meeting they attend.

Another issue related to casual participants was mentioned in discussing the voting patterns of users. It was indicated that those not deeply involved in the technical issues, who also might be characterized as casual users, have a tendency to vote "yes" on

Spring et al.

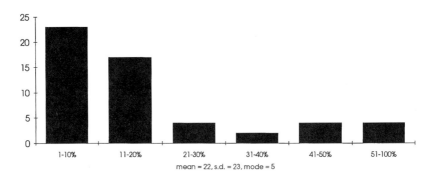

Figure 7 Percentage of Work Effort Devoted to Standards Development.

ballots to avoid having to justify a "no" answer. This results in a skewed vote. It is difficult to know what the best solution is to this problem; it may well be a matter of making individuals feel comfortable with abstaining if they are simply observing.

Appropriate Use of Technology

Without exception, those who mentioned technology were in agreement that it was underused and could be used to improve the process in one way or another. Electronic mail (e-mail) was suggested for document distribution and balloting. Using e-mail may require some due process rules to be relaxed (e.g., thirty-day balloting times and requirements of signatures in some cases). IEEE sponsored a study on the effects of e-mail on standard development while working on the IEEE 1012 standard. The study concluded that electronic mail saved more than a year in development time. The study found that there is a roller-coaster of interest generated around a standard, peaking around meetings and plummeting in between. E-mail bridged the gaps by maintaining constant contact between committee members.[15]

The IETF handles the bulk of its intra-group interaction via e-mail. Major work is no longer done at the tri-annual meetings, but rather over mailing lists. This notion of dealing principally over e-mail met with great support among interviewees. At the same time, it was noted that meetings are still the primary locus of productive activity for X3. Some concern was expressed about losing the benefits of interpersonal debate by conducting meetings in a medium that encourages users to delete anything that they wish to avoid.

It was suggested that a networked document handler that allows for multiple annotations would be invaluable to the editing process, as all participants of a given group could bind their comments to a single copy of a working paper. Both the IEEE and X3 are working on documentation automation projects. These projects may reduce the number of times information is re-keyed in new documents and save money in duplicating and distribution costs. A standard methodology for document preparation should be employed across all SDOs to insure the compatibility of the standards documents they produce. It was suggested that a defined document style would assure uniformity throughout the writing of working papers and aid in the final production of the standard.

All standards that IETF working groups produce are made electronically available. One IETF chair considered this practice critical for wide scale acceptance, indicating that having to buy a hard copy of a standard from an international organization deters user interest. Whether documents can be made available electronically by X3 and the IEEE will be a matter of organizational policy, and will have a significant impact on financing.

Interviewees were divided on the matter of tools for meetings. At the most basic level, formal rules may be viewed as a tool in meetings. One expert indicated that employing some set of parliamentary rules runs counter to the notion that standards meetings are supposed to be cooperative. For another expert, a judicious use of rules of order is the best way to ensure that everyone gets a chance to speak. He makes it clear that he does not condone "rules for rules' sake," saying that when a topic begs discussion, the protocol should be temporarily lifted.

We note that none of the interviews touched on the use of Formal Description Techniques (FDTs) as a tool for improving the process. Whether the lack of such mention is due to a lack of interest or the focus of the interviews is not clear. Future study might seek to determine the extent of the use of FDTs such as ASN.1, TTCN, LOTOS, and Estelle in committee work and the impact of such tools on the process.

A number of hardware suggestions were made, from overheads to help organize discussions, to PCs to aid in the editing of a committee's documents in real time. Similarly, a PC might be used to queue and list individuals waiting to speak to a topic. On the other hand, one expert noted that the key is to promote communication within the group and avoid a "lecture-style" presentation. In this expert's opinion, overhead slides are a mistake in that they promote a lecture style.

Techniques and Insights

We asked the experts and chairs to describe strategies they used or recommended in managing the committee process.[16] The following "rules of thumb" emerged from the discussion:

Two Hats

When the chair needs to shift from a management focus to make a technical point, put on a baseball cap with the company logo and move from the head of the table to another seat, signifying that he now wishes to be seen as taking a "company" position on a particular issue. This makes it very clear where he stands and eliminates confusion about what role he is fulfilling at the time. When at the chair's position, he is perceived as wearing the chair's hat by default.

The Duelists

When two individuals are vehemently opposed or deadlocked on an issue and it appears to be disrupting the group process, send them off to a separate room. The winner will come back to present their position, which has been "forged under fire." A similar suggestion would have the chair form ad hoc groups out of parties in conflict forcing disputing stakeholders together and charging them with resolving their disagreement as a precondition to the committee proceeding with development of the standard. This places the burden on the antagonists to subordinate their individual differences to the interests of the group.

Judicious Breaks

Break time may be used to diffuse conflict. This time can be used by the chair or third parties to address disputants and caution them to exercise restraint or otherwise cease inappropriate behavior in a manner that is non-threatening.

Meta-issues

When there are two valid points in opposition, the strategy is to move the group away from polarity. This can be done by raising the meta issue, "Does the group believe that a decision needs to be made?" Agreement on that question focuses the group on reaching consensus to resolve the impasse.

Lobbying

In contrast to separating antagonists, the chair should make efforts to minimize back room lobbying wherever possible, particularly when that discussion should be a part of the broad committee deliberations.

Hidden Agenda

Force members to bring hidden agendas into the open through "role playing," where the members have to work through an issue by stepping into the shoes of a member with a different perspective or point of view.

What It Ain't

Educate members on what standards are and are not!

Win-Win

Look for situations, issues, and positions that make everybody a winner. Avoid cornering anyone or backing an individual into an untenable position.

Focus, Focus, Focus

First define the problem fully. Only when it has been fully and clearly defined and accepted by all parties can the group define and implement the solution.

Creeping Featurism

Avoid add-ons: new features that would be "nice" as opposed to "necessary," features that get added after the die has been cast.

Summary Recommendations

Training is currently provided for X3, IEEE, and IETF committee chairpersons. This training generally takes the form of a short, focused seminar on the standardization process. Because the chair is responsible for insuring that no policy breeches occur in the meetings, training is concentrated on procedural issues and due process. This study suggests that training should be extended to provide additional information to new chairs about how to be successful in managing this intensely human activity.

Currently no formal training exists for X3 or IETF members. (The IEEE does provide an orientation session and training for committee members.) It seems that there would be some benefit in providing an orientation for new committee participants. While it may be difficult to require this training or conduct it in a special setting, it is possible that some positive impact could be achieved through paper or video based training. It was felt that a good training program could result in a 25 to 50 percent improvement in terms of time to market and quality of the standard produced. Finally, beyond improving human skills, this study highlights some potentially simple procedural changes that could have a significant impact on standards development.

In an ideal world, the selection process for chairs would seek to identify technically competent individuals with leadership, conflict management, and negotiation skills. The effectiveness of the chair can probably be increased by adding a component to their training that includes some of the techniques discussed in this paper. Video tapes might be used effectively to demonstrate various techniques for handling conflicts and managing "turtles" or "bulldogs." They would also make it easier to handle some aspects of chairperson training on an individual basis. Finally, there was some sentiment for a mentoring program that would involve an "expert" (perhaps an experienced peer) sitting in on meetings to provide advice to a new chairperson. There was an indication that this has been done before and might well be a preferred way to ease the "break-in" for new chairs who experience difficulty managing the process.

Training should be standard for members, not only for chairs. Although skills training may have its limits, it is still worthwhile to describe for all group members the nature of the enterprise in which they are involved and how it functions. Moreover, materials provided in training could serve as a continuing reference for the SDO members' most frequently asked questions. While a short orientation session might be run for new committee members, it is likely that the training will have to take the form of a video tape or paper materials.

The biggest difference between standards committees and other professional committees is the variety of concerns and perspectives that individual members bring with them. It will be important to help participants understand that the "tunnel vision" so important to specification of the standard can also be a detriment if it prevents the participant from seeing the "big picture."

Several suggestions were made for changes to the committee process. Some of the more interesting suggestions include:

1. Use a formal decision log to keep track of all decisions made by the committee and use this as a mechanism for orienting new participants.

2. Use PC-based technology to display documents and decision logs to the group in real time to reduce disagreements and speed the process.

3. Encourage the use of e-mail to reduce the down time between meetings and to speed up the communications process, potentially relaxing the burden of thirty-day balloting and meeting announcement times.

4. Make documents available online, thus reducing publication costs and increasing access.

5. Provide an option in voting that addresses the issue of casual participants voting "yes" to avoid having to explain a "no" vote.

6. Allow the chairperson/editor to make minor editorial changes to the standards document after balloting without requiring a reballoting.

7. Provide for a reaffirmation vote that permits a brief explanation by the voter of what it would take to make it a "yes." This would help avoid delays as the standard is recycled again through the lengthy process and would reduce the chance of poor market acceptance that may occur by "ramming" it through the process.

Recommendations for Further Research

One of the difficulties in conducting research on standards is the lack of data related to operationally defined terms. How many different categories of standards are there? What constitutes an anticipatory standard, a reference standard, etc.? By what measures do we establish that a standard is "successful?" What is the optimal committee size? How long should it take to develop a standard? How much should it cost? How should the committee be composed? While several studies (Weiss and Sirbu, 1990, Bonino and Spring, 1991, Weiss and Toyofuku, 1993, Lehr, 1992) have begun to address issues in this area, there is much work yet to be done (Spring, 1991a,b).

At the start of this study, we were aware of the lack of precisely defined terms. For example, the term "user" has many different meanings, even among the very knowledgeable group we interviewed. In some cases during our interviews, "user" referred to individual end users. In other cases, "user" was applied generically, describing interests on a spectrum from single consumers to multinational corporations. The consequence of applying a term with such broad application to dissimilar groups creates the appearance that their interests coincide. Certainly, no one would argue that the individual user of a database program has the same interest in standardization as General Motors. Therefore, if the topic of "user" involvement in standards development is to receive serious investigation, the term must have its definition established and specified to the interviewees in the course of questioning.

Beyond the issue of more precise definition of terms, we make four suggestions for further research:

1. Revise the questionnaire for use with a larger group of participants involved over time in a single standards effort. In such an effort, it would be important to ensure that a broad cross section is included and to track changes in the opinions expressed over time.

2. Revise the questionnaire in line with the techniques and strategies identified and survey a broader cross section of chairs to ascertain its relevance.

3. Structure a study to try to determine the impact of good and bad practices by the chair. This might be done by a retrospective study of successful and unsuccessful standardization efforts with an eye to determining what if any impact the role of the chair had along the dimensions identified in this study.

4. Work with selected chairs to incorporate the recommendations of this study and see if any difference in development time or participant satisfaction is noted in comparison to committees that continue to operate as before.

Notes

[1] Among other topics, the committee discussed how the academic research community might help in developing a better understanding of the process. Attending the meeting with the X3 members were Drs. Marvin Sirbu from Carnegie Mellon, Joseph Farrell from the University of California at Berkeley, and Martin Weiss and Michael Spring from the University of Pittsburgh. Drs. William Lehr from Columbia and Shane Greenstein from the University of Illinois, Urbana-Champaign made written contributions, but were unable to attend the meeting.

[2] The investigators wish to thank the X3 Long Range Planning Committee and its chair, Carl Cargill of SunSoft, for supporting this effort. The study would not have been possible without the interest, support, and hours of work put in by Don Loughry of Hewlett-Packard. He not only provided the introductions and endorsement that opened the doors to many of the very busy individuals who agreed to talk with us because of his request, but he spent time with the researchers reviewing early versions of the questionnaires and later with the interview teams as one of the interviewees.

[3] A full copy of the study is available from the Department of Information Science, University of Pittsburgh, Pittsburgh, PA 15260.

⁴ While public specifications look attractive, there is some concern that there is no explicit or implicit commitment in the public specification to maintenance of the standard.

⁵ On the negative side, there is concern that government involvement may inhibit the development of competitive alternatives by industrial segments.

⁶ It should be noted that there is growing data to suggest that the rapid rate of technological change is seldom accounted for by anticipatory standards. For example, OSI was based on a set of assumptions that were established before the birth of the PC and that clearly did not anticipate the significant impact of personal computers and workstations.

⁷ Throughout this paper, the term technical committee refers to an X3 technical committee or an IETF working group. When a distinction is important in how operational committees function in these two organizations, specific reference to the differences will be made.

⁸ The questions used in the various surveys are available on request.

⁹ Particular problems related to delays and voting were noted in terms of users, observers, and casual participants. These are addressed in the sections on casual participants and users.

¹⁰ For example, a mail ballot must be allocated 30 days for review. Similar limitations exist on how much notice is required to schedule a meeting.

¹¹ Only in very rare cases is there a covert attempt to add features to a document after it is approved but before it is published.

¹² The research team was convinced that at least during the conduct of the current study, we were considered one of the few exceptions!

¹³ This has been done to a limited extent in the past with excellent results. The expert would be available but would only sit in if a chairperson requests the assistance. The mentor approach might serve to ease the "break-in" for new chairs.

¹⁴ After conflict, the most significant issue mentioned was the slowness of the process, which is addressed elsewhere in this report.

¹⁵ One of the issues that will have to be addressed with e-mail is the cost. When, at the end of the study, the IEEE decided to no longer reimburse members for e-mail charges, the usage of e-mail plummeted.

¹⁶ The researchers sought out these techniques as a result of initial discussions with Donald Loughry, who impressed the research team with a number of ideas about effective management including "two hats" and "focus-focus-focus." The technical committee chairs, including Don Loughry, Richard Steinbrenner, Roger Fujii, and David Crocker, were particularly helpful in developing these ideas.

References

Besen, Stanley M. (1990). The European Telecommunications Standards Institute: A Preliminary Analysis. *Telecommunications Policy* 14, 521–530.

Besen, Stanley M., and Joseph Farrell (1991). The Role of the ITU in Standardization. *Telecommunications Policy* 15, 311–321.

Bonino, Michal, and Michael B. Spring (1991). Standards as Change Agents in the Information Technology Market. *Computer Standards and Interfaces* 12, 97–107.

Cargill, Carl F. (1989). *Information Technology Standardization: Theory, Process, and Organizations*. Bedford MA: Digital Press.

David, Paul A., and Shane M. Greenstein (1990). The Economics of Compatibility Standards: An Introduction to Recent Research. *Economics of Innovation and New Technology* 1(1), 3–42.

Didio, Leuta (1993). Standards Bodies: How Effective Are They? *LAN Times* (10), 1–7.

Dolberg, Stanley H. (1993). X/Open in the 1990s. *Open Information Systems* 8, 3–16.

Farrell, Joseph (1993). Choosing the Rules for Formal Standardization. Berkeley: University of California.

Farrell, Joseph, and Garth Saloner (1988). Coordination through Committees and Markets. *RAND Journal of Economics* (19), pp. 235–251.

Garcia, D. Linda. (1992). Standards Setting in the United States: Public and Private Sector Roles. *Journal of the American Society for Information Science* Vol. 43(8).

Greenstein, Shane M. (1992). Invisible Hands and Visible Advisors: An Economic Interpretation of Standardization. *Journal of the American Society for Information Science* Vol. 43(8).

Lehr, William (1992). Standardization: Understanding the Process. *Journal of the American Society for Information Science* Vol. 43(8).

Meek, B. C. (1988). Is Standardization Just Regularization? *Computer Standards and Interfaces* (7), pp. 257–269.

Robinson, Gary S. (1988). Accredited Standards Committee for Information Processing Systems, X3. *Computer Standards and Interfaces* (5), pp. 3–17.

Rutkowski, A. M. (1991). Networking the Telecom Standards Bodies. gopher: IETF@ISI.EDU.

Spring, Michael B. (1991a). Information Technology Standards. *Annual Review of Information Science and Technology* 26, 78–110.

Spring, Michael B. (1991b). Models, Musings, and Managers. Report to the X3 Strategic Planning Committee.

Weiss, Martin B. H., and Carl Cargill (1992). Consortia in the Standards Development Process. *Journal of the American Society for Information Science* 43(8).

Weiss, Martin B. H., and Marvin Sirbu (1990). Technological Choice in Voluntary Standards Committees: An Empirical Analysis. *Economics of Innovation and New Technology* 1(1), 111–134.

Weiss, Martin B. H., and Ronald T. Toyofuku (1993). Free Ridership in the Standards-Setting Process: The Case of 10BaseT. Pittsburgh, PA: University of Pittsburgh. Draft.

The Role of Government

When Are Standards Too Much of a Good Thing? Will They Provide Interoperability for the National Information Infrastructure?

Robert J. Aiken and John S. Cavallini

Introduction

The administration's goal of a ubiquitous and empowering National Information Infrastructure (NII) will require the interconnection and interoperability of both services and applications. The identification and deployment of appropriate standards on a nationwide basis appears to many to be the obvious solution [5, 17]. In addition to the deployment of an NII, the Administration has strongly committed itself to "reinventing government" and has indicated the need for a seamless Federal Information Infrastructure which will play a pivotal role in achieving the goal of a reinvented and invigorated government [7, 10]. The Administration, through the Information Infrastructure Task Force (IITF) and other forums, will attempt to identify standards, systems, and software products that will be used by the federal government for interagency cooperative activities and for interacting with industry and academia [7, 13, 14].

In its drive to create an interworkable NII, the U.S. federal government will identify and specify many standards [17], both formal and de facto, which the federal agencies will have to implement and deploy. Some of these will be successful and therefore aid the development of the NII, while others may impede the progress of the NII and thus place the U.S. at an international competitive disadvantage. These standards will be determined and established through a combination of informal and formal standards processes, mandates, and the sheer purchasing power of the U.S. federal government through its acquisition of specific technologies or solutions. Various industries, businesses (both national and international), and academia will be directly affected by these choices since they will be required to use them for any business activities they conduct with the U.S. government [11, 12]. A difficult dilemma exists: should the standards chosen for use by the U.S. government be chosen through a process that attempts to anticipate widespread usage and testing, or should the standards and technologies be given time "to be shaken out" by individual agencies, industry, academia, and the public, relying upon Darwin's theory as applied to technological and standards processes?

This paper will discuss these complex issues from the perspective of a user "mission" agency program, whose interactions span the globe and entail both multinational and multiprotocol collaborations with industry, academia, other nations, and its sister agencies. The Office of Energy Research's (ER) Office of Scientific Computing (OSC) and its programs, within the Department of Energy (DOE), will provide the backdrop for this treatise. In particular the Energy Sciences Network (ESnet), since it is a major component of the National Research and Education Network (NREN) and the NII, has already had to address the conundrum of a multi-standard based environment and its implications for the need for interoperability and its attainment. We will provide some instructional examples of successes and failures in adopting and using standards, and draw some conclusions about the process of choosing and using standards for satisfying agency mission objectives and the broader goals of the administration.

Standards can be either beneficial or a hindrance, depending on how they are developed, adopted and implemented. Only by using a combination of various standards (be they formal, de facto, or de jure), at different levels of maturity and from different standards development organizations (SDOs), can an organization address its requirements in a timely and efficient manner and provide interoperability with other organizations. The key to a rich and affordable information and knowledge based economy and society, including the government and the NII, is the prudent development and use of a diverse and competing set of alternatives and solutions.

Standards: Needs and Perceptions

A discussion of standards, in any computer or information sciences and technology context, is usually accompanied by spirited debate over which protocol or standard is superior. Many currently believe standards to be the only way to achieve, or the panacea for, interoperability, which will pave the way to a ubiquitous NII and strong economy [15]. This latter opinion was evidenced at a recent workshop, "Information Infrastructure Forum on Interoperability" (sponsored by the Science, Technology and Public Policy Program and hosted by Annenberg Washington D.C.), where a discussion on interoperability quickly led into a discussion on the adoption of standards as the primary means for achieving interoperability and establishing a healthy information-based economy. Most people, in fact, equate the concepts of standards and interoperability. These positions are usually based on the belief that there always exists or will exist a superior standard that will achieve interoperability on a technical or political (trade and treaty) basis, or some combination of both. Although standards have been applied to all aspects of the NII, the need for standards is probably evidenced most at the opposite ends of the technology spectrum. At one end of the spectrum, the users desire one familiar user interface and set of tools, such as a word processor or graphical user interface (GUI), while at the other end of the technology spectrum the service providers desire a small set of physical media interfaces, such as the Personal Computer Memory Card International Association (PCMCIA) or Narrowband Integrated Services Data Network (N-ISDN), on which they can develop their services and products.

Many of the Information Infrastructure Task Force (IITF) Committee on Application and Technology (CAT) working groups, including Health Care and Manufacturing, have issued white papers that identify standards as a prerequisite for making advances on the National Challenges and in other areas. The NII and standards are inextricably intertwined. Some prominent analysts, such as Brian Kahin, not only see standards affecting the success of the NII but also see the NII and its networks as a vehicle "that enables more efficient standards development" [1]. The majority of people involved in the development and deployment of technology relevant to the NII would probably agree that some base sets of standards are necessary for interoperability and for the success of the NII. However, when trying to identify which and how many standards are necessary to achieve these goals, many issues arise, such as:

• What standards exist and need to be developed and enforced? (e.g., physical layer network standards or application standards such as Sonet and Health Level 7, also known as HL-7)

• How should standards be chosen? (e.g., what process, what involvement by industry, federal government procurement, formal standards bodies, and consortia)

• Who chooses the standards for defense and civilian federal agencies? (e.g., can each agency or organization be allowed to make its own choice or do they have to follow the directives of NIST/OMB/GSA?)

• Who are the people actually developing and mandating standards? (e.g., do they have real-life operational experience in the area they are so greatly influencing?)

• What are the professional and ethical responsibilities of those persons and organizations who set standards? (e.g., is short term cost benefit or conformity more important than diversity and competition?)

• Should the U.S. Government formally require and mandate standards? (e.g., Ada, Government Open Systems Intereconnection Profile–GOSIP, Clipper Chip)

• Should multiple standards be allowed to coexist? (e.g., at the network layer are IP and OSI allowed to coexist?)

• What is the real practical life cycle of a technology and/or standard and how is it phased out or replaced when appropriate?

• How do government purchasing practices (e.g., two Federal Telecommunications Services 2000 network providers for all federal agencies) affect both the standards process and the competitive technology and services based marketplace?

• Should the government use its awesome purchasing power (e.g., FTS2000) to set procurement-induced standards and then seek to create a market for those standards to ensure interoperability and lower its own costs?

Standards and Interoperability

Standards have traditionally been adopted to achieve interoperability and to provide a common base for multiple applications. However, standards do not necessarily guarantee interoperability. Some organizations have tried to use X.400 compliant products for their electronic mail only to find that two different vendors' X.400 compliant systems do not interoperate since each uses a different portion of the X.400 address for routing purposes. Narrowband Integrated Services Data Networks (N-ISDN) is a standard that has been implemented in many regions, yet there has been a lack of inter-vendor ISDN interoperability at a national level. Even different versions of the same standard may have interoperability problems such as a loss of functionality (e.g., X.400 1984 and X.400 1988).

Many standards have been created based on the widespread acceptance and use of formerly proprietary standards (such as the Network File System (NFS)) or novel tools or applications, such as Wide Area Information Services (WAIS) and the World Wide Web (WWW). These latter examples were not specifically designed for the purpose of interoperability and yet they have become de facto standards for their respective applications by satisfying an urgent need. In addition, interoperability can be and has been achieved by cooperating organizations based on agreement(s) to use specific technologies (some are standards based, some are not) for the purpose of interoperating.

There are many valid reasons and ways to choose standards, and a variety of forums or methods for developing them. It is clear that the formal standards arena is not, and should not be considered, the only means of achieving interoperability. The realistic approach to attaining interoperability is based on the use of a combination of various formal, de facto, de jure, consortia, and even proprietary standards, all at different maturity levels in their respective technology and standards life cycles.

Technology and Standards Continuum

When discussing standards and analyzing their possible use, consideration of the technology and standards continuum is important since it will affect the ability of any organization or individual to identify, design, adopt, or affect a technology standard and any operational services based on that standard. The technology and standards time continuum is composed of many technologies and standards at different maturity and evolution stages. At any given time, the life cycle of a technology will intersect and possibly parallel the life cycle of a relevant standard associated with that technology, and likely overlap with that technology's and standard's predecessor(s) and successor(s). To further complicate matters, this process is non-linear. The successor to a particular standard or technology may come from a non-traditional source; and having no known lineage on the continuum it is a newcomer and therefore introduces a bit of chaos into the continuum. Since there exists more than one SDO, multiple standards activities parallel, overlap, and intersect each other on the technology time continuum.

Current standards processes are usually based on the concept of a single formal SDO and a linear technology and standards continuum. Yet reality has proven otherwise, as evidenced by the failure of so many anticipatory standards. The continuum is non-linear and multi-dimensional. The short cycle associated with current computer and telecommunications technologies makes long term forecasting a very challenging endeavor. As an example, neither the OSI nor the TCP/IP network layer protocols were originally designed to support the real time resource management necessary for videoconferencing, live simulations, and other demanding real time applications that are becoming popular today [6]. Many sectors, such as the manufacturing sector, the power and utility sector, government administration, and others, invest a lot of capital in equipment. Their investments have traditionally been made with the expectation that they will usefully serve their organizations' requirements for long periods of time and can be gradually depreciated. In addition, many of these large industries operate globally and are critically dependent on computers, telecommunications, and information services to remain competitive. These industries are now facing very challenging issues when deciding which technologies and standards they should employ as part of their strategy, since many of their investments are now more tightly coupled to the fast paced evolution cycle of the computer and information areas. Prior reliance by these sectors on international and slower-paced standards is now being augmented and in some cases supplanted by standards from the de facto and consortia standards arenas, which at times can seem random and chaotic in contrast to the slower pace of the formal standards process.

By the time a standard has been identified for use in any arena, its replacement or a competing solution is already in the pipeline and being tested somewhere. The leading edge standard of today is tomorrow's legacy standard and system. The technology standards continuum comprises both anticipated and surprise developments. Just as e-mail was the surprise application that arose from the ARPANET testbed, there lurks another such application(s) in the near future (talk radio internet or packet video?) that may drive us in a direction we had not anticipated with respect to standards planning and development. For this reason, exclusively mandated anticipatory standards (e.g., GOSIP/OSI) are not likely to succeed, even when the government tries to create a market for these products through procurement policy. The old standards paradigm, which was based on long drawn out, formal, and exclusive standards processes, no longer seems relevant given today's fast paced and seemingly chaotic technological advances.

One of the major reasons that standards such as GOSIP, OSI, Ada and others have never achieved their full potential is that standards development takes too long. These standards were overcome by events and overtaken by fast track de facto implementations such as TCP/IP and C/C++. The methods and processes for developing OSI and other formal standards are too long and complex and therefore can no longer keep up with the fast-paced technology time continuum. It is interesting to note that the growth of the Internet Engineering Task Force (IETF) has recently strained the capability of its consensus process to resolve major standards issues in a timely fashion (e.g., the problems encountered with IPng, the next generation of IP) and it is now enduring some of the same problems and issues normally associated with the formal standards organizations.

Since the formal standards processes are slow, it is natural to assume that faster-paced responses from other sources (de facto, consortia, etc.) will develop. Given that situation, and the fact that any standard will have versions that may or may not interoperate, coexistence is a reality that must be addressed. The Federal Information Requirements Panel (FIRP) is currently attempting to reconcile such coexistence issues—which are a direct result of the natural and nondeterministic technology and standards continuum—through the strategy of adopting new standards (e.g., making TCP/IP part of GOSIP). This does not solve the problem, since the issue is rooted in the ongoing and competitive cycle of the technology and standards continuum, and will therefore arise again. Although this attempt to address the coexistence of TCP/IP and OSI was noble, it would have been more effective and efficient for the FIRP to recommend that no one standard or SDO be given policy preference. The current process of mandating or specifying standards no longer works since there will always be yet another standard or technology in the pipeline that will need to coexist with and eventually replace the existing standards. The standards continuum will always comprise the past (legacy systems, proprietary e-mail, etc.), the present (TCP/IP and GOSIP, SMTP and X.400, etc.), and the future (IPng, MIME, etc.), with the time intervals on the continuum remaining short and overlapping one another. A standard whose conceptual design and implementation responds to the fast-paced technological development and the application-level demand is a "Just In Time Standard" (JITS) whose probability of successful adoption and implementation is very high. Yet no matter how hard we strive to develop standards, including just in time standards, that allow for evolution and change (version numbers, etc.), we must realize that any standard will ultimately be overcome; the only question is, how quickly? Given today's fast-paced technological and standards cycles, the time between innovative advances is very short and this means that standards from multiple SDOs will need to be developed and replaced quickly if standards are to be effective or even contribute to solving interoperability issues.

Measured Response

The authors believe that some base set of standards is essential to the success of any technological endeavor, especially the NII, but that these standards need to be applied in measured doses at the proper time in the technology life cycle continuum. We believe that the overzealous creation and use of standards, either through formal standards processes or by government purchasing practices, poses the risk of impeding the introduction of necessary new technologies and services for use in the NII and can adversely affect the competitive marketplace, whose healthy existence is essential for the success of the NII and for achieving the administration's goals for national competitiveness. In addition, the "technology and innovation gene pool" of the future is jeopardized when choices are made for short term benefits that can be achieved in other ways, especially when mandated anticipatory standards prematurely prune a viable branch from the evolutionary tree of technology. The achievements and health of U.S. technology are primarily due to the rich diversity of competitive techniques, ideas, and solutions that have been fostered in the past. The explosion of the Internet and its information discovery and retrieval tools (WAIS, MOSAIC, Gopher, etc.) is a testament to this concept. These tools, which all branches of the federal government are using today to reach out to the public, might never have existed had everyone exclusively used the federal government's choice of OSI/GOSIP protocols and products.

The way in which industry and government view and use standards and their processes needs to undergo a paradigm shift. The technological life cycle and the interval between the introduction of new ideas is very short (6–18 months), and therefore old standards-setting processes and paradigms are no longer valid. Kuhn [8] identified and described the cycle of scientific revolution and its importance in the evolution of science. The same metaphor applies to the technological and standards continuum, and we are currently at one of those revolutionary junctions in the continuum with the golden opportunity to effect the necessary paradigm shift with respect to standards and their processes. Evidence of this juncture point is identified in Clifford Lynch's [9] treatise on libraries and relevant standards, and Brian Kahin's [1] assertion that we are already in the transition to a Knowledge Information Infrastructure that will require a new look at standards and how they affect our ability to function in a knowledge and information based society. Drucker [4] also asserts that we are undergoing a transition to an information society that will require all of us to dramatically change the way we interact and do business on both a national and international basis.

Much of the current attention to standards and their processes has focused on "fixing" or "reengineering" the current standards process. The new paradigm should be based on the pragmatic reality that no one standard or SDO will satisfactorily address our requirements in this fast-moving technological evolution to the information and knowledge society. Competitive diversity, with a small bit of chaos, is beneficial and encourages alternatives for current and future requirements. Competition among SDOs will ensure that they remain responsive to the needs of their communities and constituents or else be replaced by more adaptive and responsive SDOs. Also, the concept of one standard satisfying all requirements within a given area is a fallacy. There will always be new versions of standards as they evolve, in addition to new or alternative standards and technologies developed to satisfy requirements and needs not addressed by current standards for whatever reason. Therefore, the new paradigm should be based on the realization that the support and exploitation of multiple standards and technologies will provide a healthier technological future, since any agreed upon standard will have been chosen through the natural selection process from among its competitive peers, and consequently will more likely address the needs of the community affected.

Standards and Interoperability in Action

Bearing in mind that the technology and standards utilized by DOE programs have very short life spans and can become eclipsed by newer and usually better technologies, we will attempt to further elucidate the above issues with some real life examples. The Energy Sciences network (ESnet) evolved out of the Magnetic Fusion network (MFENET), High Energy Physics network (HEPnet) and other energy research community networking activities. HEPnet was predominately based on DECNET and MFENET used protocols that were developed in 1974–1975 by the National Energy Research Supercomputer Center (NERSC) (formerly the National Magnetic Fusion Energy Computer Center) to provide remote access to the center's resources. The MFENET protocols were based on a draft version of the DECNET protocols that preceded the first release of a DECNET product. Yet as both DECNET and MFENET evolved, they did so on different paths. This difference in direction, coupled with the need to provide for the network protocols on its supercomputers, left MFENET the task of supporting its own proprietary protocol stack for a very long time.

Clearly, at the time the MFENET was originally designed the center made the correct choice to implement its own protocols, since there existed no other viable solution for a satellite-based network connecting users and supercomputers at that time. One problem encountered later was that MFENET did not transition to an open standards-based network protocol as quickly as was prudent. This was mainly due to an installed user base that was reluctant to change, even to achieve interoperability, and to the large effort required to ensure a smooth transition from MFENET to a new network architecture. Therefore, MFENET did not cease to exist until sometime in 1991, thereby requiring staff and effort to support it and to provide for the transition to the current multi-protocol ESnet. Pre-standards or niche application solutions can and should be used to satisfy time-critical requirements, yet they can also create problems if the transition to new standards, whether formal or de facto, is slow to follow. However, the coexistence of different protocols in this case satisfied the evolving and varied requirements of the user community and provided the capability for a smooth transition from older solutions.

In 1987, the ESnet staff had already decided to implement the TCP/IP protocols as the main basis for ER's networks, while still pragmatically supporting other protocols where appropriate. In 1989 a peer review of ESnet supported the choice to move to a TCP/IP based protocol suite as a replacement for the MFENET protocols. ESnet chose to acquire commercial routers that would provide the capability for supporting TCP/IP, DECNET IV, OSI/CLNP, X.25, and other protocols. At that time, a nation?

multiprotocol router-based network was a fairly new concept and some were skeptical about ESnet's success. However, ESnet is a customer-driven network service and therefore needed to provide both national and international support and access to a variety of sites whose applications required different sets of protocols. Contrary to the popular belief that a single standard is the only means to successfully support a diversified community (e.g., NII), ESnet has demonstrated that the support of multiple standards-based services addresses the users' needs and provides for the coexistence necessary to allow the natural selection process to occur. Coexistence provides the "shake out" period necessary to fully test and implement alternate solutions and eases the transition from older solutions to new ones. Interoperability is achieved through application-based gateways that support each constituency's current requirements and provide a transition path to future standards and systems. By not exclusively focusing on or choosing a single standard—either the federally mandated GOSIP or the popular de facto TCP/IP standards—ESnet continues to satisfy the varied international requirements of its user base while providing transition avenues for applications based on the older proprietary and legacy protocols.

When the new multiprotocol ESnet came into existence during the latter half of the 1980s, it became evident that network management needed to change. ESnet chose to use a pre-commercial version of a Digital Equipment Corporation (DEC) network management tool that handled both the IETF de facto standard Simple Network Management Protocol (SNMP) and the DECNET IV management protocol. Although the OSI Common Management Information Protocol (CMIP) existed as a standard and was being recommended by NIST as the government standard, there were no viable products available, so ESnet used SNMP as the basis for its network management solution and continues to do so today. The ESnet sites also chose to implement SNMP in order to be interoperable with ESnet and to provide an ESnet-wide network management framework. That decision was arrived at by consensus, not by mandate, and has been vindicated by the enormous selection of commercial SNMP products and the number of networks, including government networks, that currently use SNMP as their primary management tool. The Government Network Management Protocol (GNMP) is the successor of and a derivative of CMIP and is being championed by NIST as the network management protocol to be used by the federal government. Whatever its technical merit, its fate is yet to be determined. Meanwhile, had ESnet not adopted the de facto standard of SNMP as its network management framework, it would not have been able to deliver quality operational networking services to its customers during the "shake out time" in the network management arena. This is an example of the successful use of "just in time standards" to achieve interoperability.

Many times there is no choice but to adopt innovative pre-standard tools and applications in order to address the user's requirements and to provide some base level of interoperability. Information search and retrieval tools, such as WAIS, WWW, MOSAIC, and Gopher have no formal (OSI) counterpart. ESnet, in the context of providing the richest production-oriented environment that meets the needs of its users, has implemented these tools in lieu of waiting for formal standards or Federal Information Processing Standards (FIPS) solutions or alternatives. It is these tools that have captured the imagination of the Clinton Administration and the public when describing the NII. If all agencies' activities, including DOE's ESnet, had implemented only the mandated formal GOSIP/OSI standards and the procurement standards of GSA, these enabling technologies would not be available to our researchers and administrators today and the reality of a FII and NII would be much more distant. Thus it is clear that treating standards as a means, and not as an end in itself, enhances not only the chances of addressing the user's requirements but also those of achieving interoperability.

Systems and standards use versions to allow for evolution by either adding new features or for correcting "bugs." Even if only one standard or system is chosen there will still be interoperability issues due to the existence of different versions. One such example is the use of X.500 for providing user-based directory services for ESnet and its users. When ESnet implemented its X.500 services in 1990, there were no commercially available standard-based products. ESnet used the publicly available QUIPU X.500 directory software to provide such services over both the TCP/IP and OSI/GOSIP stacks. The early adoption of this technology has given

ESnet users operational directory services many years ahead of those still waiting for pure standards-based vendor directory services. However, there are a few interoperability issues between QUIPU and other X.500 services mainly due to the fact that the 1988 version of X.500 was lacking many essential management capabilities such as replication, access control, and distributed operations. Therefore QUIPU had to implement its own version of these capabilities in order to deploy an operational solution before 1992, when these issues were to be addressed by the formal standards process. As QUIPU and other products implement the 1992 X.500 standard these interoperability problems are expected to be ameliorated. Meanwhile, ESnet is using X.500 with NASA, Control Data Corporation, and others. This is a clear example of the standards process taking too long (the 1988 version did not address necessary operational issues) and also shows that adhering to standards (1988 X.500) is not the panacea for interoperability and functionality that many believe it to be.

ESnet has also implemented an X.400 gateway that provides X.400 and SMTP interoperability for the ESnet community. This early deployment of services has provided the ESnet community and the DOE important X.400 and SMTP e-mail capabilities by pragmatically providing interoperable multi-protocol services instead of needlessly awaiting resolution of a philosophical standards debate. Again, the focus on interoperability and functionality, rather than exclusively choosing one standard, has provided interoperability among the DOE community.

Interoperability is not always achieved through the implementation of a single standard. ESnet peers with other Federal Research and Education (R&E) Entities at the Federal Internet eXchange (FIX), where they use inter-network peering protocols such as Exterior Gateway Protocol (EGP) and Border Gateway Protocol (BGP) exchange routing and connectivity information and provide for the interconnection and interoperability of federal agency R&E networks. The FIX can be considered a standard for interoperability, at least for the sake of connecting the federal R&E networks [2]. It is important to note that the FIX concept is not bound to any one protocol (standard); it supports DECNET IV, TCP/IP, and OSI/CLNP, and others as needed. Even the medium used for interconnection, originally Ethernet, is not exclusive. The two FIXes now in operation have implemented FDDI and can easily provide a hybrid media interconnection point. The success of the FIX concept has been repeated in other instances, albeit with added or different functionality, such as the Commercial Internet eXchange (CIX), Network Access Points (NAPs), and the Global Internet eXchange (GIX) as exemplified in the Washington D.C. MAE-EAST implementation. We suggest that the success of the FIX and its successors is due to the fact that they focused on providing a collection of usable solutions, both standard and non-standard, for achieving interoperability, rather than focusing on the identification and exclusive use of a single mandated de jure standard.

An exclusive standard arrived at through federal acquisition policy can impede interoperability between the government and non-government organizations. In the late 1980s and early 1990s, for example, many ER programs were pursuing the use of videoconferencing to augment their existing communications mechanisms. Several sites selected video solutions that were not based on FTS2000 Compressed Video Teleconferencing Systems (CVTS). The DOE mandate at that time was to use the GSA Provided Service (a procurement and use standard) that used a non-standards-based codec. The ESnet sites had to seek exemption from this mandate in order to acquire a product that could conform to the international video standards (H.261 and other appropriate standards). In order to satisfy its videoconferencing and collaborative workspace requirements, the ESnet community developed and is implementing a plan that promotes H.200 and H.300 standard-based videoconferencing, dedicated room video solutions, and desktop solutions, which include workstation-based packetized video and audio capabilities across the Internet (e.g., MBONE). Neither point-to-point standards-based videoconferencing systems nor packet based desktop systems were by themselves a viable solution for addressing the requirements of the ER community. A plan that incorporated both solutions, including the support of MBONE across ESnet, was the only answer for ER's international and multi-organizational collaborations. OSC is currently funding research that will provide for interoperability between these videoconferencing systems.

The technology life cycle constantly demands the re-evaluation of past decisions and the transition to newer standards and technologies as they evolve. The National Energy Research Super-computer Center has hosted many serial 1 and "early shipment" supercomputers. In order to provide users with a production environment, NERSC had to design and implement its own oper-ating system (Cray Time Share System or CTSS) and libraries. This was labor intensive, but given the lack of commercial operating systems available for supercomputers at the time, it was the proper choice. In fact, some of the NSF supercomputer centers bootstrapped themselves into operation by using the NERSC and other DOE supercomputer center operating systems and system software. A tough decision presented itself when a commercial UNIX operating system became available for the supercomputers. The users had become accustomed to features available only in the NERSC-developed system and the support staff felt that their system was superior to the UNIX-based commercial software. However, the rest of the world, including the NSF supercomputer centers, was now using UNIX and the design of POSIX had commenced, thereby creating problems of data and code interoperability between the NERSC and other supercomputer centers. NERSC finally adopted UNIX as its systems level software base in 1992 and went through a painful transition process to UNIX. Although the CTSS system may have been superior to the UNIX system in many respects, the transition should have occurred sooner in order to provide better interoperability between NERSC users and those using other supercomputing facilities, including other agency funded centers. This same scenario is likely to arise again at all sites, not just NERSC, when the transition to Open Software Foundation (OSF) solutions and POSIX-compliant sys-tems is enacted, and it will occur again when the move from POSIX or OSF to their successors is made. Evolution demands constant re-evaluation and adaptation.

OSC and other areas of DOE have long recognized the value of standards when they are realistically designed and implemented in a timely fashion, and they have directly funded development of necessary standards in addition to participating in standards fo-rums such as the Internet Engineering Task Force (IETF), the Comité Consultatif Internationale de Telegraphique et Telephonique (CCITT, now ITU-T), the Institute of Electrical and

Electronics Engineering (IEEE), the Asynchronous Transfer Mode (ATM) Forum, and others. The OSC has funded research in many advanced technology areas including collaborative work environments and high-speed network access. The research and development of high-speed networking technologies includes the development of high-speed interfaces such as HIPPI for use in connecting high-end cycle and storage servers at gigabit speeds and the investigation of access from high-speed LANs, such as Fiber Channel, HIPPI, ATM and others, to high-speed wide area ATM network services. OSC's support of standards development in niche areas, such as HIPPI or packetized audio, has helped to provide necessary standards and solutions for areas not normally pursued by industry due to their perceived small customer base. It is interesting to note that DOE funds the research and development (and associated standards activities) of diverse and competing solutions, such as HIPPI, ATM, and Fiber Channel, without prejudging or pre-selecting the winners. The end result is that the standards and solutions that have garnered outside support, address real user requirements, and have lived through the natural selection process are chosen and implemented. Supporting multiple standards and technologies, and not prematurely pruning a branch off the technology evolution tree, provides DOE with a choice from among a set of competitive alternatives to best address its varied requirements.

The federal government should not think of itself as an island when choosing standards and solutions. The use of federally mandated standards in a multi-organizational (including non-government organizations), widely dispersed, and collaborative environment such as the Internet introduces many issues not encountered in an intra-governmental situation. For example, the DOE has been instructed that it must use hardware-based DES to encrypt unclassified but sensitive information. Strict adherence to this directive has precluded the use of other security techniques, such as Privacy Enhanced Mail (PEM), for the purpose of notifying DOE sites, principle investigators, and collaborators at both DOE and non-DOE facilities of suspected or known viruses, worms, and other attacks. Adherence to this directive impedes DOE efforts to communicate known security breaches to its non-DOE and non-

Governmental collaborators in a timely fashion, thereby increasing the other sites' risk of being compromised. Governmental directives and guidelines for computer and telecommunications standards should take into account that government agencies and the FII must be an integral part of the NII, in which agencies will collaborate or serve a multitude of non-government entities and organizations. The choice of one exclusive security solution (hardware-based DES) has hindered the government's ability to interoperate with both the private and public sectors.

The above real-life examples show that waiting for formal standards or implementing one set of mandated standards does not necessarily provide interoperability or an operational system. They also show that interoperability is sometimes achieved by means other than exclusively using standards. Success is achieved by implementing a full array of standards and solutions at different maturity levels and at different times on the technology and standards continuum.

Many areas that could greatly benefit from standards are overlooked. Naming and addressing are a very important part of any infrastructure, yet they are often overlooked or addressed as an afterthought. One of successes of the Internet was the availability of a known name and address space that covered anyone, including the federal government and other nations. In contrast, the OSI naming infrastructure in the United States was fragmented, with a set of rules and regulations established and mandated for the federal government but none for the private sector. We believe that the lack of a U.S. wide OSI name and address registrar, complete with standards arrived at by a wide consensus, was another major impediment to the success of OSI in the United States. Even today, there is still no U.S. registrar for X.400 management domain names and X.500 top level directory domain servers. A standard for handling and administering OSI names and addresses, including those for operational purposes, is more important for interoperability than the standards used by the mail transfer agents as described in CCITT standards documents. Many users and suppliers of the NII would benefit from an architecture that supports a standard, cheap, and easily used process for name and address management, which would further simplify the user interface to the system.

Procurement Standards

Procurement policies and practices, such as FTS2000, set standards indirectly by requiring agencies to exclusively acquire and use certain services, standards, hardware, software and systems. When government- wide contracts, such as FTS2000, are let they usually result in one or two winners and consequently reduce the number of alternative, and possibly innovative, technological solutions and competitive service providers available to the federal government. The "gene pool" of future technologies is enhanced by the availability of multiple solutions and offerings. The raw purchasing power of the federal government, as enacted through a single agency such as GSA, strongly affects—and the authors believe it to be an adverse effect—the competitive marketplace and indirectly establishes standards (e.g., FTS2000 CVTS). Recipients of large government-wide contracts are guaranteed both customers and a profit over a long period of time and therefore have little incentive to introduce new technologies at a rate commensurate with technology evolution (e.g., standards based videoconferencing codecs) or to provide interoperability (e.g., interoperability between FTS2000 networks A and B and from FTS2000 to the Internet). This impairs the agencies' abilities to interoperate with non-government organizations (e.g., the government was using FTS2000 X.400 or proprietary services while the rest of the nation used TCP/IP). Future procurement policies, such as POST FTS2000 [16], need to be defined such that services and standards are chosen from among those that will provide interoperability with the rest of the nation and allow for a multitude of service providers in order to ensure competition and the injection of new and innovative technologies into the government workplace.

Conclusion

As seen in the above examples, the DOE (especially those programs funded and sponsored by the OSC) has been a proponent of standards for the purpose of enhancing interoperability between its users, other agencies, academia, industry, and the public sector on both a national and international basis. Yet its adoption and use of these standards has been driven from a pragmatic perspective that acknowledges that new requirements and solutions will continue to be introduced into the technology and standards continuum. A rational approach to adoption and use includes: 1) participating in SDOs and developing new standards when necessary (e.g., HIPPI), 2) adopting pre-standard implementations (e.g., MFENET, packet video) in lieu of subscribing to the *Waiting for Godot* [2] standards scenario in which someone or some organization will wait forever for an event that either takes an inordinate amount of time or will not occur at all, 3) assuming and planning for the coexistence of multiple standards (e.g., TCP/IP and OSI), whether they are different protocols or versions thereof, 4) having the conviction and insight to substitute a new set of standards for an existing one when appropriate (e.g., TCP/IP for MFENET), and 5) adopting standards-based commercial products when they are easily obtainable and satisfy requirements (e.g., multi-protocol routers). It is the combined use of multiple standards from multiple SDOs and in different states of maturity that has proven successful in addressing the needs and requirements of the user community.

The old standards-setting process is obsolete. We agree with Cliff Lynch's statement that "the era of Standards as an end product has ended" [9]. We should embrace this technology and standards based (r)evolution and use it as leverage to redefine the method by which the federal government specifies, uses, and relies on standards. The authors believe that the natural selection process found in the technology and standards continuum, which is sometimes perceived as random and chaotic, is not necessarily a bad condition and that competition between diverse approaches, ideas, and technologies can ensure a rich intellectual and technological future, and thereby provide for a healthy technology and information based economy. As is found in the biological world, the natural selection process applied to a wide variety of alternatives is part of the normal evolution cycle and enhances the probability that the best solution(s) survive. If the Internet had not been developed and used we could be currently constrained to using X.25 services. It is hard to imagine how today's information innovations, such as multimedia, World Wide Web, Gopher, and others, would have been introduced if the agencies had exclusively implemented OSI.

The Government OSI Profile (GOSIP) is a procurement profile that references OSI and other protocols to be acquired by Government Agencies. GOSIP does not preclude the use or acquisition of other protocols; however, there has been an interpretation by Information Resources Management (IRM) officials at all levels that since the GOSIP is a procurement specification it was also intended to be the primary choice for implementation, with little room for exceptions. This attitude has had the same effect as if GOSIP were exclusively mandated for use, with the noted exception of the Research and Education communities within the agencies that have been successfully using the Internet and TCP/IP. This overzealous mandate has impeded the government's ability to interoperate with the non-federal community and will also impede the deployment of the NII. Let's not add our current "dominant" technological gene pool to the endangered species list by subjugating it to exclusive long-drawn-out formal standards processes.

Pending legislation, S.4, The National Competitiveness Bill, states that "federal government contribution of resources and more active participation in the voluntary standards process in the U.S. can increase their compatibility with the standards of other countries, and ease access of products manufactured in U.S. manufacturers to foreign markets." It adds that "the federal government, working in cooperation with private sector organizations including trade associations, engineering societies, technical organizations, and other standards-setting bodies can effectively promote Federal Government use of United States consensus standards and, where appropriate, the adoption and Federal Government use of international standards." The need to compete on an international basis, and therefore use international standards, is a viable strategy for enhancing U.S. businesses options; however, we should not let these perceived benefits prevent us from forging ahead in those areas where we can continue to be leaders, especially in the areas of science and technology.

The selection of technologies and standards may have a strong impact on many lives and businesses. Therefore, it is incumbent upon the analysts and federal employees who affect policy [18] in these areas and establish standards-setting processes to make sure that they consider the issues in a holistic manner and do not focus solely on short-term financial and efficiency issues. Specifically, they need to understand that they cannot truly benefit the federal government process without taking into consideration other variables and their affect on the future of our nation. As an example, anticipatory standards may prematurely prune a branch from the technology evolution tree and kill a technology that might otherwise prove to be very economical and save the government a lot of money in the future, or be an enabler technology necessary for solving national challenges such as finding a cure for cancer. The standards makers must also resist the temptation to treat standards in a simple fashion where they are viewed as being only technical or political. Since standards eventually move from paper to implementation, it is imperative that the process involve persons with recent real life operational experience to provide the necessary insight for choosing standards wisely—not just making a politically correct choice. The Government's current practice is to set standards (e.g., Clipper Chip, Ada, GOSIP, FTS2000) with the intent of creating supportive markets that will save the government money, provide interoperability, and satisfy security agencies' programs. This practice needs to be examined in the context of this moral dilemma, since those making the decisions create winners and losers in addition to possibly prematurely affecting the technological gene pool of the future. These are economic, societal, and ethical issues, in addition to being both political and technical issues.

Acknowledgment

This paper was first published in *Connexions: The Interoperability Report*, August 1994; it will also appear in *ACM StandardView* sometime in 1995.

References

1. "20/20 Vision: The Development of a National Information Infrastructure," U.S. Department of Commerce, Washington, DC, 1994.

2. Aiken, Robert J., Hans-Werner Braun, and Peter Ford. "NSF Implementation Plan for Interagency Interim NREN," *Journal for High Speed Networks*, Vol. 2, No. 1, 1993.

3. Beckett, Samuel. *Waiting for Godot*, New York: Grove Press, 1954.

4. Drucker, Peter F. *Post-Capitalist Society*, New York: HarperCollins, 1993.

5. "Global Standards: Building Blocks for the Future," U.S. Congress, Office of Technology Assessment, 1992.

6. "High Performance Computing and Communications: Toward a National Information Infrastructure," Committee on Physical, Mathematical, and Engineering, and Technology, Office of Science and Technology Policy, 1993.

7. Information Infrastructure Task Force. "The National Information Infrastructure: Agenda for Action," National Telecommunications and Information Administration, Washington, DC, 1993.

8. Kuhn, Thomas S. *The Structure of Scientific Revolutions*, Chicago: University of Chicago Press, 1962.

9. Lynch, Clifford. "Interoperability: The Standards Challenge for the 1990s," *Wilson Library Bulletin*, 1993.

10. "National Performance Review: Reengineering Through Information Technology," Office of the President, Washington, DC, 1993.

11. National Research Council. *Crossroads of Information Technology Standards*, Washington, DC: National Academy Press, 1990.

12. National Research Council. *Keeping the U.S. Computer Industry Competitive*, Washington, DC: National Academy Press, 1992.

13. Office of Management and Budget. " Government Electronic Mail for the Federal Government," Washington, DC, 1994.

14. Office of the President of the United States. "Streamlining Procurement Through Electronic Commerce," Executive Memorandum, Washington, DC, 1993.

15. "Perspectives on the National Information Infrastructure: Ensuring Interoperability," Computer Systems Policy Project, Washington DC, 1994.

16. "Post-FTS2000 Acquisition Alternatives White Paper," Acquisition Working Group of the Interagency Management Council, Washington DC, 1994.

17. Tassey, Greg. "The Roles of Standards as Technology Infrastructure," National Institute of Standards and Technology, 1993.

18. Tong, Rosemarie. *Ethics in Policy Analysis*, Englewood Cliffs, NJ: Prentice-Hall, 1986.

The Government's Role in the HDTV Standards Process: Model or Aberration?

Suzanne Neil, Lee McKnight, and Joseph Bailey

Introduction

The development of high definition television standards within the United States, Europe, and Japan and at the international level has been the subject of substantial debate and confusion in the media, government, and industry, and among the public. In this paper, we will review the critical factors and policies that have shaped outcomes in this cross-industry standards arena. The key U.S. public policy achievement was inclusion of the principles of interoperability, extensibility, scalability, and flexibility into HDTV standards development. This result occurred because of government, industry, and academic partnership.

Whether the HDTV process is a model for future federal efforts to encourage standards in the public interest is a difficult question. Certain elements of the process (in particular, the government-industry-academic partnerships) are obviously applicable in other standards arenas; other elements indicate that HDTV is a special case and may be the wrong place to look for guidance for information infrastructure standards development. However, careful analysis of HDTV standardization gives us a model where government does not sit in judgment of these standards but rather participates in a multiplicity of extremely important roles forming the new standards.

Although it is impossible to analyze high definition television without making reference to HDTV developments in other countries, this paper is not a comparative analysis and instead focuses primarily on developments in the United States. The rapid, turbulent development and convergence of computer and television technologies occurred first and primarily in this country. Focusing on the U.S. case shows in its most stark form forces that shape new technologies. However, it is important to review HDTV developments worldwide to understand the history of HDTV in the United States.

The story of HDTV begins in Japan, where the Japanese broadcast company, NHK, began research in the late 1960s on the successor to color television. NHK, together with MPT, the Japanese Ministry of Post and Telecommunications, worked with Japanese consumer electronic companies to design the standard and an entire line of production and receiver equipment. By the late 1970s, this effort had culminated in a new television system known as 1125/60 or simply 1125; the name comes from the number of scanning lines in the new picture (1125) and the 60 Hz frame rate. At the same time, the international organization responsible for formulating television standards, the International Telecommunication Union (ITU), included the question of advanced television in its study program. As was normal for the ITU, this question would go through rounds of negotiations and come before the final and formal standards setting forum in 1986.

There was a tight working relationship between NHK and the U.S. broadcast network CBS, with engineers in both research laboratories working on the 1125 system; there was also a close relationship between CBS and the U.S. State Department, focused on ensuring adoption of 1125 as a global standard. This partnership played a role in both U.S. domestic and international negotiations over the standard. While the partnership was successful at forging an apparent consensus within the United States, it was not successful at the international level: the 1986 ITU meeting voted to delay a standards vote until the next full meeting, in 1990.

One of the main reasons for delaying this vote was resistance not from the United States but more importantly from Western Europe. The anxiety in Europe over Japanese domination of the consumer electronics industry propelled the Europeans to develop their own HDTV effort. This effort was not as highly developed as the Japanese effort, which by then was fifteen years old, and in fact, the European HDTV technology was just a "tweaking" of the Japanese technology.

In the United States, the effect of the postponed ITU vote was profound. First, it destroyed pre-existing agreements among broadcasters and consumer electronics companies; second, it changed the forum for standards setting from the private to the public sector, incidentally basically displacing the State Department as a major actor; and third, it offered previously uninvolved industries the possibility of designing a standard useful to those industries. These changes were so great that by the end of 1990, an entirely new kind of standard was under consideration: the language, purpose, and many of the players were new.

The events of those four tumultuous years for HDTV technology and standards development falls into three phases. The first phase runs from the defeat of 1125 in the ITU in 1986 through the summer of 1988. During that period the state acted as an arbiter. The center of activity was the Federal Communication Commission (FCC), which, in response to private mobile communications companies, used its congressionally mandated authority to ensure order in the electromagnetic spectrum to open an Inquiry into Advanced Television. The purpose of this inquiry was to solicit opinions from the private sector. To provide more information, the Commission established an Advisory Committee on Advanced Television Systems (ACATS) composed of representatives of communication service providers, manufacturing companies, and academics. ACATS built links with private laboratories established by the broadcasting and cable industries to test the systems under FCC consideration. The model here is one of the state acting as arbiter within clearly defined boundaries. The state's authority came not only from its congressional mandate but also from tradition. Both the public and private sector actors were following the conventional path for broadcast standardization. Many of the people, organizations, and most of all the pattern of advice and the decision-making were the same for advanced television as they had been for past broadcast standardization.

Just after Labor Day 1988, Representative Edward Markey, Chair of the House Telecommunications Subcommittee, held a Congressional Hearing on Advanced Television. With his opening speech, in which he characterized high definition television as a question of international industrial competitiveness and national security, he signaled the beginning of the second phase. During this phase, the state acted on balance as a change agent and fundamentally broadened the definition of advanced television to include other applications than home entertainment and to emphasize the economic aspects of the technology.

The FCC continued with its on-going Inquiry; the new state actors were Congress, particularly the House Subcommittees on Telecommunications and Science Competitiveness, and the Advanced Research Projects Agency (ARPA).[1] The Department of Commerce, through the Secretary's Office and two other bureaus, was also briefly important. The Congressional committees used their authority to formulate policies of broad societal importance to hold hearings on a number of aspects of advanced television. The Commerce Department briefly used its authority to support U.S. industry as justification for promoting HDTV. Last, ARPA used its authority to underwrite development of critical new military technologies, its highly educated and streamlined administrative cadre knowledgeable about new technologies, and its history of successfully supporting broadly useful new technologies to spearhead the creation of a flexible advanced video system, one application of which was high definition television.

The effect of the state as change agent was to delay the FCC process enough so that old proponent companies could design new technologies and new companies could enter the FCC process. More importantly, through the long-standing ties between state actors and the computer industry, the state sought to bring computer technologies and standardization techniques into the FCC process.

During the third phase, which covers the end of 1988 through 1990, the computer companies became active within the FCC process, infusing the standardization procedures with new considerations. By late 1990, all the serious proponent systems before the FCC were digital, and the language the United States supported in international broadcast standardization fora was familiar to anyone working on advanced video in a computer company but entirely new to broadcasters.

During this debate, the future U.S. High Definition Television (HDTV) standard focused as much on the economics as on the technology. A 1989 American Electronics Association report projected that the cumulative U.S. sales of HDTV receivers, VCRs, and camcorders over the initial 20 year period after the standard was set would be $500 billion[2]. The National Telecommunications and Information Administration (NTIA) of the Department of Commerce sponsored a report, called the Darby Report, which forecast that Americans would spend $16.2 billion on advanced television and VCRs by 2010. Dr. Robert Cohen of the Economic Strategy Institute found that an investment in broadband communications could add as much as $321 billion dollars in net new GNP growth to the U.S. economy, while an Office of Technology Assessment report concluded that HDTV might drive developments in many industries including semiconductors (signal processing and memory), semiconductor manufacturing, display, storage, and communications.[3] Clearly, an HDTV standard was expected to have long-term and far-reaching implications.

Meanwhile, between 1986 and 1990, Europe and Japan were developing and demonstrating HDTV standards and prototype systems. Under pressure from their consumer electronics companies, European governments subsidized but did not direct technical work on HDTV. It was the short-sightedness of the existing European television manufacturing industries that led them to focus on the same obsolescent analog interlaced techniques employed by all current television systems. These techniques were state-of-the-art fifty years ago. They were abandoned by the computer industry more than a decade ago as inadequate for high-resolution imaging. Similarly, Japanese firms aimed at a short-term boost for their stagnant consumer electronics market and persuaded their government to coordinate over a billion dollars of corporate funding to develop NHK's analog M.U.S.E. system.

In their haste to rush to market, Japanese and European firms designed HDTV systems that failed. Their primary intent was to serve and protect existing consumer electronics industries and not to advance technology. The United States took a longer term view. Europeans and Japanese are now trying to copy U.S. technology, but they still do not understand that it is our process of involving government and academia with industry that is our main advantage. The U.S. competitive secret is to develop long-range R&D and allow private industry to compete on ideas; centralized decision-making by government-backed private monopolies only produces old solutions for new problems.

The U.S. Government's Role

The central part of this paper is an abstraction of the U.S. attempt to create a standard for HDTV. Rather than simply an attempt to explain why consumers can buy certain kinds of television sets, today and in the future, the case is a vehicle for shedding light on relationships among a variety of actors and institutions in an arena of increasing importance in the international distribution of political and economic power: the development of new communication and information network technologies. The story provides an opportunity to examine the interactions among government organizations, industries, and professional associations as each tries to shape a new technology. The state, far from being a neutral observer or arbiter among choices developed in the private sector, in fact affected both the timing of the standardization process and the fundamental nature of the standard that emerged. The new technology was far from being the outcome of an inexorable and internally technologically determined process, but was instead the outcome of a complex process in which historically conditioned relationships among people and institutions have been centrally, crucially important.

Creating new technologies during periods of rapid technological development and industrial change requires long-term vision. Long-term vision is necessary because it is hard to develop new technologies that cross industry borders. The normal incentive is for each industry simply to continue producing new (and presumably more refined) versions of existing products. One of the places in a society we look for long-term (or at least longer-term) vision is the state. However, state agencies and organizations themselves have interests and alliances and are themselves actors. Thus public as well as private sector actors have conflicting and often limited ideas of possible futures. The result of this (usually unarticulated)

institutional myopia coupled with rapid, cross-industrial technological development can be a very real impediment to technology
development.

However, not all U.S. agencies created impediments to HDTV
development; agencies like ARPA helped provide long-term vision
by spending approximately $200 million from 1988–1992. They
funded research with very good results for future flat panel manufacturing, high-density recording devices for HDTV, compression
technology superior to anything in Europe and Japan, and high-
performance computer networking. In fact, this long-range, $200
million investment bought much more than the $2 billion or so
spent by the Europeans and Japanese for short-term solutions.

The development of a high definition television standard was
constrained by rapid and fundamental changes along two dimensions. The first grew out of the rapidly changing technologies
themselves and applies to the components as well as to the end use
products. The second concerns the shape of the communications
and information industry: what now constitutes the "communication" or the "home entertainment" or even the "computer" industry? Where are the borders of those industries? One of the major
issues confronting the telephone industry during the 1970s and
1980s was the convergence of point-to-point communications and
computers: where did the boundary lie between transmission and
manipulation of information when computer chips were part of
office switchboards as well as of phone company switches? Since
digital signals look the same whether representing voice or data,
the problem compounds as electronic technologies become increasingly digital, and these digital technologies promise and have
begun to deliver an extraordinary cornucopia of new, flexible
products at decreasing unit costs. To deal with these new relationships, scholars have developed new models, such as Pool's convergence of modes.[4] Now this same convergence is occurring among
video-based industries, i.e., those that design, manufacture or
deliver moving images on an electronic monitor. This development most obviously affects the broadcast television and computer
industries, but it also affects the cable, satellite broadcasting,
telephony, medical imaging, publishing, education and training,
motion picture and film industries.[5]

Since the late 1970s, there have been two strands of development in video technologies: one has focused on increasing the capability of computers to handle motion video, the other has focused on using digital technologies to improve traditional television pictures. Until the late 1980s, these two strands of development occurred on parallel tracks that were almost totally separate from each other.[6] Even cursory analysis shows that combining television and computer technologies would provide obvious benefits for broad classes of end users, including not just residential television viewers but also medical professionals, manufacturers, product designers, educators, students and others. Despite this clarity, decision-makers in the U.S. television industry (both researchers and front office executives) focused on traditional television technologies and ignored the developments in the computer industry up to the end of the decade. Similarly, the computer industry became involved in advanced television research quite late in the standardization process, and when it did, the influence of computer technologies was much smaller than the size and importance of the industry would have suggested. These turbulent conditions set up an appropriate instance for state action, for the state to represent a "public interest" broader than a single industry. Instead, the state became involved on a fragmented level, promoting the interests of departments, agencies, and their allies.

Explanations that focus on traditional interest group factors partially explain this outcome. To explain it more completely, to understand the process of convergence among related technologies and industries, it is also necessary to focus on the role of institutions, particularly those concerning standardization. Doing so brings to light an essentially conservative force that provided order by controlling study questions, agendas, rules and procedures, language, and participants.

In the efforts to "standardize" high definition television—that is, to agree on the specific technical components of the new video technology—there were two separate standardization paths, one for computers and one for television. These paths involved different organizations, people and procedures, and they were isolated from each other, with no bridges between them. What existed instead were partnerships or alliances between industry groups and government organizations, but these partnerships reinforced the institutional separation between the two industry processes. This paper, then, is an attempt to understand the forces that eventually permitted creating a standard that was a bridge between the two camps, in the midst of technological and industrial turbulence.

The path-breaking American proposals for all-digital HDTV did not develop only in the commercial sector, as is often touted, but originated from a uniquely American partnership. For the past 20 years, ARPA, DOD, NSF, and other Federal agencies have explicitly supported work at U.S. universities and research centers in underlying technologies. This technology forms the basis for the U.S. digital HDTV proposals. The critical work includes image compression, high speed computing, communications, encryption, flat panel displays, and viewer requirements.

U.S. HDTV Standardization Abstractions

Technical standardization is important because the choice of one standard over another can have a major effect on the development of entire industries, with effects on jobs, trade, and standard of living. There is well-developed literature on standardization, but it focuses very little on the role of the state, and when it does, it assigns the state a very marginal role. Yet in reading and observation, one keeps bumping up against the state—so much so, and so often, that it is clear that the state does play a major role in technical standardization.

What is that role? Analysis of the attempt to establish a U.S. high definition television standard shows that the state is centrally involved in the standardization process at a number of points. To understand the nature and importance of state involvement, it is necessary to disaggregate the state into component parts—the FCC, Departments of Commerce and Defense, and Congress, because different agencies and departments had different forms of involvement.

We argue that there was state involvement in the standards process which made a difference. The state roles here are complicated and sometimes internally contradictory (right hand helps while left hurts) and operate across a number of levels, beginning at a very basic level of establishing legitimacy and moving to the most obvious level of funding. Finally, we argue that the state involvement took the form of regular, discernible patterns. (We are not saying that the FCC always has a specific kind of interaction with such and such industry; rather we are saying that in this case, it *did have* a particular role.) The roles we found are the following:

Funder. Either directly, through grants, loans, etc., or indirectly, through tax credits, loan guarantees, etc.

Facilitator. State actors consciously choose goals and set about enabling the private sector to realize them. The most obvious example of this role is legislation, but the executive branch also has the capacity. The most immediate example of the latter is the state's role in developing interoperability—developing digital cameras and the administrative infrastructure for a digital image architecture. The role is quite powerful and equally overlooked

Judge or arbiter. Traditional role in communications standardization. The state chooses between two or more proposed standards, deciding cases in the courts (FCC and ATV proponents)

Partner. Obvious example is the development of military equipment (ARPA and signal processing/display underwriting)

Legitimizer. FCC and Commerce as giving blessing to computer company demands

State involvement here had the effects of:

1. Equalizing power between different industries
2. Bestowing legitimacy on certain questions
3. Funding new products
4. Prolonging the standardization process in such a manner that the debate could widen and encompass new groups with new technologies—without multi-faceted state involvement, we might not be looking at HDTV at all, and we certainly would not be looking, at this time, at digital proponents

Conclusion

The U.S. government does more than just sit in judgment of a technical standard. Rather, the government is a key player that through a number of its bodies funds, facilitates, and coordinates technology development. The standardization process is not a "bake off" of technologies; it is a more complex model in which governments are very much participants.

In fact, this model of government participation at various levels can be seen in other technology developments, such as the ARPANET (now the Internet). Perhaps the HDTV standardization process is not an aberration at all. This study suggests that the U.S. government has often participated in the standardization, though in subtle and differing ways. The perception that a technology like HDTV is the result of only a commercial effort, and that government is only an observer, is incorrect. Government participates at various levels to shape the future of technology standards.

Notes

[1] The Defense Advanced Research Projects Agency (DARPA) changed its name back to its original name, Advanced Research Projects Agency (ARPA), to emphasize the dual-use nature of its technology development mission.

[2] American Electronics Association (1992), p. 2.

[3] Cohen and Donow (1989) and OTA (1990).

[4] Pool (1984).

[5] Submission to US CCIR National Committee Interim Working Group 11/9, September 1990

[6] Negroponte (1991).

Bibliography

American Electronics Association, 1992. Press Background Information—Development of a U.S.-based ATV Industry, May 9.

Besen, Stanley M., and Leland L. Johnson, 1986. "Compatibility Standards, Competition and Innovation in the Broadcasting Industry," Rand Corporation, Santa Monica, CA.

Bove, V. M., and A. B. Lippman, 1992. "Scalable Open-Architecture Television," *SMPTE Journal*, January.

Birkmaier, Craig, 1993. "The Future of Video," Television Broadcast Special Report, March.

Cawson, Alan, 1993. "High Definition Television in Europe: Why the Flagship of European Technology Policy Hit the Rocks," unpublished manuscript, University of Sussex, July.

Cohen, Robert, and Kenneth Donow, 1989. "Telecommunications Policy, High Definition Television and U.S. Competitiveness," Economic Policy Institute, ISBN 0-944826-10-5.

Davidson, Alan, 1993. "Collective Action and the Development of Technical Standards in U.S. Industry," S.M. Thesis, Massachusetts Institute of Technology, Technology and Policy Program.

Demos, Gary, 1994. "A Scalable Family of Formats for U.S. Advanced Television," unpublished manuscript, second draft, January.

Farrell, Joseph, and Garth Saloner, 1985. "Economic Issues in Standardization," Management in the 1990s, Sloan School of Management, Massachusetts Institute of Technology.

Jacobson, Bruce, 1993. "The Economics of Interoperability: Modeling High Resolution Imaging in the Computer, Consumer Electronics, Broadcast and Cable Television Industries," S.M. Thesis, Massachusetts Institute of Technology, Sloan School of Management.

Johnson, C., L. McKnight, S. Neil, R. Neuman, and R. Solomon, 1993. "America's Approach to HDTV: A Government-Industry Success Story," memorandum for Congressman George Brown, May 10, MIT DOHRS Program.

Katz, M. L., and C. Shapiro, 1985. "Network Externalities, Competition and Compatibility," *American Economic Review,* June.

Lehr, William, 1994. "Economics of Anticipatory Standard Setting," working paper, Columbia University, Graduate School of Business, presented at the Murrow Center, Tufts University, April 8.

Lippman, A., 1989. "Forget Television Sets, An Action Memo for Rep. Markey," MIT Media Lab.

Lippman, A., V. M. Bove, R. J. Solomon, and D. Tennenhouse, 1990. "Extensibility in Raster Arrays," unpublished manuscript, Massachusetts Institute of Technology, January.

McKnight, L., and S. Neil, 1987. "The HDTV War: The Politics of HDTV Standardization," presentation at the Third International Colloquium on Advanced Television Systems, "HDTV '87: From Studio to Viewer," Ottawa, Canada, October 4–8.

McKnight, L., R. Neuman, S. Downs, and R. Cohen, 1992. "Estimating the Economic Costs and Benefits of Interoperability," Draft Report for the FCC's Advisory Committee on Advanced Television Service, Planning Subcommittee–Working Party 4, April 23.

Negroponte, Nicholas, 1991. "Vanishing Point," *NEXTWORLD,* January/February.

Neuman, W. R., 1990. "Beyond HDTV: Exploring Subjective Responses to Very High Definition Television," Research Report for GTE Labs and the TVOT Consortium, MIT Media Laboratory, July.

Neuman, W. R., L. McKnight, and R. Solomon, 1996. *The Gordian Knot: Political Gridlock and the Communications Revolution,* Cambridge: MIT Press (forthcoming).

Office of Technology Assessment, U.S. Congress, 1990. "The Big Picture: HDTV and High-Resolution Systems," OTA-BP-CIT-64, Washington DC: U.S. Government Printing Office.

Office of Technology Assessment, U.S. Congress, 1992. "Global Standards: Building Blocks for the Future," TCT-512, Washington, DC: U.S. Government Printing Office.

Pool, Ithiel de Sola, 1984. *Technologies of Freedom,* Cambridge, MA: Harvard University Press.

Schreiber, William, 1990. "The Economics and Politics of High-Definition Television," unpublished manuscript, Massachusetts Institute of Technology, March.

Schreiber, William, 1993. "Advanced Television in the United States," report to the European Commission, Massachusetts Institute of Technology, July.

Sirbu, M., and L. E. Zwimpfer, 1995. "Standards Setting for Computer Communication: The Case of X.25," *IEEE Communications Magazine,* Vol. 23, March, pp. 35–45.

Solomon, R., 1989. "The Demand for High-Resolution Systems," Hearings on the Scope of the HDTV Market and its Implications for Competitiveness, Testimony before the Committee on Governmental Affairs, U.S. Senate, August 1.

Solomon, Richard, and Anthony Rutkowski, 1992. "Standards-making for IT: Old vs. New Models," paper presented at the Conference on the Economic Dimension of Standards-Users and Governments in IT Standardization, November 18.

Financing the Standards Development Process

Michael B. Spring and Martin B. H. Weiss

Introduction

In the decade since scholarly work on standards began, the basic dynamics of standards in the marketplace have been reasonably well described (see [11], [15] and [30] for surveys of this literature). Some empirical studies have been performed to examine the actual behavior of the marketplace and of committees [12, 25, 33] (even though this sampling is far short of what is necessary to fully understand standards), and preliminary attention has been paid to modeling the standards development process [8, 18]. Much anecdotal literature exists addressing changes in the standards process [6], although little has been done to quantify this (see [5, 31] for attempts at quantification). The properties, attributes, and related marketplace behavior of different kinds of standards, such as software standards vs. hardware standards, have not yet been researched.

/ The question of how to finance the standards process was been raised by the Office of Technology Assessment report [29] *Global Standards: Building Blocks for the Future.* Weiss and Spring [34] began to address selected issues of financing in the context of intellectual property issues. This paper provides a broad analytic framework for addressing financing issues through an examination of the specific, detailed pattern of costs and benefits of standards.[1]

This kind of study is pertinent in light of the numerous discussions that have occurred in recent years on restructuring the U.S. standards process. Several different kinds of standards are developed in the United States under the auspices of a multitude of professional and industrial organizations [6, 29]. Garcia [14] shows that this approach developed in the early part of this century because of a policy preference for private enterprise over government-directed activity.[2] As a result, numerous Standards Development Organizations (SDOs) emerged, none with a clear, centralized authority. The situation is compounded today by the growing popularity of consortia [32] and the increasing use of public specifications developed by dominant producers such as Microsoft. Each SDO, consortium, and industrial organization has different rules, procedures, and motivations for developing standards.

The OTA report [29] suggests that the lack of a single authoritative SDO hampers United States efforts in the international standards arena. The report was critical of the market driven, decentralized process that is in place, particularly given the planned and organized approach used by our major trading partners. While there has been increased support for chartering the American National Standards Institute to serve as the official United States voice on standards, it is difficult to see how such a charter will improve the fundamental problems of funding the development of high quality standards that serve the interests of both the nation's industrial and commercial sectors and the nation as a whole. Even without considering the issue of external pressure, Weiss and Toyofuku [36] have raised questions about the sustainability of the current process in light of "free riders."

In terms of funding, the situation in the United States generally mirrors the situation internationally. In the International Telecommunications Union Telecommunications Standardization Sector (ITU-T),

each organization bears the direct cost of participation of its experts in ITU-T meetings, including travel, hotel accommodations, etc. Such costs are quite substantial, particularly if one considers the costs arising from preparatory work (developing proposals, harmonizing them on a national and regional level, drafting the contributions, etc.). All this work prior to a meeting costs money, to be spent by each participating organization. . . . The costs incurred by TSB [Telecommunications Standardization Board] for providing logistical support, for translation, interpretation, printing, and mailing all paperwork, for salaries of TSB staff, etc., are covered by financial contributions by Administrations and other organizations admitted to take part in ITU-T activities [17].

Private financing is not the only funding strategy. The European Telecommunications Standards Institute (ETSI) pays some standards developers in order to accelerate their work [3, 24]. Colleen Preston, Deputy Undersecretary of Defense for Acquisition Reform, reported at the National Research Council Conference on Standards and Trade that as a part of acquisitions reform, DOD will be looking to pay for the development of public standards where none exist as an alternative to Milspecs and Milstds. Similarly the very high costs associated with some consortia may be viewed as upfront costs by the corporate sponsors to accelerate the standards development process. Even though the free market approach seems to be gaining favor in Europe, there remain numerous examples of standards development that is more heavily government supported than is the case in the United States. While the private sector has resisted increased government involvement, even that limited to funding, there have been recent signs of a willingness on the part of some to accept government support so long as it does not imply increased regulation and bureaucracy [22]. However, no analysis exists that provides a grounded explanation of what funding *should* be provided. In order to do that, one needs an analytic framework that articulates the costs and benefits accruing to the various stakeholders.

Framework for Analysis

At a global level, it is difficult to compare the costs and benefits of the 3.5 inch floppy disk standard with the costs and benefits of the TCP/IP standard. Even closely related standards such as IEEE 802.3 (Ethernet) and IEEE 802.3i (10BaseT) vary significantly in complexity, time required for development, cost of related product development, and length of use. All of these are factors in the cost of standardization. On the benefits side, the situation is equally complex. There are both direct and indirect benefits to the developers and users of a standard. This section provides a framework for the analysis of the costs and benefits of standards.

While any number of different dimensions might be selected as the basis for cost analysis, three stand out in the literature.

1. The type of standard
2. The nature of the development process
3. The scope of the standard

Types of Standards

David [10] suggests that standards might be classified as behavioral or technical, and within these classes further typed as basic measurement, quality assurance, or compatibility standards. While it is a sound general classification scheme, it fails to adequately discriminate among the many information technology (IT) standards that fall into the technical compatibility group. Bonino and Spring [4] and Bonino [5] identify two broad subclasses of technical compatibility standards: traditional and anticipatory. Traditional standards are those based upon products or prototypes that have been tested in the laboratory or marketplace, while anticipatory standards are those that are developed before products exist.

Cargill [6] identifies standards as conceptual or implementation and product or process. Spring and Bearman [27] describe two possible subclassification schemes for IT standards: standards may be grouped into the information technology function they perform (interconnection, interface, interchange [of data], or interoperability) or they may be grouped into the information process they relate to (creation, dissemination, storage, or access). Spring [26] has also suggested that standards may be classified as reference models, base standards, syntax standards, or implementation/derivative standards:

1. Reference models serve to organize an area and serve to constrain and focus other standards. They are not implemented directly, but through the base standards they call for. Perhaps the most famous reference standard is International Standards Organization (ISO) 7498, The Open Systems Interconnection Reference Model.

2. Base standards form a measurable and implementable product or process description. These form the majority of the standards

developed by traditional SDOs. IEEE 802.3 would be an example of such a standard.

3. Syntax standards specify a language or procedure that may be used to develop other standards. Thus while a computer language standard is a base standard (because programs developed in the language are not themselves standards), a standard such as ISO 8879—Standard Generalized Markup Language (SGML) is intended to spawn implementations of the language that are themselves standards, such as CALS or Z39.592 .[3]

4. Implementation or derivative standards are standards developed from syntax standards or those with a significant dependence on a base standard. Clearly Z39.59 is an implementation of SGML. 10BaseT may be defined as a derivative standard of 802.3, i.e. it is critically dependent on 802.3.

The costs (and benefits) of developing a standard before products are developed will be different—in distribution if not magnitude—from the costs of developing a standard based on existing products. Similarly, there are different costs and cost distributions for reference, base, syntax, and implementation standards. While different, the anticipatory-traditional and reference-base-syntax-implementation dimensions are not fully orthogonal. Reference models are almost always anticipatory. Similarly, derivative standards are frequently based on successful products. In contrast, base or syntax standards may be anticipatory (ISDN) or traditional (Ethernet). The qualified marriage of these two dimensions yields the following classification for standards by type:

1. Reference

2. Anticipatory Syntax

3. Traditional Syntax

4. Anticipatory Base

5. Traditional Base

6. Implementation

We would suggest that costs and benefits will be significantly different for each of these types of standards. Analyses that do not factor out the different costs and benefits will not provide a fair picture.

Jumping ahead in the analysis, it is not hard to imagine that it might be possible to justify government support for reference models more easily than it would be to justify it for implementation standards. Considering the long period of time involved in development of a reference standard, it is easy to see that a reference model that has heavy upfront costs might require a different funding strategy than an implementation standard. In addition, it is reasonable to expect that those who invest in a standard for the long term will have to expect a higher rate of return if the benefits do not accrue until ten years after the investment has been made. Since the benefits accruing from implementation standards will be realized more quickly than those accruing from the development of a reference standard, private funding is easier to justify. In order to see how these costs are arrayed, we suggest that the costs be determined for each of the major phases in the life cycle of a standard.

Phases of Standardization

Over the last several years, there have been several efforts to better define the steps in the standards development process. Weiss and Spring [35] suggest specification, distribution, and implementation as important phases for examining issues of intellectual property rights. The X3 Strategic Planning Committee [28] defined a five step life cycle, consisting of the following phases:

1. Initial requirements

2. Base standards development

3. Profiles/product development

4. Testing

5. User implementation/feedback

In a similar fashion, Committee T1 [23] has identified five stages:

1. An initial set of requirements for a standards project is developed based on inputs from users, manufacturers, service providers, etc.

2. Base standards are developed.[4]

3. Standards are implemented through two related activities:

(a) Within the committee process, user profiles and implementation agreements are developed.

(b) Products are developed based on the base standard and the user profiles.

4. Products are tested for conformance to the standard and profile.

5. Products are delivered to users.

For purposes of this analysis, none of the models described provides the scope and detail required. The T1 model provides reasonable scope and the X3 model a reasonable level of detail within the traditional SDO process. However, both tend to ignore the increasing importance of conformance test development and certification. Similarly, they tend not to address issues such as the need for registration agencies for implementation standards. With these concerns in mind, we suggest the following phases of standards development:

1. Requirements analysis

2. Document development

   (a) Objective setting

   (b) Development

   (c) Specification:

      i. of interface, characteristics, etc.

      ii. of conformance requirements

3. Standard approval

4. Document dissemination

5. Implementation:

   (a) of products

   (b) of conformance tests

   (c) of derivations of the base standards

6. Management

   (a) Maintenance of the standard

   (b) Establishment of certification procedures

   (c) Development of registry agents and conventions

7. Certification of products and registration of standards

Three points need to be made about this model. First, the phases are not necessarily linear. The use of formal description techniques (FDTs) in the specification phase may obviate the need for, or significantly reduce the cost of, the development of test suites in the implementation phase. At the same time, the use of an FDT is likely to increase the cost of the specification phase. Second, the expanded model defines a scope that spans organizational boundaries as they exist today. Third, not all phases apply to all standards types or to all the standards within a type. For example, it is generally meaningless to talk about conformance to a reference model. Standards that can generate conformance tests based on FDTs and that are subject to self certification will not have steps for review and certification of testing agencies. Similarly, a registration facility is only necessary where it is required by a base standard.[5]

Scope

Assigning costs to the phases of standardization, while useful, is not complete. Other factors must be considered that can impact the cost of a standard. These are perhaps best described by defining the scope of a standard. There are a number of hints in the literature as to how the scope of a standard might be defined:

 1. Cargill [6] defines one of the characteristics of a standard as its importance—"measured by the dollar impact in both the users' and providers' world . . . . For the users it is the cost of time *before* implementation of the standard; for the providers it is the cost of implementation itself" (p. 27). To operationalize Cargill's definition, one needs to define the providers and users. The provider side is accounted for in the previous two sections, but the user assessment of cost is more difficult. At a first level of analysis, we argue that the size of the user community provides one measure of scope. For instance, the users of a standard like ISDN—the owners of phones—are likely a much larger group than the users of a standard such as SCSI—the manufactures of computers and peripherals. With this in mind, it may be possible to assess the costs associated with lost opportunity given the time to develop one or another standard. From the provider perspective, one might look

at the financial impact a standard is likely to have. A change in the DOS operating system will have a far more significant financial impact than a change in SCSI.

2. Another aspect of scope has to do with the percentage of the total community involved. For example, while the United States commercial sector might well be satisfied with a POSIX standard with a strong bias toward UNIX and C, it is not acceptable to the U.S. military community or the broader European community. In this wider operating system community, it is more critical that an expanded array of operating system features (security, real time functions) and language bindings (ADA, FORTRAN) be specified. Often it will be possible to meaningfully define this aspect of scope in terms of whether the standard is intended for an industry grouping or enterprise, a nation, a region, or a global community.

3. Finally, one might examine the expected temporal scope of a given standard. A standard that is intended as a temporary fix can, or should, be developed more quickly than one requiring a commitment of many years. Similarly, developers may expect a longer period of return on their investment. As with the issue of cost to users, there are issues related to lock-in costs for standards that have longevity. David [9] has discussed the costs of lock-in for the QWERTY keyboard standard.

The scope of a standard, then, involves three measures. We operationalize them as follows:

1. Community impacted:

(a) General population—all or a large segment of the population

(b) Population segment—only one group within the population, such as the publishing community, or the service sector

(c) Development segment—a population segment that includes only the kinds of individuals involved in developing the standard

(d) Developers—the standard affects only that group directly involved in the development of the standard

2. Scope of Agreement:

(a) Industry or enterprise group defines the scope of agreement

(b) National bounds define the scope of the agreement

(c) A regional group of nations defines the scope of agreement

(d) The global community defines the scope of agreement

3. Period of commitment:

(a) The commitment is temporary for either political or technical reasons

(b) The commitment is indeterminate, and while expiration is anticipated, no fixed time period is set

(c) The commitment is considered to be indefinite, and no change is anticipated, or the commitment is made to observe the standard for a long period of time—more than 10 years from adoption, even if change might be desired

Assignment of Costs

Table 1 provides a framework within which to assign costs for each kind of standard. This table crosses type of standard with phase of standardization. It is reasonable to expect that different costs can be expected in different phases for the different types. Areas of high cost will require careful examination and elaboration while areas of low or no cost may generally be ignored. Added to this analysis will be additional lost opportunity costs based upon an assessment of the scope of the standard. For limited scope standards, the costs are simply those of development. For standards that have significant scope in terms of impact, community, or period, additional direct costs or indirect costs must be added. The indirect costs will include lost opportunity, compromise, and commitment costs.

To develop accurate cost analysis, costs must be attributed to each area in Table 1. To obtain the direct costs for even a single step can be a daunting task. For example, a detailed examination of the development process must account for the different costs of different categories of participants. Weiss and Toyofuku [36] define five categories of individuals involved with standards: developers, Type 1 free riders, Type 2 free riders, observers, and interested parties.[6] While all of these groups benefit from standards, Type 1 free riders incur no significant costs related to the development of the stan-

Table 1 Cost Breakdown by Type of Standard

		Syntax		Base		
	Reference	Anticip.	Trad.	Anticip.	Trad.	Implementation
Analysis						
Development						
design						
specification						
Approval						
Dissemination						
Implementation						
products						
tests						
derivations						
Management						
maintenance						
certification						
registration						
Certification						

dard (see Table 2). Beyond these direct costs to participants, SDOs must also pay for various administrative support costs such as photocopying, mailing, meeting rooms, preparation of minutes, procedural support, and verification.

Similarly, conformance testing costs have to be calculated. The "classical" method for conducting a conformance test is to build an apparatus to which implementations of the standard (typically referred to as the Implementation Under Test, or IUT) are attached. The apparatus stimulates or "exercises" the IUT and observes its responses. The responses and their timing are measured by the conformance test apparatus and compared to those specified in the standard (see Linn [19, 20] for a more detailed discussion of conformance testing). Alternatively, manufacturers can connect their implementations to existing implementations (normally from other vendors) in the marketplace. If they interoperate properly, then the new implementation is thought to conform to the standard.[7] This approach is sometimes called *interoperability testing* to distinguish it from conformance testing,

Table 2 Costs by Type of Participant

	Costs
Developers	Time and Travel General R&D Product R&D Conformance/Interoperability Tests
Type 2 Free Riders	Time and Travel Product R&D Conformance/Interoperability Tests
Type 1 Free Riders	Product R&D Conformance/Interoperability Tests
Observers	Time and Travel
Interested Parties	Time and Travel

since it focuses on product interoperability instead of conformance to the standard. This is arguably what end users want. Finally, there is *self certification* as a conformance test process. Here, vendors conduct their own conformance tests instead of relying on a third party to conduct them. An end user may challenge the conformance to the standard, and only at that time does the vendor have to produce the conformance test results. In each case, *any* organization that manufactures products conforming to the standard incurs these costs, regardless of the organization's participation strategy. Type 1 free riders must build conformant products even if they did not participate in the development process. Thus, this cost is relatively evenly distributed. There are some costs that might be borne by an SDO if it is involved in administering the conformance test. It is assumed here that the development of the conformance test was part of the standards development process.

To estimate the cost by phase for classes of standards without hard data from many cases is a difficult task. Nonetheless, Table 3 is an attempt to characterize these costs based on our observations and anecdotal data about the standards process. These assignments represent research hypotheses that must be tested. The rationale for the cost assignments are outlined below:

Reference Reference standards are usually designed to be applicable over long periods of time. As a result, the development of

Table 3 Development Cost Estimates by Type of Standard

	Reference	Syntax Anticip.	Trad.	Base Anticip.	Trad.	Implementation
Analysis	high	high	med.	high	low	NA
Development						
design	high	high	med.	high	med.	low
specification	high	high	low or high	high	med.	low
Approval	high	high	med.	high	med.	low
Dissemination	low	low	low	low	low	low
Implementation						
products	NA	NA	NA	high	med.	low
tests	NA	high	high	med.	med.	low
derivations	NA	high	high	NA	NA	NA
Management						
maintenance	low	low	low	med.	med.	low or high
certification	NA	low	low	low	low	low
registration	NA	high	high	NA	NA	med.
Certification	NA	NA	NA	high	med.	med.

such a standard requires that the developers have good foresight about technical capabilities and market demand. As this kind of projection in a committee forum comes as the result of extensive discussion and debate, we label the analysis and development as high cost activities. Since the standard will affect the relevant markets for a long time, it is expected that approval will also be time consuming, hence a high cost activity. The remaining phases of the standards life cycle are not applicable with the exception of maintenance, which is low cost. Note that it does not make sense to consider the implementation, certification, or registration of reference standards.

Anticipatory Syntax Like reference standards, anticipatory standards lead the market, which requires market and engineering foresight on the part of the developers, making the first several phases high cost activities. Syntax standards, by definition, require derivative standards and tests to certify the derivative standards, thus these costs are high. They also require the development and maintenance of a registry. As a result, all of these are high cost phases as well. Since syntax standards (both anticipatory and traditional) are not directly implemented in products, it is not appropriate to consider the product implementation or certification costs associated with these types of standards. The standard serves as the absolute reference for the development of tests for the derivative/implementation standards based on it.

Traditional Syntax Traditional standards are developed after the marketplace has been involved, so the development costs are generally lower. One significant exception to this is specification in the presence of competing standards in the marketplace. Finding a technical position palatable to all (or a majority of) participants is sometimes quite challenging. One example of this problem may be the development of standard mail note formats where there is currently competition between X.400 syntax specification and SMTP/MIME specification. Thus, the table shows the development costs being either low or high, with the actual cost being dependent on whether this is a single dominating standard or one of multiple competing standards. The remaining costs of syntax standards mirror the costs of the anticipatory syntax standards.

Anticipatory Base Like anticipatory syntax standards, the analysis, development, and approval phases of anticipatory base standards are high cost phases. Unlike anticipatory syntax standards, there are no registration costs, but instead there are product testing costs that will be high as product developers work to implement the standard specification. These costs are high because to date vendors have found anticipatory standards to be critically ambiguous, thus increasing development time and cost. Note that base standards typically do not require registration, and that derivative standards are typically base standards in their own right (such as the relationship between 10Base5, 10Base2, and 10BaseT Ethernet), so these are labeled as not applicable (N/A) in the table.

Traditional Base As with traditional syntax standards, traditional base standards have lower analysis, development, and approval costs, in general, than their anticipatory counterparts, largely because their definition occurs after compatible products enter the marketplace. One example of this is the development of a standard page description language in the face of three significant market standards—HPGL, PostScript, and Interpress. Also due to the marketplace presence, these standards may be subject to lower product testing costs because the testing may be an informal interoperability assessment rather than a formal conformance test.

Implementation The overall costs for these standards are low, because they are implementations or derivatives of other types of standards. Since implementation standards are based on another standard, there is minimal analysis required and development is rather straight forward. Derivative standards may have low or high maintenance costs. On the one hand, derivative standards may simply replace them. On the other hand, implementation standards may involve obtaining agreement from a large user community. Thus, maintenance of Milstd 28001 (CALS) or Z39.59—both based on SGML, will be high because large numbers of users must be involved in the revision and respecification process. Consequently, the maintenance costs of the new standard should be low *or* high.

Analysis of Benefits

While any number of different dimensions might be selected as the basis for benefit analysis, we suggest that as with costs, benefits differ based on three factors. As with costs, benefits differ based on the type of standard and the scope of the standard. Rather that assigning benefits by development phase, however, benefits are best analyzed by examining the groups to which the benefits accrue.

Three groups benefit from the development of a standard: the developers, the SDOs, and the users. Each of these groups may be further subdivided as shown below.

1. Developers
   (a) Active developers
   (b) Type 1 free riders
   (c) Type 2 free riders
2. Standards Development Organizations
   (a) Sponsoring SDO
   (b) Liaison SDO

3. Users
   (a) Producer users
   (b) Consumer users
   (c) Nation states

While it is theoretically straightforward, even if practically difficult,[8] to attribute monetary costs for standards developers, it is more difficult to evaluate benefits. For developers, net revenues (revenues beyond the cost of developing the standard and developing, producing, and certifying the subsequent product) may be a reasonable metric of benefits.[9] For SDOs, gross revenues may be a better metric.[10] For users, at the level of the nation state, the *existence* of a standard may meet some social goal, and benefits may not be directly measurable in monetary terms.

Developers

Developers have three major avenues for recovering their investment in the standards development process:

1. Profits from products based on the standard
2. Consulting with other companies based on the expertise they developed in the development process
3. Royalties and licensing fees based on intellectual property owned by the developer that was incorporated into the standard.[11]

In addition, developers may receive an indirect benefit from the prestige and industry leadership associated with active standards participation. There may also be some strategic benefits to actively participating even if the developer does not intend to manufacture and produce products conforming to the standard [31].

From a marketing standpoint, active developers must be able to recover their investment in the standard by being an early entrant to the market for compatible products, by building subcomponents (such as integrated circuits) that other product developers would likely use,[12] or through other means. If the standard is delayed sufficiently to void their product leadership capability, it will be difficult for a firm to justify continued participation in the standards process, as it will be a money losing operation.

☞

Table 4 Revenues from Sales for Selected SDOs (Source: US Congress, Office of Technology Assessment [29])

Organization	% Revenues
American National Standards Institute	28
American Society for Testing and Materials	80
National Fire Protection Association	66

Standards Development Organizations

The OTA [29] has shown that many SDOs seek to recover the costs of standards development through the sale of standards documents. In fact, this revenue has become a significant fraction of their overall operating budget in some cases (see Table 4). Other revenues for these organizations are typically derived from membership dues and other sources. Thus, the administrative portion of the standards development process is supported by all who purchase standards documents. The other major source of revenues comes from the membership dues of the participating companies. As the OTA pointed out, competition for revenues has led to hostilities within the standards development community [29].

Liaison SDOs also receive benefits from standards developed by other SDOs. They may benefit from not having to develop infrastructure standards, which may simply be referenced. More dramatically the development costs for other types of standards may be all but eliminated, particularly in the case of national standards adopted from the international arena or international standards based upon national standards. Adopting SDOs achieve all of the benefits of the sponsoring SDO with the caveat that their sales of the adopted standard will not be as high.

Users

Three categories of users are suggested: producer users, consumer users, and nation states. Producer users provide products or services that are related to the products or services directly based upon the standard. Developers of test suites are a prime example of this category. Another example might be a developer of database systems who uses an SQL compliant front end, produced by a developer, to make their database system more attractive to potential customers. Consumer users make use of products that in some way depend upon the standard. Thus corporations that build client server database systems with SQL front ends derive benefits from the standard nature of the database interface. Similarly, many users derive significant benefits in terms of product cost and system design flexibility from reliance on products that use Postscript as the interchange standard between software and display devices. These consumer users may be small or large groups. They may be vertically integrated corporations or groups of corporations engaged in an enterprise; the largest single group is often the United States government.

The last category of user is the most difficult to define. By referring to it as the nation state we intend to suggest that it is the collection of individuals who benefit from a standard even if they don't make use of it, even indirectly. As a user, the government can play an important role in supporting the emergence of a "bandwagon" around potentially strategic or important technologies [2]. It can be argued that the United States government played this role with internetworking technologies by supporting the ARPANET (and later the Internet) or by supporting other technologies such as commercial aircraft manufacturing. While the active picking of "winners" and "losers" is often decried as industrial policy, the United States has a tradition of doing this, albeit often for defense reasons.[13] Other countries are more open about their support for emerging standards and technologies.

Assignment of Benefits

As with costs, for each kind of standard, the benefits that accrue to different categories vary. Areas of high benefit will require careful examination and elaboration. As shown in Table 5, benefits can be expected to be different for each group depending upon the type of standard. For limited scope standards, the benefits accrue almost exclusively to the developers. For standards that have significant scope in terms of impact, community, or period, significant benefits will accrue to other groups. As with Table 3, the benefits summarized in Table 5 are hypotheses based on informal observation and anecdotal data from the standards development process that must be rigorously tested. The arguments for these hypotheses are stated below:

Reference   The benefit of reference standards is indirect at best for developers of all types. There is perhaps a modest benefit for active developers because reference standards can sometimes reduce the cost of developing base and syntax standards in the area, since they provide a consistent framework for standards development. Most of the benefits of reference standards, though, apply to SDOs that make use of them, and to nation states because they simplify and therefore reduce the overall cost of standards development.

Anticipatory Syntax   The benefits of anticipatory syntax standards are high, with developers in all categories receiving the benefit of shared committee research and development. Type 1 free riders may be expected to miss the benefit of the advance intelligence on issues related to product development. Sponsoring SDOs can expect higher circulation of the standards document if it is the sole or main source of information. While there will be some benefits in guiding the development of implementation standards through liaison SDOs, these are accounted for under the implementation/ derivative standards. As with reference models, syntax standards guide the development of other standards, thus reducing the overall costs for nation states.

Traditional Syntax   For developers, the benefits of traditional syntax standards are less than those of anticipatory. Rather than spawning new products, the standards likely will require changes to existing products, thus reducing benefits. The benefits to SDOs and users are generally the same as for anticipatory syntax standards with the exception of producer users who, like developers, are likely to see fewer benefits since the traditional syntax standard is likely to imply a change to existing products rather than the production of a new product.

Anticipatory Base   The net benefit of these standards varies based on the type of participation. Because of the impact of reduced R&D costs for the anticipatory standard, active developers and Type 2 free riders will benefit the most. The need to come up to speed on the technical issues and problems will likely reduce the benefits for Type 1 free riders. Sponsoring and adopting SDOs benefit because they sell many standards documents, hence improving their revenue stream. Users of all kinds benefit because a costly standards rivalry is avoided—costly in the sense that users would have risked being orphaned by adopting a standard that later turned out to be non-dominant or unsuccessful. However, producers will generally have benefits constrained because competition in the market place will increase based on the standardized products.

Traditional Base   The net benefits of traditional base standards depend heavily on whether one's preferred technology was successful. If it was, then the net benefit is very high; if not, the net benefit is low. For both Type 1 and Type 2 free riders, the net benefit is high because the development cost is relatively low. SDOs, however, have a lower benefit because the specification may already be relatively well known in the market, so that document sales may be off.

Implementation   Because implementation or derivative standards are based on other existing standards, the benefits accruing to Type 1 free riders will be high in that they may simply implement the standard, which is less likely to require significant re-engineering to understand. The developer's benefit, though, is less in light of the cost of development. Since the impact of the standard is very limited, it is of negligible benefit to liaison SDOs. Adopting SDOs may see significant benefit if the standard provides sales with no cost. (It is likely that an international SDO adopting a national standard will benefit more than a national SDO adopting an international standard unless there is a compelling reason to buy the version of the standard produced by the national SDO.) Again, because the scope of the standard is limited, the social benefits are likely to be negligible. Because implementation standards are generally more focused on user-related issues, the benefits to consumers are higher.

Approaches to Financing the Standards Process

The framework discussed above can be used to assess the funding of the standards development process. By carefully examining the

Table 5 Benefit Breakdown by Type of Standard

| | Reference | Syntax | | Base | | Implementation |
		Anticip.	Trad.	Anticip.	Trad.	
Developers						
active	med.	high	med.	high	med. or high	med.
T2 free riders	low	high	med.	high	med. or high	med.
T1 free riders	med.	med.	low	med.	low or high	high
SDOs						
sponsoring	med.	high	med.	high	med.	high
liaison	high	low	low	low	low	NA
adopting	high	NA	NA	high	high	low or med.
Users						
producer	NA	med.	low	med.	low or med.	NA
consumer	NA	med.	med.	high	high	high
nation state	high	high	high	low	low	low

costs incurred by each participant in each phase of the standards development process for different types of standards, and by comparing these to the benefits achieved by groups for each type of standard, we can assess how each group fares for each type of standard. This provides clues as to which phases of which types of standards are suitable for different standards funding methodologies. This analysis also allows for prediction of which standards with significant social benefits might be under-provided under the current funding scheme.

Table 6 is an initial attempt at constructing such a matrix. This table was constructed using information from the previous tables; note that the cost data is a result of mapping the costs of the phases defined in Table 3 onto the user communities of Table 5, using Table 2 as a guideline. As outlined in Table 2, active developers incur relatively high costs for all of their activities, Type 2 free riders incur "medium" costs, and Type 1 free riders incur low costs. Similarly, it seems reasonable to assume that sponsoring SDOs incur high cost in general (except with implementation stan-

Table 6 Cost and Benefit Analysis by Type of Standard[a]

	Reference	Syntax		Base		Implementation
		Anticip.	Trad.	Anticip.	Trad.	
Developers						
active	h/m	h/h	h/m	h/h	h/m–h	h/m
T2 free riders	m/l	m/h	m/m	m/h	m/m–h	m/m
T1 free riders	NA/m	l/m	l/l	NA/m	l/l–h	l/h
SDOs						
sponsoring	h/m	h/h	l/m	h/h	l–h/m	l/h
liaison	l/h	l/l	l/l	l/l	l/l	l/NA
adopting	l/h	NA/NA	NA/NA	l/h	l/h	l/l–m
Users						
producer	NA/NA	l/m	l/l	l/m	l/l–m	NA/NA
consumer	NA/NA	l/m	l/m	l/h	l/h	l/h
nation state	h/h	h/h	h/h	h/l	h/l	h/l

[a] In each entry the level of cost precedes the slash and the level of benefit follows. NA = not applicable.

dards), with liaison SDOs incurring medium costs (because they attend the sponsoring SDO's meetings), and adopting SDOs low costs, since they simply adopt the work of another SDO. Generally speaking, users incur low costs because they generally do not attend the standards meetings. Producer users are more likely to incur higher costs than consumer users, because the economic consequences of the standard are higher, so they are more likely to attend the committee meetings. Assigning costs for the nation state is quite difficult. To do this properly requires some concept of national investment in a standard, efficiency losses for not having a standard, and the actual direct expenditures of government. This is quite difficult to assess accurately, but is most likely to be high across the board.

It is also important to briefly discuss what is labeled as "benefits" in Table 6. The benefits presented in Table 5 were net benefits, that is, benefits beyond costs. Thus, in a sense, costs are considered twice. The other factor that must be considered is the "specificity" of the benefits. That is, are the benefits of the standard easily identifiable to developers (specific) or are they less realizable in particular products (diffuse)? An example of a diffuse benefit would be the benefits attributable to a reference model. Firms that contributed to the development of the OSI reference model could not ship products containing the reference model. Benefits would exist, however, because the *structure* of different vendors' data communications systems would be similar, allowing for easier interoperation. Furthermore, if a developer of the reference model intended to develop subsequent base or syntax standards consistent with the reference model, presumably this development would be expedited because a framework for the base standards would exist. Hence, diffuse benefits do not imply absence of benefits; diffuse benefits merely imply difficulty in *measuring* benefits, which can reduce the *apparent* benefit.

To identify areas that might be fruitful for alternative funding approaches, it is appropriate to examine those where the development costs are high but the net benefits are low to medium. Examining Table 6, it is clear that reference standards fit that category, as do traditional syntax standards, traditional base standards, and implementation standards. It is also clear that sponsoring SDOs must be provided some form of compensation for the development of high-benefit standards. These standards are likely candidates for adoption by other SDOs; while this is a good thing from the standpoint of public policy, it is something that must be addressed on the compensation side to ensure the continual development of high benefit standards.

Before policy decisions are made, it is necessary to validate the authors' assessment of the relative magnitudes of costs and benefits for various types of standards. This framework may be used to collect data on a large enough sample of standards that predictions of actual costs and benefits can be made with a degree of confidence. Because of the distributed private nature of the funding, it is difficult to quantify the costs—no one wishes to be the first to acknowledge the cost.[14] A thorough analysis of the costs and benefits will, we believe, lead to a less charged and more productive discussion of alternative structures and funding for standards setting in the United States in a era of rapid change in a global economy. We can then begin to consider experiments that will allow us to compare actual standards provision behavior with hypothesized under-provision of standards. If we are able to show that some standards are under-provided, then we can consider alternatives for financing these socially desirable standards. Below, we examine the current approach to funding standardization and suggest two possible modifications, one based on a "standards fee" and the other based on government funding.

An Analysis of the Present Approach to Standardization

Under the current system (in the United States), the costs are borne privately, but not necessarily in proportion to the benefits. It is possible for firms to free ride and still have access to the public good.[15] Nonetheless the current system attempts to recover administrative costs through profits on the sale of standards documents. Anyone who purchases the document subsidizes the system, even though those who incur the bulk of the cost—the developers—are not reimbursed directly for their investment except through the sale of products, licensing fees, and consulting fees, as described above.

The major advantage of this approach to financing standards is that those who stand to gain the most from a standard have the strongest incentive to contribute at the highest level. Thus, the system naturally allocates the development costs among the potential beneficiaries. In terms of the model proposed above, the weaknesses of the current system include:

1. If no firm anticipates a significant benefit, then the standard will not be developed, despite the social benefit of having the standard. This is particularly problematic for standards or standards-related activities where the benefit is less tangible, such as reference standards, long range planning, and executive functions.

2. The firms act on *expected* benefits. If their expectations are wrong because of delays in implementation of the standard (as with ISDN), because of free riders, or for other reasons, then the firm may be less willing to invest in standards development in the future.

3. Due to network and public good effects, the benefits of the standard may be distributed disproportionately to the costs incurred to develop it. This results in a net welfare loss to society if the standard is not developed.

4. Recovering the cost of standards development via document sales leads to competition among SDOs instead of coordination [29]. As the cost of the standards documents increase, the dissemination of the standard decreases. Thus, it is not clear that the benefits of standards are completely realized.[16]

5. There is no central authority for coordinating the efforts of the various SDOs. While the Information Systems Standards Board of ANSI makes an effort to avoid and resolve disputes between various SDOs, this does not coordinate strategic planning for the SDOs, nor does it serve to coordinate submissions to the SDOs. Thus, planning and requirements analysis are carried out in a vacuum.

6. The conformance test development, certification, and registry functions are not directly accounted for in the model. While an SDO produces the standard, other organizations are responsible for developing test suites. For example, in the case of POSIX, while the base standard is developed by the IEEE, conformance tests have been developed by National Institute for Standards and Technology and X/OPEN. The situation is complicated further by the fact that certification of conformance in accord with the suites may be by the developer under self certification, or by yet another party— an accredited certification agency such as Corporation for Open Systems. In a simple world, such an arrangement might be workable. In the real world, the development of conformance test suites may uncover errors in the standard, and the certification process may mandate changes to both the standard and the conformance tests. All of this requires cross-organizational communication under the current model and greatly increases the total cost (see Cashin [7]).

7. Perhaps more disturbing from a national point of view, dissemination of standards is driven by market demand. There is no coordinated effort to "sell" a given approach. This is particularly important for anticipatory standards, which are at heart marketing devices. This attitude is changing, and one sees encouraging developments in the telecommunications field (see Matute [21]). At the same time, important standards in the IT arena continue to languish in part for lack of marketing effort. SGML serves as one example in this area (for a discussion of SGML's development and adoption, see Adler [1]).

These shortcomings may be overcome in part by establishing additional mechanisms for funding standards. By imposing a "standards fee" or tax, those using products that rely on the standard would finance its development. In some ways, this approach attempts to recoup the cost of intellectual property embodied in the standards. While this may be conceptually sensible, significant distributional problems exist. A more extreme approach recognizes that standards are a public good, and would use public funds collected through general taxation to pay for the process, as is done in some countries. This approach relies on the taxation system for fairness and appropriate cost allocation.

In the standards fee approach, each product conforming to a standard would be subject to a surcharge to assist in the recovery of the cost of developing the standard(s) on which it is based. The fee would be collected and distributed to all developers of the standard until the costs that they incurred in developing the standard were covered. Thus, standards development is funded directly by users, as it is today, except that free riders' products would not be exempt from the cost of developing the standard. Thus, the cost differential of developers' and free riders' products would be based solely on the underlying production costs and not on the existence or absence of standards development costs. While this addresses the issue of the free ridership, it would require the development of guidelines to insure that fees are distributed in an equitable fashion. Further, policy would be required to balance and distribute the fees from widely adopted, profitable standards among those that are less profitable.

 One can also make a case for direct government financing. Garcia [13, 14] has studied the role of government in standards at some length. In [13], she argued that the current standards process had its roots in the early 1900s, and reflects the market realities of that time, as well as the pluralistic tradition of the United States In [14], she argued for the rationality of a stronger government role in U.S. standards setting given the present market realities. In particular, she pointed out that:

- It is well known that all economic transactions have *transaction costs* associated with them [37]. Standards can reduce transaction costs, so government involvement to ensure an adequate supply of standards (that is, to ensure that they are not under-provided by our current market-based approach) results in increased economic efficiency, which generally meets economic and social goals.

- The lack of an active, coordinated standards development strategy could be a disadvantage vis-à-vis our competitors who have such a strategy. By failing to set the standards-setting agenda, we can be at a disadvantage in global markets, which reduces our overall competitiveness as a nation.

- The failure to support standards development processes in emerging economies, such as Mexico, India, and China, even as our most significant trading partners are doing so, leaves the United States at a significant future disadvantage in potentially important markets.

None of this addresses the role of government as a *financier* of the standards process. Garcia tends to argue that government should take a more active role in coordinating the activities of various organizations, and perhaps in setting the agenda for them, but stops short of proposing and analyzing a government-funded standards development process. What effect would government financing of the standards process have? How would it be carried out? These are but a few of the questions that emerge as such a proposal is considered.

In this approach, standards are viewed as a public good, and broadly based government revenues are used to reimburse the developers of standards. This can be done either through direct payments or through tax credits. While this is the standard approach to financing public goods, it is potentially distortive because it is not sector specific. That is, everyone's taxes contribute to finance standards even if someone never makes use of a standard, either directly or indirectly. The difficulties that were raised in the previous section apply as well.

This is the approach, indirectly, taken by ETSI. In ETSI, *paid* standards developers are used to accelerate the development of a standard (as was noted above). The money for this expense comes from member countries, hence from a general tax levied on the citizens for the standards development process. Thus, this approach is not without precedent.

Summary

We have presented a preliminary framework for considering standards financing. Clearly much work must still be done in this area, particularly to establish an empirical basis for the conclusions. Nonetheless, it seems that some alternative financing mechanism must be found for some types of standards, lest they be underprovided. We have proposed two alternative financing mechanisms as a basis for the continuing discussion in this area. While the details must still be worked out for both of the alternatives, we believe that they would solve the under-provision problem, even though they might raise other problems.

Notes

[1] The authors welcome comments. They may be reached via the internet (spring@pitt.edu and mbw@pitt.edu) or at the Department of Information Science and the Telecommunications Program at the University of Pittsburgh, Pittsburgh, PA 15260.

[2] Garcia points out that the early predecessor to the National Institutes of Standards and Technology (NIST) was financially and politically crippled in the face of active lobbying and concern over government meddling in this "commercial" activity.

[3] ISO 8824-ASN.1 would be another example of a syntax standard.

[4] T1 defines a base standard as "a minimum set of requirements for interworking and interoperability that provides an opportunity for individual manufacturers and service providers to innovate in providing price, performance and additional features to attract and satisfy users." [23]

[5] For example, since ISO8879—Standards Generalized Markup Language (SGML) assumes the development of shared Document Type Definitions (DTDs), it was necessary to specify Registration Procedures for Public Text Owner Identifiers—ISO 9070 to allow for the registry and availability of DTDs, which are in essence derivative standards or conventions.

[6] "Free Riders" are firms that benefit from standards but do not contribute to their development; hence they get a "free ride" from the developers of the standard. To be a free rider, a firm sells compatible products after the standard is developed. Type 1 free riders are firms that wait until the standard is complete before developing compatible products. Thus, they make *no* investment in the development of the standard. Type 2 free riders attend standards committee meetings, thereby incurring costs, and gain advance information on the standard. Observers are firms or individuals who have an interest in the development process of a particular standard but who have no intention of developing

products that conform to the standard. Finally, interested parties are all others who attend meetings.

[7] Actually, the implementation conforms to those implementations of the standard. If an implementation of the standard is different from the standard but dominates the market, a *de facto* implementation of the standard could well emerge that may not conform to the actual standard.

[8] Studies by Weiss, Bonino, Toyofuku, have encountered tremendous difficulties in quantifying the costs associated with participation in the standardization process.

[9] Gross revenues may be inappropriate because it is difficult to consider revenues that do not meet or exceed a product's total development costs a benefit.

[10] SDOs are frequently not-for-profit corporations, so gross revenues may be more appropriate. Shortfalls in gross revenues with respect to costs may be made up via other sources, such as membership dues, as long as the goals of the membership are satisfied.

[11] This has been an area of some controversy. Firms are required to come up with fair and non-discriminatory terms for all intellectual property that they contributed to the committee. The European Telecommunications Standards Institute (ETSI) has developed a policy that *prohibits* firms from collecting any such royalties. This has been a bone of contention between the European Community and the United States.

[12] Weiss and Toyofuku [36] found that semiconductor manufacturers, as opposed to developers of end products, were among the most active participants in the development of the IEEE 10BaseT standard.

[13] In the early days of telegraphy and railroads, the government actively supported the efforts of these new companies by granting them special privileges. The Post Roads Act (1866) gave Western Union the permission to use public rights of way and they could fell trees for poles at no charge [16].

[14] One way to view consortia is as an effort to exclude from the benefits of standardization those who are not willing to pay the costs. Thus, the high cost of consortia membership may be viewed as a cheaper alternative than the cost of participating in the traditional SDO process.

[15] For example, a firm could refuse to pay membership fees to the SDOs and still participate in the process. SDOs are afraid of limiting participation because of the antitrust liabilities raised in the Hydrolevel vs. ASME case.

[16] A common argument in the Internet community today is that the success of IETF standards is at least in part attributable to the low cost of obtaining these standards.

References

[1] Sharon Adler. The birth of a standard. *Journal of the American Society for Information Science* 43(8), September 1992.

[2] Samuel Anderson and Jinhong Xie. An innovation rate model for markets affected by network externalities. In *19th Annual Telecommunications Policy Research Conference*, Solomons MD, September 1991.

[3] Phyllis Bernt and Martin B. H. Weiss. *International Telecommunications*. Indianapolis IN: Howard Sams, 1993.

[4] Michal Bonino and Michael B. Spring. Standards as change agents in the information technology market. Computer Standards and *Interfaces* 12:97–107, 1991.

[5] Michal J. Bonino. An exploration of anticipatory information technology standards. Master's thesis, University of Pittsburgh, Department of Information Science, Pittsburgh PA, 1991.

[6] Carl F. Cargill. *Information Technology Standardization: Theory, Process, and Organizations*. Bedford, MA: Digital Press, 1989.

[7] Jerry Cashin. Bloom fading from POSIX rose as open focus shifts. *Software Magazine*, pp. 87–97, March 1994.

[8] Rhonda J. Crane. Th*e Politics of International Standards*. Ablex, 1979.

[9] Paul A. David. Clio and the economics of qwerty. *American Economic Review* 75(2):332–337, May 1985.

[10] Paul A. David. Some new standards for the economics of standardization in the information age. In Partha Dasgupta and P. L. Stoneman, editors, *Economic Policy and Technological Performance* (Cambridge: Cambridge University Press, 1987).

[11] Paul A. David and Shane M. Greenstein. The economics of compatibility standards: An introduction to recent research. Economics *of Innovation and New Technology* 1(1):3–42, 1990.

[12] Neil Gandal. Hedonic price indices for spreadsheets and empirical test of the network externalities hypothesis. *RAND Journal of Economics* Forthcoming 1994.

[13] D. Linda Garcia. Standards setting in the United States: Public and private sector roles. *Journal of the American Society for Information Science* 43(8), September 1992.

[14] D. Linda Garcia. A new role for government in standards setting? *ACM StandardView* 1(2), December 1993.

[15] Shane M. Greenstein. Invisible hands and visible advisors: An economic interpretation of standardization. *Journal of the American Society for Information Science* 43(8), September 1992.

[16] Robert Britt Horwitz. *The Irony of Regulatory Reform*. New York: Oxford University Press, 1989.

[17] Theodor Irmer. Shaping future telecommunications: The challenge of global standardization. IEEE Communications M*agazine* 32(1):20–29, January 1994.

[18] William Lehr. Standardization: Understanding the process. *Journal of the American Society for Information Science* 43(8), September 1992.

[19] Richard J. Linn, Jr. Conformance evaluation methodology and protocol testing. *IEEE Journal on Selected Areas in Communications* 7(7):1143–1158, September 1989.

[20] Richard J. Linn, Jr. Conformance testing for OSI protocols. *Computer Networks and ISDN Systems* 18:203–219, 1990.

[21] Miguel Angel Matute. CITEL: Formulating telecommunications in the Americas. *IEEE Communications Magazine* 32(1):38–39, January 1994.

[22] Stephen P. Oksala. Remarks on "Sectoral Case Study: Information Technology and Telecommunications." Presented at the National Research Council Conference on International Standards and Global Trade, March 30, 1994.

[23] Arthur K. Reilly. A U.S. perspective on standards. *IEEE Communications Magazine* 32(1):30–36, January 1994.

[24] Gerard Robin. The European perspective for telecommunications standards. *IEEE Communications Magazine* 32(1):40–45, January 1994.

[25] Mark Shurmer. An investigation into sources of network externalities in the packaged PC software market. *Information Economics and Policy* 5(3), 1993.

[26] Michael B. Spring. Models, musings, and managers. Report to the X3 Strategic Planning Committee, April 1991.

[27] Michael B. Spring and Toni Carbo Bearman. Information standards: Models for future development. *Book Research Quarterly* 4(3):38–47, 1988.

[28] Accredited Standards Committee X3. Master Plan (Strategic). X3/SDC-C, 1993.

[29] US Congress, Office of Technology Assessment. *Global Standards: Building Blocks for the Future.* US Government Printing Office, Washington DC, March 1992. TCT-512.

[30] Martin B. H. Weiss. Communications standards. In Fritz E. Froehlich and Allen Kent, editors, *The Froehlich/Kent Encyclopedia of Telecommunications*, volume 4, pages 59–91. Marcel Dekker Inc., New York, 1991.

[31] Martin B. H. Weiss. Compatibility standards and product development strategy: A review of data modem developments. *Computer Standards and Interfaces* 12:109–122, 1991.

[32] Martin B. H. Weiss and Carl Cargill. Consortia in the standards development process. *Journal of the American Society for Information Science* 43(8), September 1992.

[33] Martin B. H. Weiss and Marvin Sirbu. Technological choice in voluntary standards committees: An empirical analysis. *Economics of Innovation and New Technology* 1(1):111–134, 1990.

[34] Martin B. H. Weiss and Michael B. Spring. Selected intellectual property issues in the standards development process. In *20th Annual Telecommunications*

Policy Research Conference, Solomons MD, September 1992.

[35] Martin B. H. Weiss and Michael B. Spring. Selected intellectual property issues in the standards development process. *Computer Standards and Interfaces* 1994. Forthcoming.

[36] Martin B. H. Weiss and Ronald T. Toyofuku. Free ridership in the standards-setting process: The case of 10BaseT. Technical report, University of Pittsburgh, Pittsburgh PA 15260, July 6, 1993. Draft.

[37] Oliver E. Williamson. *Markets and Hierarchies: Analysis and Antitrust Implications.* Free Press, 1975.

Consortia and the Role of the Government
in Standard Setting

Andrew Updegrove

So many industry associations were formed in 1988 that a number of commentators dubbed it "The Year of the Consortium." Few of these organizations were intended to develop true *de jure* standards. Instead, they were most often formed as a species of marketing partnership in response to intense competition among the largest computer companies, each jockeying to dominate (or at least maintain their position) in volatile market segments such as Unix platform sales. Despite such overtly commercial purposes, these organizations frequently found that the development of *de facto* standards and specifications provided a crucial method for achieving their ends.

Less noticeably, a far greater number of consortia have been formed over the last ten years that have had a less public but more pervasive impact on the computer, information, and communications industries. These consortia have often been formed specifically to create a single standard of common need throughout the industry. Although proprietary interests may at times influence the operations of such consortia, these interests manifest themselves as often as not as skirmishes regarding small components of the central standard, rather than concerted efforts to drive the standard itself to overtly favor a single company or concentration of companies.

Remaining prominent on the standards landscape are the well-known *de jure* standard-setting bodies, such as the American National Standards Institute (ANSI) and the Institute of Electrical and

Electronic Engineers (IEEE), whose mission it continues to be to set standards through well-evolved, representative processes relating to a larger standards set of goals.

The types of consortia and standard-setting bodies just described, and others discussed at length below, form a loosely coordinated, available, and existing "national standards infrastructure," which operates in an interlinked but independent fashion, and is both a product of and responsive to broad vendor and customer forces. Unlike the state-operated standards systems which exist in many other countries, the standard-setting process in the United States is both organic and dynamic, and is based on an evolutionary process that reaches back to pre-Civil War times.

Building the national information infrastructure (NII) will require the development of many new standards and interfaces, the adaptation of old standards and specifications, and the coordination of many standard-setting organizations. It is not feasible, and, this writer believes, not desirable, to seek to preempt or radically reform the existing method of standard setting in the course of facilitating the development of the NII. While such intervention in the past has quite appropriately led to the evolution of regulatory bodies and regulations in other areas, it is preferable in the current context for government to seek to understand, support, and—to use a computer industry term—"optimize" the existing technology standard-setting infrastructure through judicious participation and stimulation. This conclusion derives from several factors:

• First, time is short, and cooperation is needed across a vast array of industries, interests and individuals. The existing standards infrastructure has grown up in response to these realities, and is responsive to the needs and demands of various commercial constituencies.

• Second, aggressively redirecting the market forces that have created this infrastructure would not be likely to succeed if the effort was not supported by the vendors affected (in this case, a daunting percentage of the commercial base of the entire country).

• Third, the breadth of standards (new and existing) necessary to "stitch" the information superhighway together would be excessively difficult to bring under the developmental (as compared to the coordinating) control of a single standard-setting body.

• Fourth, because the budgets of the vast majority of standard-setting consortia are small (typically $25,000 to $3,000,000), the existing process of standards development is highly cost-effective. Very small infusions of funding (by government standards) could have a profound impact in this area, and in most cases no government funding would be required at all.

• Finally, standards have often evolved from the vision of a small group of companies, acting before large vendors have produced products that those vendors then seek to form standards around to their individual proprietary advantage. To overly institutionalize the standard-setting process in order to facilitate the formation of the NII might well stifle valuable standards initiatives and related technology development, and might permit the most powerful companies to exercise greater influence in the process.

For all of these reasons, it is the view of the author that the appropriate activities of government in the standard setting area over the coming years are:

• Most importantly, assisting in coordinating the operations of standard-setting bodies to ensure that a cohesive, coordinated, and timely set of standards are developed to accomplish the task at hand.

• Participating directly in standard-setting consortia as a member, through appropriate agencies.

• Taking action to seek the direct or indirect participation of appropriate non-commercial interests (e.g., educational institutions) that may not otherwise be represented in the standard-setting activities of some consortia.

• Where appropriate, commissioning (through the traditional Request for Technology and similar processes) the development of standards or components of standards, with the task being awarded to the most appropriate responding consortium.

• Where necessary, supporting the establishment of new consortia to create component standards necessary to complete the NII.

In undertaking these activities, government can effectively further national goals such as internationally promoting the U.S. industrial and services base, representing the rights and interests of those elements of society that lack an effective voice in commercial decisions, and, not least, promoting the interests of government itself as the nation's largest single purchaser of technology and services.

The purpose of this paper is to assist in understanding the types, motives, efficacy, and methods of the various types of consortia that may become involved (either by invitation or market force) in the development of the NII, and, in so doing, to provide insight to government useful in choosing appropriate partners for the task ahead. Similarly, this paper will seek to identify the factors necessary to take into account in forming new consortia necessary to complete the task of creating the NII.

With a better understanding of the dynamics that influence how standards evolve within different types of consortia and the factors essential to forming effective consortia, government will be better able to decide when to lead (perhaps by commissioning development by a given consortia of a standard, or by providing seed funding for the formation of a new consortium), when to follow (perhaps by causing one or more agencies to become members and financial supporters of a given consortium), and when to get out of the way (by recognizing that an existing consortium is an appropriate vehicle for supplying a necessary technology, and refraining from sponsoring a competing standard).

Standards and "Standards": What's in a Name?

Although the word "standards" is much bandied about in a way that would seem to indicate common agreement on its meaning, in fact there is considerable divergence of opinion on what measure of respect is to be accorded to any given standard. Some would draw distinctions based on the source of the standard, reserving the highest level of respect to "de jure" standards promulgated by organizations such as ANSI, and relegating standards maintained by industry associations to the lesser status of "*de facto*" standards. While some purists would not call consortia-developed specifications true "standards" at all, the impact of such *de facto* standards has often been as strong or stronger than *de jure* standards, and the role of market power-based *de facto* standards (such as DOS and Windows) can be most powerful of all.

Further complicating the issue is the fact that one kind of standard will often be dependent on, or incorporate, another. For example, *de facto* standards often incorporate *de jure* standards (e.g., the X Window System incorporates certain IEEE standards), and in some cases *de jure* standards bodies accept *de facto* standards or link to them, such as Object Management Group's widely recognized Common Object Request Broker (CORBA) specification. Finally, organizations like X/Open seek to develop environments that use a mix of *de jure* and widely supported *de facto* standards.

As a result, the role of *de facto* standard-setting consortia is relevant and important to true *de jure* standard-setting organizations such as ANSI and IEEE. On the one hand, as a practical matter, a *de jure* organization may opt not to develop a competing standard if it is satisfied that the *de facto* organization is providing a useful standard. As a result, a *de facto* standard-setting organization is effectively permitted to control an important area of technology. On the other hand, the endorsement or incorporation by *de facto* bodies of *de jure* standards augments the effectiveness of the latter standards.

For these reasons, a high level of sensitivity should accompany increased government involvement in what has become a complex and largely successful interlocking web of organizations, standards, and environments. At the same time, government needs to thoroughly understand the degree of proprietary influence that may exist within a given consortium and that may affect its standard-setting activities.

Developing a Taxonomy of Consortia

Consortia are to a degree merely new wine in old bottles. Trade associations have been formed for many years to promote the interests of their members; in the building trades, for example, this promotion has often involved influencing the development and promotion of building standards for local adoption, thereby benefiting the membership. However, these associations also have frequently engaged in lobbying and other activities primarily intended to protect the membership's business and market their collective wares. In the era of high technology, this traditional role has not been entirely abandoned. For example, the X Industry Association (XIA) was formed to promote the X Window System technology, simultaneously with and independently from the spinning out from MIT of a new organization, the X Consortium, which was created to continue the development of the standard itself outside of MIT. Today, XIA (and its marketing budget) is being merged into the X Consortium, as concerns mount over the avowed intention of Microsoft to supplant the Unix operating system with Windows NT.

Of greater interest than traditional trade associations are the following new types of consortia, many of which have had the development of standards or the development of new technology as their primary focus, albeit for varying strategic purposes.

Research Consortia

A number of high-profile consortia (such as SemaTech and MCC) have been formed largely as a result of heightened national pro-competitive concerns. Some have succeeded, some have failed to coalesce, and some have wandered from their original purposes as they have sought to sustain themselves. In some cases the concerns (e.g., national paranoia over loss of dominance in DRAM chip production) that helped launch the enterprises have already abated to a degree, and smaller groupings of companies (sometimes including Japanese or European partners) have since entered into joint ventures to produce specific products without the high-profile, highly political trappings of their predecessors.

Although there may prove to be instances where government should play a role in forming additional high-budget, special-purpose consortia that would develop actual technology in addition, or incident to, creating standards, it is worth noting that by far the greatest number of standards have come from more modest cooperative sources. As the focus of the current discussion is standards and not technology development per se, research consortia are not analyzed in detail in this paper.

Specification Groups

Existing groups such as the VXIbus Consortium (VXI) and the MIDI Manufacturers Association (MMA), and numerous new consortia currently being formed such as the Distributed-Computer Telephony Group and GO-MVIP, the Global Organization for Multi-Vendor Integration Protocol, are primarily concerned with assuring the development and maintenance of a usable, robust standard for the benefit of the industry generally. Essentially apolitical, they direct the greatest part of their efforts to evolving and supporting a standard, and have low budgets in consequence. Where they work best, they successfully avoid proprietary influences and pressures and implement the best technological methods to produce sensible, robust, practically implemented standards. While many such groups are formed and funded by vendors, some (such as the CAD Framework Initiative) are formed through the efforts of end-users, in order to lower acquisition costs of tools or other products that would otherwise too often be based on proprietary, non-interoperable technologies. Such groups are often formed to develop a standard to fill an important niche-industry technical gap that is not large enough to merit the attention of a recognized standard-setting body like IEEE, for example, MMA was formed to provide an essential interface standard so that the electronic music industry could develop in an accelerated and orderly fashion.

Among all types of consortia, these may be the most appropriate for the government to work with, or create, in the course of coordinating and setting NII standards. Due to the comparative absence of proprietary pressures, the work product of these consortia tends to be the most responsive to broad practical and economic needs, and most often represents a broad consensus of the industry (both direct participants and non-participants, such as end-users, alike). For similar reasons, the standards implemented by this type of consortium may often be better technically, since there is no reason to artificially select or support a given technology or architecture.

It is worth noting that these consortia tend to have not only the smallest budgets (as little as $15,000 a year), but one of the highest success rates in creating standards that are widely followed by the industry. Accordingly, they represent unusually cost-effective vehicles for standards development. However, budget sizes may constrain the activities of these organizations, and the infusion of very modest amounts of government funding in this area could have dramatic effects in both speeding and guiding the pace of standards development. By way of example, all operations of such consortia are typically volunteer in nature. Employer time demands, communication inefficiencies, and increasingly tight travel budgets all slow progress. Small amounts of funding could subsidize meeting expenses, document production, and interaction with other standards-setting bodies, thus accelerating progress.

Strategic Consortia

For purposes of this discussion, "strategic consortia" are deemed to be consortia initially formed and funded by a limited number of companies for their individual benefit in order to promote the adoption of certain technology (such as a chip architecture) as "open" technology. The primary mechanism of many such consortia for seeking to achieve this end has been the development and promotion of some type of standard, the efficacy (as compared to the marketing) of which has varied widely in practice.

Perhaps the greatest and most interesting flowering of consortia of this type has occurred in the Unix marketplace, relating not only to the operating system itself (Unix International and The Open Software Foundation, or OSF), but with respect to chip architectures (e.g., in the RISC chip market, 88open, the Advanced Computing Environment (ACE), SPARC International, PowerOpen, etc.) and software environments (the X Consortium) as well. These consortia commonly were formed with one or more of the following specific characteristics and objectives:

• They were usually formed by hardware vendors or chip manufacturers seeking market share, either by attempting to control (or avoid a competitor's controlling) the evolution of Unix or by seeking to foster rapid porting of massive amounts of software to a specific chip environment in order to foster the adoption of that chip by as many computer manufacturers as possible.

• They sought "hard" marketing objectives, such as avoiding the potential adoption of a proprietary standard controlled by a competitor. Prominent examples of such efforts include the overnight industry adoption of the MIT X Window System standard to parry the threatened spreading of Sun's NeWS technology, and the formation of the massively funded OSF to counter the perceived benefit which Sun Microsystems might reap from AT&T's ownership of Unix, following AT&T's purchase of a significant block of Sun stock (later sold). (The latter example demonstrates the parlous life cycle of a consortium: AT&T eventually conveyed Unix to Unix Systems Labs and formed another consortium, Unix International, to more publicly control and promote the operating system; most recently, USL was acquired by Novell, and OSF—with a budget in the tens of millions of dollars and license fee income popularly assumed to cover less than half that amount—is today down-sizing and contracting out development work as its long-term goals evolve).

• They sought "soft" marketing objectives, such as claiming (accurately or otherwise): the development of standards, the existence of large amounts of software embodying those standards, and the achievement of real interoperability and open systems status.

In some cases, consortia have had roots of one type and have grown branches of another: the X Consortium, as noted, was formally born in 1988 out of concern over a Sun Microsystems software product initiative. The technology itself had been under development within MIT since 1984, and the industry began adopting it as a standard in 1987. The organization and the standard then enjoyed over five years of comparatively ecumenical existence dedicated to the continued evolution of a usable standard. Today, this consortium has left its home at MIT to become an independent entity, and the imminent release of Windows NT gives new significance to this organization as a vehicle for collectively asserting and promoting the continued vitality of Unix and the X Window System standard. Recently, it has decided to merge with XIA, as mentioned above, and has entered into discussions with OSF to take over further development of two other crucial components of the Unix desktop: Motif, a graphical user interface, and CDE.

Similarly, Object Management Group (OMG) was initially founded to develop a family of standards to facilitate the adoption of object oriented programming methods and products. Today, the organization has broadened into a wide range of activities dedicated to nurturing and promoting the evolving OOP industry, including development of six major annual trade shows in five countries on four continents, development of training sessions and publishing ventures, and evolution of innovative joint marketing and electronic distribution projects. At the same time, OMG has been successful in becoming recognized as the preferred source of many types of specifications for the OOP industry, and therefore the focal point for industry efforts in this area.

A hallmark of the success of several consortia has been their good fortune (or good foresight) in being "ahead of the curve"; in OMG's case, by seeking to establish a standard before any significant company had obtained a vested interest in promoting its own proprietary technology for adoption as a standard. As a result, the industry could follow OMG's lead, and cooperate to achieve the best technical result for mutual, rather than individual, benefit.

The reverse, unfortunately, has also been true. 88open, the first RISC chip consortium, was brilliantly successful on the technical level, achieving the highest degree of true interoperability of any of the competing organizations. Nevertheless, its technical success was insufficient to overcome certain other handicaps, such as the fact that the chip technology upon which it was based was introduced too late into the marketplace to achieve the momentum of adoption from which it otherwise might have benefited. The new PowerOpen Consortium (styled in many ways on the earlier 88open Consortium) is virtually assured of avoiding this fate, since both IBM and Apple (among others) have already announced products based on the PowerPC series RISC chips being produced by Motorola, and the sales momentum that those companies represent should be more than sufficient to ensure speedy and efficient porting of significant amounts of software.

However, the success of a consortium tends to correlate strongly and inversely to the degree of proprietary advantage that its founders sought to gain. This results from a variety of factors: not only are there more losers than winners in industries dominated by a small number of large players, but the word "standard," stretched to the limit of anyone's most liberal commercial definition (e.g, VCR formats or PC operating systems), cannot usually accommodate more than one or two major instantiations on a long term basis. Again, many strategic consortia were formed as much for publicity as for actual technological purposes, or were announced before a clear plan of action had been evolved, or fell apart as the shifting strategic sands upon which they were based continued to move (e.g., the ACE Consortium, which suffered from other problems as well). Finally, strategic consortia are more likely to be formed by companies that perceive that they are already at a disadvantage, and the odds are therefore often against success from the beginning.

Conversely, the success of consortia correlates highly and directly to the absence of perceived proprietary advantage to any individual company (e.g., VXI, discussed above, or OMG, which was formed long before any significant number of object oriented products were available or even in the design phase) or, in some cases, with a very high degree of agreement among a critical mass of companies as to the existence of a common enemy (e.g., the wholesale and rapid adoption of the X Window System Standard in response to Sun).

Working with strategic consortia must necessarily involve more careful investigation on the part of government than supporting purely specification-oriented organizations. Important in this regard are the following:

• Does the government wish to influence the rough and tumble evolution of the technology marketplace in ways beyond simple standards creation? Where two (or more) competing camps are involved, the *de facto* endorsement of one architecture over another will necessarily have an influence on the fortunes of each camp, whether that was a government objective or not. While the Department of Justice (DOJ) on July 15, 1994 entered into a consent decree with Microsoft that seems to have shied away from seeking to reduce that company's market impact, it was within DOJ's power to do so. In fact, many Microsoft competitors were profoundly disappointed by DOJ's forebearance. It is not obvious that other agencies of government, not regulated by the rules of due process and procedure that govern DOJ and Federal Trade Commission (the two agencies charged with enforcing federal antitrust laws), should support or refuse to support standards or consortia with an eye toward affecting the market power of individual companies or groups of companies. While all standards are likely to impact some vendors disproportionately (both favorably and unfavorably), this result should be incidental rather than deliberate on the part of government.

• Similarly, some consortia promote standards and reap a large portion of their income through licensing and publishing revenues relating to those standards. They may also compete with other consortia or other product offerings. By endorsement of one consortium, another consortium may be placed at an economic as well as a technical disadvantage.

• By definition, strategic consortia have strategic goals. Even absent government concerns relating to incidentally favoring one group over another, government needs to be aware of and account for the motives of those who control consortia. Those motives will often impact the work and the results of these groups, and the resulting standards may be less fair, less efficacious, and less extensible than standards developed by less proprietary organizations.

• As noted above, consortia formed for strategic purposes may also be less successful, notwithstanding government participation, with attendant consequences for furthering government goals.

If government wishes to play a comparatively passive, rather than a heavy-handed role in working with consortia, it may therefore wish to evaluate at the outset, and weigh in the balance of its decisions, whether a given strategic consortium is wide-based in its support or has competitors in the marketplace, whether it is promoting or supports a technology which is succeeding or failing, and whether its management's and its members' goals are conducive to the national interest. It may be that adversely weighting proprietary purpose may be more desirable than imposing heavy layers of regulation on the activities of consortia that accept government funding. How such a comparatively *ad hoc* judgment would be formulated is admittedly not without its own problems, and may best be left to the judgment of the governing body of a "Consortium of Consortia," as discussed below.

Weighing Consortia as Government Partners

In weighing whether to support the activities of a given consortium, or to facilitate the formation of new consortia, government should also be mindful of the factors that lead a consortium to flourish or fail. For example, government will not wish to become involved with groups that are not operating with due regard for applicable antitrust law. In addition, any successful consortium must carefully address a number of structural issues in order to succeed and avoid adverse consequences. The approach to these issues will vary for a given organization depending on the goals, competitive position, and other unique features of the particular group of companies involved.

Funding Issues

Frequently, the first reality that the organizers of a consortium must confront is economic. Where goals are ambitious, such as mounting certification as well as standards development programs, funding needs can be extreme and can only be satisfied either by enrolling very large memberships (e.g., the X Consortium or OMG) or by requiring very large contributions from individual members (e.g., OSF and PowerOpen). Typically, large-budget consortia have been strategic consortia, with proprietary vendors (i.e., computer or chip manufacturers) contributing the lion's share of funding.

Substantial aid (and, where perceived to be necessary, substantial diminution of the influence of large companies, which usually receive a disproportionate number of board seats in exchange for funding) could be provided by government assistance of modest size. Using 200 as a rough estimate of the number of all computer and related industry consortia which are currently active and $200,000 as an estimate of average annual aggregate cash contributions ($50,000 may be closer to a median number) yields a total funding requirement for the consortium portion of the national standards infrastructure of only $40,000,000. Accordingly, the magnitude and cost-effectiveness of this in-place resource, and the degree of influence that comparatively modest amounts of funding might produce, should not be ignored.

A second economic concern is to ensure that those companies become members whose participation is essential in order to achieve success. Accordingly, a consortium's dues structure commonly reflects this concern, with some classes of members often bearing a disproportionate contribution obligation. The motivation of certain types of members to take up this burden is to increase the likelihood of those members later reaping a disproportionately high economic benefit in the marketplace. For example, while sponsor-level membership in PowerOpen (a significant goal of which is to foster rapid porting of software to the PowerPC environment) requires $250,000 in annual fees and initiation dues of $750,000, ISVs may participate at a limited level for only $100 a year.

Conversely (as discussed in greater detail below under "Governance"), all types of consortia are likely to maximize revenue income by offering various levels of membership, with higher dues being required of those levels of membership that receive early access to technology and other benefits. Many consortia also charge different rates for companies with different revenue levels, in order to permit smaller companies to participate (or in order to charge more to their larger members, depending on your point of view). (See Table 1.)

Although many consortia might not be formed at all if there were no strategic advantage to be gained by those who take the initiative to form them, it is also true that only those interest groups will be invited to join at what amount to subsidized rates whose participation the founding and funding members deem to be essential to achieving the sponsor members' own ends. Accordingly, government funding might be conditioned on giving membership to other interest groups, or used to fund such membership, and therefore input, in the standards process.

Besides problematic membership profiles, large-budget strategic consortia suffer from a number of other diseases peculiar to the species, one of which may be described as the "cliff syndrome." Simply put, the larger the budget, the greater the likelihood that

Table 1 Typical Dues Structure

Type of Consortium	Member Company's Annual Revenues ($MM)/Dues ($K)		
Strategic Consortium	**<50**	**50–500**	**>500**
Type of Member			
Sponsor	750 (regardless of revenues)		
Principal	50	150	350
Associate	10	15	25
End User	10	10	10
ISV	2	2	2

Total Budget: $4MM per year (3 sponsors, 10 Principals, balance of income from other members, publications, etc.)

Large Standard-Setting Consortium	**<50**	**>50**
Type of Member		
Full	25	50
Associate	5	10
End User	5	5
Individual, University, etc.	.1	.1

Total Budget: $2MM per year (30 full, 100 Associate, balance of income from other members, publications, meeting fees, cooperative advertising, etc.)

Small Standard-Setting Consortium	**<50**	**>50**
Type of Member		
Full	1	5
Associate	.5	.5

Total Budget: $50,000 per year (10 Full, 30 Associate)

such an organization will find itself unable or unwilling to downsize when its grand objective has succeeded or failed. In such a situation, such an organization tends to hurtle at full budget speed off a financial cliff of its own making and into oblivion. The origin of the problem is that while the grand objective remains the focus of the dues-paying members, little attention is given to whether their collective investment in the consortium merits the development of any long-term, less dramatic goals as well.

Often, in fact, it does not, and the consortium should be promptly and efficiently wound down when the major objective has been achieved or failed. However, in other cases, such organizations could have useful long-term lives as user groups, providers of certification services and the like, some of which may be of greater importance to the public. Unfortunately, when the pursuit of the major objective has passed into history, or if the marketplace or technology shifts have made the objective irrelevant, it is often too late to downsize the organization to a sustainable level, since the original strategic proponents are no longer interested in providing the funding necessary to transition the organization to fulfill more humble objectives. Organizations that successfully make the transition are those that have used their high-profile years to quietly backfill their budgets with income and services by establishing more humble activities, such as publishing and joint marketing programs.

The most stable and longest-lived consortia therefore tend to be those that require "modest" annual fees (modest being defined for such purposes as being on the order of $5,000 for a company with under $10 million in sales, and up to $50,000 for companies with sales of over $500 million). In this case, members tend not to send upper-level management to meetings or to examine the benefits received as aggressively or frequently. In consequence, management of the consortium can usually take a more aggressive part in the steering of the organization. Human nature being what it is, the direction of that guidance will usually be toward building a long-term, expanding organization.

Where this process works best, innovative executive directors roll out new programs on a regular basis to keep members happy and renewing. Where the process works poorly, the organization rightfully withers and dies.

In the middle case, where due to a failure of forethought or other reasons a transition has not been achieved, government funding might either assist in a down-sizing transition (where, for example, a standard remains important and requires continuing maintenance) or aid in the transfer of these duties and the underlying technology and staff to another consortium.

As with the evaluation of strategic pressures, a careful review of funding structures will therefore also assist government in assessing the appropriateness of a given consortium as a partner in standards development. Those consortia that have modest budgets and broad-based financial support are likely to be better long-term

Table 2 Sources of Technology (standards, specifications, test suites, etc.)

Organization	In-House	Member Contributions	General RFT	Contract	Contributed Employees
88open	X				
OMG		X	X	X	
X Consortium	X	X			X
Sparc Intl.	X	X		X	

partners than those whose funding is highly dependent on the goals and economic viability of a small number of large hardware companies. /

Technological Development

There are numerous models for developing technology, each with its own advantages (Table 2). The spectrum of methods runs from the very expensive method of total in-house development (88open designed and built almost all of its own test suites), through use of contract parties (such as UniSoft or ApTest, an 88open spin-off company) and contributed employees (used by CAD Framework Initiative), to employment of an RFT (Request for Technology) process (the OSF and OMG model). Other consortia, such as the X Consortium, use a mix of techniques, including reliance on member labor externally, internal staff, and contributions of technology.

Comparing the principal advantages and disadvantages of these methods, the following features stand out: In-house development can maximize control and planning and minimize time to completion, but requires the highest level of funding. Contributed employees are sometimes hard to motivate, may be preoccupied with what is going on at the home office (if they are on site at the consortium), and are often not given ample time or credit by their employers to properly complete their assigned consortium tasks. Issuing an RFT can reap a rich offering of responses, but working through to a final acceptance can be a laborious and sometimes tendentious process to operate and administer. It also requires the most scrupulous legal scrutiny to avoid anti-trust problems.

Again, where a particularly important piece of the standards mosaic may be involved, judicious economic support from government sources may facilitate production by permitting greater flexibility in choosing the mode of development.

Governance

Effective, efficient and representative evolution of standards by consortia is impossible without an appropriate structure of administration and technical decision making. When the author's law firm first began representing consortia, it performed a wide examination of possible forms under various jurisdictions, and settled eventually on the Delaware not-for-profit, non-stock membership corporation. This structure permits members to join and leave with ease, provides members (and their counsel) with a convenient and familiar body of corporate law to rely upon, and provides a unique degree of flexibility of operation. Most of the largest East Coast-based consortia are now formed on this model, while many consortia formed on the West Coast use a similar format under California law. This structure has stood up extremely well in practice.

The heart and soul of any consortium may be found in a humble home: its bylaws and charter. Although a few important rules may come to rest in a membership application, most of the regulations and rights of the organization will be found in these legal documents. Whether or not they are carefully conceived will determine whether the organization is easily managed, whether it incurs needless exposure to its members under the antitrust laws, whether its members feel themselves fairly represented and therefore renew their membership, and whether or not the organization is sufficiently flexible to evolve and flourish.

A crucial factor in reaching a stable and sustaining organization is determining the appropriate method of representing members on the Board of Directors. Organizations that we have represented have developed a variety of radically different formulae (sometimes several divergent methods have been adopted by the same organization at different points in its evolution) that have worked. These have included avowedly economic models (those who pay the highest dues get the Board seats), arbitrary solutions (the first

Table 3 Selected Membership Class Rights

	88open	PowerOpen	X Cons.	OMG	Sparc
Automatic board seat (for highest fee level)	yes	yes	no	no	yes
General voting (number of classes eligible/total number of classes of membership)	2/4	2/3	2/3	1/5	3/5
Automatic technical committee seat or shared seats (number of classes eligible/ total number of classes)	2/4	2/3	3/3	2/5	3/5
Early access (in some form) to technology	no	yes	yes	yes	yes

members to join receive the seats, while later members may stand in line for a turn-over opportunity), as well as models which place a premium on democratic values (seats are allocated to types of members—ISVs, hardware manufacturers and academics—in order to ensure that all interest groups are heard from) or neutral objectives (e.g., only non-members can be directors, to ensure that standards adopted are "pure").

Most (but not all) consortia have different categories of membership, with differing classes having different rights (Table 3). These rights may include voting for (or nominating) directors, the right to participate in technical or other committees, early access to technology or standards, and reduced (or free) access to standards, certification or other services. In some cases, access to such rights is deliberately conditioned on paying higher dues, in order to boost funding levels. In all cases, setting the benefits appropriately in relation to the dues is essential in order for the enterprise to succeed, and some trial and error is sometimes engaged in before the appropriate formula is found by a given organization. Similarly, periodic readjustments are often necessary to keep members satisfied; many consortia have gone through periods of declining membership before realizing that recalibration of dues and services was necessary.

Typically, the actual activities of consortia are implemented by technical committees, work groups, and special interest groups, as well as by non-technical governing bodies, such as business, audit and executive committees. In some consortia, most technical activities take place primarily or exclusively by electronic mail interchange rather than at face to face meetings.

Based on the experience of this author, it would be quite workable for most consortia to either accommodate government agencies as members within existing member classes, or to create or amend a class to permit government participation.

Although this author would not advocate that extensive regulations or a stringent "litmus test" be imposed on consortia before government involvement would become possible, government should nevertheless be entitled to exercise the same degree of review and influence that any other member would be granted to ensure that the vehicle that it was funding met its objectives.

Trademark Protection

Should government become involved in the development of standards through consortia, it will come into contact with issues of ownership, protection, and control that superficially appear to be philosophically counter to certain traditional government objectives. For example, although government will presumably have no interest in assisting in the creation of any standards that are not manifestly available to all, it will still share the concerns of profit-making consortium participants in making sure that such standards are effective. Should vendors falsely claim that a product is compliant with a standard, then the standard will lose credibility in the marketplace, and the standard-setting effort will be in vain. Similarly, if there are competing specifications in the marketplace, each claiming to be a standard and each using the same name, confusion will follow.

To truly control standards, a rigorous program to select, register, and maintain trademarks, service marks, and/or membership marks is therefore often advisable. Where certification is intended, registration of certification marks is even more important.

Technology Ownership

Consortia may or may not plan to develop technology when they are formed, but they often nevertheless find themselves creating intellectual property as they evolve. Since members may come and go, and the organization itself may at some point dissolve, careful consideration must be given to the current and eventual ownership of technology. Where government funding is involved, the analysis will require another dimension, and any participation by government should address this concern at the outset. Whether or not traditional rules of government funding and ownership will be appropriate will depend on the situation, and therefore the mode of actual participation by government (e.g., membership, grant support or actual contract development) will be highly relevant, due to the requirements of existing law and regulations.

A related issue arises where consortia make use of contributed employees (a frequent practice). Usually, those employees will be subject to agreements with their employers that provide that all developments created by them will belong to the employer. Similarly, many consortia permit the contribution of technology that becomes part of a specification, a standard, or an implementation of a standard, which is then made freely available to the world. In situations where technology is developed over time as a result of the contributions of many individuals and corporate members, unscrambling the ownership of that technology and the ultimate liability for any error or infringement can become nightmarish (see the "Sources of Technology" chart above).

To give one example of how complicated such matters can become, the X Window System Standard was initially developed within the Massachusetts Institute of Technology by university staff, and then supported by industry financial contributions. Member (and other) technical contributions were then often accepted, modified, and incorporated into the standard (although actual ownership of the technology contributed was not necessarily transferred), at the same time that further technology was being developed within the X Consortium (still by MIT staff). Since certain software representing the standard is licensed by the Consortium to the world at large at a minimal fee, actual code is thus released to commercial users, who then incorporate it into their products. The software distributed by the Consortium also includes third party commercial software (such as fonts), which is similarly distributed and reused. To complete this complex picture, MIT has now transferred its ownership rights to the new, independent X Consortium.

Where the avowed goal of a consortium (and the government) is to develop and support an open, non-proprietary standard, any actual ambiguity about ownership and control are much to be avoided, even if developmental convolutions like those described above may prove to be unavoidable. As a result, every consortium should institute a careful program of technology procurement, documentation, protection and labeling, as well as the inclusion of conclusive warranty disclaimers.

Similarly, a consortium must decide whether or not to throw its standards into the public domain, or copyright them and make them freely available. Usually, the latter is the better course, since it permits the consortium to maintain better control of the standard. The interests of government and industry are congruent on this point.

Tax Issues

Although taxation of consortia will not be a matter of primary concern to government in evaluating consortia as partners, government will need to be sensitive to the reality of tax planning by those who form consortia, and the way in which tax concerns affect how consortia structure themselves and operate.

Many consortia elect to operate as tax-exempt trade associations under Section 501(c)(6) of the Internal Revenue Code; a few register under Section 501(c)(3) as public charities (see Table 4). As tax-exempt organizations, most of the activities of these consortia may be carried on without payment of income taxes on dues or related income. However, a number of activities (such as the inclusion of paid advertising in consortium publications) are

Consortia and the Government in Standard Setting

Table 4 Regulatory Exemptions

Organization	Tax Exempt	NCRPA Registered
88open	no	no
OMG	yes	no
X Consortium	yes	yes
Sparc International	no	no

deemed by the IRS to stand outside the tax-exempt purposes of the organization, and to constitute "unrelated business taxable income." The income from these activities is taxable, and if too great a level of this type of income develops it may endanger the tax-exempt status of the entire consortium. Accordingly, if it is important for the consortium to engage in some taxable activities, it often decides to carry on those activities through a separate corporation. However, many common consortium fee-generating activities that are of greatest relevance here, such as certification testing and standards publishing, will usually be deemed to be related to the purpose of the consortium and thus fall within tax exempt parameters.

Although tax avoidance (as compared to tax evasion) is a legal and hallowed part of the American psyche, it is unfortunate that those forming a consortium often fail to remember that tax avoidance was not their primary purpose for forming the organization to begin with. Where a consortium has an admittedly strong proprietary purpose, that purpose or affiliation will usually make obtaining tax-exempt status impossible without crippling the purposes of the organization. Similarly, where an organization intends to embark upon many taxable activities anyway, the amount of tax structuring that may be necessary to avoid taxation of other activities can rise to a level of artificiality and inconvenience that ultimately outweighs the benefit of carrying on its other activities on a tax-exempt basis.

In balance, where an organization is a true standards-setting organization, seeking tax-exempt status will usually be well worthwhile. Securing tax-exempt status facilitates budgeting and financial management, and permits management to ignore the possibility of taxable year-end profits. Where the purpose is proprietary or the plans complex, it sometimes proves to be better to forgo filing, or to later abandon tax-exempt status, if this can be accomplished without adverse consequences. Where tax-exempt status is not sought or is surrendered, taxes may be minimized or eliminated by managing the budget as closely as possible to a break-even point annually. Where feasible, multi-year member commitments are often sought to facilitate long-term planning relating to issues such as hiring of management and entering into leases (OSF's multimillion dollar, multi-year commitments led the pack in this regard for some time). Obviously, long-term issues are most problematic for the "cliff syndrome" consortia mentioned above, and least troublesome for stable, large member base consortia with smaller annual dues, such as OMG, which is now the world's largest software consortium with over 400 members.

Antitrust Issues

As with tax issues, antitrust concerns (quite properly) affect the way consortia structure themselves and operate. By definition, consortia are combinations of competitors. As such, they must operate with careful regard to the federal and state laws that they are subject to, as well as to the threat of treble damages suits from private parties.

At times, consortia seek to carry out new practices for which there are no (or only poorly analogous) precedents, and careful analysis must then be undertaken to ensure that risks are not inadvertently taken. In such cases, consortia encounter legal expense and uncertainty that may impede their actions. Happily, standard setting is presumptively deemed to be an appropriate activity for joint activity. Engaging in certification services, while less explicitly favored, may be carried on so long as proper controls are established to ensure non-discriminatory pricing and access to testing.

As a generality, the legal community believes that non-members may be charged higher fees for certification testing and other services and products than members, so long as there is a rational relation between these fees and dues already paid by members and expended on the establishment of the services or products in question. The reason that these practices are engaged in is that some incentives must be given to the companies that fund the activities of the consortium. The alternative is "free ridership," where individual companies see no advantage to funding what they hope others will pay for. Government support for the standards development activities of consortia would help remove the advantage that well-to-do companies have over those whose budgets do not permit participation in multiple consortia.

Government assistance in the antitrust area to date has been most marked through passage of the recently augmented and renamed National Cooperative Research and Production Act of 1993 (the NCRPA; originally, the National Cooperative Research Act of 1984). Under the NCRPA, certain types of activities (such as, arguably, the development of standards) are protected from the risk of treble damages and liability for a plaintiff's attorneys' fees.

However, the NCRPA is not without problems and limitations. Although the amendments enacted in June of 1993 expand the activities that the NCRPA covers, there is still doubt as to the exact coverage involved. Also, public disclosure of members is required, and this is not always acceptable for a strategic consortium where members may not yet have announced their commitment to a given technology or architecture; in such a case, the ability of their competitors to discover their strategic direction as a result of their membership in the consortium may be seen to outweigh the benefits of registration under the NCRPA. Finally, as with many pieces of legislation, there are also a number of unartful, or politically influenced, aspects to the NCRPA which make it difficult to tell whether liability may be eliminated in a given situation or for a given member or activity. For example, the ability of some non-US members of a consortium to take advantage of certain aspects of the NCRPA's protection will probably be impossible to reliably determine. Although it is doubtless too soon to look for further amendment of the NCRPA, there remain areas where amendment, or at least clarification, would be of material benefit to the effective advancement of standards development through consortia.[1]

Finally, the industry is waiting to see to what degree the predominantly laissez-faire antitrust policies of the two preceding administrations will abate, and to what extent consortia will be under increased scrutiny. It was rumored some three years ago that the federal antitrust agencies were undertaking a broad investigation of high-technology consortia at the time that OSF came under examination, but no public announcement or other enforcement action followed. As a result, although industry hopes that the pro-competitive activities of consortia will continue to receive at least some measure of government sympathy, if not outright legislative encouragement, the potential for suit by private litigants (such as competitors) remains a concern, especially where NCRPA protection does not extend, or where registration was not deemed to be feasible. In that regard, it is worthy of note that OSF was sued by private parties concurrently with the commencement of the government investigation, and it is popularly believed that the government inquiry was inspired by private party complaints.

Conclusions

Participation by government in consortium standard setting activities can (and should) occur at more than one level, such as: coordination of consortia standard-setting activities, funding of standards development and conformance testing, direct membership in consortia as a consumer of goods and services, and active promotion and participation in the founding of new consortia, where necessary.

One method whereby government could more dramatically facilitate the evolution and coordination of standards to support the development of the NII might be to promote and help fund the formation of a national clearing house, or "Consortium of Consortia." This would bring together consortia with an interest in the technological areas that comprise necessary components of the information superhighway. Such a body could:

• Facilitate cooperation and coordination of existing consortia, and formation of new consortia

• Act as a mechanism for requesting bids from those consortia that it deems to be appropriate and eligible for development of new standards, and for the creation of test suites

• Conduct or contract for certification testing of necessary technological components of the NII

• Provide support services (e.g., administrative, communications)
on a contract basis for small, standard-setting consortia that typically have no paid staff, thus facilitating and speeding their activities, and leveraging member funding in the process

• Invite participation of heretofore unrepresented, or under-
represented, interest groups (e.g., representatives of academic
institutions) in the standard setting process at the highest level.

As a first step, such an organization could catalogue the areas of
expertise and interest of existing consortia with an eye toward
assessing their utility in developing standards for the NII. More
intelligent government decisions could then be made based on this
foundation.

Although the appropriateness of the more proprietary of the
strategic consortia for government partnership may vary, the utility
of formal standards bodies, specification consortia and the "less
strategic" consortia such as the X Consortium for establishment of
useful standards can scarcely be seriously questioned (otherwise,
why would so many of their standards and specifications be recognized by the *de jure* standard-setting organizations?). To ignore this
ready, available, and (somewhat) coordinated standard-setting
infrastructure of responsive organizations would be to neglect a
resource of importance. Those responsible for the formation and
implementation of NII policy should work to thoroughly involve
existing consortia in the standard-setting process, and should
promote the formation of new consortia, where appropriate, to
develop and maintain those standards components of the NII for
which no existing organization is an appropriate choice.

Note

[1] A current private antitrust suit brought by a private company against the Open
Software Foundation (OSF) is also worth watching since it challenges the
applicability of the NCRPA to OSF. This is perhaps the first occasion where a
federal court will have the opportunity to give an expansive or a restrictive
interpretation of the NCRPA's applicability.

References

For two different treatments by this author of some of the same material contained in the above article, see:

"Forming, Funding, and Operating Standard Setting Consortia," *IEEE MICRO*, December 1993, pp. 52–61. This was a special issue dedicated to the analysis of standards setting issues in high technology industries. This article does not address government issues, and focuses more heavily on organizational issues and concerns.

"Forming and Representing High-Technology Consortia: Legal and Strategic Issues," *Computer Lawyer*, March 1994, pp. 8–17. This article focuses more heavily on intellectual property, organizational, antitrust and other legal issues important to the formation and operation of consortia.

The strategic consortia discussed in this article are of recent enough vintage that there has been (as yet) little academic or other thorough analysis of them. Consequently, most sources are to be found in the trade press and in information disseminated by the consortia themselves. However, the following are useful sources for data:

The World of Standards, 2nd edition (San Jose, CA: 88open Consortium Ltd., 1991). This is an excellent source book, containing detailed descriptions of over 100 important recognized standards and the organizations which sponsor them, as well as various products which are significant in the industry, such as WINDOWS, Motif, PostScript, SVR4, etc.

Softwars: The Legal Battles for Control of the Global Software Industry. Anthony Lawrence Clapes (Westport, CT: Quorum Books, 1993), pp. 261–274. This interesting and opinionated book has an excellent chapter on the Open Systems debate and the way that it has played out in the consortia trenches.

The Evolution of Open Systems. (San Jose, CA: 88open Consortium Ltd., 1992). Good, concise review of the history and evolution of open systems, with some emphasis on the current role of binary compatibility standards.

Interoperability and Intellectual Property

Competing Definitions of "Openness" on the NII

Jonathan Band

Introduction

In the early 1990s, the computer, entertainment, and communications trade press began to devote increasing attention to the "information infrastructure." Although no one vision for the information infrastructure emerged, the dominant metaphor was the "information superhighway." Just as the federal interstate highway program of the 1950s and 1960s created a vast road network that facilitated automobile travel throughout the United States, so would the information superhighway create a vast communications network that would facilitate the movement of digital information throughout the United States.

With the election in 1992 of Vice President Gore, an early champion of the information infrastructure, Washington also began to focus more attention on the information infrastructure. The Clinton Administration in 1993 issued "The National Information Infrastructure: Agenda for Action," which sketched out its basic vision for the National Information Infrastructure (NII). One of the Administration's goals was to "promote seamless, interactive, user-driven operation of the NII." The Administration recognized that this goal could be accomplished only through interoperability:

Because the NII will be a network of networks, information must be transferable over the disparate networks easily, accurately, and without compromising the content of the messages. Moreover, the NII will be of maximum value to users if it is sufficiently "open" and interactive so that users can develop new services and applications or exchange information among themselves, without waiting for services to be offered by the firms that operate the NII.[1]

The Administration further recognized that interoperability could be achieved only through standardization:

To assure interoperability and openness of the many components of an efficient, high capacity NII, standards for voice, video, data, and multimedia services must be developed. Those standards also must be compatible with the large installed base of communications technologies, and flexible and adaptable enough to meet user needs at an affordable cost.[2]

While recognizing the importance of standardization, the Administration also conceded that in the information and communications industries, the standards process "has not always worked to speed technological innovation and serve end-users well."[3] Once it identified this critical problem, however, the Administration failed to offer a meaningful solution. It simply charged the National Institute for Standards and Technology to "review and clarify the standards process to speed NII applications."[4]

It soon became apparent to the Administration, Congress, and industry that interoperability and openness required more than NIST's review and clarification of the standards process. Since the issuance of the "Agenda for Action" in 1993, the issues of interoperability, openness, and standardization on the NII have been debated heatedly inside the Beltway. A broad consensus has emerged that the government should not establish NII standards but rather facilitate their establishment by the private sector. The government, in other words, should help define the rules of the road. At the same time, no consensus has emerged concerning those rules of the road. Everyone supports "openness," but each firm seeking to participate in the NII has its own definition of "openness" that supports its narrow commercial interest. The differences between the varying definitions of openness are particularly pronounced with respect to software interfaces. This paper examines some of the definitions of openness that have emerged during the course of the debate.

The Working Group on Intellectual Property Rights

The Agenda for Action established the National Information Infrastructure Task Force under the chairmanship of Commerce Secretary Ron Brown. The Task Force included an Information Policy Committee, which in turn included a Working Group on Intellectual Property Rights. This Working Group, under the chairmanship of Patent Commissioner Bruce Lehman, was initially charged with the task of determining the adequacy of existing copyright law to protect content distributed on the NII. In October 1993, however, the Working Group requested comments from the public on a wider range of intellectual property issues relating to the NII, including: "Should standards be established to encourage or require the intercommunication or exchange of information and the interoperability of the different types of computer software and systems supporting or utilizing the NII?"[5] This question introduced the possibility that the government may require software interoperability on the NII. Virtually all parties submitting comments agreed with the government's basic goals of interoperability and standardization, but they disagreed on how to achieve these goals.

Joint comments filed by the Business Software Alliance (BSA)[6] and the Alliance to Promote Software Innovation (APSI) recognized the central role of software in the NII:

While much of the talk about the NII revolves around hardware, it is essential to understand that what makes the whole system work is software. Fiber optic networks and digital information hardware without software are incapable of responding to even the simplest command or forwarding the simplest message. The hardware may serve as the "muscle" but it is the software that will operate as the "brains" of the NII. Software transforms the raw power of the high capacity networks and computers into information that helps people at work, school, and home.[7]

APSI and BSA then asserted that "the elimination of incompatibilities is in everyone's best interests."[8] Because compatibility was in "everyone's best interests," the market would achieve it efficiently without government interference.

The American Committee for Interoperable Systems (ACIS)[9] agreed that the market would select standards, but cautioned that the software developers whose interface specifications became de facto standards would try to assert copyrights in those standards in an effort restrict competition and extract monopoly rents. ACIS noted that the U.S. Court of Appeals for the Second Circuit in Computer Associates Int.'l, Inc. v. Altai, Inc., 982 F.2d 693 (2d Cir. 1992) had ruled that copyright protection did not extend to interface specifications, but observed that many circuits had not yet considered the issue. In those circuits, "competing vendors who develop products conforming to th[e] de facto specifications would face costly litigation as well as the possibility the a court might erroneously refuse to follow the Second Circuit's lead."[10]

ACIS also addressed the software reverse engineering technique known as disassembly.[11] In certain circumstances, a competitor may be able to discern the de facto NII standard interface specifications only by engaging in disassembly. ACIS was confident that the other circuits would agree with the Ninth and Federal Circuits that disassembly was a fair use; nonetheless, "until all circuits adopt this rule, vendors whose interface specifications become de facto NII standards may challenge the disassembly of their software products."[12]

ACIS concluded that

there is a substantial possibility that vendors will assert proprietary rights in interface specifications which become de facto NII standards. This danger is magnified by the wave of mergers and joint ventures sweeping the computer, communications, cable, entertainment, and consumer electronics industries. Several powerful companies working together may well have the market power to set a de facto NII standard over which they will exercise proprietary control to the exclusion of all competitors.[13]

To eliminate the threat posed by proprietary control over de facto standards, ACIS proposed (1) that the government specifically endorse the Computer Associates and Sega decisions, and file amicus briefs urging other courts to follow suit; and (2) that the Antitrust Division of the Justice Department approve mergers and joint ventures relating to the NII only if the parties to the transaction waive any proprietary claim to de facto NII standard interface specifications. ACIS, however, acknowledged that some software interfaces might be patentable subject matter, and did not oppose patent protection for such interfaces provided they met the statutory requirements of novelty and non-obviousness.

In July 1994, the Working Group issued a preliminary draft report styled as a Green Paper. In the introduction, the Green Paper explicitly stated that it would not address "the current debate over whether or to what extent certain aspects of computer programs are or should be protected under copyright laws."[14] Instead, the Green Paper focussed primarily on copyright protection for content flowing through the NII.

In its closing pages, however, the Green Paper turned briefly to the issue of intellectual property protection for NII-related standards. The Green Paper noted that "Interoperability and interconnectivity of networks, systems, services and products operating within the NII will enhance its development and success."[15] The Green Paper then signalled its support for intellectual property protection of NII-related standards. Specifically, the Green Paper stated that

in the case of standards to be established, by the government or the private sector, the owner of any intellectual property rights involved must be able to decline to have its property used in the standard, if such use would result in the unauthorized exercise of those rights. If the rights holder wishes to have its intellectual property as part of the standard, an agreement to license the necessary rights on a nondiscriminatory basis and on reasonable terms may be required. In the case of de facto standards, arising out of market domination by an intellectual property rights holder, unfair licensing practices can be dealt with through the antitrust laws.[16]

While the Green Paper approved of intellectual protection for NII-related standards generally, it took no position on the narrower issue of whether NII software interface specification standards should receive copyright protection. Rather, it referred to a broader category of NII standards, such as copyright management systems and encryption technologies, which properly are the subject matter of patents. Indeed, the Green Paper referenced the FCC's recent adoption of a patented AM radio stereophonic transmitting system as a technical standard as an example of proprietary rights in standards. Thus, the Green Paper's recognition of proprietary rights in NII standards should not be construed as endorsement of copyright protection for NII interface specification standards.

The Set-Top Box Debate

While the Working Group was preparing its report, Congressman Markey of Massachusetts entered the fray. Markey, Chairman of the House Telecommunications and Finance Subcommittee, had introduced legislation breaking down the barriers between the telecommunications and cable industries as a means of facilitating the development of the NII. While studying the issue, he began to appreciate the significance of the television set top convertor box (set-top box). The set-top box is envisioned as the entry point of the NII into the individual home or business. The hardware and software in the box will have to be compatible with the information superhighway outside the home as well as the television, computer, and application software inside the home. Markey soon understood that proprietary control over the set-top box interfaces would bestow control over access to the entire NII.

On February 1, 1994, Markey held a hearing on the set-top box issue. Witnesses from Microsoft and Sun Microsystems presented conflicting visions of proprietary control of set-top box interfaces, and, by implication, all critical NII interfaces.

Nathan Myhrvold, Microsoft's Senior Vice President for Advanced Technology, began by describing three necessary characteristics any set-top box (or any NII appliance) operating system must possess: (1) "it must be an open system which encourages independent third parties to participate in creating applications, services, and other products to work in concert with it";[17] (2) "it must ensure sufficient compatibility for information appliances to work with each other, while at the same time not requiring such great conformity and similarity so as to stifle innovation";[18] and (3) it must be neutral to different types of communications networks, e.g., telephone and cable television. Significantly, Microsoft viewed the openness and compatibility of the operating system only in terms of the ability of other vendors to attach to the operating system, not in terms of the ability of other vendors to compete with the operating system.

Myhrvold stated that "consumer demand and market forces will force companies to ensure that their systems have such characteristics."[19] Market forces also will lead to "maximum innovation" and "the best quality products at lowest prices."[20] By contrast, if the government set the standards, "development will be slowed, innovation inhibited, and technology frozen at current levels."[21]

Myhrvold explained that "Microsoft is pursuing an open systems strategy with its own products. Thus, any Microsoft [interactive television] operating system would be made readily and widely available. Microsoft is committed to communicate with, include, and listen to, the content providers and independent software vendors that will be developing the applications to run in . . . NII information appliances."[22] For Microsoft, "open" meant open for attaching, but not competing, products.

Myhrvold acknowledged "that there are some who would go further and say that a system is not truly 'open' unless its implementation or interfaces are in the public domain."[23] Myhrvold disagreed with such a definition of openness, and provided a vigorous defense of proprietary interfaces:

Without the incentive offered by the ability to license intellectual property, the information infrastructure would not get built. R&D of the type needed to develop complex products like interactive television requires the investment of hundreds of millions of dollars. Companies must be able to recoup those investments by licensing the rights to use the fruits of those investments. In addition, public domain standards give international competitors a free ride on technology and intellectual property developed here in the U.S.[24]

This passage combines two of the principal tenets of the "maximalist" intellectual property position. Protection for interface specifications is necessary (1) to provide adequate incentive for innovation and (2) to enable U.S. firms to withstand foreign competition. The passage neglects to mention, however, that protection for the set-top box operating system interface specifications would give Microsoft control of a multi-billion dollar market, leading to profits orders of magnitude larger than its R&D investment. The passage also neglects to mention that many foreign competitors have become so technologically sophisticated that they may well develop critical interfaces needed by U.S. firms.

Myhrvold's testimony also reflects the maximalist tendency to misrepresent the position of the interoperable developers. The interoperable developers did not want the government to set standards nor did they they want to place interface implementations in the public domain. The testimony of Wayne Rosing, Corporate Executive Officer of Sun Microsystems, made these points clearly.

At the outset, Rosing emphasized the importance of interoperability to the success of the NII:

Interoperability is what allows systems with multiple components to work together, and it creates the opportunity for the existence of competing, interchangeable implementations. Interoperability assures a level playing field for businesses interested in providing products and services for the NII; it also guarantees consumers the widest possible range of choices at competitive prices.[25]

It is worth noting that Rosing's "interoperability" is different from Myhrvold's "openness" or "compatibility." Rosing spoke of "competing, interchangable implementations," while Myhrvold referred to independently developed applications attaching to Microsoft's operating system.

Rosing explained that interoperability depended on standard interface specifications, and took pains to distinguish specifications from implementations: "Interface specifications are pieces of paper; implementations are actual products or services."[26] He also observed that "the distinction between an interface specification and an implementation is important because the former provides the basis for interoperability, while the latter provides the basis for competition."[27]

Rosing then discussed the dangers of permitting ownership of interface specifications:

Monopoly control of interfaces might make specifications unavailable to third parties, or it might allow access only to a select group of suppliers, thereby limiting competition. A similar anti-competitive impact would occur if interface specifications were only available for excessive license fees, by effectively prohibiting new entrants. Incomplete or untimely disclosure of interface specifications might also make true interoperability difficult, and stymie new, smaller entrants.[28]

Rosing analogized proprietary interface specifications to barriers on the information superhighway.

Rosing next described his view of the government's proper role in the NII. He stressed that the government should not set standards: "That would freeze innovation and greatly limit all the benefits of competition."[29] Further, he did not want the government to interfere with intellectual property protection for interface implementations. He did, however, advocate government mandated barrier-free interface specifications. He proposed two sets of government actions to achieve this goal. First, the government should "designate critical NII interfaces as barrier-free."[30] Second, the government should define certain requirements relating to these interfaces, including: a fully and publicly documented specification; availability to all developers; no license fees; no intellectual property restrictions; alteration only with timely notice; and openness on both sides of the interface, i.e., for attaching and competing products.

In short, Microsoft and Sun articulated two radically different visions of the NII. In Microsoft's view, the interface specifications to critical operating systems would be proprietary, but the proprietor would allow other vendors to attach their products to the proprietor's operating system. In Sun's view, the interface specifications would be in the public domain, and any vendor would be permitted to develop its own implementation of any product conforming to those specifications, including operating systems. Microsoft's vision would require a reversal of Computer Associates, because Microsoft seeks copyright protection for interface specifications. Sun's vision, conversely, went beyond Sega. Sun not only wanted the interface specifications unprotected, it wanted them published, thereby obviating the need to reverse engineer. Sun also seemed to suggest that critical NII interface specifications should not be eligible for patent protection.

After the hearing, Congressman Markey amended his telecommunications bill to provide for a Federal Communications Commission (FCC) study of set-top box interfaces. Markey's provision included the following Congressional findings:

(1) the convergence of communications, computing, and video technologies will permit improvements in interoperability be-

tween and among those technologies;

(2) in the public switched telecommunications network, open protocols and technical requirements for connection between the network and the consumer, and the availability of unbundled customer equipment through retailers and other third party vendors, have served to broaden consumer choice, lower prices, and spur competition and innovation in the customer equipment industry;

(3) set-top boxes and other interactive communications devices could similarly serve as a critical gateway between American homes and businesses and advanced telecommunications and video programming networks;

(4) American consumers have benefited from the ability to own or rent customer premises equipment obtained from retailers and other vendors and the ability to access the network with portable, compatible equipment;

(5) in order to promote diversity, competition, and technology innovation among suppliers of equipment and services, it may be necessary to make certain critical interfaces with such networks open and accessible to a broad range of equipment manufacturers and information providers;

(6) the identification of critical interfaces with such networks and the assessment of their openness must be accomplished with due recognition that open and accessible systems may include standards that involve both nonproprietary and proprietary technologies.[31]

The language of the sixth finding was carefully crafted to remain neutral on the issue of whether software interface specifications could be protected by copyright: the interfaces referred to in the paragraph could include both software and hardware interfaces; the form of ownership could include patents or copyrights; and "standards that involve ... proprietary technologies" could mean either standards that include proprietary technologies or standards that apply to proprietary implementations.

The provision also included a finding concerning the government's role with respect to standard setting: "whenever possible, standards in dynamic industries such as interactive systems are best set by the marketplace or by private sector standard-setting bodies."[32] This finding emphasized Markey's aversion to having the government establish the standards for the NII.

Markey did, however, envision a critical role for the FCC concerning these standards:

(A) to identify, in consultation with industry groups, consumer interests, and independent experts, critical interfaces with such networks (i) to ensure that end users can connect information devices to such networks, and (ii) to ensure that information service providers are able to transmit information to end users, and

(B) as necessary, to take steps to ensure these networks and services are accessible to a broad range of equipment manufactures, information providers, and program suppliers.

This language suggests that Markey envisioned competition at each juncture of the NII, including, presumably, the set-top box operating system. The provision was silent on how the FCC was to ensure such competition.

The provision then required the FCC to commence an inquiry:

(1) to examine the impact of the convergence of technologies on cable, telephone, satellite, and wireless and other communications technologies likely to offer interactive communications services;

(2) to ascertain the importance of maintaining open and accessible systems in interactive communications services;

(3) to examine the costs and benefits of maintaining varying levels of interoperability between and among interactive communications services;

(4) to examine the costs and benefits of establishing open interfaces (A) between the network provider and the set-top box or other interactive communications devices used in the home or office, and (B) between network providers and information service providers, and to determine how best to establish such interfaces;
* * *

(7) to ascertain the conditions necessary to ensure that any critical interface is available to information and content providers and others who seek to design, build, and distribute interoperability

devices for these networks so as to ensure network access and fair competition for independent information providers and consumers.

The seventh paragraph appears to contemplate competition on either side of each critical interface. The provision left it to the FCC to determine how to ensure such competition.

Not surprisingly, maximalist organizations such as the Computers Systems Policy Project (CSPP)[33] found this language extremely troubling. In their lobbying effort to defeat it, they misrepresented the proposed FCC inquiry as a government standard-setting exercise, notwithstanding the explicit finding opposed to government standard setting. They also tried to eliminate the need for the entire provision by making three "concessions," two true and the third false. The first true concession was that open interfaces should mean interface specifications readily available to all vendors so that they could "build products that are compatible with both sides of the interface,"[34] i.e., attaching and competing products. The second true concession was that open interfaces should mean specifications revised only with timely notice or public process.[35] These concessions reflected the CSPP members' desire to limit Microsoft's ability to dominate the NII.

Notwithstanding these concessions, the CSPP still insisted that an open interface could involve proprietary technology. "Developers of specifications for interfaces must be able to retain ownership of and benefit from the intellectual property that goes into the specifications, in order to maintain incentives to develop new technologies."[36] The false concession concerned a voluntary industry-wide licensing policy: "When a developer of an NII system proposes proprietary technologies for incorporation in critical NII interface standards, the developer of the technology should be prepared to license the technology on reasonable terms and conditions, demonstrably free of discrimination."[37]

This language, modelled on the patent policy of most standards organizations, has a fundamental flaw in the NII context: it lacks an enforcement mechanism. When a firm joins a standards organization, it agrees to abide by the patent policy. If the firm refuses to license its technology on reasonable and non-discriminatory terms, the organization can refuse to include the technology in a standard. Further, most standards organizations have adopted dispute resolution processes to resolve quickly licensing disputes between organization members.

There is, by contrast, no single standards organization for the NII. Thus, there will be no means of enforcing a voluntary "reasonable and non-discriminatory" licensing policy. Even if such a licensing policy were enacted into law, it would simply lead to endless litigation; a license fee that seems "reasonable" to Microsoft or IBM, for example, may not seem "reasonable" to a small competitor.

The CSPP itself appeared to recognize the shortcomings of its voluntary licensing policy. In a House hearing on "Electronic Commerce in the National Information Infrastructure," its witness acknowledged that "in markets that are not competitive," the government would have to "provid[e] oversight, and interven[e] when necessary to ensure that critical interfaces are open."[38]

At the same hearing, Computer and Communications Industry Association (CCIA) President Allan Arlow explained the benefits of non- propriety NII interfaces:

It is my belief that sooner or later, we will have an open, non-proprietary NII. The question we will answer in the next few years is whether we will have this open, competitive system in the near future—with it[s] attendant economic and social benefits—or only in the distant future, after numerous ugly antitrust suits and regulatory and legal squabbling . . . . Make the critical interfaces open, and you can rest assured that the genius of competition and free enterprise will deliver the best NII in the shortest possible time.[39]

The Four Definitions of Openness

Thus far, at least four definitions of openness on the NII have emerged. Following is a description of these four views, proceeding from the most proprietary to the least proprietary.

1. Microsoft believes that interface specifications should be proprietary, but will permit openness by licensing the specifications to firms developing attaching (but not competing) products. At least with respect to software interfaces, this position will require reversal of the Second Circuit's Computer Associates decision.

2. CSPP also believes that interfaces specifications can be proprietary, but will permit openness by licensing the specifications on reasonable and non-discriminatory terms for the development of products on either side of the interface. This position, too, would require reversal of Computer Associates.

3. ACIS believes that software interface specifications are not protectable under copyright, and that therefore reverse engineering (including dissassembly) to discern those specifications does not infringe the author's copyright. Software and hardware interface specifications, however, may receive patent protection if they meet the statutory requirements.

4. Sun believes that critical NII software and hardware interface specifications should receive neither copyright nor patent protection. Further, the interface specifications should be published, obviating the need for reverse engineering.

These different definitions of openness reflect the difficulties inherent in the convergence of two conflicting cultures: telecommunications and computers. The telecommunications industry historically has been extremely open, in part because of government regulation of the AT&T monopoly, and in part because of the obvious network externalities flowing from a universal system. In contrast, the computer industry historically has been relatively closed, with incompatible stand-alone systems. The profit margins in closed systems are much higher, and the computer industry has reluctantly become more open over the past decade only in response to consumer demand. The computer industry realizes that it will have to become even more open to participate in the telecommunications-oriented world of the NII, but many firms will remain as closed as possible in an effort to extract additional profits.

Openness on the NII is as American as motherhood and apple pie. But just as there are many different types of apple pie, so too are there many different types of "openness." When a firm representative states that the firm supports openness on the NII, the firm representative should be required to define openness. Does she mean non-proprietary or proprietary with licensing? Does she mean licensing for the development of attaching products, or for competing products as well? Is she referring to software interfaces, or hardware interfaces, too?

The ultimate form of "openness" selected for the NII will have a significant impact on the nature of competition in the NII, which, in turn, will have far reaching implications for both our economy and our society. Accordingly, we must pay close attention to the definition of openness on the NII.

Notes

1 "The National Information Infrastructure: Agenda for Action," 9.

2 Ibid., 10.

3 Ibid.

4 Ibid.

5 58 Fed. Reg. 53917 (October 19, 1993) (emphasis added).

6 The BSA represents several large independent software houses, including Microsoft, Lotus, and WordPerfect.

7 Joint Statement of the Business Software Alliance and the Alliance to Promote Software Innovation, November 18, 1993, 4–5.

8 Ibid., 9.

9 ACIS represents firms such as Sun Microsystems, Storage Technology Corporation, and AT&T Global Information Solutions (formerly NCR), whose computer hardware and software products interoperate with systems developed by other vendors.

10 "ACIS Comments on Intellectual Property Issues Involved in the National Information Infrastructure Initiative," December 10, 1993, 5.

11 Disassembly is the translations of the 0's and 1's of machine readable object code into a higher-level, human-readable form. Unauthorized translations typically infringe the author's exclusive rights, but the U.S. Courts of Appeals for the Ninth and Federal Circuits found that software disassembly, when performed for a legitimate purpose and when necessary to discern unprotectable elements of a computer program, was a non-infringing "fair use." *Sega v. Accolade*, 977 F.2d 1510 (9th Cir. 1992); *Atari v. Nintendo*, 975 F.2d 832 (Fed. Cir. 1992).

12 Ibid., 6.

13 Ibid., 6–7.

14 "Intellectual Property and the National Information Infrastructure," July 1994 ("Green Paper"), 2.

15 Ibid., 139.

Band

[16] Ibid., 140.

[17] Nathan P. Myhrvold, Statement of February 1, 1994, 5.

[18] bid.

[19] Ibid.

[20] Ibid., 6.

[21] Ibid.

[22] Ibid., 15.

[23] Ibid.

[24] Ibid., 23.

[25] Wayne Rosing, Testimony, February 1, 1994, 2.

[26] Ibid.

[27] Ibid., 3.

[28] Ibid., 4–5.

[29] Ibid., 6.

[30] Ibid.

[31] H.R. 3636, §205(a).

[32] §205(a)(8).

[33] §205(a)(9).

[34] §205(b).

[35] The CSPP represents many of the large computer systems vendors, including IBM, Apple, and Hewlett-Packard.

[36] Computer Systems Policy Project, "Perspectives on the National Information Infrastructure: Ensuring Interoperability," February 1994, 7 (CSPP Report).

[37] Ibid.

[38] Ellwood R. Kerkeslager, AT&T Vice President, Technology & Infrastructure, Statement, May 26, 1994, 3.

[39] CSPP Report (see note 36), 10.

[40] Kerkeslager, Statement, 8.

[41] Allan J. Arlow, CCIA President and CEO, Statement, May 26, 1994, 5.

[42] Oracle shares Sun's views. See Tim Hyland, "Standardization on the Information Highway," April 21, 1994.

References

Position Papers

"ACIS Comments on Intellectual Property Issues Involved in the National Information Infrastructure Initiative," December 10, 1993.

Arlow, Allan J., May 26, 1994, Statement.

Business Software Alliance and the Alliance to Promote Software Innovation, November 18, 1993, Joint Statement.

Computer Systems Policy Project, "Perspectives on the National Information Infrastructure: Ensuring Interoperability," February 1994.

Hyland, Tim, "Standardization on the Information Highway," April 21, 1994.

Kerkeslager, Ellwood R., May 26, 1994, Statement.

Myhrvold, Nathan P., February 1, 1994, Statement.

"The National Information Infrastruction: Agenda for Action."

Rosing, Wayne, February 1, 1994, Statement.

Working Group on Intellectual Property, "Intellectual Property and the National Information Infrastructure," July 1994 ("Green Paper")

Cases

Atari v. Nintendo, 975 F.2d 832 (Fed. Cir. 1992).

Computer Associates v. Altai, 982 F.2d 693 (2d Cir. 1992)

Sega v. Accolade, 977 F.2d 1510 (9th Cir. 1992)

Other Authorities

58 Fed. Reg. 53917 (October 19, 1993)

H.R. 3636, §205

Arguments for Weaker Intellectual Property Protection in Network Industries

Joseph Farrell

Economists view intellectual property policy as a tradeoff (isn't everything?)—a tradeoff between the goal of rewarding and thus encouraging innovators, and the goal of "efficient diffusion" embodied in marginal-cost pricing. By protecting intellectual property from imitators, society raises the price of innovative products above cost and above what it would have been with no protection. This causes inefficiencies as some people refrain from using a useful idea because the price is too high, but it also rewards the innovator and thus encourages innovation. Many economists believe that encouraging innovation is more important *in general* than encouraging efficient diffusion, suggesting that the balance should tilt somewhat towards protection and encouragement of innovation rather than towards encouraging low prices for existing innovations.

"Network effects"—the considerations that make each user value a good more highly if more other users adopt it—are common in the information industries. For example, a telephone is useless unless people you want to talk to also have telephones; a TV set is useless unless enough people have them that someone decides to broadcast witty, uplifting, and intelligent programming; and a computer is much more useful if enough people have compatible computers that a large variety of software is available. In this paper I give some economic arguments suggesting that the intellectual property tradeoff should be more than usually tilted towards efficient diffusion—that intellectual property should be less strongly protected—when the innovation is subject to network effects. This observation may qualify the general economic view that the balance should tilt towards stronger protection.

Why You Want Weak Protection in Network Markets

The simplest argument for weak(er) intellectual property protection in network industries is that when network effects are present, each user deterred by a price above cost not only loses the benefit of the innovation for himself but also reduces the benefit to all those who do adopt. So a given reduction in demand is more harmful when network effects are important. Of course, it does not automatically follow that (once an innovation is made) a given degree of intellectual property protection is more harmful in such a market: a protected innovator's pricing policy might be very different when network effects arise. But simple calculations suggest that, indeed, the efficiency loss due to monopoly is a larger fraction of the total potential social benefit from an innovation if network effects are more important.[1] So, when we balance those "deadweight losses" from allowing above-cost pricing against the (harder to measure) losses from innovations not made because the incentives were too small, we should tilt more in the direction of keeping prices close to cost—we should not protect intellectual property as strongly as we should for innovations without network effects.[2]

Thus intellectual property protection is especially *costly* when network effects are strong, so we should cut back on it. At the same time, intellectual property protection is often especially *powerful* in network markets, since a *de facto* standard can control a market, so the legal protection is leveraged and confers stronger effective protection than in other markets.

Much of the reward to innovation is not directly provided by the legal protections of intellectual property law, but legal protection helps get it going.[3] Perhaps the chief channel for this to happen is the *first-mover advantage*: the first firm in a market tends to retain advantages over later entrants (for instance, users associate the innovation with the innovator; the innovator may have an advantage in buying up inputs needed for the innovation; the innovator gets a head start down any learning curve).[4] These effects can be powerful and long-lasting; Bayer still seems to have a big advantage in the market for aspirin, for instance. So, when first-mover advantages are strong, a little temporary intellectual property protection—a honeymoon period—that lets an innovator establish a market position can be leveraged into a substantial and long-lasting advantage.

Thus, intellectual property protection is extra-concentrated when first-mover advantages are powerful: and they typically are powerful when network effects are important. The installed base of users built up during the honeymoon period provides a powerful motive for future users to stick with the innovator—if the latter refuses to allow imitators' products full compatibility with its own. In this way, for example, the early Bell system leveraged its seventeen-year basic patent protection into a prolonged dominance of the telephone market in the United States.[5] An innovator may thus keep imitators at bay beyond the legally specified protection period, effectively prolonging the protection.

Similarly, protection may be expanded in dimensions other than time. For instance, a patent's horizontal *scope* or "breadth" specifies how different a competing product must be in order not to infringe.[6] Network effects may expand the effective horizontal scope of a patent: for instance, if a patent or copyright explicitly covers only one particular way of doing things, network effects may make users reluctant to buy a different product, even if it is not inherently inferior. Thus the effective scope might cover a whole market, even if the ostensible scope covers only a narrowly defined product. For example, although Lotus's 123 software copyright ostensibly covers only Lotus' implementation of a spreadsheet and not the idea, Lotus's first-mover position built enough of an installed base that Lotus-compatibility became an important factor in selling a competing spreadsheet.[7] An innovator that can deny the ability to be compatible may have greater *effective* protection than it deserved or than anyone intended.

A further leveraging comes from the ability to control or prevent subsequent innovation. In fast-moving markets, the effective lifetime and scope of intellectual property may be limited more by superior superseding innovations than by the legal life and scope.

Absent network effects, an innovation may be valuable only until a competitor invents something better. Indeed, one goal of patent law is precisely to encourage such leapfrogging innovation: if the new idea is sufficiently better than the old (as defined by a "vertical" aspect of the scope of protection) then it should supplant it.[8] But it is notoriously hard for an incompatible product to supplant an established standard.[9] Once again, as a standard gets established in its honeymoon period, the effective degree of intellectual property protection can rise beyond what the law explicitly provides or what the innovation deserves.[10]

Excessive protection is particularly likely if the standard was not an impressive work to begin with. Then, network effects may confer a large reward on an invention that was perhaps almost obvious. It may take little creativity to choose an interface (it's obvious that there must be one, and the choice may be quite arbitrary), but the choice, if protected, may confer power over a large market. Perversely, copyright law makes arbitrariness a point in favor of strong protection, and (unlike patent law) does not insist that an innovation be "non-obvious."[11]

Excessive protection may also be likely when several potential innovators are competing for a market. The reward to a winner of such a competition should be related to its incremental contribution, relative to the hypothetical case in which the other contestants competed in the absence of the actual winner. If a narrow winner can take the whole market and be relatively unconstrained by the presence of a near runner-up, as may well be the case in network markets, especially if the standard is chosen administratively (as at the FCC or in other formal standards processes) rather than by marketplace competition, then the winner may well get an excessive reward. Economists are familiar with essentially this point in the context of patent races. If several firms are racing to realize an innovation, the first to complete it has made a social contribution equal to the value of having the innovation somewhat (often, not much) sooner: Elisha Gray filed a patent caveat for a telephone-like device ("harmonic telegraph") on the same day that Alexander Graham Bell applied for his basic telephone patent. The patent system, however, rewards the innovator as if the contribution were the value of having the innovation at all—a much larger quantity.

Thus, with network effects, an innovator may control the market more firmly than it could without network effects. Obviously, the innovator has more chance to build an installed base advantage if its legal intellectual property protection is stronger. So there is still a relationship between legal protection and effective protection: it is just a relationship with a big multiplier! Between this and the fact that effective intellectual property protection is more costly in terms of efficient diffusion once an innovation is made, there is a two-fold case for weakening legal intellectual property protection for products with big network effects. You don't want much such protection, and a little goes a long way.

How Does Policy Match Up with These Arguments?

I am no lawyer, but I don't think these policy arguments are clearly reflected in the law. Two places where we might look for exceptions are the essential-facility doctrine of antitrust and the merger doctrine of copyright law.

Essential Facility

When a firm or group of firms owns an asset that is or becomes "essential" for competing in a market and cannot reasonably be duplicated by a competitor, courts may sometimes order that the facility be made available to the owner's competitors. Potentially, the "facility" could be a *de facto* standard. One (loose) example is the settlement of the European Community's early 1980s antitrust investigation of IBM: IBM's proprietary interfaces had spawned an industry that had to use those interfaces, and IBM agreed to publish details of any changes in advance so that its plug-compatible competitors had access to the interface technology.[12] Another example is the settlement of the American case of *Bell & Howell vs Kodak*, in which Kodak agreed to sell data on the design of amateur photo equipment before introducing it into the market.[13]

Economists often find the essential facility doctrine perverse: it has the taste of saying to a successful investor or innovator, "You have created something so useful that with it you can totally outperform your competitors. If it were merely useful, we would let you keep the benefits, but since it is so *very* useful you must share." This may seem especially weird in the context of intellectual property, where the grant of a temporary monopoly is explicitly intended. I think also that part of the pained reaction comes from economists' sense that incentives for innovation are generally weaker than they should be,[14] so weakening them by means of compulsory licensing seems perverse. But if protection is excessive, as I suggest it can be here, the policy makes more sense.

Merger Doctrine

In copyright law, an aspect of a creation is not protected where it is the only reasonable way to achieve a useful end.[15] An apparently open question is whether this provision can be applied to an originally arbitrary and protectable part of a creation that, through popularity, becomes a *de facto* standard and *thus becomes* the only commercially reasonable way to compete. One recent software copyright ruling was decidedly hostile to this view,[16] while another (Computer Associates versus Altai) seems to have favored it.

Bad Law Can Be Overcome—Some Days

While the law often provides strong intellectual property protection for network products, such protection is often undone by agreements or unilateral commitments of the parties concerned. Innovators abjure some available protection in order to compete for market acceptance of their products.[17] In the case of the National Television Standards Committee (NTSC) color TV standard, RCA followed such a strategy for several years; there are also many recent examples in the computer industry, notably Intel's second-sourcing of early generations of its iAPX architecture.

More formally, many standard-setting organizations require an innovator to agree to license on "reasonable" terms before they will incorporate proprietary technology into an official standard.[18] The FCC set up such a policy in its standard-setting process for HDTV.[19] The International Organization for Standardization (ISO) and the American National Standards Institute (ANSI) both have such policies,[20] which are followed by many organizations such as the Electronic Industries Association that work under ANSI rules.

These provisions tend to make market adoption of standards smoother, faster, and more likely. This may well be a move in the right direction even if it reduces the rewards to innovation, but it need not do so. In fact, given the nature of the consensus standards process, reducing real or perceived vested interests in particular solutions—such as particular technologies—will tend to make consensus easier to reach. Elsewhere (Farrell 1991) I have reported calculations suggesting that this benefit may overwhelm the "direct" reduction in rewards to innovation: that is, innovators themselves may prefer these licensing policies. As confirmation, note that even if an *ad hoc* informal standards-choosing forum has no binding policy, participants often offer to license key technology in order to make it more likely that the technology will be accepted as a standard.[21]

Where Does This Leave Us?

I have argued that in industries where standards and network externalities are important, there are good economic arguments for protecting intellectual property somewhat less strongly than is usually desirable. While the law seems unresponsive to these arguments, market mechanisms and organizational policies may provide some response. Though that's some relief, it hardly seems a good reason to continue overprotecting some network-intensive intellectual property. If excessive protection were *always* given back, it wouldn't matter whether protection was excessive. But surely it's only sometimes, not always, that this happens.

Indeed, one could argue that these "giveaways" show that legal protection of intellectual property in those cases is superfluous: the market already provides so much (through first-mover advantages, for instance) that even the owner wants little more.

These are complex issues, and my analysis here is quite preliminary. Incentives for innovation are very important, and intellectual property protection should not be reduced casually; but while the case for loosening intellectual property protection in network industries is surely not proven, I think there is enough of a case to bring the matter to intellectual trial.

Acknowledgment

I thank Suzanne Scotchmer, Carl Shapiro, Pamela Samuelson, and especially Paul Klemperer for helpful discussions on this and related topics. Comments are very welcome.

Notes

[1] See Farrell and Shapiro (1992), pages 40–42. Note, however, that this calculation was done in a static model; an unresolved issue is whether a firm with market power in a network innovation (perhaps conferred by IPP) might engage in socially desirable penetration pricing.

[2] Other "costs of monopoly"—in particular the possibility that the innovator is not the most efficient distributor of an innovation and that licensing contracts work imperfectly—may not vary as much with network effects, which may blunt the force of this argument.

[3] See for instance Levin, Klevorick, Nelson, and Winter (1987).

[4] For a survey of theory and empirical findings on first-mover advantages, see Lieberman and Montgomery (1988). See also Caves, Whinston, and Hurwitz (1991).

[5] See the illuminating history by Brock (1981), for instance.

[6] Klemperer (1990) stresses this aspect of patent scope.

[7] See for instance Gandal (1994).

[8] Scotchmer (1991) stresses this aspect of intellectual property policy.

[9] Of course, it should be hard: it is socially costly to shift to a new incompatible technology. But it may be even harder than it "should" be, as Farrell and Saloner (1986) and Katz and Shapiro (1986) show. Even if it is only "appropriately" difficult, the difficulty is still an added source of advantage for the established firm.

[10] We should not expect that subsequent innovations will be blatantly stifled. Rather, since the original innovator has veto power over their introduction, they will be introduced but with licensing arrangements that make the introduction benefit rather than displace the original innovator. That is good in its way, but can go too far: see Scotchmer and Green (1990) and Scotchmer (1991/93). Brock (1981) describes how Western Union, and later Bell, bought up relevant inventions in telecommunications.

[11] Plausibly, this makes copyright a bad mode of protection for computer software. See Menell (1987), Samuelson (1989), Farrell (1989), and others.

[12] "Undertaking Given by IBM," *Bulletin of the European Community*, 10 (1984), 96–103.

[13] "Bell & Howell Believes Kodak Suit Settlement Will Help its Business," *Wall Street Journal*, July 18, 1974, page 29; *Chemical Week*, July 17, 1974, page 24.

[14] Of course, this sense is based on a particular analysis (one potential innovator). Economists are aware that with competition to innovate there may be excessive incentives for R&D. But few think that this is typical in practice.

[15] See e.g. Strong (1990).

[16] Samuelson (1992a, note 170) reports Judge Keeton's derisive comments on this idea in the *Paperback* case.

[17] See Farrell and Gallini (1988) and Economides (1992) for models of this.

[18] Surprisingly, there has apparently been very little trouble with the definition of "reasonable."

[19] See Farrell and Shapiro (1992), page 42, and references there.

[20] For some details and analysis see Farrell (1991). Recently the European Telecommunications Standards Institute (ETSI) has proposed a stronger policy, which has become very controversial. For a recent discussion, see for instance Shurmer and Lea (1994).

[21] Do these policies confiscate intellectual property rights? I think not, both because participation in these processes is generally voluntary (this is where the ETSI policy becomes controversial) and also (relatedly) because patent-holders benefit from the more rapid standardization process that is likely to result with these licensing policies. See Farrell (1991), for instance.

References

Brock, Gerald, 1981. *The Telecommunications Industry*, Cambridge: Harvard University Press.

Caves, Richard, Michael Whinston, and Mark Hurwitz, 1991. "Patent Expiration, Entry, and Competition in the U.S. Pharmaceutical Industry," *Brookings Papers on Economic Activity: Microeconomics*, 1–66.

Economides, Nicholas, 1992. "Invitations to Enter," mimeo, New York University.

Farrell, Joseph, 1989. "Standardization and Intellectual Property," *Jurimetrics Journal*.

Farrell, Joseph, 1991. "Choosing the Rules for Formal Standardization," mimeo, Berkeley.

Farrell, Joseph, and Nancy Gallini, 1988. "Second-Sourcing as a Commitment: Monopoly Incentives to Invite Competition," *Quarterly Journal of Economics*, November.

Farrell, Joseph, and Garth Saloner, 1986. "Installed Base and Compatibility: Innovation, Product Preannouncement, and Predation," *American Economic Review*, December.

Farrell, Joseph, and Carl Shapiro, 1992. "Standard-Setting in High-Definition Television," *Brookings Papers on Economic Activity: Microeconomics.*

Gandal, Neil, 1994. "Hedonic Price Indexes for Spreadsheets and an Empirical Test for Network Externalities," *RAND Journal of Economics* 25: 160–170.

Katz, Michael, and Carl Shapiro, 1986. "Adoption of Technologies with Network Externalities," *Journal of Political Economy.*

Klemperer, Paul, 1990. "How Broad Should the Scope of Patent Protection Be?" *RAND Journal of Economics.*

Levin, Richard, Alvin Klevorick, Richard Nelson, and Sidney Winter, 1987. "Appropriating the Returns from Industrial Research and Development," *Brookings Papers on Economic Activity*, 3, Special Issue on Microeconomics, 783–832.

Lieberman, Marvin, and David Montgomery, 1988. "First-Mover Advantages," *Strategic Management Journal* 9: 41–58.

Menell, Peter, 1997. "Tailoring Legal Protection for Computer Software," *Stanford Law Review* 39.

Samuelson, Pamela, 1989. "Why the Look and Feel of Software User Interfaces Should Not Be Protected by Copyright Law," *Communications of the ACM*, 32.

Samuelson, Pamela, 1992a. "A Critique of *Paperback*," *Law and Contemporary Problems*, 55.

Samuelson, Pamela, 1992b. "Legally Speaking: Update on the Copyright Look & Feel Lawsuits," *Communications of the ACM.*

Scotchmer, Suzanne, and Jerry Green, 1990. "Novelty and Disclosure in Patent Law," *RAND Journal of Economics.*

Scotchmer, Suzanne, 1991. "Standing on the Shoulders of Giants," *Journal of Economic Perspectives.*

Scotchmer, Suzanne, 1991/93. "Protecting Early Innovators: Should Second-Generation Products Be Patentable?" GSPP working paper, Berkeley, January 1991 (revised 1993).

Shurmer, Mark, and Gary Lea, 1994. "Telecommunications Standardization and Intellectual Property Rights: A Fundamental Dilemma?," paper presented at Telecommunications Policy Research Conference, October.

Strong, William, 1990. *The Copyright Book*, 3rd edition. Cambridge: MIT Press.

Telecommunications Standardization and Intellectual Property Rights: A Fundamental Dilemma?

Mark Shurmer and Gary Lea

Introduction

The vital importance of standards for compatibility and inter-operability across a wide range of network industries is clear. Equally apparent is that the growing rewards from winning, or at least controlling to some degree, the outcome of the standardization process has made reaching consensus on standards much more difficult, at the very time when such agreements are essential if society is to enjoy the full benefits of global information and communications networks. Not surprisingly, concerns that the existing standards-setting infrastructure is ill-equipped to deal with the challenges posed have led to increasing calls for reform.[1] This paper considers one aspect of this debate, the potential for conflict between the standards process and the intellectual property (IP) system, and examines reforms proposed by the European Telecommunications Standards Institute (ETSI).

Protection of intellectual property rights (IPRs) is, of course, seen as necessary in creating sufficient incentives for firms to engage in innovation. At the same time, strong legal protection may exacerbate the problems of vested interest that complicate the formal (institutional) standards process. The dilemma for policy makers is how far IPRs should be overridden in the public interest of common standards.

In one sense, the basic economics of the issue seems quite straightforward, even if rather more complex issues arise in practice. The existing IP system is already a reflection of the need to balance two conflicting objectives: (i) the desire for the widespread diffusion of new products and processes; and (ii) the need to create sufficient incentives for firms to engage in innovation. The application of IP law thus serves to ameliorate to some extent the "all or nothing" nature of the IPR versus standardization conflict. However, compatibility raises a number of problems not adequately dealt with by existing IP law. Moreover, rapid technological advance, which is increasing both the importance and the complexity of the standards process, means that without reforms these problems will become ever more apparent.

The paper focuses in detail on specific reforms proposed by ETSI. Since compatibility is the very essence of value in a telecommunications network, it is not surprising that the most far-reaching proposals for reform have emanated from this sector. The paper considers to what extent these proposals serve to resolve the potential IPR/standards conflict.

Standards and Standardization Outlined

Technical standards, formerly considered an arcane area best relegated to the attention of engineers, have only lately begun to emerge as matters of strategic importance. Today, even the most casual of observations will reveal their growing economic importance—recent high-profile examples include the acrimonious political wranglings over the setting of high definition television standards (see Cave and Shurmer, 1990; Shurmer, Cave et al., 1992) and concern over Microsoft's alleged use of standards to dominate the world market for personal computers, leading to unprecedented cooperation between competition authorities in the United States and Europe. More historical examples include the battle for video cassette recorder standards, fought primarily between VHS and Betamax, and the case of the QWERTY keyboard, which remains the *de facto* standard despite the later invention of more ergonomically efficient arrangements (David, 1985).

Generically, a "standard" can be defined as a set of technical specifications adhered to by a producer either tacitly or as a result of a formal agreement. We shall restrict our present analysis to the consideration of compatibility or interoperability standards. A product that conforms to such a standard can serve as a subsystem within a larger system built from numerous components and subsystems.

There is now a substantial and growing literature examining economic processes affecting the formation of compatibility standards.[2] This literature suggests that a product emerges as a standard not only because of its intrinsic features but also because of the benefits deriving from a large installed base. The nature of these benefits, termed network externalities, plays a key role in determining the degree of product standardization that occurs.

Direct network externalities are simply generated from the growing number of users adopting the product. As additional users join a telephone network, for example, consumers' utility clearly increases. Indirect network externalities are derived from features extrinsic to the product, which increase with the number of adopters, and which add value to the core product. For example, the growing installed base of a product may generate a greater range of complementary products. As the number of users of VHS video-recorders increased, so did the supply of pre-recorded cassettes. This complementary link applies to many other products, from the supply of software for a particular computer standard to the supply of television programmes (in terms of both numbers and quality) for a given television standard.[3]

Compatibility can also offer significant cost savings. On the supply side, standardization allows firms to benefit from greater economies of scale, for instance from allowing the use of interchangeable parts. Without a standards agreement, firms may have to manufacture to a number of different standards; thus production runs are smaller.

Common standards can serve to *enhance* levels of competition and international trade. In essence, they serve to unify market requirements so that competition can be established amongst producers and service providers for the benefit of both producers and consumers. Producers, for example, benefit from the enhanced value of their products ensuing from compatibility. Consumers benefit from being able to freely choose between different producers with the confidence of compatibility between different systems components (Matutes and Reigbeau [1987] term this "mix and match compatibility.") Common standards can also *lower* barriers to international trade and *promote* innovation (the latter by avoiding wasteful duplication of R&D effort and by allowing faster product development).

Standardization is not, however, without its negative aspects. Divergent standards can be used to *create* trade barriers as well as to lift them. They can also serve to *restrict* competition by reducing variety. More significantly, standardization can *retard* innovation: continued long-term acceptance of a standard can breed undue reliance on technology that has, in fact, been superseded by technically superior products or systems. New users are often faced with a choice between the benefits of compatibility and the benefits of new technology; the former often wins even when it should not.

It is these competing and conflicting positive and negative aspects that help explain why standardization does not occur even when it is socially desirable. The literature suggests, for example, that standardization may be more beneficial for small firms than for large firms (Katz and Shapiro, 1985, 1986). The sheer size of the latter's sales may be sufficient to generate positive network effects without compatibility with other firms. For smaller firms, however, compatibility often assumes great significance in yielding these network effects. More particularly, it is that fact that the costs and benefits of standards may be unevenly distributed among participants in the standards process, so that each may favour different solutions and have different views on the optimal timing of standards decisions. Once established, standards can dictate the nature and intensity of competition within product markets for many years to come. Control of the outcome, and/or its timing, can therefore yield significant economic advantage on the sale of both core and related products. The timing, nature, and degree of product standardization thus depends on the complex interaction of the (often conflicting) interests of its participants.

Just as there are many different types of standards, so they can emerge in a number of different ways. We distinguish between two distinct processes. The first is entirely market mediated, whereby a product emerges as the industry or *de facto* standard. Such a process assumes characteristics something akin to a race, with products competing to gain installed base more rapidly than their rivals. Alternatively, a standard may be determined through a *formal* process of political ("committee") deliberations or administrative procedures, which may be influenced by the market processes without reflecting them in any simple way. The formal committee process encompasses a variegated collection of organisations known as standards institutions. These bodies have long remained conspicuous and little understood by outsiders, but they underlie much of the standardization activity. It is within these institutions that the conflict between standardization and IPRs is becoming increasingly apparent.

Intellectual Property Rights

The term "intellectual property" covers a wide range of subject matter including items such as trade marks and performers' rights. In this context, we are mainly concerned with the oldest[4] and truest[5] forms of IPRs—patents and copyright. Patents protect innovations ("inventions") in the scientific and technical field—typically chemical/biological substances, machinery or processes—which are the result of the application of knowledge[6] to an industrial or technical problem and which are, in themselves, novel and indicative of some inventive step over and above the "prior art."[7] Copyright, by contrast, covers cultural artifacts from the areas of education, entertainment, and the arts. The main aim of copyright is the protection of original literary, artistic, and musical works.

In broad terms, IPRs create (temporary) monopolies over their subject matter. The IPR holder acquires a bundle of rights to exploit his/her invention or work.[8] In the case of a patented invention, this will typically contain exclusive rights to use the specified process or produce the specified substance. In the case of a copyright, the holder has exclusive rights to reproduce the work or issue copies thereof.

There are, however, a number of important differences between patent and copyright law. For example, the duration of a patent is typically 20 years from grant,[9] whereas copyright will last for at least the duration of the author's life plus 50 years from the start of the year following his/her death.[10] Moreover, in most countries (with the limited exception of the Untied States[11]) copyright is automatically acquired without formality, whereas a patent has to be applied for from a recognised state or regional authority (such as the European Patents Office); the patent application process is lengthy,[12] involves substantive examination of novelty and inventive advance, and may result in refusal where the aforementioned criteria are not met.

Despite its shorter duration, the strength of the bundle of rights granted under a patent is greater than the rights granted by copyright. The latter is often described as a "weak monopoly" because it will only protect the actual expression of a work and not the underlying idea, concept or system (Pessa, 1991)—a restriction clearly not present in patent law. Furthermore, copyright is subject to a number of *automatic* exceptions (colloquially known as "fair uses") whereby acts that would otherwise be infringing are permitted for the public good (e.g., the reproduction of passages from literary works for educational purposes).[13]

Orthodox economic theory has long suggested that monopolies should be avoided *unless* some "special case" can be made out for the monopoly under examination. In essence, monopoly power enables firms to raise price above the competitive level by cutting output. The absence of competition may also permit slack and inefficiencies that raise costs (Liebenstein, 1966). As a result, antitrust policy towards monopoly market structure is well developed in most modern economies.

What then, is the "special case" for IPR monopolies? The economic rationale for the granting of temporary monopoly rights to IPR holders is to reward those who invest their time and money in technological invention and innovation. Such activity is inherently risky and success is by no means guaranteed. Research and development (R&D) expenditures represent front-end sunk costs, which once incurred are irrecoverable. In order to make such investments, innovators must expect post-innovation prices to remain high enough to recoup these initial expenditures: i.e., they must expect to maintain some degree of monopoly power. IP law is designed to heighten this expectation.

Herein lies the dilemma. For once a new product or process emerges, the socially optimal outcome is for its widespread diffusion through the economy. However, in order to create sufficient incentives for innovation, some degree of monopoly power is required. The aim of IPR protection is therefore to achieve the optimal balance between these two conflicting objectives.[14]

It should be noted that IPRs are only one possible incentive for innovation, and others have been used or proposed. Marxist systems of law, for example, have largely denied IPRs in favour of state posts and preferences for scientists and authors.[15] Similarly, Breyer (1970) has argued in favour of the abolition of copyright (at least for certain classes of work such as educational books and computer programs) on the basis that unprotected products will enjoy lead time over copies and that producers will be voluntarily constrained by fears of a "trade war." In any event, imitation requires knowledge about the innovation, and this knowledge is seldom perfect. Firms may therefore seek to additionally protect innovations through means of commercial secrecy. (This is particularly true in the case of process innovations). Indeed, in certain instances, this may be a preferable approach since it avoids the need for disclosure inherent in a patent application.[16]

It remains true to say, however, that on a global basis IPRs are now generally recognised as the most effective mechanism for achieving the balance between the desire for widespread diffusion of new innovations and the need to create sufficient incentives for innovations. As a result, IP law is well-established in most countries. Recently, however, concern has been expressed about the ability of existing IP law to support innovation. One particular aspect of this debate is the growing concern over the potential for conflict between IPR and standards.

The Conflict Between Standardization and IPRs

In the very broadest sense, standardization and IPRs share the same economic objective—namely, to ensure that society benefits to the full from innovation. However, the approaches adopted to achieve this objective are very different. IPRs are orientated toward producers and reflect the trade-off between the need to create sufficient incentives for innovation and the public good nature of an innovation once it has been discovered. Standardization, on the other hand, is much more consumer orientated and seeks to encourage a common platform whereby users benefit from enhanced competition and trade.

It is because of these differing approaches that standardization and IPRs can conflict. Standards inevitably encompass a whole host of IP often owned by numerous companies. The impact of strong IPRs is to significantly increase vested interests in the timing and outcome of the formal standards process. This may in turn may make consensus impossible, or at least prolong the negotiations. It may also mean that the outcome is a reflection more of the participants' relative bargaining power than of any objective technical considerations (Farrell, 1989).

Indeed, the simple presence of IPRs inevitably slows the formal process. The right of the IPR holder to refuse to allow its inclusion in a standard means that standards institutions must obtain agreement from IPR holders at each stage of the drafting process. Alternatively, they risk having to repeat the process following refusal.

In practice, the theoretical "all-or-nothing" nature of the IPRs versus standardization conflict is to some extent ameliorated by IPR licensing provisions and by the possible application of competition law. Participants can, and indeed often do, choose to limit their rights to IP embodied in formal standards. Much of the standardization process relies on such voluntary undertakings, including most importantly the licensing of IPRs. A licence is a permission to do that which would otherwise be prohibited; in the case of IPRs, this would be the right to carry out the acts prohibited by virtue of the exclusive rights an IPR owner has. Save those comparatively rare instances where the state or other responsible body has powers to force licensing on terms (see below), licensing is a power solely reserved to the IPR holder. That is, under normal circumstances:

(i) An IPR owner is not obliged to licence out an IPR

(ii) An IPR licence may discriminate amongst potential licensees

(iii) Where an IPR holder does issue a licence, it is entitled to secure any such monetary or other consideration (such as a cross licence of the other party's IPR) that it is able to extract from the licensee(s) selected.

Standardization, however, is not a "normal circumstance." In this area, IPR owners will typically offer up licences (i) for a fair sum, (ii) on reasonable terms and conditions, and (iii) on a non-discriminatory basis. Such a decision involves a trade-off between the benefits of compatibility and the prospect of at least influencing the final outcome against the potential losses arising from partly relinquishing IPR.

There are, however, two problems with this approach to standardization. First of all, the voluntary nature of the scheme means that producers still have a great degree of control, particularly in the area of information disclosure—it has to be taken on trust that a producer is disclosing "best available means" on the deployment, use, or manufacture of a particular product or technique. More importantly, it must be remembered that there is no guarantee that a producer can be cajoled into licensing—if it perceives the net benefits of non-licensing or limited, private licensing to be greater, then it will naturally choose one of those options. Moreover, it remains unclear whether the correct incentives for licensing exist.

There is mounting evidence to suggest that the process of agreeing fair, reasonable and non-discriminatory terms and conditions for licences of IPR encompassed within standards is becoming ever more complex and problematic. Among recent high-profile cases are fears of legal wrangles between the companies who have contributed IPR to the MPEG 1 and 2 digital compression standards[17] and growing concern in the United States over attempts to patent computer program source code.[18] At the very least, as the importance and complexity of standards and the value of IPRs grow, the incentives for the strategic use of IPRs to control the direction of the standards process can only increase. Even if agreement is eventually reached through private negotiations, it is arguable that the growing period of time necessary to reach such agreement threatens to undermine the formal standards process.[19] The public policy concern is that while wrangles over licensing terms and conditions ensue, the market may "lock-in" to an inferior proprietary standard, with the consequent adverse welfare and competition effects (Swann and Shurmer, 1994).

Given that an IPR holder refuses to licence IP encompassed within a standard, a standards body is faced with the dilemma of what to do next. It may be possible to design around the IPR, though this clearly lengthens the standards process once more. If, however, this proves impossible, at present two possible course of action are open, though neither is entirely satisfactory.

One potential way forward is the imposition of compulsory licensing arrangements. Although strictly speaking a contradiction in terms, such officially sanctioned appropriation of material protected by IPRs *is* possible. Indeed, in the case of standardization, one might think it desirable when an IPR holder can effectively hold the international business community to ransom. However, the constraining economic factor for such application is possible damage to the incentive to create.

Moreover, there are significant legal obstacles in the shape of provisions in the international treaties protecting intellectual property:

(i) In the patent field, for example, the Paris Convention 1883 states that compulsory licences are not allowed in the first three years after grant.[20]

(ii) The Berne and Universal Copyright Conventions place very severe substantive limitations on the practice—the Berne Convention, in particular, is firmly based on "exclusive rights," specifies a limited number of "free uses," and says that other exceptions shall only be permitted under signatories' legislation where these do not prejudice the legitimate interests of the author.[21]

Thus, until such time as the IP conventions and implementing laws are amended to include standardization as a recognised class of activity and provide appropriate rules for the necessary licensing, the application of compulsory licensing is circumscribed and piecemeal in scope. However, an interesting example of an apparently valid, express standardization provision within copyright does now exist: the recently implemented EC Directive on the Legal Protection of Computer Programs[22] introduces a limited right of "decompilation" whereby otherwise infringing acts that occur during the course of decompiling a program (i.e., copying files, translating object code back into source code) are permitted where they are necessary to gain information to allow software/hardware interoperability (see Schmidtchen and Kobolt, 1993).

Competition law might also be used to resolve the non-licence scenario. A prime example is the IBM System/370 agreement thrashed out between IBM and the EC Commission in the period 1981–1984:

(i) Various manufacturers, including disk drive builders, complained that, among other things, IBM refused to disclose information that would allow them to attach ("interface") their products to System/370 mainframe CPUs.

(ii) IBM countered by claiming that System/370 was "proprietary" (partly because of claimed IPRs attached to it, e.g., copyright in the operating system).

(iii) The Commission countered that IBM's failure to disclose interface details was an abuse of monopoly under Article 86 of the EEC Treaty.

(iv) The matter was settled with IBM agreeing to release the necessary information.

Thus, by application of competition law, the EC Commission was able to establish a *de facto* "plug and play" standard for IBM peripherals. However, competition law is a crude instrument for this sort of task, and recognising the pitfalls (e.g., possible damage to the incentive to innovate), the EC Commission has now issued its Communication on "Intellectual Property Rights and Standardisation."[23] The Communication sets out more detailed policy controls and considerations on use of the various competition provisions of the Treaty.

In general, the Commission views standards setting as a matter of negotiation in good faith between producers and regulators (para. 6.2.1), but reserves the right to apply EC competition articles in specific cases (para 6.3.1), particularly where such intervention is necessary to ensure compliance with standards that are either mandatory or enjoy some other "particular status" under Community law (para. 6.3.2). However, competition law's application to IPR problems is limited by a policy constraint against undercutting the incentive to innovate and by virtue of international treaties creating IPR protection (see above).[24]

The potential for conflict between standards and IPRs has typically been overcome within standards bodies by members agreeing to licence IPRs on fair, reasonable, and non-discriminatory terms and conditions. This, however, is achieved on a purely voluntary basis, and clearly involves the firms concerned weighing up the relative costs and benefits of the licence versus non-licence decision. The growing importance of standards may help tip the balance in favour of the non-licence decision, or may at least prolong the process of reaching IPR, and consequently standards, agreement. Current IP and competition policy provisions provide only partial solutions to the non-licence decision.

The extent to which it is possible to preserve IPRs and promote standards is a dilemma confronted by standards bodies and manufacturers every day. Technological advance, which is increasing both the importance and the complexity of standards, can only serve to accentuate IPR problems. In the light of such difficulties, growing attention has focused on possible reforms to the IP system. We now turn our discussion to events in the telecommunications arena, and detail European proposals for change.

Standards and IPRs in Telecommunications

It seems scarcely necessary to note the huge strategic and economic significance of standards in the telecommunications arena. Traditionally, telecommunications standards were established in one of two ways. At a national level, standards were set on a *de facto* basis by the dominant telecommunications carrier. Coordination problems did not arise because of its monopoly position and/or its status as a public utility. At an international level, compatibility between autonomous national networks was achieved through bilateral government agreements. Much of this work took place within the framework of the International Telecommunications Union (ITU).[25]

As is well known, the telecommunications sector has experienced major structural changes, and this process continues apace today. Market liberalisation, in part a response to rapid technological change which means that the industry is no longer seen as a natural monopoly, has significantly increased the number of players.[26] In the UK, for example, the government has issued telecommunications licences to over 40 firms (not all of whom are operating yet). As a result, it is now appropriate to talk of a telecommunications market—a market for which standardization has assumed even greater importance as a mechanism with which to achieve a "level playing field" for competition, so ensuring that the full benefits of deregulation can be realised.

At the same time as the importance of standards for telecommunications has increased, so the process of achieving standardization has become more complex. National and international standards bodies now face the coordination problems posed by an ever growing membership. Moreover, rapid technological advance has increased the breadth and complexity of the work they undertake.[27] There is evidence of growing concern within both industry and government that the existing institutional infrastructure is unable to deliver high quality standards at the pace demanded by the market. As a result, the telecommunications standards-setting process is currently in something of a state of flux,[28] with the various institutions embarked on a range of reforms designed to improve their responsiveness to the market.[29]

The potential adverse effect of strong IPRs has been the subject of much concern in the formal standards arena. This is particularly true of telecommunications, where the widespread introduction of digital technology has heightened the importance of IPRs. Taking the example of a new digital mobile telephone system, one might find the following bundle of IPRs attached to it:

(i) A patent or patents on elements of the system architecture (e.g, a novel, inventive way of packing more data into each block transmitted)

(ii) Copyright in computer programs in embedded electronic systems (e.g., handset controllers) or other hardware

(iii) Miscellaneous design rights[30] in items ranging from handset cases through to connector plugs, circuit diagrams, and semiconductor topographies.[31]

The importance of IPRs in protecting producers' R&D investments in hardware, software, and systems is likely to grow still further in the immediate future as the growing convergence of telecommunications with the information technology and broadcasting industries brings closer the much heralded "multimedia age."[32]

ETSI and IPRs

The growing importance of IPRs is exacerbating the problems of telecommunications standards setting. While a range of reforms have been proposed, the practical lead has been set by ETSI, which has recently detailed bold and controversial plans to effectively place certain limits on IPRs. ETSI's origins lie in the European Community's desires to create a common market for telecommunications equipment and services. Common standards were seen as vital in achieving this objective, and the EC's 1987 Green Paper[33] called for the establishment of a new European telecommunications standardization body. In March 1988, in response to the EC call, ETSI was created by the European Conference of Postal and Telecommunications Administrations (CEPT).[34]

The EC is linked to ETSI in a number of ways including (i) an EC Council Resolution of 27 April 1989 whereby the EC standards bodies (CEN & CENELEC), Member States, and the Commission were invited to cooperate with ETSI[35]; (ii) the Joint Presidents Group, which coordinates ETSI, CEN and CENELEC activities; and (iii) the appointment of the EC Commission as an advisory body ("Counsellor") to ETSI. By 1992, ETSI had set 140 European Telecommunications Standards ("ETS") and interim standards ("I-ETS"), many of which derive from CCIR and CCITT recommendations; the organisation now sets standards in an area (the "Standards Application Area" or "SAA") stretching from Iceland to Turkey.

ETSI is unusual among telecommunications and IT standards-setting bodies in that its voting membership includes producers in addition to the usual range of PTTs and trade organisations. It is this inclusion of manufacturers that allows ETSI an extraordinary degree of leverage in creating standards: in addition to its standards policy, ETSI can (and has) created IPR licensing terms and conditions (collectively, the "Undertaking"), which producer-members ("PMs") must abide by as a precondition for membership. In short, the would-be PM has to weigh up the burden of ETSI licensing policy against the "golden opportunity" of direct participation in standards setting.

ETSI's IPR undertaking has been the subject of intense negotiations since 1989. Its objective has been to move beyond the traditional approach to resolving the potential IPR/standards conflict by placing certain limits on the rights of IPR holders. Specifically, ETSI has been concerned to avoid the situation whereby it develops a standard only to find it cannot be adopted since the holder of IP encompassed within that standard refuses to license it on fair, reasonable, and non-discriminatory grounds.

In its original form, ETSI proposed that PMs should automatically grant patent and computer program copyright licences on such terms (in effect, compulsory licensing), with a waiver of copyright in documentary material. This strict compulsory licensing was subsequently rejected on the grounds that it was inconsistent with existing IP law. ETSI's widely publicised first draft Undertaking of February 1991 modified the position thus (see Good, 1992):

(i) Only IPRs deemed "essential" by the relevant standards working party in the design phase came within the licensing scheme

(ii) The IPR holder was entitled to "opt out" of licensing essential IPRs if an objection was lodged within 90 (originally 60) days of identification.

This approach was generally welcomed by governments and PTTs, which, by virtue of their relatively small R&D budgets, typically own few IPRs. In contrast, the proposals met with strong resistance from large IPR holders such as the major IT and consumer electronics firms. Led notably by IBM, Digital Equipment, and Motorola from the United States and the Dutch giant Philips, a major campaign was mounted to block the proposed ETSI reforms (Cane, 1993).

On 18 March 1993, following much wrangling, the ETSI General Assembly finally approved the "IPR Policy" document, which sets out the objectives and general framework for resolving IPR/standards conflicts, and the annexed IPR Undertaking. The rules adopted are interim arrangements with a minimum duration of two years from 1 April 1993 and are subject to review and alteration thereafter (para 14).

Under this policy, PMs and associates are generally bound by their Undertakings to notify ETSI of any IPRs that may affect standards (para 6.1), and have specific duties of IPR ascertainment (para 6.2), notification of maximum royalty rate (para 6.5), etc. Moreover, PMs and their associates are required to license on fair, reasonable, and non-discriminatory terms (see paras 3.1–3.5) any essential IPR they own or control subject to: (i) the defined "right to withhold" and (ii) the would-be licensee having observed the principle of "licence reciprocity" (see paras 5.1–5.3). The "right to withhold" (paras. 4.1–4.5) basically allows a PM or associate to withhold an IPR licence if it notifies ETSI of the IPR and related (draft) standard in question within 180 days of the Technical Assembly's approval of the (draft) standard's work programme or change thereof, whichever comes later (para. 4.1). Thus, while recognising the IP holder's inalienable right to refuse to licence, the "right to withhold" effectively places a time limit on exercising that right.

If a licence is withheld, the Policy dictates that such refusal (and, indeed, a refusal to license by any third parties) be dealt with as follows:

(i) Efforts will be made by the Technical Assembly to find an alternative (para 8.1.1)

(ii) If these are not successful, ETSI shall request reconsideration (para 8.1.2)

(iii) If this results in a second refusal, the matter will be turned over to the EC Commission (para. 8.1.3).

The EC Commission might, presumably, deploy competition law to ensure licensing, but this will only be possible in those sections of the SAA that fall within its jurisdiction. A similar procedure is adopted when ETSI becomes aware of an IPR held by a third party that is not available (para. 8.2). It should further be noted that the Policy extends the SAA to any country in which an officially recognised national standardization body has formally adopted the standard and implemented it (para 14).

A final point to note is that, wherever possible, arbitration will be used to resolve Undertakings problems between PMs and/or associates (paras. 19.1–19.11). A mediation procedure is also built into dealings with third parties from whom licences are not available.

Analysis of ETSI IPR Policy

In its present form, there can be little doubt that the ETSI IPR Policy and Undertaking represents an ambitious attempt to avoid potential IPR/standard conflicts. In individual member weighted voting it was approved by 88% to 12%, and the national vote resulted in unanimity (with one abstention). However, it is important to note that strong objections to the ETSI proposals remain, and it is significant that among the 12% voting against the Policy number some of the world's major IPR holders. Furthermore, US IT companies have, under the auspices of CBEMA (a trade association), filed a complaint with the EC about the Policy and Undertaking. Concern has, in particular, focused upon four areas that depart significantly from existing practice.

(a) The Opt-out Period

As noted above, the provisions of the "right to withhold" require an IP holder to notify ETSI of its refusal to license IPR within 180 days of the IP's inclusion on the Technical Assembly's work programme. The purpose of this provision is one of risk reduction—it prevents ETSI from working toward a standard that encompasses IPR that is not available to license on fair, reasonable, and non-discriminatory terms (and which therefore could not be adopted). The 180 day time limit is no longer of particular concern to companies—indeed, it represents a compromise over previously proposed 60 and 90 day limits.

Of rather more concern is the issue of when the clock starts ticking. Critics have expressed concern that mere mention in the Technical Assembly's work programme may not provide sufficient information to conduct an IPR search. Indeed, the Policy has been criticised in that it places no express general duty on ETSI to conduct IPR investigations (Prins and Schiessl, 1993); rather, it relies on disclosure by all parties. One possible way forward is to place the onus of proof that sufficient information was available to conduct a search on ETSI.

(b) Monetary Consideration

The ETSI Policy and Undertaking has further been criticised in that it limits the freedom of parties to set their own licensing terms and conditions by explicitly setting out in advance details of what constitutes a fair, reasonable, and non-discriminatory agreement. This represents a break with existing practice under which such details are left to negotiation on a case by case basis. Assessment of the need for reform of the present system is problematic for there exists little systematic evidence on the matter. Further research in this area would be most valuable.

Even if it proves desirable to set out in advance more explicit details of the permissable scope of licences than is presently the case, it is not clear that the ETSI proposals represent an appropriate way forward. Particular attention has, for example, focused upon the requirement that licences be granted for monetary consideration unless otherwise agreed by both licensee and licensor. ETSI's intention is to avoid the following type of scenario:

A small electronics company seeks to license a specific IPR from a large multinational IT company. The larger company responds by demanding to cross-licence some of the smaller company's IPR, the concern being that this IPR may represent the life-blood of the smaller company. Alternatively, the smaller company might offer to cross-licence IPR that is of little use to the larger company.

It is hard to see, however, why the above situation would not be ruled out by simple application of the existing fair, reasonable, and non-discriminatory principle. Moreover, it is not difficult to cite examples whereby monetary consideration alone might not constitute appropriate licensing terms. For example, consider the case of the manufacturer of a mobile telephone base station who requires connection to the network switch. A simple licence for monetary consideration from the switch manufacturer may, without further technical assistance, be insufficient to ensure compatibility.

(c) SAA

Concern has also focused upon the territorial jurisdiction of the ETSI IPR Policy and Undertaking. Essentially, this is limited to the SAA, with the provision that this be extended to include any other country in which: (i) an officially recognised national standardization body has formally adopted an ETSI standard and implemented it, or (ii) a major telecommunications network operator has procured or is about to procure on a substantial scale equipment to a specification compliant with that standard.

ETSI's aim is clearly to promote the adoption of its standards worldwide. However, concern has been expressed that companies are effectively forced to licence wherever ETSI standards have been adopted. Furthermore, critics suggest that such conditions deprive other countries of their sovereignty—if an ETSI standard is adopted in the United States, for example, then ETSI IPR rules would apply. This not unnaturally has provoked opposition from other standards bodies, and the legal position of such a move remains unclear. Thus there exists a very real danger that, far from promoting worldwide sales of ETSI standards, the provision may actually inhibit sales.

Most of the problems over territorial jurisdiction arise because the proposed IPR reforms are occurring at a regional level. This has led to the inevitable turf battles between the regional telecommunications standards bodies. A move towards a coordinated international approach to IPRs would help avoid many of the current jurisdictional disputes and prevent the development of regionally fragmented IPR regimes.

(d) Arbitration

A final area of concern focuses on provisions for disputes to be settled by arbitration. The Undertaking stipulates that where agreement cannot be reached by the parties within a period of three months, the matter will be settled by arbitration. Concern has been expressed that this time period is too short to allow fruitful and conclusive private negotiations. Moreover, it is argued that arbitration is an unsuitable means of solving certain IPR disputes. For example, it is suggested that infringement of validity essential can only be conclusively determined by the courts.

Summary and Conclusions

This paper has analyzed the potential for conflict between standards and IPRs, particularly within the context of the formal standards process. The dilemma is that while strong legal protection of IPRs can exacerbate the difficulties of reaching standards agreement, such protection is seen as necessary if we are to preserve the incentives to innovate. This problem is to some extent ameliorated by the provisions of IP law, which itself tries to balance the competing objectives of promoting the widespread diffusion of new products and processes and of protecting the incentives for innovation. The analysis of this paper, however, suggests that the growing importance of standards raises new questions about where the appropriate balance should be drawn.

Meanwhile, the extent to which it is possible to preserve IPRs and promote standards is a dilemma facing the formal standards bodies every day. Moreover, the growing importance of IPRs threatens to slow, or arguably in some cases halt, the standards process at the very same time as the market is demanding ever quicker standardization agreements. The use of the existing legal framework, encompassing voluntary licensing arrangements and competition law, offers only a partial and increasingly inadequate solution. As the value of standards grows, so the incentives for firms to use IPRs as a strategic tool with which to attempt to control the pace and direction of the standards process can only increase. Even where IPR agreement is eventually reached, the concern is that an inferior proprietary standard may have already been established in the market.

Some reform of the treatment of IPRs seems therefore inevitable if the formal standards bodies are to remain responsive to the demands of the market. In this respect, the ETSI proposals are a welcome step in the right direction. ETSI's decision to set a strict time limit on the right to withhold essential IPRs should help to speed up the standards process. Many questions remain, however, about some of the finer details of the policy and about its consistency with wider IP and competition law. Moreover, it is apparent that a coordinated international approach to IPR reform would be preferable to separate regional initiatives. These issues form part of our ongoing research. One thing is clear: the ETSI proposals represent clear evidence of the growing concern over potential conflicts between standards and IPRs and of the increasing dissatisfaction with the solution offered by the existing IP system.

Acknowledgment

We are grateful to Frede Ask, David Hendon, Harry Ibbotson and Ron Nicholson for illuminating discussions about the ETSI IPR policy. They are not responsible for any remaining errors. Shurmer gratefully acknowledges the support of the Economic and Social Research Council (ESRC) under award number L120 25 1003.

Notes

[1] Such calls have come from industry, from standards practitioners, and from governments. See, for example, DTI (1994), OTA (1992), OECD (1991) and Ergas (1987).

[2] For an excellent discussion of this and a number of other cases see Grindley (1992).

[3] Other types of standards include reference or measurement standards and minimum quality standards; see David (1987) for a discussion of this taxonomy.

[4] Farrell and Saloner (1985, 1986), Katz and Shapiro (1985, 1986) and David (1985, 1987) represent some of the seminal papers; see also David and Greenstein (1990) for an excellent survey.

[5] For an empirical analysis of sources of network externalities in the packaged PC software market, see Shurmer (1993a).

[6] For a typology see David and Greenstein (1990).

[7] The first patents were granted in fifteenth-century Italy (Scherer and Ross, 1990).

[8] That is, more truly representative of intellectual effort (Cornish, 1989).

[9] Mere mathematical methods, scientific theories and discoveries such as laws of nature are not patentable—they must be applied in some way; see for example s1(2) UK Patents Act, 1977.

[10] "Prior art" is the state of applied scientific knowledge at the point in time of invention.

[11] Subject to any special rules such as those governing the acquisition of rights by third parties. For example, an employer is entitled to copyright in literary, musical, dramatic or artistic works if an employee creates them in the course of employment; s11(2) Copyright, Design & Patents Act 1988.

[12] Within the EC, a limited exception has been devised that may eventually allow a special form of protection to pharmaceutical products in order to allow 20 years from test approval; OJ 1992 L182/1 & ECJ Case C-350/92.

[13] Copyright duration in the EC will eventually be harmonised at life plus 70 years; OJ 1993 C27/7 adopted.

[14] The U.S. Copyright Office registers work, but since the passing of the Berne Convention Implementation Act 1989, the penalties for non-registration have been diminished.

[15] A UK patent will typically take 40–42 months from application to grant, with an upper limit of 54 months being set.

[16] See S36 CDP 1988 & Art. 10(2) Berne Convention.

[17] In the United States, for example, the principal policy instrument (other than merger laws) is section 2 of the Sherman Act. In the UK, the main competition body is the Monopolies and Mergers Commission. In the European Union, Article 86 of the European Economic Community Treaty, adopted in 1957, prohibits "any improper exploiting...of a dominant position".

[18] There is now a large literature which seeks to determine the optimal patent life trade-off. This stems from the pioneering work of Nordhaus (1969).

[19] For example, there was no copyright law in the People's Republic of China until 1987.

[20] The optimal choice between protection by patent, by commercial secrecy, or by a combination of both, depends upon the particular circumstance under consideration. The empirical evidence highlights the wide diversity of the propensity to patent across industries (Scherer, 1983).

[21] This formula was first adopted by the International Electrotechnical Commission (IEC) for patent licensing.

[22] See *Electronic Times*, March 1994 and Birkmaier (1994).

[23] See "Softwares", *The Economist*, 23 April 1994.

[24] Reaching the licensing agreements for the Global System for Mobile communications (GSM), for example, took some two to three years.

[25] In order to give the patentee a fair chance to exploit the patented invention.

[26] Art. 9(2).

[27] Council Directive 91/250/EEC (14/0591).

[28] See IBM v Commission (1981) 3 CMLR 635, (1984) 3 CMLR 147.

[29] Intellectual Property Rights and Standardisation COM(92)–445 final, adopted 27 October 1992.

[30] Indeed, this latter point formed one of the grounds of appeal in the *Magill* case on licensing of TV listings (see reports at (1991) 4 CMLR 586 et seq).

[31] Besen and Farrell (1991) present a detailed account of the changing nature of the ITU's standards work.

[32] For a concise account of deregulation in the EC see Amory (1991).

[33] For example, phase 1 of the GSM standard runs to over 5,000 pages.

[34] For a detailed account of the changing institutional infrastructure, see Shurmer (1993b).

[35] Concern at the slow pace of reforms at the international level partly explain the growing preeminence of regional standards organisations (Besen and Farrell, 1991).

[36] The extent to which designs are covered by copyright or separate design rights varies from country to country.

[37] A separate class of sui generis design rights first created by the U.S. Semiconductor Chip Protection Act, 1984.

[38] The potential of these new multimedia remains unclear, but substantial investment programs have already begun. For example, BT plans to invest £20 million in the second trials stage of its "video on demand" service. While at the other end of the spectrum, the estimated cost of MCI's proposals to upgrade its network to act as an "information superhighway" for advanced television, telephone and computer applications tops $20 billion.

[39] Communication of the Commission, Towards a Dynamic European Economy, Green Paper on the Development of the Common Market for Telecommunications Services and Equipment, COM(87)290 of 30/6/1987.

[40] CEPT had formerly coordinated the activities of the national PTTs in Europe. ETSI, in effect, became its successor.

[41] OJ 1989 C117/1.

[42] Essential IPRs represent the only viable technical solution for obtaining compliance with the specifications stipulated in the standard in question.

References

Amory, B., 1991. Telecommunications in the European Communities: The New Regulatory Framework, *International Computer Law Adviser*, Dec 91–Jan 92, 4–20.

Besen, S. M., and J. Farrell, 1991. The Role of the ITU in Standardization, *Telecommunications Policy*, August, 311–321.

Birkmaier, C., 1994. Another Tollbooth on the Information Highway?, *Videography*, June.

Breyer, S. G., 1970. The Uneasy Case for Copyright, *Harvard Law Review*, 84, 281.

Cane, A., 1993. Setting Standards for Telecommunications, *Financial Times*, 20 February, p. 8.

Cave, M., and M. Shurmer, 1990. Standardization Issues for HDTV, in J.P. Chamoux (ed.) *Deregulating Regulators? Communications Policies for the 90's* (IOS Press).

Cornish, W. R., 1989. *Intellectual Property*, Sweet and Maxwell.

David, P. A., 1985. Clio and the Economics of QWERTY, *American Economic Review*, 75, 332–336.

David, P. A., 1987. Some New Standards for the Economics of Standardization in the Information Age, in P. Dasgupta and P. Stoneman (eds.) *Economic Policy and Technological Performance*, Cambridge University Press.

David, P. A., and S. Greenstein, 1990. The Economics of Compatibility Standards: An Introduction to Recent Research, *Economics of Innovation and New Technology* 1(1/2), 3–41.

DTI, 1994. *Future Resourcing of the Preparation of Standards*, London: Department of Trade and Industry.

Ergas, H., 1987. Does Technology Policy Matter? in Guile and Books (eds.) *Technology and Global Industry: Companies and Nations in the World Economy*, 191–245, Washington DC: National Academy Press.

Farrell, J., 1989. Standardization and Intellectual Property, *Jurimetrics Journal*, 30(Fall), 35–50.

Farrell J., and G. Saloner, 1985. Standardization, Compatibility and Innovation, *Rand Journal of Economics* 16 (1), 70–83.

Farrell, J., and G. Saloner, 1986. Installed Base and Compatibility: Innovations, Product Pre-announcements, and Predation, *American Economic Review* 76, 940–955.

Good, D., 1992. How Far Should IP Rights Have to Give Way to Standardisation, *European Intellectual Property Review*, 9, 225.

Grindley, P., 1992. *Standards, Business Strategy and Policy: A Casebook*, London Business School.

Katz, M., and C. Shapiro, 1985. Network Externalities, Competition and Compatibility, *American Economic Review* 75(3), 424–440.

Katz, M., and C. Shapiro, 1986. Technology Adoption in the Presence of Network Externalities, *Journal of Political Economy* 94(4), 822–841.

Kaufer, E., 1988. *The Economics of the Patent System*, Harwood.

Liebenstein, H., 1966. Allocative Efficiency v. X-Efficiency, *American Economic Review*, 56, 392–415.

Matutes, C., and P. Regibeau, 1987. Standardization in Multi-Component Industries, in H.L. Gabel (ed.) *Product Standardization and Competitive Strategy*, North Holland.

Nordhaus, W. D., 1969. *Invention, Growth, and Welfare: A Theoretical Treatment of Technological Change*, Cambridge: MIT Press.

OECD, 1991. *Information Technology Standards: The Economic Dimension*, Information Computer and Communications Policy Report 25; Paris: OECD.

OTA, 1992. *Global Standards: Building Blocks for the Future*, Congress of the United States Office of Technology Assessment, Washington DC: US Govt. Printing Office.

Pessa, P., 1991. Evaluating the Idea/Expression Dichotomy: Rhetoric or a Legal Principle, *Computer Law and Policy*, 166.

Prins, C., and M. Schiessl, 1993. The New European Telecommunications Standards Policy, *EIPR*, 8, 263–266.

Scherer, F. M., 1983. The Propensity to Patent, *International Journal of Industrial Organisation*, Vol 1, 107–128.

Scherer, F. M., and D. Ross, 1990. *Industrial Market Structure and Economic Performance*, Boston: Houghton Mifflin.

Schmidtchen, D., and C. Kobolt, 1993. A Pacemaker that Stops Halfway, *International Review of Law and Economics*, 413–430.

Shurmer, M., 1993a. An Investigation into Sources of Network Externalities in the Packaged PC Software Market, *Information Economics and Policy*, 5, 231–251.

Shurmer, M., 1993b. International Telecommunications Standardization: An Overview of the Institutional Framework and Evaluation of Standards Policy, paper presented to the 1993 *International Telecommunications Society (ITS) European Regional Conference*, Marstrand, Sweden, June.

Shurmer, M., M. Cave et al., 1992. *HDTV: High Definition, High Stakes, High Risks*, NERA, Brunel University.

Swann, P., and M. Shurmer, 1994. The Emergence of Standards in PC Software: Who Would Benefit from Institutional Intervention?, *Information Economics and Policy*, forthcoming.

Position Papers

Interoperability and Intellectual Property

Frede Ask
European Telecommunications Standards Institute

The Role of ETSI

The European Telecommunications Standards Institute (ETSI) was established in 1988, with its headquarters in Sophia Antipolis in southern France. The ETSI membership list now contains 347 Members and 65 Observers, including the administrations of 28 CEPT countries and the leading European public network operators, manufacturers, users, private service providers, and research bodies. The EC (European Commission) and the EFTA (European Free Trade Association) Secretariat hold the status of special Counsellors.

ETSI standardization work is mainly carried out by Technical Committees and Sub-Committees, which are based on voluntary participation of ETSI Members. Every Member has the right to be represented in any of these bodies. For certain areas of standardization, however, it is necessary to speed up the work by using other methods than voluntary participation of Members. Here we have the Project Team model. At the ETSI headquarters in Sophia Antipolis, a number of Project Teams are working according to Terms of Reference established by the Technical Assembly. A Project Team typically consists of five or six experts working on a full-time or part-time basis for a period of six months to two or three years. Since the creation of ETSI about 100 Project Teams, made up of approximately 400 experts, have been at work. Some teams have already accomplished their mission of producing standards. At the moment ETSI has 30 active Project Teams made up of about 100 experts. The standards production of ETSI has been very successful. Approximately 500 deliverables (standards and technical reports) have been produced and adopted since ETSI was established.

The standards devised by the ETSI Project Teams and Technical Committees must be approved by the ETSI Technical Assembly in order to obtain status as ETS (European Telecommunications Standards). These are voluntary standards. However, ETSI has also undertaken to produce the technical content of the so-called Common Technical Regulations (CTRs). CTRs are regulations issued by the Technical Recommendations Applications Committee (TRAC). When TRAC wants ETSI to produce the technical content of a CTR, this will be done in accordance with an EC mandate. This mandate will make it clear that the standard in question will be a mandatory one. The output from ETSI is in this case called TBR (Technical Basis for a Regulation).

It can thus be said that ETSI is still only making voluntary standards. On the other hand, ETSI is prepared to take up the obligation of contributing to the necessary mandatory standards. But it will be TRAC who transforms the ETSI output, the TBR, into a CTR, by adding the administrative clauses and other necessary details. The arrangement between the European Commission, TRAC, and ETSI regarding the production of CTRs should be seen as a special application of the New Approach (described in Council Resolution of 7 May 1985, 85/C 136/01); i.e., an EC Directive refers to existing standards. It should also be mentioned that before ETSI issues a standard, the standard will be approved and implemented according to a procedure respecting the governing principles for standards making (standstill period, public enquiry, approval by national weighted voting, and other national handling). It goes without saying that the European national standardization bodies play an important role in this area.

Until recently, Europe was far from being a single market. Each national telecommunications network had its own technical specifications and approval process. This state of affairs contributed to the protection of national industries, and non-European companies had to market their products individually to each European country. Thus, it was extremely difficult to gain access to the whole

European market. With the creation of the European Single Market, the European Telecommunications Standards (ETSs) have begun to play a very important role, for the following reasons:

• Interoperability of networks: Standards assure that the telecommunications networks (be they public or private) can work together. Here it is worth mentioning that many standards, which by definition are voluntary, contain a number of technical specifications that in practical terms are mandatory.

• Free movements of goods and services: In theory, free movement of telecommunications products and services could be introduced between the countries without having standards. There would be, however, a risk of some countries denying the import of certain types of equipment by "inventing" technical or safety reasons. If, on the other hand, the vendor or service provider can prove conformity to standards, then free movement is better secured.

• Liberalization: Liberalization of the telecommunications sector means that customers can buy their products and services wherever they want. The free movement of products and services is necessary to make liberalization more than an illusion. Consequently, standards also play an important role in liberalization.

• Public Procurement: In spite of liberalization, substantial parts of the telecommunications infrastructure will be run by public or semi-public bodies. Here public procurement plays an important role. In order to avoid protection of national industries, it is necessary to establish rules to make sure that foreign manufacturers have a chance to deliver their equipment. Here again, standards are the tool to ensure that public procurements are run in a correct and transparent way.

Intellectual Property and Standards

The issue of Intellectual Property Rights (IPR) will undoubtedly play an increasing role in telecommunications standardization in the coming years. This is due partly to the high number of patents within this high technology sector and partly to the fact that many telecommunications standards are mandatory, either formally or in practice. ETSI is in the process of attempting to solve the problems of IPR by means of its adopted but not yet implemented IPR Policy and Undertaking.

ETSI wants to avoid the following situation: ETSI's Technical Assembly decides that a standard shall be made regarding a certain telecommunications product. A technical working group is then established with the goal of elaborating that standard. After, for instance, three years of work, the standard is ready for adoption (to be sent out for public inquiry followed by a vote). At a certain point in time before the adoption of the standard, an ETSI Member informs the ETSI Director that it has an IPR (typically a patent) that covers the technical solution described in the said standard. In other words: In order to design or produce equipment in accordance with the standard, it is necessary to ask for a license from the patent holder. If the latter refuses to grant a license on fair, reasonable, and non-discriminatory terms, it would then be the only manufacturer who could deliver products that meet the standard. It goes without saying that such a monopoly situation is neither acceptable to ETSI nor to society as a whole.

The EC Communication on IPR states (clause 6.2.1.6) that as a general principle "Intellectual Property Right holders should use best efforts to identify in a timely manner any IPR which they hold which is relevant to a standard which is being developed and to confirm or refuse permission for its incorporation in that standard promptly." This principle is reflected in the ETSI IPR arrangement in the form of an obligation for Members (or non-Members who have signed the Undertaking) to disclose to ETSI in good faith whether they have IPRs that might become essential, and to inform ETSI whether they will exercise their right to refuse to grant licenses. By "essential" it is understood that the IPR represents the only viable solution to obtain compliance with the specifications stipulated in the standard in question.

This obligation to disclose, in a timely manner, potentially essential IPRs protects the standardizers from spending significant time and manpower resources only to discover that their standard is blocked by an IPR holder who refuses to grant licenses. Considering that the cost of a technical working party over a period of three years, for example, could be close three MECU (corresponding to approximately three million US dollars), it seems reasonable to protect society as well as the standardizers against such futile investments.

In order to allow a reasonable period of time for IPR holders to identify their own portfolios of IPRs, the ETSI IPR Undertaking allows a period of 180 days for IPR holders to notify ETSI if they are willing to grant licenses for a specific IPR. This 180-day period begins on the date the ETSI Technical Assembly has decided to put into its Work Program a work item related to the standard which is going to be elaborated. It should be underlined that the work item in question has to be defined with enough clarity for the IPR holder to carry out a meaningful search. The 180-day period only counts from the day this condition is fulfilled.

The IPR Holders' inalienable right to refuse to grant licenses is reflected in the EC Communication on IPR, Clause 4.3.5, which says: "The freedom of the right holder to refuse to license is, at the present time, absolute, since his exclusive intellectual property rights cannot be subject to expropriation or compulsory licensing except in exceptional circumstances such as reasons of national security or over-riding public interest." It should also be underlined that there are no consequences for the IPR holder if it refuses to grant licenses provided that the notification is given within the 180-day period.

The ETSI IPR Policy and Undertaking stipulate a number of requirements to the licensing terms once the IPR holder has granted a license. These terms—as well as the arrangement for the identification of the IPRs—are currently being debated among the Members of ETSI in a special committee established by the ETSI General Assembly.

The Standards Development Process and the NII: A View from the Trenches

S. N. Baron
Society of Motion Picture and Television Engineers

Background

The standards system in the United States consists of a number of standards developers including government agencies, professional societies, trade associations, and technical advisory groups. Thousands of individuals, corporations, and government agencies contribute their efforts to the process of standards development. The bulk of these standards are developed as part of a voluntary standards system that is based on the principles of openness and due process and leads to consensus on the content of the standard.

Much of the voluntary standards development system is administered through the American National Standards Institute (ANSI) which is recognized as the central coordinating body by many of the United States voluntary standards developers. ANSI and member standards developers work under a defined set of procedures that provide criteria, requirements, and guidelines for coordinating and developing consensus on voluntary standards. Approval of the standards indicates that "the principles of openness and due process have been followed in the approval procedure and that a consensus of those directly and materially affected by the standards has been achieved."[1] ANSI also provides a gateway to international standards organizations. ANSI coordinates United States activities with international groups like the International Organization for Standardization (ISO) and the International Electrotechnical Commission (IEC).

The due process and openness requirements of the voluntary standards development system are of particular importance. Due process means that any "person" with a direct and material interest in the activity's outcome has a right to participate in the activity. In this context, a "person" is an organization, corporation, government agency, or individual. Participation includes the right to express a position and its basis, have the position considered, and appeal the decision if adversely affected. Openness means that participation is open to all persons directly and materially affected by the activity in question without them having to overcome any undue financial barrier, be a member in any organization, or be restricted on the basis of their technical qualifications or other similar requirements.[2] Openness also implies the timely and adequate notice of the initiation and process of standards development and the establishment and progress of a consensus-developing group.[3]

Consensus is established when substantial agreement has been reached by those directly and materially affected. Substantial agreement is understood to imply much more than a simple majority but not necessarily unanimity. Consensus requires that all views and objections be considered and that a concerted effort be made toward their resolution.[4]

In addition to the principles of openness, due process, and consensus is the unstated but implied principle of timeliness. Rapid changes in technology have dramatically shortened the lifetime of standards. The U.S. voluntary standards development process recognizes the impact of change, and the process provides for all standards to be revisited and reaffirmed every five years.[5] Timeliness is, therefore, a critical issue. A standard must be available in a timely manner. If introduced too quickly, the standard may represent a state of the art that is insufficiently mature to be sustained: in other words, the standard is rendered inadequate soon after its introduction. If introduced too slowly, the standard may represent a state of the art that has already been overcome by more advanced developments: in other words, the standard is made obsolete before its introduction.

Timeliness is driven by the practical realities of the marketplace. For example, the Society of Motion Picture and Television Engineers (SMPTE), a recognized U.S. voluntary standards developer since 1916, restructured its standards development practices some half-dozen years ago and reduced the minimum formal standards documentation cycle from 2 1/4 years to less than 6 months. This decision was made in response to industry need and the impact of technology on the voluntary standards development environment.

The United States is fortunate in having a voluntary standards development program in place that is private sector-administered yet draws upon the strengths of both the public and private sectors. There is a need, however, to revisit the standardization process on a regular basis for the purpose of maintaining its relevancy in light of developments in technology and changes in the international standards-setting environment. The National Institute of Standards and Technology (NIST) provides an oversight function and fora for the discussion of the process, particularly when dramatic changes in the standards development environment occur. Excellent examples are a public hearing on U.S. participation in international standards activities held in April 1990, and a workshop in June 1994 on the impact of the NII which produced this book.

The impact of the NII (and more importantly, the Global Information Infrastructure or GII) on the voluntary standards development process is the subject of this paper.

Standards Development Process

There are six stages in the process of developing a standard (see Figure 1):

1. Determination of a need

2. Discovery, in which information necessary to the development is acquired

3. Development of the standards document by a group of individuals with expertise in the area

4. Public review, which includes distribution for public comment prior to approval

5. Determination of consensus, which includes resolution of any objections or problems raised during the process

6. Publication and distribution for public use.

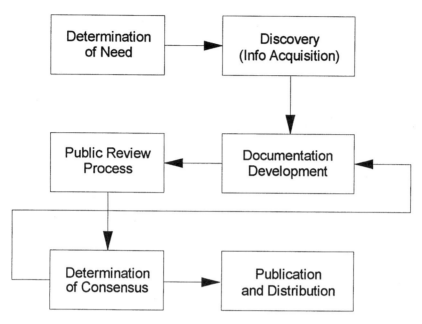

Figure 1 The Standards Process.

Table 1 illustrates the current standardization process and the NII's influence on that process.

The SMPTE Documentation Program

SMPTE standards activities are focused on multimedia "info-tainment" services, moving image sequences and associated sound that are geared to the mass market. In most of its activities, SMPTE is concerned with technologies and practices that are international in scope. SMPTE has developed a documentation program that defines three levels of documentation (standards, recommended practices, and engineering guidelines)[6] and a list of criteria that all documents must meet.[7]

The SMPTE documentation program provides for the process shown in Figure 2. SMPTE provides an acceptable public forum where multiple service providers and multiple service users who are usually competitors can meet to discuss technology and its application and to develop consensus on standards.

Table 1 Navigating the Process

Stage	Current Process	Possible Improvement
1a. Determination of Need	Draft request for standards development.	
1b. Finding the Right Standards Developer	Know which standards-developing society has jurisdiction and make appropriate request for development.	A list of authorized standards developers made available through the NII or through NIST, the Library of Congress, ANSI, etc.
2. Discovery	Call for input of relevant information. Public notification (ANSI PIN).	Put ANSI PIN on Internet. SMPTE SEEC exists on CompuServe. Expand to include non-ANSI efforts.
3. Documentation Development	Standards developer charges a group with developing standard. Documents are generated and communicated to interested parties.	A standard means of transporting text and drawings is required.
4. Public Review Process	Reviewed at meetings called for that purpose. Published for public comment in appropriate media (SMPTE *Journal*, SMPTE SEEC). This is currently an "expert" review process.	Create special bulletin board(s) for public comment. This may prolong the consensus determination process.
5. Determination of Consensus	Resolution of challenges and objections.	Publication of resolution on bulletin boards.

Standards development work begins with both a determination of need and consideration of the probability that the process will produce a document that will meet the criteria. The request for standards development requires support by multiple parties and usually includes multiple providers and users. Sufficient statement of support indicates that the proposal may generate a market and thus some possible competitive response. SMPTE also provides a mechanism for public review of the standards developed by consortia to allow user input prior to final approval of the standards

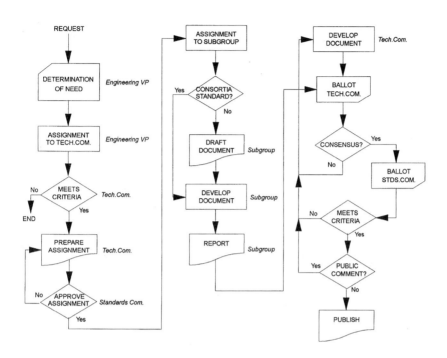

Figure 2 The SMPTE Document Development Process.

document. The 35 mm film format, SMPTE 125 (the precursor to ITU/R 601), and the D1 tape format are examples of standards developed by SMPTE. The D2 and D3 tape formats are examples of standards developed by consortia and processed by SMPTE.

Work is assigned to Technology Committees in the SMPTE documentation process. These committees are organized according to areas of expertise, such as recording technology, film laboratory technology, projection technology, or electronic signal interface technology. The requirement for public notification that work has begun is met by publication of an announcement in the SMPTE *Journal*, a notice posted on the SMPTE SEEC Bulletin Board, and submission of the PIN form to ANSI.

The Technology Committee prepares a plan of work that stipulates the work to be done, a timeline for that work, and the form of the final output including reporting requirements. If the body of knowledge pertaining to a specific request for documentation is sufficient to begin work, a small drafting group may be assigned to create a straw man document or, in the case of a request by a consortium, distribution of its existing documentation. If the body of knowledge pertaining to a specific request for documentation is not sufficient to begin work, a Study Group may be formed to develop a report on the state of the art, requirements for further development in technology, and areas where documentation might begin.

The SMPTE process has shown electronic communication to be an effective means of both alerting interested parties that a project has been identified and providing a mechanism to request input from an informed audience. Electronic communication is also a useful means of providing interested parties with access to the documents during development stages. The major obstruction to this access is the lack of a common means of transporting formatted text and engineering drawings across the interface. This lack of a common transport mechanism, particularly with respect to engineering drawings, also impedes progress in developing the standards documents.

The Technology Committees meet at regular intervals to discuss project work in progress. Most of the committees' communication is through electronic and paper mail. The Technology Committee is assigned responsibility of developing consensus on a document (lower level groups need not reach consensus and may file majority and minority reports). The consensus process is currently handled by letter ballots, followed by electronic communication of the results. Any objections during the balloting process are also handled by electronic or paper mail. SMPTE has considered the use of electronic balloting in order to shorten the balloting process. However, electronic balloting requires a secure validation process, and the decrease in processing time would not be significant since the balloting period must allow adequate time for members to review and comment on the document.

Once consensus is achieved, the document is forwarded to the SMPTE's Standards Committee for administrative approval. Administrative approval verifies that the request for work was properly administered and that any objections were properly handled. The document is then published in the Society's *Journal*. Editorial comments received at any stage are considered by the Chair of the

Technology Committee in consultation with SMPTE Engineering department staff and the Engineering Vice President. Comments that might require a technical change to the document are returned to the Technology Committee for further consideration. The comments are reported by electronic and paper mail.

Impact of the NII on the Four Principles

Openness and Due Process

A NII makes universal "openness" a distinct possibility. We have defined openness as open participation for all persons directly and materially affected by the activity in question. Furthermore, everyone can participate without having to overcome any undue barriers, conditions, or restriction. A bulletin-board approach to announcements and requests for comment ensures that the requirements will be met for the timely and adequate notice of initiation of standards development and the general public's access to information on the consensus process. A bulletin-board approach to posting the standards' contents helps facilitate the due process requirements.

However, while an increase in public awareness and participation is "good news," its impact on the standardization process could become "disastrous." ANSI considers the "user-consumer" to be directly and materially affected by the outcome of the standards process,[8] and that an individual user of the goods and/or services is therefore an appropriate participant in this process. Imagine the impact on a voluntary standards developer if he or she had to review the comments of a few hundred thousand NII commentators on the subject of professional studio lighting colorimetry standards, for example. That developer would then have to address these issues and objections (whether they be informed or not) to the contents of a standard placed on the NII for public comment. The impact on the developer's resources would be overwhelming.

Clearly, there must be a balance between the benefits of universal openness and those of achieving meaningful standards in a timely manner. Again, the definition of "open" in an NII environment needs to be addressed.

Consensus

Consensus is established when those affected by the standardization have reached substantial agreement. Consensus requires that
all views and objections be considered and that a concerted effort
be made toward their resolution. Often objections are not relevant
to the issue and can be easily eliminated. Take for example, a
committee determining the technical adequacy of an electronic
information interchange protocol. A member raises marketplace
objections. SMPTE standards are argued on technical merits, and
because they are voluntary standards, marketplace arguments are
deemed to be invalid.[9]

The consensus process does, however, provide for appeals, and
thousands of NII participants could lead to such an overload in
administration of comments and responses to appeals that the final
approval of a standard would be delayed. Such delay could have an
impact on the practical implementation of the standard, with
serious economic impact.

Timeliness

A standard must be available in a timely manner. Voluntary standards developers are continually challenged by the need to introduce standards after the technology has become sufficiently mature
to sustain the standard but before it becomes obsolete. A standardization process prolonged by massive numbers of interventions
may consistently produce standards that are obsolete before their
introduction.

Conclusions

Digital compression techniques applied to the transport of images,
sound, and data are providing the catalyst to make a digital
information infrastructure economically viable. Digital packetized
communications systems provide flexibility, economy, and compatibility across a broad spectrum of distribution media. They allow
the development of new services and the practical possibility of
interactive services in the areas of entertainment, education, information, and business transactions.

Administration

The United States is fortunate to have a private sector–administered voluntary standards development program that draws upon the strengths of both the public and private sectors. The introduction of a NII will require greater cooperation between all interested parties to maintain the system. Major issues to be resolved include the means of supporting universal access to the NII and protection of intellectual property rights. We must respect and protect the property rights of the content providers. In the absence of such protection, the NII's content will be restricted by the owners of that content. We must deploy both legislative and technical mechanisms to ensure these rights. Mechanisms to be developed include access control, systems for payment and audit, security and traceability, and respect of privacy (the ability to limit access).

Possible Benefits Derived from the NII

The NII could facilitate meeting openness and due-process requirements of the voluntary standards process by providing:

1. A directory of authorized standards developers, stating their areas of jurisdiction

2. Bulletin board services (similar to IEEE on the Internet and SMPTE SEEC on CompuServe) to post projects underway and facilitate a mechanism for input to the process

3. A standard means of transporting text and drawings across the interface

4. An document archive with titles, abstracts with key-word access, and document contents, with protection of intellectual property rights and payment to standards developer for access to documents

5. Assurance that any new tools developed are designed to shorten the development process.

The development and use of voluntary standards would be facilitated by establishment of a universal archive. A virtual universal archive could be created by providing appropriate tools on the NII.

Notes

[1] "American National Standards Institute, Procedures for the Development and Coordination of American National Standards," *Foreword*, September 9, 1987.

[2] SMPTE Administrative Practices, Section XIII.H.3, *Due Process Requirements*, July 2, 1991, p. 12.

[3] SMPTE Administrative Practices, Section XIII.H.4, *Consensus*, July 2, 1991, p. 12.

[4] "American National Standards Institute Procedures for the Development and Coordination of American National Standards," *Section 1.3 Criteria for Approval and Withdrawal of American National Standards*, pp. 8–9, September 9, 1987.

[5] "American National Standards Institute Procedures for Development and Coordination of American National Standards," *Section 4.4.1 Periodic Review of American National Standards*, September 9, 1987, p. 13.

[6] *Standards* are documents that state basic specifications and criteria necessary for interchange or interconnection including form and/or function requirements. *Recommended Practices* are documents that state specifications, dimensions, criteria, and form and/or function but are not absolutely necessary for effective interchange or interconnection. A Recommended Practice may provide information on test products or procedures. *Engineering Guidelines* are basically tutorial and may provide information to guide design preliminary to standardization.

[7] The criteria include: evidence of potential for use, lack of significant conflict with existing documents, no evidence that the document is contrary to the public interest, resolution of proprietary issues and conformance with rules on format and content.

[8] "American National Standards Institute Procedures for the Development and Coordination of American National Standards," Section 1.2.3.1. User-Consumer, September 9, 1987, p. 7.

[9] SMPTE Administrative Practices, Section XIII.K, *Engineering Documentation Program*, pp. 21–23.

The Current Debate on IT Standardization Policy in the European Union

Paola Bucciarelli
European Commission

Like other industrial regions of the world, the European Union[1] is preparing its evolution towards the Global Information Society and expects great opportunities from it in terms of economic progress, employment, quality of life, and improved public services. At the request of the European Council, a task force composed of top representatives of industry, operators, and users delivered their vision of the Global Information Society and the broad lines of an action plan that will make it possible.[2] *Interconnection of networks* and *interoperability of services and applications* are recommended among the primary actions that will facilitate evolution toward the Information Society. *Open systems standards* are considered to be essential for interconnectivity and interoperability. Consequently, it is recommended that the European standardization process be reviewed in order to increase its speed of action and responsiveness to the market.

The Global Information Society has increased pressure on the standardization process, and has attracted more attention to the role of standardization policy. In fact, standardization policy has always been important in the achievement of other important European economic objectives, such as the single market. During recent months, however, the need for refocusing standardization policy on user requirements has been clearly expressed. The debate had already been opened in specialized circles when the impetus of the Information Society arrived, widening the debate on standardization and making the improvement of its performance more urgent.

Although initiated earlier, standardization policy in the Information Technology (IT) field was given momentum ten years ago by Council Decision 87/95[3], which set the legal reference for its main pillars:

- Alignment with international standards

- The production of European profiles to reduce options and improve interoperability

- Measures to support the application of standards, such as testing services to assure a degree of discipline in the implementation of product standards and procurement guidance to create a critical mass. In particular, it is noteworthy that an article of this Council Decision requires reference to European and international standards for the purchase of systems with interoperability requirements.

Over the ten years from 1985 to 1995 all the necessary elements will have been developed to meet the policy objective of providing multivendor systems interoperability for the exchange of data and information to support the operation of the Single Market and the economic and social cohesion of the European Union. EWOS and ETSI have been created to speed up production of European standards and to increase participation by all interested parties. The CTS[4] program has supplied technical means for assessing the correct implementation of the standards. EPHOS[5] has provided detailed guidance on the selection of options to best meet the needs of public administration; it has also been expected to provide advance information to suppliers.

The major developed countries have embraced a similar policy and have promoted similar initiatives for its implementation (such as GOSIP in the United States and OSI policy in Japan). Other countries have been willing to follow their example.

Current Issues

Across the world, public administrations, private sectors, users' associations, academia, and large and small suppliers, having recognized the benefit of open communication through standardized specifications, have committed themselves to adoption of the

Open Systems Interconnection (OSI) specifications. These were expected to displace any other public or proprietary specification because they are the result of an international standardizing process and are expected to be implemented worldwide.

After ten years, the concept of Open Systems has "taken off." The popularity achieved by the Open Systems concept constitutes a remarkable success for standardization policy. However, "openness" is not necessarily achieved through official standards. Despite the fact that the concepts of interoperability and portability through Open Systems have become a "must" for customers and vendors, products based on official standards have not been widely implemented. On the contrary, they have often been displaced by so-called "de facto" standardised products, i.e., products successful in the market whose technology is based on either public or private specifications. Such specifications may be very satisfactory from the technical point of view, but using them raises the risk of creating "islands of incompatibility" resulting from each community being able to choose its own technical solution.

While everyone agrees on the advantage of standards over private or public specifications, nobody is willing to wait for the effective fully standardized solutions that have been promised for years. Conversely, the demand for them has never been really firm and wide enough to push manufacturers to a genuine commitment to standards. Standardization policy has thus far failed to result in a wide implementation of standardized products. Four major areas appear to face serious problems :

• The capacity of the present standardization system to keep pace with technological evolution and to deliver the required specifications on time and with the appropriate level of detail

• The possibility of implementing such specifications with enough discipline to avoid divergence and to enable interoperability

• The market availability of standards-conforming products

• The ability of purchasers (public or private) to refer to standards for buying and building interoperable systems without difficulty.

These difficulties are especially evident in networking, where large groups are using different protocol suites to meet their open systems requirements. In particular, the IPS (Internet Protocol

Suite) specifications are playing an increasing role. However, they have been unable to displace the OSI standards, as the two protocol suites address different needs. The IPS solutions are simple, cost-effective, and widely available. OSI solutions compete with IPS for richness and flexibility, and find supporters among those communities that have requirements that IPS is unable to satisfy. For those communities OSI represents the only possible non-proprietary solution. The result is a lack of interoperability, which may be partially overcome by the implementation of gateways, through these will inevitably add cost, complexity, and degradation of service.

This OSI-IPS duality, which is hard to reconcile, is only one example illustrating how a difficult situation can evolve if the relationship between standardization and the market is not straight-forward, well understood or well accepted. Competing standards are painful to users, costly to manufacturers, confusing to managers, and detrimental to the construction of worldwide interoperable information infrastructures. The IPS-OSI case offers a test for the global infrastructure: if the most developed regions are not able to agree with one another and to set up unified, basic services (starting from e-mail), a Global Information Society will not be feasible.

The European Union's standardization policy has been applied for more than ten years. During this time, so many changes have occurred that its role, or at any rate its mechanisms, require a review. Major changes have occurred in the technological domain, and standardization should be adapted to keep pace with them. Moreover, the promise of a Global Information Society is adding new opportunities and requirements to the role and mechanisms of standardization. Such challenges cannot be faced by a system that is suffering from the weaknesses mentioned above. The Commission therefore believes that refocusing IT standardization policy is a primary concern. It has opened a debate on the different aspects of standardization policy, which will culminate in November 1994[6] with a Workshop in Brussels. At this Workshop the European Commission will ask its partners to make recommendations on how and where to reshape IT standardization policy so as better to serve the European Union's social and economic objectives.

The Point of View of the European Commission

The Commission is responsible for the definition of standardization policy for the European Union, but it is not within its capacity to solve the standardization problems facing the information society. The Commission can be more than policy maker—it can influence and support the evolution of the system by playing the roles of user, customer, regulator, arbiter, sponsor, and facilitator—but the main initiatives remain under the responsibility of other players. The recommendations of the Report on the Global Information Society clearly illustrate the distinction between the roles of different organizations. The standardization organizations, for example, are responsible for improving their planning and their production mechanisms to meet the requirements of the information society.

Although the Commission is open to debate and will reflect on its policy and decisions and on the interests of the involved parties, its point of view remains firm on certain principles:

1. The Definition of the Word "Standard"

The Commission favors the adoption of a unified worldwide terminology, and considers that *Standards* are only those developed by recognized standardization organizations. At the international level, ISO and IEC are such organizations; at the European level they are CEN, CENELEC, and ETSI. Standards are drawn up on the basis of defined rules, and are subject to an open comment and voting process. The word *Specifications,* with further qualifier, should be used for the other kind of documents. In particular, a *Publicly Available Specification* (PAS) is a document that meets certain criteria making it suitable for possible processing as a formal standard.

2. A Policy Based on Standards

The standardization policy of the European Union favors the application of international and European standards. Preference should be given to standards whenever they provide efficient solutions to technical problems. Delivering timely and accurate standards is of the utmost importance for the provision of information infrastructure, and represents a major challenge to the standardization system. Transposition into standards (e.g., by use of "fast track procedures") of Publicly Available Specifications established by industry, professional organizations, or consortia may speed up the process and should be encouraged, provided that three conditions are met:

- The consensus ought to be able to withstand the test of a public enquiry
- The situation regarding intellectual property rights (IPRs) should be clear
- Such standards should evolve with a sufficiently broad participation by the various players to ensure they can be properly maintained.

Conflicting standards risk creating islands of incompatibility, and should be discouraged. When they cannot be avoided, a sufficient level of interoperability among them should be a requirement. This is the case with the IPS and OSI protocol suites, for which *co-existence* and *convergence* should be the recommended guidelines.

3. Conformance Testing and Interoperability

Conformance testing remains strictly associated with rigorous implementation of standard specifications and their unambiguous interpretation. This is to provide business assurance of operability as well as technical integrity. A larger deployment of standard-based products will allow better appreciation of this need and, in consequence, a better shaping of the conformance services, which today appear to be a solution waiting for a problem. The requirements for the testing process have to be reformulated and clearly expressed by the market, and then the services will be adapted to fit them. For example, testing services might be engineered to be better integrated in the product development process by manufacturers or shaped in a way that can be used on customer premises.

The immense problem of producing and maintaining abstract test suites and related test technologies should be faced by sharing the workload at the international level and by investing in automated tools, which reduce the need for human intervention in the design and execution of tests. Public investment aid for conformance testing in the European Union has been be refocused in this direction.

Interoperability testing should be application driven and based on internationally developed reference implementations. Interoperability testing, however, should not be approached without prior conformance testing unless standards are delivered with a high degree of accuracy and completeness.

4. Public Procurement Guidance

The need to refer to standards to ensure exchange of information and portability of applications has become obvious to all levels of administration. Purchasers are aware of their responsibility in this area. Purchasers are, however, under pressure to adopt shorter-term cost-effective solutions rather than create a market for longer-term solutions based on standards. The difficulty for suppliers is that there is an insufficient market to encourage them to offer cost-effective, well integrated, and high-performance solutions based on standards. Existing means of public procurement coordination through mandatory reference to standards or profiles will not be effective, due in part to a technology and education gap between the technical standards and customers. Emerging cooperation between public procurers to produce common procurement guidelines such as EPHOS addresses this problem. Its success will depend on reaching a threshold sufficient to convince the suppliers that the market has grown enough to justify further investment in standard-conformant products.

5. Maintaining the International Alignment

Industrial countries should align their policies to standards, and should provide an example to developing countries. This has been done in the past on the basis of ISO standards and, although possibly refocused, coherence in such policies should be mantained to avoid fragmentation of economies and to promote and secure worldwide interoperability. Without this interoperability, the Global Information Society will not exist.

Conclusion

After more than 10 years of stable standardization policy, the European Commission has opened a debate on major policy issues culminating in an open Workshop in November 1994. The objective of the policy is not under discussion. The essential objective, interoperability through open standards, is still valid and, at least conceptually, has been attained. The popularity achieved by the concept of open communication through standardized specifications represents a remarkable success of standardization policies worldwide. This objective has become even more serious and urgent in the context of the Global Information Society. What needs to be rethought are the strategies and practical measures to achieve the policy objective. The standardization process seems to be the most challenged. The European Commission is willing to support and facilitate the evolution of the standardization process and to accompany it with adequate measures for testing, procurement, and R&D. However, the responsibility for the transformation of the process remains with the standards organizations, and these are encouraged to act in synergy with industry. Finally, the importance of maintaining alignment of standardization policies worldwide should be restated and further implemented by the industrialized regions, through common thinking and common actions whenever possible.

Notes

[1] Formerly "the European Community".

[2] "Europe and the global information society" Recommendation to the European Council . Brussels, May 26, 1994.

[3] Council Decision of December 22, 1986 on Standardization in the Field of Information Technology and Telecommunications (87/95/EEC).

[4] CTS is the acronym for "Conformance Testing Services," a program launched by the Commission in 1986 to develop testing tools and set up testing services in the Union. The CTS program is still in progress. The last call for proposal was issued in 1993.

[5] EPHOS is the European Handbook for Open Systems.

[6] "How to choose the right ICT standardization policy," Brussels, November 28–30, 1994.

Excerpts from *Realizing the Information Future: The Internet and Beyond*

Computer Science and Telecommunications Board, National Research Council, with an introduction by Marjory Blumenthal and David Clark

The development of standards to support the emerging National Information Infrastructure will be shaped by expectations about the technical framework or architecture for the NII and by the social and organizational processes by which different perspectives are considered, captured, and balanced. These issues are addressed in the following excerpts from a report prepared by the interdisciplinary, industrial-academic NRENAISSANCE study committee of the Computer Science and Telecommunications Board of the National Research Council.

The report in full contains three major sections. The first section sets a vision for the NII, translates that vision into a technical framework, and identifies key issues that must be addressed for the successful realization of an advanced, integrated NII. The second section of the report considers the experiences, perspectives, and concerns of the research, education, and library communities. The last section of the report details issues and recommendations for government action.

As part of the discussion of architectural and deployment issues for a national information infrastructure, the report considers a set of issues, including security, convergence of industry sectors, scale, open research problems, and issues and concerns with the setting of standards. The report discusses how the setting of standards fits into the larger picture of translating a vision of the NII into deployed technology. The excerpted material briefly describes the current state of standards setting in the NII context, and identifies some of the current stresses and pressures on the standards-setting process. Overall, it concludes that the current processes for setting standards are facing increasing pressures from the pace of technological advance, the growing number of industry sectors involved, and the lack of coherent leadership to set a long-range direction for emerging standards.

Standards

Role of Network Standards

To make the vision of an integrated NII a reality and to define NII compliance, it is necessary to specify the technical details of the network. This is the role of standards, the conventions that permit the successful and harmonious implementation of interoperable networks and services. That standards serve to translate a high-level concept into operational terms-and that the process of standards definition is thus key to success in achieving an NII-is well understood in many sectors; indeed, the latter half of the 1980s seemed as much preoccupied with standards as it was with product differentiation. This was true in both the computer and communications industries.

Today, network standards relevant to the NII are being discussed in many different, sometimes competing contexts, such as the following:

• The Internet standards are formulated by the Internet Engineering Task Force (IETF), an open-membership body that currently operates under the auspices of the Internet Society and with support from research agencies of the U.S. federal government.

• The Open Systems Interconnection (OSI) network protocols, which offer an alternative set of protocols somewhat similar to the Internet protocols, have been formulated by the International Organization for Standardization (ISO) internationally, with U.S. contributions coordinated by the American National Standards Institute. A U.S. government version, GOSIP, has been promulgated by the National Institute of Standards and Technology (NIST).[24] ISO is broadening the OSI framework (see Appendix E).

• Standards for local area and metropolitan area networks such as Ethernet, Token Ring, or distributed queue dual bus (DQDB) are formulated by committees under the auspices of the Institute for Electrical and Electronics Engineers.

• Asynchronous transfer mode, an important emerging standard at the lower levels of network service, is being defined by at least two organizations, the ATM Forum and the International Telecommunications Union (ITU) Telecommunications Sector (formerly referred to as the CCITT).

• Standards for the television industry are formulated by a number of organizations, including the Society of Motion Picture and Television Engineers, the Advanced Television Systems Committee, and the ITU.

These sometimes discordant processes are shaped by commercial interests, professional societies, governmental involvement, international negotiation, and technical developments. The recent explosion of commercial involvement in networking has had a major impact on standards definition, as standards have become a vehicle for introducing products rapidly and for gaining competitive advantage.

Factors That Complicate Setting Standards

The committee believes that the critical process of setting standards is currently at risk. Historical approaches to setting standards may not apply in the future, and we lack known alternatives to carry us forward to the NII. The committee discusses below a number of forces that it sees as acting to stress the process.[25]

Network function has moved outside the network

As noted above, much of the user-visible functionality of information networks such as the Internet is accomplished through software running on users' end-node equipment, such as a computer. The network itself only implements the basic bearer service, and this causes changes in the standards- setting process. When function moved outside the network, the traditional network standards bodies no longer controlled the process of setting standards for new services based on this functionality. The interests of a much larger group, representing the computer vendors and the applications developers, needed to be heard. This situation is rather different from that in the traditional telephone network, where most of the function was implemented in the interior of the network, and the user equipment, the telephone itself, had characteristics dictated largely by the telephone company. With the advent of computer networks in the 1970s and the strong coupling to computer research, the clear demarcation between users' systems and the network began to blur, and uncontrolled equipment appeared more frequently at user sites, to be attached directly to data networks. Some of this equipment was experimental, and the network could make few assumptions about its proper behavior.

One thing that is clear now is that much of the capability and equipment of connectivity is moving to the "periphery" of the networking infrastructure; for example, there is tremendous penetration of private local area networks on customer premises. This emphasis on the periphery implies that a single entity, or even a single industry, will be incapable of controlling the deployment of the networking infrastructure. Thus the need for an ODN architecture is clear.

It is hard to set standards without a recognized mandate

The controlled nature of the early telephone system essentially gave the recognized standards bodies a mandate to set the relevant standards. Historically, the telephone network was designed and implemented by a small group that controlled the standards-setting process because it controlled the network. (In most countries outside the United States, the telephone system is an arm of the government.) Similarly, in the early days of the Internet, the standards were set by a body established and funded by the Department of Defense, which (for the DOD) had a mandate to provide data network standards.[26] No such mandate exists in the larger network context of today. For the Internet, for example, the explicit government directive to set standards has been replaced by a process driven by vendor and market pressures, with essentially no top-down control.

A bottom-up process cannot easily set long-term direction

As can be seen in the Internet community, the absence of a mandate to set and impose standards has led to a bottom-up approach, a process in which the development community experiments with new possibilities that become candidates for standardization after they have been subject to considerable experimentation and use. Standardization is thus akin to ratification of what is the generally accepted practice. The paradigm of translating operational experience into a proposed standard imposes at least one measure of quality on a set of competing proposals. It has proved successful compared to the relatively more controlled and top-down processes occurring in the ISO. But the bottom-up approach to setting standards is not without fault.

Although setting standards by negotiation, compromise, and selection in the marketplace has been largely effective for the Internet, it is important to recall that the Internet had its early success in the context of overall direction and guidance being provided by a small group of highly motivated researchers. This indirect setting of direction seems to have faltered as the Internet community has become larger and more fragmented by commercial interests. Currently, the Internet community seems to make short-range decisions with some success, but long-range decisions, which reflect not only immediate commercial interests but also broader societal goals, may not get an effective hearing. The Internet Architecture Board (IAB) has the charter to develop longer-range architectural recommendations on behalf of the Internet community, but it cannot impose these recommendations on anyone.

A top-down approach no longer appears workable

Many people consider the bottom-up approach to be too much like a free-market model in which the final result is due to individual enterprise and competition, that is to say, is not sufficiently managed. The top-down approach appears to be more manageable to many observers, particularly those with extensive experience in managing large-scale networks to meet commercial expectations for performance. However, the classical top-down approach has not succeeded in the current environment, whereas the bottom-up Internet process, which has directly embraced diverse approaches and objectives in its bottom-up process, is a phenomenal success that must be applauded and respected. Although there may be merit in considering how to integrate the top-down and bottom-up approaches, there is little experience to suggest that either approach alone will work easily in the larger context of the future NII.

Commercial forces may distort the standards-setting process

A vendor, especially one with a large market share, can attempt to set a unilateral standard by implementing it and shipping it in a product. Some of the most widespread "standards" of the Internet are not actually formal standards of the community, but rather designs that have been distributed by one vendor and accepted as a necessity by the competition. This approach can lead to a very effective product if the vendor has good judgment; it may open the market to innovation and diversity at a higher level based on the standard. However, the objectives of the vendor may not match the larger objectives of the community. The resulting standard may be short-sighted, it may be structured to inhibit competition and to close the market, it may simply be proprietary, and it may inhibit evolution.

Setting Standards for the NII—Planning for Change Is Difficult But Necessary

Managing the process by which the NII network environment evolves is one of the most critical issues to be addressed. Planning for change requires an overall architecture and constant attention to ensure that any standard, at any level of the architecture, is designed to permit incremental evolution, backward compatibility, and modular replacement to the extent possible. Unfortunately, as the committee has noted above, the current standards-setting processes seem least effective in setting a long-term direction or guiding the development of standards according to an overall vision of the future. Thus there is some need to find a middle ground whereby an overall vision of the NII can inform standards selection and also allow for competing interests and approaches to be evaluated in an open process. *The critical question is not what the exact vision is, but how it will be promulgated and integrated into the various ongoing standards activities.*

The second excerpt is from the final section of the report, which discusses the various roles that the government should play in fostering the NII. The report recognizes that the private sector will finance the deployment of the NII and thus should take the lead in setting the standards that define it. It stresses that it is not the role of the government to set NII standards, but that the government has a number of critical responsibilities in this area. Governmental involvement can provide a long-term vision, can balance interests and ensure that competing perspectives are heard, and can help to connect the private sector to the range of international standards-setting organizations. The report urges that government participate in the NII standards-setting process as a partner to the other interests represented there. The material excerpted below recommends actions by the government to foster and stabilize NII standards setting in the future, complementing and contributing to private-sector standards-setting activities.

Influencing the Shape of the Information Infrastructure

The federal government can influence the shape of the NII in terms of both architecture and deployment. In both instances, standards, procurement, regulation, and investment incentives are key mechanisms. This report focuses on standards and procurement, in addition to related research investments, as tools for shaping NII architecture and deployment; full consideration of regulations, which are effectively a more formal approach to standards, and investment incentives was beyond the scope of the committee.

Although most of the public debate over the NII has addressed issues specific to the U.S. context, the NREN program has demonstrated the benefits of easy international connectivity, including international information sharing, collaboration in research, and educational exchanges at all levels; it has also illustrated how difficult it can be, in some parts of the world, to achieve even physical connectivity. Expanded international interconnection will require bilateral and multilateral agreements, involving the Department of State, other agencies, and perhaps other bodies, most likely building on existing and prior law (although physical implementation will be effected with private investment[21]). See Appendix E.

Even more importantly, the prospect of broader international connection underscores the need to address issues that will arise with information-oriented applications, which will be affected by differences in legal regimes, values, and so on. Intellectual property rights, transborder data flow,[22] privacy, and security are among the areas that will present challenges for the international information infrastructure, challenges that U.S. information policy making should anticipate.

Influence on Architecture and Standards

As discussed in Chapter 2, the committee's vision of an Open Data Network entails achieving a more general and flexible architecture than appears likely to emerge independently from private-sector actions. In part for this reason, a central activity will be the development of appropriate standards and guidelines. *The process of setting standards is the only way that a high-level vision of the NII can be translated into a useful deployed infrastructure.* This report attempts to sketch a vision, but clearly this vision is partial and must be translated into a concrete architecture and a set of defining standards. Thus defining the vision and creating standards must be to some extent interdependent. Of course, setting standards is not the same as getting them adopted. However, the history of the Internet standards-setting process, characterized by vision and leadership by ARPA program managers and creativity among those in the research community that they funded, illustrates that sometimes the two activities can go hand-in-hand.

The committee sees the involvement of the government as critical in shaping future network standards. If the NII is to succeed, the government must stay involved in the process and find some better way than now exists to represent the broad interests of society in the standards-setting process.

Setting standards for infrastructure involves a broad range of entities with different competencies, constituencies, time scales, and effectiveness, all of which interact in a context in which standards setting is largely voluntary. Thus, part of the jurisdiction lies with the Federal Communications Commission, part with domestic voluntary standards committees (the American National Standards Institute, Institute for Electrical and Electronics Engineers, and so on), part in international bodies (the International Telecommunications Union (ITU) Telecommunications Sector (formerly CCITT), part with such voluntary groups as the Internet Engineering Task Force (IETF), and part with a variety of ad hoc and more formal industry consortia. The situation is complicated by the fact that, particularly in areas such as information infrastructure, U.S. actions must relate to a larger, international standards-setting process.

No organization at the moment holds the charter to set a global vision of the NII. The Internet Society represents one effort to provide coherence in this dimension. It reflects a bottom-up grass-roots approach that has so far marked the growth and evolution of the Internet; it is also moving toward more formal, liaison relationships with the International Organization for Standardization and the ITU, steps that would enhance its involvement in international standards setting (although within the Internet Society, the IETF has traditionally focused on lower-level protocol and architecture issues, and as characterized in Chapter 2, upcoming challenges relate to the middle and higher levels). Since the current broad base of stakeholders precludes direct control by the government, the government must decide what organizations it will support to bring into existence a vision for the NII as well as the supporting standards, and it must work internationally to establish the working relationships and the mandates that can make the NII a reality.

The committee is not recommending that the government charter one of its standards-setting agencies, such as NIST, to directly set or mandate all of the standards anticipated for the Open Data Network. Indeed, past attempts to influence the process directly in this way have not been effective. The attempt to force the use of Open Systems Interconnection (OSI) protocols by the promulgation of a federal government version, GOSIP, must be seen as a misguided attempt to exercise a governmental mandate. In the commercial marketplace, the contest between the OSI and TCP/IP protocol suites is over: the OSI market has largely disappeared,[23] and vendors who invested enormous sums in trying to develop this market are understandably upset. The difficulties of both abandoning previously chosen directions and deciding on standards for future directions are illustrated by the winter 1994 controversy over the draft report of the FIRP, which suggested that NIST abandon its position mandating the procurement of technologies implementing the OSI suite.[24]

Against this backdrop comes an administration effort to strengthen the involvement of NIST in the NII initiative. This can be seen in the significant expansion proposed for the FY95 NIST budget, the prominent role of NIST's director in the IITF activities, and the FIRP's draft recommendation that NIST identify federal preferred standards profiles and aim "to converge the Government to a single interconnected, interoperable standards based internetworking environment."[25] NIST manages the development of Federal Information Processing Standards (FIPS), and the FIPS system would be a vehicle to promote NII-compliant technology as suggested in Chapter 2.

The issue of a more active government role in setting standards is controversial. Many standards are being set in industry, particularly at the applications level (such as data standards emerging from the PC applications software environment). Many in industry believe that the ad hoc bottom-up standards-setting process that has characterized the U.S. computer industry and Internet context has been key to today's global leadership in those arenas. There is also concern in the business community about the ability of government officials to make the right choices (whether for standards or regulations), a view captured in a Wall Street Journal editorial contending that "it is truly hubris for these politicians to think they can somehow fine tune or stage manage the rapidly developing world of advanced technologies."[26] Even within government, opinions differ as to the appropriate timing and direction of standards setting. For example, a Federal Communications Commission official participating in a forum on wireless communications observed that the FCC preferred encouraging to mandating standards in a new industry, while an NTIA official was quoted as asking whether the FCC should do more than provide encouragement.[27]

On the other hand, standardization has been immature and conflict or lack of consensus has been apparent in such cross-cutting concerns as management, security, and network naming, areas where industry-driven standardization may be neither sufficient nor sufficiently timely. Moreover, the objective of providing a truly national, consumer-oriented set of services increases the decision-making stakes because consumer-oriented standards tend to be slow to change-the consequences of these decisions are evident for relatively long periods of time.[28] These are among the factors arguing for explicit attention to the direction, degree, and consistency of standards-setting actions across government.

Readers interested in the full report can contact the National Academy Press at 1-800-624-6242 or via the Internet at amerchan@nas.edu. The full report is available on the Internet at [www, gopher, ftp].nas.edu.

Notes

[24] The current status of the GOSIP is in doubt. NIST has convened the Federal Internetworking Requirements Panel to advise it on options for dealing with the GOSIP. At this writing, the draft report of this panel, opened for comments, was not yet final. However, the overall direction of the report appears to be to abandon the current GOSIP, which mandates one required protocol suite (the OSI suite), and to move to a more open approach based on multiple suites and an explicit acceptance of the Internet protocols.

[25] See also U.S. Congress, Office of Technology Assessment, *Global Standards: Building Blocks of the Future.* TCT-512. Government Printing Office, Washington, DC, March 1992.

[26] In the early 1970s, ARPA undertook the development of TCP/IP for the specific purpose of providing a standard approach to interoperation of DOD

networks. The technical development was done by a working group convened and funded by ARPA, with academic and industrial research participants. In the late 1970s, ARPA worked with the Defense Communications Agency (DCA) to mandate TCP/IP as a preliminary standard for internetworked DOD systems. The DCA and ARPA cooperated on the establishment of a more formal review committee to oversee the establishment and deployment of TCP/IP within the DOD.

[21] In an address to a United Nations conference on telecommunications, Vice President Gore referred to an expectation for a "planetary information network" that would be achieved without U.S. funding, through private investment. See Nathaniel C. Nash, "Gore Sees Privatization of Global Data Links," *New York Times*, March 22, 1994, p. D2.

[22] A new National Research Council study, "Bits of Power," is examining some of these issues in the context of research networking.

[23] X.400 and X.500, part of the OSI suite, are in some use.

[24] Comments on the draft included criticisms by aerospace firms, manufacturers, and foreign governments of the prospect of OSI abandonment given investments to date in support of OSI as well as criticism that individual agency choices of protocols could be anarchic; overall, however, comments from U.S. parties supported the draft FIRP report by a factor of two to one. See Ellen Messmer, "Critics Assail Plan to End Fed's OSI Policy," *Network World*, March 21, 1994, pp. 1 and 63; and Sam Masud, "Agencies Question Wisdom of Opening up GOSIP," *Government Computer News*, March 21, 1994, pp. 1 and 104. The two-to-one support figure was reported by FIRP member Milo Medin at an IETF meeting in March 1994.

[25] "Draft Report of the Federal Internetworking Requirements Panel," prepared for the National Institute of Standards and Technology, January 14, 1994, p. vi.

[26] *Wall Street Journal*, "Blocking the Information Highway," April 8, 1994, p. A14.

[27] Florence Olsen, "Feds Define Wireless Needs As Spectrum Auction Nears," *Government Computer News*, February 21, 1994, pp. 48–49.

[28] According to Scott Shenker, in a discussion on the challenge of making the "right decisions" about network service interfaces, "Once a home consumer standard becomes widely adopted, there is tremendous consumer pressure for that standard to remain stable." See Scott Shenker, "Service Models and Pricing Policies for an Integrated Services Internet," prepared for a conference, Public Access to the Internet, John F. Kennedy School of Government, Harvard University, May 26–27, 1993, draft dated June 8.

Multimedia Standards Development Issues

Philip V. W. Dodds
Interactive Multimedia Association

The field of multimedia technology is fraught with opportunity, confusion, and consternation. It is alluring and attractive, and yet it is elusive and seemingly always sailing just over the horizon. Even the word "multimedia" has multiple definitions within the entertainment, information, and communications industries. To clarify this puzzle, a model of multimedia businesses will be presented that provides a framework for understanding the various economic forces behind multimedia products and services. This model will illustrate the relationships among multimedia technologies such as cable television, computer games, home computing, business desktop computing, enterprise-wide computing, and telecommunications, and will explore areas of actual and potential standardization in this period of global convergence.

Defining what multimedia is and what it can do is very difficult. It certainly means different things to different people; it also means different things to different industries. There is, however, a common denominator: *change*. The computer industry's stunning advances in performance and cost reduction have created opportunities for digital technologies to invade new and previously unrelated industries. These changes mean that existing standards may well become obsolete or irrelevant as new standards emerge to connect previously isolated industries.

A wholesale shift is underway from analog media, such as composite television and vinyl records, to precisely calculated digital representations, like high definition TV and compact discs. Once in digital form, information is no longer captive to one industrial

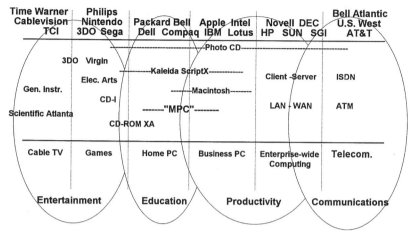

Figure 1 The Multimedia "Continuum."

distribution system. In theory, the same digital information stream can be viewed at home, in a car, at your office, or anywhere, thus potentially uniting isolated information systems and industries. However, standard formats for these streams, as well as common interfaces and protocols, must be established for the dream of "information everywhere" to be even partially realized.

In order to better understand the economics of the various participants in the multimedia arena, each player and the relationship they have to their respective markets will be described. The multimedia "continuum" has six major areas: television, games, home computing, business computing, enterprise-wide computing, and telecommunications. The companies in each of these areas are involved in "multimedia" business, though with different products, distribution, and end user expectations. Standards are more important to some companies than others, and standards are in some cases regulated by law or age-old industry practice.

Entertainment

On the left-most side of the continuum chart are broadcast and cable television. Both of these services are rooted in the entertainment industry, and both deliver entertainment content in one direction (at least for now): from one source out to many "receivers." Next, we find consumer games, such as Sega, Nintendo, and 3DO. These devices also deliver entertainment to the home via the television receiver.

Education

Home computing, a relatively new but sizzling hot market in the United States, is a close cousin to the consumer game category, since both are primarily aimed toward school children and both have been driven primarily by interactive multimedia games. An increasing number of title publishers are aiming to publish for game machines designed for television as well as for desktop computers. Major tool makers such as Macromedia now offer authoring tools that are specifically designed to map to a variety of quite different delivery systems.

The home computing sector is felt by many to be the best hope for the effective application of technology to education. Many of the new titles that have been issued over the past year have been educationally oriented, presumably appealing to concerned parents who want to give their child the best possible educational advantage. One has to believe that many parents like playing games too, and that that is at least a *part* of the purchase rationale.

Business Productivity

In the U.S. market, home computers are simply stripped down, commoditized versions of business desktop computers with sound cards and CD-ROM drives. Junior's computer is architecturally identical to work-place computers—as are most of the productivity software tools—but with lower raw performance. At work the computers tend to be faster and more sophisticated, since they are built and bought to improve productivity, and (perhaps) because they are purchased on the basis of competitive need, using "other people's money." The business desktop has always been the place for tools; business computers, therefore, are the vessel into which one pours work for manipulation, representation, or recalculation. The sequence is usually the same: the user puts information in, which is then manipulated, massaged, and put into a final form for presentation.

More recently, desktop computers have become communications vehicles. Often starting as small local area networks, desktop computers are now connected to an immense web of communications capabilities. In the past, most business desktop systems were connected to file servers primarily to ease document flow and management. The development of connected personal computers emphasized the growth of enterprise-wide computing, where systems and software have been tuned to provide core information and messaging services within organizations. Thus, the continuum inherits a communications component.

Communications

Communications systems are designed to transport information quickly and reliably. The bulk of the telecommunications infrastructure was created principally to support real time voice communications. Enterprise-wide computing is now pushing more digital information through telecommunications systems, with the effect of converting "plain old telephone" service into a sophisticated set of transport services capable of supporting high quality interactive multimedia applications.

Multiple "Econo-Structures"

What distinguishes these six categories are the economic forces that fuel each industry and the distribution systems and infrastructures that have historically guaranteed their isolation from one another. The coupling of economic forces with the existence of stable distribution systems, such as wires, radio spectrum, and CDs, has formed fairly rigid "econo-structures" that have retarded the merging of technologies in these diverse industries. Different standards have evolved in each of these industries that cannot and will not easily be abandoned, although there are changes on the horizon that make these old rules less likely to remain in effect.

With the transition to all-digital information formats, the distribution system barriers are quickly falling. Nonetheless, it is clear that many of these industries, such as cable television and business computing, have served utterly different customer profiles. These paying customers aren't changing as quickly as technology changes.

Users change their habits slowly, and new distribution systems and the standards upon which they are built cannot be shifted overnight. Therefore, we can expect that new products in any one of these example industries are highly likely to resemble products that have been in existence for some time already, and will likely be based on or extensions of existing distribution standards that consumers are already accustomed to. One example of this is the audio Compact Disc from which nearly all multimedia formats are derived.

User Expectations

Multimedia markets can be mapped to (at least) four different categories of users: Entertainment (broadcast television, cable), Education (home computing), Productivity (business desktop and enterprise-wide computing), and Communications (telecommunications). These four categories define the *primary* justification for purchase and use. Certainly the various industries are adding capabilities of their "neighbor" industries in the hopes of expanding their market. These purchaser justifications, in turn, drive sets of expectations that arise from the experiences and needs of the user group.

In the entertainment markets, important factors include: a high entertainment component (escapism), good visual and aural effects, action, and low cost. Education applications, on the other hand, are expected to contain high quality material and be primarily user-driven. In these applications, cost is less an issue than for, say, games or movies. Productivity tools used in the office may be quite expensive; the cost per "seat" for employees at a connected workstation is much higher than an individual is willing to pay at home. Finally, users generally place a much higher priority on multimedia quality (i.e., video or audio) than on service reliability, and most people expect to pay a fair amount for their communications services, due to the importance of timely information transfer.

The standards adopted for the distribution and delivery of multimedia content are, therefore, governed or defined in large part by the requirements of the consumers who purchase and use

Usage		
Entertainment	Productivity	Communications
Quality		
High (e.g., "virtual reality")	Application dependent	Relatively Low (e.g., "voice quality")
Cost		
Low (< $500)	Application dependent	High
Priority		
Low (off duty)	High during work	Real time (now)

Figure 2 End User (Purchaser) Expectations.

the technology. It does no good, for example, to attempt to apply a standard for content distribution to the entertainment industry that lacks good quality audio or video. Similarly, a standard that provides high fidelity audio to cellular phone systems but requires very wide bandwidth channels would be of little use to phone service providers.

Standards Groups

Standards come from many different types of organizations, each with their own agenda and purpose. The technical quality of a standard, though important, is not the determining factor for success or failure of a particular standards group. In fact, the origin and history of a particular standards group often provide important insights into the likelihood of long term acceptance by an industry group. Some of the types of standards groups include:

- *De facto* (literally, "in reality") Market Acceptance
- Partnership/Joint Venture
- Consortia
- Trade Association/Professional Society
- Formal Standards Bodies (ISO, ANSI, IEEE)

De facto standards are declared winners after the fact; by definition, such standards may not be claimed until a majority of the market has accepted the standard through use and purchase. Partnerships and joint ventures are usually made up of two or three companies who believe that through their joint marketing efforts they will be able to quickly establish a *de facto* standard. Such efforts fail as often as they succeed. Consortia composed of four or more organizations usually form in response to the perception of a joint competitive threat. Often such groups find themselves attempting to compete with *de facto* standards held by competing organizations.

Trade associations, like the Interactive Multimedia Association (IMA), are required to represent their entire membership, so their efforts tend to focus on those enabling areas of agreement that will benefit the whole industry. While this often limits the scope of work that can effectively be done, the end result can be extremely helpful as members of associations unite in "enlightened self interest."

Finally, formal or *de jure* standards bodies are the means by which durable and irrefutable standards are firmly established. The mere existence of a *de jure* standard does not mean that the standard will be used or be useful, however. As with all standards, formal standards are important to the industry in which they were developed. Since such standards take a very, very long time to develop (sometimes six or more years), some feel that the process is not very useful in the fast-moving high technology field.

Many have observed that the interest on the part of manufacturers in cooperating on formal standards is least on the entertainment end of the continuum and most toward communications. Cooperation on standards is greater in communications in part due to the distributed nature of network solutions and the fact that there are many players in this area of the market. Consumer products, on the other hand, tend to be offered by one company, or a few companies, in a more or less complete form. Consensus among consumer products companies is usually not necessary, or deemed desirable, in that highly competitive, winner-take-all environment.

While government rules, such as those promulgated by the FCC for broadcasters, force consumer companies to attend to some standards issues on a consensus basis, their usual preference is to

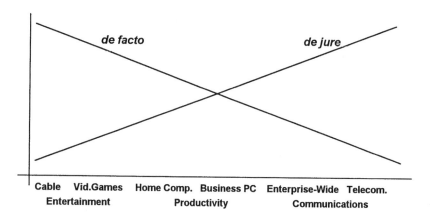

Figure 3 Degree of Standards Group Effectiveness.

attempt to set standards on their own, or to partner with one or two other companies to gain market leadership. Winning a *de facto* standard is the best defense against competition in the consumer market; helping to establish and then abiding by *de jure* standards is the best way to gain entry and maintain a presence in the telecommunications market.

The Role of the Interactive Multimedia Association

The multimedia industry brings together people from many diverse backgrounds and talents. While this diversity gives multimedia its vitality, the absence of a common frame of knowledge and understanding among the key players in the emerging field can act as an obstacle preventing smooth communication within the development community. The IMA was formed in order to foster effective communication and common understanding of the business issues that impact technology companies, publishers and developers, and their target markets.

The IMA is an international trade association representing the entire spectrum of the multimedia industry: applications developers; suppliers of hardware and software; system integrators, publishers and distributors; educators; and users. About 20% of IMA members are outside the United States; Pacific Rim representation is strong and growing, particularly among computer and consumer electronics manufacturers. IMA's mission is to promote the development of interactive multimedia applications and reduce existing barriers to the widespread use of multimedia technology. The IMA's scope of activities has recently expanded to include the development of baseline market data that establishes the sizes of various components of the multimedia publishing market. The development of reliable and independently developed data that establishes installed base figures provides essential information to developers making important investment decisions.

The IMA's Compatibility Project focuses on the development and adoption of technology that permits cross-platform interoperability of multimedia applications. Through this effort, the leading providers of multimedia technology come together to debate, refine, and ultimately adopt recommendations that are designed to enlarge the market and provide wide access to the entire industry. For example, the IMA established a "fast track" method for reaching agreement among industry players called a *Request For Technology (RFT),* which solicits existing solutions to cross-platform compatibility as candidates for standardization. Three such RFTs are currently in process: Multimedia Services, focusing on distributed multimedia applications over networks; Data Exchange, which provides mechanisms for cross-platform portability of multimedia content; and a Scripting Language for multimedia titles, which will permit interactive applications to be published in a platform-neutral way. By examining scripting languages and other technologies like networked multimedia services and multimedia data exchange formats, the IMA is taking the lead in making multimedia a content-dependent, rather than platform-dependent, industry.

In addition to these RFTs, the IMA sponsors projects and forums designed to both protect and educate multimedia designers and vendors. The Intellectual Property Project was organized to address problems that inhibit the acquisition and use of content in multimedia applications and services. This project covers topics ranging from licensing paradigms and strategies to legal and policy issues. The IMA has also created a number of forums and Special Interest Groups (SIGs) that may be of interest to developers. Designed to pursue focused objectives within the multimedia community, SIGs focus on topics such as interactive multimedia formats and markets and high-quality digital video.

Externally, the IMA works to educate the public about multimedia through speakers and by jointly sponsoring conferences with other industry groups like the National Association of Broadcasters (NAB) and the International Information Communications Society (IICS). These opportunities ensure that IMA members are taking an active role in shaping the future of multimedia computing by working with others to advance the industry and establish a strong and profitable marketplace.

Intellectual Property Rights and High Technology Standards

William Ellis
International Business Machines Corporation

CBEMA, the Computer and Business Equipment Manufacturers Association, is an association of companies that live or die based on their innovation. So we take very seriously threats to our intellectual property rights, such as the European Telecommunications Standards Institute (ETSI) IPR Policy and Undertaking. We find what ETSI has done to be unacceptable. It completely ignores the decades of experience that went into the formation of the intellectual property policies of all other major standards-developing organizations. We are also disturbed by others who share ETSI's view of intellectual property rights—those who believe that policy makers, standards bodies, or whoever can override intellectual property rights in the public interest of common standards. Those of us whose businesses thrive on the development of patented technologies find the notion that these patents can sometimes be ignored astonishing.

There is a delicate balance between IPR and standards. The right balance enhances both. That balance directly impacts innovation in a given industry: it impacts manufacturing and R&D jobs, and ultimately the consumer. Missteps in this area can very quickly kill research in a technology. You do need standards, but over-reaching in standards can quickly turn the network industry into the television industry of the 1990s, where everything becomes a commodity. As we all know, the manufacturing of high-volume, low-profit commodities quickly migrates out of the United States.

Now supporters of the ETSI policy want to dismantle the very thing that maintains a discipline over this process: the fact that the inclusion of IPRs into a standard is ultimately done on a voluntary basis. There are tremendous advantages to having your technology selected for a standard. But there are significant pitfalls as well, and that must be recognized.

Some argue that a primary problem with voluntary licensing is that the IPR holder may not have disclosed every detail of his product design and manufacturing technique. But over-detailed standards down to the last screw are precisely what cause technology products to become commodities. Standards bodies have perfected a process that uses specifications that set out the functions to be accomplished, rather than detailed design specifications that leave no room for innovation. The voluntary nature of the negotiation between the IPR owner and others in the standards body provides the discipline that prevents over-standardization and resulting commodization from happening. In an open standards process, the presence of competitors and users should put the emphasis on finding solutions where using IP is not essential, but rather just one alternative.

Some assume that more control by standards bodies increases the common good and that decisions of standards bodies are always benign and inherently in the best interest of all. But standards bodies are made up of individuals from companies and other organizations, each with varying degrees of influence. In any standards body there will always be technology have-not companies who advocate standardizing down to the last screw. Whether they are successful depends on the balance of power in the standards body. Giving them, as in the ETSI policy, compulsory license rights strips out the checks and balances in the system.

There are international barriers to compulsory licensing, such as the Paris Convention and Berne Convention strictures. There are also strictures in the recently signed GATT World Trade Organization Treaty text. Those restrictions are in place because of simply horrendous compulsory licensing abuses that took place in the developing world. Providing compulsory license authority for standards would set a truly awful precedent for the developing world, and it would make compulsory licensing in standardization the method of choice for stripping out the patents of foreign companies. Ultimately, the United States would be the loser.

Some critics of the voluntary standards system criticize the provision that an IPR owner may, in fact, refuse to license. Although this provision does exist, I am not aware of any patent holders, at least in the ANSI, IEC or ISO standards bodies, who have participated in the process and have refused to permit their technology to be standardized. Ultimately, agreeing to license means that their manufactured products will be in demand, and may give them some manufacturing advantages. The true problems arise with IPR holders that are small companies or universities. In many cases, a patent is a small company's only asset, and they want to make significant revenue from the standard. Likewise, universities don't manufacture products. Their entire benefit comes from licensing revenues, and they want those revenues maximized. They have no interest in taking part of their compensation in a right to use other patents; they simply want money. Ultimately these problems are best resolved by the marketplace, not by some select group of companies or a standards organization.

It is said that the devil is in the details. This is certainly the case with the ETSI IPR Policy and Undertaking. On the surface, it appears to be simply a very bureaucratic expansion of the straight-forward policies of other standards-developing organizations. But closer examination reveals several problems with the ETSI policy:

1. ETSI is based on a system of weighted voting. Although it is primarily U.S. technology that is implicated in the IPR Policy and Undertaking, U.S. companies have only 3.6% of the weighted vote. The demonstrated result is control through the weighted voting by a select group of telecommunications operators.

2. Non-members are potentially shut out of the EU telecommunications market because (a) there is no requirement in the ETSI Undertaking for members to license the IPR incorporated into their standards to non-ETSI members, and (b) non-members will have no ability to influence the technology used in the ETSI standards, so they will be put in a weakened position relative to their competitors in ETSI.

In essence, the ETSI Undertaking constitutes a framework to facilitate a collective boycott to eliminate non-member competitors from the EU market.

I should also mention that although ETSI is chartered to set standards for the European Union, it grants a compulsory license to European members for worldwide sales to major telecommunications operators. I said "European members" because there is no requirement allowing U.S. members to manufacture in the United States to supply telecommunications operators in the European market.

3. The ETSI Undertaking is a license-by-default system. Inaction means you lose your right to prevent your IPR from being licensed in the ETSI standard.

Now, that type of provision is a penalty or a quid pro quo that you might apply to someone who proposes his own technology for a standard and then refuses to license. But to apply it against a company that merely sends a representative to a committee meeting, or to apply it to non-members, is a travesty.

This is not only a license-by-default system: no formal or even informal notice goes out to the IPR owner that specific patents it owns are implicated by a proposed ETSI standard. There is simply no notice given. It is argued that the approval of the 6-12 line work program, which sets out the area to be standardized and initiates the running of ETSI's proposed 180-day withdrawal period, provides notice. A 6-line summary, whether or not it ever gets distributed to all of the ETSI members (which is questionable), gives no notice of anything. The 6-line summary can evolve over the several years of standards development along any number of diverse technical paths. The end result will be a finished standard embodied in a many-page technical specification that could not possibly have been divined from a 6-line summary. And after the 180-day withdrawal period has lapsed, your competitors can freely propose your technology for a standard, with no recourse left to your company. You can't stop them. Nor are you are dealing with just a single standard under development. ETSI has approximately 1200 ongoing standards work programs, each one with a 6-12 line approved work program. What company can afford to monitor all of that activity?

ETSI supporters argue that the voluntary system used by other standards-developing organizations is bad because of delays in implementing the standard caused by a need to reach agreement with the IPR owner. They point out that with the rapid rate of technological change, the standard may be obsolete before agreement is reached. If that's really true, they have no business standardizing on that technology in the first place.

Often cited as an example of this wrangling is the two to three years it took to reach agreement on the Global System for Mobile Communication (GSM) digital telephone standard (which, incidentally, is not obsolete). The GSM negotiation illustrates why discipline is required. In GSM, Motorola technology was proposed for the standard by a Motorola competitor. Motorola was not even a member of the standards committee and was given no notice that its technology was even under consideration. The GSM committee then approached Motorola and demanded a royalty-free license. This is precisely the situation that U.S. industry is concerned about, and precisely the reason why CBEMA objects so vehemently to the ETSI proposal. (Incidentally, Motorola did ultimately agree to allow its patents to be used in the GSM standard.)

CBEMA has always supported standardization efforts. We support telecommunications standardization in Europe. But we staunchly oppose dropping the consensus process used to formulate standards in all other standards bodies. That process provides checks and balances against abuse and international commodization of innovative technologies by those companies and countries that do not do R&D.

Information Technology Standardization and Users: International Challenges Move the Process Forward

Georges Ferné
Organization for Economic Cooperation and Development

The globalization of the world economy is characterized by the growing interdependence of firms and countries worldwide. Information and telecommunications infrastructure have played, and will continue to play, a key role in the globalization process by creating new networking opportunities. This will obviously have an enormous impact on the demands for, and the priorities in, information technology standardization. It may well be that the increasing weight of international considerations will drive national policies and adjustments. This paper uses the example of the demands for users' involvement in information technology (IT) standardization to suggest that the limited prospects for progress in this area in national settings may change drastically as a result of international challenges and competition.

Concern about difficulties in the diffusion of new technologies and about apparent inefficiencies in the standardization process have prompted standards makers to raise questions about the role of users more and more frequently. But can standardization in information technology become more efficient, technological dead-ends be avoided, and the diffusion of new technologies be assisted by involving users more closely in standard setting? The idea is attractive, but is it realistic?[1]

Standardization of information technologies to introduce coherence among computer systems could have an enormous impact. A common bedrock of coherent systems, effectively interconnected and allowing communication from computer to computer with ease, is vital for the future of industrial and trade infrastructure. IT users should be freed from dependency on a single manufacturer so that they can use heterogeneous systems with hardware and software that will still be compatible even though it is supplied by different firms—IBM, DEC, Apple, and so on. Unless this comes about, the world system for data processing, transfer, and access will remain fragmented and will not allow new industries and services to evolve.

The difficulty is that IT standardization involves many different parties as well as huge costs. For instance, the total cost of developing the Open System Interconnection (OSI) set of standards has been estimated at over $4 billion over the past fifteen years. In 1984 the start-up budget for one of the bodies concerned (X-Open, a consortium of large firms) totaled some $90 million.

Manufacturers and Users

IT standardization involves two groups whose interests occasionally clash. First, there are the computer hardware and software manufacturers and distributors and the service firms working in product design, manufacturing, and marketing. They have tended to follow monopolistic strategies and to divide the market into captive customer groups for specific systems (MS-DOS, Apple, and so on). Then there are the users, who are concerned with standardization only to the extent that it specifies the nature and precise characteristics of the products available, raises expectations of new applications and functions, and diversifies their sources of supply.

Users have a tremendous hold over the industry, even though they may not be aware of it. Their choices can spell out life or death for a standard.[2] In information technology, standards mostly concern networks, and the capacity of networks to attract customers depends on size. The more users who adopt a standard (VHS versus Betamax, for example), the more the standard will be attractive to other potential users (VHS is favored because more films will be available, because it will be easier to exchange and borrow cassettes, and so on).

IT standardization is hampered by the fact that its products (standards) do not match customer requirements (functions). Inevitably, there is a feeling that if producers and users consulted one another more, many of these problems could be resolved, or at any rate mitigated. But this kind of consultation is especially difficult, since IT users form a highly heterogeneous body of distinct groups that often change. Users can be divided into four categories:

• Major user groups (often multinational),[3] each representing sufficient market share to enable them to negotiate on an equal footing with equipment suppliers or service firms, sometimes even setting their own standards (as have General Motors, Boeing, British Airways, Electricité de France, Reuters, and others)

• Public administrations, which can sway decisions in their capacity as IT users (as has the Department of Defense in the United States, for instance)

• Professional or trade associations (for example, food distributors in the United States, who developed bar codes in distribution)

• Individuals using microcomputers, who can only influence standardization through their purchasing decisions.

In spite of these differences, users by and large share a common core of expectations about standardization. First, standardization should help avoid technological dead ends, where incompatible options trap users in a doomed technology. That has happened to people who purchased computers that were subsequently cast aside by software designers (the failure of PS/2, launched by IBM in the late 1980s, shows that even the biggest users can suffer this mishap), or who chose video recorders that met Betamax and not VHS standards. Second, standardization should promote universality by making it easy to communicate between all kinds of hardware and software from different sources.

Obstacles to Standardization

Although in favor of standardization, and on good grounds, each group of users—if not each user—wishes to have access to technical systems as closely tailored to its own requirements as possible. The search for universality thus counteracts that for specificity. This is a vital point, as it illustrates the frequent clash of interests between users and sellers. Sellers obviously prefer "captive" users, who have no other option than the hardware and software offered to them by a single vendor, because this secures the seller's market share or market lead. On the other hand, users have everything to gain from an open environment that enables them to turn to any supplier they wish for each component of their computer systems and therefore derive the full benefit of competitive advantages; for users to gain this benefit, each product should comply with a system of compatible standards.

Standardization is therefore the source of countless clashes between numerous actors with varying ambitions: imposing the use of the standards they control, breaking into a monopoly to acquire a foothold, or escaping these constraints to obtain "customized" standards compatible with as many other standards as possible. These conflicts and contradictions are bound to flare up sooner or later. For instance, a dispute with considerable implications arose at the European Telecommunications Standardization Institute (ETSI) on the subject of intellectual property rights. A standard may include technological components that are owned by a firm. Should the firm then be free to choose the size of the fees to be paid for the use of such a standard—say, the GSM mobile telephone standard, which can cover the whole of continental Europe (at least)—or should this right be limited? This example is all the more significant because it underlines that the issue of user participation raises questions and creates difficulties that are even more drastic at international than at national levels.

Other obstacles may arise whenever users in various sectors decide to develop their own systems while official procedures are being laboriously followed to develop more general standards. Once users' own standards have been introduced, the diffusion of general standards in that sector is in practice hampered by the existence of many incompatible variants. Such is the case in Electronic Data Interchange (EDI), where the general standard, EDIFACT, now has rivals in the form of "customized" standards in road and air transport and various industrial and trade sectors.

Finally, users may be the victims of their own choices or of the mistakes made by manufacturers. When Wang missed the turn taken by office automation, many users found they had no other option than to convert to radically new systems at considerable cost.

The price to pay can be very high both for users and for suppliers when protracted and expensive standardization work is brought to a halt by such obstacles. Hence the idea of trying to achieve, in the early stages of standardization, consensus solutions through user participation, so that the use of new products can spread more easily.

Standardization: Where?

Producer-sellers and users lie on either side of the market where standards compete and of an institutional system that in recent years has considerably branched out in the IT field. Rapid technological progress and increasing integration of IT and communications have spawned many official and non-official bodies nationally, regionally, and internationally. In Europe, for instance (although similar bodies exist elsewhere), there are the European Workshop for Open Systems (EWOS) and the Open Systems Interconnection/Technical and Office Protocol (OSITOP) on the user side, and on the manufacturer side there are the European Computer Manufacturers' Association (ECMA) and the Standards Promotion and Application Group (SPAG).[4] Various firms have joined together to defend specific interests or to move faster than the official channels: internationally, there is the International Standards Organization (ISO), the International Electrotechnical Committee (IEC), and the International Telecommunications Union (ITU); in Europe, there is the European Committee for Electrotechnical Standardization (CENELEC) and the European Telecommunications Standardization Institute (ETSI).

The many different roles of government in the standardization process muddy the picture even more. By shaping the "profiles" of the technologies it wishes to acquire, and therefore by having a direct influence on the choices made by equipment manufacturers, the public sector can exert strong influence over the adoption of standards in high-tech activities such as defense. The impact will be significantly greater when such influences take on an international dimension. An example is the European Procurement Handbook for Open Systems (EPHOS), and there are equivalents in other regions.

Public administrations have also become large users of IT in all areas and participate as such in the activities of the various standardization bodies without necessarily coordinating their positions. In many countries, government gives financial support to the standardization system, which therefore usually relies on public subsidies as well as on voluntary contributions by industry. The appropriate balance between the two modes of financing is the subject of much debate in most countries.

At national levels, governments have occasionally been tempted to intervene in the standardization of IT by promoting a given standard either in the general interest (for open systems, for instance) or for the purpose of championing a national standard. This move has not always been successful. Moreover, the "perfectionism" of official systems clashes with the uncontrolled spontaneous changes occurring worldwide in the field in response to user choices. The official setting of X400 electronic mail standards is in practice hampered by the uncontrolled but extraordinarily rapid worldwide growth of the Internet network, which diversifies to suit individual users.

The *ad hoc* combinations that come and go as all these public and private interests fluctuate have—to the dismay of all concerned—made it more difficult to monitor standardization in IT so as to prevent duplication of activities by the various bodies and introduce minimum coordination. Producers complain about the huge costs and questionable efficiency of participating in these various bodies; in the case of a multinational several hundred experts may be involved. Secretarial services and the chairmanship of many working parties have to be provided, and participation fees must be paid to every consortium that aims at producing a family of standards (such as UNIX, which covers at least seven divergent variants). And users complain because they are acutely aware of the slow and inadequate progress of institutions that do not meet their expectations for compatibility between different types of equipment, and because when they participate more directly in the discussions they have to contend with institutional opacity, not to mention the considerable expenses entailed.

Ways of Participating

Some users, of course, are highly organized and already participate in the standardization of IT, sometimes with considerable impact. Most of these users are so big that they can set their own standards and impose their requirements on producers to ensure the development of systems that meet general requirements while addressing their specific needs. Examples are banking groups, who have set standards for the exchange of data on financial transactions, and air carriers, who have created standards for ticket-booking systems.

Large firms are increasingly coming together in semi-official associations or working parties such as EWOS, SPAG, OSITOP or X-OPEN. Their objective is to draw up unofficial standards quickly on a consensus basis, which the parties concerned can introduce without waiting for the approval of official institutions through cumbersome and protracted procedures. The rapid evolution of IT favors this type of approach, especially to encourage the setting of application standards for open systems aimed at facilitating exchanges between different configurations. The aim of this work is to establish a system of standards for interfaces between computer systems, which would apply to computer equipment and operating systems and to communication protocols that specify data access modes. The framework thus defined should act as a reference for identifying more limited applications in response to actual requirements in the field.

The problem is that in a period of rapid technological growth, this kind of general framework is bound to be approximate, and therefore leaves so much room for maneuver that the applications covered by the framework are not necessarily compatible with one another. Throughout the world there are many groups trying to raise the degree of compatibility between computers operating under UNIX or to develop the basis for computer-assisted transactions systems such as Electronic Data Interchange (EDI). But the final outcome of this work often generates new barriers to communication among families of standards that are supposed to be close to one another. In the hope of overcoming these barriers, groups and bodies that are more specialized than ever before are being created without others ever being phased out, so that the overall standardization system is becoming ever more complex, opaque and poorly coordinated, resulting in an "institutional jungle."

Small users could indeed join forces with one another, in the same way that large users do, so as to spread the costs of attending the many meetings of the legions of national and international bodies involved in, say, the setting of EDI standards in transport or real estate, which are tending to acquire new network structures. But many users decide not to join, in the knowledge that the benefits of any standardization will eventually be freely available to all. Official institutions—in Europe, CEN-CENELEC (the European Standardization Committee-European Electrotechnical Standardization Committee) for information technologies and ETSI for telecommunications, or at global level, the ISO, IEC and ITU— are full of good intentions and are prepared to accept the representatives of smaller users. But even assuming they are willing to come forward, small users realize that the actual decisions are taken elsewhere and, here again, they have to face the costs.

User participation becomes difficult or not depending on the types of standard concerned:

• National or international: A small or medium-sized enterprise might sacrifice resources to take part in the proceedings of a national technical group working on a standard liable to bring specific benefits, but will hesitate to become involved in regional or worldwide proceedings.

• Product or functional standards (those governing teletex, videotex, mobile telephones, modems, and so on): Here again, the more the potential benefits are limited to a specific product, the more direct participation of specific, well-identified users might be expected.

• *Ex post, ex ante* or anticipatory standards: It can be easier to obtain a consensus for setting a standard for a product undergoing development than for one that is already marketed; this is the path increasingly followed by standardization bodies (the GSM standard for the next generation of mobile telephones has been drawn up in this way). The problem is that a product that is not yet in existence does not have any clearly identified users.

The Impact of Globalization

The current economic globalization process is making all users, whether large or small, more aware of what is at stake: small firms now feel involved in world markets. Although current standardization mechanisms generate multiple variants and complex fragmentation (as with EDI standards), advancing globalization means that these problems have to be overcome. IT producers are not going to introduce a high degree of coherence and compatibility unprompted, since that would stimulate competition and they wish to retain their market shares under the protection of their own technologies. Pressure from users alone can make them do so.

In 1991, the first signs appeared: a group of large firms that use IT (initially composed of American Airlines, Boeing, DuPont de Nemours, General Motors, Kodak, McDonell Douglas and Merck) drew up a "menu" of requests, providing a kind of framework for future standardization work for the IT industry. More recently, a group of industrial experts on IT standardization was set up by the OECD Committee for Information Computer and Communications Policy to draw up a report on the mechanisms, procedures, and products of standardization. Although very large multinational firms are the most overtly active at this stage, the movement is bound to spread, especially through the relations between these firms and their suppliers.

The recent conclusion of the GATT Uruguay Round in December 1993 reflects the increasing importance attached to standards internationally as an important ingredient in the developing infrastructure of the new global economy—which in itself will be strengthened, since the Uruguay Round agreements apply to 115 members against the 40 or so signatories of the current GATT's "voluntary standard code." In addition:

• The accord encourages countries to join and actively participate in the standardization work of the international standards bodies.

• The agreement calls on countries to use International Standards when they exist.

• A new dispute settlement mechanism will be available to combat standards being used as disguised trade barriers.

These developments are all the more significant in view of the fact that industry increasingly aims at the design of international standards, without necessarily going through an intermediate stage of national (and often divergent) standards. Globalization is instrumental here, because it compels multinational firms that have traditionally been very decentralized and diversified to establish greater coordination and to develop alliances with others. The demand for international standards is thus bound to increase significantly—all the more so in view of the integration of former communist countries into the world trading system.

At the present time, many governments try to define and introduce measures to stimulate and facilitate the participation of a wider range of users. Government intervention in standardization may take different forms, including informing a wide range of users about the benefits of competitiveness; more active participation of government bodies in fields where collective interests are at stake; and efforts to ensure equal access to strategic information, transparency of procedures, and the general economics of institutional mechanisms. However, at national levels, these efforts rapidly encounter the limits outlined above, which drastically reduce the levels of users participation that can be realistically expected.

Globalization, however, may have a more profound and decisive influence, because no firm, large or small, can afford to ignore the new networking opportunities that have become a key to maintaining and increasing competitiveness even in one's domestic market. Can governments provide a framework that will ensure more coherent standards development? Should they attempt to streamline the world institutional structure of standards making in IT? Should they even attempt to promote "meta-standards" at the international level to influence the standardization process in more coherent and economical directions?

There is no doubt that new technologies—today information technology, tomorrow materials and biotechnology—require new approaches to keep costs under control and avoid wasted technical efforts. From their own viewpoints, users can bring a new dimension to IT standardization that is closer to the concerns of competitiveness and efficiency prevailing throughout the industrial fabric. International developments set these questions against a radically new background and open an unprecedented debate on the role of governments—as custodians of the public interest and as users— in shaping the future path of IT standardization at the world level.

Notes

[1] "The Economic Dimension of IT Standards—Users and IT Standards," ICCP series, Paris: OECD Publications, 1994. This paper is chiefly based on the study conducted by Dominique Foray, Professor of Economics at the Ecole Centrale de Paris, on "The Economic Dimension of Standards—The Role of Users in Information Technology Standardization" (unpublished).

[2] *Information Technology Standards: The Economic Dimension*, Paris: OECD Publications, 1991.

[3] Computer equipment or service distributors that also happen to be users are ignored here, since this category concerns buyers of IT products only.

[4] Georges Ferné, "The Economic Stakes in Computer Standardization," *The OECD Observer*, No. 164, June/July 1990.

The Global Standards Process: A Balance of the Old and the New

Richard B. Gibson
Joint ISO-IEC Technical Committee 1 on Information Technology

Introduction

The JTC 1 TAG (Technical Advisory Group for Joint Technical Committee 1 of the ISO/IEC) is the U.S. position development body that relates to the Plenary group of JTC 1. It is administered by the Computer Business Equipment Manufacturers Association (CBEMA). Other U.S. TAGs, administered by several U.S. Standards Developing Organizations (CBEMA, IEEE, TIA), relate to the various subsidiary bodies of JTC 1 (Subcommittees, Working Groups) and to specific JTC 1 projects. The family of JTC 1-related U.S. TAGs operate in concert under a Memorandum of Agreement sponsored by the Information Systems Standards Board of ANSI. In addition to the organizations holding specific TAG assignments, the family of U.S. groups having an interest in JTC 1 work includes EIA, T1, X9, X12 and others. While the author has been invited to submit this paper as the Chairman of the JTC 1 TAG, for timing reasons, this document has not received committee approval. The views expressed here are, therefore, those of the author.

The title of this paper reflects several themes that will be developed further. The two most important are represented by the terms "global" and "process." Standards must serve the marketplace. When the marketplace is global, so must be the standards. Marketplace acceptability, however, is not the sole criterion by which one judges the value of a standard. One can find many examples of practices/specifications that have found wide market acceptance (so-called de facto standards) but do not have many important attributes one would look for in a standard. Thus, the notion of a standards development process. The standards development process is what ensures the achievement of standards goals that go beyond market acceptability.

Another key term is "balance." A process that produces standards must seek a balance between conflicting objectives. Most people want standards work to be done more quickly; standardizing new technologies *too* quickly can inhibit technical growth and innovation. The intellectual property employed in standards must be widely available; the rights of the intellectual property holders must be protected. To promote fair competition, standards should not be imposed by a single entity; the more stakeholders involved in a standard's development, the longer it will take. Standards should promote compatibility; standards should encourage technical innovation.

The private sector process for development and approval of voluntary consensus standards has evolved over the years to deal with these conflicting demands. Is it perfect? Certainly not. Is it static in its approach to dealing with the difficult demands? Certainly not. Is it our best hope for meeting the difficult demands before us? Definitely. What we need is not radical change, but rather continuous improvement of the global system in place today.

In dealing with changes to the standardization process, one must keep in mind the objectives of the process and the need to keep in balance these objectives. For example, a single-minded quest for lower cycle time could destroy the system's ability to meet other important objectives. The challenge before us is to find the means to meet important new requirements while preserving old requirements that continue to be important.

The global standardization system is undergoing major changes. Foremost among these changes is an orientation toward global rather than national standards. This change is progressing at different rates in different sectors; however, in fields where the technology is changing rapidly (e.g., information technology, telecommunications) the shift to a global orientation is nearly complete. This shift in orientation has produced a number of changes in the U.S. process, including the synchronization of national and international activities and the adoption of national standards only after the international work is complete.

The same global market forces that have led to a focus on global standards have also led to a much stronger marketplace orientation. Increasingly, participants in the standards process are recognizing the strategic importance of standardization. Governments begin to develop the same awareness as standards are linked to trade matters and national priorities such as the NII. These factors have led to a stronger orientation toward user requirements within the standards process and a substantial reduction in the average time required to produce a standard.

Another development of the last five years is the relative explosion in the number of organizations that are not formal standards groups but do standards-related work. These organizations, loosely referred to as consortia, perform a great variety of standards-related functions. Early consortia focused heavily on creating implementation agreements for individual standards, and defining "profiles" of standards to perform specific functions (e.g., OSI transport). Thus, their focus has been on post-standardization issues. The international standards process responded to these needs by creating a means whereby profiles (functional standards) developed by various organizations could be quickly processed within the formal system and adopted with the stature of an international standard (International Standardized Profile—ISP). This process is now being generalized for use thoughout ISO.

Other consortia, while generally making use of existing standardization, address pre-standardization needs. There is much speculation and debate within the industry as to the role and the necessity for such groups. Some argue the groups exist because the formal standards process is too slow to meet their needs. This is certainly true for the small, market-oriented groups that attempt to reach rapid agreement on how to deploy a new technology with minimal market risk. On the other hand, there are some consortia that are quite large in membership and more general in scope. Such organizations tend to have more of the qualities traditionally associated with formal standards groups. There is truth in the rule of thumb that the development time of a standard is proportional to the breadth of the consensus achieved.

Another valid argument is that the process of making standards is itself a competitive business. Administration of the voluntary standards process is largely financed by dues paid to the various membership organizations that administer standards development and by the sale of completed standards.[1] Competition either for dues or for document sales may lead to a desire for organizational independence from the formal standards process.

Whatever the role or motivation for consortia, it seems clear that rapidly changing technology and market forces will maintain consortia as an important part of the standards landscape. This is viewed by the author as a positive development, since consortia have created a considerable body of technically sound, market-accepted work. This work is beginning to find its way into the formal standards process. Indeed, there is evidence that a significant portion of standards technical development is done outside of formal standards committees and is later brought into the system for technical consensus building and formal approval. In the author's view, this practice should be a model for achieving synergy between the formal standards process and the various organizations doing standards-related work.

The Global Standardization System

The private sector process for development and approval of voluntary consensus standards has existed for many years on both a national and a global level.[2] Organizationally, the process includes National Standards Bodies in each country (one per country) and three global standard bodies, the International Organization for Standardization (ISO), the International Electrotechnical Commission (IEC), and the International Telecommunications Union (ITU). The ISO and IEC are private sector organizations and relate to private sector National Bodies in each country. The ITU is a treaty organization in the public sector and relates to national administrations in each country. Each National Standards Body can be a "member" of the global standards bodies and each has established a system for standardization within its country. These national systems determine positions for use within the global bodies and, in the case of the private sector standards bodies, also provide for the creation and adoption of National Standards.

Many national systems are centralized, with the National Standards Body having direct organizational control over the committees that develop and approve standards and national positions. In the United States, with the exception of the national position development associated with the ITU (centralized under the auspices of the U.S. Department of State), the standardization system is decentralized.[3] The U.S. National Body, ANSI, accredits over 250 independent standards-developing organizations (SDOs) to develop national standards and to determine positions for use in the international arena (Technical Advisory Groups—TAGS).

Goals

The goals of a standardization system should be distinguished from the goals of a standard. While the general goals of individual standards are well known (e.g., promote compatibility/interoperability, lower cost through competition, etc.), a standardization system must go beyond the obvious goals of efficiently and effectively producing standards.

One relatively simple but extremely important goal is an inherent characteristic of a standard. A standardization system serves to *limit the choices* available in the marketplace to those that promote the common good. For example, U.S. standards for electrical plugs and receptacles permit a wide variety of electrical appliances to be used universally throughout the United States. If each jurisdiction in the United States were to create its own "standard" for electrical fixtures, the overall common good would be sacrificed. While there is considerable opportunity for multiple, autonomous organizations to participate in a standardization system, the final approval process must bring diverse interests together. Multiple peer organizations, all producing standards with the same stature, is equivalent to having no standardization system at all.

Because of both the necessity of selecting only one solution and the market consequences of that decision, a standardization system must provide some basic safeguards to protect the rights of those affected by the standards. Information about new standards developments must be publicly available. Development groups must be open to all interests and free from dominance by a single interest. Decisions should be made by consensus. A formal dispute resolution process should exist and the rights of intellectual property holders should be protected.

The goals of a standardization system relate to the *confidence* that the public can place in the standards produced. This confidence is not measured by the market success of the standards. Confidence in a standard means that the standard is above reproach in terms of being fairly developed and widely supported (supported in a consensual sense). Certain uses of standards (e.g., government procurements, standards used as the basis for regulation) require that the chosen standard not unfairly discriminate against any affected interest. In these cases, the standardization system must through its basic processes assure standards users that there is no other technical specification that has a broader level of consensus support. In practice, this is achieved by strict adherence to the due process principles reflected in the above discussion of safeguards.

National Body Process

The standardization principles mentioned above are the basis for accreditation of U.S. standards developers by ANSI. Internationally, these principles are endorsed by the three pre-eminent global standards bodies: ISO, IEC, and ITU. These three organizations differ at the operational level but are very similar at a broad policy level. For instance, all three organizations share a common notion of membership, looking to nations as their principal members. The National Body process addresses the issue of membership in these global standardization bodies.

Despite the case for a single approval point for standards, three separate organizations have evolved. It should be noted, however, that the process and standardization principles, not the organizations themselves, are the basis for confidence in the result. Each new organization creates additional coordination problems that siphon resources away from actual standards development. In the case of ISO, IEC, and ITU, extensive cooperation mechanisms exist to ensure both minimal overlap and collaboration on projects of mutual interest.

The National Body process is an international form of governance for standards development with nation-state representatives. While not perfect, National Body membership does recognize the political institutions that society has given sovereign powers. One might argue that a representative form of governance is not needed in the case of standards making, but it is no more practical to allow individual representation at the international level than it would be to allow it in the U.N. or in the U.S. Congress.[4] One might also argue that the National Body memberships should be supplemented with organizational memberships, but this would dilute the influence of National Bodies since a very large set of organizations would become eligible for membership if this were allowed.

Membership can also be viewed as a staged consensus process. As a national consensus on an issue is reached in each country, these agreements form the basis for the international stage of the consensus process. Such a system has its pros and cons. If the two consensus-making stages were completely decoupled (i.e., each country works in isolation and then attempts to obtain agreement at the international level after its work is complete) the system could become very inefficient. Fortunately, in most fields, and certainly in the IT field, there is a high degree of coupling between national and international activities. Not only are there good formal communications within the process, but many national development groups (particularly in the United States) benefit from significant international participation. Magnetic and optical media, programming languages, and local area networks are major examples.

There are two major arguments for staging the consensus process. The first argument relates to defining (protecting) national interests, which can be cultural, commercial, or security-related. While most standards work is technically oriented, and good technical solutions are desired, there are many non-technical factors that must be considered in developing a standard. Manufacturers, users, and governments often take intense economic interest in standards. Standards making is no longer the exclusive domain of expert technicians. In light of the debate last year over NAFTA, it seems unlikely that many would find it politically attractive to relinquish a national voice in standards, since standards affect trade,[5] commerce and, therefore, the U.S. economy.

The second argument concerns the enfranchisement of smaller economic interests. The cost of international meetings (participants' travel and living expenses) is significantly higher than that of domestic meetings. This is a deterrent for smaller stakeholders. However, in most cases, the national preparatory process allows all U.S. points of view to contribute to the shaping of the U.S. national position without the necessity for international travel.

The JTC 1 Process

Conventional wisdom about the formal standards process creates a picture of technical committees endlessly debating technical minutia and a bureaucratic process that creates monstrous delays in producing results. Unfortunately, even ardent supporters of the system would have to admit to elements of truth in this portrayal. This picture was even more true before standards were viewed as having strategic importance. However, this view does not do justice to today's overall system, particularly in important fields such as information technology. The system is driven by the collective views of its participants and as the participants have become more market-focused, so also has the standards process. This change is perhaps most evident in Joint Technical Committee 1 of the ISO and IEC.

JTC 1 was created in 1987 to combine the information technology work of the ISO and IEC. The committee operates under its own procedures (subject to the approval of ISO and IEC and generally consistent with ISO/IEC procedures) and has a collaboration agreement with the ITU for the progression of joint work. JTC 1 is made up of a Plenary body and 17 Subcommittees. Most of the Subcommittees have Working Groups to deal with specific aspects of the technical program. Membership in the Plenary body and in the Subcommittees is by National Body (either Participating or Observer), but several types of non-voting Liaison memberships exist. Individual expert participation is authorized at the Working Group level, where it is presumed that most of the technical development work will be done.

From a process standpoint, JTC 1 has three ways to progress work to the status of an International Standard (IS): the five-stage development process, the fast-track process and, for ISPs, the ISP process. Of the three standards processes, the five-stage process is

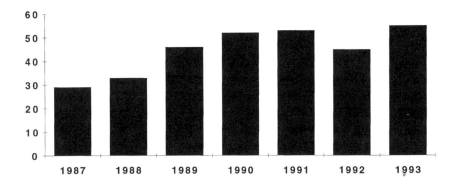

Figure 1 Number of JTC 1 International Standards Produced, 1987–1993 (the total number is 458).

most general purpose and the one most often used. The fast-track and ISP processes play an important role but they are more narrowly defined and less frequently employed.[6]

JTC 1 produces two types of standards documents: the International Standard (IS) and the International Standardized Profile (ISP). It also creates Technical Reports and several types of maintenance documents. JTC 1 is a very productive group, accounting for about 30% of ISO's standards output. As shown in Figure 1, JTC 1 has produced 458 ISs through the end of 1993 and is currently at an annual production rate of over 50 ISs per year.

As shown in Figure 2, JTC 1 produced 24 ISPs through the end of 1993. Since each ISP may include more than one Profile, the number of Profiles per year is also shown. The ISP process was completed in 1989 and the first ISP approved in 1990. The number of ISPs/Profiles has increased year by year, and in late 1993-early 1994 a very large number of Profiles were submitted. The 1994 figures (May 1994) shown reflect Profiles being processed but not yet approved.

There is considerable flexibility in the five-stage process (methods are covered in Appendix A). Through this flexibility, and in response to the need to accelerate standards development, JTC 1 has significantly reduced the time required to produce a standard. Figure 3 shows how the overall development interval has been reduced by over 10 months, to just over 40 months, since 1988. This is two-thirds the average time for all ISO committees. The average

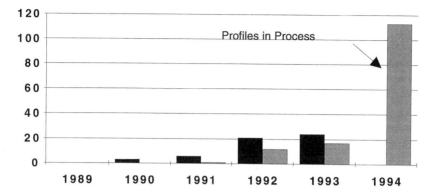

Figure 2 Cumulative Number of ISPs (solid) and Profiles (gray) per Year.

time to reach the DIS decision point has also declined over 60%, to about 12 months. This decline is significant since at this point the technical content of the standard is usually stable enough for implementation efforts to begin. Unfortunately, in some cases the DIS decision is made too soon. This results in a substantial number of technical comments being received during the DIS ballot. This lengthens the DIS preparation period (with a possible second DIS ballot) and substantially delays the point at which implementations may safely begin.

The short DIS decision interval also provides a good indication that much of the actual technical development work is being brought into the process from outside sources, rather than being developed inside the committee structure.

Two years ago, a U.S. proposal for a new C-Liaison category was accepted. The purpose of these liaisons is to facilitate the direct interchange of technical information on specific projects between consortia and the technical committees of JTC 1. After a slow start (which parallels the slow start of usage of the ISP process), over a dozen requests for such liaisons were approved by JTC 1 in early 1994.

A Process Model

In the process employed by all three global standardization organizations, the development of a standard takes place in three major

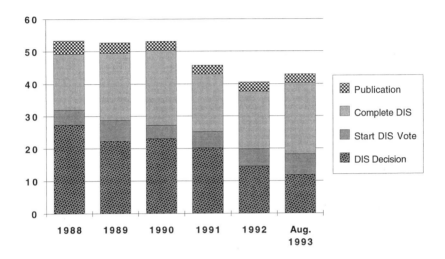

Figure 3 JTC 1 Development Time (in Months).

phases.[7] In Phase One the basic technical work is completed. This work may be done by an international standards committee (e.g., a JTC 1 Working Group), national standards committee, consortia, or individual participant. Phase Two involves building a technical consensus for the work and occurs within the technical committee (e.g., a Subcommittee in JTC 1). Phase Two concludes with a vote of Subcommittee National Body members. Phase Three involves formal standards approval. In the case of JTC 1, this is done by a letter ballot vote by the JTC 1 Plenary group's National Body members. This final vote provides a means to judge whether due process was followed in the development of the standard (in JTC 1, technical comments are still allowed during this vote). The National Body process relates primarily to phases Two and Three: technical consensus building and final approval. It is much less concerned with the standard's actual development.

Those who would use the standardization process wisely must first recognize that the objective of the process is to achieve the broadest possible consensus for the work. Process inputs can occur at the national level (in one or more nations) and at the international level. However, a consensus of National Bodies will ultimately be required for approval. The formula for success is to build the broadest possible international consensus for the work, at the earliest opportunity. U.S. groups having substantial international participation have an edge over those that do not have such participation. International consortia also have this advantage. Furthermore, it is counterproductive to surprise an international group with new work. Having one or more National Bodies (in the case of JTC 1, particularly the U.S. National Body) as advocate for a given piece of work clearly improves the chances for success.

Success in the standardization system is earned, not conferred by an authority. There is no mechanism at the international level to make organizational-level endorsements (such mechanisms are, however, under study). The focus should be on the work, not on the organization that produced it. Over the years, several organizations have achieved a high success rate for their work (e.g., IEEE for Local Area Network standards, ECMA for magnetic media work). There is no guarantee that work by the same organizations in other areas would have met with the same degree of acceptance.

Many consortia question the value added by their participation in the formal standards process. Some consortia possess high-quality technical specifications (publicly available specifications—PAS), often market accepted, that were developed in a rigorous process. While such organizations would understandably prefer to operate as the peer of the three global standards bodies, a multiple peer paradigm is not a practical way to operate the global standardization system. Furthermore, the mechanisms necessary to facilitate a multiple peer system (e.g., accreditation, elimination of overlap and work duplication, etc.) would likely be more onerous to the consortia than the current system.

It is critical to producers, users, and PAS owners that the body of good technical work existing outside of the formal standards process be integrated with existing standards. Only if this integration occurs can the standards process keep pace with technology and market demands. This integration is also essential if the technology is to be within the reach of those requiring the confidence afforded by the formal standards process. This integration translates into a wider market for standards and lower cost for standards users.

A solution to improving the standardization process lies in making use of the flexibility that the formal process provides at the technical development level. Both the United States and Europe have suggested relaxing government procurement regulations to permit procurement based upon PASs. Such a move would withdraw a critical element of support for the private-sector standards process, and has questionable long-term consequences for government procurements. We need not invent a back-door path—the front door is wide open.

As the public and private sectors come together to deal with these complex issues, we must keep in mind that no system of standardization can hope to live up to all expectations. The system must balance many conflicting objectives and different interests may view this balance in different ways. If standards were to become a prerequisite for market entry, technical growth and competition would be stifled. Thus, there will always be attractive technology in the marketplace which has not yet been "standardized." While one could argue that this is a failure of the standardization system, a better argument would recognize that without the incentive of free market entry, the technology would not likely be produced. Standards cannot be viewed in isolation of market forces. Standards making is not a pristine technical endeavor; it is a process that must reflect the diverse interests of the market. As a consequence, we must be prepared to accept that there are aspects of the standardization system that cannot be "fixed" because they represent a market sensitivity that must be retained.

Appendix A: JTC 1 Standards Processes

JTC 1 has three ways to progress work to the status of an International Standard (IS): the five-stage development process, the fast-track process and, for ISPs, the ISP process. The five-stage process is clearly the most general purpose of the three and the one most often used. The fast-track and ISP processes play an important role but they are more narrowly defined and less frequently employed.

The Five-Stage Process

This is the mainstream ISO/IEC process that has been adopted by JTC 1. The five stages (six if you count Stage 0) are, in time sequence:

Stage 0 (Preliminary Stage): A study period is underway. Such a study may lead to one or more NPs (New Proposals). In some cases (e.g., large new work areas) there is a formal, approved study period. More often, however, study periods are relatively informal.

Stage 1 (Proposal Stage): An NP is under consideration. A proposal for new work must be approved by JTC 1 before work can begin but this approval is on default basis for minor extensions of existing projects. A minimum of five National Body members of the Subcommittee (SC) must agree to actively participate in the work.

Stage 2 (Preparatory Stage): A WD (Working Draft) is under consideration. Successive WDs record the technical evolution of a standard. When a WD has reached a reasonable level of completeness, it may be registered as a Committee Draft (CD). The CD is given a number and sent out for three-month ballot of National Body members of the SC.

Stage 3 (Committee Stage): A CD is under consideration. Consideration of successive CDs continues until substantial support is reached, at which time the CD may be advanced to DIS (Draft International Standard) status.

Stage 4 (Approval Stage): A DIS is under consideration. DIS ballot periods have just been reduced to a four-month interval and are voted on by the JTC 1. While successive DIS ballots are allowed, ISO and IEC are increasing the pressure to move to a simple up-down, two-month vote on DISs. JTC 1 has not yet adopted this "confirmation" ballot approach, since many JTC 1 DISs are not as stable as they should be.

Stage 5 (Publication Stage): An IS (International Standard) is being prepared for publication. This stage follows the passage of the DIS to allow for ISO/IEC final publication.

Fast-Track Processing

The fast-track process was created to handle completed standards from either a National Body or an A-Liaison organization at the JTC 1 level. Under this process, the submitter of the proposed IS submits the document to JTC 1 at what is essentially Stage 4. The proposed standard does not have to be in ISO format. Also, the proposed standard does not have to be aligned with an existing project; rather the project is created with the approval of the fast-track. The document submitter may or may not indicate which SC should have responsibility for the document; the Secretariat of JTC 1 must make this determination at the time of submission. JTC 1 initiates a four-month ballot on the document, and if the ballot passes and comments are received, the task of resolving the ballot comments is given to the SC (or group) designated for that purpose. Following ballot resolution, the text is modified in accordance with the comments and progressed to Stage 5. Maintenance responsibility for the IS is assigned to a designated JTC 1 group. If the ballot fails, the document is withdrawn.

This process can be effective if there is a high degree of consensus and if the assignment issue is clear and not controversial (e.g., as in the case of magnetic media standards). If either of these conditions is not met, experience has shown that the fast-track will likely fail. Typically, submitters of a fast-track document need to work informally for quite some time to build support for the document in the SCs before its submission. Fast-track is a nice capability to have available in the process, but it is far from a general-purpose standards approval mechanism.

ISP Processing

The ISP process was established in the late 1980s to deal with functional standards and functional profiles. JTC 1 recognized that a significant effort was being made in Regional Workshops to establish implementation agreements for collections, or profiles, of JTC 1 base standards. These implementation agreements fix parameters and define the options left open within the base standards. Recognizing the importance of this work, JTC 1, in concert with S-Liaison organizations, defined a new document type (ISP) and defined a new process for producing ISPs.

A new work item (NP) does not have to be approved for an ISP. However, a profile must be included in a taxonomy of profiles before the ISP's submission. A proposed ISP may be submitted to JTC 1 (with an explanatory report) by a National Body, an SC or Technical Committee within ISO, or an S-Liaison (to the Special Group on Functional Standards—SGFS) organization. To qualify for submission, three basic criteria must be met: the proposed ISP must have been internationally harmonized, developed in an open environment, and consistent with the base standards referenced. After a short review by experts appointed for the task, a review report is produced and the entire package (explanatory report, review report, and proposed ISP) is submitted to JTC 1 for a four-month ballot. If the ballot passes, and comments are received, the submitter must agree to any changes suggested during the ballot resolution process. The submitter retains ownership of the document, both for changes requested and for continuing maintenance. Unless agreement is reached (in which case the document becomes an ISP), the document is returned to the submitter. This process was set up to deal with aggregations of existing base standards, not to create new ones.

Processing Flexibility in the Five-Stage Process

Generating NPs (Stages 0–1)

The first two stages of the process (0 and 1) are usually the simplest and typically do not require a great deal of time. Except for large new work areas (major new initiatives), NPs are typically originated with National Body contributions to a WG or SC. If the group agrees, the submitting National Body is usually asked to prepare the NP, which the committee then progresses as an SC-originated NP. In some cases, the National Body will submit the NP directly to JTC 1. After completing a project, the SC/WG sometimes decides that a further piece of work is required and will originate an NP at a meeting.

The National Body's role in the NP process varies. While NPs originated by the U.S. National Body (at the JTC 1 level) require JTC 1 TAG approval, U.S. TAGs at the WG and SC level may (through contributions) cause NPs to be originated by SCs. Most NPs go through the SC-level route.

Working Drafts (Stage 2)

In the straightforward development process, Stage 2 includes the opportunity to spend the most time on the work. If the working draft is developed by the international meetings of the WG (driven by expert and National Body contributions), many meetings may be required. This time-consuming mode of operation, however, is being used less and less. The key to progressing any standards work in this stage is to focus the committee on the first working draft. To expedite this procedure, typically one or more committee members undertake to produce a first draft and present it to the committee. Increasingly, however, the first draft exists at the time, or close to the time, the NP is prepared by virtue of work that has been done in another organization. Depending upon the nature of this work and the degree of international consensus on it, the time spent in Stage 2 could be reduced to zero. Virtually eliminating Stage 2 work is the greatest opportunity to accelerate the process.

There is the opportunity to identify on the NP form whether or not there exists a working draft suitable for CD processing. If the NP is approved by JTC 1, and the SC agrees that the draft is suitable for registration/ballot as a CD, it may be progressed immediately to Stage 3. Similarly, if some time after an NP is approved, National Body or Liaison members of the committee produce a draft text that the committee finds acceptable, the SC can progress the document to Stage 3. A number of techniques to accomplish this progression are currently in use.

Example 1: A National Body has completed a standard but is not convinced that there is sufficient support to risk a fast-track. In this case, the National Body could originate an NP that indicates that the document is available. Assuming a reasonable level of international support, the SC could register the document as a CD and work out any problems during the CD ballot and its resolution.

Example 2: A given National Body formally agrees with the SC to do the actual technical development work in their national committee (which may be in a national or an international organization[8]), and to be sensitive to all comments received from members of the international committee. In effect, the national committee becomes like a WG of the SC. Such an arrangement has been called a Hague agreement and is widely used in SC 22 for programming language development. As documents progress under this arrangement, however, national views might develop that are not in concert with the views of the international committee (for example, the parent of the national group doing the development work may insist upon some position at odds with the international organization). Such issues are worked out on a case-by-case basis.

Example 3: Another method is similar to the Hague agreement described above except that a formal agreement is not reached. The international community recognizes and agrees that most of the formative technical work on a subject is being done in another group. By appointing a project editor from the other group and referring technical issues to the project editor the technical control of the document is in effect transferred to the other group. It is under this arrangement that IEEE 802 relates to SC6 for LAN work. The key to the success of such arrangements is the confidence that the international community places in the other organization. This confidence is earned over a period of time and is created by the degree of international participation allowed in the development group and its sensitivity to comments received from the international community via the SC. Arrangements, such as the one between IEEE 802 and SC 6, are associated with a National Body. That is, IEEE 802, while sponsored by an international organization, is accredited by ANSI, and ANSI is thus viewed as the National Body responsible for the arrangement.

There exists an increasing number of internationally oriented Liaison organizations (A & C) at the SC level. Although these organizations have relatively complete work suitable for standardization, it is not clear under what conditions an arrangement between the SC and the Liaison organization (such as that between IEEE 802 and SC6) could be established. It is of key importance whether or not the international community would entrust the work to an organization if the community did not have recourse to a National Body. In other words, international organizations may want the group to be nationally sponsored.

Given that a consensus of National Bodies is required to progress the work, it is in the interest of any submitting organization to secure international support early on. For example, IEEE 802 progresses its work nationally through the SC 6 TAG (X3S3). Typically, this TAG forwards the work to SC6 with a U.S. National Body endorsement. The favorable endorsement by the SC 6 TAG virtually ensures that the U.S. National Body will support the work at all levels in the process. While an A- or C- Liaison to an SC may directly submit its work to the SC/WG, bypassing the national level committees, it would forego a valuable opportunity to obtain national support for the work.

Example 4: In the recorded media field, standards are needed very quickly, so consensus on solutions is reached more rapidly than in other areas. After SC-level agreement on a working draft, the SC essentially turns the document over to ECMA, which then fast-tracks it. This bypasses the CD ballot stage and shortens the overall process by several months. Obviously, this method only works when there is a high degree of consensus and a high degree of cooperation between the SC members and ECMA. This procedure is most often employed by the magnetic and optical media committees to, in effect, bypass Stage 3.

Approval (Stages 3–4)

Completing a single CD ballot followed by a DIS ballot takes 12-18 months (allowing for mailing, ballot resolution, etc.). In addition to Example 4, a few things that can be done to shorten this period. For instance, the cleaner the draft text, the faster the resolution of comments process. If major technical comments are received with the DIS ballot, technical changes to the DIS may require a second DIS ballot (this is a current problem area for JTC 1). Multiple CD ballots to resolve technical differences are preferable since the CD ballot period is shorter and the ballot group directly involves members of the SC. Also, if documents do not progress to the DIS level until their technical content is stable, the general ISO/IEC procedure, which allows no technical comments on a two-month DIS ballot, could be used. Electronic distribution might also shorten the mailing delays. There is, however, a limit to how much the ballot periods can be shortened and still give time for the national committees to agree upon their votes.

Publication (Stage 5)

There is time required between ballot resolution and ISO/IEC's publication of the standard for the editor to complete the final draft and the Information Technology Task Force (ITTF, the joint ISO/IEC staff group responsible for JTC 1) to publish the document. Unfortunately, this interval has been increasing in the last year or so. ITTF helps the process by having its editors work with project editors early on to understand drafting requirements. The main problem, however, is technical editors not committing the resources necessary to complete the work on a timely basis after the final vote has been taken.

Notes

[1] In some countries, the government funds a portion of the private-sector system.

[2] Part of the difficulty in discussing standards and standards processes is the widespread use of the term "standard" to mean substantially different things. For the purpose of this paper, the following conventions will be adopted: The terms "standard" or "formal standard" will refer to specifications that have been processed through the consensus process for voluntary standards and formally adopted by a recognized national (ANSI) or international (ISO, IEC or ITU) standards body. Specifications that have been made public and that have some measure of consensus support short of formal adoption by the bodies mentioned above will be called "Publicly Available Specifications (PASs)" or with the name of the adopting organization as a modifier for the term "standard" (e.g., Internet standard). The term "de facto standard" refers to a specification/practice that has found wide market acceptance. Specifications for de facto standards may or may not be in the public domain and the "owner" of the defacto standard may be a single organizational entity (e.g., a single supplier) or may be a membership organization.

[3] The State Department committee, however, often makes use of positions developed within the decentralized structure.

[4] In addition to TAGs, IEC position development makes use of other mechanisms associated with the U.S. National Committee for the IEC operating under the umbrella of general ANSI policy.

[5] It is important to note that we are talking about the governance of the standards system (making the rules, approving the standards, etc.) as opposed to the system for producing the technical content of the standards. While the National Body process within ISO, for example, extends down to the Subcommittee level, expert participation is allowed at the Working Group level, where it is presumed that most of the technical development work will be done.

[6] In addition to voluntary standards as the basis for national regulations, treaties such as NAFTA and GATT contain language that gives preference to international standards in proving that a given regulation is not a technical barrier to trade.

[7] See Appendix A for a more detailed description of JTC 1 standards processes.

[8] For simplification, it is assumed that agreement exists to undertake the work; that is, a new project has been authorized. In the case of JTC 1, this involves a National Body vote of the JTC 1 Plenary body.

[9] The actual responsibility is given to the national body, but the group that the National Body looks to for the work may reside in either a national organization (e.g., X3) or in an international organization (e.g., IEEE).

Standards and the Information Infrastructure

William F. Hanrahan
Computer and Business Equipment Manufacturers Association

Introduction

Assisting in the rapid implementation of an information infrastructure (II) is a high priority for CBEMA. CBEMA recognizes that interoperability is key to a successful information infrastructure in the United States, and equally essential to a global II. Accordingly, CBEMA is engaged in an extensive effort to develop a coherent set of voluntary information infrastructure standards that will be necessary as well as sufficient for achieving access to networks on a broad, consumer-friendly basis and that will also protect individual privacy, security, and intellectual property.

Development of the II is a massive undertaking. Transforming the vision into reality will require unprecedented international cooperation among business, government, and academic communities. Strong active participation by vendors and users in the II voluntary standards development process will help ensure that as the II evolves the vision articulated last fall by the Administration's Information Infrastructure Task Force will indeed be transformed into reality.

Although there is still some debate among experts on the precise definition of "information infrastructure"—indeed, on the definition of "interoperability" itself—there seems to be consensus on what informed users expect: an infrastructure where information flows across different systems and competing networks. Interoperability will allow diverse systems made by different vendors to communicate with each other, so users don't have to make major adjustments to account for differences in products and services.

Standards are essential to achieving the interoperability that users will demand of the II. CBEMA believes that the best approach to developing standards is one that seeks to identify and restrict standards to a sufficient minimum, leaving maximum room for providing present and future choices for vendors and users.

This paper outlines the characteristics of II standards and the II standards development process that CBEMA believes are fundamental to achieving a system that is as open, interactive, and flexible as is technically possible:

- The need for international standards
- The scope of standardization
- Timeliness of standards development
- Interoperability and extensibility
- Open systems
- Networking and applications
- Voluntary consensus standards
- Intellectual property rights protection
- Privacy and security considerations
- Public and private sector roles in II standards development

CBEMA welcomes comments on our perspective on standards development and the information infrastructure. We look forward to a continuing, productive dialogue among all parties with an interest in II standards development.

International Standards Are Increasingly Important

In today's global economy, internationally recognized standards are increasingly vital. The standards adopted for the II must be compatible with the standards used throughout the world to ensure that information can flow easily across national and regional borders. II standards need to be international. The U.S. Government and U.S. voluntary standards-developing organizations cannot unilaterally set II standards for the world, even though many international standards are adopted from standards or technology first developed in the United States. Because we're really dealing with a Global Information Infrastructure (GII), the standards for the information infrastructure need to be developed in, or adopted by, the recognized international standardization bodies: the International Electrotechnical Commission (IEC), the International Organization for Standardization (ISO), and the International Telecommunications Union (ITU).

The Scope Needs to Include a Realistic Perspective of Marketplace Needs

In addition to the need to develop international II standards, the scope of such standardization needs to be broad enough to include a realistic perspective of the marketplace and the needs of the user. CBEMA supports the establishment of the ANSI Information Infrastructure Standards Panel (IISP) to accelerate development of standards critical to the National Information Infrastructure (NII) and the GII. The mission of the Panel is to promote, accelerate and coordinate the timely development of II standards within the national and international voluntary standards systems. The requirements for standardization of critical interfaces and other attributes will be based upon competitive models of the architecture for the II. The open competitive architectural models will be defined by user requirements and driven by market forces. In this regard II is no different than other areas of standardization. The market will determine what will be used, taking all factors (such as user requirements, intellectual property rights, and security) into account.

Standards Development Is Taking Less Time

While conscious of the need to spend sufficient time to develop complex technical standards, standards developers, in response to market demand for new standards for interoperability, are taking positive steps to accelerate the standards process. These steps have already paid off. Average development time for all standards in the

ISO has been reduced by one-third over the last five years. During this period, output of technical standards pages increased 20 percent annually. Ongoing process improvement programs in ANSI and the IEC have also reduced standards development times and continue to show progress. ANSI is making changes to allow standards-developing organizations (SDOs) to approve American National Standards without going through the additional procedural step of submitting the standard to ANSI's Board of Standards Review for approval; this reduces the procedural time by several weeks. By the end of 1992, committee JTC1, which develops information technology standards for ISO and IEC, had reduced the time to reach consensus on a stable draft standard to an average of under 20 months. At this point, when the draft standard is stable, companies often begin implementing the standard. The increasing acceptance of e-mail as a vehicle for inter-company, international communications among technical professionals is expected to further accelerate the process by making dissemination and discussions of proposed standards almost instantaneous. Parts of the ISO-IEC-ANSI process should not be given up; they should be used by others. To be internationally acceptable, standards with marketplace impact require not only openness but also due process, as several Supreme Court decisions and international disputes have taught us.

Interoperability and Extensibility Will Stimulate Investment by the IT Industry

The appropriate role of interoperability is another area of concern to CBEMA. We believe that role is to identify and restrict required protocols to a minimum, leaving maximum room for providing consumers choice and building competitive advantage in the marketplace. The benefits of an interoperable and extensible system are clear. Such a system will allow high technology to be used for interactive education, expand the availability of advanced health care, promote productivity, and enhance the efficiency and effectiveness of government institutions. More generally, it will enable data, images, and video information to be widely available across the full range of consumer and business settings in a form that is easily conveyed, manipulated, and viewed. In addition, an interoperable and extensible system will stimulate investment by U.S. computer and business equipment manufacturers in products and services that utilize digital display technology. The resulting economies of scale will reduce the unit cost of converting signals across disparate environments, lowering expenses for broadcasters and likely expediting the deployment of Advanced Television (ATV) and other technologies.

Open Systems Should Be the Solution of Choice

Open Systems should be the solution of choice. They are important to workers in and managers of information systems who are dealing with major integration problems that have far reaching financial implications. Systems should be open at the key interface levels, e.g., at the generic platform interface level.

To their credit, the phone companies have long been champions of open systems, to which everyone who can pay has equal access. For example, AT&T and the Bell Operating Companies are common carriers. They act as pipelines connecting everyone. They have applied the same open approach to their technology, long ago surrendering control of equipment used in the home. The result? A raft of innovation, from call waiting to inexpensive answering machines that allow users to retrieve their messages by using any touchtone phone. On the other hand, it is clear they thought Open Network Architecture went too far and have opposed it. In contrast, cable companies decide what is transmitted over their wires. They continue to own the TV converter box in each home and thus control the technology that passes through the TV. That's a lot of power. Whoever controls the box controls this interface between the consumer and the marketplace. A central challenge is including cable in the II. A closed approach to technology in any part of the II would only slow the development of the Information Infrastructure and delay the new services consumers might want. If there is going to be one guiding principle for the Information Infrastructure, it should be: Keep it open for innovation.

All industries are moving toward open systems as defined by formal standards. There is a need to provide incentives to providers of equipment and services to be "II compliant." Regardless of whether the origins of a standard are de facto, developed in committee, or mandated, the primary requirement is to avoid establishing arbitrarily non-compliant system features when an existing or emerging standard that largely addresses the same needs is available or can be influenced. (For example, ISO is nearing closure on MPEG2, which is largely similar to the ATV proponents' compression/decompression techniques. An international standard would preclude anti-competitive efforts to partition world markets.)

Networking and Applications Are the Backbone of the II

II is an evolutionary concept that has been evolving and will continue to evolve for a long time. There are two separate areas related to standards and technology: networking and applications. Many of the needed standards exist today or are currently under development. Most, if not all, of the technology is here today.

In the area of networking, convergence of existing standards and protocols is important. In our comments on the January 14, 1994 draft report of the Federal Internetworking Requirements Panel, we stated that CBEMA members believe some level of convergence between the Internet Protocol Suite (IPS) and the Open Systems Interconnection (OSI) protocol suite is possible, is ultimately in the best interests of vendors and users, and warrants immediate and urgent action. We responded to the report's implication that minimal OSI (mOSI) is narrowly focused and must be tailored to specific applications by stating that mOSI is a fully conformant subset of OSI upper layers 5, 6 and 7, yet it contains only 5% of the size/complexity/functionality of a full OSI upper layer stack. Despite its minimal size, a mOSI configuration is believed to support well over 95% of the applications now in widespread use throughout the OSI and Internet context. Use of mOSI has the potential for removing or minimizing some of the major objections and impediments to the use of OSI, e.g., that it is too complex, too slow, too expensive. In fact, mOSI can play a significant role in facilitating the "convergence" process addressed throughout the FIRP report.

Much work that must be coordinated is going on in other networking technologies. For example, the first network equipment built to Synchronous Optical Networks (SONET) standards was introduced in 1989, and by the end of 1992 over 20,000 SONET add-drop mulitplexers had been deployed in U.S. point-to-point architectures. Today, SONET is transforming telecommunications and making broadband, fiber-based systems available to millions of people. It has been estimated that by 1998, business and government use of data communications will exceed their use of voice services. Data communications already are undergoing great changes as the power of the intelligent network is put into the hands of users via standardized technologies such as Local Area Networks (LANs), Wide Area Networks (WANs), Asynchronous Transfer Mode (ATM), and Frame Relay. These technologies are providing capabilities for such important applications as file transfers, imaging, collaborative desktop conferencing, electronic mail, and electronic data interchange, all of which will greatly enhance the ability to serve both domestic and international users. The point here is not that there must be one solution, but rather that a range of technologies that can interoperate will provide the best solution through competition.

Application portability is a strong and consistent requirement of most users across a broad spectrum of application domains. The real key to achieving Application portability from the users' perspective is to have an integrated set of base standards that apply to services required by and offered to users' applications. Such an integrated set of base standards with selected options and parameters is known as a profile. Although some ISO/IEC Joint Technical Committee 1, Information Technology (JTC1) standards are related to Application Portability, many application standards are the responsibility of other ISO and/or IEC Technical Committees. JTC1 collaborates with Users Groups to develop Application Environment Profiles (AEPs). A consequence of this collaboration is the identification of any deficiencies that might exist in the standards or standards activities. The Technical Study Group 1 (TSG-1 of JTC1) report recommended that the standardization of Interfaces for Application Portability (IAP) be achieved through the specification of an Open System Environment (OSE) framework for profiling concepts and procedures, hereafter called "OSE Standardization." The TSG-1 report identified a fundamental difference in this type of standardization: as opposed to (bottom-up) base standards and profiling, OSE requires a top-down approach. While profiles defined in the OSI world are built with a bottom-up approach (one or more available standards with a choice of options), the OSE concepts lead to a top-down approach (defining a profile from the user requirements). Such differences should be seen as a need to take two broad views of OSE standardization: (1) the technical view and (2) the presentation view. The JTC1 Special Group on Functional Standards (SGFS) has expanded its scope to include Open Systems, not just Interconnection. A complete set of standards is a key point for application portability. For example, software portability would not be possible if two platforms have the same operating system interface and the same Application Programming Interface (API) to transport services but two different User Interfaces.

Voluntary Standards, Consortia, and Proprietary Standards Each Have a Role

CBEMA strongly supports the use of voluntary standards, both national and international, where appropriate (for instance, in the interest of promoting trade). The voluntary standards process is open to all interested parties, large and small, in both the private and public sectors. Voluntary standards provide producers and users the opportunity to choose how and when to use standards based on the pressures and consequences of marketplace activity. Thus, voluntary standards, by allowing freedom of choice, permit users and suppliers to best meet their common interests. Consensus standards benefit from a wide range of thinking and ensure that individuals and organizations have the opportunity to affect standards that in turn will affect them. (The tradeoff is that it takes time to achieve consensus.) Voluntary standards also permit technological innovations to proceed, unlike mandatory standards, which are more likely to freeze technology and inhibit innovation. Advances are very difficult when laws must be changed to take advantage of new technology.

The January 14, 1994 draft report of the Federal Internetworking Requirements Panel (FIRP) recommended that federal internetworking should be based on the following hierarchy of standards: first, open international voluntary standards; second, national voluntary or consortia standards; third, proprietary standards with multinational commercial prevalence. CBEMA submitted the following comments on this recommendation:

• First, FIRP's report recommends broadening the criteria for an "international standards organization." CBEMA does not believe this is in the best interests of the users or vendors. Each incremental addition to the ISO, IEC and ITU as acceptable international standards organizations adds to user confusion, introduces significant possibilities for multiple peer standards that are incompatible or in conflict with each other, makes achieving interoperability objectives more difficult, and undermines the established and recognized standards organizations.

• Second, CBEMA does not believe it is valuable to recognize consortia-developed standards and specifications to be at the same level as national standards. American National Standards have been put through the open ANSI process to ensure equitable consideration, due process, and consensus. Though consortia-developed standards may have wide acceptance, they have not been put through the same rigorous development and scrutiny as national standards, and therefore should not be included in the same category as national standards. On the other hand, we support mechanisms to expedite the work of consortia or others who are willing to make the final commitments required for voluntary standardization.

• Third, CBEMA believes it is contrary to basic federal procurement policy to consider endorsing proprietary standards or protocols except in exceptional circumstances. Using proprietary standards or protocols gives special and unfair advantage to a single vendor or limited number of vendors. We agree that criteria need to be developed to define these proprietary standards or protocols as "open." However, using "multinational commercial prevalence" as this criterion is insufficient to ensure openness.

Intellectual Property Rights Must Be Protected

The voluntary, private-sector-led standards system provides for inclusion of intellectual property in standards, and for nondiscriminatory access to that intellectual property. For a standard to be adopted, the owner of any patent rights involved must agree to license the patents on fair, reasonable, and nondiscriminatory terms and conditions. Any owner who does not agree to license patents on these fair terms has little chance of seeing the technology adopted as part of a formally recognized standard. This policy is followed by all ANSI-accredited standards-developing organizations, the IEC, the ISO, and the ITU, as well as most other national and regional standards-developing organizations in the world. Standards organizations thus act to ensure availability and usability of their standards, while further encouraging innovation by recognizing past creativity.

The existing voluntary standards process provides fair access to standards required for interoperability and allows competition to flourish, while providing inventors and innovators the incentive they need to invest money, take risks, and devote time and effort to creating new technology. These benefits are realized without the need for government intervention. The patent policy common to all major standards-setting organizations appropriately balances the needs of users and the rights of technology creators. This policy has worked very well for many years and CBEMA believes there is no need to change it.

There are many examples of successful standards that incorporate proprietary technology licensed on reasonable and nondiscriminatory terms. The patented modular telephone jack is incorporated in Federal Communications Commission (FCC) Part 68 Rules and is the basis of an IEC standard. North American Philips licenses its audio compact disc patent to over 100 manufacturers. A teleconferencing and refresh coding standard adopted by the ITU uses AT&T-patented technology. Xerox and IBM offer reasonable licensing terms on patents needed to implement Institute for Electrical and Electronics Engineers (IEEE) standards for their respective Ethernet and Token Ring Local Area Networks. The fact that reasonable license fees have been collected for the relevant patents has not prevented the above standards from being widely implemented in a competitive market.

If there is any concern that a particular company might not reasonably license rights to its property, the standards-setting organization is free to not include that technology in a standard. This simple safeguard is a product of allowing all interested parties to participate in the consensus standards development process.

Privacy and Security Are Essential for Users

Standards and technological development will be critical to achieve privacy and security for individuals and service providers interacting on the II. The II will carry many kinds of information that users will expect to be kept private. Providers of information and entertainment programming certainly will need to receive proper compensation for value delivered to consumers and to be protected from theft of service. This protection will need to be accomplished in such a way that consumers will still have the free use of their consumer equipment. Open access to open, secure networks must be the goal.

Consumers also need to be assured that they will receive and pay for only services of their own choosing. Customer choice and willingness to pay for that choice, after all, should be the basis for II. New technologies such as smart cards need to be developed and implemented in a standardized way so that II security is clearly established and protected. We live and work in a global environment. Communications and the need for privacy cross national and regional borders.

Finally, consumers should have the right not to interact with the system. People ought to be able to insulate themselves from unwanted communication. They deserve the right to be able to exit from the II at any time, and to not be monitored in their homes.

Multiple, overlapping networks, some of which will be virtual networks, make development of a common security architecture difficult. Business must have confidence that sensitive commercial information transmitted over the II can be adequately protected from disclosure to, or corruption or alteration by, unauthorized users. Encryption is the technique most commonly used by businesses to protect networked data. The II must provide the flexibility for business to utilize a full range of techniques and technologies according to user needs. II standards must be developed with everyone's security concerns in mind. Standards should be based upon the following criteria:

- Standards must be internationally accepted
- Users must be free to choose the security technology (e.g., encryption) that best fits their needs, without unnecessary export restrictions
- Users must be able to implement security in either hardware or software
- The responsibility and accountability for security management of owners, providers, and users should be defined.

In particular, encryption policy for the II should be flexible and based upon algorithms that are unclassified, implementable in hardware and software, and usable in globally interconnected networks. The preferred approach is to use algorithms that are standards, such as DES and RSA, and that can be used for digital signature, message authentication, encryption, and key management where the key management system is controlled by its user. Moreover, the encryption standards used should neither be subject to special export control restrictions nor incompatible with existing worldwide encryption systems. The U.S. Government should work together with other governments, as well as U.S. and foreign producers and users, in an open forum to develop an encryption policy that is internationally workable. Alternatives that satisfy the requirements of both public and private sectors should be evaluated.

Government Has Two Roles: User and Regulator

Finally, government, in its role as an II user, participates in many standards-developing organizations, working cooperatively with industry and with other user organizations. As a major purchaser of information technology and other products, government plays an important role in helping to develop standards that will impact its use of these goods. In certain limited cases, the government sets technical regulations—for example, the federal government sets public health and safety requirements for medical devices and in areas such as electromagnetic emissions—but for the information technology and telecommunications industries the government does not set standards for commercial interoperability. The Government also sets requirements for its own procurement of computer and communications equipment. Consistent with the 1979 Trade Act and as directed by OMB Circular A-119, the Federal Government establishes its standards by adopting private-sector consensus standards.

An issue with public policy makers in government is that the number of industries coming together in the II, combined with the number of technologies, produces an appearance of confusion. This leads them to think regulatory solutions may be needed when actually the marketplace is sorting things out. The industry-led process to establish technical standards for high definition television (HDTV) demonstrates the benefits of limited government involvement. Even though the Federal Communications Commission (FCC) has the statutory authority to set terrestrial broadcasting standards, the FCC wisely chose to apply its leadership in support of a process that is led and funded by the private sector. In contrast, the governments of Japan and the European Union took much stronger roles in funding and determining HDTV standards. The result has been that the United States, in an open, consensus-based process combining the best elements of competition and collaboration, has developed world-leading technology far superior to the government-planned and subsidized system overseas. Thus, government intervention has been shown to be unnecessary and potentially detrimental to standards development efforts. Any expansion of the government's role to one of controlling or mandating U.S. industry standards could slow the process, stifle innovation, and place a greater burden on taxpayers, thereby hurting U.S. international competitiveness. The expertise in commercial technology and market demand needed to create interoperable systems for the II exists in the many thousands of private-sector professionals who design products and write software to meet customers' needs. The voluntary consensus process in which these private sector personnel work with interested users and academic and government experts will continue to create successful, open standards to meet the needs of the information infrastructure.

The Public and Private Sectors Need to Work Together

CBEMA understands the short-term needs of users to achieve interconnection and interoperability of computers and systems from products, services, and infrastructure that are available now and in the near-term. Nevertheless, in satisfying their short-term needs, users should exercise great care not to impede their ability to achieve their ultimate aim to converge to a single, interconnected, interoperable, standards-based internetworking environment. CBEMA also recognizes that, while a single standard is preferable, the reality is that there may be multiple solutions in networking as in other areas of information technology. The critical point is not the number of solutions employed but their compatibility in an interconnection sense.

The current industry/government cooperation and partnership has proved beneficial to all parties and we encourage its continuation. The government should expand and coordinate its participation in voluntary standards development and encourage convergence toward a single standard. All groups should work together to achieve a single set of non-duplicating, non-conflicting, compatible standards by:

• Identifying the core standards (formal and de facto) already in place that potentially support the II based on a proposed architecture and related service

• Identifying those standards that are not yet being developed and, via the voluntary process, initiate development projects to address these new standards

• Continuing to encourage dramatic improvement in the business process of standards development.

Commercial users, vendors, and governments need to work together in an open international forum for the preparation and approval of global standards. Globally recognized standards bodies (ISO/IEC JTC1 and ITU-T) should set the standards for the internationally required set of standards.

Note

[1] *Interoperability:* The ability of two or more systems (for the purposes of this definition, "systems" includes devices, databases, networks, or technologies) to interact with one another in accordance with a prescribed method so as to achieve a predictable result—for example, the extent to which TV transmission technology can work effectively with telecommunications and computer technologies; the extent to which the ATV system will permit the exchange of information among television, computer and communication technologies.

Extensibility: The ability of II systems and applications to support and incorporate new functions and technological advances—for example, the ability of an ATV transmission system to support and incorporate new functions and future technological advances.

Standards for the Information Infrastructure: Barriers and Obstacles

Jerry L. Johnson
The State of Texas

Introduction

Every citizen has a stake in the deployment of an advanced Information Infrastructure. The new jobs market is moving from large manufacturing facilities to a distributed framework of medium and small industries that form alliances to create products, information, and services. This new framework, which will influence where businesses and people locate, depends on the availability of a robust Information Infrastructure that is accessible for every citizen.

Universal service was the goal of the Communications Act of 1934. However, universal service only addressed plain old telephone service. Other government initiatives have provided access to postal services, electric power, and public television. The convergence of new and evolving technologies will affect all four service areas.

This paper addresses some of the key barriers, obstacles, and issues related to developing the Information Infrastructure. We should not place our initial focus on technical solutions, but discuss the impact of technology and define the capabilities required for improving information access and service. The policies regarding information access and service delivery by federal, state, and local governments must change in order to stimulate the development and deployment of the Information Infrastructure. While some government agencies are beginning to provide public access to information, several of these initiatives have required specialized "terminal" equipment such as kiosks. These non-standards based systems do not provide access to all government information and increase the cost to the taxpayer.

The United States must develop an architecture framework for the National Information Infrastructure (NII) in partnership with other nations to create the Global Information Infrastructure (GII) required for open competition in all markets and seamless electronic commerce across all national borders. The NII/GII will require new standards to facilitate the transition from the current analog infrastructure to the ubiquitous switched, broadband digital infrastructure required for the future. However, the technical standards development process must change and be more responsive to user requirements.

The NII/GII, built with public/private partnerships and based on open, standards-based technology, holds the promise to improve service delivery to every citizen; it will also help businesses compete in the global marketplace and increase the quality of life.

Barriers/Obstacles and Recommendations

Citizens currently have limited access to government information and services

Current governmental laws and agency rules require the submission of paper documents and some even specify a form of payment (e.g., cashier's check). This information is then keyed into the requesting agency's computer system and often printed out on paper for further processing. Agency services may only be available at a central location or field office. State, local and federal government agencies operate multiple offices and service centers in the same community. Very few offices serve rural America. Citizens may have to make multiple trips to various offices to transact business and receive services from government entities.

Electronic access can empower every citizen and help generate demand for the information infrastructure. An Interagency Working Group of federal government agencies recently published "Public Access to Government Electronic Information: A Policy

Framework." The State of California has enacted legislation to make government information available on line; it is currently available on the Internet. The proposed Government Information Locator Service (GILS) initiative recommends a decentralized approach to locating information through a common indexing standard. In July 1994, the National Institute of Standards and Technology (NIST) issued a solicitation for comments on the GILS proposal. Comments are due back to the NIST in October 1994. These initiatives reflect the growing need for facilitating access to government information, and prove that government can change the way it does business by recognizing its citizens as its customers.

In July 1994, The Office of Management and Budget (OMB) published a new revision to Circular No. A-130, Management of Federal Information Resources. The new version address agencies' management practices for information systems and technology. The major recommendations of that circular are as follows:

1. To promote agency investments in information technologies that improve service delivery to the public, reduce burden on the public, and lower the cost of federal program administration

2. To encourage agencies to use information technology as a strategic resource in promoting fundamental reevaluation of federal agency work processes, organizational structures, and means of interacting with the public

3. To recognize the changes in the technical, legal, and operational environment that agencies face when managing information technology.

All government agencies need to establish a consistent policy for access to information and services. The federal government's "Policy Framework" and GILS documents should address these requirements. State and local governments must take an active role in commenting on the GILS standards and, when approved, these standards should be adopted by all government entities. Payment by individuals or organizations of any required fees for information and service access must allow electronic funds transfer or payment by credit card.

Lack of consistent regulation for communications providers limits competition and access to services

Federal, state, and local governments each play different roles in regulating service providers. Regulation has focused on four different kinds of information or transmission media:

• The press are not regulated because of the First Amendment.

• Telephone companies or Local Exchange Carriers (LECs) are regulated by States. Congress allowed telephone service to be operated by a monopoly in return for stringent government oversight of rates and regulation of access.

• Cable television companies are regulated by the Federal government, local communities, and sometimes at the state level.

• Wireless communications providers are regulated by the Federal Communications Commission (FCC) through the frequency licensing process.

Currently not all service providers contribute to the Universal Service Fund. The frequency spectrum is a limited national resource, but wireless service providers and private users do not contribute to the Universal Fund. Only LECs receive money from the Universal Service fund. Merging telecommunications technologies are requiring a redefinition of universal service.

New legislation proposed by the federal government will preempt some state and local government regulation authority. However, such legislation may not pass this congressional session and does not address a process for implementing competition. Funding for universal service is not addressed in this legislation, and state oversight and regulatory authority will still be required. In the future, all service providers should contribute to the new Universal Service/Access fund. Administration of this fund will require federal and state oversight, but should be implemented by local governments. Local governments will identify needs for infrastructure improvements, business development, and citizen eligibility. An electronic voucher authorized for eligible users could be given to any qualified service provider.

State governments should expand oversight and regulatory authority to all communications service providers. This would include LECs, cable, cellular (land-based and satellite), long distance, and wireless service providers (PCN/PCS and paging), and industry that has private wireless networks. Regulatory oversight would not need to address rate regulation in competitive markets, but instead ensure the infrastructure's equal access and deployment. Duties of the regulatory authority would include:

• Establishing the amounts to be contributed to the Universal Service/Access Fund. This could include fees based on a percentage of profits, service access fees, and/or fees for each device (e.g., $0.25 monthly fee on paging devices and cellular phones).

• Requiring that service providers collect fees for 911 or other N11 public service operations.

• Establishing rules and guidelines for equal access and deployment of the switched-broadband infrastructure.

Competition would build on the proposed federal legislation initiatives and could start with any service provider. The service provider would be required to install switching equipment and could initially compete for residential services. After achieving 15% share of the available residential market (divided by the number of service providers, should others enter the market), LECs and the new service provider would be subject to reduced regulation and could offer any information service to all customers. Service providers would be required to connect to anyone and could not limit service only to the business community. Any reduction in service fees to business users would also apply to residential users. Service providers would all be connected to one another and would need to demonstrate interoperability for communications and directory services.

Printed telephone directories can limit competition and increase demand on waste/landfill requirements

Currently LECs own the information and content of their respective telephone directories. Publication of the directories is subsidized through advertising in the Yellow Pages. Increased service competition would require additional directories. This could lead to information overload and increased demand on community landfill facilities.

Directory issues are not covered in the current federal legislation. Directory information must be available in a useful manner to all. Accessibility of information and services is critical to the deployment of the Information Infrastructure. While the cost of personal computers (PCs) has and continues to drop, less than 50% of the households in America have a PC. The French government has eliminated this problem by making directory services available and issuing a device to every household.

In order for LECs to be required to stop publication of directories, telephone numbers would have to be made available on line. Under these conditions, LECs would have a specified period of time before ending current publication (e.g., four years). If the community still found a need for a printed directory, anyone could publish a consolidated directory and would have reasonable access to service provider number information. Publishers could charge a fee to customers, but would be required to charge a deposit fee for each directory (e.g., five cents per printed page). Directory publishers would be required to establish procedures for collecting and recycling old directories.

Another option would be for the government to fund research and development of an inexpensive appliance to access electronic directory information. The new universal service/access fund could help qualified users obtain the new appliance, a PC, or other means of accessing social services. Interoperable Directory Services are critical to the success of the NII initiative, and the federal government should fund a public domain version of the X.500 standard for them.[1]

Lack of consistent and user friendly access to public information and services adds to the cost of providing voice and electronic access

Federal and state agencies currently fund 800 numbers for the public to access voice and electronic-based information. Multiple 800 and local numbers, however, do not provide consistent and useful access to information and services; in fact, 800 numbers add to the cost of making information available. Some states and federal agencies have tried using electronic kiosks to access information and services, but this effort has not been very successful. The United States Postal Service itself terminated a contract for Postal Buddy after the Postal Buddy Corporation lost $40 million in only three years. Only the State of Texas is evaluating the use of a standard local number for consistent and user friendly access.

Technology is available to access both voice and data through a single telephone number. 911 access to emergency services is a success because the number is easy to remember and is being deployed nationwide. Florida allowed Southern Bell to issue the five unassigned N11 numbers (211, 311, 511, 711,[2] and 811) to private industry; the lottery was open to anyone willing to pay $10,000 a month for each N11 number. The lottery approach, however limits consumer choice of information providers. Just as the frequency spectrum should be considered a national resource, so should the five remaining N11 numbers. State and federal regulators should not issue any of the five remaining N11 numbers until those numbers are evaluated for providing access to government information and services. If the Texas N11 test is successful, state and federal regulation would provide general guidance and direction for other N11 numbers in the U.S. The government will identify technical standards and requirements for a consistent user interface, and the N11 numbers will then be issued to local governments for providing public access to community and government information and services. Local governments could operate or outsource operation of the N11 delivery service on a two-to-five-year cycle. Providers would offer free Internet access to government information, collect fees for special government services, and market access to advertising and other services. A percentage of the fees would then help fund universal service/access.

Lack of policy and infrastructure to support digital signatures and secure transactions

Eliminating or changing laws and agency rules that require paper forms and documents is a first step, but government does not have a viable policy for digital signatures and the secure transmission of information. The National Institute of Standards and Technology (NIST) has been working on a Digital Signature Standard (DSS) for several years. Once this is resolved, federal, state, and local governments will need to establish procedures and identify responsibility for distributing public keys for DSS.

In June 1994, the U.S. Public Policy Committee of the Association for Computing Machinery urged the administration to withdraw the "Clipper Chip" encryption proposal. The current policy for an Escrowed Encryption Standard (EES) held by the U.S. government would limit acceptance in the global marketplace. While NIST approved the DSS in May 1994, its version is not compatible with the public domain version, and may violate existing patents. Public Key distribution issues have not yet been addressed. Although the International standard for Directory Services (X.500) includes public key distribution, the Directory Services standards and products have not progressed as expected, though DSS public keys can be distributed over the Internet. At least one federal agency is working with the United States Postal Service (USPS) to register and distribute keys.

NIST must resolve the DSS and EES issues and provide guidelines for key distribution. Each state should allow DSS documents to be used as official transactions between agencies and the public. The American National Standards Institute (ANSI) has delegated responsibility for Directory Service registration to each Secretary of State. State governments should thus establish policy and procedures for issuance and distribution of DSS keys. The policy should also allow delegation of DSS authority to state agencies and local governments.

Laws and rules prevent public/private partnerships that could help develop applications to improve access to information and services

The federal government has identified funding for public/private partnerships that implement the goals of the National Information Infrastructure. However, many state agencies are restricted by law and by rules that prohibit their participation in industry partnerships. Furthermore, ownership and use of shared technical resources are restricted by grant programs and government rules, and these regulations must be altered in order to facilitate partnerships between government agencies and industry.

Federal grant programs require matching funds for up to 50% of these program costs. The National Telecommunications and Information Administration (NTIA) has identified $26 million in its current grants budget and proposed $100 million for FY 1995 and $150 million for FY 1996. These grant programs are designed to encourage public/private partnerships. Texas created a state match fund in 1993, but continued funding for this program is uncertain.

States should remove restrictions on public and private industry partnerships that improve electronic information access and service delivery. They should continue to contribute to the state match pool out of the new state Universal Service/Access fund described above, as well as new taxes on paging and cellular/PCN/PCS devices. All levels of government should reward those agencies who instigate partnership projects. Rather than reducing an agency's budget by projected savings, the agency should retain a high percentage of those savings to expand partnerships and innovative programs.

The current standards process for information technology is outdated and not responsive to user requirements

Information Technology (IT) standards are often developed by national bodies. These standards are then submitted to International Standards Development Organizations (SDOs), or the national bodies may participate in SDO committees. National and international organizations have in the past only developed paper standards and have not required reference implementations as a demonstration of the standardized technology's viability. This was not a problem when technology was only changing every 10-15 years. Technology is now advancing at intervals of 18-24 months.

National and international SDOs rely on the sale of paper standards documents to fund organizational operations. Standards have copyright restrictions that limit distribution to users and institutes of higher education. In contrast, Internet users require reference implementations of technical solutions before a standard is approved, and all standards along with working documents are available on-line at no cost.

The State of Texas has addressed standards development in comments on proposed FIPS and in the Open Systems Environment (OSE) Implementor's Workshop (OIW). The state has recommended a five-step process to fix the current standards development process. The OSE Technical Committee (OSE-TC) forwarded these concerns to the SDOs in 1993. In March 1994, the OIW approved changes to its procedures manual that would implement the recommended changes.

The SDOs need to implement the OSE-TC recommendations to improve the development process. When the SDOs require reference implementations, at least one implementation should be in the public domain. The public domain version could carry copyright and patent provisions where the SDO would receive a portion of the royalties if the implementation were used for commercial products. This condition could offset the revenues currently obtained from the sale of paper standards. The States, through the OIW, should take a more proactive role in the standards process.

Rural America is not getting the most cost-effective form of information access and service delivery

Federal, state and local agencies operate wireless networks in rural areas for law enforcement, emergency services, fire protection, and other specific services. The FCC has never required standards for the two-way radio communications systems used in these networks. Once a system was purchased, users could only obtain additional equipment from the same vendor; different agencies operating in the same areas often have systems that do not interoperate with one another. This has proved a critical shortcoming during major natural disasters, when additional resources deployed to the area have proved inadequate. Current cellular telephone systems are analog, and few systems are deployed in rural areas.

Between 1987 and 1989, Southwestern Bell evaluated and tested the application of radio loops for basic local exchange telephone services. One test site included Ft. Davis, Texas. This site covered eight customers who were served on a open wire facility, 47 years old, and used a analog carrier system, 15 years old. The customers were ranchers in a mountainous area 18 to 36 miles from the Bell central office. The test was successful and demonstrated that wireless service cost less than half the projected price of upgraded wired services. The radio-linked customers were charged the same standard rates as wired customers, and only incurred a small additional charge for the new telephone company equipment installed at each house (approximately $12 per year).

New digital cellular technology could provide a suitable replacement for both wired and private wireless services in rural America. The FCC is currently reallocating frequencies from current users to additional spectrum allocations for new digital services. However, the FCC may not be fully addressing rural America's requirements for access to information and services. Digital cellular technology that could meet public and private sector requirements in rural areas is presently available. Digital cellular systems could insure privacy for users, and priority access for law enforcement and emergency services. The same technology and systems could serve citizen needs for residential and mobile access.

The Office of Technology Assessment (OTA), the FCC, and the NIST must address rural America's requirements for government and public access to information and services. The FCC should not issue new frequency licenses until these requirements have been addressed and technical solutions developed and tested. Current licenses for two-way radio systems would then be subject to the same review as those proposed for federal users under the Spectrum Reallocation initiative.

New standards and appliances are needed to make the transition from the current analog based infrastructure to the NII's broadband digital infrastructure

The telephone only achieved "appliance" status after the 1982 Modification of Final Judgement (MFJ) decree. The decree broke up the Bell system into seven regional companies and prevented the Bell companies from manufacturing telephone equipment. Telephone appliances with a wide variety of features are now available from multiple vendors. This rich selection of appliances provides users with voice messaging, call screening, portability, and many other features. However, just as people did not immediately replace their rotary dial phones, so they will not just throw away their current telephone appliances.

The current analog telephone system requires battery power from the phone company's central office to provide ring current and signaling. Fiberoptic and coax cable systems will not provide battery power. Coax transmission systems operate on a one-to-many methodology and each end device must contain the logic to recognize when it is being addressed. The analog system, however has one advantage over digital systems: only the central office requires backup power to ensure access to 911 emergency services.

The primary advantage of broadband digital service is to access multimedia and computer network applications, information, and services. The current analog telephone appliances may continue to serve basic voice communications if an interface device can also be developed. This interface device would contain the logic for address recognition, signaling, and possibly battery backup. The key question for battery backup, however is defining the design criteria: How many telephone appliances will the backup be required to power and how long must it operate without electric power? Battery backup provisions could be the sole responsibility of the end user. Backup power devices have been developed for the PC industry and already meet a wide variety of consumer and business needs.

The FCC, NIST, and NTIA should determine the feasibility of an interface device to aid in the transition from analog to digital networks. If feasible[3], federal grants could facilitate its design and deployment. Service providers should not be allowed to implement systems with a non-standard interface. The government should establish new standards for residential house wiring and evaluate communications access standards for new community development.

The United States lacks a forum to address development, deployment and policy discussions on the NII

The Clinton Administration has established the Information Infrastructure Task Force (IITF) and several subcommittees to address various issues related to the National Information Infrastructure (NII) initiative. The NTIA has established a Bulletin Board System (BBS) and Internet connectivity, which allow users to access information about the NII initiatives and current work by the IITF and its subcommittees. However, postings of committee meeting minutes are often late or not available in electronic form. The one exception is the IITF Committee on Applications and Technology.

This task force posted early drafts of documents and made available in electronic form any published report.

Participation by state and local government representatives has thus far been severely limited. The federal government, through the Federation of Government Information Processing Councils (FGIPC), has established a forum for federal, state and local government participation. This forum, called Interchange, will host the first workshop and conference in 1994. Interchange '94 will provide an opportunity to demonstrate intergovernmental cooperation and projects regarding the NII. State and local governments should actively participate in Interchange '94. NTIA and the IITF should also participate, and solicit open discussion of the issues addressed in this paper and others related to the development and deployment of the NII.

In May 1994, the State of Texas published the Architecture Framework for Information Resources Management (AFIRM). AFIRM provides guidance to govern the evolution of the state infrastructure. It is also the foundation for introducing and promoting the interoperability, portability, and scalability of state information systems. All levels and entities of government agencies should develop an AFIRM for the NII.

Notes

[1] The current public domain version of the X.500 standard for Directory Service does not comply with the current X500 standards.

[2] 711 is used in several states for deaf relay, and should be reserved for this service nationwide.

[3] Cable companies in Europe are providing both telephone and TV services. Several joint initiatives have been announced in the U.S., however information on a standards-based interface was not available at this time.

References

Architecture Framework for Information Resources Management (AFIRM), Volume 1: Overview, May 1994, State of Texas Department of Information Resources.

Architecture Framework for Information Resources Management (AFIRM), Volume 2: Technical Reference Model and Standards Profile, May 1994, State of Texas Department of Information Resources.

Architecture Framework for Information Resources Management (AFIRM), Volume 3: Architecture Concepts and Design Guidance, May 1994, State of Texas Department of Information Resources.

Public Access to Government Electronic Information, A Policy Framework, February 10, 1994, Interagency Working Group.

The Government Information Locator Service (GILS), Report to the Information Infrastructure Task Force, May 2, 1994.

The Role of ANSI in Standards Development for the Information Infrastructure

Sergio Mazza
American National Standards Institute

The Information Age

Vice President Al Gore, the National Information Infrastructure (NII) Task Force and others have rightly focused on the strategic importance that information-related technology, industries and activities have for the United States today. The business of America is, increasingly, the creation of the technologies that manage, transmit, and use information that drives our economy. How well that is accomplished is the ultimate barometer of how economically healthy and safe we are as a nation.

Fortunately, we are witnessing an incredible surge of technological breakthroughs in the information arena here in the United States. But information technology that had no way to connect or operate with other systems and users, a technology without standardization, without widespread universal access, without certain proprietary guarantees, would be turbocharging down the information highway to nowhere.

Since "information infrastructure" encompasses such a vast array of services and communication modalities—everything from data bits, parities, switches, optical fiber transmission lines, and satellites to video on demand—there has to be a system of standards established that will facilitate their interconnectivity and interoperability. Otherwise, sounds become silence and pictures only invisible images. In short, the technology has to be channeled properly for everyone's benefit—the user, the maker, and the provider. Only through a workable system of standards will all

Americans—and people everywhere—be guaranteed access to information and have the possibility of communicating any time, anywhere, with anyone, using voice, data, images, or video transmission.

The National Information Infrastructure is not a new invention. It signifies what has been developing for some time now, an enormous undertaking that is meeting the challenges of the information age. Most of the interfaces that enable NII's interoperability have already been developed by the national voluntary standards system. The NII is not starting from ground zero; it is extending an existing process.

The Standards-Setting Process

How standards are developed and established is a more critical question than which standards may result. The process of standards development is crucial. If the process for developing standards is in harmony with the needs of users, makers, and providers alike, as well as those of society as a whole, the outcomes will be optimal.

In the information technology world of today, we have to avoid sub-optimal processes of standards development. Spur-of-the-moment, shortcut substitutes could be counterproductive. Experience in other fields of standardization has demonstrated that voluntary consensus has been the best method since the first standards were set for the thread sizes of machine bolts during the industrial revolution last century—certainly since the founding of the voluntary, not-for-profit American National Standards Institute in 1918.

Already there are many examples of successful voluntary standards development in the information technology field. It was a voluntary process that established the computer standards for 5.25 inch and 3.5 inch floppy disks and diskettes, local (single) area network standards, computer programming languages, and communications protocols for computer modems, to name but a few. Moreover, standards were set and implemented without sacrificing intellectual property rights.

Time and again, experience has proven that in the United States the standards that have been developed through an open, nondiscriminatory, voluntary, private-sector-led, consensus process are the standards that have found the widest acceptance and the greatest utility, especially because they were generated to meet user needs. Ideally, the standards development process for the government's NII initiative and policy goals will include the active participation of both customers and providers of technology:

• Customer associations (consumer protection organizations, user groups, etc.)

• Information experts from academic institutions and research centers .

• Private industry (information processors, communication equipment manufacturers, software manufacturers and vendors, cable, phone and communication transmission providers, database developers and entertainment producers, etc.)

• Government (NIST, FCC, DOD, etc.)

• Voluntary Standards Developers (such as the Accredited Standards Committee X3 on Information Technology, the Telecommunications Industry Association, the Society of Motion Picture and Television Engineers, the Electronic Industries Association, and the Institute of Electrical and Electronics Engineers)

• ANSI, which provides both a forum for coordination and a system for accreditation.

Without question, these sectors have already been involved to one degree or another in the voluntary process that is setting standards for the information highway of today and the twenty-first century. The question raised is whether the current process is keeping pace with the speed of technology's challenge.

Roadblocks in the Standardization Process

In spite of almost hyperspeed advances in the voluntary information standardization process, there have been complaints both in private industry and in government that the current standardization process for the National Information Infrastructure is too slow, too disconnected, too unresponsive to user needs, and/or unable to extract an appropriate commitment from the key participants, i.e., manufacturers, vendors, users, etc. In fact, a complete body of work that faces no controversy can speed through the international system in six months and through the domestic system in four months. Additional time is invested precisely because the system is responsive to the need to reconcile diversity among all directly and materially affected parties.

An alternative proposal is for the government to determine what standards are needed, create and set new interoperability standards, and establish deadlines for industry to meet the standards. Such proposals overlook that the technical expertise is in the private sector, the investment of funds is in the private sector, and the vast majority of customers will be individuals making their choices. Imposing government control or oversight also would likely add even more time and create more roadblocks. The NII Task Force's "Agenda for Action" did complain that the "standards process is critical and has not always worked to speed technological innovation and serve end-users well." Nevertheless, the Task Force was careful to add that government can help by "participating more actively in private-sector standards-writing bodies." It did not recommend that government take control.

Government intervention and control could perhaps accelerate some of the process but would likely alienate a significant sector of industry, fail to elicit an optimal involvement from the other participants, and run the risk of becoming the biggest obstacle to creative advancement. Any process as complex as standardizing information technology has to allow for competing interests and compromise, which requires time and patience with a democratic process in which the government should be an active participant.

Moreover, government intervention would fly in the face of U.S. practice and tradition. FCC Chairman Reed Hundt did not hesitate to advocate a traditional role for government in his address to the National Press Club on May 2, 1994.

"I do not believe," said Chairman Hundt, "that the public wants government to pick its favorite network for development. The public does not want government to choose among different proposals for technological innovation of the networks. I agree with the public. Instead, competition should determine who wins. Our role is to referee the game. As a referee, I prefer—just as they do in the NBA playoffs—to let the players play."

Mr. Hundt observed that difficult issues of "interconnection, standard-setting, and tariffing ... will have to be debated." And he called for the adoption of three key principles as a framework for competition: "choice, opportunity, and fairness."

Another alternative is for there to be no policy seeking interconnectivity and interoperability except through the serial decisions of customers opting for whatever technology best meets their current needs. This goes too far in the other direction. It might result in a universally usable system, but likely one based on monopolization, not choice.

Voluntary Standardization Initiatives

ANSI can document the fact that the debate has been under way for some time in the voluntary standards-setting forum, and in most instances the results have been nothing short of astounding.

Two ANSI-accredited standards development organization (SDO) committees in particular have blazed remarkable paths for the information age: Committee T1—Telecommunications, administered by the Alliance for Telecommunications Industry Solutions (ATIS), and Committee X3—Information Technology, administered by the Computer and Business Equipment Manufacturers Association (CBEMA). T1 was formed in 1984 after the Bell System divestiture. X3 was created in 1959, even before the information computer chip "big bang." Another key SDO laying the foundation for the NII environment is the Institute of Electrical and Electronics Engineers (IEEE).

Committee T1

T1's dual role as a U.S. standards developer and an initiator of global standards harmonization is making a vital contribution to the realization of communication any time, anywhere. The key technologies of asynchronous transfer mode (ATM), personal communications services (PCS), and synchronous optical networks (SONET) are but a few of the subjects for which standards have been developed in Committee T1. T1 is the primary U.S. technology source in the International Telecommunication Union (ITU), where its openness and consensus process ensures an extremely high degree of acceptance of U.S. positions. On an annual basis, 500 to 1000 T1 contributions are approved as U.S. positions to the ITU.

These standards have been developed and set in record time. But T1 is working even harder to make the process faster and more efficient. For example, it has a parallel balloting procedure that enables standards to be voted on by the full committee and the technical committee simultaneously. By an arrangement with ANSI, new standards proposals are published and distributed widely even before they receive ANSI's final approval, and not a single one of the 100-plus proposals has failed to get final approval. In recent years, Committee T1 has focused on:

• Improving the quality and timeliness of T1 outputs to meet user needs (the pace of T1 outputs has more than doubled in the last two years—for many areas the contributions are one hundred percent electronically presented).

• Building and utilizing liaisons with other organizations to increase standards harmonization (e.g., T1 chair is a member of the IEEE Standards Board. In addition, T1 participates in cross-documentation with many groups such as meeting with a Telecommunications Industry Association group monthly to progress PCS standards development).

• Increasing industry awareness of the role and importance of standards (resulting in high-level workshops and fuller industry participation).

Committee X3

Committee X3's work in setting standards for information technology has been no less spectacular. Much of X3's earliest work was in the promulgation of American standards for coding of character sets, programming languages, and data communications. Everyone involved in today's discussions of a National Information Infrastructure is familiar with such standards as the American Standard Code for Information Interchange (ASCII), the C programming language, and the series of standards for data transmission rates, networks, and performance.

From its early standards of the 1960s, X3 has expanded its scope to encompass the storage, processing, transfer, display, management, organization, and retrieval of information through the use of new and emerging technologies. In leading the shift from proprietary, stand-alone information systems, X3 and its more than 2,000 volunteers from over 900 organizations now produce standards intended to provide interoperability and transportability of services across disparate information systems. Leading areas of work include high-density digital and optical storage media, geographic and spatial data systems, multimedia and hypermedia information coding, security techniques, open systems interconnection, and distributed computing.

Like its T1 counterpart, X3 has led or participated in a number of initiatives to speed the adoption of international standards. One such example is the adoption of a "fast track" procedure. Through its cooperative dealings with other SDOs and its work as a major Technical Advisory Group to the ISO/IEC Joint Technical Committee 1 on Information Technology, X3 has fostered those standards that provide for worldwide information development and dissemination in what is to become a voluntary standards-based "Global Information Infrastructure."

IEEE

IEEE has established POSIX standards that provide for application portability between diverse computer systems. This complements work being accomplished in other information technology areas such as computer languages and database access. The result is a convergence of computer operating system capabilities to provide for portable applications.

IEEE's work has been adopted by the U.S. and European governments as procurement standards. Certification programs have been established, and all major computer vendors now offer the POSIX-certified system. Most recently, Microsoft's NT was certified. This standard provides a basis for multivendor competitive supply of computer systems, access to new technology as it emerges, and the ability to execute existing applications software. It is the core of today's "servers" and "workstations," and can be applied from "set-top" devices to supercomputers. The POSIX work has been adopted as ISO/IEC standards and EN (European Norms), and also is being translated into Japanese by Japan's national body for use in that country.

The Portable Applications Standards Committee in IEEE, where POSIX was developed, has also developed application program interface (API) standards for x.400 and x.500 applications, which have already formed the basis for NIST's Application Portability Profile and similar work in Europe.

Also, IEEE's 802 Standards Committee has provided the Local Area Network (LAN) standards that are the foundation for Internet, OSI, and private networks worldwide. This includes the "Ethernet" standard (802.3), which is the most prevalent LAN environment in industry.

These are only a few examples of the many SDOs from consumer electronics to electronic commerce that are rapidly advancing the information highway standards-setting process in step with the pace and content of technological change. They are ensuring that standards are not onerous or burdensome but rather are user-friendly, purposeful, and efficient. T1, X3, and IEEE all have differing procedures but they are all open, voluntary, balanced, consensus-based, and due-process–oriented development processes—and thus have all the attributes of Reed Hundt's key principles of choice, opportunity, and fairness.

Government's Key Role

This is not to say that government does not have a key role to play as a fellow participant in the standards-setting process. Obviously, it is a major user and purchaser of information technology and information products. It can and does help develop the standards that will affect its use of these products and technology. Government has been and is a welcome major player on the T1, IEEE, and X3 committees and on many other standards-setting bodies. Moreover, it does need to unilaterally set technical regulations in certain limited areas that affect public health and safety requirements. And it certainly has a role in the establishment and adoption of international standards, especially where treaties are involved.

However, given the interdependence of national and international development of information technology and communications standards, it would be, as the Computer & Business Equipment Manufacturers Association (CBEMA) emphasized, "unworkable for the U.S. Government to mandate these standards." The process for establishing internationally recognized standards is voluntary, reflects many different concerns and interests, and generally requires more time than is needed for a U.S.-only standard. In the international arena, the federal government wisely relies on ANSI and specific U.S. commissions already collaborating with international organizations such as the International Organization for Standardization (ISO).

Federal, state, and local governments have been strong supporters of and participants in the voluntary process for establishing national and international standards for over 75 years and there is no reason to propose that their role should become less democratic and more autocratic in the information age. The short-term needs of the government to achieve interconnection and inter-operability of systems, products, services, and infrastructure now available are understandable. Nevertheless, as CBEMA pointed out in its evaluation of a Federal Internetworking Requirements Panel Report, "the government should exercise great care, in satisfying its short-term needs, not to impede its ability to achieve its ultimate aim to converge the government to a single interconnected, interoperable standards-based internetworking environment."

Government's own institutional internetworking needs do not stand alone. It interfaces with and cannot ignore the broader interests of the total NII environment, which must be integrated and compatible so that citizens and business alike can communicate with the government. The informational needs of the country should be the all-pervasive, primary driving force for NII standards development.

ANSI's Role in Standardization

The American National Standards Institute is not anticipating any significant role change in the standardization process on the part of government. Nor does it envision any change in its own relationship to government. It has not been the private sector's role through ANSI to tell the government what it should do. ANSI serves a far better purpose in helping the government know what it needs. Government agencies have been indispensable team players in setting standards in all of the areas contributing to the development of information communication. There is no wish on the part of other ANSI members for that to change.

America's culture and free enterprise system have been the guiding principles of the ANSI Federation of 1,300 companies, 250 professional, technical, trade, labor, and consumer organizations, and some 30 government agencies. Since 1918, the U.S. voluntary standards system has been administered successfully by the private sector, via ANSI, with the cooperation of federal, state, and local governments.

The process that ANSI has promoted and coordinated has established standards in industries across the board, including telecommunications, safety and health, information processing, petroleum, banking, household appliances, and many more. In all of these areas, ANSI and its members have been setting technical standards that support market expansion as one of their driving principles. Attention to the marketplace is a key component of the process.

In addition, ANSI is a major contributor in the development of the global information network. It administers the Joint International Organization for Standardization–International Electrotechnical Commission (ISO-IEC) Committee on Information Technology (JTC 1) and four of its subcommittees. ANSI recently provided the opportunity for its members to participate in key meetings in Mexico in anticipation of NAFTA. It has worked jointly with government in representing U.S. concerns over the Intellectual Property Rights policy of the European Telecommunications Standards Institute (ETSI), which pose a serious threat to U.S. competitiveness. As a direct result of the access ANSI provides, U.S. companies are able to compete more effectively in the global market.

Reflecting ANSI's partnership role, the federal government, through the Technology Reinvestment Project (TRP), has invited ANSI to negotiate a cooperative agreement with the National Institute of Standards and Technology (NIST) to begin the development of an electronic information infrastructure, the National Standards Systems Network (NSSN), linking the databases of the hundreds of organizations involved in the development, production, distribution, and use of technical standards in the United States. The system will reduce standards development time, minimize duplication of effort, and decrease production costs. The NSSN will also provide cataloging, indexing, searching, and routing capabilities to facilitate end-user access to the entire range of regional, national, and international standards.

Domestically, the diverse interest groups that compose the standards developing community are coming even closer together under the Institute's umbrella, further strengthening the U.S. private sector voluntary standards system. Perhaps this has been most visibly demonstrated in the field of health care informatics, an activity that is a major application of NII. Since the announcement of NII's creation, ANSI's members have been researching, discussing, and debating how best the goals of NII might be carried out and how the voluntary standards development process could assist in this all-important task.

Information Infrastructure Standards Panel

Realizing the urgency of working to facilitate an accelerated standardization process that addresses the information and communication revolution in full progress, ANSI has more recently undertaken a new initiative that reflects the thinking of the best minds in the fields of information processing and communication technology without imposing a further burden on our nation's taxpaying public.

To ensure the continuance of an open, consensus-based process combining the best elements of competition and collaboration that has facilitated the United States global leadership in developing information technology, ANSI is establishing an Information Infrastructure Standards Panel (IISP) within the National Voluntary Standards System to support accelerated deployment of the National Information Infrastructure and the Global Information Infrastructure.

The IISP's Mission

The IISP has as its mission to promote, accelerate and coordinate the timely development of required NII standards within the National and International Voluntary Standards System. The terms of reference for the IISP are to:

• Catalog requirements for standardization of critical interfaces and other attributes, based on open, competitive models of the architecture for the NII;

• Catalog existing national and international voluntary standards, and de facto standards that address the identified requirements above;

• Seek to obtain agreement from a standards developer to develop the standard in a timely manner, where one does not exist;

• Bring individual industries and standards developing organizations together to establish work plans and priorities for updating standards or creating new standards as deemed necessary;

• Promote ongoing collaborative efforts between SDOs to establish work plans and develop joint and/or complementary standards;

• Accelerate standards development and approval through the appropriate investment of resources;

• Solicit participation in, and promote understanding of, the voluntary standards effort by those sectors that have not traditionally used the national and international voluntary standards system if they have a substantial role to play in providing standards;

• Establish and maintain liaison with other national, regional, and international information infrastructure standards efforts so as to harmonize the resulting standards; and

• Make widely available the results of the Panel's work.

Panel Membership

Participation on the IISP is open to representatives of all directly and materially affected parties of the NII. The only requirement is that participants have some form of public electronic mail access.

Panel Infrastructure

The program is staffed by a senior level program director and an administrative assistant. The director is responsible for providing executive and secretarial support for the Panel, the active solicitation of participation by those sectors not traditionally involved in the voluntary standards process, providing a liaison with other national, regional, and international information infrastructure efforts, and providing press liaison on the Panel's work.

Funding is being provided by the participants. The initial seed money is coming from several industry sectors and is to be supplemented by others as they join. To achieve the terms of reference, the Panel will be engaged in a gross analysis of standards inventories against preferred models, determining the "gaps" and promoting their completion through the appropriate sources, coordinating with federal government agencies, assuring representative membership in the standards-setting process, etc.

SDO Responsibility

In order for the Panel to function with maximum utility, ANSI, building upon the initiatives already undertaken in several SDOs, is calling for each NII-related SDO to designate (or form) an appropriate group as its focal point for NII standardization work. This group is to be responsible for:

• Identifying work within the SDO that is responsive to NII needs and making this visible in useful ways to the IISP and interested parties. (The "lists of standards" indicate the benefits they provide and how they relate to NII needs.)

• Receiving requirements for NII standards, identifying the appropriate forums within the SDO, and providing feedback on action taken with respect to such requirements

• Providing a forum for liaison with other groups, including consortia that are identifying requirements, developing specifications, engaged in actual implementation experience, or seeking reference specifications

• Providing liaison to other SDOs in this topic area, not only in terms of appropriate participation but also in terms of collaboration on programs of work and presentation of capabilities and deliverables

• Utilizing electronic tools wherever applicable to improve the effectiveness of this collaboration, and to communicate NII standards information through channels being developed in the NII community.

Some of the guidelines already identified by SDOs will be proposed for a modus operandi. For example, the Computer Systems Policy Project (CSPP), whose membership includes major players like Apple, AT&T, IBM, Unisys, and others, is proposing an industry-led strategy to ensure interoperability in the NII. Instead of suggesting an architecture for the NII, CSPP has identified critical points in today's infrastructure that must be interoperable for the successful implementation of the NII vision. These critical points fall into four categories:

1. Appliance to Network: the interface between an information appliance and a network service provider

2. Appliance to Application: the APIs (Application Program Interfaces) between an information appliance and emerging NII applications

3. Application to Application: the protocols that one NII application, service, or system uses to communicate with another service or system

4. Network to Network: the interfaces among and between network service providers.

A great deal of time could be spent debating models and architectures in this area, which might be an invitation to either government intervention or preemption by external processes. On the other hand, through the IISP and the proper establishment of standards that ensure openness of the interfaces, the critical goals of NII can and will be advanced. This will allow users and providers to transmit information smoothly throughout the NII, enable wide access to information and services, and stimulate competitive markets for NII products and services.

ANSI'S Commitment

The beneficiaries and potential beneficiaries of the information highway—users, makers, providers, and society—depend on an optimally appropriate and efficient system of standards for interoperability as we hurl into an increasingly interconnected, on-line world. The system's power base is the voluntary private sector that makes NII a reality.

ANSI understands that its mission is to protect the existing investment of consumers and industry in today's information infrastructure while looking forward to future technologies and applications. The whole process of standardization involves a continuum and an evolution, not a quantum leap.

The SDOs that compose ANSI's membership have already pioneered the information standardization frontier with remarkable success and without ceasing to identify and implement new ways to improve the process. These same participants have proposed and established the Information Infrastructure Standards Panel as an all-important element for the development process. ANSI is fully committed to IISP and recommends the active participation of all interested parties to realize its full potential in NII.

In its vision for the future, ANSI sees government and industry continuing to strengthen the cooperative and mutually beneficial relationship that has existed since federal government agencies joined in the founding of ANSI in 1918. By working together in real partnership—private and public sectors jointly addressing U.S. concerns abroad with one voice, confronting the challenges brought about by a global marketplace, furthering U.S. global competitiveness, and contributing to the safety and health of the American people—the best interests of the United States will be guaranteed.

There should be no doubt that ANSI, with its long history of successful, user-oriented, standards-setting achievements, with its multifaceted and truly representative standards-setting member organizations, will be dedicated to promoting and helping to realize a seamless, interactive, user-driven information highway that puts Americans and American technology and know-how in the leadership position that will drive human communication and development to undreamed of destinations in the twentieth-first century.

The Role of Standards in the Defense Information Infrastructure

D. Burton Newlin, Jr.
Department of Defense

The Superhighway, Information Highway, Global Highway, or Data Highway, whatever it is called, will allow government, industry, and citizens to have access to global information in an electronic format. The information has always been available, but mostly on paper, stored in libraries, archives, repositories, and files that were almost impossible to find and expensive to access. Making information available in an electronic format dramatically reduces the difficulties of finding and retrieving it. The National Information Infrastructure (NII) will deliver to all Americans the information they need, when they want it and where they want it, at an affordable price.

The NII is an information transportation system consisting of a network of networks that will integrate hardware, software, and skills in order to make it easy and affordable to connect people with each other and with a vast array of services and information resources. The NII—which is to be built, owned, and run by the private sector—will use communication and information technologies including telephones, computers, networks, hardware, software, cable TV, fiber optics, electrical utilities, video services, multimedia, and teleconferencing. Traffic on the Superhighway will consist of text, graphics, images, voice, multimedia, and data. The different parts of the system must adhere to standards to effectively move this information along the highway and be interoperable.

The three major components needed to convert information technology into usable information systems are architecture, standards, and products. The construction of an Information Super-highway involves commercial or specially developed products (hardware or software), which generally conform to technical standards; these standards normally fit into an overall "blueprint" or architectural design. Sometimes proprietary or special designs are required and special products are produced in accordance with engineering drawings or requirements, but these special products are very expensive, since they are customized and not mass produced. Standards policy for the National Information Infrastructure must ensure that individual standards are integrated with the architecture framework and are embodied in conformant products so that the standards work well in the marketplace and maintain competition.

The Information Infrastructure expands beyond the nation; it includes the international community. No longer is information restricted to our shores. Most large corporations are international in nature; many of our trading partners are in the international community; and when the Department of Defense is involved in international conflicts, the communications and computer information must be exchanged in the international arena with our friends and Allies. Thus standards policy must also ensure compatibility at the international level.

The Role of Information Technology Standards

Standards are central to information interchange. Spoken language is one example: it does not really matter which language we speak as long as the group exchanging the information speaks the same language. Another example is the competition between the two standards for video cassette recordings. Many felt that the Beta standard was technically superior, but VHS had the largest market share and won out. Although standards should be cost effective, it does not matter which standard is selected, as long as a single standard satisfies the basic requirements and is agreed upon by the marketplace.

Standards shape how the Information Superhighway is constructed. Standards define the tools used by engineers to design, develop, and construct equipment, facilities, systems, and projects. Standards define the engineering processes, procedures, practices, and methods. Standards can also be used in specifications, acquisition documents that define the essential technical requirements for purchased material and the criteria for determining whether the technical requirements are met.

Standardization has traditionally allowed the use interchangeable parts and encouraged competition. In the information age, IT standards foster competition and interoperability using open systems concepts. The concept of a federal computing environment that is built on an infrastructure defined by open, consensus-based standards is well on its way to becoming the dominant model for organizing these systems. Such an infrastructure is called an Open System Environment (OSE). Vendor-specific implementations of data communications protocols have led to isolated domains of information. An open systems environment means applications that can work on any vendor's platform, using any vendor's operating system. It means applications that can have access to any vendor's database and can communicate and interoperate over any vendor's network. It means applications that are secure and manageable and interact with the user through a common human/ computer interface. Interoperability, portability, and scalability each justify the pursuit of open systems standards.

The government often imposes standards for its own use through laws, regulations or policies. This is similar to issuing traffic rules and regulations: the government has a responsibility to establish and enforce the "rules of the road." The government already does this for communications networks. The major government standards policy organizations are the Department of Defense (DoD), the National Institute of Standards and Technology (NIST), and the Federal Communications Commission (FCC). In 1960, the federal government issued OMB Circular A-71 that permitted agencies to develop their own standards if commercial efforts failed. Legislation later gave NIST the responsibility for developing computer standards, called Federal Information Processing Standards (FIPS) Publications, for government users.

Technological advances are creating a number of opportunities with respect to federal information dissemination. One example of the type of new programs that make the Internet more navigable by the user is called Mosaic. Developed at the National Center for Supercomputing Applications (NCSA) in Champaign-Urbana, Illinois, Mosaic is distributed free to any Internet user, and lets people point and click their way to information on the World Wide Web [1]. Electronic technology permits the government to disseminate information on a centralized or decentralized basis. But technology has outpaced the major governmentwide information dissemination statutes, and technological advances complicate the federal government's relationship with the commercial information industry [2]. Standards are one tool to help harness these technological advances.

Standardization is an important consideration throughout the acquisition process as a way to foster competition and reduce maintenance costs throughout a system's life-cycle. Both the Federal Acquisition Regulation (FAR) and the Defense Federal Acquisition Regulation (DFAR) Supplement require that standardization considerations be a part of the acquisition process. Standardization within the Department of Defense is required by Public Law 82-436 (1952) and Title 10 of the United States Code. This law is implemented under DoD Instruction 5000.2, "Defense Acquisition Management Policies and Procedures," and DoD 4120.3-M, "Defense Standardization Program Policies and Procedures" [3]. MIL-STD-970, "Order of Preference for the Selection of Standards and Specifications," may also be used for guidance. The general criteria are to use standards required by law or international treaty first and mandatory government standards (e.g., Federal Information Processing Standards) second. Third are the national and international non-government standards (such as those set by the International Organization for Standardization (ISO) or the American National Standards Institute (ANSI)) and DoD interest standards (such as those developed by the Institute of Electrical and Electronic Engineers (IEEE)). Fourth are standards from consortia, such as the Open Software Foundation (OSF), Network Management Foundation (NMF), and the Open Systems Environment Implementor's Workshop (OIW). Next are Commercial Item Descriptions, followed by federal specifications and standards. DoD and Military Standards that are unique to a service or agency are last.

In April of 1994, the Department of Defense issued a report of the Process Action Team on Military Specifications and Standards. It reported that specifications and standards reform is an integral part of the acquisition reform vision of the Clinton Administration, a vision intended to revolutionize the way the government does business. The Secretary of Defense issued a policy memorandum entitled, "Specifications and Standards—A New Way of Doing Business" [4]. This memorandum directs the increased use of performance and commercial specifications and standards. The policy stated that if performance specifications are not practicable, then non-government standards shall be used. It also stated that military specifications or standards shall only be used as a last resort and with a waiver.

The current standards challenge is to keep pace with the accelerating changes in information technology. Today, over fifty percent of the International Organization for Standardization (ISO) standards projects and activities involve information technology standards. The American National Standards Institute (ANSI) is reviewing how to streamline and accelerate its standards process to meet the rapid changes in information technology. Because the traditional standardization process has been so slow, numerous standards consortia and coalitions participants are meeting to accelerate and establish open systems standards to capture the technology. In addition, as organizations re-engineer and downsize, participation in standards bodies has been declining because of economics and reduced travel budgets. Nonetheless, OMB Circular A-119 states that it is the policy of the federal government to rely on voluntary standards, both domestic and international. The Circular also states that it is government policy to participate in voluntary standards bodies when such participation is in the public interest and is compatible with Agencies' missions, authority, priorities, and budget resources [5]. Department of Defense participation in non-government standards bodies' technical committees is documented in the Defense Standardization Directory SD-11 [6]. The directory lists over 2200 DoD personnel from nearly 50 organizations who participate on technical committees.

Defense Information Infrastructure

President Clinton has challenged us to make our government work better and cost less. There are several laws and management initiatives to "reinvent" the federal government, and DoD in particular, in response to President Clinton's directive to improve the management structure and efficiency of all federal agencies. These include the Government Performance and Results Act, Chief Financial Officers Act, Reinventing Government, Information Infrastructure Task Force, National Performance Review, Defense Performance Review, Bottom-Up Review, Acquisition Reform, Defense Management Report, Corporate Information Management, and DoD Plan for Streamlining the Bureaucracy. The expansion of the Superhighway will also contribute to this goal. The National Information Infrastructure (NII) is implemented under Executive Order 12864, signed by President Clinton on September 15, 1993, and amended on December 30, 1993 [7]. The President established the Advisory Council on the National Information Infrastructure to advise the Secretary of Commerce on matters related to the development of the NII.

As part of the reinvention of government, the U.S. military is undergoing a major restructuring and downsizing, using a new strategy of multinational military alliances to defeat aggressors. A Bottom-Up Review was conducted to build a multi-year plan for the strategy, force structure, modernization, and supporting industrial base and infrastructure needed in the aftermath of the Cold War. The major weapons of future conflicts will involve information warfare: knowing what, when, where, and why about the enemy. To this end, the Department of Defense is establishing a Defense Information Infrastructure (DII), an interconnected system of computers, telecommunications, and other support structure serving the DoD's local and worldwide information needs.

The DII encompasses information transfer and processing resources, including information and data storage, manipulation, retrieval, and display. More specifically, the DII is the shared or interconnected system of computers, communications, data, applications, security, people, training, and other support structure, serving the DoD's local and worldwide information needs. The Defense Information Infrastructure (1) connects DoD mission support, command and control, and intelligence computers and users through voice, data imagery, video, and multimedia services, and (2) provides information processing and value-added services to subscribers over the Defense Information System Network (DISN). Unique user data, and user applications software are not considered part of the DII [8].

The DoD must give its warfighters the right information at the right location at the right time. The Defense Information Systems Network (DISN), a subelement of the Defense Information Infrastructure, is the DoD's consolidated worldwide enterprise-level telecommunications infrastructure, which will provide the end-to-end information transfer network for supporting military operations. It will be transparent to its users, facilitate the management of information resources, and be responsive to national security and defense needs under all conditions in the most efficient manner.

The Defense Information Infrastructure is viewed as part of the National Information Infrastructure being pursued by the Clinton Administration, and will interface with the rest of the National Information Infrastructure where effective and feasible. The Defense Department is planning to join with the General Services Administration to combine its requirements with the next generation of the Federal Telecommunications System (FTS) 2000. The President has also established and directed a federal electronic commerce acquisition team to develop a plan for standardizing electronic commerce environments and applying electronic data interchange to federal procurements. The Defense Department is co-chairing the team along with the General Services Administration.

To carry out its mission and achieve interoperability, the DoD is using corporatewide open systems technical standards as part of a standards-based architecture. The Defense Department cannot afford to have one set of standards for tactical or command, control, communications, and intelligence (C3I) and another set for management information systems. Using national and international standards will keep DoD on the leading edge as we enter the Information Age. The use of standards will reduce systems costs and improve the interoperability, efficiency, and effectiveness of information systems, both internally and with external organizations such as suppliers and allies.

DoD Corporate Information Management Initiative

One of the early Department of Defense initiatives to reinvent government was a plan implementing the DoD Corporate Information Management (CIM) Initiative, which was approved by the Deputy Secretary of Defense on 14 January 1991 [9]. The plan established a Director of Defense Information who had overall responsibility for implementing the corporate information program across the Department. This included the development and implementation of information management policies, programs, and standards.

The purpose of the Corporate Information Management initiative is to improve efficiency and productivity across the Department. In order to offset declining resources, DoD must accelerate the pace at which it defines standard baseline processes to determine data requirements; selects and deploys migration systems; implements data standardization; and conducts functional process improvement reviews and business process improvement or re-engineering within and across all functions of the Department [10]. Process improvement is a management discipline applied by functional managers to redesign the Department's processes, organizations, and culture. Accelerating integration and interoperability is key to containing the functional costs of performing the DoD mission within a constrained budget [11].

To carry out this information management policy, the Assistant Secretary of Defense Command, Control, Communications and Intelligence, ASD(C3I), expanded the roles and responsibilities of the Defense Communications Agency and renamed it the Defense Information Systems Agency (DISA). Under the Defense Management Report (DMR) 918, "The Defense Information Infrastructure (DII)," the Department of Defense established an Information Technology (IT) Standards Program under DISA, and the Assistant Secretary of Defense (C3I) assigned DISA as the Executive Agent for Information Standards [12]. Under the new organization, the DISA established a Center for Architecture and a Center for Standards to support the information technology standardization program under the overall Defense Standardization Program. Responsibility for the development and maintenance of the TAFIM resides with the DISA Center for Architecture. The DISA Center for Standards has developed a Department of Defense Information Technology Standards Management Plan [13]. This plan establishes the mechanism to lead, integrate, coordinate and manage the standardization effort to adopt or develop "open systems standards" to achieve interoperability and portability. The Information Technology Standards Program Office serves as a mechanism for adopting, developing, specifying, certifying, and enforcing information technology standards. With the goal of meeting DoD needs using open systems voluntary standards, DISA's Center for Standards is focusing on the development of a single, coordinated DoD voice to external information technology standards bodies. As the DoD focal point for information technology standards, the Center for Standards is participating in several standards activities with the National Institute of Standards and Technology. DISA also established a Corporate Information Management Office to assist in the development, coordination and execution of the DoD Data Administration Program, which includes data elements standards [14]. The Corporate Information Management Program has provided oversight of all aspects of information management, technology and systems, and the integration of the principles of information management into all of the Department's functional activities.

One of the Corporate Information Management objectives is to improve business processes and integrate communications and data processing infrastructure by implementing enhanced information systems that incorporate a standards-based technology. Under the Defense Standardization Program there are 36 standardization areas. DISA is the Lead Standardization Activity for the four major information technology areas [15]: Information Processing Standards for Computers (IPSC), Information Standards and Technology (INST), Data Communications Protocol Standards (DCPS), and Telecommunication Systems Standards (TCSS). There are approximately 2000 national, international, Federal, DoD, NATO, and Service-unique standards associated with information technology and telecommunications that DISA must monitor and oversee.

The evolving DoD enterprise vision for Information Management is the implementation of a computing and communications infrastructure that will support portability, scalability, and interoperability of applications. Portability is defined as the ease with which a system or component can be transferred from one hardware or software environment to another; an example of a standard that provides portability is IEEE STD 610.12. Scalability is defined as the ability to use the same application software on many different classes of hardware/software platforms, from personal computers to supercomputers. Interoperability is defined as the ability to share information through the effective use of compatible data and technical standards; interoperability ensures successful communications between systems. These goals will be achieved through the development of a common, multi-purpose, open systems standards-based technical infrastructure. The technical infrastructure includes support applications, computing platforms, communications networks, and associated software. It imposes order on DoD information systems, improves interoperability, and facilitates upgrading technology components as missions and requirements change.

Applications Portability Profile and Technical Architecture Framework for Information Management

With approximately 2000 government and industry information technology and telecommunications standards that specify how information systems are designed and maintained, the challenge is to determine which standard to pick for a specific design. To achieve the goal of national and global interoperability, the U.S. government has selected a manageable subset of the open systems standards. This subset of open standards is defined by NIST's Applications Portability Profile (APP) and the DoD Technical Architecture Framework for Information Management (TAFIM). The NIST Applications Portability Profile is provided to assist Federal agencies in making informed choices regarding the selection and use of Open System Environment (OSE) standards. The Technical Architecture Framework for Information Management represents the Department of Defense consensus Open System Environment and provides guidance on information technology standards.

A selected suite of standards that defines the interfaces, services, protocols, and data formats for a particular class or domain of applications is called a profile. The National Institute of Standards and Technology's Applications Portability Profile (APP) integrates industry, Federal, national, international, and other standards into a federal application profile. This profile provides the functionality necessary to accommodate a broad range of federal information technology requirements. As the U.S. government's Open System Environment profile, APP guides Federal agencies in making informed choices regarding applicable Open System Environment standards. The Applications Portability Profile provides information on product availability and conformance testing for each of the standards it identifies [16]. The status of the standards in the Applications Portability Profile is constantly changing; as new standards evolve and old standards fail to gain acceptance by the marketplace or become obsolete, the APP will continue to evolve.

To guide the implementation of a worldwide Defense Information Infrastructure, the Department of Defense has implemented the federal government's Applications Portability Profile in the DoD Technical Architecture Framework for Information Management (TAFIM). The TAFIM describes the DoD migration and target open system environments and provides guidance on information technology standards applicable to fulfilling the OSE requirements. It also provides information technology standards guidance for all phases of information technology systems. The expressions of enterprise, mission, function, and application level standards guidance can be independently applied.

DoD policies that require the use of TAFIM information technology standards and standards conformance testing are contained in directives and instructions that implement the policies and assign responsibilities and procedures to achieve compatibility and interoperability of a consolidated DoD-wide, global information infrastructure. No longer will the military services develop data communications systems separately; it is "DoD policy that, for compatibility, interoperability, and integration, all command, control, communications, and intelligence (C3I) systems developed for use by U.S. forces are considered to be for joint use" [17]. The procedures for compatibility, interoperability, and integration of command, control, communications, and intelligence systems are provided in DoD Instruction 4630.8 [18].

Technical Reference Model and Standards Profile

Volume 3 of the Technical Architecture Framework for Information Management is the Reference Model and Standards Profile. The hierarchy of information technology construction starts with an architectural framework, which is divided into service areas. For each service area identified in the TAFIM, a set of technical standards has been identified from the large variety of proprietary, open systems, international, NATO, national, Federal, military, agency unique, or de facto standards that are being used in the marketplace. The Technical Reference Model defines a target framework and profile of standards for the infrastructure and the applications that it will support [19]. The 30-plus technical standards that are identified for the service areas in the Technical Reference Model are summarized as follows:

Programming	Ada, PCTE
User Interface	X-Windows, DoD HCI Guide, P1201.X
Data Management	SQL, IRDS, RDA, TDI
Data Interchange	SGML, CGM, Raster, EDI, IGES, ODA
Graphics	GKS, PHIGS
Network	GOSIP, TLSP, NLSP, ISO Security Architecture, LAN Security, TNI, MIL-STD-187-700
Operating System	POSIX.1, POSIX.2, POSIX.4, POSIX.6, GNMP
Security	TCSEC, DSS, CMW
System Management	GNMP, MIL-STD-2045-38000

The standards identified in the Programming service area include programming languages and language bindings, as well as Integrated Computer Aided Software Engineering (I-CASE) environments and tools. The DoD is required by public law to use the programming language Ada: "Where cost effective, all Department of Defense software shall be written in the programming language Ada, in the absence of special exemption by an official designated by the Secretary of Defense." The two standards identified in the TAFIM for programming services are:

Ada	Ada Programming Language, FIPS PUB 119 (Ada, ANSI/MIL-STD-1815A-1983)
PCTE	Portable Common Tool Environment, ECMA Specification 149 (ISO fast track)

The User Interface standards define the relationship between client and server processes operating within a network, particular the graphical user interface display processes. The standards identified in the TAFIM for user interface services are:

General	DoD Human Computer Interface Style Guide (February 24, 1992)
X-Windows	FIPS PUB 158-1, The User Interface Component of the Application Portability Profile
IEEE P1201.X (future)	IEEE P1201.1, Draft Standard for Information Technology Uniform Application Program Interface; IEEE 1201.2, IEEE Recommended Practices for Graphical User Interface Drivability

The Data Management service area includes the data dictionary/directory services. The data management standards identified in the TAFIM are:

IRDS	Information Resources Directory System, FIPS PUB 156
SQL	Structured Query Language, FIPS PUB 127-1
TDI	Trusted Database Interpretation, NCSC-TG-021, National Computer Security Center
RDA (future)	Remote Database Access

The Data Interchange service area includes the following standards:

SGML	Standard Generalized Markup Language, FIPS PUB 152; MIL-M-28001, "Markup Requirements and Generic Style Specification for Electronic Printed Output and Exchange of Text"
CGM	Computer Graphics Metafile, FIPS PUB 128; MIL-D-28003, "Computer Graphics Metafile (CGM)"
Raster	Raster Graphics Representation in Binary Format, Including FIPS PUB 150 and ODA Raster Document Application Profile; MIL-R-28002, "Requirements for Raster Graphics Representation in Binary Format (GRP 4 Raster Scanned Images)"
EDI	Electronic Data Interchange, FIPS PUB 161
IGES (gap filler)	Initial Graphics Exchange Specification, FIPS PUB 177; MIL-D-28000, "Digital Representation for Communications of Product Data: IGES Applications Subset"
ODA/ODIF/ODL (future)	Office Document Architecture/Office Document Interchange Format/Office Document Language, ISO 8613:1989

The Graphics standards identified in the TAFIM provide the interface for programming two and three dimensional graphics in a device independent manner. The graphics standards are:

GKS	Graphical Kernel System, FIPS PUB 120-1
PHIGS	Programmer's Hierarchical Graphics System, FIPS PUB 153

The Network service area includes standards for telecommunications, data communications, transparent file access, personal/ microcomputer support, and distributed computing support. Service areas related to telecommunications are voice telephone, data transmission, facsimile, record traffic, and video support. The network standards identified in the TAFIM are:

GOSIP	Government Open System Interconnection Profile, FIPS 146-1
MIL-STD-187-700	Interoperability and Performance Standards for the Defense Information System
ISO Security Architecture	ISO IS 7498-2, Information Processing Systems; OSI Reference Model—Part 2: Security Architecture
TNI	Trusted Network Interpretation, NCSC-TG-005
TLSP (future)	Transport Layer 4 Security Protocol
NLSP (future)	Network Layer 3 Security Protocol
LAN Security (future)	IEEE 802.10 F, Standard for Secure Data Exchange Sub-Layer Management, March 1993 (Sections A–E & G in Draft)

The Operating System service area includes kernel operations, shell and utilities, system management, and security. The TAFIM identifies the following standards:

POSIX.1	Portable Operating System Interface for Computer Environments, FIPS 151-1
POSIX.2	Portable Operating System Interface for Computer Environments
POSIX.4	IEEE Portable Operating Systems Interface Part 1, Systems Application Program Interface (API), Amendment 1: "Real Time Extensions C Language."
POSIX.6 (future)	Security Extension: Draft IEEE P1003.22, "Guide to POSIX Open Systems Environment Security Framework"; Draft IEEE P1003.6, "Security Extension to 1003.1."
GNMP	Government Network Management Profile, FIPS 179

MIL-STD-2045-38000   Network Management for DoD Communications (Draft)

Security services are required in any information system. The DoD has issued DoD 5200.28-STD, "DoD Trusted Computer System Evaluation Criteria (TCSEC)," which addresses this requirement for the Department. The other security standards referenced in the TAFIM are the Defense Intelligence Agency (DIA) series of standards, which deal with security requirements for compartmented mode workstations. The standards listed in the TAFIM are:

TCSEC	Trusted Computer System Evaluation Criteria
CMW	Compartmented Mode Workstation
DSS	Digital Signature Standard (Draft FIPS)

Under the System Management area the TAFIM identifies the following standards:

GNMP	Government Network Management Profile, FIPS 179
MIL-STD-2045-38000	Network Management for DoD Communications (Draft)

Downsizing from Legacy to Migration Information Systems

To meet the changing threats, economical realities, and challenges from the international marketplace, the DoD is in the process of downsizing and re-defining and re-engineering its mission and infrastructure. Part of this downsizing involves the streamlining and reduction of several thousand systems to a limited number (a hundred or more) of migration systems as we head for our future target systems. The DISA Center for Integration and Interoperability has pioneered the development of automated tools to help the DoD achieve the effective integration and interoperability of its mission support, command and control, and intelligence information systems. The automated tools known as the Defense Integration Support Tools, or DIST, and the "Integration Checklist for Migration Assessments" offer the technical and functional communities the help they need with the challenges of selecting migration systems, improving functional processes, and standardizing data [20].

Migration systems have been officially designated to support common processes for functional activities that can be used DoD-wide or DoD component-wide. A migration system is the initial cut in the process of identifying a limited, standardized set of systems from the total array of systems being funded and supported today. Under the downsizing effort, the DoD is selecting a limited number of migration systems to enhance and upgrade and move toward target systems compliant with the TAFIM standards over the next three years as technology advances. The migration systems will undergo transition to the standard technical environment and standard data definitions being established through the Defense Information Management (IM) Program, and must "migrate" toward compliance with the Reference Model and Standards Profile [21]. The architecture for each migration system will determine the set of TAFIM-compliant technical standards that are being used to achieve interoperability, portability, and scalability. The DISA Center for Standards is responsible for identifying the Technical Information Standards, specified in Volume 7 (Draft) of the TAFIM. The DISA Joint Interoperability Test Center (JITC) is responsible for maintaining a list of Registers of conformant and interoperable products that have been tested and approved for use in DoD information systems.

The selection of candidate migration systems by DoD is based on procedures established to guarantee a structured analysis of functional and technical adequacy in terms of system conformance to the TAFIM. Migration system assessments include technical analysis of migration candidates to ensure that legacy system migration will result in an information system baseline that is technically adequate to support subsequent functional and technical improvement activities. In order to validate the technical sufficiency of candidate migration systems, each legacy application is assessed within a functional activity or sub-activity in terms of relevant functional, technical, data handling, and programmatic criteria. Migration system assessments determine the degree to which legacy applications conform to the TAFIM and their suitability for accommodating subsequent process and data improvements. The TAFIM currently identifies over thirty technical standards for selection and use in DoD migration systems.

An analysis is being conducted under the DoD Sustaining Base Information System (SBIS) program to determine its compliance with the Technical Architecture Framework for Information Management architectural requirements, standards selected, and standards conformant products. This project is based on the standards identified in the Technical Architecture Framework for Information Management as applied to a representative sample of DoD migration systems.

The Need for Registers of Conformant Products

For each standard identified in the TAFIM there should be conformant commercial off-the-shelf (COTS) or uniquely developed products. Within the federal government, each Federal Information Processing Standard specifies whether testing is necessary to validate conformance of implementations. In implementing the National Institute of Standards and Technology Application Portability Profile, NIST has established the National Voluntary Laboratory Accreditation Program (NVLAP) to accredit laboratories for performing testing under various standards programs. The accreditation requirements are strict and different for each standard, and accreditation is good for two years. The TAFIM does not provide the additional information on conformance testing for each of the standards that is provided by NIST's Applications Portability Profile. This additional information on the availability for specific standards product is also needed by the DoD user community.

The Chairman of the Joint Chiefs of Staff Instruction 6212.01 requires the Defense Information Systems Agency to assess whether applicable standards, compatibility, interoperability, and integration requirements are considered during the requirements review process. The Joint Interoperability Test Center (JITC) at Fort Huachuca, Arizona, is a DISA organization responsible for interoperability testing across the DoD. Commercial products may conform to standards but still not be interoperable because of the leeway in interpreting the standard. The JITC has developed a draft policy that explains how interoperability certification is obtained for command, control, communications, computers and intelligence systems, and automated information equipment and systems [22]. The Joint Interoperability Test Center has been assigned as the "Department of Defense Executive for Information Systems Testing" and as such has established and maintains lists of Registers of certified products and systems that have been tested for conformance and interoperability. However, there are only Registers for conformance at present. The first interoperability Registers were being developed, but funding for these Registers has been cut because of budget reductions.

The major challenge in constructing the Information Superhighway with standards will be to select the proper standards and to identify commercial products that conform to the standards selected. Emphasis needs to be placed on ensuring that the standards identified in the National Institute of Standards and Technology Application Portability Profile and the DoD Technical Architecture Framework for Information Management have standards Registers that identify products that have been tested either formally by the government or informally by the marketplace. Registers of certified products should be established for every standard in each of the open systems environment service areas. These Registers should contain information on product availability and conformance and interoperability testing.

Internet and Open Systems Interconnection Standards

An integral part of the NII or Information Superhighway is the Internet. The origin of the Internet dates back to the early 1960s, when the Department of Defense hired the RAND Corporation to look for a command-and-control network that could survive a nuclear holocaust. At the time it was feared that a nuclear attack would reduce any conceivable network to shreds. In 1964, RAND proposed a network that resembled a spider web, with computer nodes at each intersection of the web. Messages sent across the network would be divided into packets and each packet would be separately addressed. Each packet would begin at a specific node and end up at some other specific destination node, winding its way through the network web on an individual basis. The path the packet took across the web would be unimportant, since only final results would count. This haphazard delivery system might be inefficient, but would be extremely reliable.

In 1969 the Defense Department's Advanced Research Project Agency built a network using this design, calling it the ARPANET. As time passed the APRANET became a true network of networks and grew into what is known today as the "Internet" [23]. Today the Internet is a global web of over 25,000 computer networks and to which over 20 million people now have access. There are five basic Internet "domains": gov (government), mil (military), edu (educational institutions), com (commercial), and net (nonprofit organizations). The Internet is moving away from its original base in military and research institutions and into high schools, colleges and universities, public libraries, and the commercial sector. A volunteer group, the Internet Society, manages the Internet and promotes its use. As the Internet evolves, it will form a major component of the so-called Superhighway of tomorrow.

The original standard used by the ARPANET was NCP, "Network Control Protocol." The ARPANET next changed to a higher-level, more sophisticated set of protocols called TCP/IP, which consists of two standards: the "Transmission Control Protocol," defined in MIL-STD-1778 [24], and the "Internet Protocol," specified in MIL-STD-1777 [25]. The TCP/IP software was created by the Department of Defense and became a standard in the public domain. TCP/IP was chosen to connect the systems that make up the Internet; the use of the DoD protocols for computer networking spread exponentially and is now global.

Another important step in developing network standards was the creation in the late 1970s and 1980s of the International Standards Organization's Open Systems Interconnection (OSI) Reference Model (ISO 7498). The OSI initiative is a bold attempt to avoid the haphazard evolution of incompatible protocols. It is based on a seven-layer reference model that is intended to guarantee reliable communications between computers.

The U.S. government has become the biggest player in open systems interconnection by developing its own profile, called Government Open System Interconnection Profile (GOSIP), and mandating its use on new procurements under FIPS 146. The GOSIP standard is based on the requirement for interoperability; it also includes protocols to handle security concerns absent from the original ISO model. The DoD policy states "that all new automated information systems and major upgrades requiring network services, including tactical applications, specify and use Government Open System Interconnection Profile protocols. Use of GOSIP protocols is required for all DoD data networks which have a potential for host-to-host connectivity across network or subnetwork boundaries" [26]. The Defense Information Systems Agency, Joint Interoperability Test Center, in Fort Huachuca, Arizona, is one of several facilities accredited by the National Institute of Standards and Technology to do GOSIP Conformance and Interoperability Testing and Product Registration.

Marketplace Response to Standards

Two recent standards studies by the Federal Internetworking Requirements Panel looked at competing standards: one compared the GOSIP and TCP/IP standards, and the other reviewed the Office Document Architecture (ODA) and Standard General Markup Language (SGML) standards. These studies have pointed out that just because international standards exist, that does not mean the marketplace is supporting and using them.

The DoD addressed communications standardization in the late 1970s, when it selected TCP/IP for the Defense Data Network (DDN). In 1987 the National Institute of Standards and Technology selected the Government Open System Interconnection Profile (GOSIP) suite as an experimental co-standard with the DoD protocols. However, the implementation of OSI in the Government Open System Interconnection Profile has not found much favor among commercial customers in the United States, although it is doing better in Europe. A proposal by the Federal Internetworking Requirement Panel (FIRP) to expand the government's OSI-only procurement policy has become the focus of intense debate among network planners worldwide.

One of Open Systems Interconnection's strongest standards is the X.400 package, which is used for electronic mail systems. Electronic mail has become one of the prime motivations for internetworking. The General Services Administration (GSA) has made X.400 interoperability a prerequisite for its Federal Telecommunications Systems (FTS) 2000 vendors. But like many standards, X.400 faces competition, in this case from the Simple Mail Transfer Protocol (SMTP), which was designed to work with the DoD protocols. The marketplace will determine which standard will succeed.

The National Institute of Standards and Technology chartered the Office of the Secretary of Defense (C3I) to head up the Federal Internetworking Requirements Panel. The panel determined that technology was moving faster than industry and users could assimilate it and faster than the standards process could react. The draft report provides several key recommendations to the Office of Management and Budget (OMB) and the Department of Commerce. These include that responsibilities for fostering standards should be strengthened by the Department of Commerce, that voluntary standards should be adopted and used by Federal Agencies, and that international standards should be considered in the interest of promoting trade in accordance with OMB Circular A-119 guidance [27]. The report also recommends that the current GOSIP policy be modified to reflect the wider range of international voluntary standards for internetworking, such as TCP/IP.

The data interchange service area of the TAFIM, which tries to standardize the electronic interchange of information using text and graphics, is another area that has seen competing standards. Efforts have been underway since the early 1980s to convert engineering drawings and technical manuals from paper and microfilm to an electronic format. An office was created within the Office of the Secretary of Defense to develop the standards needed to electronically interchange this technical information. The office is called CALS, which has variously stood for Computer-aided Acquisition and Logistics Support and Continuous Acquisition and Lifecycle Support. Three of the data interchange standards that the CALS office supported were the Standard General Markup Language (SGML), Initial Graphics Exchange Specification (IGES), and the Office Document Architecture (ODA) standards.

A Document Interchange Symposium was sponsored by the DISA Center for Standards in March 1993 at Airlie, Virginia. The symposium participants were tasked to review market acceptance for two of the international CALS standards identified in the National Institute of Standards and Technology Application Portability Profile and the Technical Architecture Framework for Information Management. Selected internationally known experts in document interchange were brought together to clarify the needs for document interchange; evaluate the suitability of existing de facto or propriety solutions; and assess the quality, maturity, and cost of available implementations of existing standards. The two international standards that were reviewed were the Office Document Architecture (ODA) and Standard General Markup Language (SGML). Both of these are international standards, with SGML coming from the publishing community and ODA coming from the data communications community.

The symposium participants agreed that the SGML standard should be adopted as the recommended standard for logical structure representation because of functionality, previous successful DoD use in the CALS program, widespread availability of commercial off-the-shelf (COTS) products, and near-universal adoption by industry. The key conclusion of the symposium was that for large, complex documents, containing text, graphics, images or spread sheets, the marketplace acceptance of document interchange based on SGML was overwhelming. On the other side, ODA was not a viable option for DoD specifications or procurements due to the high risk and lack of broad national and international industry support [28].

Conclusions

As the Information Superhighway is being constructed, it is being paved with a subset of standards selected from the over 2000 technical standards that are available. Some of the standards are formal, some de facto; some are too complex, and some standards have no support in the marketplace. Information technology is dynamic and in some areas is accelerating faster than standards can be developed.

The federal government has developed an initial architecture framework called the Applications Portability Profile, and the DoD

has implemented this architectural framework in the DoD Technical Architecture Framework for Information Management (TAFIM).
The use of open systems standards should foster competition and
reduce maintenance costs throughout a system's lifecycle. However, for the Information Superhighway to function effectively, the
technical standards that are adopted to construct and use the
highway must have products that implement the standards. The
true measure of a standard's success is determined in the marketplace.

References

[1] *Fortune* Magazine, "The Internet and Your Business," pages 86–96, Vol. 129, No. 5, dated March 7, 1994.

[2] Informing The Nation: Federal Information Dissemination in an Electronic Age, United States Congress, Office of Technology Assessment, dated October 1988.

[3] DoD 4120.3-M, "Defense Standardization Program Policies and Proce-dures," dated July 1993.

[4] Secretary of Defense memorandum, "Specifications and Standards—A New Way of Doing Business," dated 29 July 1994.

[5] Executive Office of the President, Office of Management and Budget Circular A-119, "Federal Participation in the Development and Use of Voluntary Standards," dated October 20, 1993.

[6] Directory of Department of Defense Participation on Non-Government Standards Technical Committees, SD-11, dated November 17, 1993.

[7] Executive Order 12864, "National Information Infrastructure," signed by President Clinton, dated September 15, 1993, amended on December 30, 1993.

[8] Assistant Secretary of Defense (C3I) Memorandum, "Information Manage-ment Definitions," dated February 25, 1994.

[9] Plan for Implementation of Corporate Information Management in DoD, Office of the Assistant Secretary of Defense (Command, Control, Communica-tions and Intelligence), dated January 10, 1991.

[10] Deputy Secretary of Defense Memorandum, "Accelerated Implementation of Migration Systems, Data Standards, and Process Improvement," dated 13 October 1993.

[11] Secretary of Defense Memorandum, "Acquisition Reform: A Mandate For Change," Secretary of Defense, Honorable William J. Perry, dated February 9, 1994.

[12] Assistant Secretary of Defense (C3I) Memorandum, "Executive Agent for DoD Information Standards," dated September 3, 1991.

555
Standards in the Defense Information Infrastructure

[13] JIEO Plan 3200, "Department of Defense Information Technology (IT) Standards Management Plan," dated November 1993.

[14] Secretary of Defense Memorandum, "Implementation of Corporate Information Management Principles," dated November 16, 1990.

[15] DoD Standardization Directory, SD-1, 1 January 1994.

[16] Application Portability Profile (APP), The US Government's Open System Environment Profile OSE/1 Version 2.0, NIST Special Publication 500-210, dated June 1993.

[17] DoD Directive 4630.5, "Compatibility, Interoperability, and Integration of Command, Control, Communications, and Intelligence (C3I) Systems," dated November 12, 1992.

[18] DoD Instruction 4630.8, "Procedures for Compatibility, Interoperability, and Integration of Command, Control, Communications, and Intelligence (C3I) Systems," dated November 18, 1992.

[19] "Department of Defense Technical Architecture Framework for Information Management," (TAFIM) Volume 3, Reference Model and Standards Profile, Version 1.3, Defense Information Systems Agency, dated December 31, 1992.

[20] "Defense Integration Support Tools (DIST)," Center for Integration and Interoperability, Defense Information Systems Agency, Suite 1501, 5201 Leesburg Pike, Falls Church, Virginia 22041-3201. Telephone 703-756-4746

[21] "Department of Defense Technical Architecture Framework for Information Management," (TAFIM) Version 1.1, Defense Information Systems Agency, dated October 21, 1992.

[22] Draft JIEO Circular 9002, Version 15, "Requirements Assessment and Interoperability Certification of C4I and AIS Equipment and Systems," dated January 21, 1994.

[23] "A Short History of the Internet," The Magazine of Fantasy and Science Fiction, February 1993, F&SF, Box 56, Cornwall, CT 06753.

[24] MIL-STD-1778, "Transmission Control Protocol," dated 12 August 1983.

[25] MIL-STD-1777, "Internet Protocol," dated 12 August 1983.

[26] Assistant Secretary of Defense(C3I) Memorandum, "DoD Policy on the GOSIP Data Communications Protocols," dated September 25, 1990.

[27] Draft Report of the Federal Internetworking Requirements Panel, Prepared for the National Institute of Standards and Technology, dated January 14, 1994.

[28] "Document Interchange Symposium Proceedings," Arlie, Virginia, March 25–26, 1993. Sponsored by Defense Information Systems Agency, Joint Interoperability Engineering Organization, Center for Standards.

Standardization and Conformity Assessment in Telecommunications and Information Technology

Stephen P. Oksala
UNISYS

Introduction

Standardization and conformity assessment activities in the telecommunications and information technology sectors share a number of characteristics. Technology is changing rapidly. At the same time, purchasers of new technology are demanding interoperability between networks, computers, applications, and people. Therefore, we also need standards. Rapid technological change and standards don't usually fit together, and these complex standards must all be compatible with each other. These changes are occurring in an intensely competitive market where new companies are offering new products and services every day.

It's worth noting that there are differences between the telecommunications and information technology industries. The telecommunications industry has a history of regulation, while the IT industry doesn't. Telecommunications is also largely a service industry, while information technology has its roots in hardware and software products. There are significant cultural differences (such as attitude toward government involvement) between the two sectors because of these factors. While they use the same technology and must deal with many of the same issues, they are not one industry and are likely to react very differently to external forces.

Impact on Industrial Development

How do standards setting and conformity assessment affect patterns of industrial development? It should be no surprise that standards drive information technology product development. Clients demand the freedom to choose between vendors, so our industry has a broad range of formal and informal standards development. This is a worldwide process because the information technology industry's interest is in international rather than national or regional standards. Unisys and other companies participate nationally because that's the path to international acceptance. The U.S. information technology industry has been extremely successful in having its standards adopted internationally through the private-sector process because of this focus.

Software conformity assessment is relatively new to the information technology industry but it is becoming as important as standardization. Of increasing concern, however, is the requirement for formal product testing in accredited laboratories, as well as process audits like ISO 9000. Government procurement has been the primary driver in this area; there has been little demand by commercial customers for anything beyond a supplier's declaration of conformance. Such testing is extremely expensive, and it is by no means clear that the benefits are worth the cost—particularly when customers or markets require duplicate testing or certification. Harmonization of testing and mutual recognition of results would go a long way toward reducing costs and expanding the range of available products.

The Impact of Consortia

Why has industry formed so many consortia? And is this a permanent change in the industrial process? Industry participants have formed consortia to complete specific technical work, promote standards, ensure implementation of standards in products, test products, and even build common software for their members. The public tends to lump all these activities together under the general term "standards." But if we focus just on consortia work on technical specifications, we see that the usual reason for consortia formation is to speed the completion of standards and ensure that they pertain to real products. Consortia have done effective and efficient work in this regard but there is no credible evidence that the consortia process is inherently faster than the formal standards process. It's worth noting that new consortia usually refer to the previous generation of consortia rather than the formal standards groups when they complain about speed. Consortia sometimes fall short of their goals because they believe that they can short-circuit the painful political process of developing broad-based consensus. Relying on the willingness of the participants to passively follow the major players has not proved to be an ideal solution.

Why, then, do consortia remain so popular? First, consortia do things other than standards development. Second, they concentrate on existing technology and product implementations to keep a greater focus on near-term success. OSI is an example of the opposite approach, and the world thinks of OSI when they think of the formal standards process. The OSI example may just be telling us that top-down, carefully architected anticipatory standards can't be successfully developed for complex environments with changing technology. De facto groups such as the Internet Society and the ATM Forum have been successful in meeting well-focused objectives with good industry consensus and a philosophy of taking small steps with proven implementations.

Consortia also seem to have effective methodologies. They work more intensively than formal standards groups; in some cases, participating organizations provide full-time people to expedite the work. They also make better use of technology. Therefore, they have the potential to be more efficient, but they may also exclude the small participant because of the higher level of resources required. The formal standards process has always placed "due process" and "openness" ahead of efficiency; it has catered to the least endowed person, company, or nation. In the future, formal standards groups will probably have to adopt similar methodologies to the consortia, even if participation becomes more difficult for individuals or small companies.

Consortia add value and are easy to form, so they will continue to be a factor in our industry. Unfortunately, the number of consortia is becoming so large that there is often considerable confusion. We don't know which standards are the best technical solutions, we can't judge the credibility of any particular standard or standards group, and we don't have a clue about how to deal with mutually exclusive standards. Vendors react to this by participating in all the groups and implementing everything, while users express their frustration by demanding the formation of yet another new consortium to "do it right." This means added cost and time for everybody. Even more disturbing is the tendency for consortia to compete with one another after their initial missions are completed and they move toward expanding their scope in order to stay in business. The most likely outcome of this competition, if allowed to continue, is a new level of proprietary systems. Customers would have to choose both their consortia and their vendors since the likelihood of interoperability problems would be high.

We need to efficiently take advantage of these groups by doing two things. First, we need to recognize that the formal processes are preferred at the national and international levels. One rationale for standardization is the elimination of "low value" product differentiation and its associated costs to vendor and user. Competition in standards at the results level is not of benefit to either side. Given the number of independent groups in the process, the only way to establish a final winner is for a top level process to "bless" one or a very few standards for any given function and/or to bless (accredit) organizations as being competent. This process is currently provided by the formal process through accredited standards developers, through ANSI (in the USA) and on to ISO, IEC, and ITU. The only alternatives to using this process are to endorse chaos or turn over the blessing process to the U.S. government. Chaos is not the answer, and the problems with the government are discussed below. The answer is that the formal standards process still represents the best method for coherency in IT standardization.

The second thing that needs to be done is to separate technical development from formal approval in the formal standardization system. This will take advantage of the good work being done while maintaining a system for establishing legitimacy and minimizing confusion. Changes in the standards process may be required; for example, giving international consortia non-voting membership in the international organizations. It is unlikely that consortia will disappear given our inclination to create and use them and their ability to exist independent of their members. It is therefore necessary to maximize the benefit that can be gained from the technical work gaining consensus in these other fora.

The Role of the U.S. Government

The U.S. government's role in the standardization process has been the subject of intense debate for a number of years. There is general recognition that government will continue regulatory oversight where health and safety are important. In other areas we hope to continue our successful history of minimal regulation and see telecommunications regulation diminish accordingly. Where regulation is necessary government should use the voluntary system to the extent feasible. The European Union's approach of establishing general requirements and referencing voluntary standards for technical detail could be a useful model for American implementation.

Beyond regulation, there are a number of roles government might play in information technology standards and conformity assessment. Government is both a large user and a developer of technology; its agencies have significant technical expertise and a substantial stake in the outcome of the process. Government should therefore continue to actively participate in the voluntary standards process on the same basis as other interested parties. This will ensure the widest possible input to and acceptance of the resulting standards.

Government can also play a greater funding role in standardization. The formal standards infrastructure is largely dependent on voluntary funding. ANSI manages the US infrastructure and pays the U.S.'s share of ISO and IEC costs. However, many companies and public sector entities that benefit from the standards process and participate in detailed technical standardization are not members of ANSI; they are freeloaders in the national and international systems. Government could help alleviate this problem through significantly greater dues payments, coverage of specific infrastructure items such as ISO and IEC membership dues, or hosting international meetings in the U.S. Government can also support specific process improvements through grants such as the recent ARPA grant for the National Standards System Network project. Finally, government could support R&D tax credits for standardization activities.

Government can also take actions in the area of conformity assessment. Where required, government can negotiate mutual recognition agreements so that industry can test products once and sell them everywhere. Government can also offer services such as accreditation of laboratories or recognition of private sector accreditation programs. These roles support industry by providing needed services based on industry requests.

Government can help the standardization process through participation, funding, and other support mechanisms. However, despite a steady diet of studies and hearings, the government's potential role in managing the process continues to draw the most attention. The information technology industry has been successful in standardization, so what added value could government bring to the management process?

One commonly heard reason for government management is to "represent the national interest." This sounds good—but how can anyone independently determine the "national interest" in technical work? The U.S. standards system allows all affected parties to represent their own interests. The sum of these interests can reasonably be considered to be the national interest. Government participants can represent the interests of their own agencies or a broader government constituency. Like participants from other organizations, each government employee brings to the process a mixture of personal technical beliefs, organizational interests, and concern for the overall success of standardization. Government participants do as well as others in properly managing their work, and appear to be under no illusions that they represent the technical interests of the general population.

Some people believe that the standardization process would be more effective and efficient under government management, but the arguments for this are not compelling. A major criticism of the formal standards process is the procedural overhead that sometimes seems designed to prevent accomplishments. A government-managed system would have even more stringent rules and greater delays. There may also be other constraints. Unrelated diplomatic and political considerations have affected government technical decisions in the past, and will presumably continue to do so in the future. The most recent example of this is the Clipper Chip controversy, in which the federal government, despite almost unanimous opposition, is pushing ahead with its new encryption system.

The government can't do a better job unless it establishes a mechanism to dictate solutions when the interested parties have difficulty reaching consensus. We don't need this kind of "improvement." The current system may seem chaotic, but it's designed for maximum sensitivity to the wishes of the participants. Because of this, vendors and users will accept a solution once it surfaces. Forcing solutions will eventually result in a private-sector advisory function to a governmental standards organization. Those who believe such an organization would always be responsive to vendors and users need look no further than the Clipper Chip controversy to realize that an advisory function provides the right to comment, not the right to decide. Our system is based on a neutral administration of the process, facilitating consensus decisions by the participants. (Or no decisions—a standard may be desirable but not achievable because the necessary consensus doesn't exist.)

Government could help unite the process by formally recognizing the existing private sector system. It could do so by granting a "Federal Charter" to ANSI to firmly establish a clear and consistent path for national and international recognition. This is commonly done in other countries. Such an agreement will require mutual responsibilities; in the vernacular, there may be "strings" attached. But reasonable dependencies would be a fair price to pay for the benefits gained from this new partnership. Some will oppose this partnership, feeling that any ties to government will irreparably damage the standards process. However, the standards world is changing and we are seeing those changes reflected first in information technology. Partnership will allow the U.S. private sector to continue to provide coherent and coordinated technical leadership at both the national and international levels and offer government the opportunity to take greater advantage of the system in lieu of internally generated standards and detailed technical regulations.

Users in Standardization

Another currently fashionable topic among standardizers is users and their role in standardization. The current IT standards focus is in large measure due to user demands at several levels. Some users want to participate in developing technical solutions or advocating specific products or technologies, and are already active in the process. However, most users want standards but don't care about the technical content. We frustrate them when we take forever to agree, or when we provide incompatible but apparently equally credible standards. Users should participate in the standardization process: even those who don't care about technical details can help define requirements, drive other participants toward completion, and buy standardized products. The latter is important because it tells the vendors that the desire for such products is real. As the GOSIP program has shown with remarkable clarity, there is a big difference between endorsing the principle of standards and using them.

Summary

In summary, information technology standardization can be characterized through the following points.

• The development process is largely driven by international standards.

• Consortia will continue, and the formal standards process needs to make changes to recognize their work and adopt some of their methodologies.

• Government can participate in the process, provide additional funding, and establish other support mechanisms. It can also minimize regulation, establish sensible testing requirements, and work for mutual recognition worldwide. Most importantly, it can help establish a coherent national system supporting the international system by formally recognizing the existing private sector system and encouraging everyone to use it.

• Users can participate in many ways, but the system will not really work until purchases are consistent with principles.

Do We Need a New Standards System?

L. John Rankine
Rankine Associates

When I was invited to present this position paper I gained the strong impression that I was expected to call for change in our current standards system and to suggest that it be restructured to meet our needs better. Let me rise to that challenge by proposing that we wipe the national slate clean by getting rid of the American National Standards Institute (ANSI). With ANSI out of the way, we can put in place the ideal standards system for the United States and then begin to set the international house in order. The question is, what system do we put in place?

Only a few years ago, the approach of having a National Standards Council analogous to the Standards Council of Canada was being talked about. While any country can always learn from and even adopt the methods of another, it does not necessarily follow that because it works well there it should be adopted here—if indeed, it works well there. Often it does not. Based on my own observations of the U.S. standards scene and the national character and culture of the United States, it would appear vital to have something along the following lines:

• A National Standards Institute (NSI) largely supported by private sector industry and organizations, with a Board of Directors that truly represents, in proper proportion to the support given and the work performed, the needs of U.S. industry, users, government, labor, and general interest groups. The fee structure would have to ensure that all who benefit bear their fair share of the costs. The NSI would provide the national coordination procedures under which voluntary consensus standards are written as well as the U.S. interface to the ISO and the IEC. In addition to a properly representative Board of Directors, it would have a balanced representative Executive Committee, Finance Committee, and Strategic Planning Committee. The foregoing would draw on advice from a General Advisory Council open to all NSI members and an International Advisory Council appointed by NSI to bring together the best available expertise in international affairs and strategy from whatever source.

• As needed (e.g., for information technology) there can also be created Industry Sector Councils, which would be open to all NSI members interested in a specific industry and would assist NSI in serving the needs of that industry.

• There should be a Standards Associations Council, open to the standards-writing associations, to promote unity of national and international purpose and advise the NSI accordingly. Associations providing key services such as secretariats would also participate.

• There should be a Government Advisory Council to advise and coordinate with the U.S. Government on key issues. This Council would draw upon the best expertise from all sectors as needed for the issue or issues at hand.

• The chairs of the all of the above should report directly to the NSI Board of Directors and advise the NSI Executive Committee of the Board of Directors as needed.

The underlying purpose of NSI would be to serve the national and international interests of the United States in the voluntary consensus standards-making process and to be officially recognized and supported as such by all participating U.S. interests.

Surely you will grant that this is a reasonable and politically correct proposal. (Note, for example, how NSI uses 75% of the letters in both NIST and ANSI.) The only thing wrong with my proposal is that we do not need it! All the ingredients it offers are already within the scope of the ANSI structure, with some fine tuning. The point I want to make is that if ANSI did not exist, we would most probably have to reinvent it.

At the international level, given the ubiquitous nature of today's information technology, we would probably not reinvent both the

ISO and IEC. They came into being at different times to meet different needs. But, if we were to do away with both, we most surely would end up creating something like an Organization for International Standards. Again, especially as far as information technology goes, there is no need to do this. We have already done it in the creation of the ISO/IEC Joint Technical Committee 1 for Information Technology.

I am sorry if I disappoint you by not calling for a re-structuring of the national and international standards system, but I am very skeptical about reinventing wheels when there is no clear-cut need to do so. Furthermore, one of the fundamental theorems of bureaucracy is that new organizations do not necessarily make old ones disappear: they merely make the pile higher and deeper, and this we definitely do not need. My first point therefore is that we get on with what we have. NIST, ANSI, ISO, IEC, CCITT, ASME, IEEE, ASTM, JTC1, T1, X3, etc., etc. are doing the job. By and large the standards we have needed have been produced, and they continue to be produced as new needs arise. This is not to claim that the present system is perfect. It never was and never will be, but rack it up against any other system in the world and you will find the United States to be away out in front in regard to leadership in information technology standardization.

Some of the More Common Complaints about the Current System

Having just admitted that our system is less than perfect, let me now turn to some of the most common complaints that we hear about it.

The system is too slow.

Given the protection offered by our antitrust laws and the need for the voluntary standards system to reconcile all affected and often opposing interests (users, manufacturers, government, academe), the system has by definition to be "slow." However, as a chairman of the key international committees dealing with information technology standards (ISO TC 97 and later ISO/IEC JTC1) for more than twenty years, I have been struck by the fact that those who most often complain about the slowness of the system are frequently among the first to complain when a sincere attempt is made to speed it up. Furthermore, these same people are often the cause of the delays. We should bear in mind that when opinions on an international standard do not differ widely it can be processed in less than a year domestically and internationally. Next time you hear the system is too slow I recommend that you look into the situation. You will probably find that the problem is with the people involved and not with the system.

The users are not sufficiently involved.

This is a subject that the OECD has taken under consideration over the past few years. In a study I performed for the OECD in 1992, my findings were:

1. Users exert considerable influence over information technology standards.

2. User needs are represented by direct participation in standards committees and also via user groups, the media, and manufacturers' understanding of user needs.

3. Government understanding and representation of user needs can often be distorted by political objectives as well as by the abuse of government procurement powers.

4. The larger and more sophisticated users have greater influence over standards than the smaller, less sophisticated users.

5. User participation is a vital and constructive element of developing truly useful information technology standards.

6. Negative participation by users, user groups, and consumer groups to combat and delay standards development and revision has been infrequent and has stemmed, in some cases, from lack of understanding of the standards process.

7. The IT standards process is increasingly complex, difficult to understand, and subject to a proliferation of organizations, all of which is costly to users and all other participants.

Given the above findings, my recommendations were as follows:

1. With rare exceptions, such as to acquire unique expertise, user participation in information technology standards development does not need to be specially funded by governments.

2. Standards education at managerial and executive levels in both the private and public sectors is needed to ensure higher quality participation in the standards process and reduce the proliferation of duplicate organizations and efforts. Universities and business schools have a major void to fill in this regard.

3. The role of governments and government departments and agencies in the IT standardization process should be to reflect their own needs as users, rather than to attempt to speak for the needs of non-governmental users.

4. Governments should refrain from using their procurement powers to achieve political and other objectives through IT standardization.

5. Computer networking and CD-ROM technologies should be exploited to make standards information more readily available to users and to facilitate user input.

6. Standards organizations at national, regional, and international levels need to continue their efforts to avoid overlap and duplication of efforts. The International Electrotechnical Commission (IEC) and the International Standards Organization (ISO) have set an example by combining their IT standardization to create the Joint Technical Committee 1 for Information Technology (JTC1).

7. The standards organizations at national, regional, and international levels need to educate the management and executive levels of the user community, both governmental and non-governmental, as to their existence and the value of their services in meeting user needs expeditiously.

Since the completion of this report in 1992, new developments have occurred in regard to putting the standards development, publication, and distribution process on-line, the Standards Project Automation effort at the Institute for Electrical and Electronics Engineers being one example. This should further enhance the user's ability to participate in the IT standards process.

In order to further examine the needs of users, the OECD has established a Group of Industrial Experts on IT Standardization, which held its first meeting in Paris in January 1994. This meeting brought together ten executives from several large industrial organizations; three computer manufacturers; four expert advisors; and three key executives of the OECD. While the OECD is not interested in entering the standards-making process, it is interested in the effects of standards on the economies of the 24 major industrial nations that constitute its membership. A special OECD concern is user needs for standards and whether or not these are adequately considered in the current standards structure. OECD findings generally result in policy recommendations that can be implemented by the member nations of the OECD in varying degrees.

The January 1994 meeting was a first attempt to put some form into a somewhat amorphous subject and to reach some tentative conclusions to be formalized into a report after a second meeting of the Group on October 18-19, 1994 in Paris. While a considerable amount of time was consumed at this first meeting in understanding the current standards system, certain ideas emerged. Among these is that the OECD is now seeking the views of the industrial sector before the fact rather than after the fact in formulating policy-related recommendations. Also of significance is that neither the industrial users nor the OECD staff see government control as an answer. Both understand that governments tend to look inward, whereas the issues before the Group require looking outward in order to derive international solutions. There is also no desire on the part of the user element of the Group to see standardization of product design, as this is viewed as counterproductive to innovation and creativity. The preference is for compatibility among hardware and software products achieved via standardized interfaces.

It appears at this stage that the main output of the Group will be to identify specific user needs, many on a very fundamental level, to be maintained and communicated to the standards community, quite probably on an on-line basis. There appears to be no desire at this stage to create new standards organizations, the view being that there are already too many, some of which are obsolescent in light of current technology and convergences as characterized by multimedia. My own contributions and recommendations to the Group are largely embodied in my 1992 report to the OECD entitled "The Role of Users in IT Standardization."

U.S. competitiveness is damaged by organizational disputes.

Distracting as some of the frictions between the standards-writing organizations in the United States may be, they are largely irrelevant to the issues of trade and competitiveness. To put it another way, if the standards-writing bodies of the United States were in total harmony, U.S. trade and competitiveness would be neither improved nor diminished. Furthermore, the apparent preoccupation of the U.S. government with restructuring the U.S. standards system, as evidenced by the NIST hearings in 1990 and again in 1993, is perceived by other nations as diminishing the credibility of the current U.S. interfaces with the international system. This is not in the national interest.

The prime national need in regard to the U.S. standards system at this stage is a much higher level of executive awareness and understanding within government and industry of the strategic significance of the standards process. If this were to come about it could solve many of the problems that currently plague the system. Among the solutions needed are proper funding of standardization efforts; resolution of petty differences between persons and organizations; better coordination of standards development and distribution; and, most important of all, much closer government and industry cooperation and coordination overseas.

The challenge to U.S. competitiveness in world markets is not going to be met by hand-wringing over imagined standards issues nor by changing standards structures. It has to be met by educational capability, innovation, product and service excellence, intelligent and direct involvement, and quality salesmanship in a world community that is going to be increasingly populated by a lot of people making the most of all of these qualities.

In other countries the standards bodies are government-run.

This is a common fallacy, especially in the case of IT standards development. In the key countries of the democratic and industrial world, industry is the backbone of participation in key standards-setting organizations such as ISO and IEC. For example, in the computer industry, Olivetti is a major factor in Italian representation; Siemens in German representation; Bull in French representation; ICL in U.K. representation; Fujitsu, Hitachi, and NEC in Japanese representation; Philips in Dutch representation; and DEC, UNISYS, NCR, and IBM in U.S. representation. Many standards bodies in other nations bristle at the suggestion that they are government-run. DIN (Germany), BSI (the United Kingdom), and AFNOR (France) are examples. Furthermore, in the case of the CCITT, U.S. participation is managed by the Department of State, whereas in the case of the other countries participation is by their PTTs, an increasing number of which are now in the private sector due to increasing liberalization and deregulation in the field of telecommunications.

The U.S. government doesn't play a strong enough role.

The U.S. government is definitely a key and valuable player in the standards arena. In IT standards development it has played a strong role, especially since the passage of the Brooks Bill. In addition to the then National Bureau of Standards (NBS), now NIST, the Department of State, Department of Defense, NTIA, NIOSH, OSHA, OTA, FCC, and others have been actively involved.

Like other governments, the U.S. government has been tempted from time to time to try to achieve political and non-technical objectives by forcing certain directions in standardization, often by use of its procurement power. For the most part, such attempts have failed to achieve their objectives or, even worse, have backfired.

I submit the following as examples of the role the U.S. government should play in the standards process so as to promote U.S. interests domestically and internationally:

1. The government should monitor the standards process for fairness and dangers to life and limb.

2. The government should participate in standards writing primarily as a user and should use voluntary consensus standards wherever possible.

3. The government should refrain from using and abusing its procurement powers to force political objectives via standards writing.

4. The government should have close liaison with the private sector, and together they should define which are the government spheres (e.g., GATT, EEC, EFTA), which are the private spheres (e.g., CEN/CENELEC, ISO, IEC, Pacific Area Standards Congress (PASC)), and which are jointly shared (e.g., CCITT).

5. The government should assist as called upon by the private sector, and the private sector should likewise help the government as needed, within their respective spheres.

6. The government should ensure that when a U.S. delegation is being dispatched to governmental discussions overseas to deal with issues crucial to a U.S. industry, the best available talent from the industry itself is embodied in the delegation. Industry association executives alone are not enough.

7. The government should cooperate with the private sector in timely recording, updating, and distribution of standards and standards-related information so that U.S. manufacturers are not caught unawares as to international market requirements.

8. The government should encourage programs that raise the level of education on standardization at managerial and executive levels in both the public and private sectors.

9. The government should cooperate with industry, each using their respective channels of authority, to propagate a broad international understanding of U.S. approaches to standards setting and to test methods and procedures.

10. The government should refrain from ill-conceived attempts to restructure or impose new structures on a system that has evolved over the years to meet U.S. needs. To do so, particularly at this time, could be detrimental to U.S. interests in world markets.

Change by Evolution Rather Than by Revolution

Although I do not recommend restructuring the standards system, certain market forces and technological advances will cause evolutionary changes. Given today's technology, the possibility of putting on-line, nationally and internationally, the entire process of proposing, developing, publishing, distributing, and updating standards is an enticing one. There are several immediately apparent benefits:

1. Standards could be developed more rapidly, thus overcoming the frequent criticism that the standards process is too slow, particularly in areas involving the faster-moving technologies.

2. The expense of standards making could be vastly reduced. Scarce and expert talent would not have to waste time and travel expense in attending meetings in distant and often expensive locations.

3. The standards process could be more accessible to users and other interest groups. Presumably, this would increase the utility of standards and make their adoption more widespread.

4. The costs of purchasing standards could be significantly reduced, again benefiting users.

5. By allowing immediate access to the latest version of a standard or the draft of a proposed standard, costly mistakes could be avoided and public safety enhanced.

6. The need for standards organizations could be reduced, together with disagreements among them, which are often viewed today as hindering the standardization process.

While for the most part the technology available is capable of handling the "start-to-finish" standards process, there are certain factors that have to be reckoned with. Some of these are as follows:

1. Many involved in the current system, especially those who are not computer literate, will resist the on-line development of standards. Some like to go to standards meetings. They will claim that "the personal touch" will be lost. Coffee break conversations, so often helpful in breaking deadlocks, will no longer be possible. Good faith understanding and agreement (or disagreement) will be lost.

2. While the process may become more open, it will also invite many to be involved who have little vested interest in the process, and this will create a "Tower of Babel" effect that could extend the development times involved.

3. Those who are not "computer literate" could complain that they are now being excluded and that, as a result, many vital views and arguments will not be heard.

4. Reliability will come into question. The international communication services most likely to be used do not necessarily certify that documents sent were ever received. Data transmission times may preclude "last minute" documents being distributed on a timely basis during working sessions on developing the standard.

5. Voting procedures may become more complex on legal and other administrative grounds. Is the vote coming in being made by the proper person or by someone masquerading as him or her?

6. System security will be challenged. Can a "hacker" disrupt and even ruin years of work? What happens if such work is inadvertently lost by an innocent error or oversight in the system? Who is accountable? What are the audit capabilities and legal implications?

At this stage, the following conclusions seem reasonable:

1. On-line handling of the complete standardization process (proposal, development, drafting, approval, publication, distribution, and updating) is going to happen sooner or later as a result of initiative and economic pressures.

2. A broad attempt to displace the current system is likely to flounder and set back progress several years.

3. Success is most likely to be achieved by tackling well-defined projects involving a few highly computer literate participants who are dedicated to demonstrating results.

4. An on-line system will not quickly displace existing institutions, but it will hasten the obsolescence of these institutions, particularly the standards development organizations.

5. Consortia in the high-tech field are most likely to produce successful results using on-line systems.

6. Newer media for distributing, accessing, and updating standards, such as CD-ROM, are likely to continue to play a key but increasingly ancillary role.

The Standards Project Automation (SPA) currently underway at the IEEE is a leadership effort that will give valuable insight and experience in the viability of on-line standards development. SPA is a key element of the National Standards Systems Network being promoted by an ANSI committee in conjunction with NIST. This work comprises input from over eighty organizations, among whom are the leading standards-developing organizations and many large companies interested in the development and distribution of standards and standards information. All of this is an excellent example of a coordinated and cooperative effort to support the work of the private sector and government.

Avoid Hasty Adoption of International Management Systems

Traditionally the national and international standards organizations have been dedicated to the task of reaching international consensus on standards. Over the past several years, however, there has been a distinct trend towards defining management systems. This trend ushers in a whole new series of considerations.

There is little doubt of the sincerity of the International Standards Organization (ISO) in bringing about its series of international standards for quality management, commonly known as ISO 9000. Nor is there doubt that some suppliers of products and services have learned better ways of managing their quality systems as a result of implementing ISO 9000. The doubts about ISO 9000 arise from a lack of country-to-country acceptance, questionable implementation practices, and the fact that it is based on what some view as an obsolete quality-management philosophyæit is a system dealing with process rather than with product.

A bureaucratic burden arises from the strong impression that suppliers to the European Economic Community of nations will not have their products or services accepted unless they can demonstrate that they conform to ISO 9000. This has resulted in a rush to get certified under ISO 9000 and the emergence of a whole new cadre of certifiers who vary widely in capability, experience, and ethical practices. Reputable certifiers can do a thorough and impartial job. Others are less than thorough, to the point that even some of the key players in the development of ISO 9000 are concerned. For example, a certifier may ask the question, "Do you follow this ISO 9000 requirement?" The answer "No, we don't" may be quickly followed by the certifier asking, "But of course you will, won't you?" An affirmative answer may be enough to ensure certification under ISO 9000, especially in view of the fact that the certifier is being paid by the supplier. The top executive of a large manufacturer's organization has confided that their "particular problem is the uneven application of quality management standards, country by country, and indeed firm by firm, which puts the party in the most rigorous application at a cost and competitive disadvantage." Another aspect of the bureaucratic burden being imposed is that certification under ISO 9000 in one country does not mean acceptance under ISO 9000 in another, even within the community of EEC nations. Many are plunging into ISO 9000 with no knowledge of this, and those who discover it are frequently told the problem is being fixed. "By whom and by when?" is the question. Nations frequently guard their standards and industrial practices jealously for reasons of trade, regulatory requirements, and other vested interests.

The cost of conformance to the ISO 9000 quality management system is a crucial and often crippling issue. Even the larger multinationals, many well-known for their quality products and practices, can incur initial costs of over a hundred million dollars. At the other end of the scale, a small and highly innovative supplier can be put out of business by being faced by a hundred thousand dollar cost, his only option being to forego acceptance under ISO 9000 and suffer the consequent loss of market. This may drive some of the most innovative, high-quality suppliers out of business. An attendant issue in ISO 9000 inspection is the protection of intellectual property rights. Divulging highly valuable trade practices and secrets to inspectors in the course of ISO 9000 certification may, if the information becomes known by competitors, offset any benefits to be obtained.

A paradox of the ISO 9000 situation is that, while many suppliers are aware of many of the concerns being expressed here, they are nonetheless rushing to get through the ISO 9000 door so as to avoid market losses. The small companies are often driven by their relationships as suppliers to the large ones. An executive of a large

European advanced technology company has also commented to me that ISO 9000 provides a crutch to the mediocre manager of quality in an organization. If ever accused of having a poor quality program, the manager in charge is in a stronger position if he can state that his operation is qualified under ISO 9000. Accordingly, ISO 9000 is being driven by such thinking and by standards bodies and inspection authorities who see it as a money maker. The other drivers are the industrial companies who, as one executive put it, see it as "an added cost of doing business which amounts to paying protection money to avoid loss of market."

The overriding questions about ISO 9000 are threefold: First, will it bring about better products and services? Second, will it foster innovation and creativity? Thirdly, will the benefits ever offset the costs? As it stands, the answers to those questions are largely "no" because the ISO 9000 quality management system is itself a system too often lacking in management quality. Unless that problem is solved soon, the key results of ISO 9000 will be primarily added costs of doing business for suppliers and higher prices for consumers.

What has been said above in regard to ISO 9000 applies also to the current quest for a similar standardized management system for environmental issues. The problem in all of this begins not with the actual work in ISO, but with the adoption of the results by governments and others who demand adherence to the management system standards by suppliers. Many suppliers, particularly in the IT industry, may well have quality management and environmental control systems superior to those being adopted as the international standard. Indeed, some may be national prize winners in this regard. Nonetheless, they have to go to considerable expense to adjust to what may be in many cases inferior management systems if they wish to stay in business.

Summary and Conclusions

Restructuring the national and international system for the development of IT standards will accomplish little other than laying new structures over existing ones and involving more people, many of whom will have little or no knowledge of the real world of standardization. The frictions that have plagued the standards system in the past have been largely a function of people and their personalities. The key players now involved with the system from government, industry, users, and the standards-writing organizations nationally and internationally are, for the most part, a new breed much more dedicated to making the system work. In the final essence, this is perhaps the most important consideration of all, because good people will make a bad system work and a perfect system will fail with the wrong people calling the shots.

The changes that are required in the system will occur on an evolutionary basis. If the standards bodies and standards-writing organizations do not meet the challenges facing them, they will become irrelevant and will be replaced by consortia and on-line standards development systems. If manufacturers choose not to be involved or embark on wrong directions, they will pay the penalty in the marketplace. Unfortunately, if the government decides to use standards to achieve political ends or dictate technological options by abuse of procurement powers or any other means, it will not go out of business, but everybody will suffer. This makes the government's behavior in the national and international standards arena especially important. If its participation is dedicated to contributing its vast experience as a user of IT and to ensuring fairness in the system worldwide, it will further the development of the information infrastructure.

In conclusion, I would just mention a luncheon conversation I had in Europe last year with the Director General of one of the world's most prestigious national standards bodies. He said, "The U.S. is an unmatched force in international standardization. The power resident in your unique structure of ANSI, ASME, ASTM, IEEE, and the many, many other standards organizations you have is unmatchable and unstoppable, especially when it is backed up by your government. You so clearly have the leadership, and the standards world depends on it."

Defining the U.S. Telecommunications Network of the Future

Arthur K. Reilly
Committee T1

Open, voluntary, consensus-based standards will be critical to achieving efficient access to and transport of information within the National Information Infrastructure (NII) [1]. Such standards can provide the minimum requirements necessary for interoperability while promoting innovation (new services and capabilities) and reducing costs (multiple vendors, multiple service providers). Open, voluntary, consensus-based standards have broad industry acceptance, are robust and forward-looking, and are widely implemented.

Extensive use of future telecommunications and information services will depend upon the evolution, extension, and enhancement of the U.S. national telecommunications "network of networks" to transport information. The promise of the convergence and/or merger of the communications, computer, entertainment, and information industries necessitates interface standards that provide both the flexibility for innovation within each industry and interconnection/interworking between industries [2, 3].

Since 1984, Committee T1–Telecommunications has developed telecommunications network standards within the United States. This paper describes:

- Committee T1's efforts to improve the quality and timeliness of T1 standards products to meet user needs while working with other organizations nationally, regionally and globally
- Committee T1's relationship with government

• Conclusions/recommendations to continue quality efforts, create a partnership between private-sector standards bodies and government, and increase user and industry awareness of the importance of the private-sector standards process.

Origins and Role of Committee T1

In the United States prior to 1984, the Bell System was the de facto U.S. telecommunications standards developer. The Bell System, which then provided service to approximately 85 percent of the subscribers in the United States, described the interface specifications necessary for interconnection in various technical publications and compatibility bulletins.

As the Bell System breakup approached, segments of the industry recognized that the previous de facto standards process was no longer appropriate or even practical in the United States. In August 1983, the Exchange Carriers Standards Association (ECSA—in 1993 renamed the Alliance for Telecommunications Industry Solutions[1]) was formed as a non-profit organization. One of the first acts of ECSA was to propose the formation of a consensus-based industry committee to develop telecommunications network interconnection standards.

Committee T1–Telecommunications was formed on February 2, 1984. Its mission was to develop standards and technical reports related to U.S. telecommunications network interfaces and to develop positions on related subjects under consideration in international standards bodies. Four membership interest groups were established: Users/General Interest, Manufacturers, Interexchange Carriers, and Exchange Carriers. The industry accepted the ECSA offer to sponsor the committee, and the committee initiated efforts to gain American National Standards Institute (ANSI) accreditation. ANSI accreditation was received in October 1984.

One of Committee T1's initial priorities was to provide technical specifications needed to keep the existing set of U.S. telephone technologies and services working. A more forward-looking priority was to ensure that the U.S. "network of networks" could grow to introduce new telecommunications technologies and services. The committee could not focus on just one technology or capability but had to recognize the need for interworking many technologies and capabilities. Over the years, Committee T1's objectives and results have become global in scope [4, 5] and now cover development of standards and technical reports that apply to:

• Network Interfaces (analog [4 kHz] and digital [56 kb/s to 10 Gb/s])

• Services, Architecture, and Signaling

• Digital Hierarchy and Synchronization

• Performance

• Systems Engineering, Standards Planning, and Program Management

• Environmental Considerations

• Signal Processing

• Internetwork Operations, Administration, Maintenance, and Provisioning

In 1992, Committee T1 had approved its 100th Standard or Technical Report. By the end of 1994, Committee T1 is expected to have approved its 200th Standard or Technical Report. The increased rate of standards development is, of course, due to many factors, including the increased pace of technological progress. However, this progress in the face of general industry downsizing was possible only through continuous attention to quality and process improvements, and the hard work and dedication of Committee T1's approximately 1200 engineers and scientists. There are T1 standards meetings almost every week somewhere in North America.

"Standards are too slow. Standards have too many options. / Standards are not responsive to market needs." This refrain is often heard or read throughout the conglomerate information/communications/computer/entertainment industry. It is particularly unfortunate that these statements are applied as though they are universal constants. Conventional wisdom makes no distinctions regarding standards organization, industry segment, specific technical topic, or geographical extent. The unconditional form of the statements suggests that even time may not be a factor. But the reality of standards, certainly in the area of telecommunications network standards, contrasts sharply with negative generalizations regarding them.

The importance of telecommunications standards to the industry, the United States, and the global economy is all around us. The Clinton Administration's "National Information Infrastructure—Agenda for Action," NAFTA [6, 7], and GATT [8] all cite the importance of telecommunications standards and promote their development and use to facilitate markets, economic growth, and an improved quality of life.

While this theme is trumpeted loudly in the national discourse on the NII, one fundamental question remains: "What is the NII?" Today, we still do not know except in the broadest of terms. The NII of the year 2000, however, will most likely depend upon a national telecommunications "network of networks" whose technical standards will have been developed by the end of 1995.

Quick development of standards does not portend a limited NII with only a few telecommunications network technologies or capabilities. Committee T1 does not have an unrealistic crash program to develop all the needed standards in the next 18 months. Innovation and new capabilities will not cease in 1995 once these standards have been completed.

Rather, Committee T1's work program will continue to focus its resources on the key telecommunications network technologies that will provide the roadbed for the "Information Superhighway." These include:

• Digital Access Technologies—Narrowband ISDN, Broadband ISDN/Asynchronous Transfer Mode (ATM), Asymmetrical Digital Subscriber Lines (ADSL), Frame Relay, and associated network and signaling capabilities

• Multimedia Capabilities

• Synchronous Optical NETwork (SONET)

• Personal Communications—wireless access and network capabilities to provide personal mobility

• Intelligent Network

• Common Channel Signaling (Signaling System #7 (SS7))

• Network Survivability

• Network Management

A broad range of Committee T1 Standards and Technical Reports (or ITU Recommendations driven by U.S. contributions originating in T1) exists in all these areas. Furthermore, the Committee recognizes the importance of interoperability. Current Committee T1 work focuses on reducing options in the individual base standards. It also addresses interworking between the multiplicity of past and present standardized technologies and capabilities.

Quality Standards Development in a Rapidly Changing Industry

The nature of the telecommunications industry is dynamic. Change and transitions are constant. Thus, at any point in time new technologies and additional capabilities will always be considered for standardization. Independent of the stage of standards development, Committee T1 realizes that industry needs for timely standards drive the standards process.

Committee T1 and the standards process in general are continually being improved. Certainly, Committee T1 has viewed the "quality process" as a journey without end. A Standing Committee on Standards Process Management works to identify and address quality issues. Committee T1's consensus-based standards process does not limit industry's or T1 participants' ability to develop timely, high-quality standards. Standards leaders and participants must, however, always be attentive not to limit themselves by imposing restrictions that the process does not require. T1 has made significant progress in focusing its technical efforts to target present and future industry needs, and in streamlining operations in such areas as standards development and liaison, balloting, electronic document handling, and publication. Is the job done? Certainly not. But Committee T1's standards process is neither slow nor unresponsive to market needs. Open, deliberate, fair to all regardless of size, consensus-based, and user-oriented, yes.

Committee T1's Quality Improvement Program includes an annual T1 Leadership Workshop where the T1 Advisory Group (T1AG) steps back and analyzes the T1 process and operations. It also includes creation of a biannual Five-Year Strategic Plan. The Leadership Workshop, with its brainstorming format, provides a creative atmosphere and gives life to some of the best and most productive T1 initiatives. The Five-Year Strategic Plan provides a clear direction as to the issues and the priorities within Committee T1. An important part of this plan is an Implementation Plan that identifies areas for effort, specific actions to be undertaken, and the Committee T1 entity that is responsible for pursuing the action. Periodic reviews of progress on Strategic Plan items is part of the T1 Program. A 1995 Committee T1 Strategic Plan is now under development.

As noted already, the production of Committee T1 Standards and Technical Reports has increased significantly. To meet industry requirements of timeliness, high-quality, and interoperability, T1 resources must be utilized efficiently. Examples of specific actions taken to improve this portion of the T1 process include establishment of Technical Focus Areas, an electronic Bulletin Board System (T1BBS), and T1 Training Programs.

Committee T1 has 140 individual projects approved and active. However, the eight "Technical Focus" areas previously highlighted have been specifically identified by Committee T1 as critical to the future U.S. "network of networks" and are certain to be important elements of the National Information Infrastructure. With the exception of Network Survivability and SS7 Interconnection, these topics have also been identified as areas of continuing high mutual interest by T1 and its counterparts in Australia, Canada, Europe, Korea, and Japan. This Global Standards Collaboration (GSC) process, which Committee T1 initiated, provides a framework for global telecommunications network standards coordination.

In each of the eight technical focus areas, Committee T1 has given special attention to building liaisons with other organizations, especially user groups. T1 representatives working with colleagues in other U.S. standards bodies and industry forums have identified the flow of the telecommunications process referred to as the "Standards Life Cycle." This flow (shown in Figure 1 and described in Table 1) outlines the stages of developing and evolving standardized products.

If standards development is to be effective and if standards are to be implemented, development can not be viewed as an isolated process. Standards bodies must communicate with other interested parties in the process. Users Groups with whom Committee T1 has close liaison include the North American ISDN Users

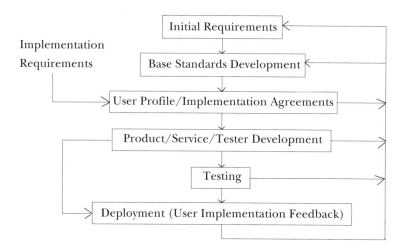

Figure 1 The Standards Life Cycle.

Table 1 Stages of the Standards Life Cycle

The standards life-cycle process is cyclic and so could theoretically begin at any stage. In general, a flow from the top to the bottom in Figure 1, with feedback as shown, may provide the most orderly introduction of a service or technology interface.

Stage 1: An initial set of requirements. Inputs from users, manufacturers, or service providers that can provide a initial, perhaps high-level, basis for defining the service or technology interface.

Stage 2: Base standards. A minimum set of requirements for interworking and interoperability that provides an opportunity for individual manufacturers and service providers to compete on price, performance, and additional features to attract and satisfy users. This standards stage may involve multiple standards development organizations within the United States (e.g., T1, TIA, IEEE, X3) and harmonization with other standards bodies around the world.

Stage 3: User profile and implementation agreement development. Standards may be forward-looking and provide a longer-term target to determine the features of a specific technology or service interface. Sometimes it is beneficial to identify how a new technology or service interface standard can be used with other standards in order to provide an application that meets a user's need. In addition, with new technologies or services it may be difficult to provide all capabilities immediately.

Stages 4, 5 and 6: Development, Testing and Deployment. Implementation agreements between a group of vendors, service providers, and users may provide a sufficiently large implementation of the technology or service for it to be tested and deployed. In this way, valuable experience and feedback can be gained to be provided back to iterations of other stages.

Forum, the ATM Forum, the Frame Relay Forum, the Multimedia Communications Forum, the Personal Communications Industry Association (PCIA, formerly Telocator), the Internet Engineering Task Force, the Network Management Forum, the Network Reliability Council (and the Network Reliability Steering Committee), and the Industry Numbering Committee (INC). Each of these groups is focusing on a specific topic and promoting the use of that technology or issue based on standards [9–16]. Committee T1 is responsible for standards that integrate these standards with other emerging technologies and service capabilities. To benefit the industry, Committee T1 works with these individual groups to identify their standardization needs and developing a program to respond to them. These efforts are consistent with Committee T1's Vision Statement, which goes beyond developing standards documents and addresses quality, implementation, and standards harmonization.

Committee T1 has close ties to many other standards development organizations in the United States and around the world. We have already mentioned the Global Standards Collaboration process. In the United States, T1 and its Technical Subcommittees also work very closely with other ANSI-accredited standards organizations such as the Telecommunications Industry Association (TIA), the Institute of Electrical and Electronics Engineers (IEEE), and Committee X3. Examples of these close relationships can be seen in the T1/TIA Joint Technical Committee on Wireless Access, the Statement of Cooperation between Committee T1 and TIA's Mobile and Personal Communications Division, and a PCS Standards Program Management Plan developed jointly by T1, TIA, the IEEE, and PCIA.

Committee T1 believes that Electronic Data Handling (EDH) is critical to the future success of standardization. EDH can facilitate both standards development and standards dissemination. The T1 Bulletin Board System (T1BBS) has dialup access over the public telephone network (without access restrictions) and Internet Telnet access. In addition, File Transfer Protocol (FTP) and a self-subscribing e-mail mailing list (Majordomo) facilitate the availability of T1BBS information and the dissemination of topic group electronic contributions/messages to anyone interested. Multiple processors and backup systems ensure near continuous access to users for e-mail and file uploading and downloading. T1BBS is accessed by people and organizations around the world. Internet "Gopher" capabilities for T1BBS are currently under study.

The EDH effort has included a program and timetable to stimulate utilization of the system. To encourage progress in this area, an award is presented at each Committee T1 meeting to the individual, T1 group, or company that has done the most to promote T1 EDH. For example, one PCS working group is meeting monthly and is using T1BBS extensively to advance their work. They already have more than 90% of their contributions distributed electronically prior to the meetings.

T1 holds an annual T1 Leadership Training Workshop for leaders at all levels of the organization. The workshop reviews T1 principles, procedures, and legal issues. Included in the workshop are case studies and skits to assist the learning experience and provide practical techniques for expediting consensus building and standards development.

EDH Training Seminars have been held at meetings of Committee T1 and its Technical Subcommittees (TSCs). In addition, the position of Information Director (to answer questions and conduct special programs) has been established for Committee T1, T1AG, and each of the individual TSCs.

Committee T1 is concluding a very successful one-year trial of a simultaneous T1 and TSC letter ballot process, which is used in addition to the sequential process used previously. The trial gave each TSC Chairman the option of using this process to approve T1 Standards and Technical Reports. The simultaneous process was chosen for approximately one-half of the documents balloted. The simultaneous standards approval process cut the standards development period by three to six months.

ANSI publishes Committee T1 Standards, and ATIS (the T1 Secretariat and sponsor) publishes Committee T1 Technical Reports. Until 1993, the ANSI Board of Standards Review had to approve T1 Standards (based on process rather than technical content) before ANSI initiated publication. The quality of and the strong consensus supporting T1's documents has led to ANSI approving all T1 documents. Based on this experience, ANSI agreed in 1993 to initiate T1's publication process upon initial receipt of a draft T1 standard. This system saves about one to two months in the standards publication process. ATIS now publishes Committee T1 Technical Reports in-house using equipment that produces a high-quality bound report with print-quality covers. This publication process is very quick and flexible; when special industry needs have required it, this process has been used to publish Technical Reports within one day.

Committee T1 Relationship to Government

Committee T1 is a private-sector standards organization. This contrasts with telecommunications network standards processes in some other parts of the world, where all or part of the standards work program is funded and directed by government. In many nations the global trend toward privatization has gained significant momentum. The U.S. standards process serves as a successful model that other nations are emulating. The telecommunications industry, characterized in the United States by regulation and an international treaty between nations, has been served well by a telecommunications network standards process that involves a partnership between Committee T1 and the U.S. government. This partnership provides flexible industry dynamics to meet user needs that are consistent with the "statutory" U.S. government roles.

A number of federal agencies and departments are valued, proactive members of Committee T1 and its Technical Subcommittees. These government organizations represent users and implementers of standards in the private-sector. Their standards participation is subject to the same obligations and privileges that apply to all other members of the subcommittees.

International telecommunications network standards are developed in the International Telecommunication Union (ITU) [17], a specialized agency of the United Nations that has been established as a treaty organization. By virtue of this treaty status, the U.S. Department of State administers the U.S. ITU membership. However, the State Department depends heavily on the technical expertise of the American private sector in establishing its delegation. In this way, Committee T1 has served as the primary developer of technical contributions approved by the State Department process and destined for the ITU. Each year 500 to 1,000 such contributions are originated in Committee T1. Committee T1 representatives also play active roles in the U.S. National Committee and the U.S. delegation to the ITU Telecommunication Standardization Advisory Group.

While the U.S. telecommunications industry is regulated, the U.S. telecommunications network standards process in Committee T1 is not. Individual Committee T1 standards participants contribute to the process as they feel is appropriate. The T1 standards process focuses on the technical aspects of contributions. The open, consensus-based process leads to a technical solution that meets consumer and industry needs without direct regulation.

Committee T1 has provided inputs to organizations such as the FCC in response to specific requests, as well as at T1's initiation. Because of the special role of regulators and the impact of their decisions on the industry, special care is taken by Committee T1 in such situations. Committee T1 is a technical organization and as such does not advocate policy positions.

Committee T1's partnership with government is evident in the case of several current topics. One area specifically identified as important to the NII is Network Reliability. Committee T1 standards and related work were identified as "Best Practices" and Recommendations in "A Report to the Nation" issued by the FCC's Network Reliability Council (NRC) June 1993. Currently, Committee T1 is working closely with the Network Reliability Steering Committee. A "Technical Report on Analysis of FCC-Reportable Service Outage Data," which began with the August 1993 identification of the need for such an effort, has an expected publication date of August 1994.

Personal communications is another area receiving a great deal of attention. The Committee T1 PCS framework Technical Reports and Network Architecture/Services Description standards provide the industry with the necessary information for planning and implementing these services. Additional technical reports and standards providing further details and capabilities are complete or in progress to meet the next stages of industry needs.

Technical specifications of candidate PCS air interfaces are being developed in collaboration with the Telecommunications Industry Association (TIA). Initial air interface standards are expected to be approved beginning in the fourth quarter of 1994, which is also the current FCC schedule for beginning the 2-GHz PCS spectrum auction process. Additional signaling standards beyond the base PCS capability will follow. Periodic reports have been provided to the FCC staff on PCS standards progress, issues, and work program schedule.

Global and regional trade discussions have highlighted the important role of standards in international commerce. This, combined with the trend toward privatization within telecommunications networks, has led U.S. government agencies to request assistance from representatives from Committee T1 to share their private-sector standards processes and experiences with others around the world.

Committee T1 representatives have led technical efforts within the Organization of American States' (OAS) Commission on InterAmerican Telecommunications (CITEL) and its Permanent Consultative Committee 1 (PCC1) to coordinate standards throughout the Americas. Committee T1 also hosted the first Americas Telecommunications Standards Symposium in April 1992. Committee T1 and TIA are among the U.S. charter members of the Canada/Mexico/U.S. private-sector initiated Consultative Committee on Telecommunications (CCT). TIA provides the U.S. Secretariat for this group, which was established to work toward compliance with the "Standards-Related Measures" provisions of the North American Free Trade Agreement (NAFTA). A T1 representative is the U.S. facilitator of the CCT working group on Service Providers/Telecommunications Networks, and an advisor to U.S. Government delegates to NAFTA's Telecommunications Standards Subcommittee.

Conclusion and Recommendations

Committee T1 believes that voluntary, consensus-based telecommunications network standards, developed in a private-sector process with the principles of openness, fairness, balance, and due process, have served the United States well, and should be endorsed and promoted. This process can provide timely, high-quality, collaborative standards within the United States and strong American technical leadership and contributions abroad. Such a process can quickly identify and respond to changes needed to improve the process and to address user and industry needs.

The convergence of the dynamic telecommunications, computer, information, and entertainment industries will continue to require a standards process that stimulates competition and innovation. This is being achieved through a voluntary industry standards-development process. The process provides the minimum technical requirements to be forward-looking, and also provides a consensus view on the future directions of a technology or capability. All of these characteristics are essential to meet user needs in technology's dynamic, multi-industry environment.

The Committee T1–U.S. Government partnership has been and continues to be exemplary. Continued technical participation by various government agencies is essential for Committee T1 to ensure that its special user needs are considered in the standards development process in general, and that its skills in such areas as timing and synchronization (NIST), performance assessment (e.g., of ATM and video (NTIA/ITS) [18]), and network reliability (DISA and NCS) are available to the standards process.

The relationship between Committee T1 and the U.S. government in its roles as regulator and trade advocate has been a partnership that has permitted each to carry out its individual responsibilities and complement the other. The success of this partnership can be attributed to Committee T1's broad vision of its role as well as government's willingness to recognize the technical and leadership strength of the private sector.

Standards bodies must continue their broad vision, and government must continue to recognize the contributions of standards bodies, in order for this partnership to continue to benefit users and industry. In addition, it is recommended that public and private sectors work to increase user and industry awareness of the standards bodies, their processes, and the essential contributions they make to users, from the individual to the global network. Without clear and consistent recognition of the importance of these efforts, the resources necessary for base standards development may not be available.

The success and progress that Committee T1 has achieved are due to the contributions of the approximately 1,200 individual participants, the innovative technical leaders at all levels of T1's Technical Subcommittees, and the T1 Secretariat (ATIS). T1's strength has been and continues to be world-class technical expertise, exemplary dedication and hard work, and commitment to the Committee T1 principles outlined in this paper.

Notes

[1] In October 1993, ECSA broadened its membership eligibility to include, in addition to exchange carriers, all telecommunications service providers with a plant investment in transport and/or switching equipment. This adds interexchange carriers, cellular providers, CATV companies, as well as other alternate access service providers to the membership of the newly-named Alliance for Telecommunications Industry Solutions (ATIS).

[2] The Telecommunications Industry Association (TIA) is an ANSI-accredited standards development organization that issues standards in the telecommunications field. TIA was created from the 1988 merger of the Information and Telecommunications Technologies Group of the Electronic Industry Association (EIA) and the United States Telecommunications Suppliers Association. Since TIA's telecommunications standards-writing activities originally started with EIA, TIA now has over 50 years of experience in these standards efforts. Whereas Committee T1 focuses on network standards and interface standards, TIA focuses on equipment and systems standards that work with those Committee T1 standards. TIA organizes its standards-writing activities to support its four main Divisions: Fiber Optics, User Premises Equipment, Mobile and Personal Communications, and Network Equipment. In these four Divisions of TIA, approximately 70 Engineering Committees and Subcommittees are staffed by industry subject-matter experts and create these TIA voluntary industry standards.

References

[1] National Information Infrastructure: Agenda for Action, Clinton Administration, September 1993.

[2] R. Amy, "Standard By Consensus," *IEEE Communications*, January 1994, pp. 52–55.

[3] W. Bailey, "Cable Television Architecture of the Future," IEEE-USA Information Policy Forum, May 1993.

[4] A. Reilly, "A U.S. Perspective on Standards Development," *IEEE Communications*, January 1994, pp. 30–36.

[5] G. Peterson and C. Dvorak, "Global Standards," *IEEE Communications*, January 1994, pp. 68–70.

[6] North American Free Trade Agreement, Chapter Nine: "Standards-Related Measures," October 1992.

[7] North American Free Trade Agreement, Chapter Thirteen: "Telecommunications," October 1992.

[8] Final Act Embodying the Results of the Uruguay Round of Multilateral Trade Negotiations (General Agreement on Tariffs and Trade—GATT), December 15, 1993.

[9] F. Sammartino, "A Year in Review 1992," ATM Forum Annual Report, March 1993.

[10] F. Sammartino, "The ATM Forum," Presentation at Committee T1 Annual Meeting, February 1993.

[11] R. Kemper, "The Multimedia Communications Forum," Presentation at Committee T1 Meeting, November 1993.

[12] J. Warner, "Network Management Forum," Presentation at Committee T1 Meeting, November 1993.

[13] D. Stokesbury, "The North American ISDN Users' Forum," Presentation at Committee T1 Meeting, June 1992.

[14] S. Wakid and K. Roberts, "North American Agreements on ISDN," *IEEE Communications*, August 1992, pp. 42–47.

[15] FCC Network Reliability Council, "Report to the Nation," June 1993.

[16] Network Reliability Steering Committee, "Annual Report," September 1994.

[17] T. Irmer, "Shaping Future Telecommunications: The Challenge of Global Standardization," *IEEE Communications*, January 1994, pp. 20–28.

[18] N. Seitz, S. Wolf, S. Voran, and R. Bloomfield, "User-Oriented Measures of Telecommunications Quality," *IEEE Communications*, January 1994, pp. 56–66.

Today's Cooperative Competitive Standards Environment and the Internet Standards-Making Model

Anthony M. Rutkowski
Internet Society

Today's Standards-Making Architecture

The architecture of standards-making organizations in the tele-communication and information fields has undergone fundamental change over the past decade. The old architecture was simple and well-bounded around a handful of bodies with explicit international, regional, national, and subject matter jurisdictions. These standards-making bodies were virtually sovereign, following slow, deliberate, time-honored processes that had remained essentially unchanged during the 130 years since the first multilateral telecom standards conference, and they engaged legions of standards professionals whose careers often began and ended in a single committee.

Over the past ten years, that old architecture has been fundamentally altered. Constellations of new bodies now exist with diverse new constituencies and boundaries, and all are competing in a global standards marketplace. Even the form of these new bodies differs dramatically from traditional organizations. Their range includes: (1) industry aggregations around a vendor specification, (2) ad hoc global initiatives around a specific technology, (3) national or regional bodies created to bring about a competitive marketplace, and (4) global hyperdynamic developmental and technology transfer "engines" like the Internet Engineering Task Force. Meanwhile, the traditional bodies struggle to evolve within a standards marketplace that finds their products largely unacceptable, yet still run processes that incur collective costs of tens of millions of dollars per year.

This transition hasn't been simple or easy. The notion of competition in standards making—like competition in a rigid monopoly provisioning environment or socialist economy—is not accomplished without considerable angst and difficult accommodation by those relinquishing power centers and jobs.[1]

Why Is This Rapid Transition Occuring?

The reasons for the transition fall into several categories:

• Moore's Law: Electronic technologies are changing dramatically on an average of every two years. Furthermore, in the highly dynamic environment of the Internet, fundamental rates of change are measured in months (Rutkowski's Law).

• Most telecommunication and information markets are very competitive. The marketplace, not institutions and government, decides winners and losers. A good current example is Open Systems Interconnection (OSI). The publisher of *Communications Week International,* at a 1993 industry forum of CEOs, chided European Union leaders about "effectively killing advanced data networks in Europe through single-minded pursuit of OSI solutions."[2]

• Most of the information infrastructure has passed from being a public good to being a private commodity. Millions of individuals and organizations now own and design a collective national and global infrastructure. The Interop trade shows, now the largest industry events in the world, are a manifestation of this transition. They are also an example of a new kind of industry-based institution that implements interoperable solutions far more effectively than government mandates.

• An increasingly global competitive environment effectively precludes solutions favoring a particular country or market segment. Attempts by governments to mandate specific directions that are at odds with the global marketplace will likely only disadvantage that nation or market by limiting both the quality and performance of products and services available to users and the scale of the market available to vendors.

- The requisite manner in which standards are developed, promulgated, and implemented for computer network environments is fundamentally different from hardware-oriented fields. Although not quantifiable, the development of computer software appears to require a rather different "culture"—a handy reference that captures the kinds of individuals, institutions, and processes necessary for success in this environment.

- Time-to-market has become the single most compelling factor for both service providers and product vendors. This concern is a byproduct of rapid technology change, a robust competitive marketplace, and a globally competitive environment. Time-to-market encompasses not only rapid development of standards, but also implementability and meeting real user needs.

- The last twenty years have been an expensive collective learning experience about "bottom up" versus "top down" initiatives. Top down initiatives are characterized by grand telecommunication and information infrastructure standards programs begun through traditional international organizations. In these organizations, long-term concepts and plans are developed after years of deliberation and then pursued and implemented at regional, national, and local levels. This process can sometimes take decades. Meanwhile, the real revolutions in the telecommunication and information fields have occurred from the bottom up. Personal computers and workstations, local area networks, cost-oriented leased lines, routers, network operating systems, the Internet, and other capabilities have empowered individuals and organizations to develop their own infrastructures and control their own information destiny.

These factors have produced a very different standards-making architecture. Today, direct government involvement in picking winners and losers is likely to be the kiss of death for the unlucky recipient. With few exceptions, every direct governmental intrusion into the standards marketplace over the past decade has had major adverse consequences. On the other hand, minimal government involvement, designed primarily to foster research, collaboration, and technology transfer among developers and rapid dissemination of standards, appears to work well.

Stature of Standards-Making Organizations

Recently, many attempts have been made to aggrandize some organizations and their products by referring to them as *de jure*. This term is usually used in contrast with other organizations and their products that they characterize as *de facto*. It is not clear how this *de jure* versus *de facto* notion was started, but the terms have fairly specific meanings in law that are wholly inapplicable to our voluntary systems of standards. *De jure* means legitimate, just, or imposed as a matter of law. *De facto* is a contrasting condition characterized as illegitimate, condoned, or accepted for practical purposes.

In a world of heterogeneous, voluntary standards-making bodies, no organization has a right to claim its standards are more legitimate or legally binding or even "preeminent" than those produced by any others, including individual corporations that have obtained adoption of their standards in an open marketplace. The ISO, for example, is a private—not a treaty—organization. Even the ITU-T, which is an international body under a public intergovernmental organization, does not produce legally binding standards. Indeed, at decades of formal international conferences, great care has been taken to assure that standards remain purely voluntary, on a par with all other organizations.

Internet Standards Making as a Model

The Internet standards development process is by far the best in the business. More than just a standards process, it is a distributed collaboration and innovation engine that has produced a thriving new field of electronic communication and a ten-billion-dollar global marketplace growing faster than any communications technology yet devised. Its very uniqueness, however, suggests that it may not be easily applied to existing standards-making organizations and their proceedings.

It is worth examining the attributes of the Internet standards and the associated processes.

• **Individual participation.** From the outset, the Internet standards process was based on individual as opposed to organizational participation. In fact, organizational views are not introduced or discussed. This significantly alters behavior at meetings and emphasizes substantive issues.

• **Direct open participation by experts and innovators**. Anyone may immediately access all relevant information and standards or may participate in any Internet standards-making activity. This may be done via the global Internet at no cost, or by attending any of the triannual meetings at nominal cost. These meetings are also multicasted live on two audio and video channels to more than 500 sites in nearly 20 countries. This exceptional accessibility has proven a magnet for experts and enthusiastic innovators, who freely share their ideas, expertise, and even their computer code. Many students and low-level researchers who freely invent, criticize, and produce concepts and products are also drawn into the activity. Much of the work progresses on the Internet itself—day and night.

• **Output consists of demonstrated working standards**. Before Internet standards reach a certain point, at least two independent implementations must have been completed. This emphasis on working code and demonstrated interoperability is considered central to the process.

• **Emphasis on meeting real user needs.** The use of preliminary interest groups to initiate a standards-making activity combined with participants who actually use the technology and the development of real implementations produces standards that generally meet actual user needs. This occurs predominantly through "bottom up" rather than "top down" standards making.

• **A well-managed development process**. Standards making is closely followed by Area Chairs and forced to proceed rapidly or face termination.

• **Minimum institutional ossification**. Working groups are created easily and terminated quickly upon completion of their specific tasks. This constant turnover prevents permanent committees, rigid institutional infrastructure, or semi-permanent individual roles.

• **Standards are approved via a robust expert review process**. Internet standards must be accepted by both the Internet Engineering Steering Group and the Internet Architecture Board. This peer consensus is reached by people who are intimately familiar with the technology and have one principal motivation—making sure the standard will work. All formal standards actions are published electronically and on paper by the Internet Society, which also takes international responsibility for the standards and for peer liaison with other international organizations.

• **Standards and related materials are universally and instantly accessible and browsable.** Internet standards (and frequently the associated code) are distributed and made available instantly on international Internet servers by mail-based and ftp services. Recently, the IETF Secretariat has advanced the state of the art in standards-making support by providing Gopher-based and WWW-Mosaic hypertext browsing capabilities.

• **Activities are network-based.** Standards making on the network also involves considerable support requirements. For each Internet Standards meeting, this support includes constructing a rather substantial enterprise internet, obtaining scores of computers, providing docking stations, and assembling a multicasting facility. However, this allows attendees not only to accomplish their work but also to continue their personal professional endeavors.

• **Creating the right culture**. Having the right institutional ambiance is very important for attracting the best and the brightest in computer programming and networking. The right ambiance includes informality, network access, and the presence of a large peer group. Culture is also occasionally troublesome, as programmers and networkers have low thresholds of tolerance for controls and influences perceived as unnecessary. Nevertheless, culture is often a critical factor in determining productivity and innovation.

The Internet standards process—although close to an ideal development model—is quite different from most existing standards-making bodies. While it might be possible to adopt many of these Internet practices for a new organization, it is quite different to make over existing organizations to assume these attributes. Standards bodies are more often homes for specialized industry or government constituents than they are neutral technological forums. As a result, even "open" governmental standards forums are usually effectively closed, with no incentives to admit outsiders. All of these factors limit propagation of the Internet model, even though its adoption would clearly be beneficial.

The Government Role

The appropriate role of government in standards making is one that encourages generic open information systems platforms and processes; promotes open technology transfers among the broadest possible range of innovators, developers, and users; and allows a robust competitive marketplace to determine winners and losers. An appropriate international role is to assure that these same values are applied to multilateral and national forums.

How government accomplishes these goals is critical to their success. Fortunately, we have nearly 20 years of benchmarks to gauge what works and what doesn't. Avoiding picking winners and losers extends to forums as well—although providing support to open up the processes does seem to produce significant benefits.

Perhaps one of the principal roles of government in this environment is simply to follow and understand what is occurring both domestically and worldwide. This information can be made publicly available and used to enhance another important role—effecting the open "technology transfer" noted above. A great deal can be done to encourage more open standards processes throughout the world, which will become increasingly important as a robust global marketplace emerges and WTO trade rules apply to the information infrastructure.

Notes

[1] A chart of the Standards Making Universe (popularly known as the Rosetta Stone) was prepared for the first Standards Summit in 1990 and has been revised continually since that time to reflect the changing architecture. It shows a complex multitude of organizations divided into traditional-model telco, radio, and information systems bodies and new-model telco and information systems bodies. It is included in the electronic version of this paper, which can be accessed on the World Wide Web at the URL http://www.isoc.org/amr-on-standards.html.

[2] D. Gilhooley, at the Networked Economy Conference, Washington DC, October 20–21, 1993.

Interoperability and Standards in the NII: The Infrastructure's "Infrastructure"

Douglas W. Schoenberger
AT&T

Introduction: Running a Railroad

In the late 19th century, railroads were the major mode of transport in America for both people and goods. Stations, tracks, depots, and schedules were all in place to serve a growing country. Unfortunately, one major element was hampering the use of railroads: the lack of a uniform standard for time. Communities ran on "solar time." Twelve o'clock noon was determined by individual communities when the sun was deemed to be directly overhead. For example, when it was 12:04 p.m. in New York, it was 12:16 p.m. in Boston, 11:40 a.m. in Pittsburgh, and 11:22 a.m. in Cincinnati. Although significant rail infrastructure was in place, a key non-standardized infrastructure component was hampering rail use. Our 20th century National Information Infrastructure (NII) also requires a supporting infrastructure: *interoperability via open critical interfaces enabled by industry-developed standards.*

This historical example gives lessons to those who seek to enhance the National Information Infrastructure and indicates the importance of interoperability and standards as the infrastructure's "infrastructure." This paper will broadly define the NII, introduce the concept of interoperability and its importance, and discuss the appropriate standards-setting environment and how standards can help insure interoperability.

Defining the National Information Infrastructure

Much of the discussion on the NII has centered on the "information superhighway" and therefore focused solely on the switching and transmission capabilities of communications networks. Such a view inappropriately limits the capabilities, services, and applications that an enhanced NII can offer. In fact, the National Information Infrastructure consists of four separate elements:

• *Information Appliances* include computers, from mainframes to laptops; telephone sets; television sets; fax machines; and personal communicators. These are the devices people use to generate, send, and receive voice messages, data, video, and multimedia information, as well as simply communicate with one another.

• *Communications Networks* include local area networks; local exchanges, including local exchange telephone companies; cellular and PCS carriers; cable TV providers; alternate access vendors; TV and radio broadcasters; and long distance networks, including terrestrial and satellite.

• *Information Resources* are the databases and applications offered by information service and content providers. These may range from large electronic databases accessed by phone or personal computer to simple disks slipped into personal computers or television game sets. Other examples include information on public and government services, educational programs, and medical information.

• *Skilled, well-trained people* produce, transmit, access, and manipulate an ever-expanding flow of information. These human resources and support services will enable users to conduct business by locating and retrieving information, authenticating the information that is accessed, and ensuring security for stored data. Ironically, although people are key to tapping the power of the other NII components, they are often last to be considered in today's NII discussions.

Interoperability: Critical for Enhancing the NII

This broader view of the National Information Infrastructure, and ultimately the Global Information Infrastructure, has significant ramifications for determining how best to enhance it. Because these different aspects of the NII are being built, supplied, and maintained by hundreds of different vendors, as well as by individuals and government agencies, *interoperability* is essential. Interoperability allows diverse systems made by different vendors to communicate with each other, facilitating access and ease of use. Simply stated, *interoperability is the ability of different systems to work together.*

Interoperability among the NII information appliances, applications, communications networks, and information services is essential for several reasons. Interoperability will maximize end user choice of individual products and services that are assured to function together transparently on an end-to-end basis. Interoperability will ensure that information service and content providers have access to all end users in any targeted market regardless of users' choice of individual products and services. Users will not be limited to a particular vendor's offerings based on their information appliance or geographic location.

Interoperability will also promote competitive markets for NII information products and services. This, in turn, will stimulate innovation and increase customer choice and responsiveness to the market and yield lower prices. By making the NII accessible to the greatest number of competing providers, interoperability will lead to improved availability and affordability. Also, interoperability will increase network accessibility for individuals and institutions. Everyone should have the opportunity to access the NII consistent with their individual requirements. "Critical mass" points, such as libraries, community centers, and schools are locations where access to advanced NII services and information resources must be made available. (Significantly, the thirteen largest domestic computer corporations have also recognized the importance of interoperability and have published their position in a Computer Systems Policy Project (CSPP) paper entitled "Perspectives on the National Information Infrastructure: Ensuring Interoperability" released in February 1994.)

Implementing Interoperability

The benefits of interoperability are clear, but how can interoperability be implemented? *The key to interoperability is the development and implementation of open interfaces.* An *interface* is a connection between two systems that is specified in physical (electrical or mechanical) and/or logical (message format and exchange procedure) terms. The interface specification provides the information and technical parameters for how systems communicate with each other, but should be limited to that information necessary to enable communications between the systems, allowing suppliers to develop different implementations with distinguishing characteristics.

Interoperability requires *open* interfaces. An interface is physically and logically open if its specifications are readily available to all vendors, service providers, and users, and if such specifications are not revised without timely notice or public process. Interfaces critical to the interoperability of the NII should be open, thereby allowing manufacturers and vendors to provide, in compliance with reasonable licensing terms and conditions, equipment and software to meet the interface specifications.

Thousands of interfaces, both open and closed, exist in today's NII. However, a much smaller set of these interfaces, located at key "high leverage" points, is critical for enhancing the NII. These interfaces enable or catalyze the development and interworking of a broad array of existing or new products and services built and operated by multiple, competing providers and users. Conversely, they can also hinder competition, growth, and open access. Critical interfaces that are open ensure commonalities needed for interoperability, without stifling technological innovation.

Figure 1 shows a chart of four critical interface families that deserve special attention and are defined below.

• *Category 1: Appliance to Network.* This interface links information appliances and local access providers, including telephone company, cable television service providers, or competitive access providers. This interface is critical because it will allow users and providers of information services to connect information appliances of their choice to any access networks. For example, a user will be able to plug any type of information appliance, such as a television, computer, or telephone, into an outlet provided by the chosen local access provider to access any relevant service.

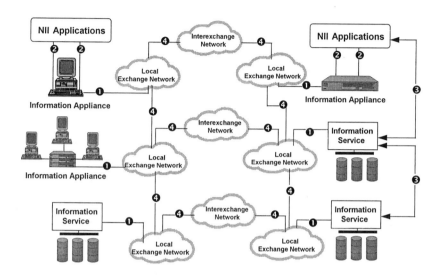

Figure 1 Critical Interfaces for Interoperability in the NII (circled numbers indicate categories).

- *Category 2: Appliance to Application.* This interface provides application programming interfaces (API) between information appliances and emerging NII applications. APIs are well-defined protocols used between a platform and existing and emerging applications. Examples include telephony, database access, multimedia applications, and X.400. Open APIs will enable applications programmers to write new applications that are platform independent and therefore portable.

- *Category 3: Application to Application.* This interface consists of the protocols that one NII application, service, or system uses to communicate with another application, service, or system. This will enable users to generate and receive information in various formats and media without having to make special adjustments to translate between different implementations.

- *Category 4: Network to Network.* These are the interfaces between and among network service providers. For example, this would include the interface between the switches of an access provider and the switches of an interexchange carrier (IXC) or enhanced service provider (ESP). This interface is critical because it will allow customers to access and connect with all IXCs and ESPs. In turn, each IXC and ESP must be able to reach its end customers through a variety of competing access providers.

These categories of interfaces provide a basis to promote and evaluate the progress of interoperability. Unfortunately, several critical interfaces are not being opened quickly enough for a variety of reasons. Some interfaces are not defined, or no interface specification has been developed. For example, while technical specifications exist for connecting different telecommunications switches, interface specifications do not exist between cable companies and competitive access providers. In other cases an interface specification exists, but it is not open. For instance, the interfaces between a set-top box and the networks of local exchange companies, cable TV providers, and competitive access providers are currently closed. This is an important interface to be open, since it would allow consumer electronics vendors to compete, resulting in choice, features, innovations, and reduced prices for consumers. Occasionally multiple open interface specifications exist, which impedes interoperability, or the open interface specification is too complex and/or expensive to be widely deployed and adopted. For example, the many "dialects" of SQL prevent users from realizing the benefits of a common and consistent set of commands and database queries.

These thorny problems must be addressed by NII component suppliers and users to insure interoperability and unlock the power of the NII. Fortunately, a process already exists that folds marketplace forces and technical expertise with open participation by NII component providers and users that can and should address these problems: *today's industry-driven standards process*. The following sections briefly address the importance of standards, the impact of international standards, intellectual property rights issues, and the appropriate government role in the standards process.

Standards: Enabling Interoperability

Implementing interoperability via open interfaces hinges on using the existing industry-led, market-driven standards process. Unfortunately, the word "standards" is widely used in many different contexts. Formal *standard* interfaces are those that are formally recognized by a national or international standards body. Standard interfaces are formulated in open, consensus-based processes where all parties with an interest have an opportunity to participate. These processes greatly facilitate open interfaces. Formal standards are different than *publicly available specifications*. Although these specifications are available to all, they are controlled by a limited set of entities, such as a company or a consortium, and are not formulated via a full consensus process. Importantly, these specifications often may be unilaterally changed by these controlling entities. As a result, they often do not result in open interfaces. *De facto standards* result when the marketplace accepts a particular implementation of a product, service, or application, which leads to its wide deployment. However, these offerings are often controlled by one supplier, are not formally developed via an open, industry-based consensus process, and are often unilaterally changed by the controlling entities. Furthermore, de facto standards are often short-lived as new and innovative offerings are introduced and accepted by the marketplace.

In summary, formal standardized interfaces are key to removing many of the interoperability issues discussed above. Formal standards facilitate interoperability by allowing two or more systems to interact with one another using agreed-upon methods to achieve a predictable result. This compatibility, in turn, encourages the development and introduction of differentiated products and services by multiple suppliers.

Furthermore, marketplace forces continue to drive the NII toward open standards. Today's NII users are increasingly demanding that products and services interoperate so they can access the resources they need. In NII markets that are competitive (such as the interexchange communications market), competitive forces are allowing customers to choose between multiple suppliers. This provides a clear and strong incentive for suppliers to define open interfaces and to disseminate industry-developed standards.

Importance of International Standards

In today's global economy, internationally recognized standards are increasingly important. This is especially true for technology-rich and communications-oriented services provided via NII applications. Although developing international standards may require more time than would a domestic-only standard, national and international standards processes are increasingly becoming synchronized, adding little, if any, additional time to develop global standards. Clearly, the U.S. standards bodies cannot set standards for the world, but many international standards are based on standards or technology developed in the United States. Furthermore, global standards ultimately offer greater compatibility and economic benefits by reducing barriers to trade, lowering product development costs, and improving U.S. overall global competitiveness.

Intellectual Property

Today's voluntary, private-sector-led standards development process provides for nondiscriminatory access to standard interface specifications. When a proprietary technology is incorporated into a standard, the developer must voluntarily agree to license the technology on reasonable terms and conditions, demonstrably free of discrimination. Any proposal to prohibit intellectual property rights and licensing fees for critical NII interfaces would discourage companies and entrepreneurs from innovation and remove any incentive to develop new technologies. This could cripple the NII, which in turn would lead to significant economic harm for the United States. In the international arena, the interdependence of national and international development of NII standards requires an industry-led public standards-setting process; standards mandated by the U.S. government would be untenable in today's international marketplace.

Appropriate Government Role

Proposals that recommend a dominant role for government in the standards development process would seriously risk the adoption of inadequate or inappropriate standards. The voluntary standards process is driven by marketplace forces, which require flexibility and innovation to compete in fast-paced technology products and services. Any government action that would override the existing voluntary consensus process could easily lead to adoption of technology with little or lagging market demand. Furthermore, this inappropriate government role would eventually lead to the removal of incentives for innovation and invention, as the private sector would be frozen, waiting for government decisions on what technologies would be adopted as standards.

While the development of standards should be both led and implemented by industry, the government should play a role in interoperability standards. As a major user of computer and communications products and services, the government should actively participate in the existing standards development process. Furthermore, the government, as directed by OMB Circular A-119, establishes standards for procurement purposes by adopting private-sector-developed standards whenever possible. In markets that are not fully competitive, the government, in some cases, should help stimulate the opening of critical interfaces to ensure interoperability via industry-approved standards. The government should also play a key role in representing the nation's interests in treaty-based standardization organizations, while allowing the private sector to play the dominant technical role.

Conclusion: "Running" an Infrastructure

In 1883, the U.S. and Canadian railroad authorities adopted a proposal by Charles F. Dowd, a Saratoga Springs, NY school principal, and Sir Sandford Fleming, a Canadian civil engineer, to adopt "time zones" so trains could move from town to town without operating under local "solar time." This "standard," developed by the private sector, coupled with concurrent work on standard track width, brakes, couplers, and wheels, fostered the development of the railroad industry and subsequent national economic growth. Like the 19th century railroad example, enhancing today's national information infrastructure and realizing subsequent national economic growth will depend upon leveraging the infrastructure's "infrastructure," specifically by ensuring interoperability via open NII interfaces based upon the existing industry-led, market driven standards process.

OMG: Building Industry Consensus

Richard Mark Soley
Object Management Group

Introduction

The free market, those with a capitalist bent believe, is a powerful instigator of the creativity that produces jobs. Since the beginning of the computer era in the late 1940s, giant leaps have been made by enterprising thinkers and builders from Watson to Jobs, Kapor, and Gates. The freedom to discern a business problem that could be solved with some form of automation, and then do something about it, created the hardware and software giants of today. Lotus 1-2-3 and Autocad were created with scant controls on creativity.

On the other hand, for at least one hundred years (and more vigorously so since the close of World War II), national and international organizations have sought to agree proactively on standard interfaces and descriptions for everything from screw threads and fabric weights to electrical power transmission and data communications. Some governments and corporations have then used these standards to set procurement guidelines, hoping to save money on training, redundant purchasing, and the other fallout of incompatible materials and systems.

But standardization has a built-in balancing problem: while standards promote compatibility (and thus lower overhead), they have a tendency to stall technological progress and limit creativity to solve real business problems. In addition, the cumbersome wheels of the international standards process (as exercised by ISO, ITU, and other international organizations, and supported by national standards bodies such as ANSI) do not move quickly; this has often, in the world of hardware and software, led to useless (and ignored) standards. Eight to twelve years to standardize on programming languages, to take a real example, is ludicrous in a software marketplace in which companies ship new compilers annually—or even more often. Nevertheless, the international standardization process is, and will always be, an important way to create wide, lasting consensus in industry.

Largely due to the tension between the benefits of the standardization process and the speed of technological innovation, the 1980s saw a great surge in the consortium business. In retrospect, it is clear the organizations such as OMG, OSF, UI, IMA, X/Open and so forth were all trying to find a point on the line between a totally open free market and a completely proactive standards-based requirements market. All of the consortia chose processes that moved faster than the ISO process (the OMG process, for example, typically takes 18 months), but which preserved a strong measure of competitiveness to ensure creativity, a better solution, and a fair, legal openness.

OMG Principles and Process

OMG set to work in 1989 with one overall goal: to enable the creation of a Global Information Appliance. Put simply, computer users ought to be able to plug into the world's information services as easily as they plug into the world's power systems today. The industry is certainly still far from that goal, but moving in the right direction. OMG chose three bedrock foundations for its process:

• Object Technology, and in particular Distributed Object Computing, is the best way to build interoperable systems, particularly in the presence of complicating factors such as multiple vendors, varying hardware and software architectures, and geographically separated systems.

• A standard with no implementation is not worth the paper on which it's printed; therefore, OMG will never promulgate a standard with no existing implementation.

• OMG itself will never build, sell, or even resell software, but instead will provide only specifications of standards.

These foundations imply a competitive selection process for object-oriented frameworks, interfaces, and languages to support interoperable applications executing on a wide range of hardware, operating, and network systems.

In 1989, OMG chose a working process that centered around public Requests to gather information from the worldwide computer software industry before setting forth standards. In order to provide guidance for the standardization process, OMG first developed an architecture for interoperability. That "reference model," termed the Object Management Architecture (OMA), was outlined in OMG's first publication, the Object Management Architecture Guide (OMAG). The OMA has since made possible a structured, incremental refinement process for developing the standard interfaces necessary to build and maintain distributed systems.

The first step in the process is taken by OMG's Technical Committee (TC). Based on the overall roadmap provided by the OMA, the TC chooses a general area of standardization on which to work; it also charters a Task Force (TF) to carry out studies in that area, generate a roadmap for work and internal architecture if necessary, and carry out the required work. For example, in 1990 the TC chartered an Object Request Broker Task Force (ORB TF) to fill out the most important portion of the OMA, the main communications backbone.

The first task carried out by any TF is to issue a Request for Information (RFI). This very general request asks for any interested party (e.g., vendors, users, or academics) to provide feedback to the TF about likely standardization requirements. Responses to RFIs have historically varied from worries about standardization occurring too early in an area to complete internal architectures for systems in a particular area. This is the most open phase of the OMG process, since any party is invited to comment on the OMG technology adoption process.

Based on responses to the initial RFI, the TF then decides on a direction of standardization and a priority of work items. The efforts of the Object Services Task Force, for example, often center on likely constraints of the various Services to be adopted and thus the order in which Services should be adopted. A common result of reviewing of RFI responses is a set of architecture and roadmap documents.

Based on what is learned in the RFI step, a TF then begins issuing Requests for Proposals (RFPs). In this step, the TF is not requesting general guidance, but instead is looking for specific application programming interfaces (APIs), protocols, and languages necessary to fulfill both a general set of guidelines (called Technical Objectives) and a technology-specific set of requirements generated by the TF. As prospective respondents (who must be corporate OMG members) begin the preparation of their responses, the TF develops evaluation guidelines to handle the submissions.

The first, unique step of the RFP process is a requirement for a Letter of Intent to Respond (LOI). Companies that plan to respond to an RFP must submit a LOI to OMG by a published deadline. This must be signed by a corporate officer or managing director of the company. It not only states the company's intent to take part in the Request selection process, but also guarantees that the company will make an implementation of the provided specification commercially available. This step also provides a public statement of companies' commercial intents.

Then the submissions begin to flow in. A submission to an OMG RFP process comprises not only any required technical specifications, but also the answers to a set of questions put forth by the OMG Business Committee, to help guarantee that the provided specifications will be available in a commercial product. Based on those guarantees and the provided specifications, the TF that issued the RFP begins the technical evaluation process—which it seldom finishes.

To understand why initial evaluation processes are generally not completed, it's important to realize that submitters of technology often take advantage of an RFP process to learn what their competitors are up to. They then use that information not just to compete with one another but also to create technology mergers. In every technology selection process to date, at least one initial submission has come from a consortium of companies, and at least one group of submitters has merged during the initial evaluation process.

These exigencies require another submission deadline. The "players" from the first deadline submit new (and usually merged) submissions, generally taking into account what they have learned from the evaluation process. Leeway for such mergers is now built into every OMG technology adoption process. While the actual corporate agreements to effect mergers happen outside the OMG process and without prodding from OMG staff or committees, mergers have had an important effect in creating the industry consensus for which OMG strives.

In the next step, evaluations begin in earnest, leading to a one company–one vote ballot vote by the TF for recommendation to the TC. The TC then must ratify that recommendation by a two-thirds margin of the full Corporate OMG membership in order for the Board of Directors to make its final decision. The Board makes its decision based not only on the TC technical review but also upon examination of the commercial availability review by the Business Committee and a review by the OMG End-User Special Interest Group, to ensure that the planned standard meets or exceeds real end-user requirements.

In early 1993 it occurred to a group of OMG members and staff that while the stiff requirements for submission and evaluation ensured that consensus would be built around widely-applicable technology solutions, more narrow technology areas might never be served by the OMG Request process. In particular, commercial users of OMG standards requiring technology- or domain-specific extensions (such as less-widely-used programming languages or particular vertical markets) might desire a standardized solution in their particular area. However, despite the fact that multiple competitive solutions might not even exist in an area, that need might never be served due to OMG's lack of interest in that technology area.

To allow service to a wider community, at the end of 1993 the OMG inaugurated a new Request for Comments (RFC) "fast-track" adoption process. This process allows OMG Corporate members to submit technology specifications for which no Request is outstanding (i.e., unsolicited submissions). Routed to the appropriate Task Force for consideration, these submissions may then be presented for public comment (i.e., to the entire industry) as potential OMG standards.

During this public comment period, *any* person or company may respond. Responses may vary from outright support to statements of inadequacy of the proposal. Any significant negative comments on the proposal "derail" it, forcing the proposal through the usual, competitive selection process. However, if there are no significant negative responses, the proposal follows the usual TC and Board of Directors voting procedure to become an OMG standard.

This new "fast track" process has yet to be used at this writing, but has been welcomed warmly by various groups of users of existing OMG standards as a way to embrace their specific markets. The RFC process is expected to widen the user base of OMG standards significantly in 1994 and beyond.

In sum, the OMG technology adoption process is fast, but takes into account the need for competitive proposals to solve real user problems. The dual-response system allows for time to build consensus among OMG members, which also helps build acceptance throughout the industry.

The OMG process to date has already produced the widely acclaimed Common Object Request Broker Architecture (CORBA, see [CORBA]) Object Request Broker, the foundation for interoperability across all computing platforms. In addition, a rigorous Object Model and a growing set of layered Object Services standards have built upon the CORBA baseline (see [COSSI]), and at this writing the OMG is beginning to build domain-specific vertical market standard interfaces through the Common Facilities adoption process. OMG and its standards are now well accepted in the computing industry, and as OMG passes its fifth birthday the world of OMG technology users is expanding rapidly. OMG goals for the future include not only maintenance and growth of the existing suite of standards, but more layered standards to continue to build the Global Information Appliance.

Someday you'll plug your wristwatch into a socket in New York and order a telephone number from the directory system in Sydney. And though you won't see it, the transaction will rely on OMG standards.

References

[OMAG] Richard Soley (ed.), *Object Management Architecture Guide, Second Revision,* New York: John Wiley, 1992.

[CORBA] *Common Object Request Broker Architecture Specification, Version 1.2,* New York: John Wiley, 1992.

[COSSI] Jon Siegel (ed.), *Common Object Services Specification,* Volume 1, New York: John Wiley, 1994.

Glossary of Acronyms

ACIS	American Committee for Interoperable Systems
ACS	Accredited Standards Committee
AFIRM	Architecture Framework for Information Resource Management
ANDF	Architecturally Neutral Distribution Format
ANS	Advanced Network and Services, Inc.
ANSI	American National Standards Institute
API	Application Program Interface
APSI	Alliance to Promote Software Innovation
ARPA	Advanced Research Projects Agency, Department of Defense (formerly DARPA)
ASCII	American Standard Character Information Interchange
ASME	American Society for Mechanical Engineers
AT&T	American Telephone and Telegraph
ATM	Asynchronous Transfer Mode
ATV	Advanced Television
BBS	Bulletin Board System
BGP	Border Gateway Protocol
BIOS	Basic Input-Output System
BSA	Business Software Alliance
BSI	British Standards Institute
CAD	Computer-Aided Design
CALS	Continuous Acquisition and Life-cycle Support
CAM	Computer-Aided Manufacturing
CAT	IITF Committee on Applications and Technology

CBEMA	Computer and Business Equipment Manufacturers' Association (now Information Technology Industrial Council)
CCITT	Consultative Committee for International Telegraphy and Telephony (now ITU-T)
CCS	Cargo Community Systems
CEN	Committee of European Normalization
CENELEC	CEN, Electro-technology
CEPT	Conference of Postal and Telecommunications Administrations
CIX	Commercial Internet Exchange
CLNP	Connectionless Network Protocol
CMIP	Common Management Information Protocol
CNRI	Corporation for National Research Initiatives
CORBA	Common Object Request Broker Architecture
COS	Corporation for Open Systems
COSS	Common Object Services Specification
CSPP	Computer Systems Policy Project
CTR	Common Technical Regulation
CTS	Conformance Testing Services
CVTS	Compressed Video Teleconferencing System
DEC	Digital Equipment Corporation
DISA	Defense Information Systems Administration
DNS	Domain Name System
DOD	Department of Defense
DOE	Department of Energy
DOS	Disk Operating System
DSS	Digital Signature Standard
EBU	European Broadcasting Union
EC	Electronic Commerce
EC	European Commission
ECMA	European Computer Manufacturers' Association
EDI	Electronic Data Interchange
EDIFACT	Electronic Data Interchange For Administration, Commerce, and Transport
EES	Escrowed Encryption Standard
EFT	Electronic Funds Transfer
EFTA	European Free Trade Agreement

EGP	External Gateway Protocol
EI	Enterprise Integration
EIA	Electrical Industry Association
EPHOS	European Handbook for Open Systems
ESP	Enhanced Service Provider
ETS	European Telecommunications Standard
ETSI	European Telecommunications Standards Institute
EU	European Union
EWOS	European Workshop on Open Systems
FCC	Federal Communications Commission
FCCSET	Federal Coordinating Council on Science, Engineering and Technology
FDDI	Fiber Data Distributed Interface
FDT	Formal Description Technique
FGIPC	Federation of Government Information Processing Councils
FII	Federal Information Infrastructure
FIRP	Federal Internetworking Requirements Panel
FIX	Federal Internet Exchange
FTP	File Transfer Protocol
FTS2000	Federal Telecommunications System 2000
GATT	General Agreement on Tariffs and Trade
GII	Global Information Infrastructure
GILS	Government Information Locator Service
GIS	Geographical Information Systems
GIX	Global Internet Exchange
GOSIP	Government Open Systems Interconnection Protocol
GSA	General Services Administration
GUI	Graphical User Interface
HDTV	High-Definition Television
HPCCIT	High-Performance Computer and Communications Information Technology
IAB	Internet Advisory Board
IANA	Internet Assigned Number Authority
IATA	International Air Transport Association
IBM	International Business Machines
IEC	International Electrotechnical Commission
IEEE	Institute for Electrical and Electronics Engineers

IESG	Internet Engineering Steering Group
IETF	Internet Engineering Task Force
IGES	Initial Geometric Exchange Specification
IICS	International Information Communications Society
IISP	Information Infrastructure Standards Panel
IITF	Information Infrastructure Task Force
IMA	Interactive Multimedia Association
INSEAD	European Institute of Business Administration
IP	Internet Protocol
IP	Intellectual Property
IPR	Intellectual Property Rights
IRM	Information Resources Management
IRTF	Internet Research Task Force
IS	International Standard
ISDN	Integrated Systems Digital Network
ISO	International Standards Organization
ISOC	Internet Society
ISP	International Standardized Profile
IT	Information Technology
ITI	Industrial Technology Institute
ITSB	Image Technology Standards Board
ITU	International Telecommunications Union
ITU-T	ITU committee on telecommunications (formerly CCITT)
IXC	Inter-exchange Carrier
JTC1	Joint ISO-IEC Technical Committee 1 on information technology standards
LAN	Local Area Network
LAP	Link Access Protocol
LEC	Local Exchange Carrier
LOI	Letter of Intent
MAP	Manufacturing Applications Protocol
MFS	Modification of Final Judgment
MITI	Ministry of International Trade and Industry
MPEG	Motion Picture Experts Group
NAB	National Association of Broadcasters
NAP	Network Access Point
NASA	National Aeronautics and Space Administration

NBS	National Bureau of Standards (now NIST)
NCR	National Cash Register
NCTA	National Cable Television Association
NFS	Network File System
NIC	Network Information Center
NII	National Information Infrastructure
NIOSH	National Institute for Occupational Health and Safety
NISO	National Information Standards Organization
NIST	National Institute for Standards and Technology
NP	New Proposal
NRC	National Research Council
NREN	National Research and Education Network
NSA	National Security Agency
NSF	National Science Foundation
NTIA	National Telecommunications and Information Agency
NTSC	National Television Systems Committee
OECD	Organization for Economic Cooperation and Development
OEM	Original Equipment Manufacturer
OMA	Object Management Architecture
OMAG	Object Management Architecture Guide
OMB	Office of Management and Budget
OMG	Object Management Group
OOP	Object-Oriented Programming
ORB	Object Request Broker
OS	Operating System
OSC	Office of Scientific Computing
OSE	Open Systems Environment
OSF	Open Software Foundation
OSHA	Occupational Safety and Health Administration
OSI	Open Systems Interconnection
OSTP	Office of Science and Technology Policy
OTA	Office of Technology Assessment
PAS	Publicly Available Specifications
PASC	Pacific Area Standards Congress
PC	Personal Computer
PCMCIA	Personal Computer Memory Card International Association

PCS	Personal Communication System
PDES	Product Data Exchange using STEP
PM	Producer-Member
POSIX	Portable Operating System Interface for Computer Environments
PTT	Post, Telegraph and Telephone administration
QFD	Quality Function Deployment
RFC	Request For Comments
RFI	Request For Information
RFP	Request For Proposals
RFT	Request For Technology
RISC	Reduced Instruction Set Computer
SAA	Standards Application Area
SCSI	Small Computer System Interface
SDO	Standards Development Organization
SGML	Standard Graphic Mark-up Language
SMC	Standards Management Committee
SMPTE	Society of Motion Picture and Television Engineers
SMTP	Simple Mail Transfer Protocol
SNA	Systems Network Architecture
SONET	Synchronous Optical Network
SPA	Standards Project Automation
SPARC	Standards Planning and Requirements Committee
SPC	Strategic Planning Committee
SQL	Structured Query Language
STEP	Standard for Exchange of Product Model Data
T1-ANSI	ANSI committee for telecommunications standards
TAG	Technical Advisory Group
TBR	Technical Basis for a Regulation
TCP/IP	Transmission Control Protocol/Internet Protocol
TF	Task Force
TIA	Telecommunications Industry Association
TOP	Technical and Office Protocol
TP4	Transport Protocol 4
TRAC	Technical Recommendations Applications Committee
UAOS	User Alliance for Open Systems
UI	User Interface

USPS	United States Postal Service
VCR	Video Cassette Recorder
WAIS	Wide-Area Information Server
WAN	Wide-Area Network
WWMCCS	World-Wide Military Command and Control System
WWW	World Wide Web
X.n	CCITT data communications standards
XIA	Cross-Industry Association

Contributors

Robert J. Aiken (aiken@es.net) works for the Lawrence Livermore National Laboratory on special assignment to the U.S. Department of Energy.

Frede Ask is an engineer and lawyer from the University of Copenhagen. In 1988, after various posts in Danish industry, he was elected Deputy Director of ETSI (the European Telecommunications Standards Institute).

Joseph P. Bailey (bailey@rpcp.mit.edu) is a Research Assistant at the Research Program on Communications Policy at the Center for Technology, Policy, and Industrial Development, Massachusetts Institute of Technology.

Jonathan Band (JXB1@Mofo.COM) is a Partner at Morrison & Foerster, Washington, D.C.

S. N. Baron (baron@oepandd.nbc.com) is NBC's Managing Director of Television Technology. He is currently President of the Society of Motion Picture and Television Engineers (SMPTE).

Marjory S. Blumenthal (mblument@nas.edu) is Executive Director of the Computer Science and Telecommunications Board of the National Research Council. She directed the project that resulted in *Realizing the Information Future.*

Lewis M. Branscomb (lewisb@ksgrsch.harvard.edu) is the Albert Pratt Public Service Professor at Harvard University. He is Director of the Program on Science, Technology, and Public Policy at Harvard's John F. Kennedy School of Government and is Principal Investigator of the Information Infrastructure Project.

Paola Bucciarelli works in the European Commission department responsible for defining and implementing the standardization policy in information technology and telecommunications.

Carl F. Cargill (carl.cargill@eng.sun.com) is the Standards Strategist for Sun Microsystems, the author of *Information Technology Standardization: Theory, Process, and Organizations,* and Editor-in-Chief of the ACM Journal *StandardView.*

John S. Cavallini (cavallini@nersc.gov) is the Acting Associate Director of the Office of Scientific Computing, Office of Energy Research, at the U.S. Department of Energy.

David D. Clark (ddc@lcs.mit.edu) is a Senior Research Scientist at the M.I.T. Laboratory for Computer Science. He has been involved in the development of Internet standards since 1975, and was a principal author of the NRC/CSTB report *Realizing the Information Future.*

Philip V. W. Dodds (pdodds@ima.org) is President of the Interactive Multimedia Association.

William Ellis is the Intellectual Property Counsel for IBM Corporation in Arlington, Virginia.

Joseph Farrell (farrell@econ.Berkeley.edu) is Professor of Economics and Affiliated Professor of Business, University of California, Berkeley.

Georges Ferné is with the Standardization Section of the OECD.

Paul W. Forster (pforster@ics.uci.edu) is a graduate student at the Department of Information and Computer Science, University of California, Irvine.

Richard B. Gibson (rgibson@attmail.com) is Chairman of the U.S. Technical Advisory Group for Joint Technical Committee 1 of the International Organization for Standardization and the International Electrotechnical Commission (ISO/IEC JTC 1).

William F. Hanrahan (bhanrahan@itic.nw.dc.us) is a member of the Information Technology Industrial Council (formerly CBEMA).

Jim Isaak (Isaak@csac.enet.dec.com) is the Director of Information Infrastructure Standards with Digital Equipment Corporation's Corporate Standards and Consortia group, chair of IEEE SCC 33 (Information Infrastructure), and member of ANSI IISP.

Jerry L. Johnson (jerry.johnson@dir.texas.gov) is Senior Policy Analyst, Statewide Planning Division, Department of Information Resources, State of Texas.

Brian Kahin (kahin@harvard.edu) is Adjunct Lecturer in Public Policy and Director of the Information Infrastructure Project in the Science, Technology, and Public Policy Program at the John F. Kennedy School of Government, Harvard University. He is also General Counsel for the Annapolis-based Interactive Multimedia Association.

John Leslie King (king@ics.uci.edu) is Professor of Information and Computer Science and Management at the University of California, Irvine.

Gary Lea (g.r.lea@reading.ac.uk) is a Lecturer in the Department of Law at the University of Reading.

William Lehr (Wlehr@research.gsb.columbia.edu) is Assistant Professor of Finance and Economics at Columbia University.

Martin C. Libicki (libicki@ndu.edu) has been a Senior Fellow at the Institute for National Strategic Studies, National Defense University, since 1986. His present field of interest is the relationship between information technology and national security.

Sergio Mazza (mmaas@attmail.com) is president of the American National Standards Institute (ANSI), a not-for-profit membership organization that coordinates the U.S. voluntary standards system and represents the United States to the International Organization for Standardization (ISO) and the International Electrotechnical Commission (IEC).

Lee McKnight (mcknight@farnsworth.mit.edu) is a Lecturer in the MIT Technology and Policy Program, a Principal Research Associate at the MIT Center for Technology, Policy and Industrial Development, and Associate Director of the MIT Research Program on Communications Policy.

Jonathan A. Morell (jam@iti.org) is Principal Member of the Technical Staff at the Center for Electronic Commerce of the Industrial Technology Institute.

Suzanne Neil (scn@rpcp.mit.edu) is Associate Director of the Research Program on Communications Policy at the Center for

Technology, Policy and Industrial Development at the Massachusetts Institute of Technology.

D. Burton Newlin (burt.newlin@osd.mil) is a Computer Specialist at the Office of the Assistant Secretary of Defense, Command, Control, Communications and Intelligence, Information Management.

Stephen Oksala (soksala@corp.bb.unisys.com) is Director of Corporate Standards at UNISYS.

Arati Prabhakar (director@micf.nist.gov) is Director of the National Institute of Standards and Technology.

John Rankine (j.rankine@ieee.org) is President of Rankine Associates and a former Chairman of ANSI and of ISO/IEC JTC1. He acts in an advisory capacity on standardization for the OECD, the International Chamber of Commerce, and the IEEE Standards Board.

Arthur K. Reilly (cc.bellcore.com!akr) is Chairman of Committee T1–Telecommunications, Washington, D.C.

Anthony M. Rutkowski (amr@isoc.org) is Executive Director of the Internet Society. He has participated in, studied, and managed standards making bodies and processes for twenty years in the U.S. government, private-sector companies, academic institutions, and international organizations.

Douglas W. Schoenberger (schoenberger@attmail.com) works in AT&T's Government Affairs organization, where he is responsible for developing and advocating policies regarding technology and infrastructure issues.

Mark Shurmer (Mark.Shurmer@brunel.ac.uk) is Lecturer in Industrial Economics at Brunel University.

Anna Slomovic (Anna_Slomovic@rand.org) is a Senior Policy Analyst at RAND working principally with the Critical Technologies Institute in Washington DC.

Richard Mark Soley (soley@omg.org) is Vice President and Technical Director of the Object Management Group, Inc.

Michael B. Spring (spring@pitt.edu) is an Assistant Professor of Information Science at the University of Pittsburgh. He also serves on the Long Range Planning Committee of X3 and co-chairs the

NRC Review Board for the Information Technology Laboratory of the National Institute of Standards and Technology.

S. L. Stewart (sstewart@nist.gov) is a computer scientist at NIST.

Andrew Updegrove (73314.3215@compuserve.com) is a partner in the Boston law firm of Lucash, Gesmer & Updegrove, which concentrates its practice in the representation of high technology companies and consortia.

Caroline S. Wagner (cwagner@rand.org) is a Senior Policy Analyst at RAND working principally with the Critical Technologies Institute in Washington DC.

Martin B. H. Weiss (mbw@pitt.edu) is Associate Professor of Telecommunications and Information Science and Co-Director of the Telecommunications Program at the University of Pittsburgh.

Index

value of, 227
and view of standards, 90
voting patterns of, 239–240
User alliances
development of, 183–189
for open systems (UAOS), 90, 185
User Interface standards, 543
User Procurements, 94, 95
User Requirements, 94, 95
Users Groups, on Committee T1,
584, 586

Validation, of standardization model,
94, 95
Vendors, 10–11
consortia of, 182–183
and open system standards, 178
and proprietary systems, 189
role of, in standard setting, 88–89,
91, 434
and self-certification, 223, 300
tool technology transfer to, 210–
211
Very high-speed integrated circuit
(VHSIC), 65
Video cassette recorder, standards
for, 379
Video technologies, strands of
development in, 283–284
Voluntary consensus process, 499–
500, 517
Voluntary consensus standards,
development of, 222–223
Voluntary standardization initiatives,
520–523
Voluntary standards, role of, 494–495
Voluntary standards developers, 518
Volunteer labor, assessment of value
of, 215, 216
Volunteer standards process, 106,
107–108
Voting, options in, 246
Voting rules
purpose of, 133
supramajority, 133, 139
VXI bus Consortium (VXI), 327

Wang, 458
WANs, 48, 493
Weighted voting, problems with, 452
See also Majority weighted voting
Wide Area Information Services
(WAIS), 257
Wide area networks. See WANs
Willingness-to-pay (w-t-p), 126
Windows NT, 326, 329
Wireless communications providers,
regulated, 505
Working Draft (WD), 479, 481–484
Working Group (WG), 473, 481
World Wide Web (WWW), 257, 534
Writing stage, 83

X Consortium, 326, 329
X Industry Association (XIA), 326,
329
X/OPEN, 461
and Microsoft, 223
X/Open Company, Ltd., 87
XPG, 44–45
X3 Strategic Planning Committee,
84–85
composition of, 230–235
data from, 228–229
and life cycle standards, 294
standardization style of, 223
study, 221, 225–250
and voluntary consensus standards,
222
X9, 466
X12, 466
and SDO, 222
success of, 54
X400 electronic mail standards, 460,
551
See also Electronic mail
X.400 gateway, 266
X Window System Standard, and
technology ownership, 342–343

Z39, as SDO, 222